Using Harvard Graphics®

2nd Edition

Stephen W. Sagman
Jane Graver Sandlar

QUE® CORPORATION
LEADING COMPUTER KNOWLEDGE

Using
Harvard Graphics®

2nd Edition

Copyright © 1990 by Que® Corporation.

Library of Congress Catalog No.: 90-62069

ISBN 0-88022-608-0

93 92 91 90   4 3 2

Interpretation of the printing code: the rightmost double-digit number is the year of the book's printing; the rightmost single-digit number, the number of the book's printing. For example, a printing code of 90-1 shows that the first printing of the book occurred in 1990.

Using Harvard Graphics, 2nd Edition, is based on Harvard Graphics through Version 2.3.

DEDICATION ▼

To Eric Weinberger and Artie and Holden Sandlar for their love and support.

Publishing Director

Lloyd J. Short

Acquisitions Editor

Karen A. Bluestein

Product Director

Shelley O'Hara

Project Manager

Paul Boger

Production Editors

Sandra Blackthorn
Kelly D. Dobbs

Editors

Kelly Currie
Lori A. Lyons
Heidi Weas Muller
Daniel Schnake

Technical Editor

Ron Holmes

Indexer

Jill D. Bomaster

Editorial Assistant

Patricia J. Brooks

Book Design and Production

Dan Armstrong
Bill Basham
Claudia Bell
Brad Chinn
Don Clemons
Sally Copenhaver
Travia Davis
Denny Hager
Susan Hill
Tami Hughes
Bill Hurley
Chuck Hutchinson
Betty Kish
Bob LaRoche
Larry Lynch
Diana Moore
Cindy L. Phipps
Joe Ramon
Dennis Sheehan
Louise Shinault
Bruce Steed
Mary Beth Wakefield
Vickie West

*Composed in Goudy Old Style and Excellent No. 47
by Que Corporation.*

ABOUT THE AUTHORS

Stephen W. Sagman

Stephen W. Sagman is a free-lance technical writer and PC educator based in New York City. He has written hundreds of articles and product reviews, often relating to graphics, which have appeared in *PC Week*, *PC/Computing*, *PC Magazine*, and others. Mr. Sagman has written documentation, user's guides, marketing materials, and custom training materials. He has taught students and executives on a variety of computer topics, such as the basics, advanced graphics, desktop publishing, and, of course, Harvard Graphics.

Prior to technical writing, Mr. Sagman edited *MIDI Marketer*, an electronic musical instrument marketing newsletter, and served as marketing manager for several high-technology companies.

Mr. Sagman graduated from Hamilton College and has an M.B.A. from the City University of New York. He is the president of Computer Music Marketing, Inc., and is the author of Que's *1-2-3 Graphics Techniques*.

Jane Graver Sandlar

Jane Graver Sandlar is the president of Support Our Systems, Inc., a documentation and training company based in Red Bank, New Jersey. She has taught students in many corporate environments to use Harvard Graphics. Ms. Sandlar's company produces print-based and on-line user's guides, training guides, quick reference guides, and other documentation for corporate and government audiences. In addition, SOS trains users on a variety of personal computer and mainframe software packages.

Prior to starting SOS, Ms. Sandlar worked for several large and midsize corporations, developing and delivering training and documentation. She received her bachelor's degree from Northwestern University and earned her master's degree in Instructional Technology and Information Science from Syracuse University.

Support Our Systems, Inc., 10 Mechanic St., Red Bank, NJ 07701, offers customized symbol libraries of documentation symbols for technical writers. Please contact Support Our Systems for more information.

Contents at a Glance

Part IV   Simplifying Your Work

Part V   Wrapping Up

TABLE OF CONTENTS ▼

▼

I Learning the Basics

3   **Quick Start: Taking a Guided Tour of Harvard**
    Graphics..

II   Making Charts

4   Creating Text Charts 97

III Adding Pizzazz

ACKNOWLEDGMENTS

The authors want to thank Mary Jane Reiter, Helen Kendrick, Don Bragg, Ira Kaye, and Lisa Christopher at Software Publishing Corporation for their invaluable assistance.

The authors especially want to thank Sandy Blackthorn for her tireless and consummate editing and reediting, Shelley O'Hara, Karen Bluestein, Paul Boger, Lloyd Short, Ron Holmes, and the many other editors at Que for their support during the development, writing, and production of this book. Additional thanks go to Terry Simboli and Ted Lewis for their help with editing and graphics.

TRADEMARK
ACKNOWLEDGMENTS

Que Corporation has made every effort to supply trademark information about company names, products, and services mentioned in this book. Trademarks indicated below were derived from various sources. Que Corporation cannot attest to the accuracy of this information.

1-2-3, Freelance Plus, Lotus, Symphony, and VisiCalc are registered trademarks of Lotus Development Corporation.

COMPAQ is a registered trademark of COMPAQ Computer Corporation.

dBASE IV is a trademark of Ashton-Tate Corporation.

Encapsulated PostScript and PostScript are registered trademarks of Adobe Systems, Inc.

Hewlett-Packard is a registered trademark and LaserJet is a trademark of Hewlett-Packard Co.

IBM is a registered trademark and PS/2 is a trademark of International Business Machines Corporation.

Micrografx is a registered trademark and Windows Draw is a trademark of Micrografx, Inc.

Microsoft, Microsoft Excel, Microsoft Windows, and PowerPaint are registered trademarks of Microsoft Corporation.

PageMaker is a registered trademark of Aldus Corporation.

PFS is a registered trademark and Harvard Graphics and Professional Plan are trademarks of Software Publishing Corporation.

Quattro and Quattro Pro are registered trademarks of Borland International, Inc.

Ventura Publisher is a registered trademark of Ventura Software Publishing Corporation.

Xerox is a registered trademark of Xerox Corporation.

CONVENTIONS USED IN THIS BOOK ▼

The conventions used in this book have been established to help you learn to use the program quickly and easily.

Names of commands, menus, modes, options, overlays, and screens are written with initial capital letters.

On-screen messages are written in a `special typeface` and capitalized exactly as they appear on-screen.

Words and letters the user types are set off on a separate line or are written in *italic*.

Introduction

If you draw graphs by hand or use a typewriter to type overhead projections, you will be amazed at the helping hand a computer can provide. Whether or not you already use a computer, you will be delighted when you try Software Publishing Corporation's Harvard Graphics. No other business graphics software can give you a larger helping hand in creating interesting and expressive business presentations.

Harvard Graphics is one of the computer industry's most popular business software packages because it makes creating professional-looking, expressive business charts as easy as choosing a few options from your computer's screen. When you try Harvard Graphics, you find that you have a host of easy-to-use tools for creating charts and equally easy methods for presenting your masterpieces on paper, on slides, or in animated desktop presentations.

Harvard Graphics can create just about any visual aid you can imagine to enhance a business presentation. Many people use Harvard Graphics to make slides, transparencies, and printed handouts, but you may want to use the program to create a printed agenda for your meeting or to draw a map that directs attendees to their locations. You also may want to use Harvard Graphics to create the cue cards you will use at the podium during your speech and to create the awards you will present at the conclusion of your presentation. The potential uses for Harvard Graphics are limited only by your imagination.

Harvard Graphics is certainly not the only business graphics program available, but many other graphics programs require that you be a proficient artist or an experienced computer user. Harvard Graphics imposes no such limitations. In fact, even if your formal art education stopped in the fourth grade, you can turn out well-designed and attractive business graphics with Harvard Graphics. Leaving the default options yields beautiful results for your charts.

The program's capacity to guide you in creating a chart makes Harvard Graphics unusual. By following its built-in chart recipes, you allow the program to make many of the aesthetic decisions—both major and minor—that may otherwise confront you when designing a chart. If you decide to create a bar chart, for example, Harvard Graphics picks an appealing combination of colors, adds descriptive information to the chart's axes and legend, and even scales the size of the chart title to fit your needs. If you are happy with the scheme Harvard Graphics uses, and the chart looks satisfactory, you can stop there. To complete your work, you can save the chart on disk and reproduce it with your printer, plotter, or slide maker. If your sense of aesthetics suggests a few changes, however, you easily can edit any aspect of the chart's design. You may even want to elaborate on the design by adding lines, boxes, arrows, or predrawn pictures from the included libraries of available symbols. All these possibilities and more are at your fingertips with Harvard Graphics.

What Is in This Book?

In the chapters that follow, you will find detailed information about how to accomplish specific charting tasks and how to control the many features of Harvard Graphics. Topics are organized logically, so that they build on the information contained in previous chapters.

Part I of this book, "Learning the Basics," examines the basics of Harvard Graphics. Chapter 1, "Introducing Harvard Graphics," provides information on the benefits of Harvard Graphics, the applications of the program, and the other graphics packages available on today's market.

Chapter 2, "Getting Started," provides all the information you need to install and start the program.

Chapter 3, "Quick Start: Taking a Guided Tour of Harvard Graphics," takes you on a comprehensive tour of the program's most important capabilities. In this quick tour, you try your hand at making a text, bar, and pie chart.

Part II, "Making Charts," provides in-depth information about making charts. Chapter 4, "Creating Text Charts;" Chapter 5, "Creating Graph Charts: Bar and Line;" and Chapter 6, "Creating Graph Charts: Area, High/Low/Close, and Pie," provide detailed descriptions of the options available for making text and graph charts.

Chapter 7, "Calculating Data," includes the information you need to know to calculate new information based on the data you enter in Harvard Graphics.

Chapter 8, "Importing and Exporting Data," teaches you what you need to know about importing text and numbers from other software applications and about exporting completed Harvard Graphics charts to other applications.

Part III, "Adding Pizzazz," covers the ways in which Harvard Graphics can enhance the text and graphic charts you create. Chapter 9, "Drawing with Harvard Graphics: Draw/Annotate," focuses on the pizzazz you can add to charts with the Draw/Annotate feature.

Chapter 10, "Quick Start: Using Draw Partner;" Chapter 11, "Adding Graphic Objects in Draw Partner;" and Chapter 12, "Modifying Graphic Objects in Draw Partner;" cover Draw Partner thoroughly, teaching you everything you need to know about this superb drawing utility.

Part IV, "Simplifying Your Work," covers two Harvard Graphics features that can make your work faster and easier. Chapter 13, "Using Step-Savers: Templates," covers how to use Templates in Harvard Graphics.

Chapter 14, "Using Step-Savers: Macros," covers the Harvard Graphics macro utility, which can record your keystrokes and play them back.

Part V, "Wrapping Up," includes chapters that describe producing both printed and on-screen output. Chapter 15, "Producing Stellar Output," covers the techniques you should know to get printed, plotted, or recorded output.

Chapter 16, "Creating Slide Shows and Screenshows," describes everything you should know about making slide shows and producing on-screen desktop presentations called screenshows.

Appendix A, "Adding Flair with Symbols," contains an alphabetical listing of all the symbols included with Harvard Graphics.

Appendix B, "Harvard Graphics Quick Reference," provides reference information about text charts, graph charts, Draw/Annotate, Draw Partner, and templates.

Appendix C, "What's New in Harvard Graphics 2.3," summarizes the revisions to Version 2.13. These revisions include changes to Draw Partner and new features such as the chart gallery, color palettes, and hypershow.

Appendix D, "Harvard Graphics Accessory Programs," covers five new accessories that Harvard Graphics offers: Quick Charts, Designer Galleries, Business Symbols, Military Symbols, and U.S. MapMaker. Two additional accessory products, Draw Partner and Screenshow Utilities, are included in Version 2.3 and no longer sold as separate utilities.

Who Should Use This Book?

Even if you never have used a computer, you can follow the simple step-by-step instructions that this book provides. If you have used other software, such as a word processor or database manager, this book shows you what makes Harvard Graphics different. And if you have used other graphics software, or if you have been using Harvard Graphics already, you will find details about getting the most out of the more sophisticated capabilities of Harvard Graphics.

How To Use This Book

All learning is done best in small, frequent doses. Don't try to get through this book or learn everything that is in it in one sitting. Do try to find time to work with this book and your computer when you are not distracted by the routine uproar of your business or home.

You will learn the most if you have the chance to try the procedures and exercises in each chapter while you are sitting at your computer. When you finish *Using Harvard Graphics*, keep the book handy as a ready reference. This book's comprehensive index and table of contents are helpful guides when you want quick refreshers about how to accomplish specific tasks.

Part I

Learning the Basics

Includes

Introducing Harvard Graphics

Getting Started

Quick Start: Taking a Guided Tour
of Harvard Graphics

1

Introducing Harvard Graphics

Harvard Graphics is so versatile that the program can create a virtually unlimited array of custom charts. Even so, you may fall back on one of the program's popular, built-in business chart styles and color schemes. Harvard Graphics offers the freedom for you to quickly and easily base an eye-catching chart on a proven format.

This chapter presents an overview of the basic chart styles you can create with Harvard Graphics. In addition, Harvard Graphics introduces some of the advanced tasks you can perform, such as drawing and enhancing charts, creating slide shows and screenshows, and combining chart types on one page. In this chapter, you also learn about the benefits of Harvard Graphics and how the program stacks up against other graphics software packages on the market. Finally, you examine the Harvard Graphics approach to creating charts—an approach that makes Harvard Graphics easy and fun to use.

Making Text Charts

Text charts, covered in Chapter 4, make useful handouts or slides in a presentation when concepts are conveyed better with words than with pictures. Text charts can relate a presenter's key points or show lists of goals and objectives. Text charts also are ideal for making comparisons or for presenting the benefits and drawbacks of an issue.

Text charts can be simple and unadorned, or they can include numbered lists of items or bulleted points to emphasize the items on a list. Text charts also can contain two or three columns to help the viewer compare information side by side. Figure 1.1 shows a sample text chart used for eliciting contributions to a nonprofit organization.

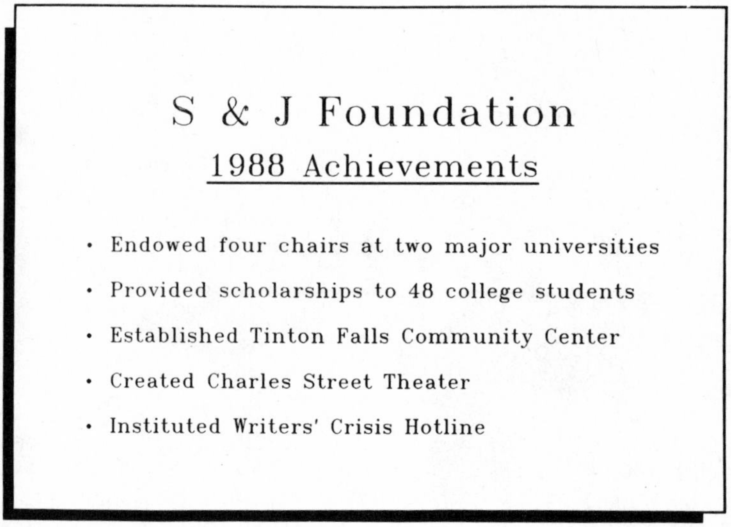

Fig. 1.1.

A sample text chart.

S & J Foundation
1988 Achievements

- Endowed four chairs at two major universities
- Provided scholarships to 48 college students
- Established Tinton Falls Community Center
- Created Charles Street Theater
- Instituted Writers' Crisis Hotline

Creating Graph Charts

Graph charts, covered in Chapters 5 and 6, come in a variety of familiar designs. They are ideal for conveying numeric information. *Bar charts* depict the relationships among discrete numbers, and *line charts* eloquently express trends. *Pie charts* and *column charts*, which show the breakdown of a total, also are popular.

Harvard Graphics provides other graph chart types. *Point charts*, known among statisticians as scattergrams, show the correlation between two sets of results. *Area charts* emphasize total quantities. *High/low/close charts* fulfill the needs of Wall Street watchers and other financial professionals by tracking the high, low, and closing prices of stocks and bonds and other financial instruments. High/low/close charts also can illustrate numeric measurements that have a high and low during an interval, such as temperature or barometric pressure.

With Harvard Graphics, you can create unlimited variations of these basic charts. By making changes such as altering the scale of a chart's axes or altering the bar style, you can create a never-ending variety of charts to satisfy any need. Figure 1.2 shows some of the basic Harvard Graphics chart types.

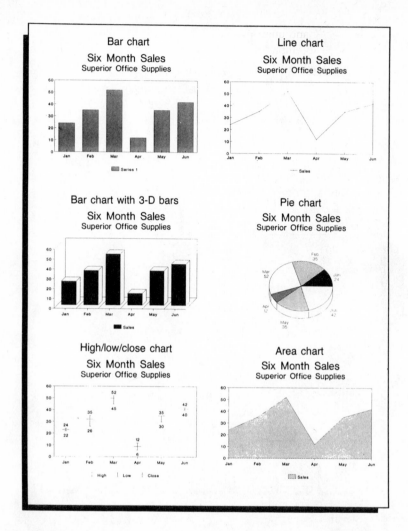

Fig. 1.2.

An assortment of Harvard Graphics graph charts.

With Harvard Graphics, you can chart numbers you have calculated, or you can enter raw data and instruct the program to perform calculations and graph the results. Harvard Graphics provides nearly two dozen mathematical and statistical calculations that you can use to make your data more meaningful. For statisticians, the statistical calculations Harvard Graphics performs are primarily linear, but a number of standard regression curves also are included. Calculating data with Harvard Graphics charts is covered in Chapter 7.

Creating Organization Charts

Keeping track of the ever-changing personnel in most companies is a task that only a computer can manage. Using the special *organization chart* feature of Harvard Graphics, described in Chapter 4, you can depict the reporting structure among employees or among the divisions of an organization.

With Harvard Graphics organization charts, setting up hierarchical diagrams with multiple levels and complex relationships is easy. You enter a list of managers, each manager's subordinates, and any staff assistants level by level until the entire division or organization is diagrammed. Figure 1.3 shows a typical organization chart for a small company or department.

Fig. 1.3.

A typical organization chart.

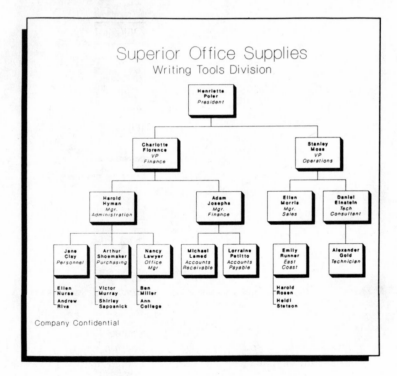

Drawing and Enhancing Charts

After you create a text or graph chart, you can embellish the chart by using two special Harvard Graphics features called *Draw/Annotate* and *Draw Partner*. Figure 1.4 shows a chart before and after the chart has been enhanced with

Draw/Annotate. You also can use Draw/Annotate to draw an illustration from scratch.

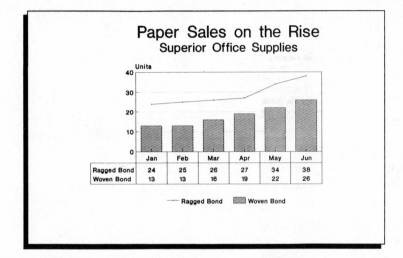

Fig. 1.4.

A chart before and after Draw/ Annotate was used.

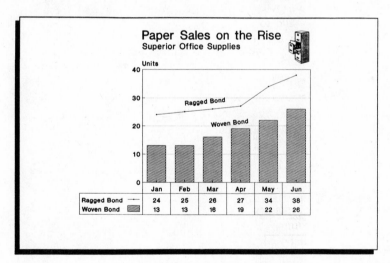

The Draw/Annotate feature, described in Chapter 9, provides you with a basic set of drawing tools. You can add lines, arrows, boxes, circles, and other shapes to a chart. With Draw/Annotate, you can move, copy, or resize any of the chart's components. You also can add text to comment on any aspect of the chart.

Perhaps the most useful feature of Draw/Annotate is its capacity to adorn charts with preexisting drawings, called *symbols*. You can use symbols to dress up charts and add meaning with pictures. You also can use symbols as the starting point from which to create your own custom graphics files for later use with desktop publishing programs. Harvard Graphics comes with a comprehensive starter set of symbols in a variety of libraries, each pertaining to a specific theme—buildings, cities, people, industry, and so on. You can add more symbols by creating your own symbols in Harvard Graphics or by purchasing additional symbol libraries from the makers of Harvard Graphics (Software Publishing Corporation) and from third-party companies that produce graphics files that you can import into Harvard Graphics.

For more sophisticated drawing capabilities, you can summon the special powers of Draw Partner, an attachment to Harvard Graphics that provides a variety of special drawing features. For example, with Draw Partner, you can rotate objects, add perspective, or zoom in for closer editing on a portion of a chart. Draw Partner is described in detail in Chapters 10, 11, and 12.

Creating Slide Shows

Most often, you create and reproduce charts one by one. Harvard Graphics, however, provides *slide shows* for reproducing or viewing charts a group at a time.

By collecting several charts into a slide show, you can display the charts one after another on the computer's screen or send them consecutively to an output device for reproduction. If you're planning to use the charts you create as part of a stand-up presentation, you can make practice cards for rehearsing your speech or cue cards for use at the podium. Practice cards can hold notes and comments about the charts in your presentation. You also can use slide shows to create screenshows.

Creating Screenshows

Many people use Harvard Graphics to produce only printed pages, overhead transparencies, and slides. But you can go beyond these commonplace tasks and create a dazzling desktop presentation called a *screenshow*.

Instead of using photographic slides, which are projected on a screen one after another, you can create an animated presentation on your computer screen, using television-like special effects to change from one chart to the next. At your disposal is an entire arsenal of wipes, fades, overlays, and weaves that provides spectacular transitions among images. For a boardroom meeting or small presentation, you can use a large-screen monitor to display your screenshow. For large audiences, you can project a screenshow onto a large screen with a high-resolution computer projector.

You even can use a screenshow to create a presentation that the viewer can control. A screenshow can display different segments based on the keystroke input of the viewer. Screenshows used in this fashion are ideal for demonstrations and sales presentations and even for rudimentary computer-based training. Slide shows and screenshows are covered in Chapter 16.

Mixing Chart Types on a Page

With Harvard Graphics, you can include more than one chart on each page or slide, allowing readers to compare charts easily. You also can prepare a handout of your slides with up to six charts on each page. In Harvard Graphics, a chart composed of two or more existing charts on a page is called a *multiple chart* (even if you're mixing chart types). After you create a multiple chart (see Chapter 15), you can pull the chart into Draw/Annotate to add text comments and arrows that point out the similarities among charts. Figure 1.5 shows a typical multiple chart.

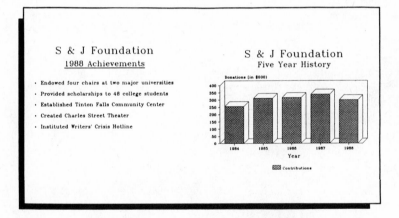

Fig. 1.5.

A typical multiple chart.

Examining the Benefits of Using Harvard Graphics

The flexibility of Harvard Graphics for creating top-quality presentation graphics is enough to make Harvard Graphics the leading business-graphics software for IBM-standard computers. But Harvard Graphics offers added benefits—elegance of design and ease of operation.

Harvard Graphics is designed to blend effortlessly into a preexisting computer setup, regardless of the combination of hardware in use. Harvard Graphics is well known for its remarkably broad selection of drivers for the bewildering array of printers, plotters, slide makers, graphics displays, and other output devices available. Unless you own truly obscure (and probably obsolete) equipment, Harvard Graphics should be ready to exercise the maximum capabilities of your graphics display and output devices.

Harvard Graphics also provides carefree compatibility with a variety of other software. To avoid retyping existing data into a chart, you easily can pull data from a 1-2-3 spreadsheet, an ASCII file, or the files of other Software Publishing Corporation products, such as PFS: Professional Plan. Harvard Graphics also directly imports and exports one of the most popular computer graphics file formats: Computer Graphics Metafiles (CGM). Popular desktop publishing software such as Xerox Ventura Publisher and Aldus PageMaker and graphical word processors such as Samna's Ami Professional can read CGM files directly. You can use Harvard Graphics to create the illustrations and graphs used in newsletters, brochures, and other documents. For software that does not accept CGM files, Harvard Graphics offers you a choice between two other output file formats: Encapsulated PostScript (EPS) files and Hewlett-Packard Graphics Language files.

These methods of interchanging files among software have in common their object-oriented graphics file formats. *Object-oriented graphics programs*, also known as vector-based graphics software, create images out of dozens, hundreds, or even thousands of individual lines, boxes, and curves. For example, a bar chart is composed of a tremendous number of individual lines, each forming a segment of one of the bars or one of the axes. Any text added to a chart, in its title or legend, for example, also is composed of objects that are combinations of curves and straight lines.

Paint programs, the alternative to object-oriented graphics programs, act on a representation of your display in the computer's memory. In this representation, called a *bit map*, each point on the screen (a *pixel*) corresponds to one computer "bit" of information. Each pixel is mapped to 1 bit—hence the name bit-mapped graphics. When drawing an image on-screen, bit-mapped graphics programs illuminate patterns of pixels in a specific shape. To draw a box, for example, a bit-mapped program illuminates a box-shaped pattern of pixels.

Object-oriented graphics programs, like Harvard Graphics, provide several benefits over bit-mapped graphics software. First, because all the figures on-screen are composed of individual objects, you can modify each object with ease. For example, if an arrow pointing to a chart needs adjustment, you can shorten or lengthen the arrow or change its position on-screen without affecting the chart's other components. With bit-mapped graphics, you need to turn off the pixels that form the arrow's shape by using an "eraser" tool. In the process, you easily may erase pixels that form part of another chart component underneath the arrow.

Object-oriented graphics also maintain their crisp resolution even if you vary the size of the overall chart or use a different output device. To increase the size of a bit-mapped image, a graphics program needs to add new pixels by calculating their position mathematically. For example, to lengthen a box by 20 percent, a bit-mapped program needs to add 20 percent more pixels, positioning them according to the program's calculations. A new, larger image is created from the existing image. Moreover, as a bit-mapped program increases the size of an image, the program thickens the lines of the image to magnify everything proportionally.

To lengthen the same box, an object-oriented program needs only to increase the length of the box's four lines by 20 percent. The object-oriented program's modification is precise, adding no distortion to the image. The new, longer lines maintain the same thickness as before, so that the lines look as thin and crisp as they did before the change. Figure 1.6 gives you a simple illustration of the difference between using these two approaches.

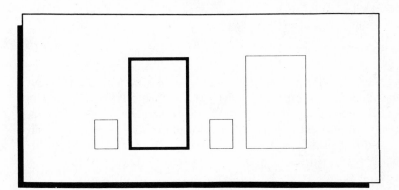

Fig. 1.6.

A box magnified by a bit-mapped program (left) and an object-oriented program (right).

Harvard Graphics offers other technical benefits you can read about in the chapters that follow. You learn that Harvard Graphics operates quickly. Harvard Graphics is designed to incorporate a quick and responsive feel, just as a sports car has been designed for power and agility. The menus and screens appear on-screen with a satisfying snap instead of the sluggishness of other graphics programs. In addition, the authors of Harvard Graphics designed its menus and program options while considering the ease of use. You can pick any of several methods available for selecting from a menu. As you work with Harvard Graphics, you can choose the method that is easiest and most convenient at the time.

Harvard Graphics also is impressive for its myriad of charting options. The program offers you a broad array of ready-made charts and graphs and enormous flexibility for tailoring its preexisting designs to your needs.

The people who designed Harvard Graphics knew good graphics design, and they incorporated their knowledge into the program. The built-in intelligence of Harvard Graphics has captured the imaginations of more users and reviewers than any other graphics program. Start a bar chart, for example, and Harvard Graphics chooses a color scheme, positions the legend, sizes the axes, and arranges the titles. The program also performs all these tasks with what appears to be unerring judgment. Thus, Harvard Graphics is a graphics tool and a graphics authority. In fact, one reviewer commented accurately that it is "hard to be tasteless" with Harvard Graphics.

This built-in, safety-net approach has two advantages. First, the graphics design feature can keep you from embarrassing yourself by creating a chart that is less than attractive. Second, this feature enables you to create a chart quickly because the program does much of the work.

To augment the capabilities Harvard Graphics provides, you can purchase six enhancements from Software Publishing Corporation: ScreenShow Utilities, Quick-Charts, Designer Galleries, US MapMaker, Business Symbols, and Military Symbols. Many of the capabilities of Quick Charts, Designer Galleries, and Screenshow Utilities are incorporated into the newest release, Harvard Graphics Version 2.3.

ScreenShow Utilities adds a capture program that can copy any screen display (even from another program) to a bit-mapped PCX-format file for incorporation into a screenshow. ScreenShow Utilities also provides methods for you to manage slide show files on disk and a tool to project Harvard Graphics slide shows easily and quickly without using Harvard Graphics. Quick-Charts and Designer Galleries offer popular predefined charts and templates that you can use by supplying your own data.

Designer Galleries provides 12 special, attractively designed, color-coordinated palettes not available in the standard Harvard Graphics package. US MapMaker enables you to create color-coded maps that can display financial or statistical data by region. You can display all the United States, select regions, and choose from 32,000 major cities and towns. Business Symbols provides more than 300 predrawn symbols grouped into 20 libraries. Military Symbols adds more than 200 military symbols (like aircraft and ships) in 15 libraries.

Learning about the Competition

Now that you know some of the background and benefits of the Harvard Graphics package, you may be interested in how the program stacks up against its competition. This section examines some of the other graphics software packages available on today's market.

Other Business Graphics Software

Although Harvard Graphics is one of a dozen or more business graphics packages, Harvard Graphics generally is regarded as the leader in the category. Even if another program handles one or another charting aspect with slightly more aplomb, Harvard Graphics outperforms its competitors with its well-rounded strengths and generous assortment of features.

Harvard Graphics' prime competitor is perhaps Freelance Plus from 1-2-3's progenitors, Lotus Development Corporation. Freelance Plus offers more typefaces for chart text than Harvard Graphics and a horizontal bar menu that mimics the well-known 1-2-3 menu system. But the Harvard Graphics user interface is more logical and, in our opinion, simpler to use. Furthermore, Harvard Graphics offers a wider variety of statistical functions and text and graph chart types than Freelance Plus, and Harvard Graphics' symbol libraries are far more diverse and attractive.

The other business graphics software offered by Lotus Development Corporation, Graphwriter II, excels in gathering data from a 1-2-3 spreadsheet and graphing the data visually. Graphwriter II also uses a highly automated approach to generating charts in volume. But Harvard Graphics offers Graphwriter-like data links to 1-2-3 charts as well, and Harvard Graphics surpasses Graphwriter's features that enable you to embellish charts and draw charts and graphics from scratch. You would need to use both Graphwriter and Freelance Plus to do all that Harvard Graphics does in one package.

Perhaps the most formidable competition in flexibility and ease of use are the new graphical charting programs that run under the Microsoft Windows graphical environment. Micrografx Charisma and Microsoft PowerPoint are two examples. Their presentations on-screen are highly visual. You can modify a graphical representation of a chart on-screen.

Windows, however, requires a significant amount of disk space to operate and a high-performance computer to run its graphics. With Windows, you should have at least an IBM AT-class computer with its fast 80286 microprocessor computer chip. Harvard Graphics runs as comfortably on a less expensive PC or XT as it does on a faster AT or even a fast 80386 computer. The only requirement

Harvard Graphics imposes is the use of a display system (a graphics card and monitor) capable of graphics. Such limited requirements enable you to set up a low-cost but effective graphics workstation.

Two other popular entrants into the business graphics software category are distinguished by their use of three-dimensional graphics to impart real pizzazz to a presentation. Boeing Graph and Enertronics' EnerGraphics enable you to graph numeric data in three dimensions by plotting information along a third axis rather than along the usual two axes offered by most graphing programs. As a result, the depth of bars or lines is a measure of the data they represent. The three-dimensional effect offered by Harvard Graphics adds the appearance of depth to objects on-screen to give them a more interesting appearance. In Harvard Graphics, the depth of bars or lines has no significance; data is still graphed on only two axes. For all the spectacular output these other packages can create, they are incapable of making plotters produce three-dimensional graphics (plotters, by nature, cannot reproduce 3-D graphics). Users with plotters, therefore, can create and reproduce two-dimensional graphics only; for two-dimensional graphics Harvard Graphics offers more options.

Harvard Graphics stacks up well against other programs dedicated to the task of creating business charts and graphs. Harvard Graphics also compares remarkably well with graphics software in several other categories, discussed next.

Draw Packages

Although most purchasers probably buy Harvard Graphics for its capacity to create business charts, many purchasers now also rely on the program's drawing capabilities. Before Harvard Graphics, the most popular method of freehand drawing on a computer was with "draw" programs, such as Windows Draw from Micrografx and GEM Draw from Digital Research. Draw programs offer the same object-oriented graphics offered by Harvard Graphics.

Harvard Graphics incorporates the essential elements of draw software in its Draw/Annotate and Draw Partner modules, which are accessible from the main menu. If you are purchasing graphics software to gain draw features, Harvard Graphics provides complete charting and desktop presentation capabilities as no-cost extras. If your goal is to produce business charts or desktop presentations, you will acquire superb draw capabilities in Harvard Graphics.

Spreadsheet Graphics

When 1-2-3 first appeared, one of its most valued attributes was the addition of database management and graphing capabilities to the electronic spreadsheet design introduced by VisiCalc. At the time, the ability to graph data in the same package in which you managed data sounded like a promising idea.

But the 1-2-3 graphics module paled in comparison to the dedicated graphics programs that soon appeared—some designed solely to create charts based on 1-2-3 spreadsheet data. These programs offered more graphics versatility and power than 1-2-3 (even 1-2-3 Releases 2.2 and 3.0) and created charts with far more style and appeal.

More recent spreadsheets, such as Microsoft Excel and Borland Quattro Pro, offer charting capabilities far superior to those that 1-2-3 delivers. Some of these spreadsheets' charts even compare favorably with the charts generated by the graph chart module of Harvard Graphics. But Harvard Graphics enables you to embellish these basic charts considerably by using the Draw/Annotate and Draw Partner features. With these two modules, you can adorn and transform bland charts that are simply communicative into stylish graphics that are truly expressive. Moreover, with Harvard Graphics you get complete text layout capabilities, described next.

Text Layout Packages

When software authors recognized that computers and printers were quickly replacing typewriters on corporate desks, they decided to create software that has one of the typewriter's more uncommon but indispensable features: the capacity to produce text pages that can be turned into overhead transparencies or slides.

A number of software packages dedicated to the task of word charting have appeared, but none are easier to use than the text charting capabilities of Harvard Graphics. Creating text charts in Harvard Graphics means that you can bring the charts into the Draw/Annotate portion of the program and add embellishments, eliminating the need to physically "cut and paste" pages to combine pictures and words.

With the incorporation of complete text charting capabilities into many business graphics programs, word charting software has become outmoded.

Slide Show Packages

Unlike word charting programs, slide show packages are growing in popularity. Slide show packages enable users to capture bit-mapped graphics images from the screens of other programs or to assemble the output files of other graphics software into fun desktop presentations. IBM's PC Storyboard kicked off the category with its simple paint program capabilities and rudimentary charting skills.

What truly distinguished PC Storyboard and distinguishes its current version, Storyboard Plus, is the capacity to create animated presentations that combine images and provide movie-like transitions from one screen to the next. PC Storyboard offers an entire arsenal of wipes, pans, fades, weaves, and other transition effects. Show Partner FX, another slide show presentation package, provides superior graphics capabilities and the same animation capabilities as PC Storyboard.

Harvard Graphics screenshows provide similar eye-catching special effects, but the images can be full-blown Harvard Graphics charts, with all their bells and whistles. If you have created bit-mapped graphics in paint programs, you can incorporate those graphics into a screenshow, perhaps as the background for a Harvard Graphics chart.

Understanding the Approach of Harvard Graphics

To better understand why people find Harvard Graphics so logically organized and easy to use, you should understand more about the Harvard Graphics approach to creating charts.

Every graphic that Harvard Graphics creates is called a chart. A *chart* is a screen of text, a screen of graphics, or a screen that combines both. You begin a new Harvard Graphics chart by entering text or numbers onto a data screen or by importing the data from another program. You can press the F2 (Draw Chart) function key to preview the simple chart Harvard Graphics creates automatically.

Inevitably, you will think of a few changes and additions to the appearance of the basic chart Harvard Graphics produces. If you are working with a text chart, you can make changes on the data screen you have filled in. If you are working with a graph chart, you choose the alterations you want by changing the selections on the chart's Titles & Options pages. Each graph chart type has its own set of options on its Titles & Options pages that governs the appearance of the chart. After you make changes on the Titles & Options pages, your chart can be far more informative, embellished with labels, legends, special formatting, and other additions. Charts carried to this stage are sophisticated and have the quality you expect in a professional business presentation. So far, you have done no actual drawing, but you have created professional-looking charts just by entering data and modifying the chart's appearance with the Titles & Options pages.

If you have the time and inclination to adorn your chart with more graphics, or if you need to highlight some aspect of the information that the chart conveys, you can pull a text or graphic chart into the special Draw/Annotate or Draw

Partner feature of Harvard Graphics. Of course, those of you who are truly artistic can skip the earlier steps and jump right to Draw/Annotate or Draw Partner to create a chart from scratch. Most people, however, use these two drawing programs to add lines, boxes, arrows, text comments, or predrawn graphics to a text or graphic chart.

Finally, you can send your chart to a printer, plotter, or slide maker. Or you can create shows that display your chart on-screen.

Using Harvard Graphics involves four principal activities:

❑ Making text charts

❑ Making graph charts

❑ Drawing new charts or annotating existing charts in Draw/Annotate or Draw Partner

❑ Producing output by reproducing charts on paper, on film, or on-screen

All other uses for Harvard Graphics embody some variation of one of these four activities. In fact, Harvard Graphics offers so many variations that it is the great chameleon of business graphics programs, blending inconspicuously into any environment. Put Harvard Graphics in a corporate art department and churn out professional slides and graphs. Use Harvard Graphics in a marketing department and generate superb sales presentations. Integrate Harvard Graphics into a desktop publishing workstation and serve up professional-quality illustrations and graphics for newsletters and brochures.

Before you finish reading this book, you will become expert at all four activities and you will be ready to discover your own variations. The makers of Harvard Graphics have done an extraordinary job of automating the type of artistry that once required the services of a trained professional. But Harvard Graphics, like any fine computer software, is an instrument that you must learn to use. Only after you have mastered the basics can you take advantage of the program's subtleties and nuances.

Chapter Summary

In this chapter, you have learned about the capabilities of Harvard Graphics. In the next chapter, "Getting Started," you learn important information about setting up, starting, and using Harvard Graphics. In Chapter 3, you take a comprehensive tour through the program.

2

Getting Started

Chapter 1 describes the benefits of using Harvard Graphics and some of the philosophies that underlie the program's design. This chapter provides much more pragmatic information—from how to install and start Harvard Graphics to how to navigate through the Harvard Graphics menu structure.

Harvard Graphics is highly regarded because of its simple, intuitive user interface. *User interface*, one of the computer vernacular's newest additions, refers to the methods a software package offers you to control its operation. Some software packages require that you use your keyboard's function keys to issue commands. Some programs provide menus of choices that appear on-screen. Harvard Graphics provides you with a combination of approaches to issue commands. You can use several techniques to tell Harvard Graphics what to do next. Later in this chapter, you learn about the various ways you can control Harvard Graphics. Which method you decide to use depends on your personal style.

This chapter also presents a detailed look at other aspects of the Harvard Graphics user interface, such as summoning help information to the screen. You learn some fundamentals that you will find helpful when joining the Harvard Graphics quick-start tour in the next chapter.

Installing Harvard Graphics

The complete Harvard Graphics 2.3 software system, ready for installation, comes on ten 5 1/4-inch disks or five 3 1/2-inch disks. You can use the INSTALL program on the disk labeled Disk #1. (If you are still using Harvard Graphics 2.13 or earlier, the INSTALL program is on the Utilities disk.)

Although you can run Harvard Graphics 2.13 and earlier versions on a computer without a hard disk, you must have a hard disk to run Harvard Graphics 2.3. In fact, you will find that being able to keep all your Harvard Graphics files readily accessible on a hard disk accelerates your work dramatically. Hard disks have become relatively inexpensive, so acquiring one is almost certainly worth the cost. Other program requirements are

- An IBM or compatible system
- At least 512K RAM, but 640K is recommended
- DOS 2.1 or later version
- An 80-column display with appropriate adapter

To start INSTALL, insert Disk #1 into drive A (or insert the Utilities disk if you are installing Harvard Graphics Version 2.13 or earlier), type *a:* at the C:\> prompt, and press Enter. Then type

INSTALL

When you start INSTALL, the program first asks which drive you want to hold the Harvard Graphics files. If you have more than one hard disk or a large hard disk with several partitions, you see a list of the available drives. If you have only drive C, you see only one choice.

Use the up- or down-arrow key to move the small rectangular pointer to the drive you want and then press Enter.

Harvard Graphics asks in which directory all its files should be installed. The default is the \HG directory (shown as \HG\). If you want to put Harvard Graphics in a different directory (for example, if you want to keep the old version of Harvard Graphics in \HG on your hard disk), you must backspace to delete the suggested directory name and then type a new directory name. Be sure to put a backslash before and after the directory name. If you want to install the program in a directory called \HG23, for example, type *hg23*\ and then press Enter. To accept the recommended directory name (\HG\), press Enter without changing it.

The INSTALL program displays a menu with six options. Use the up- and down-arrow keys to move the pointer to the option you want and then press Enter. The options available to you follow:

Option	Function
All Files Except VDI Devices	Installs the program files, tutorial files, and sample files but does not install the VDI device files
Program Files Only	Installs only the files needed to get Harvard Graphics 2.3 up and running

Option	Function
Tutorial Only	Installs only the tutorial files
Sample Files Only	Installs only the sample files (shown in the Harvard Graphics manual)
VDI Device Files	Copies the VDI files to your hard disk but does not modify the CONFIG.SYS or AUTOEXEC.BAT file. To properly install the VDI files, you must make these modifications manually. Later in this chapter, you receive information about installing the VDI files
Exit	Stops the INSTALL program and returns to the DOS prompt

If you are installing Harvard Graphics 2.3 for the first time, you should select All Files Except VDI Devices. If you are using an installed version of Harvard Graphics 2.3 that is missing certain files, you can run the INSTALL program to copy just the category of files you want (only the VDI device files, for example).

When you select an option from this menu, Harvard Graphics starts the installation process. The program tells you each time you need to insert a different disk into the disk drive. To stop the INSTALL program while it is working, press the Esc key.

If you are using Harvard Graphics 2.13 or an earlier version, you can run the INSTALL program on the Utilities disk. The INSTALL program copies all the Harvard Graphics files to the hard disk directory you specify.

The INSTALL program makes Harvard Graphics do most of the work of setting itself up on your computer's disk drives.

When you install Harvard Graphics, you may want to create a separate directory in which to store the actual charts you create. By setting up a separate directory for your work—C:\HGDATA, for example—you can use DOS commands to back up or archive your data files easily. In addition, Harvard Graphics can quickly present a list of the charts you create, because the program does not need to search through as many files, including its own program files, to pull out your charts.

To create a special directory for your work, follow these steps:

1. Make sure that the DOS prompt is on-screen.

2. Type *cd * and press Enter to be sure that you are at your hard disk's root directory.

3. Type *md \hgdata* and press Enter to create a directory for your work. (If you want to name the directory something other than HGDATA, type the name you want after the backslash.)

Figure 2.1 shows how your screen appears as you carry out this sequence of steps. After you create a directory, the screen doesn't appear any different, but a new directory now exists to store your data files.

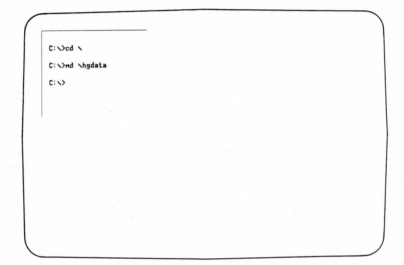

Fig. 2.1.

Creating a directory for your work.

```
C:\>cd \
C:\>md \hgdata
C:\>
```

Placing your data files in a subdirectory of the Harvard Graphics program directory provides an additional measure of protection from the hands of inexperienced DOS users. By hiding your work two directory levels deep, you keep others from accidentally wiping out your work because they cannot go near your files in their day-to-day use.

To make a subdirectory for your work under the Harvard Graphics directory, follow these steps:

1. Make sure that you are at the DOS prompt after installing Harvard Graphics with the INSTALL utility.

2. Type *cd \hg* and press Enter to change to the Harvard Graphics directory. (If you chose a name other than \HG for your Harvard Graphics directory, substitute that name.)

3. Type *md \hgdata* and press Enter to create a directory for your work called HGDATA under the current directory (C:\HG).

4. Type *cd * and press Enter to return to the root directory.

Figure 2.2 shows how your screen appears as you carry out this sequence of steps.

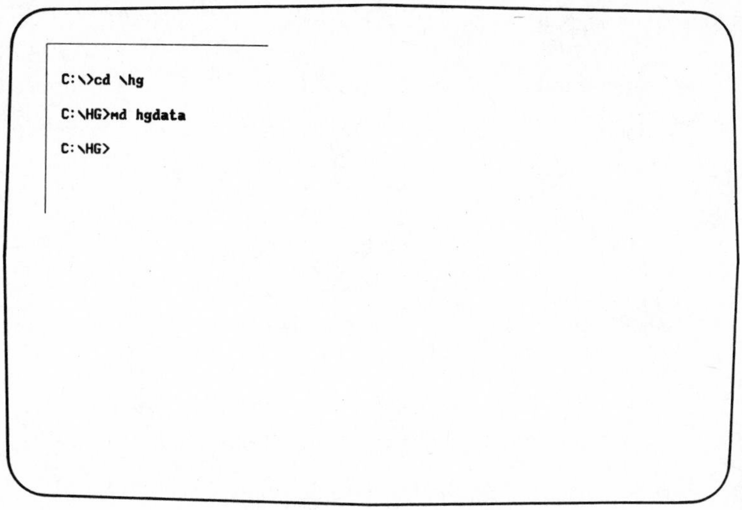

```
C:\>cd \hg
C:\HG>md hgdata
C:\HG>
```

Fig. 2.2.

Creating a subdirectory for your work.

If you set up \HGDATA under C:\HG, the new directory name is C:\HG\HGDATA. If you choose to place all your charts in a special directory, such as C:\HGDATA or C:\HG\HGDATA, you should modify the Harvard Graphics defaults so that the program always uses that directory to retrieve files or to save new files. To specify a directory as the default data directory, see the section called "Setting Up Defaults" later in this chapter.

Certain output devices require that you install special Virtual Device Interface (VDI) files. The VDI is special software written to manage the exchange of data between software like Harvard Graphics and certain output devices. If your output device requires the VDI, its operating instructions will say so. You also need to carry out the VDI installation if you plan to create Computer Graphics Metafile (CGM) files for export to other graphics programs or to desktop publishing software. CGM files are discussed in Chapter 9.

Setting up the VDI device files is an option of the INSTALL program. If you are just starting with Harvard Graphics, you probably do not need the VDI files installed yet. If you are a Harvard Graphics veteran, you can return to the INSTALL program later and select VDI Device Files from the list of available files to install.

After you run the INSTALL program and select VDI Device Files to install, the INSTALL program automatically sets up a VDI directory under the directory in which you installed the Harvard Graphics program files. If you installed the program files in \HG, for example, the VDI files are copied to \HG\VDI.

Next, you must edit the CONFIG.SYS file in the root directory of your boot disk. To install the VDI device drivers, add two lines to the end of the

CONFIG.SYS file. These two lines depend on the VDI hardware you have. Use the information in the list that follows to determine the correct two lines. If the VDI files are installed in a directory other than C:\HG\VDI, type the correct directory name instead.

VDI Device	Lines Added to CONFIG.SYS
AST TurboLaser	device=c:\hg\vdi\ll.sys
	device=c:\hg\vdi\gsscgi.sys
Bell & Howell Color Digital Imager IV and Quintar 1080	device=c:\hg\vdi\bellhowl.sys
	device=c:\hg\vdi\gsscgi.sys
CalComp ColorMaster	device=c:\hg\vdi\clrmstr.sys
	device=c:\hg\vdi\gsscgi.sys
Lasergraphics PFR and LFT	device=c:\hg\vdi\ll.sys
	device=c:\hg\vdi\gsscgi.sys
Matrix PCR, QCR, and TT200	device=c:\hg\vdi\mtxscodl.sys
	device=c:\hg\vdi\gsscgi.sys
Metafiles	device=c:\hg\vdi\meta.sys
	device=c:\hg\vdi\gsscgi.sys

To export CGM files, for example, you must include in your CONFIG.SYS file the two lines listed with Metafiles in the preceding list.

In the \VDI subdirectory, you will find a sample CONFIG.SYS file; you can copy this file to the root directory of your hard disk and then edit it according to the preceding information.

Advanced users should note that the VDI device drivers occupy as much as 60K of memory, depending on which drivers you use. The Harvard Graphics program requires 420K of memory to run. Therefore, 480K of memory is needed for the program and the VDI device drivers. Some computers—especially those with network device drivers loaded—may not have enough memory to have both the network drivers and the VDI device files loaded. In this case, you must create two CONFIG.SYS files—one with the network device drivers and one with the VDI device drivers. Use one CONFIG.SYS or the other, depending on whether you want to use a VDI output device or work on the network.

Users of 80386 computers may be able to use an 80386 support program that can run certain device drivers in high RAM, above the 640K mark. QEMM and 386-to-the-Max are two examples of such programs.

Starting Harvard Graphics

After you install Harvard Graphics, you can start the program by changing to the directory that contains Harvard Graphics and typing *hg*. Assuming that you have a hard disk, follow these instructions when you see the C:\> or C> DOS prompt:

1. Type *cd \hg* and press Enter to change to the Harvard Graphics directory.

2. Type *hg* and press Enter to start Harvard Graphics.

Note: You can use upper- or lowercase letters or a combination of the two when typing commands.

Those of you who know DOS well may prefer to set up a batch file that changes to the data directory and then loads Harvard Graphics from its own directory. Assuming that the data directory is C:\HGDATA and the Harvard Graphics directory is C:\HG, such a batch file may look like the following:

```
ECHO OFF        ;Turns off DOS echo
CD \HGDATA      ;Changes to the HGDATA directory
C:\HG\HG        ;Loads HG from the C:\HG directory
CD \            ;Returns to the root directory after you quit ;
                Harvard Graphics
```

The comments to the right, preceded by semicolons, are optional. The Harvard Graphics opening screen, shown in figure 2.3, leaves little doubt about whether you started the program successfully. After the opening screen appears, the Harvard Graphics main menu appears (see fig. 2.4).

Fig. 2.3.

The Harvard Graphics opening display.

Fig. 2.4.

The Harvard Graphics main menu.

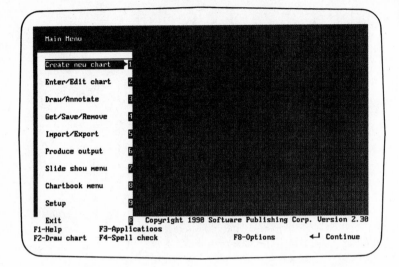

```
Main Menu

  Create new chart      1

  Enter/Edit chart      2

  Draw/Annotate         3

  Get/Save/Remove       4

  Import/Export         5

  Produce output        6

  Slide show menu       7

  Chartbook menu        8

  Setup                 9

  Exit                  0    Copyright 1990 Software Publishing Corp. Version 2.30
F1-Help         F3-Applicatioos
F2-Draw chart   F4-Spell check              F8-Options       ↵ Continue
```

Using the Harvard Graphics Menus

User interfaces of many other programs offer only one method for you to choose program commands. You use the arrow keys to pick an on-screen option, select from a menu by pressing the number corresponding to your choice, or press a function key to run a command. With Harvard Graphics menus, you can use a combination of all these techniques, and you can decide which techniques to use as you work.

After you pick a menu option, you can press Esc to return to the main menu. Then you can try any of the following approaches:

❑ *Selecting with the arrow keys.* Move the highlight up and down the menu until your choice is highlighted. Then press Enter.

❑ *Selecting with the space bar.* Press the space bar to move the highlight down the list and then press Enter to select an option. If you continue to press the space bar, the highlight cycles back to the top of the menu.

❑ *Selecting with numbers/letters.* Press the number (or letter) to the right of each menu option. With this approach, you don't need to press Enter after selecting a menu option.

❑ *Selecting with the first letter of the menu option.* Press the first letter of the menu option you want to choose and then press Enter. If more than one option share the same first character, press the same key again to move to the next option with the same first letter.

As you work with Harvard Graphics, you will find a surprising intelligence at work in its menus. When you first start Harvard Graphics, for example, the highlight is positioned on the Create New Chart option because that option is the next logical choice. After you retrieve a chart you have already made, the highlight is positioned on the Enter/Edit Chart option. Most Harvard Graphics menus are in the same vertical list format as the main menu.

Most Harvard Graphics screens also include a separate horizontal menu of function key choices across the bottom of the screen. Each function key option includes a one- or two-word reminder of that key's purpose. As you work with Harvard Graphics, you will see that the F1-Help option nearly always calls up help information and the F2-Draw Chart option nearly always previews the current chart on-screen. But most other function key options perform only short-stint jobs, such as setting the size and placement of text or changing from one file directory to another. What a function key does and, therefore, what the menu at the bottom of the screen shows, depends on the current activity you are performing in Harvard Graphics.

Using a Mouse

If you have a mouse, you have even more ways to use Harvard Graphics menus. By moving the highlight with the mouse and pressing the left mouse button, you can select from among menu options. Pressing the left button is equivalent to pressing the Enter key. To back out of a menu and return to the preceding menu, you can press the right mouse button. Pressing the right mouse button is equivalent to pressing the Esc key.

To choose from among the function key choices at the bottom of the screen, you can press both mouse buttons simultaneously; then highlight a function key choice and press the left mouse button. Pressing both mouse buttons together switches between choosing from the vertical menu on-screen and choosing from the horizontal function key menu at the bottom of the screen. Here is a summary:

Mouse Operation	Keyboard Equivalent
Left button	Enter key
Right button	Esc key
Both buttons	Toggle to/from the function key menu

When you learn about using the Options pages, you will find that moving the mouse cursor off the top or bottom of the screen moves you to the preceding or next Options page.

Navigating through Harvard Graphics

By examining the Harvard Graphics main menu, you can get a sense of how the program is organized and how the task of creating business presentations flows logically.

Everything you do in Harvard Graphics starts at the main menu. After you leave the main menu by selecting one of its options, you may not return until you finish creating a chart, assembling a slide show, printing a series of charts, or performing any of the other tasks Harvard Graphics makes possible.

Take a look at the main menu and notice that its entries are arranged top to bottom in order of their frequency of use. Because creating charts is the task you probably carry out most frequently, the Create New Chart option is positioned at the top of the list. The task you perform least often is setting the program's defaults, and the Setup option is located at the bottom of the list.

Choosing the Create New Chart option from the main menu takes you to the Create New Chart menu, which offers a choice from among a variety of chart types. Although this list looks bewildering at first, the list holds only two basic chart types: *text charts* (text and organization charts) to communicate concepts and textual facts and *graph charts* (pie, bar/line, area, and high/low/close charts) to convey numeric information. The other three options, Multiple Charts, From Chartbook, and Clear Values, are for advanced features covered in later chapters.

Choosing the Enter/Edit Chart option enables you to make changes to the current chart in your computer's memory—usually the last chart you were working on in the current Harvard Graphics session. If you just started Harvard Graphics, you need to create a chart or retrieve (or "get") a preexisting chart from disk by first using the Get/Save/Remove option from the main menu.

After you finish a text or graph chart and save it on disk, you can bring the chart into a special Harvard Graphics mode called Draw/Annotate by choosing the Draw/Annotate option from the main menu. Draw/Annotate mode enables you to embellish your chart by adding hand-drawn graphics, text, or symbols from a library of drawings already created for you. Also, you can start at Draw/Annotate with a blank screen and draw your own chart from scratch. You also can pull your chart into Draw Partner for more sophisticated drawing and annotation. Draw Partner is not on the main menu, however. You get to Draw Partner by pressing F3 (Applications) and then selecting Draw Partner or by pressing Ctrl-D.

The next two main menu options, Import/Export and Produce Output, provide facilities for you to manage the flow of data into and out of Harvard Graphics. By choosing Import/Export, you can bring data into Harvard Graphics from other programs and create special output files to transfer Harvard Graphics charts to other software, such as desktop publishing programs. By choosing Produce Output, you can reproduce your charts on paper or on film.

Choosing the Slide Show Menu option or Chartbook Menu option gives you access to two special Harvard Graphics features. *Slide shows* enable you to create on-screen presentations called *screenshows* or send sets of charts to an output device, such as a printer, plotter, or film recorder, for reproduction. *Chartbooks* enable you to organize Harvard Graphics templates—files that you create to hold the formats for your standard charts.

Setup is the final option on the main menu (other than Exit, which ends Harvard Graphics and returns you to the DOS prompt). By choosing Setup, you can specify a variety of important settings, such as the type of output device you will use to print your charts, the type of graphics display you have, and the color palette used by your video card and slide maker. You also can set standard characteristics for all your charts, such as whether they are oriented horizontally or vertically on the page. The next section discusses the Setup options in detail.

Using Setup

Before you begin working in earnest, you should set up Harvard Graphics for your needs and for the particular combination of equipment and DOS directories you are using. You can set up these defaults by using Setup on the main menu. When you select Setup, the Setup menu appears (see fig. 2.5).

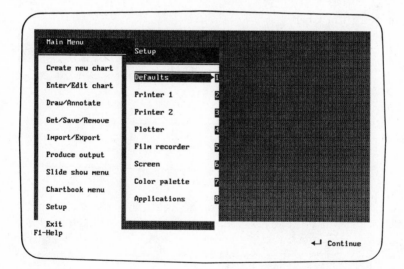

Fig. 2.5.

The Setup menu.

The Setup menu enables you to inform Harvard Graphics about the types of hardware you will use for this session and future Harvard Graphics sessions. From the Setup menu, you can specify the brand of output device you will use to reproduce your charts, the type of graphics display you have, and the variety of colors —called the *color palette*—used by your charts. You also can set up a special Applications menu so that you can start other programs from within Harvard Graphics.

This section describes all the Setup options and covers setting up Harvard Graphics for your equipment.

Setting Up Defaults

The Defaults option is the most important option on the Setup menu. When you select Defaults, the Default Settings screen appears (see fig. 2.6). The options on the Default Settings screen enable you to set certain starting conditions for all subsequent charts, such as the disk directory for chart storage, the orientation for charts (vertical or horizontal), and the typefaces used for chart text.

Fig. 2.6.

The Default Settings screen.

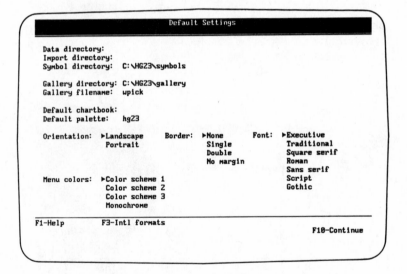

Note: If you change the defaults according to the instructions that follow and find that they don't "take" (the next time you load Harvard Graphics, the defaults are back to their original settings), you must reinstall Harvard Graphics from the disks. This condition indicates that Harvard Graphics has been moved from one directory to another on your hard disk. Therefore, Harvard Graphics no longer knows where to look for the configuration information you updated when you changed the defaults. To move the Harvard Graphics program files, you must delete them from their original directory and reinstall them in a new directory.

When you move your data files to the new directory, be sure to copy the file HG.DIR to the new directory, too. This file holds a table of contents and the descriptions you supplied for the data files on your disk.

Changing the Data Directory

Unless you specify otherwise, Harvard Graphics saves all the new charts you create in the same directory that holds the Harvard Graphics program. If your hard disk is drive C, that directory is probably C:\HG. By specifying a special data directory to store your work, you can instruct Harvard Graphics to save new charts in that directory. When you tell the program to "get" a chart (retrieve a chart that already has been created), the program also looks in that special directory.

Before you specify a new data directory for charts, that directory already must exist on your hard disk. You can create a directory by using the Make Directory (MD) DOS command or by using any of the popular disk management utilities that enable you to manage the files and directories on your hard disk. See "Installing Harvard Graphics" earlier in this chapter for a simple procedure to set up a directory for your work.

To specify a different default data directory, follow these steps:

1. Select Setup from the main menu.

2. Select Defaults from the Setup menu. The cursor is positioned next to the Data Directory prompt. Unless you already specified a different data directory, this entry is blank.

3. Type the name of the new directory for your charts—*c:\hg\hgdata*, for example—and press Enter.

Now you can make more changes to the Default Settings screen by pressing Tab to move from field to field, or you can return to the main menu by pressing F10 (Continue).

Specifying an Import Directory

When you start to build graph charts with numeric information, you will learn that you can import data from the files of other software—from a 1-2-3 worksheet or an ASCII file on your hard disk, for example. By using the Import Directory setting on the Default Settings screen, you can specify the directory in which Harvard Graphics always looks for an import data file.

To enter a default import directory, move the cursor to the Import Directory prompt by pressing the Tab key, type the appropriate entry, and press Enter.

If you regularly import data from Lotus worksheets, for example, and you keep all worksheets in a directory called C:\LOTUS, you can enter *c:\lotus* at the Import Directory prompt. When you import data into a graph chart, you can override the current Import Directory settings. But by providing defaults, you can instruct Harvard Graphics to suggest the most likely directory candidate and save yourself a little time and energy.

Setting the Symbol Directory

When you first install Harvard Graphics 2.3, the INSTALL program copies all the Harvard Graphics symbols to a special subdirectory. The INSTALL program also enters the name of that directory at the Symbol Directory prompt. If you move your symbols to another disk or directory, perhaps on a disk with more free space, you should modify the entry here to tell Harvard Graphics where to find its symbols. Modify the entry by moving the cursor next to the Symbol Directory prompt and typing a new path name, complete with the drive name. If your symbols are in D:\HGSYMBOL, for example, type *d:\hgsymbol* after the Symbol Directory prompt and then press Enter.

Setting the Gallery Directory

The Harvard Graphics 2.3 INSTALL program also installs a gallery of predefined charts in a special subdirectory. That subdirectory is shown after the Gallery Directory prompt. The default gallery (WPICK) is shown after the Gallery Filename prompt. You probably do not need to change the Gallery Directory and Gallery Filename entries, unless you use the Quick-Charts add-on program, which enables you to create your own galleries in a different directory. Then you will need to enter the directory in which you have saved the Quick-Charts galleries and the gallery file names.

Selecting the Chartbook To Open

By entering a chartbook name after Default Chartbook, you can have Harvard Graphics open a specific chartbook each time the program starts. *Chartbooks* are special Harvard Graphics files that store collections of preformatted charts, called *templates*. You will find detailed information about templates and chartbooks in Chapter 8. If you haven't created a chartbook yet, leave the Default Chartbook entry blank.

After you do create a chartbook that you want Harvard Graphics to open at the beginning of each session, move the cursor to the Default Chartbook prompt and enter the name of the chartbook to open. Harvard Graphics always looks for the chartbook in the data directory you specified on the first line of the Default Settings screen.

Setting the Default Palette

Harvard Graphics 2.3 comes with a variety of attractively coordinated color schemes, called *palettes*, for your charts. After you install the program, the default palette is HG23.PAL. You can select a different palette from the Setup menu for the current working session, or you can cycle through all the available palettes and view them on-screen when you create a chart from the Gallery. You can find information about choosing a palette for a new chart in Chapters 4 and 5.

Setting Defaults for Orientation, Border, and Font

The next three entries on the Default Settings screen enable you to establish three important starting settings for all future charts. Unless you choose a setting that differs from one of these defaults when you actually create a chart, Harvard Graphics uses these settings for all new charts.

Orientation

By establishing a default chart orientation, you can determine whether the new charts appear horizontally or vertically on the page. Figure 2.7 illustrates the difference between landscape and portrait orientation.

The Landscape option produces a chart sideways on a page. Landscape is appropriate for many printed charts and graphs and for displaying charts on-screen. Landscape is especially useful if you intend to create slides that are oriented horizontally. Unless you change the setup default when you first use Harvard Graphics, the program is preset to produce all charts in landscape orientation.

The Portrait option produces a chart vertically on a page. Portrait is particularly appropriate for text charts designed for printed handouts.

To set the default orientation, press the Tab key repeatedly until the cursor moves to the Orientation prompt on the Default Settings screen. The entry with the small pointer to its left is the current setting. Because Landscape is the initial Harvard Graphics default, the pointer should be just to the left of the Landscape option. To move the pointer to the next entry, press the space bar, press the first

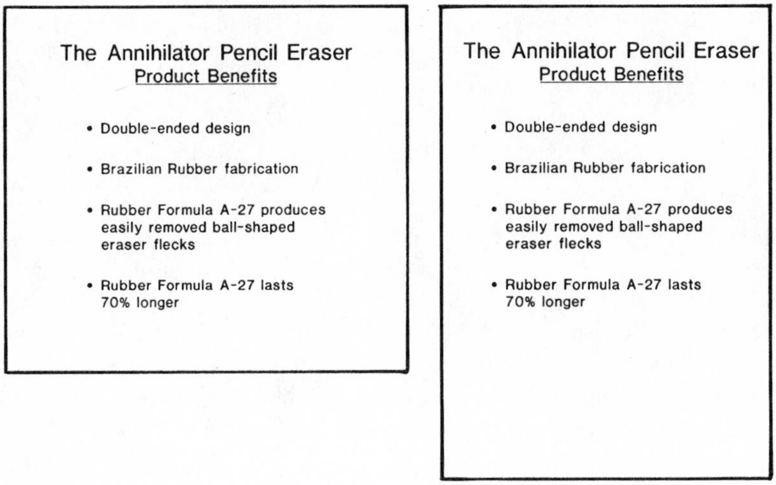

The Annihilator Pencil Eraser
<u>Product Benefits</u>

- Double-ended design

- Brazilian Rubber fabrication

- Rubber Formula A-27 produces
  easily removed ball-shaped
  eraser flecks

- Rubber Formula A-27 lasts
  70% longer

The Annihilator Pencil Eraser
<u>Product Benefits</u>

- Double-ended design

- Brazilian Rubber fabrication

- Rubber Formula A-27 produces
  easily removed ball-shaped
  eraser flecks

- Rubber Formula A-27 lasts
  70% longer

Fig. 2.7.

*Landscape and
Portrait chart
orientations.*

letter of the entry, or use the up- and down-arrow keys. When the correct entry is highlighted, press Tab or Enter to move to the next setting, or press F10 (Continue) to return to the Setup menu.

When you create a chart, you can decide to override the default orientation setting by pressing F8 (Options). Information about the F8-Options selection is provided later in this chapter.

Border

With Harvard Graphics, you can add a single- or double-line border around each chart or include no border at all. Both borders are illustrated in figure 2.8. A border is a box that encloses a chart, adding accent. The initial default is for no borders. You may choose to add a single- or double-line border by pressing Tab to move the cursor to the Border option and selecting an option by using the space bar, pressing the first character of the option, or using the up- and down-arrow keys to highlight the option.

A special option available in Harvard Graphics 2.3, No Margin, instructs Harvard Graphics to print each chart as large on the page as the printer permits. Most printers provide their own small margin around the page, however. No Margin works only with charts printed on 8 1/2-by-11-inch paper; No Margin doesn't work with VDI devices or plotters.

When you begin creating charts, you will learn that you can preview charts on-screen by pressing F2 (Draw Chart). When you preview a chart with a border, the border does not appear on-screen. To see the border, you must preview the

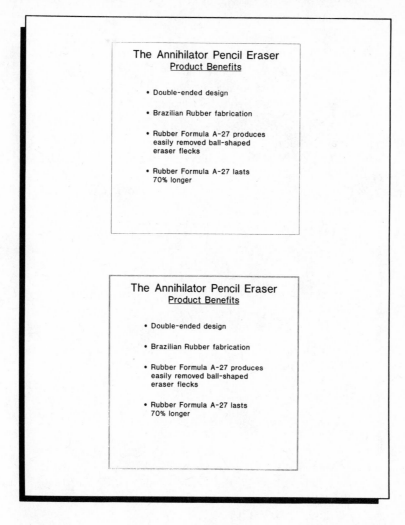

Fig. 2.8.

A single- and double-line border.

chart just before you print the chart by choosing Produce Output from the main menu and then pressing F2 (Preview). More information about printing is in Chapter 9.

Even though you have established a default on the Default Settings screen, you can override your choice for a border when you actually create a chart. To override your choice, press F8 (Options), which is discussed later in this chapter.

Font

Normally, Harvard Graphics enables you to use only one font for the text in each chart. A *font* is a particular style of character. You may be more familiar with the term *typeface*, but the two terms are interchangeable in Harvard Graphics. Harvard Graphics provides seven different fonts, illustrated in figure 2.9. The initial default font is Executive.

To choose another font for all text on future charts, move the cursor to the list of possible fonts and choose from among them by using whichever selection method you prefer. To confirm your selection, press F10 (Continue) or press Tab to move the cursor to the Menu Colors option at the bottom of the page.

Fig. 2.9.

The seven Harvard Graphics fonts.

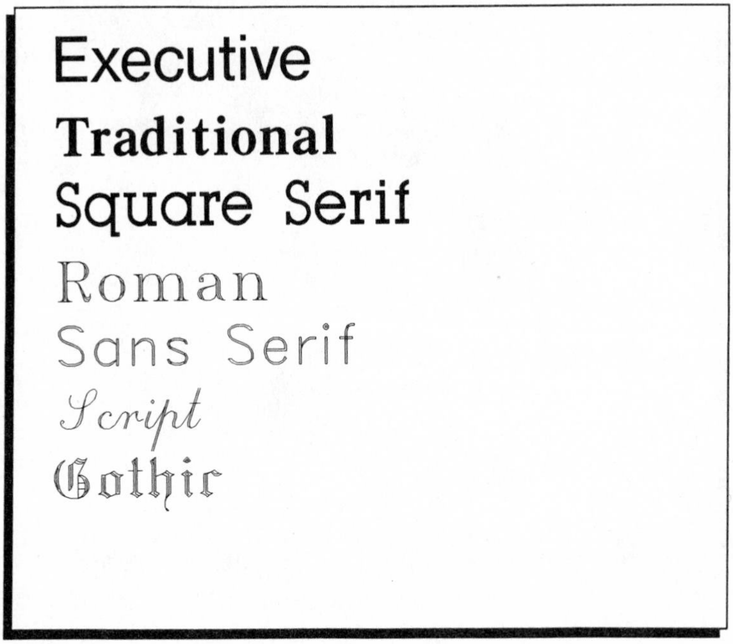

Executive
Traditional
Square Serif
Roman
Sans Serif
Script
Gothic

When you are ready to create a chart, you can select a font other than the default font by pressing F8 (Options).

Setting a Menu Color Scheme

Even if you have trouble color-coordinating the outfits you wear, you should be able to achieve a pleasing combination of menu colors on-screen, because Harvard Graphics enables you to choose from only three tastefully selected menu color schemes other than monochrome. These color schemes are for the Harvard Graphics menus only. They do not affect the colors in the charts.

To choose a color scheme, move the cursor to the Menu Colors prompt at the bottom of the Default Settings screen by pressing the Tab key repeatedly. Then select the option you want and press Enter. You see the effect of the change as soon as you press F10 to return to the Setup menu. Of course, when you leave Harvard Graphics, the screen reverts to its original colors.

You may find that Monochrome is the preferred setting, if you use a monochrome monitor with a color/graphics card. Some of the earlier COMPAQ computers use this combination.

Setting International Formats

Harvard Graphics 2.3 provides an easy method for you to set defaults for the date, time, punctuation, and currency symbols that are appropriate for the country or for charts destined for a particular country. As you install Harvard Graphics, you are asked to select a country from a list. Harvard Graphics then uses settings that suit that country. For example, many European countries customarily put the day number before the month number in a date abbreviation so that June 12, for example, is written 12/6. In the United States, 12/6 is December 6. You can adjust for these differences by setting the proper international format.

To change the defaults later, press F3 (Intl Formats) when you are working on the Default Settings screen. (You access the Default Settings screen by selecting Setup from the main menu and then Defaults from the Setup menu.) Then use the Tab key to move from setting to setting and press the space bar to select the proper setting.

The Year Format and Date Format options determine the order of the month and year numbers and the month and day numbers, respectively (6/12 or 12/6 and 5/31 or 31/5).

The Date Separator option determines the punctuation symbol placed between dates (01/01/90, 01.02.90, or 01-02-90).

The Thousands Separator option determines the punctuation used within numbers of thousands (2,630.24 or 2.630,24 or 2 630,24).

The Currency Symbol option enables you to enter a symbol other than $ for use in the axis labels and data tables. To specify British pounds, press and hold down the Alt key while typing *156* on the numeric keypad. For the yen, press Alt-157, and for the franc, press Alt-159.

The Currency Position option determines where the currency symbol is placed in relation to the currency amount—immediately before or after, or one space before or after ($195, 195$, $ 195, or 195 $).

Specifying Hardware Options

Harvard Graphics supports a wide variety of output devices and video options, but the program does not know what you have attached to your computer unless you tell it. The next four options—Printer 1, Printer 2, Plotter, and Film Recorder—on the Setup menu enable you to configure Harvard Graphics properly for the particular combination of hardware you use.

Your system may use a standard dot-matrix or laser printer to produce text and a color printer for graphics. You can configure printer 1 and printer 2 separately, if you have two different types of printer connected to your computer. When you print a chart, you can specify which of the two printers Harvard Graphics should prepare output for.

To configure Harvard Graphics for any combination of two printers, a plotter, and a film recorder, follow this approach for each device:

1. From the Setup menu, select the hardware device for which you want to set a configuration.

2. On the setup screen that appears, use the arrow keys to highlight the choice that matches the make and model of your equipment. Figure 2.10 shows the Printer 1 Setup screen. On some computer screens, you cannot see highlighting properly. If your choice does not become highlighted on your computer's screen, you can look at the bottom of the screen to see your current choice.

3. Press F10 to continue.

4. From the Parallel/Serial overlay that appears next (see fig. 2.11), choose options according to the type of printer connection you are using. Then press Enter.

If you are communicating with an output device through a standard parallel printer port, choose the appropriate port (LPT1, LPT2, or LPT3). If you are communicating with an output device through the serial port, you need to specify whether the port is COM1 or COM2, and you need to select appropriate communications parameters (baud rate, parity, data bits, and stop bits). The default communications parameters probably work with your serial output device, but you should check the device's user's manual for specific recommendations.

If your printer or plotter communicates with Harvard Graphics through the Virtual Device Interface (VDI), a communications protocol that interprets between graphics software and certain hardware, you do not see the Parallel/Serial overlay when you select VDI Printer or VDI Plotter and press F10. Your installation is not yet complete. You need to set up the VDI device driver provided with Harvard Graphics. If you are using Harvard Graphics 2.13, you can set up the VDI

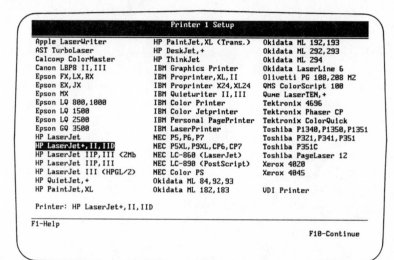

Fig. 2.10.

The Printer 1 Setup screen.

```
                         Printer 1 Setup
Apple LaserWriter        HP PaintJet,XL (Trans.)  Okidata ML 192,193
AST TurboLaser           HP DeskJet,+             Okidata ML 292,293
Calcomp ColorMaster      HP ThinkJet              Okidata ML 294
Canon LBP8 II,III        IBM Graphics Printer     Okidata LaserLine 6
Epson FX,LX,RX           IBM Proprinter,XL,II     Olivetti PG 108,208 M2
Epson EX,JX              IBM Proprinter X24,XL24  QMS ColorScript 100
Epson MX                 IBM Quieturiter II,III   Qume LaserTEN,+
Epson LQ 800,1000        IBM Color Printer        Tektronix 4696
Epson LQ 1500            IBM Color Jetprinter     Tektronix Phaser CP
Epson LQ 2500            IBM Personal PagePrinter Tektronix ColorQuick
Epson GQ 3500            IBM LaserPrinter         Toshiba P1340,P1350,P1351
HP LaserJet              NEC P5,P6,P7             Toshiba P321,P341,P351
HP LaserJet+,II,IID      NEC P5XL,P9XL,CP6,CP7    Toshiba P351C
HP LaserJet IIP,III <2Mb NEC LC-860 (LaserJet)    Toshiba PageLaser 12
HP LaserJet IIP,III      NEC LC-890 (PostScript)  Xerox 4020
HP LaserJet III (HPGL/2) NEC Color PS             Xerox 4045
HP QuietJet,+            Okidata ML 84,92,93
HP PaintJet,XL           Okidata ML 182,183       VDI Printer

Printer: HP LaserJet+,II,IID

F1-Help
                                               F10-Continue
```

Fig. 2.11.

The Parallel/Serial overlay.

```
                         Printer 1 Setup
Apple LaserWriter        HP PaintJet,XL (Trans.)  Okidata ML 192,193
AST TurboLaser           HP DeskJet,+             Okidata ML 292,293
Calcomp ColorMaster      HP ThinkJet              Okidata ML 294
Canon LBP8 II,III        IBM Graphics Printer     Okidata LaserLine 6
Epson FX,LX,RX           IBM Proprinter,XL,II     Olivetti PG 108,208 M2
Epson EX,JX              IBM Proprinter X24,XL24  QMS ColorScript 100
Epson MX                 IBM Quieturiter II,III   Qume LaserTEN,+
Epson LQ 800,1000        IBM Color Printer        Tektronix 4696
Epson LQ 1500            IBM Color Jetprinter     Tektronix Phaser CP
Epson    Parallel            Serial                      Quick
Epson                                                    1350,P1351
HP La   ►LPT1          COM1    COM2                       41,P351
HP La    LPT2     Baud rate: ►9600  4800  2400  1200  300
HP La    LPT3     Parity:    ►None  Even  Odd            er 12
HP La             Data bits: ►8     7
HP La             Stop bits: ►1     2
HP Qu
HP Pa

Printer: HP LaserJet+,II,IID

F1-Help
                                               F10-Continue
```

device files by running the INSTALL program again. For information on setting up the VDI driver in Harvard Graphics 2.13 or earlier, see Appendix D in the Harvard Graphics user's manual.

If you use a plotter for your output, bear in mind that plotters, as a rule, cannot print three-dimensional graphics. In addition, some of the symbols discussed in Chapter 7 are not supported by plotters.

Setting Up the Screen

To configure Harvard Graphics for the graphics card and monitor you are using, select Screen from the Setup menu. Harvard Graphics configures itself for the screen you are currently using and makes that screen the default screen. You need to select an alternate screen only if you have a second graphics card in your system and want to use it rather than the default screen.

You also may need to change the default screen if you plan to display screen-shows. Certain graphics card and monitor combinations do not display screen-show effects. If you have an IBM PS/2, a VGA card, or a VEGA Deluxe, you must select Default Screen from the Screen Setup screen to display screenshows properly. If you have any of the Toshiba gas-plasma portables (T3100, T3200, T5100, or T5200), you must choose CGA Color or CGA Monochrome to see screenshow effects.

If you use a VGA display system, the INSTALL program detects that you have a VGA and sets up the default screen as EGA color (640 x 350 resolution) so that you can see the transition effects in screenshows. If you select VGA on the Screen Setup screen, instead, you see graphics that are clearer (full 640 x 480 resolution) when you preview your charts on the screen, but you cannot see the transition effects in screenshows. The transition effects at full VGA resolution are too complex for the memory of most VGA cards.

To select a different screen on the Screen Setup screen, use the up- and down-arrow keys to move the highlight to the screen you want and then press Enter.

If you plan to use a monochrome card with an EGA or a VGA, you do not see screenshow effects at all. The same holds true if you use a VDI or DGIS graphics adapter.

Modifying the Color Palette

The final option on the Setup menu is Color Palette. With this option, you can alter the palette of colors Harvard Graphics uses when the program displays charts on an EGA, VGA, VEGA Deluxe, or DGIS graphics card or sends chart output to a film recorder to create slides. Or you can select one of the predefined color palettes.

To select from one of the predefined color palettes provided by Harvard Graphics 2.3, choose Color Palette from the Setup menu and then choose Select Palette from the Palette menu. Harvard Graphics displays a list of the currently available color palettes (each with a PAL file extension). Use the up- and down-arrow keys to highlight the palette you want and then press Enter.

You also can select palettes when you start a chart from the Gallery. This method is far easier and enables you to see the combinations of colors in each palette. Chapters 4 and 5 provide information about selecting a color palette when you start a chart from the Gallery.

You probably want to use the standard color palettes provided. But, if you want to modify an existing color palette to create a color combination, select Edit Palette after you have selected a palette. You see the Color Palette Setup screen, shown in figure 2.12.

```
                        Color Palette Setup
Palette file: hg23        Screen: EGA          Output: PCR,QCR
                          Red   Green  Blue     Red   Green  Blue
     1 │ White   -Title   1000  1000   1000     1000  1000   1000
     2 │ Cyan dk -Ser 1    0    660    660      660   330    330
     3 │ Blue    -Ser 2    0    330    660       0    330    825
     4 │ Blue lt -TextDK   330   660   1000      0    660    660
     5 │ Cyan LT -Labels   660  1000   1000     660   1000   1000
     6 │ Yel LT  -Ser 5    1000 1000   660      1000  1000   770
     7 │ White   -Text     1000 1000   1000     1000  1000   1000
     8 │ Black   -FrmBkg    0    0      0         0    0      0
     9 │ White   -Symbol   1000 1000   1000     1000  1000   1000
    10 │ Gray lt -Symbol   660   660   660      660   660    660
    11 │ Black   -Symbol    0    0      0         0    0      0
    12 │ Red     -Symbol   660   0      0        660   110    0
    13 │ Green   -Symbol    0    660    0        110   770    110
    14 │ Blue    -Symbol    0    0      1000      0    165    1000
    15 │ Yellow  -Symbol   1000 1000   0        1000  1000   0
    16 │ Blue DK -Bkgrnd    0    0      330       0    0      330

Background color: 16    Description: Blue bkg. with cyans and blues  = 11.PAL

F1-Help
F2-Show palette                                         F10-Continue
```

Fig. 2.12.

The Color Palette Setup screen.

Use Tab to move from option to option on the Color Palette Setup screen. Each color listed in the second column next to the color number is composed of a number for red, green, and blue. The second set of three numbers for red, green, and blue is for the output device rather than the screen. Here is a summary:

- ❏ 0-249 is none.
- ❏ 250-499 is low color intensity.
- ❏ 500-749 is medium color intensity.
- ❏ 750-1,000 is high color intensity.

To change any of the colors, type a new color name next to the color number and then enter three numbers for its red, green, and blue color component. To see the effects of your changes, press F2 (Show Palette).

You should try to match the colors specified by the three numbers under the Output heading (the colors for your output device) with the colors specified by the three numbers under the Screen heading (the colors for your screen). This way, your screen most closely reflects what you see when you produce output.

If you use a Polaroid Palette or Palette Plus as your output device, you should run the LISTKEY program that came with your Polaroid device. This program creates a table with numbers you can type in the Red, Green, and Blue columns under Output. PALETTE.EXE, another program that comes with the Polaroid Palette and Palette Plus, exposes an image of 72 colors the Polaroid Palette can create.

If you use a Matrix file recorder, the MATRIX.ASC file in the \SAMPLES directory is a text file that lists the color values you need to enter for each color the Matrix film recorder supports. MATRIX.SCD is a SCODL file you can send to your Matrix film recorder to see the colors it can create.

The PTI ImageMaker approximates the Harvard Graphics screen colors. If you select the PTI ImageMaker as your film recorder on the Setup menu, Harvard Graphics uses the PTI.PAL file that sets up colors properly. To change the background color of slides produced by the PTI ImageMaker, use the following information to set color number 16:

Color Number	Background Color
5	Dark blue
9	Light blue
13	Light gray
14	Dark red
15	Dark gray
All other numbers	Black

Setting Up the Applications Menu

Harvard Graphics 2.3 now includes a menu of applications you can call up when you press F3 (Applications). This menu allows you to start another program without having to leave Harvard Graphics. You can start most other programs that run under DOS.

To see the Applications menu, press F3 (Applications) at the main menu. The Applications menu that is automatically set up when you install Harvard Graphics 2.3 is shown in figure 2.13.

To modify the applications listed on the menu, select Applications from the Setup menu. You can modify menu items 2 through 8. For each menu item, you must enter three items of information. On the first line, after the menu item number, enter the name of the application just as you want it to appear on the Applications menu. For Lotus 1-2-3, for example, you can enter *Lotus*, *Lotus 1-2-3*, *1-2-3*, or just *123*. On the second line, next to Maximum Size (K), enter the memory amount the program requires in kilobytes. You can find this information on the program's box or in its user's manual. If you are unsure how much information a program requires, leave this entry blank. If a program requires 384K, type *384* at this option.

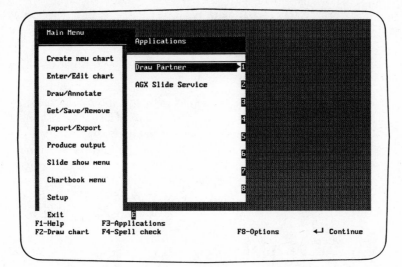

Fig. 2.13.

*The default
Applications menu.*

On the third line, next to Command, type the command you need to start the program. The best procedure is to include the full path name, including the drive and directory name in which the program is stored. To start 1-2-3 on drive C in the \LOTUS directory, for example, you should enter *c:\lotus\123*.

To install DOS as an application, enter *DOS* as the menu item and *command.com* after the Command prompt.

To set up advanced application options and the options for Draw Partner, press F8 (Options) at the Applications screen. You see the overlay shown in figure 2.14.

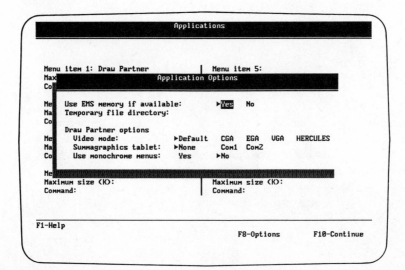

Fig. 2.14.

*The Application
Options overlay.*

If your computer has EMS (expanded) memory, you can set Use EMS Memory If Available to Yes. Harvard Graphics is stored temporarily in expanded memory while you run other programs by selecting them from the Applications menu. Be sure to set Use EMS Memory If Available to No if you include on the Applications menu programs that use EMS memory themselves.

If you use a RAM disk rather than EMS memory, you can specify the name of the RAM disk after the Temporary File Directory prompt. The RAM disk must have 600K of available memory. Harvard Graphics stores itself temporarily in the RAM disk while you run another application from the Applications menu. You also should enter a directory name at this prompt if you have set aside a special part of your hard disk as a scratch area for work files. If you have no EMS memory and you do not enter a temporary file directory, Harvard Graphics creates a temporary file with a random name in your default data directory to store itself while you use an application started from the Applications menu.

The Draw Partner options on the Application Options overlay enable you to set a default video mode for Draw Partner. Normally, Default is the best choice. The default video mode is determined when you first install Harvard Graphics 2.3 and Draw Partner. If you change video cards, you should change the video mode accordingly. If you have a VGA display system and you are working in Draw Partner without using Harvard Graphics screenshows, you should select VGA as the video mode on the Application Options overlay. Doing so provides the maximum standard IBM resolution your VGA can provide (640 x 480).

If you use a Summagraphics tablet, you can select COM1 or COM2 as its port. The default setting is None.

When the Use Monochrome Menus option is set to Yes, Draw Partner's menus are displayed in monochrome rather than colors. You may want to use this option if you use a monochrome display system that tries to emulate color with shades of gray, such as most laptop displays.

Overriding the Defaults with F8-Options

The selections you make on the Setup menu remain in effect until you change them. Suppose that you're creating a chart, and you decide that you want to vary from the orientation, border, font, or palette defaults established on the Default Settings screen. You can use the F8-Options selection to change the defaults for the current session. Pressing F8 summons the Current Chart Options overlay (see fig. 2.15). When you quit Harvard Graphics after setting the options on this overlay and start the program again later, the defaults revert to the settings on the Default Settings screen.

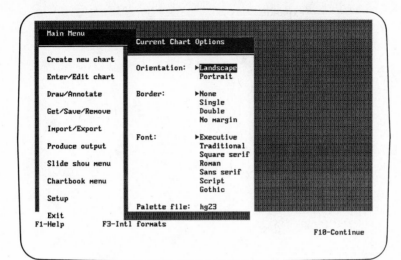

Fig. 2.15.

*The Current Chart
Options overlay.*

Make a habit of checking the F8-Options selection before starting any new chart
to make sure that these defaults are properly set for the chart you want to make
next. If someone else uses Harvard Graphics before you, that user may use the
F8-Options selection to vary the default settings for his or her charts. You do not
want to find that out when you preview the chart later.

Getting On-Line Help

At any point as you work, you may summon help information to the screen by
pressing F1 (Help). The help information that appears pertains to the current
action Harvard Graphics is carrying out. This feature is called *context-sensitive
help*. Check the bottom right corner of the help screen. If you see PgDn-More
Help, you can see more help information by pressing the PgDn key. To return to
your work and clear away the help information, press Esc.

Figure 2.16 shows the help screen that appears when you press F1 at the main
menu.

Fig. 2.16.

*The main menu
help screen.*

```
Main Menu
    To select a function:
        ■ Use the Space bar or arrow keys to move the cursor
          and press Enter.
        ■ Or, type the number next to the function.

Select:               To:
1. Create new chart   Create a chart from scratch.
2. Enter/Edit chart   Work on the current chart.
3. Draw/Annotate      Draw or add lines, shapes, or symbols.
4. Get/Save/Remove    Manipulate files on disk.
5. Import/Export      Use non-Harvard Graphics files.
6. Produce output     Print, plot, and record a chart, slide
                      show, or practice cards.
7. Slide show menu    Create and display series of charts.
8. Chartbook menu     Use templates for your charts.
9. Setup              Prepare Harvard Graphics for use with
                      your computer system.
Function keys:
   F2  Display the current chart.
   F3  Select an application without leaving Harvard Graphics.
   F4  Check spelling in the current chart.
   F7  Size and place the current chart.
   F8  Set and change current chart options.
                  Press Esc to cancel          PgDn-More help
```

Chapter Summary

In this chapter, you installed and set up Harvard Graphics. You also learned how to use the Harvard Graphics menus. That information will be invaluable to you when you join the quick-start tour of Harvard Graphics in the next chapter. The tour gets you up and running quickly and shows you how easily you can create expressive and appealing charts with Harvard Graphics.

3

Quick Start: Taking a Guided Tour of Harvard Graphics

In later chapters, you examine the nitty-gritty aspects of creating graphs and charts of all types. In this chapter, you get an overview of how Harvard Graphics works. Before you complete this guided tour, you learn some of the most appealing features of Harvard Graphics. You see the program's wide range of uses and its impressive simplicity. You also see how Harvard Graphics' gallery of charts and built-in chart blueprints can help you achieve good graphic design. In this tour, you prepare several text and graph charts, and before you're done, you enhance these charts with Harvard Graphics' special Draw/Annotate feature.

With Harvard Graphics, you can create sophisticated charts even if you don't have knowledge of computer programming or training in artistic design. In fact, even Harvard Graphics users who have never used a computer can start fashioning eye-catching charts almost immediately.

Imagine that you are on the board of a well-known office supply manufacturer. Suddenly, you learn that the presentation at tomorrow's stockholders meeting has fallen into your lap, and no one is available to assist you in your preparation. Harvard Graphics is already on the office computer's screen, however, so you decide to use the program to assemble the visuals to accompany your presentation. Good decision. Harvard Graphics is the ideal choice.

For tomorrow's speech, you need to describe (in positive tones) the following criteria:

- ❏ The corporation's objectives for the fourth quarter

- ❏ The corporation's second-quarter revenues

- ❏ The projects with the largest effect on the second quarter's profits

You decide that a list of bulleted points is perfect for your first chart, showing corporate objectives. Harvard Graphics provides a chart called a *bullet list*, which is an ideal tool for listing a series of points or summarizing the key issues that you will elaborate on in a speech.

The rest of your presentation conveys numeric information calculated from the data you have on-hand. Using the program's bar and pie charts, you can present numeric information visually in an attractive format and can even have Harvard Graphics perform financial calculations on your data as the program prepares a series of charts.

With the help of Harvard Graphics, you can prepare comprehensive and creative charts for tomorrow's presentation, a task you accomplish as you complete this quick-start tour.

(Of course, you need to set up the program before beginning, so—if you haven't already done so—follow the installation and starting procedures covered in Chapter 2. After you start Harvard Graphics, and the opening graphic display appears, you are taken to the Harvard Graphics main menu. Then you're ready to rejoin this tour.)

Selecting from the Main Menu

Harvard Graphics main menu is the starting point for nearly all the program's major functions (see fig. 3.1). The main menu appears immediately after you see the Harvard Graphics logo screen when you start the program. From the main menu, you can select the type of chart to create, save a chart on disk, send a chart to a printer or plotter, or import data files from other software applications into a chart. You also can use the main menu options to assemble charts into slide shows, create multiple charts, and produce chartbooks, which are collections of commonly used charts.

To make a selection from the Harvard Graphics main menu, you can use one of several methods:

- ❏ Using the arrow keys, move the cursor to highlight a menu choice, and then press Enter.

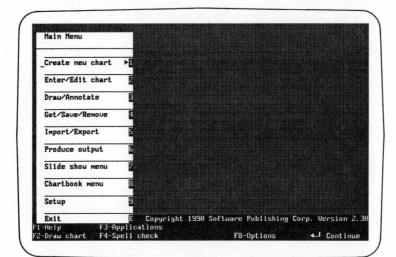

Fig. 3.1.

The main menu.

❏ Press the number or letter displayed to the right of a menu choice.

❏ Press the initial letter in the menu choice (for example, press C to choose Create New Chart). If two choices start with the same letter, Harvard Graphics cycles between them. This method works perfectly for (S)lide Show Menu and (S)etup, but with (E)nter/Edit Chart and (E)xit, you may be in for a surprise if you press E twice.

❏ Press the space bar until your menu choice is highlighted, and then press Enter.

Using the space bar to select from among options is a method that works consistently at nearly every menu and overlay that Harvard Graphics presents to you.

Using a Mouse

The assumption in this tour is that you are controlling Harvard Graphics with your keyboard only. If you want to combine a mouse with the keyboard, these three hints should help:

❏ Press the left mouse button to make a selection (same as pressing Enter).

❏ Press the right mouse button to back out of a function (same as pressing Esc).

❏ Press both mouse buttons simultaneously to select from among the function key choices at the bottom of the screen. Then point to a command and press the left mouse button to choose it.

Using the Gallery

With Harvard Graphics Version 2.3, you can select from a collection of pre-designed chart types when creating a chart. This assembly of preset chart designs is called the *gallery*. As you work with Harvard Graphics, you find that gallery selections are available for all the different chart types.

To select a chart from the gallery, you choose Create New Chart from the Harvard Graphics main menu and then choose From Gallery from the Create New Chart menu. You practice using this feature when creating the first chart in this chapter.

Creating a Text Chart

Now you are ready to create the first chart in your presentation: a bullet list showing marketing objectives for the next quarter. The marketing objectives follow:

- ❏ Increase sales of mechanical pencils by 10 percent
- ❏ Add 10 distributors to the roster
- ❏ Improve corporate image with advertising
- ❏ Increase sales by instituting a corporate training program for distributors

In the sections that follow, you learn how you can make this list into a presentable bullet chart.

Checking the Default Settings

As a rule, before you create a chart, you should examine the current session defaults by pressing F8 (Options) at the main menu.

Defaults determine how Harvard Graphics draws a chart if you do nothing more than enter data and let the program create the chart. By changing the defaults, you can determine how all subsequent charts in your current session are created. For example, you can decide whether you want all charts to be in portrait (vertical) or landscape (horizontal) format, and you can set a font—or typeface—for the text in your new charts.

For the first chart in this tour, select portrait orientation and leave all the other standard settings as they are. Portrait orientation is appropriate for the overhead transparencies you are creating. After all, you may make this same presentation at corporate regional offices later. There, you can count on having nothing more sophisticated than an overhead projector.

To select a portrait orientation, follow these steps:

1. Press F8 (Options) at the main menu. The Current Chart Options overlay appears (see fig. 3.2).

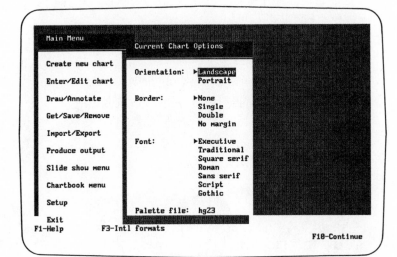

Fig. 3.2.

The Current Chart Options overlay.

2. At the Orientation field, use the space bar to highlight Portrait, and press Enter. The cursor moves to the Border field. A *border* is a line or set of lines that surrounds your chart, serving as a frame for your graphic. Suppose that for this set of charts, you do not need to include a border because your charts eventually will become transparencies, and the cardboard transparency holder hides the border. (For the curious among you who turn on the border anyway, be forewarned that it is not displayed when you use the F2 [Draw Chart] key.)

3. Press Enter to move to the Font options. The Executive option, the default, works well with the text and graph charts you create in this tour because the typeface is clean and easy to read. Therefore, leave this default Font option as is.

The Palette File field should be set at hg23, which is the default palette for Harvard Graphics Version 2.3. This option, which enables you to change color combinations, is particularly useful when you are creating slide shows to be presented on-screen or producing slides to be printed on a film recorder or by a service bureau.

4. Press F10 (Continue) to return to the main menu and save your changes.

Selecting a Bullet List

To create a bullet list, follow these steps:

1. Select Create New Chart from the main menu. The Create New Chart menu appears.

2. Select From Gallery from the Create New Chart menu. The gallery of charts appears, as shown in figure 3.3.

3. Press 1 from the main gallery to choose the text chart style. The gallery of available preset text charts appears (see fig. 3.4).

4. Press 2 to choose the bullet list (with a subtitle) style.

5. Press F10 (Edit + Clear) to summon the Bullet List screen.

Fig. 3.3.

The gallery of available predesigned charts.

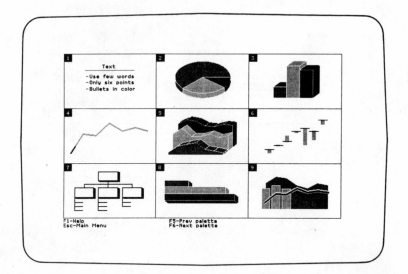

You use the Bullet List screen to type the text you plan to include in the finished chart and to make changes to the chart's appearance. Harvard Graphics enables you to change the size of the letters and their attributes (italic, boldface, underline, and so on).

Now complete the Bullet List screen so that it matches the sample completed screen shown in figure 3.5.

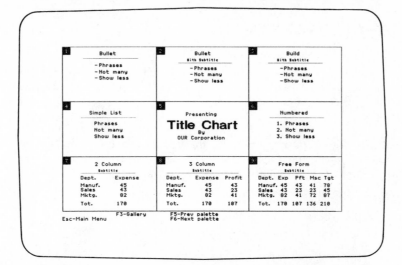

Fig. 3.4.

The text chart gallery.

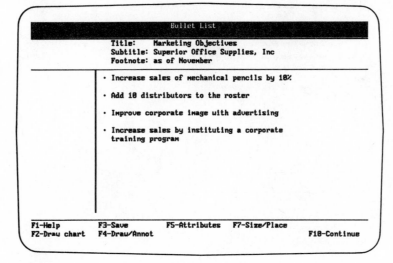

Fig. 3.5.

The Bullet List screen with text entered.

Completing the Bullet List Screen

Use the first three lines of the Bullet List screen to enter a title, subtitle, and footnote for the chart. Use the Tab key to move from line to line after you have entered each item. Because this chart lists the marketing objectives for the next year, type *Marketing Objectives* for the title. For the subtitle (which appears in a smaller type size), type *Superior Office Supplies, Inc.* Use the Footnote line to specify the date, typing *as of November.*

After entering the titles and footnote, tab down to the open area below and type your first bulleted item after the bullet that automatically appears. Bullets appear on every other line in a bullet list. To create a bullet, press Enter twice at the end of a complete bulleted item.

If a bulleted item consists of two lines (see the last item in fig. 3.5), Harvard Graphics wraps the text around to the next line. In other words, you can type the entire line, and Harvard Graphics adjusts the placement of the text as you type it, onto one line or two as necessary. This feature is new in Version 2.3.

If you make a typing mistake, use the Backspace key to delete the character you just typed or press Del to delete the character at the cursor's location.

After you finish entering text, press F2 (Draw Chart) to preview the chart with its current settings. Your chart should look like the one shown in figure 3.6.

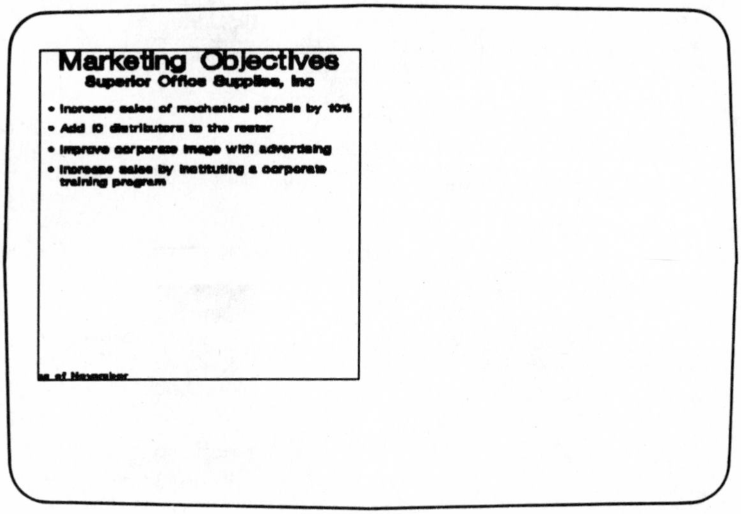

Fig. 3.6.

Previewing the chart by pressing F2 (Draw Chart).

Marketing Objectives
Superior Office Supplies, Inc

- Increase sales of mechanical pencils by 10%
- Add 10 distributors to the roster
- Improve corporate image with advertising
- Increase sales by instituting a corporate training program

as of November

After you examine your work in progress, you can press Esc to return to the Bullet List screen so that you can continue working on the chart. This procedure is the standard iterative process of creating a Harvard Graphics chart. You enter data into the data screen, preview the chart, and then return to the data screen to adjust the chart's appearance. After several iterations back and forth (previewing the chart and modifying its appearance), you decide when the chart is ready and save it on disk.

Adjusting Text Size and Bullet Type

When you preview the chart by pressing F2 (Draw Chart), you may want to change the appearance of the bullet list's text and bullets. No problem. With the F7 (Size/Place) command, you easily can adjust the size of text characters to fit the available space and can change the type of bullet used. Size in Harvard Graphics is a measure expressed as a percentage of the short side of the page. Size is a relative measure, in which 99.9 is the largest potential text size and 1 is the smallest size. The size feature is described in detail in Chapter 4.

To summon the Size/Place overlay, press Esc from the preview screen to return to the Bullet List screen. Then press F7 (Size/Place). Figure 3.7 shows the Bullet List screen with the Size/Place overlay visible.

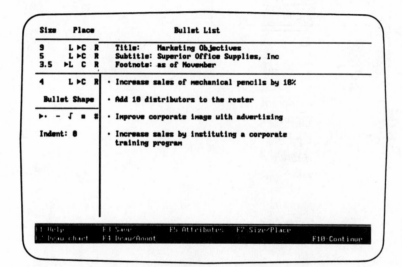

Fig. 3.7.

The Bullet List screen with the Size/Place overlay.

With the Size/Place overlay in view, follow these steps to adjust text size and bullet type:

1. The cursor begins in the Size column next to the Title line. The number in this row sets the size of the title of the list. Press Ctrl-Del to remove the number 9, and press 8 to indicate the new size. As you work with Harvard Graphics, you get a feel for the relationship between the Size settings and the actual size of the resulting text.

2. Use the Tab key to move the cursor to the first of the five possible bullet shapes on the menu, and press the space bar twice to select the check-mark bullet.

3. Press F10 (Continue).

4. Press F2 (Draw Chart) to view the chart. The result is shown in figure 3.8.

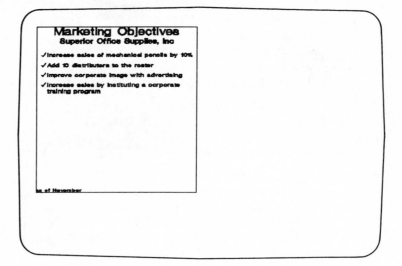

Fig. 3.8.

The bullet list after changing the title size and bullet type.

Regardless of whether you decide that the chart is now complete and ready for printing or determine that you need to make additional changes to its format, you should save the chart on disk before proceeding. Before saving the chart, return to the main menu by pressing Esc twice.

Saving the Chart

To save your chart, follow these steps at the main menu:

1. Select Get/Save/Remove.

2. Select Save Chart from the Get/Save/Remove menu. Figure 3.9 shows the Save Chart overlay that appears. The cursor is at the Chart Will Be Saved As field.

3. Type a name of up to eight characters for the chart and press Enter. An example name is OBJECTVS. Don't worry about typing the CHT file name extension. Harvard Graphics adds the extension for you when you save the chart.

4. If you want to replace the description Harvard Graphics derives from the title of your chart, type a new description over the old. For now, leave the current description.

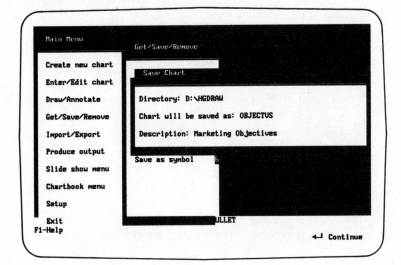

Fig. 3.9.

Saving the chart.

5. Press Enter to save the chart. The message Saving... appears in the lower center of the screen.

Now you have saved your chart, but suppose that you have forgotten to emphasize the bulleted item about increasing sales. After all, increasing sales is the point of your whole presentation. Why not italicize the words "Increase sales" for emphasis? With Harvard Graphics, you can italicize selected words easily by using the F5 (Attributes) command, discussed next.

Setting Text Attributes

Even after you save a chart, you still can revise it. As long as you have not started a new chart, the current chart is still available for immediate editing. At the main menu, select Enter/Edit Chart to modify the current chart. Then, at the Bullet List screen, follow this procedure to change the attributes of selected words to italic:

1. Tab to the first bullet, and position the cursor at the first letter of the word *Increase*.

2. Press F5 (Attributes). The Attributes menu bar appears at the bottom of the screen.

3. Use the right-arrow key to highlight the words *Increase sales* (see fig. 3.10).

Fig. 3.10.

*Highlighting the text
to change.*

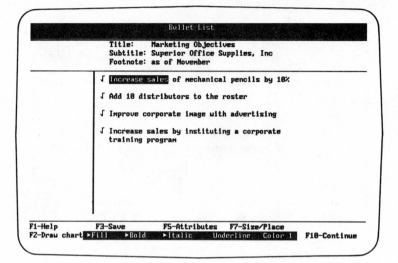

4. Press Tab to move the cursor on the Attributes menu bar to the Italic option, and press the space bar to turn on the italic attribute. A small pointer appears just to the left of the Italic option to indicate that the italic attribute is on.

5. Press F10 (Continue).

Nothing appears to happen on-screen, but when you press F2, you can see the result of the changes you made. Press F2 (Draw Chart) to see that the italic attribute really worked. Save the chart again with the same name, OBJECTVS, by pressing F3 (Save) from the Bullet List screen. The Save Chart overlay appears. This feature, the ability to save from a data screen, is new with Harvard Graphics Version 2.3. Previous versions enabled you to save only from the main menu.

Now the first chart in your presentation is complete, and you are ready to communicate your enthusiasm about a new topic, the remarkable strength of last quarter's revenues. To do that, you create a second chart, a bar chart.

Creating a Bar Chart

Bar charts are perhaps the most visually appealing and elegant charts in the repertoire of Harvard Graphics, and they are probably the most familiar type of chart, too. Bar charts provide the opportunity for the reader or audience to visualize and compare numbers displayed graphically.

In this section, you create a bar chart that displays three months of second-quarter sales for several products so that others can see easily which product was the leading seller. To create a bar chart, select Create New Chart from the main menu and then select Bar/Line from the Create New Chart menu.

Setting the X-Axis

When you select the Bar/Line option, the X Data Type Menu overlay appears. In this overlay, you make choices about how you want the X-axis data segregated. Because your sales data is organized by month, you want Harvard Graphics to display the results for month 1, month 2, and month 3 along the x-axis of your chart. Actually, because you want to display monthly results for several products, each month consists of a *set* of bars—one bar for each product in the Superior Office Supplies line.

To set the Month option on the X Data Type Menu overlay, follow these steps:

1. Use the space bar to select Month at the X Data Type prompt and press Enter. The cursor moves to the next option, Starting With.

2. Type *Apr* and press Enter. The cursor moves to the next option, Ending With.

3. Type *Jun* and press Enter.

4. Press Enter at the Increment field to leave it blank.

The Increment field determines how many units Harvard Graphics increases each new X data setting. Suppose, for example, that you set X Data Type to Day and specified Sun and Sat as your x-axis data starting and ending points. Setting the increment to 2 gives the result of Sun, Tues, Thurs, and Sat only. The x-axis is labeled with every other day rather than every day. If you leave the Increment field blank, Harvard Graphics assumes an increment of 1.

Figure 3.11 shows the completed X Data Type Menu overlay.

Entering Data and Previewing the Chart

After you complete the X Data Type Menu overlay, the Bar/Line Chart Data screen appears (see fig. 3.12). This screen performs the same function as the Bullet List screen you used when creating the text chart. The Bar/Line Chart Data screen enables you to enter the exact data you want charted.

Fig. 3.11.

The X Data Type Menu overlay.

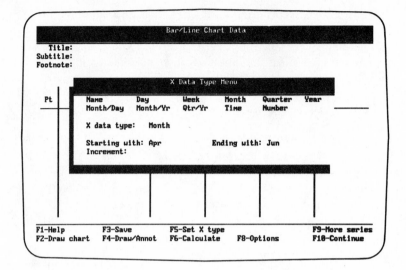

```
                        Bar/Line Chart Data
    Title:
 Subtitle:
 Footnote:
                        X Data Type Menu
 Pt      Name       Day        Week       Month      Quarter    Year
         Month/Day  Month/Yr   Qtr/Yr     Time       Number

         X data type:    Month

         Starting with: Apr             Ending with: Jun
         Increment:




 F1-Help         F3-Save        F5-Set X type                F9-More series
 F2-Draw chart   F4-Draw/Annot  F6-Calculate   F8-Options    F10-Continue
```

Fig. 3.12.

The Bar/Line Chart Data screen.

```
                        Bar/Line Chart Data
    Title:
 Subtitle:
 Footnote:

          X Axis      Series 1   Series 2   Series 3   Series 4
 Pt       Month

 1        Apr
 2        May
 3        Jun
 4
 5
 6
 7
 8
 9
 10
 11
 12
 F1-Help         F3-Save        F5-Set X type                F9-More series
 F2-Draw chart   F4-Draw/Annot  F6-Calculate   F8-Options    F10-Continue
```

Notice that the leftmost column is labeled X Axis Month. Harvard Graphics already has entered Apr through Jun based on the information you provided on the X Data Type Menu overlay. In fact, if you type the full month names on the X Data Type Menu overlay, Harvard Graphics supplies full month names (April, May, and June) rather than abbreviations.

The Title, Subtitle, and Footnote fields shown on this data screen function the same as they did for the bullet list you completed previously. Use the Title line to give the chart a title, the Subtitle line to add definition to the name, and the Footnote line to give relevant supplemental information about the chart—the date, for example.

With this chart, suppose that you want to show the second-quarter revenue from sales of these three SOS specialty products: Mechanical pencils, Swirly pens, and Annihilator erasers. You can give the chart the title *Pens, Pencils, & Accessories.* Enter the title on the data screen, but leave the Subtitle field blank because the title provides a complete description. For a footnote, type *Company Confidential.*

Next press F2 (Draw Chart) to preview the blank chart. Notice that the title, subtitle, and footnote are all in place, and a box indicates where the graph appears after you type in the graph's data.

Press Esc to return to the Bar/Line Chart Data screen so that you can type the sales data into the chart. Note the four columns labeled Series 1, Series 2, Series 3, and Series 4. Pressing F9 (More Series) shows the next four series (5 through 8). To return to Series 1, 2, 3, and 4, press F9 again. These Series columns are where you enter your sales data.

A *series* is a related set of data about one subject, such as the growth in population of a county over a period of years or the monthly sales of a particular product. In bar charts, a series is represented by a collection of bars of one color or pattern. Harvard Graphics enables you to enter eight series, so that you can graph eight separate sets of information. But using more than four or five series in a chart can make the chart look cluttered and less graphic.

In the chart that you need to produce for Superior Office Supplies, each product's sales over the course of the second quarter is one series. The set of data about Mechanical pencils is Series 1. The data about Swirly pens is Series 2. The data about Annihilator erasers is Series 3.

You assemble the data as follows:

Month	Mechanical Pencils (Series 1)	Swirly Pens (Series 2)	Annihilator Erasers (Series 3)
April	3,993	6,995	12,878
May	4,318	5,937	10,698
June	4,957	8,490	13,639

Complete the second-quarter revenue chart now by typing these numbers in the appropriate columns of the Bar/Line Chart Data screen, omitting the commas. The Tab key moves the cursor on the Bar/Line Chart Data screen from one series to the next. Press Tab to move the cursor to the right and Shift-Tab to move the cursor to the left. Pressing Enter moves the cursor down one line in the same column. Pressing the up-arrow key moves the cursor up one row. Figure 3.13 shows the completed Bar/Line Chart Data screen.

Bar/Line Chart Data
Title: Pens, Pencils, & Accessories
Subtitle:
Footnote: Company Confidential
Pt
X Axis
Month
Series 1
Series 2
Series 3
Series 4
1 Apr 3993 6995 12878
2 May 4318 5937 10698
3 Jun 4957 8490 13639
4
5
6
7
8
9
10
11
12
F1-Help
F2-Draw chart
F3-Save
F4-Draw/Annot
F5-Set X type
F6-Calculate
F8-Options
F9-More series
F10-Continue

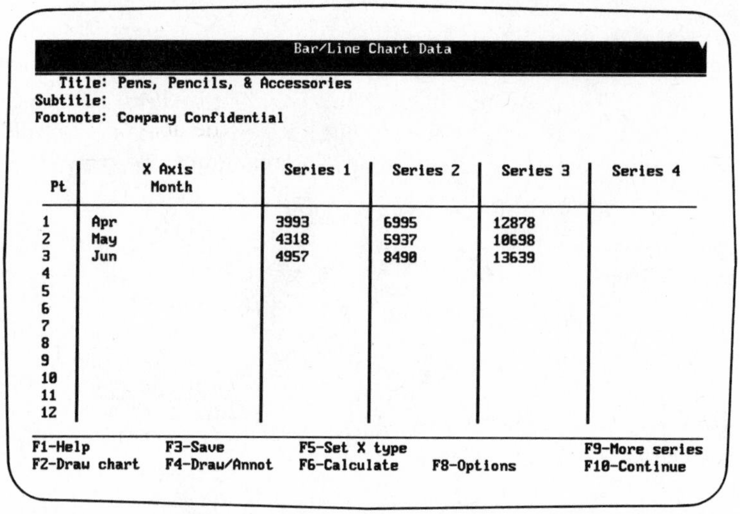

Fig. 3.13.

The second-quarter revenues entered in the Bar/Line Chart Data screen.

Next, preview the chart by pressing F2 (Draw Chart). You see the chart shown in figure 3.14, complete with x- and y-axis labels, bars, and even a legend.

Pens, Pencils, & Accessori
Thousands
16
14
12
10
8
6
4
2
0
Apr
May
Jun
Series 1
Series 2
Series 3
Company Confidential

Fig. 3.14.

The second-quarter revenues chart preview.

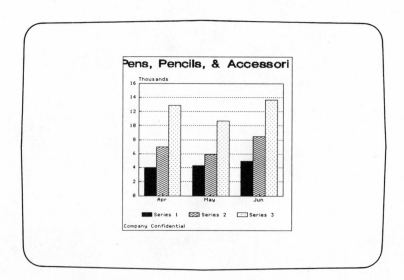

Using the Titles & Options Pages

Now that you have previewed the chart created by Harvard Graphics, you can customize the result to suit your needs and tastes. Press Esc to return to the data screen and press F8 (Options) to see the first of four Titles & Options screens. You use options in Harvard Graphics to change the appearance of the current chart. Each type of graph chart has its own series of Titles & Options pages unique to the attributes you can set for that type of chart. Titles & Options pages for bar/line charts, for example, give you the ability—among other things —to turn flat bar or line graphs into snazzy, three-dimensional charts. After setting the options to your satisfaction, you can press F2 (Draw Chart) to again preview the chart.

Right now, you should be looking at the first Titles & Options page. The top line of the page displays Page 1 of 4, and two triangular arrows on the sides of the screen point up (left side of screen) and down (right side of screen) to indicate that additional pages are available to you. You can use the PgDn and PgUp keys to move between the pages. Each page sets another visual aspect of the completed chart. Figure 3.15 shows the first Titles & Options page. Notice that Harvard Graphics interprets the data and adds the Y1 axis title automatically.

```
▲         Bar/Line Chart  Titles & Options  Page 1 of 4         ▼

              Title:        Pens, Pencils, & Accessories
              Subtitle:

              Footnote:     Company Confidential


          X  axis title:
          Y1 axis title: Thousands
          Y2 axis title:
 Legend                            Type              |Display| Y Axis
 Title:                  Bar  Line Trend Curve  Pt   |Yes  No| Y1  Y2

  1 | Series 1                     Bar              |  Yes  |  Y1
  2 | Series 2                     Bar              |  Yes  |  Y1
  3 | Series 3                     Bar              |  Yes  |  Y1
  4 | Series 4                     Bar              |  Yes  |  Y1
  5 | Series 5                     Bar              |  Yes  |  Y1
  6 | Series 6                     Bar              |  Yes  |  Y1
  7 | Series 7                     Bar              |  Yes  |  Y1
  8 | Series 8                     Bar              |  Yes  |  Y1

 F1-Help                   F5-Attributes   F7-Size/Place
 F2-Draw chart                             F8-Data      F10-Continue
```

Fig. 3.15.

The first Titles & Options page.

Using the First Titles & Options Page

The first Titles & Options page determines the overall appearance of the series in the chart. You can use this page to specify such characteristics as whether the series are shown as lines or bars. On this page, you also can name the series that appear in the legend something other than Series 1, Series 2, and so on.

Notice that the first three lines are set up much like the first three lines of the Bar/Line Chart Data and Bullet List screens, with Title, Subtitle, and Footnote lines. The current entries in these lines are borrowed from the data screen you completed a moment ago. You can change these lines by typing over them if you have changed your mind about the contents.

Complete the rest of this page so that it resembles the completed Titles & Options page shown in figure 3.16. Use the Tab, Shift-Tab, and Enter keys to move from option to option, and use the space bar to make your selections. To rename the series, tab to Series 1, and press Ctrl-Del to remove the words Series 1. Then type *Mechanical Pencils*. Continue filling out the page until it is complete with all the series names.

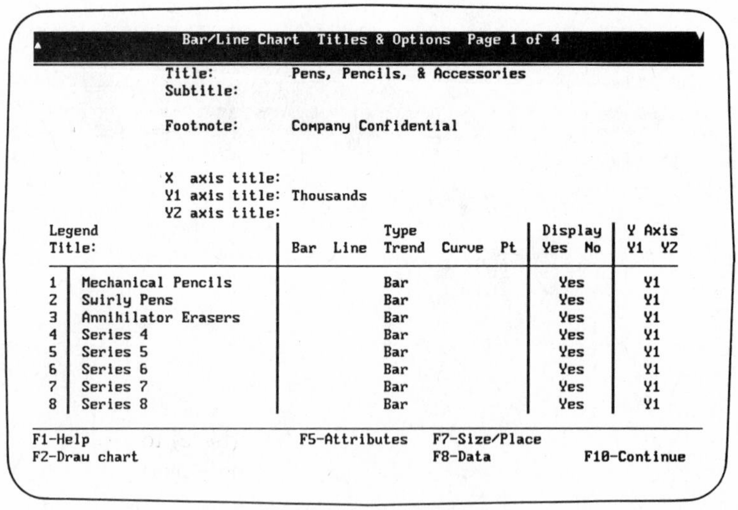

Fig. 3.16.

The completed Titles & Options page.

```
┌─────────────────────────────────────────────────────────────────────┐
│▲        Bar/Line Chart  Titles & Options  Page 1 of 4      ∨         │
│                                                                      │
│              Title:        Pens, Pencils, & Accessories              │
│              Subtitle:                                               │
│                                                                      │
│              Footnote:     Company Confidential                      │
│                                                                      │
│                                                                      │
│           X  axis title:                                            │
│           Y1 axis title:  Thousands                                 │
│           Y2 axis title:                                            │
│      Legend                        Type            Display  Y Axis  │
│      Title:              Bar  Line Trend Curve  Pt Yes  No  Y1  Y2  │
│                                                                      │
│      1 │ Mechanical Pencils        Bar              Yes      Y1     │
│      2 │ Swirly Pens               Bar              Yes      Y1     │
│      3 │ Annihilator Erasers       Bar              Yes      Y1     │
│      4 │ Series 4                  Bar              Yes      Y1     │
│      5 │ Series 5                  Bar              Yes      Y1     │
│      6 │ Series 6                  Bar              Yes      Y1     │
│      7 │ Series 7                  Bar              Yes      Y1     │
│      8 │ Series 8                  Bar              Yes      Y1     │
│                                                                      │
│      F1-Help              F5-Attributes   F7-Size/Place              │
│      F2-Draw chart                        F8-Data        F10-Continue│
└─────────────────────────────────────────────────────────────────────┘
```

You can alter the size and position of the chart's title, subtitle, and footnote by using the F7 (Size/Place) command on this page, just as you did when creating the bullet list. By changing the size of these lines, you can vary their importance on the page. Altering the size of the title lines also affects the size of the graph portion of the chart. Smaller title lines leave more room for a larger graph. The size and place are changed from the options screens in bar/line charts and from the data screen in text charts because text charts do not have related options screens.

Press F7 (Size/Place) to summon the Size/Place overlay and then change the Title line's Size setting to 6. Tab to the Subtitle line and change the settings of both of those lines to 0. (Even though no subtitle is in this chart, a setting of anything other than 0 reserves some space above the graph for a subtitle. A size setting of 0 eliminates this space and increases the size of the graph.) Figure 3.17 shows how the Size/Place overlay appears with the new Size settings. Press F10 (Continue) to save these changes.

Size	Place			Bar/Line Chart Titles & Options Page 1 of 4
6	L ►C	R	Title:	Pens, Pencils, & Accessories
8	L ►C	R	Subtitle:	
8	L ►C	R		
2.5	►L C	R	Footnote:	Company Confidential
2.5	►L C	R		
2.5	►L C	R		
4	►C		X axis title:	
3	►→ ↓		Y1 axis title:	Thousands
3	►→ ↓		Y2 axis title:	

	X labels			Type				Display		Y Axis	
	Y labels	Bar	Line	Trend	Curve	Pt	Yes	No	Y1	Y2	
1	Mechanical Pencils			Bar			Yes		Y1	
2	Swirly Pens			Bar			Yes		Y1	
3	Annihilator Erasers			Bar			Yes		Y1	
4	Series 4			Bar			Yes		Y1	
5	Series 5			Bar			Yes		Y1	
6	Series 6			Bar			Yes		Y1	
7	Series 7			Bar			Yes		Y1	
8	Series 8			Bar			Yes		Y1	

F1-Help			
F2-Draw chart	F5-Attributes	F7-Size/Place	
		F8-Data	F10-Continue

Fig. 3.17.

Using the Size/Place overlay on the first Titles & Options page.

The first Titles & Options page is complete, and now is a good time to preview the chart and admire your work. Press F2 (Draw Chart). The chart looks fine, so press Esc to return to the first Titles & Options page, press F8 (Data) to return to the Bar/Line Chart Data screen, and press F3 (Save) to save the chart. Name the chart P&P-2Q (for "pens and pencils second quarter"). Figure 3.18 shows the completed Save Chart overlay.

You move on to creating the third chart in your presentation shortly. But first, take a few minutes for a quick look at the second, third, and fourth Titles & Options pages to see what other changes you can make to a chart's appearance.

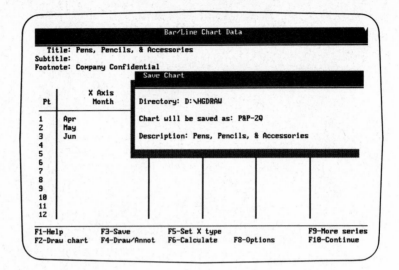

Fig. 3.18.

The Save Chart overlay for the P&P-2Q chart.

Viewing the Second Titles & Options Page

Press F8 (Options) to summon the first Titles & Options page from the Bar/Line Chart Data screen. Then press PgDn to see the second of four Titles & Options pages (see fig. 3.19). This page enables you to set many characteristics of the elements of the current chart. For example, on the second Titles & Options page, you can set the width of the bars in a bar chart and decide whether they will be displayed as three-dimensional bars. The second page also defines the appearance and positioning of the legend, which is a visual key that correlates series with their bars. With Harvard Graphics, a legend is optional. If you decide to include a legend, you can place it above, below, inside, or outside the graph.

Viewing the Third Titles & Options Page

Press PgDn at the second Titles & Options page to summon the third Titles & Options page, shown in figure 3.20. Use this Titles & Options page to change the underlying structure of the chart's appearance. You can set up grid lines behind the bars, for example, or you can set minimum and maximum values for the chart's two axes (horizontal and vertical).

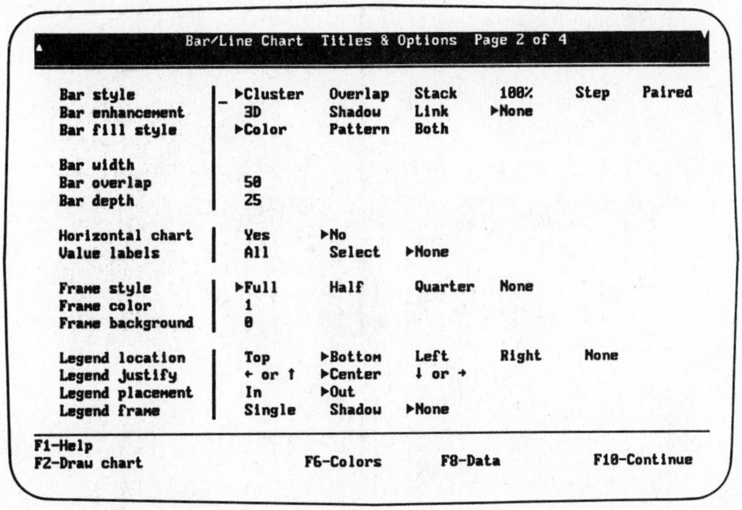

```
┌──────────────────────────────────────────────────────────────┐
│         Bar/Line Chart  Titles & Options  Page 2 of 4          │
├────────────────────────────────────────────────────────────────┤
│                                                                │
│  Bar style        _  ▸Cluster   Overlap   Stack    100%   Step   Paired │
│  Bar enhancement     3D         Shadow    Link     ▸None        │
│  Bar fill style      ▸Color     Pattern   Both                  │
│                                                                │
│  Bar width                                                     │
│  Bar overlap         50                                        │
│  Bar depth           25                                        │
│                                                                │
│  Horizontal chart    Yes        ▸No                            │
│  Value labels        All        Select    ▸None                │
│                                                                │
│  Frame style         ▸Full      Half      Quarter   None       │
│  Frame color         1                                         │
│  Frame background    0                                         │
│                                                                │
│  Legend location     Top        ▸Bottom   Left      Right  None │
│  Legend justify      ← or ↑     ▸Center   ↓ or →               │
│  Legend placement    In         ▸Out                           │
│  Legend frame        Single     Shadow    ▸None                │
│                                                                │
│ F1-Help                                                       │
│ F2-Draw chart              F6-Colors      F8-Data     F10-Continue │
└──────────────────────────────────────────────────────────────┘
```

Fig. 3.19.

The second Titles & Options page.

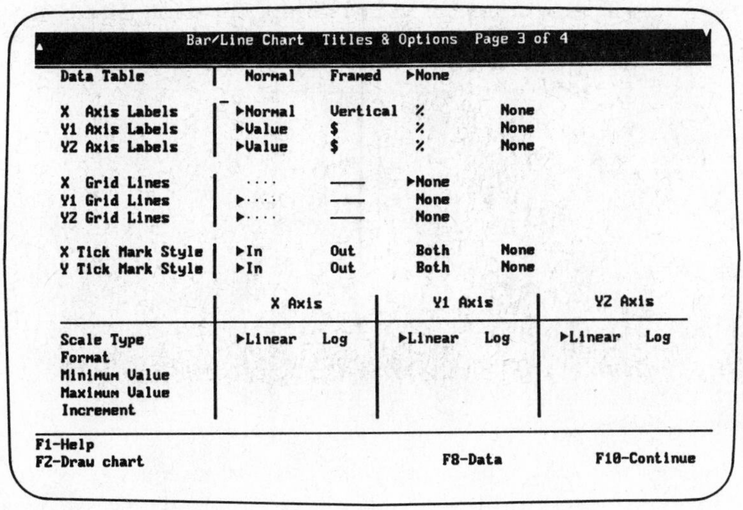

```
┌──────────────────────────────────────────────────────────────┐
│         Bar/Line Chart  Titles & Options  Page 3 of 4          │
├────────────────────────────────────────────────────────────────┤
│  Data Table       _   Normal    Framed    ▸None                │
│                                                                │
│  X  Axis Labels     ▸Normal    Vertical   %        None        │
│  Y1 Axis Labels     ▸Value     $          %        None        │
│  Y2 Axis Labels     ▸Value     $          %        None        │
│                                                                │
│  X  Grid Lines        ····       ────     ▸None                │
│  Y1 Grid Lines      ▸····        ────      None                │
│  Y2 Grid Lines      ▸····        ────      None                │
│                                                                │
│  X Tick Mark Style  ▸In         Out       Both     None        │
│  Y Tick Mark Style  ▸In         Out       Both     None        │
│                                                                │
│                       X Axis        Y1 Axis        Y2 Axis      │
│                                                                │
│  Scale Type         ▸Linear  Log   ▸Linear  Log   ▸Linear  Log │
│  Format                                                        │
│  Minimum Value                                                 │
│  Maximum Value                                                 │
│  Increment                                                     │
│                                                                │
│ F1-Help                                                       │
│ F2-Draw chart                             F8-Data     F10-Continue │
└──────────────────────────────────────────────────────────────┘
```

Fig. 3.20.

The third Titles & Options page.

Viewing the Fourth Titles & Options Page

Finally, press PgDn at the third Titles & Options page to display the fourth and last Titles & Options page. Use this page to describe titles, which are the names that you give to series, axes, and the overall chart. You also use the fourth Titles & Options page to control the specific appearance of bars and lines in a chart.

Using this page, for example, you can change the bars to show a cumulative display or change the line style on line charts. Figure 3.21 shows the fourth Titles & Options page.

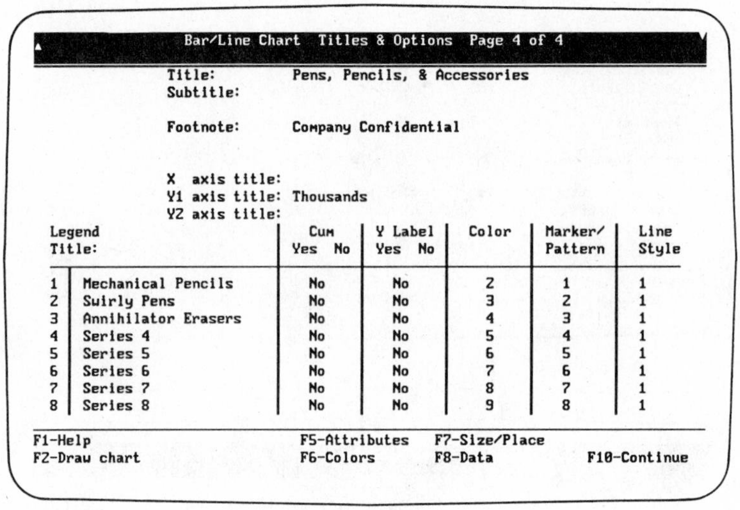

Fig. 3.21.

The fourth Titles &
Options page.

```
┌─────────────────────────────────────────────────────────────────────┐
│▲            Bar/Line Chart  Titles & Options  Page 4 of 4            │
│═══════════════════════════════════════════════════════════════════════│
│              Title:        Pens, Pencils, & Accessories             │
│              Subtitle:                                               │
│                                                                      │
│              Footnote:     Company Confidential                     │
│                                                                      │
│          X  axis title:                                             │
│          Y1 axis title: Thousands                                   │
│          Y2 axis title:                                             │
│   Legend             │ Cum    │ Y Label │ Color │ Marker/ │ Line     │
│   Title:             │ Yes No │ Yes No  │       │ Pattern │ Style    │
│   1 │ Mechanical Pencils │ No  │ No    │  2   │   1    │  1         │
│   2 │ Swirly Pens        │ No  │ No    │  3   │   2    │  1         │
│   3 │ Annihilator Erasers│ No  │ No    │  4   │   3    │  1         │
│   4 │ Series 4           │ No  │ No    │  5   │   4    │  1         │
│   5 │ Series 5           │ No  │ No    │  6   │   5    │  1         │
│   6 │ Series 6           │ No  │ No    │  7   │   6    │  1         │
│   7 │ Series 7           │ No  │ No    │  8   │   7    │  1         │
│   8 │ Series 8           │ No  │ No    │  9   │   8    │  1         │
│                                                                      │
│ F1-Help                  F5-Attributes  F7-Size/Place               │
│ F2-Draw chart            F6-Colors      F8-Data      F10-Continue    │
└─────────────────────────────────────────────────────────────────────┘
```

Creating a Pie Chart

The third chart in your presentation will show the projects with the largest effect on the second-quarter's profits. Suppose that when you assess the sales figures for the second quarter, you are happy to learn that two products new to the Superior Office Supplies line influenced revenues more than any others. These products are the designer pens and pencils and the small, personal appointment notebooks in the stationery division.

In this case, you want to compare the monthly breakdown of revenues generated by sales of pen and pencil sets with the monthly breakdown of revenues generated by sales of appointment books. From the computer-generated sales reports that the vice president of sales gave you, you pull the sales figures for the second quarter and jot them on paper. The numbers look like this:

	Pen and Pencil Sets	Appointment Books
April	$23,866	$40,676
May	$20,953	$63,800
June	$27,086	$38,539

To compare the sales of these two products, you wisely decide to graph the information as a pie chart.

Selecting the Pie Chart Data Screens

Creating a pie chart is much like creating a bar/line chart. First, you type the data into a data screen. Then you alternate between previewing the chart and modifying its appearance by using Titles & Options pages.

Follow this procedure to reach the Pie Chart 1 Data screen:

1. Select Create New Chart from the main menu.

2. Select Pie from the Create New Chart menu. The Change Chart Type overlay appears. Press the space bar to select No at the Keep Current Data field and press Enter. The Pie Chart 1 Data screen appears (see fig. 3.22).

```
              Pie Chart 1 Data  Page 1 of 2               ▼

Title:
Subtitle:
Footnote:

Slice    Label              Value         Cut Slice   Color   Pattern
         Name               Series 1      Yes  No

  1                                          No         2        1
  2                                          No         3        2
  3                                          No         4        3
  4                                          No         5        4
  5                                          No         6        5
  6                                          No         7        6
  7                                          No         8        7
  8                                          No         9        8
  9                                          No        10        9
 10                                          No        11       10
 11                                          No        12       11
 12                                          No        13       12

F1-Help          F3-Save                              F9-More series
F2-Draw chart    F4-Draw/Annot    F6-Colors    F8-Options    F10-Continue
```

Fig. 3.22.

*The Pie Chart 1
Data screen.*

Notice the similarity between the Pie Chart 1 Data screen and the Bar/Line Chart Data screen (see fig. 3.12). The Pie Chart 1 Data screen provides the same set of lines for a title, subtitle, and footnote. For a title, enter *2nd Quarter Top Performers.* For a subtitle, enter the name of the company: *Superior Office Supplies.* For a footnote, type *Company Confidential.*

To proceed further, you need to understand one significant difference between the Pie Chart 1 Data screen and the Bar/Line Chart Data screen. When the Pie Chart 1 Data screen first appears, it provides space for you to enter data for

Series 1 only. To enter a second series of data, you must press F9 (More Series). You can enter up to eight series of data by continuing to press F9.

Notice that the top line of the screen shows Pie Chart 1 Data Page 1 of 2. Two Pie Chart Data screens are available. With pie charts, you can display two pies side by side. The series displayed in the left pie is the series shown on the first screen (page 1), and the series displayed in the right pie is the series shown on the second screen (page 2). To get to the second screen, press the PgDn key. To change the series shown on the left or right side of the screen, press PgDn or PgUp to get to the appropriate page, and press F9 (More Series) until the correct series appears.

With Harvard Graphics, you can display only two pies at a time, with each pie showing one series. The key to using the Pie Chart Data screens is to match one of the two pies with one of the eight series by pressing PgDn or PgUp to choose the pie (left or right) and pressing F9 (More Series) to select a series for that pie. Figure 3.23 shows the relationship of series and pages.

Fig. 3.23.

The relationship of series and pages.

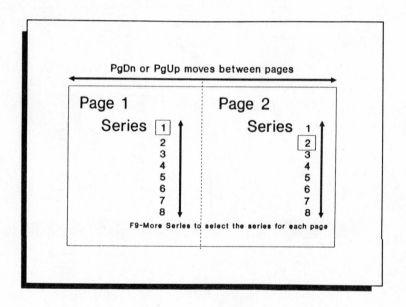

Try using the PgDn and PgUp keys to move between the two data screens for pie charts. Stop when the first data screen is displayed. Then try pressing F9 (More Series) until you see Series 1 in the Value column.

Next type the labels and data shown in figure 3.24. This data is for the sales of designer pen and pencil sets.

```
                    Pie Chart 1 Data  Page 1 of 2
Title:     2nd Quarter Top Performers
Subtitle:  Superior Office Supplies
Footnote:  Company Confidential

Slice      Label              Value        Cut Slice   Color   Pattern
           Name               Series 1     Yes  No

  1    Apr                   23866             No      2       1
  2    May                   20953             No      3       2
  3    Jun                   27086             No      4       3
  4                                            No      5       4
  5                                            No      6       5
  6                                            No      7       6
  7                                            No      8       7
  8                                            No      9       8
  9                                            No     10       9
 10                                            No     11      10
 11                                            No     12      11
 12                                            No     13      12

F1-Help        F3-Save                                 F9-More series
F2-Draw chart  F4-Draw/Annot   F6-Colors   F8-Options  F10-Continue
```

Fig. 3.24.

The Pie Chart 1 Data screen with entries.

Before you enter the second product line on the chart, press F2 (Draw Chart) to preview the left side of the chart. Figure 3.25 shows how your screen should look.

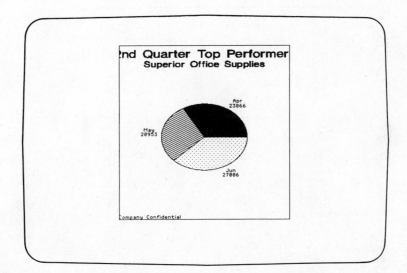

Fig. 3.25.

The pie chart before the second series is added.

Press Esc to return to the first data screen, and press PgDn to enter data for Series 2. Enter the data as shown in figure 3.26.

Fig. 3.26.

The Pie Chart 2
Data screen.

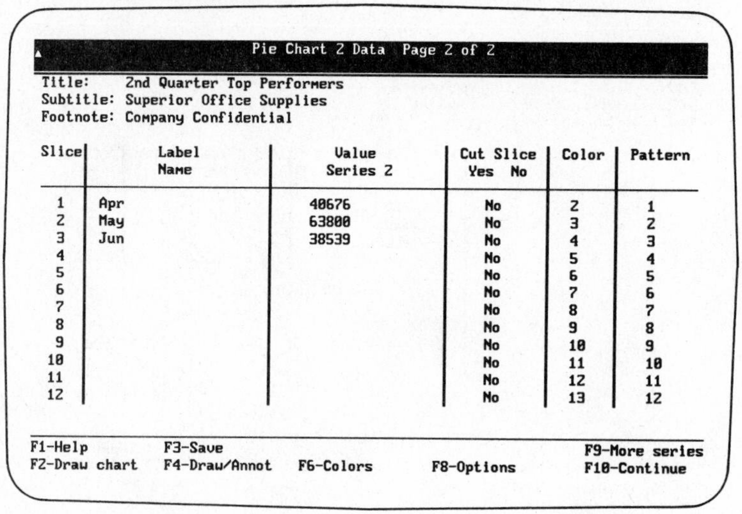

```
┌──────────────────────────────────────────────────────────────────┐
│ ▲          Pie Chart 2 Data   Page 2 of 2                          │
│ Title:    2nd Quarter Top Performers                               │
│ Subtitle: Superior Office Supplies                                 │
│ Footnote: Company Confidential                                     │
│                                                                     │
│ Slice│    Label          │   Value    │Cut Slice│ Color │ Pattern  │
│      │    Name           │  Series 2  │ Yes  No │       │          │
│      ├───────────────────┼────────────┼─────────┼───────┼──────────│
│   1  │ Apr               │   40676    │   No    │   2   │    1     │
│   2  │ May               │   63800    │   No    │   3   │    2     │
│   3  │ Jun               │   38539    │   No    │   4   │    3     │
│   4  │                   │            │   No    │   5   │    4     │
│   5  │                   │            │   No    │   6   │    5     │
│   6  │                   │            │   No    │   7   │    6     │
│   7  │                   │            │   No    │   8   │    7     │
│   8  │                   │            │   No    │   9   │    8     │
│   9  │                   │            │   No    │  10   │    9     │
│  10  │                   │            │   No    │  11   │   10     │
│  11  │                   │            │   No    │  12   │   11     │
│  12  │                   │            │   No    │  13   │   12     │
│                                                                     │
│ F1-Help         F3-Save                            F9-More series   │
│ F2-Draw chart   F4-Draw/Annot   F6-Colors   F8-Options F10-Continue │
└──────────────────────────────────────────────────────────────────┘
```

Now press F2 (Draw Chart) to preview the chart. Figure 3.27 shows the two pie
graphs side by side in a chart.

Fig. 3.27.

A pie chart with
two series.

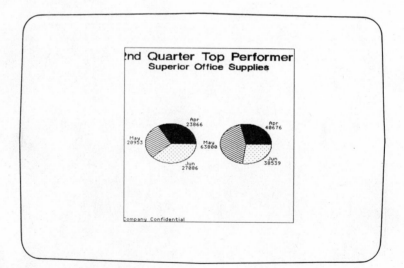

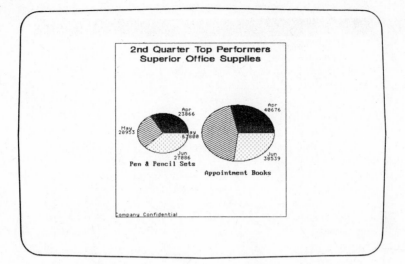

Fig. 3.31.

Drawing proportional pies.

Press Esc again to return to the first Titles & Options page, and press PgDn to examine the second Titles & Options page. This collection of options is discussed in detail in Chapter 6. For this quick tour, only two small changes are in order: you need to remove the values from the chart and replace them with the percentages for each slice of the pie.

Follow these steps to make the changes:

1. Tab to the Show Value field and press the space bar to select No in the Pie 1 column.

2. Tab to the Show Value line in the Pie 2 column and press the space bar to select No for the right pie.

3. Tab to the Show Percent field and press the space bar to select Yes for the Pie 1 column.

4. Tab to the Show Percent line in the Pie 2 column and press the space bar to select Yes for the right pie.

5. Press F10 (Continue) to confirm your choices. Figure 3.32 shows the second Pie Chart Titles & Options page with these changes completed.

6. Press F2 (Draw Chart) to see the results of your changes, which are shown in figure 3.33.

Fig. 3.32.

The second Titles & Options page with changes.

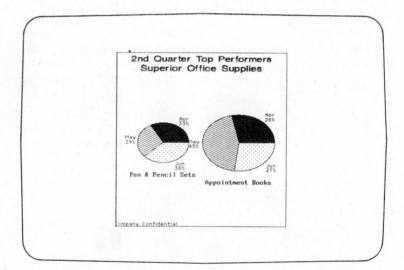

```
┌────────────────────────────────────────────────────────────────────────┐
│ ▲        Pie Chart Titles & Options   Page 2 of 2                        │
│                                                                          │
│                        Pie 1                        Pie 2                 │
│                                                                          │
│  Chart style      ▶Pie    Column         ▶Pie    Column    None          │
│  Sort slices       Yes    ▶No             Yes    ▶No                      │
│  Starting angle    0                      0                               │
│  Pie size          50                     50                             │
│                                                                          │
│  Show label       ▶Yes     No            ▶Yes     No                      │
│  Label size        3                      3                               │
│                                                                          │
│  Show value        Yes    ▶No             Yes    ▶No                      │
│  Place value      ▶Below  Adjacent Inside ▶Below  Adjacent Inside         │
│  Value format                                                            │
│  Currency          Yes    ▶No             Yes    ▶No                      │
│                                                                          │
│  Show percent     ▶Yes     No            ▶Yes     No                      │
│  Place percent    ▶Below  Adjacent Inside ▶Below  Adjacent Inside         │
│  Percent format                                                          │
│                                                                          │
│  F1-Help                                                                 │
│  F2-Draw chart                          F8-Data          F10-Continue     │
└────────────────────────────────────────────────────────────────────────┘
```

Fig. 3.33.

The finished pie chart.

Saving Your Pie Chart

Now that your chart is complete, save it on disk so that you can retrieve it later. To help remind you of the chart's purpose, try to give the chart a mnemonic name, such as PEN-APPT (a chart comparing pen and pencil sets with appointment books).

To save your chart, do the following:

1. Select Get/Save/Remove from the main menu.

2. Select Save Chart from the Get/Save/Remove menu.

3. On the Save Chart overlay, type *pen-appt* as the chart name and press Enter twice to save the chart. Harvard Graphics adds a CHT file name extension for you.

Viewing Bar and Pie Chart Galleries

Before you use Draw/Annotate to add emphasis to the charts you have just created, you may want to look quickly at the galleries of predesigned graph charts. Just as you did with the bullet list you made previously in this chapter, you can select from the galleries to pick a preformatted bar or pie chart and determine the final appearance of your chart, without having to change the choices on the Titles & Options pages. The gallery feature enables you to produce attractive output quickly. Take a look at the gallery by following this procedure:

1. Select Create New Chart from the main menu.

2. Select From Gallery from the Create New Chart menu.

3. Press 3 from the gallery to display the bar chart gallery shown in figure 3.34. (This gallery is the most commonly used bar chart gallery, but several other galleries, including those accessed by selection numbers 4, 8, and 9 from the main gallery, show different types of bar charts.)

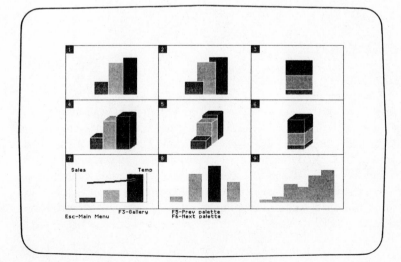

Fig. 3.34.

The bar chart gallery.

4. Press F3 (Gallery) to return to the main gallery.

5. Press 2 to view the pie chart gallery, which is shown in figure 3.35.

Fig. 3.35.

The pie chart gallery.

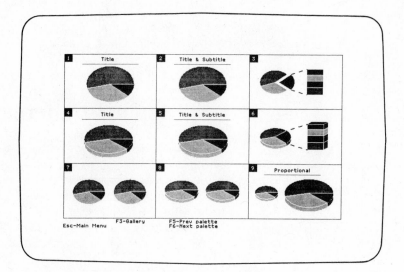

6. Press F3 (Gallery) to return to the main gallery.

7. Press Esc to return to the main menu.

You can use any of these preformatted charts without having to start a chart from scratch. After you pick a design from the chart gallery, all you have to supply is the data to complete the chart.

Using Draw/Annotate To Enhance a Chart

As you near the end of the tour, you can look back proudly at your accomplishments. In only a short while, you have created three complete charts: OBJECTVS, a bullet list; P&P-2Q, a bar chart; and PEN-APPT, a pie chart. These charts may be perfectly satisfactory as they are, but you can improve their impact dramatically with a special Harvard Graphics feature called Draw/ Annotate. Draw/Annotate enables you to enhance charts by adding pictures, any of hundreds of symbols from a symbol library, and hand-drawn arrows, boxes, circles, and text.

In this section of the tour, you retrieve the bullet list that you created previously. You then learn how to use the Draw/Annotate feature to add a box around the last bulleted item, giving it additional emphasis.

Retrieving a Text Chart

To retrieve the bullet list (OBJECTVS), follow these steps:

1. Select Get/Save/Remove from the main menu.

2. Select Get Chart from the Get/Save/Remove menu. Figure 3.36 shows the Select Chart file list, which appears so that you can pick one of the charts on disk.

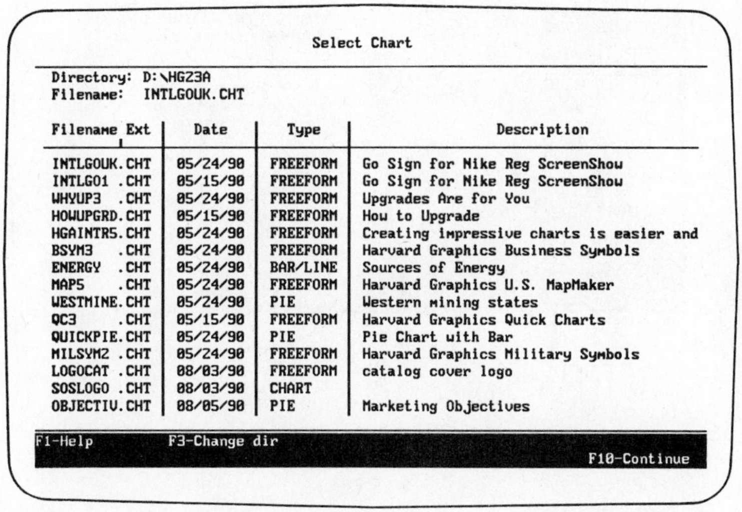

```
                        Select Chart

   Directory: D:\HG23A
   Filename:  INTLGOUK.CHT

   Filename Ext |  Date  |  Type   |         Description

   INTLGOUK.CHT | 05/24/90| FREEFORM | Go Sign for Nike Reg ScreenShow
   INTLGO1 .CHT | 05/15/90| FREEFORM | Go Sign for Nike Reg ScreenShow
   WHYUP3  .CHT | 05/24/90| FREEFORM | Upgrades Are for You
   HOWUPGRD.CHT | 05/15/90| FREEFORM | How to Upgrade
   HGAINTRS.CHT | 05/24/90| FREEFORM | Creating impressive charts is easier and
   BSYM3   .CHT | 05/24/90| FREEFORM | Harvard Graphics Business Symbols
   ENERGY  .CHT | 05/24/90| BAR/LINE | Sources of Energy
   MAP5    .CHT | 05/24/90| FREEFORM | Harvard Graphics U.S. MapMaker
   WESTMINE.CHT | 05/24/90| PIE      | Western mining states
   QC3     .CHT | 05/15/90| FREEFORM | Harvard Graphics Quick Charts
   QUICKPIE.CHT | 05/24/90| PIE      | Pie Chart with Bar
   MILSYM2 .CHT | 05/24/90| FREEFORM | Harvard Graphics Military Symbols
   LOGOCAT .CHT | 08/03/90| FREEFORM | catalog cover logo
   SOSLOGO .CHT | 08/03/90| CHART    |
   OBJECTIV.CHT | 08/05/90| PIE      | Marketing Objectives

   F1-Help        F3-Change dir
                                                    F10-Continue
```

Fig. 3.36.

The Select Chart screen.

3. Use the down-arrow key to highlight the file named OBJECTVS. Notice that highlighting the file places it after the Filename prompt at the top of the screen.

4. Press Enter to select the highlighted chart. The bullet list appears.

Switching to Draw/Annotate Mode

Now, to change to Draw/Annotate mode so that you can enhance the bullet list, follow these steps:

1. Press Esc to display the Bullet List screen.

2. Press F10 (Continue) to return to the main menu. (The bullet list remains the current chart.)

3. Select Draw/Annotate from the main menu. The Draw/Annotate screen appears (see fig. 3.37).

Fig. 3.37.

The Draw/Annotate screen.

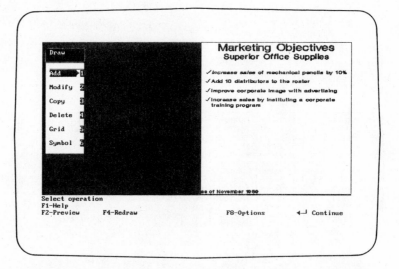

Note: If you are working with Harvard Graphics Version 2.3, you can skip step 2 and just press F4 (Draw/Annot) from the data screen to bring the chart into Draw/Annotate mode. Version 2.3 of Harvard Graphics enables you to access Draw/Annotate directly from a data screen rather than from the main menu.

Take a minute to look at the Draw/Annotate screen. On the right, the OBJECTVS bullet list appears on the drawing board, the work area on which you perform Draw/Annotate chart enhancements. On the left, the Draw menu appears. Use this menu to choose from among the available Draw/Annotate commands.

Draw/Annotate mode is different in two respects from the modes in which you create text and graph charts:

❏ The options available for modifying the chart appear on the main screen rather than on separate Options pages.

❏ The chart shown on-screen was created in another mode (Text or Graph mode) and brought into Draw/Annotate for embellishment. The only exception occurs when you want to draw with Draw/Annotate on a blank page. In that case, you start a free-form chart (Text mode chart) and bring it into Draw/Annotate without adding any data on the free-form data screen.

When you are in the middle of a Draw/Annotate operation, the left portion of the screen becomes an options panel. When you press F8 (Options), the cursor jumps to the options panel, and the F8 function key choice on the bottom line of the screen changes to F8-Draw. If you press F8 (Draw), the cursor jumps back over to the drawing board. Try this procedure several times to see how it works.

At the lower left corner of the screen, a prompt reminds you of your place in the current operation. Notice that when the screen is at the Draw menu, the instruction line displays Select operation.

Adding a Box to an Existing Chart

To add a box around the last bulleted item on this chart, follow these steps:

1. Select Add from the Draw menu. (Use the cursor to highlight the choice and then press Enter or just press the number 1 on your keyboard.)

2. Select Box from the Add menu. The cursor moves to the drawing board, and the instruction line displays the message Select first box corner.

3. Press F8 (Options) to move to the options panel.

4. Use the space bar to select No at the Square option. You need to draw a rectangle rather than a square.

5. Tab to the Style option, and press F6 (Choices) to see the types of boxes available. Figure 3.38 shows the 21 standard box types from which you can choose. Selecting and placing specific box styles is described in detail in Chapter 9. For the purposes of this quick tour, move the cursor to the rounded selection (box type 4), and press Enter.

6. Tab to the Fill choice, and press the space bar to select No.

7. Press F8 (Draw) to move the cursor back to the drawing board.

8. Position the cursor where you want the upper left corner of the box to be, and press Enter.

Fig. 3.38.

The Harvard Graphics standard box types.

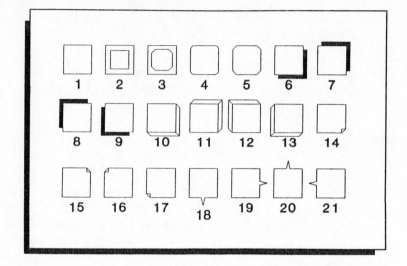

9. Use the PgDn and right-arrow keys to position the opposite corner, the lower right corner of the box, and press Enter when the box surrounds the fourth bulleted item (see fig. 3.39).

Fig. 3.39.

Completing the rounded box.

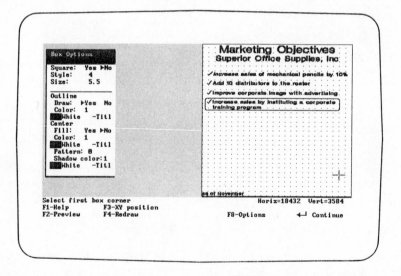

Although you can see the results of your actions on the Draw/Annotate screen, you still can use the F2 (Draw Chart) command to preview the final chart on the full screen before saving and printing it. To preview and save the chart, follow these steps:

1. Press F2 (Draw Chart) to preview the final chart.

2. After you finish examining the chart, press Esc twice to return to the Harvard Graphics main menu.

3. Select Get/Save/Remove from the main menu and save the chart with the name OBJEC1. If you use a name different from the file's original name, you end up with two charts on disk—both the original and the new version. You now can return to OBJECTVS if you need to make other changes.

To add other shapes that are in the Harvard Graphics archive (circles, ovals, squares, rectangles, lines, and arrows), you can follow similar procedures. The methods you use, however, change slightly when you create more sophisticated polygons and polylines. These procedures are explained in detail in Chapter 9.

Including Predrawn Symbols in an Existing Chart

Not everyone is an artist. If your drawing skills are less than sublime, and you hope to add anything more than simple lines, boxes, circles, and arrows to a chart, you may want to rely on the built-in Harvard Graphics library of predrawn symbols.

A *symbol* in Harvard Graphics is a special kind of picture that already has been drawn for you. Groups of symbols are stored in symbol files provided with Harvard Graphics. Each file follows a theme. The Office symbol file provides images of such standard office implements as staplers, pen and pencil sets, calendars, and filing cabinets. The Computer symbol files include pictures of computers, computer parts, and so on. Harvard Graphics includes hundreds of symbols for use in your charts and also offers you the opportunity to create symbol libraries of your own. Several optional supplementary symbol collections, such as the Business symbol utility library, are available for you to add to your collection.

To see how symbols work, try adding drawings to the pie chart you created previously in this chapter. In this exercise, you add symbols of coins to the smaller pen and pencil set pie and dollar bills to the larger appointment book pie. These symbols are from the Money symbol file.

Remember, to bring a chart into Draw/Annotate mode to add drawings, you must retrieve the chart from disk first. After you have retrieved the chart, it becomes the current chart, ready for embellishment if you enter Draw/Annotate mode. Follow the procedure in the previous section on "Retrieving a Text Chart," but this time retrieve the pie chart you called PEN-APPT so that you can enhance it with Draw/Annotate.

To place a symbol on your chart, follow these steps:

1. Select Symbol from the Draw menu.

2. Select Get from the Symbol menu.

3. Select the MONEY.SYM file from the list of file names that appears (see fig. 3.40). Press PgDn to scroll the symbol library names down one screen, highlight MONEY.SYM with the down-arrow key, and press Enter. The Money symbol library appears on your screen (see fig. 3.41).

4. Position the cursor on the symbol of the coins in the left column and press Enter.

5. Press the Backspace key so that you can determine where to position the symbol.

6. Position the cursor at the upper left corner of where you want to draw an invisible box to contain the symbol; then press Enter. In this case, position the cursor just under the P in the word Pen, and press Enter. Figure 3.42 shows the precise position for the upper left corner of the box.

Fig. 3.40.

The Select Symbol File screen.

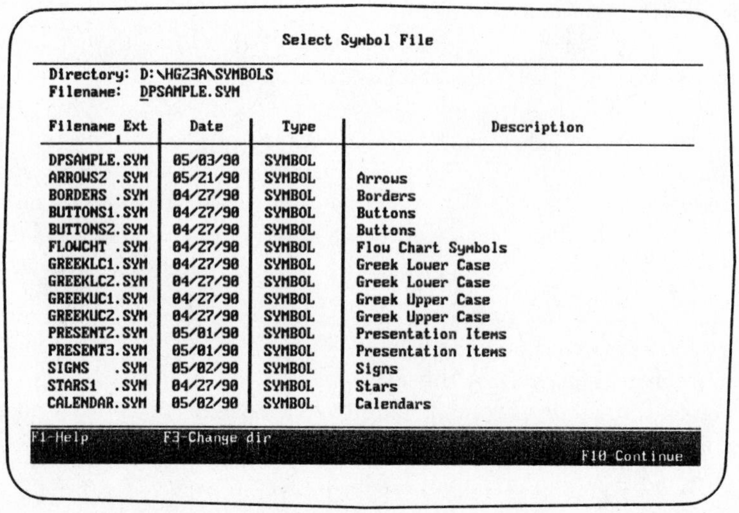

```
                          Select Symbol File

          Directory: D:\HGZ3A\SYMBOLS
          Filename:  DPSAMPLE.SYM

          Filename Ext    Date      Type              Description

          DPSAMPLE.SYM   05/03/90   SYMBOL
          ARROWS2 .SYM   05/21/90   SYMBOL    Arrows
          BORDERS .SYM   04/27/90   SYMBOL    Borders
          BUTTONS1.SYM   04/27/90   SYMBOL    Buttons
          BUTTONS2.SYM   04/27/90   SYMBOL    Buttons
          FLOWCHT .SYM   04/27/90   SYMBOL    Flow Chart Symbols
          GREEKLC1.SYM   04/27/90   SYMBOL    Greek Lower Case
          GREEKLC2.SYM   04/27/90   SYMBOL    Greek Lower Case
          GREEKUC1.SYM   04/27/90   SYMBOL    Greek Upper Case
          GREEKUC2.SYM   04/27/90   SYMBOL    Greek Upper Case
          PRESENT2.SYM   05/01/90   SYMBOL    Presentation Items
          PRESENT3.SYM   05/01/90   SYMBOL    Presentation Items
          SIGNS   .SYM   05/02/90   SYMBOL    Signs
          STARS1  .SYM   04/27/90   SYMBOL    Stars
          CALENDAR.SYM   05/02/90   SYMBOL    Calendars

          F1-Help        F3-Change dir
                                                    F10-Continue
```

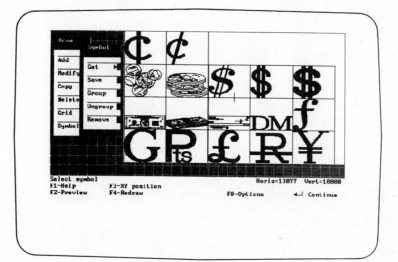

Fig. 3.41.

The MONEY.SYM symbol file.

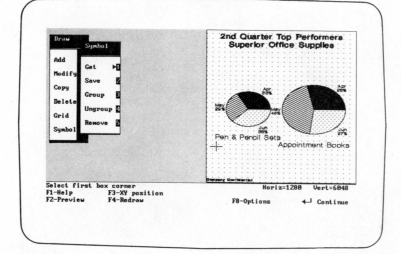

Fig. 3.42.

Positioning the coins symbol.

7. Press the PgDn key and right-arrow key repeatedly to open the box (or press PgUp to make the box smaller) until the box is the proper size for the symbol you want to place on-screen. Figure 3.43 shows how the screen looks before you press Enter again.

8. Press Enter to confirm the size and instruct Draw/Annotate to draw the symbol. Figure 3.44 shows how the chart looks with an added symbol.

Fig. 3.43.

Sizing the box to hold the symbol.

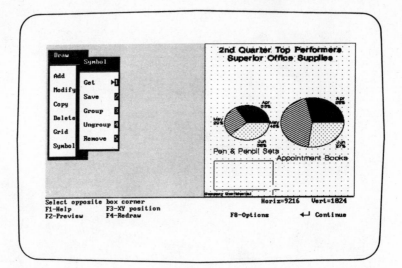

Fig. 3.44.

The pie chart with a symbol added.

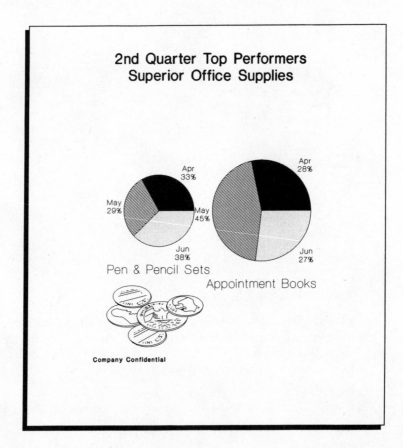

Now that you have placed the first symbol, finding and placing the second symbol should be a simple procedure. Complete this chart by placing the dollar bills symbol below the words Appointment Books. Then save the chart with the new name 2QPIESYM for "second-quarter pie chart with symbols."

Another method for adding graphic elements and symbols to your charts is to use Draw Partner, a special portion of Harvard Graphics 2.3. Draw Partner provides all the capabilities of Draw/Annotate and adds many of its own more sophisticated features. Draw Partner is so feature-packed, in fact, that this book devotes three chapters to it. You learn about Draw Partner in Chapters 10, 11, and 12.

Printing Your Charts

The visual accompaniment to your presentation is complete, so now you can accomplish one last detail: creating your final output. Harvard Graphics creates slides and plotted charts as easily as it prints to a standard printer. Because you need to make transparencies for this presentation, however, you can print on a regular printer first and photocopy the completed charts onto transparency film later.

You can start by printing the chart you completed last, because 2QPIESYM, the pie chart, is already on-screen.

Before you print for the first time, check to see that Harvard Graphics is set correctly for your printer. Chapter 2 provides important information about setting up Harvard Graphics for your output device. Chapter 15 gives detailed information about creating output.

To print your pie chart, follow these steps:

1. Press Esc twice to return to the main menu and select Produce Output.

Note: If you are using Harvard Graphics Version 2.3, you can summon the Print Chart Options overlay by pressing Esc and then pressing Ctrl-P to select Produce Output.

2. Select Printer from the Produce Output menu.

3. Use the Tab key to move between printing options, and use the space bar to highlight the option you want to select. Table 3.1 shows the available choices you can select from the Print Chart Options overlay.

4. Press F10 (Continue) to send the chart to the printer.

Table 3.1
Print Chart Options Overlay

Option	Description
Quality	Harvard Graphics provides three output qualities. Draft quality prints faster but without the sharpness of Standard quality or the extra-fine resolution of High quality. Choose the Draft option the first time you print and check your work, because this option prints the fastest.
Chart Size	Harvard Graphics enables you to print your chart in one of four sizes to accommodate your final output needs—Full, 1/2, 1/3, or 1/4. Usually, on your first try, you should print at full size so that you easily can inspect the chart.
Paper Size	Choose Letter (8 1/2-by-11-inch) to print on a standard-size page, or choose Wide (8 1/2-by-14-inch) to print on a legal-size page.
Printer	With this option, you can pick between two possible printer setups. For detailed information about setting up more than one printer for use with Harvard Graphics, see Chapter 2.
Color	If you have a color printer or another output device that is color, you can select Yes to indicate color.
Print to Disk	Select Yes for this field if you want to create a copy of the file on disk. When you print to disk, the file has a PRN extension.
Number of Copies	After Harvard Graphics constructs a chart to send to the printer, the program can print quickly as many copies as you want.

After you finish printing the pie chart, you can retrieve and print each of the other charts you created.

Chapter Summary

After completing this tour, you have only scratched the surface of the capabilities of Harvard Graphics. In this chapter, you created a text chart (a bullet list), a bar chart, and a pie chart. You used the F7 (Size/Place) command to alter the text size, and the F5 (Attributes) command to alter the characteristics of a group of words. Then, using the Draw/Annotate mode, you drew a box on a text chart, and selected symbols and placed them on a pie chart. Finally, you saved and printed all the charts you created.

In the next chapter, you learn the details of creating text charts, and you have the opportunity to create and embellish all the available text chart types.

Part II

Making Charts

Includes

4

Creating Text Charts

Text charts are indispensable tools for business presentations. Overheads, slides, or handouts with bulleted points can distill a speech's central themes into easily understood key phrases. Text charts made into slides or overheads can offer an audience relief from less-than-electrifying orators.

Of all the chart types you learn about in this book, text charts are the simplest to create. Unlike graph charts, which have many options, text charts require only that you enter and format text. Producing a basic chart, however, is only the start. With Draw/Annotate and Draw Partner, you can add hand-drawn pictures or hundreds of preexisting symbols to a plain text chart. With Harvard Graphics slide shows and screenshows, you can string a series of text and graph charts into an automated presentation.

Harvard Graphics offers four predefined text chart types: title charts, simple lists, bullet lists, and column charts. The program also offers a free-form chart type that you can use to design a page from scratch. In this chapter, you learn to create each of these text chart types.

In Harvard Graphics 2.3, you can start a new chart by selecting a text chart style and then filling in the data, or you can select a preformatted text chart from the Gallery. The *Gallery* is a library of preformatted text and graphic charts from which you can choose. Of these two approaches, selecting a chart from the Gallery is almost always preferable. By examining the Gallery, you can see before you begin entering data exactly how a chart will appear. The Gallery also enables you to choose easily from among color palettes for the chart.

As you are learning to create the various types of text charts in this chapter, however, you first learn to select chart styles from the Harvard Graphics menus. This method gives you the practice you need to become proficient with the text charts. The chapter then explains how you can use the Gallery.

Creating a Title Chart

A *title chart* is ideal for the opening slide of a presentation or the first page of a handout. Title charts provide room for a large title, a smaller subtitle, and a second subtitle. Figure 4.1 shows an example of a title chart that uses all three of these text areas.

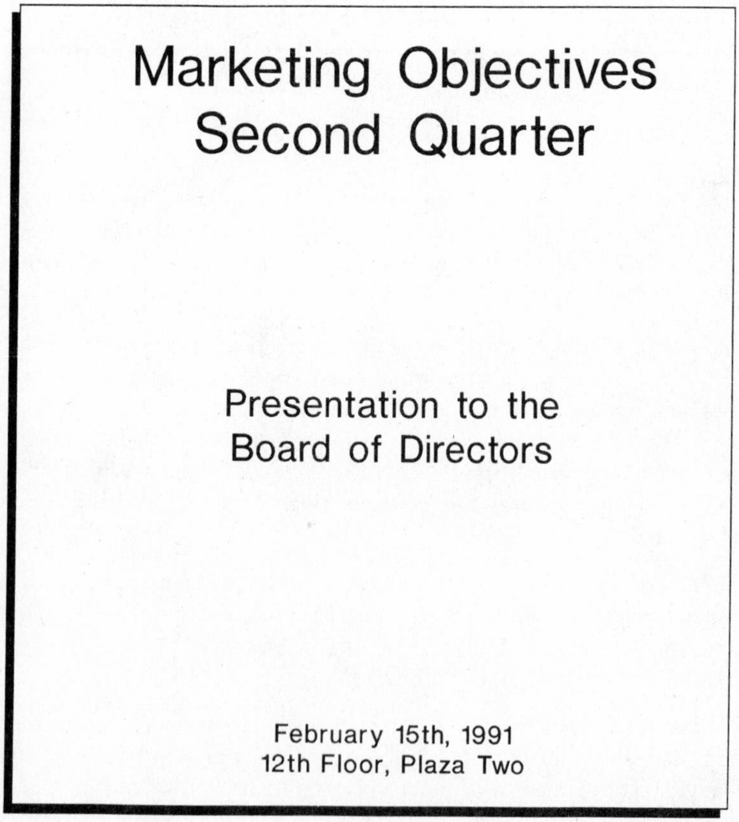

Fig. 4.1.

A sample title chart.

Marketing Objectives
Second Quarter

Presentation to the
Board of Directors

February 15th, 1991
12th Floor, Plaza Two

Checking the Options

Before you create a chart, always press F8 (Options) at the main menu to examine the current options. The Current Chart Options overlay appears (see fig. 4.2).

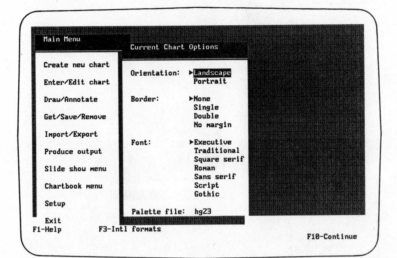

Fig. 4.2.

The Current Chart Options overlay.

When you start Harvard Graphics, the Options settings are the same as the default settings you established when you used the Setup command from the main menu. If you set the Orientation option to Portrait, for example, any chart you create starts in portrait orientation. You may want to modify the settings on the Current Chart Options overlay, however, for just this chart. For an explanation of the four options that appear on the Current Chart Options overlay, see the description of the Setup defaults in Chapter 2.

To change any of the current chart options, press the Tab key to move the cursor to the option you want to change and use the space bar to make a selection. To confirm your choice, press Enter. At any time, you can press F10 (Continue) to accept the current settings and return to the main menu. Or you can set all four options one by one. After you set the fourth option (Palette File), you are returned to the main menu.

Starting a Title Chart

To begin creating a title chart, do the following:

1. Select Create New Chart from the main menu.

2. Select Text from the Create New Chart menu.

3. Select Title Chart from the Text Chart Styles menu.

Figure 4.3 shows the menu path you take to create a title chart. When you choose Title Chart, the Title Chart screen appears. (If you have not saved the last chart you created or your latest changes, a warning message appears. Press Enter to continue.)

Fig. 4.3.

Using the menus to create a title chart.

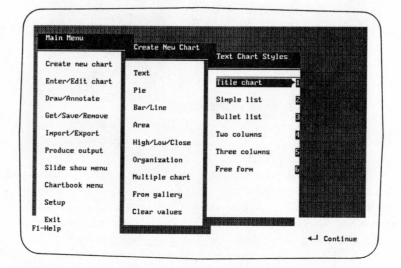

Entering Title Chart Text

The Title Chart screen that appears after you select Title Chart from the Text Chart Styles menu shows three areas labeled Top, Middle, and Bottom. The top area holds a chart title, the middle area holds a chart subtitle, and the bottom area holds a second subtitle.

To enter text, position the cursor at one of the three areas by pressing Tab. Type up to three lines of text, pressing Enter at the end of each line to advance to a new line. You may type text into any or all three of the areas. Text entered into the top area appears as a title; text entered into the middle area appears centered vertically on the page; and text entered into the bottom area appears centered across the bottom of the page.

For practice in creating a title chart, follow this example. Suppose that Superior Office Supplies needs to deliver a new product presentation to its sales force. The company plans to use a title chart as the first page of a slide presentation and as the first page of a handout distributed after the presentation.

To complete the Title Chart screen for this chart, enter *Superior Office Supplies* and *Marketing Division* in the top section, in two lines. Enter *The Annihilator* and *Pencil Eraser* in the middle section, in two lines, and enter *New Product Presentation* in the bottom area. Figure 4.4 shows the completed Title Chart screen.

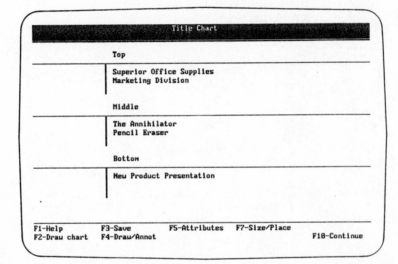

Fig. 4.4.

Entering text in the Title Chart screen.

Previewing a Title Chart

A title chart is the simplest and most easily understood example of how Harvard Graphics requests a few key ingredients and concocts a chart based on built-in chart recipes. After you have entered text in the three parts of the Title Chart screen, you can sample the finished result and preview the chart by pressing F2 (Draw Chart). Harvard Graphics draws the same chart on-screen that the program produces on paper or film.

While previewing a chart, you can make no changes to the content or format. If the chart looks satisfactory, you need only return to the Title Chart screen, save and print the chart, and continue creating the next part of your presentation.

Or, if necessary, you can return to the Title Chart screen and make alterations to customize the chart. You should become accustomed to previewing your charts often as they are developed.

Figure 4.5 shows the chart you see when you press F2 (Draw Chart) after entering the Superior Office Supplies text. Notice that each line on the chart is centered and that the top two text lines have the largest text size. The following section discusses how to modify this default setting.

**Superior Office Supplies
Marketing Division**

**The Annihilator
Pencil Eraser**

New Product Presentation

To quit previewing a chart and return to the Title Chart screen, press Esc.

Changing a Title Chart's Text Size and Placement

You can vary the size and placement of a chart's text by pressing F7 (Size/Place) when the Title Chart screen is displayed. When Size/Place is available, it is presented as one of the function key choices at the bottom of the screen. Pressing F7 summons an overlay showing two new columns of information, as shown in figure 4.6. This Size/Place overlay enables you to modify text size and alignment.

Size, the first option you can set from the Size/Place overlay, is a measure of the height of the characters in a line of text. If a line contains no characters, the

Size option determines how much space the line occupies. You can use this option to decrease or increase the height of a blank line between two lines of text if you want to move the lines closer together or farther apart.

```
                        Title Chart

   Size     Place    Top

   8      L ►C  R  | Superior Office Supplies
   8      L ►C  R  | Marketing Division
   8      L ►C  R  |

                    Middle

   6      L ►C  R  | The Annihilator
   6      L ►C  R  | Pencil Eraser
   6      L ►C  R  |

                    Bottom

   4      L ►C  R  | New Product Presentation
   4      L ►C  R  |
   4      L ►C  R  |


   F1-Help          F3-Save        F5-Attributes   F7-Size/Place
   F2-Draw chart    F4-Draw/Annot                         F10-Continue
```

Fig. 4.6.

The Size/Place overlay on the Title Chart screen.

The unit of measure for Size may seem arbitrary to users accustomed to working in inches or points, but the simplest way to think of character size is as a percentage of the largest possible character you can fit on the short side of your page or screen. The largest possible character has a size of 99.9. All other characters are measured in relation to this hypothetical character.

Without a familiar unit of measure, the results of a Size setting can be difficult to imagine. A good approach to using this option is to examine a line's current size and preview the chart. Adjust Size in increments of one or two until text characters look right when you preview. Remember that you can use tenths of a unit for small changes in character size; 6 may be too large, for example, but 5.5 may be just perfect.

Figures 4.7 and 4.8 illustrate the effect of a change in text size. A title with a Size setting of 11 overwhelms the other text on the chart shown in figure 4.7. A setting of 8, shown in figure 4.8, makes the title stand out but still blend with the rest of the text.

A Size setting of 0 removes a line. To delete a line temporarily from a chart, you can set the Size for the line to 0, print the chart, and then return the line to its earlier size. You may find this procedure handy when you want to include some information in one presentation that should be omitted in another presentation.

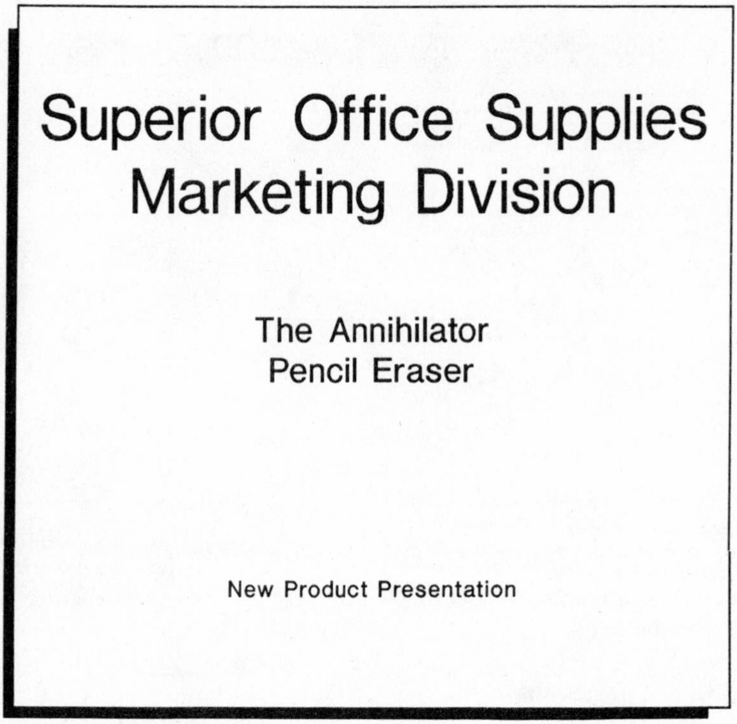

Fig. 4.7.

*Using a Size setting
of 11 for the title.*

Superior Office Supplies
Marketing Division

The Annihilator
Pencil Eraser

New Product Presentation

As you become accustomed to using Harvard Graphics, you will develop a feel for the relationship between the Size setting and the results on the printer, film recorder, or other output device.

Place, the second option you can set from the Size/Place overlay, determines the alignment of text. Text can be left-aligned, right-aligned, or centered.

Try making the Size changes shown in figure 4.9 for the sample title chart by following the procedure given here. Then the chart you preview by pressing F2 (Draw Chart) should match the chart shown in figure 4.10.

Superior Office Supplies
Marketing Division

The Annihilator
Pencil Eraser

New Product Presentation

Fig. 4.8.

Reducing the title's Size setting to 8.

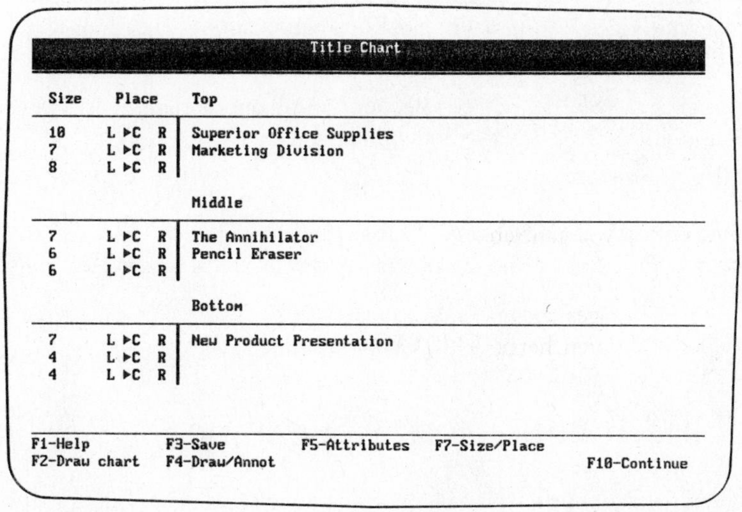

	Title Chart	
Size	**Place**	**Top**
18	L ▶C R	Superior Office Supplies
7	L ▶C R	Marketing Division
8	L ▶C R	
		Middle
7	L ▶C R	The Annihilator
6	L ▶C R	Pencil Eraser
6	L ▶C R	
		Bottom
7	L ▶C R	New Product Presentation
4	L ▶C R	
4	L ▶C R	

```
F1-Help        F3-Save        F5-Attributes   F7-Size/Place
F2-Draw chart  F4-Draw/Annot                              F10-Continue
```

Fig. 4.9.

Changing Size and Place settings.

To change the Size and Place settings, follow these steps:

1. From the Title Chart screen, press F7 (Size/Place) to show the settings of each line of your chart. (To move from setting to setting, press Tab. To cycle through the settings in reverse order, press Shift-Tab.)

2. To enter a new size, type the new number over the old number and press Enter. To change a line's place, use the Tab key to move the cursor to the place settings (L, C, and R) and then press the space bar to move the cursor from one place setting to the next. You also can press L, C, or R to make a Place selection.

3. After changing the Size and Place selections for all appropriate lines, press F10 (Continue) to return to the Title Chart screen.

4. Press F2 (Draw Chart) to preview the chart.

   If you want to make further changes to the Size/Place settings, press Esc to return to the Title Chart screen. Press F7 again and enter new sizes and places.

5. Press any key to return to the Title Chart screen.

Modifying Title Chart Text Appearance

Text size is one text characteristic you can change after you enter text into a title chart. You also can change text appearance by pressing F5 (Attributes) to display the Attributes menu bar, shown in figure 4.11.

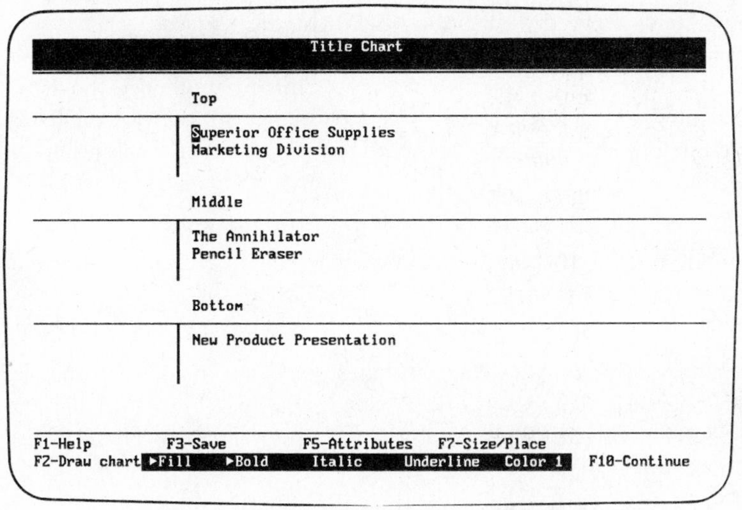

```
                    Title Chart

         Top

         Superior Office Supplies
         Marketing Division

         Middle

         The Annihilator
         Pencil Eraser

         Bottom

         New Product Presentation


F1-Help        F3-Save      F5-Attributes  F7-Size/Place
F2-Draw chart ▶Fill   ▶Bold    Italic    Underline  Color 1   F10-Continue
```

Fig. 4.11.

The Attributes bar at the bottom of the screen.

The Fill option produces solid text characters. If Fill is off, characters appear as outlines. Figure 4.12 shows the difference between characters with the Fill option toggled on and off.

Superior Office Supplies
Superior Office Supplies

Fig. 4.12.

Comparing filled characters with outlined characters.

The Bold, Italic, and Underline options format text as a word processor does. You can use any combination of these attributes.

The Color option modifies the color of text on-screen and as created by devices that produce color output, such as film recorders, color printers, and color plotters.

Before you press F5 to summon the Attributes bar, position the cursor immediately under the first character you want to modify. Then press F5 (Attributes).

Use the arrow keys to move the cursor and highlight the text you want to format. To highlight an entire line, position your cursor on the first character of the line and press the down arrow. You also can press Shift-F5 to change the attributes for one or more entire lines. Use Tab to move the cursor on the Attributes menu bar from one option to the next. Use the space bar to toggle an option on or off. (An option is on when it is preceded by a small triangular pointer.)

To set the color of selected text characters, use Tab to position the cursor on the Color option and press F6 to view a list of available colors. Select a color from the list by moving the cursor and pressing Enter when the correct color is highlighted.

To get some practice working with the Attributes menu bar, modify the sample Superior Office Supplies title chart by underlining Marketing Division, italicizing New Product Presentation, and toggling off the Fill option for New Product Presentation. Follow these steps:

1. Be sure that you are viewing the Title Chart screen.

2. Position the cursor on the first text character you want to modify, which in this example is the M in Marketing.

3. Press F5 (Attributes).

4. With the Attributes menu bar visible at the bottom of the screen, highlight the text you want to format (Marketing Division) by using the arrow keys to move the cursor across the text.

5. Press the Tab key until the cursor is at the Underline option.

6. Press the space bar to toggle on the Underline option.

7. Press F10 (Continue).

8. Position the cursor anywhere on the New Product Presentation line and press Shift-F5 to highlight the entire line.

9. Press the Tab key several times to move the cursor to the Fill option.

10. Press the space bar to turn off Fill and press Tab twice to move the cursor to Italic.

11. Press the space bar to turn on Italic.

12. Press F10 (Continue) to confirm your choice.

13. Press F2 (Draw Chart) to preview the chart.

Figure 4.13 shows the completed title chart with your changes.

Superior Office Supplies
Marketing Division

The Annihilator
Pencil Eraser

New Product Presentation

Fig. 4.13.

The results of changing the text attributes.

Saving a Title Chart

After you have fine-tuned your first chart to perfection, return to the Title Chart screen by pressing Esc. Then press F10 (Continue) to return to the Harvard Graphics main menu. From the main menu, you can save the chart on disk (or print the chart, which is covered in Chapter 15). Notice that the current chart type is displayed near the bottom of the screen. When you save the chart, the chart name you enter appears to the right of the current chart type on the same line of the main menu screen.

To save the chart so that you can modify or print it later, choose Get/Save/Remove from the main menu. The Save Chart option on the Get/Save/Remove menu already is highlighted because Harvard Graphics recognizes that you have an unsaved chart in your computer's memory.

Select Save Chart by pressing Enter, and the Save Chart overlay appears, as shown in figure 4.14. Notice that next to the Directory prompt, Harvard Graphics supplies the disk directory you specified as a default for your data and also provides a description of the chart taken from the first line on the Title Chart screen. Because the cursor already is positioned at the Chart Will Be Saved As prompt, enter a file name, using up to eight characters. For this title chart, for example, you may type *titlecht*. If you want to modify the description of the chart, press Tab or Enter to move the cursor to the Description line. You can accept the current description without changes by pressing F10. To change the description, type the new one in place of the old. Then press Enter or F10 to save the chart. As with most Harvard Graphics prompts, you can press Tab to move from one prompt to the next. Accept the current description (Superior Office Supplies, in this example) by pressing Enter to save the chart on disk.

Fig. 4.14.

The Save Chart overlay.

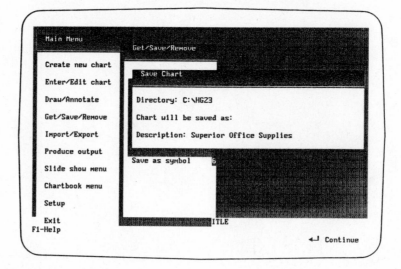

Harvard Graphics 2.3 offers two other, much faster ways to save a chart in progress. From the Title Chart screen, you can press F3 (Save) or Ctrl-S. The Save Chart overlay appears directly over the data screen. You can fill out the overlay and quickly save the chart without having to return to the Harvard Graphics main menu.

Making a Simple List

A *simple list* is ideal for presenting items arranged in no particular order and with each item given equal emphasis. The items of a simple list are displayed one under another and centered, unless you specify otherwise.

Use a simple list to identify the central subjects or themes of a presentation. For example, use a simple list as part of the overview of your sales presentation to show the products you plan to discuss.

By default, simple lists have a title centered at the top of the page, usually in a larger text size, followed by a list of centered items below the title and an optional footnote in the lower left corner. Figure 4.15 shows an example of a simple list.

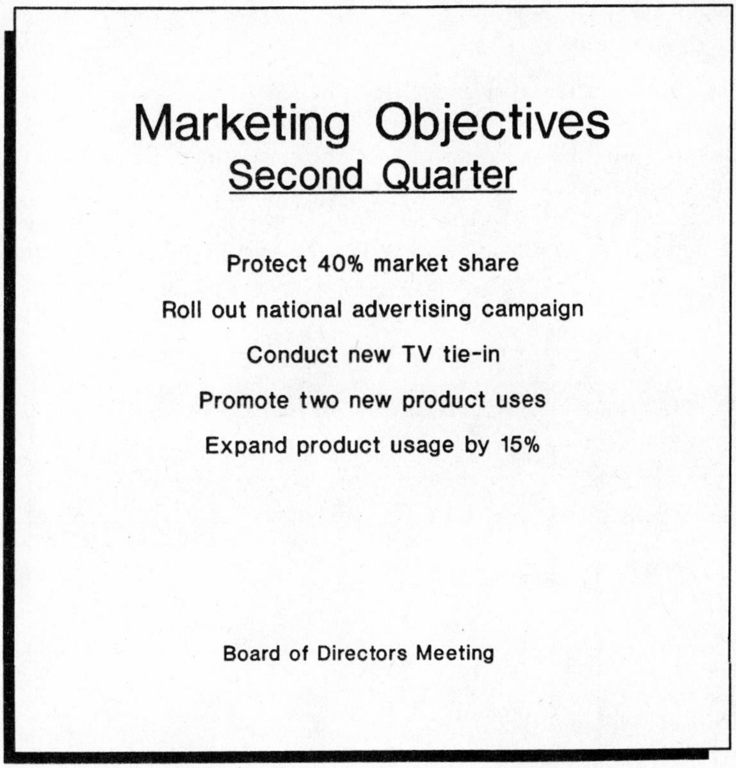

Marketing Objectives
Second Quarter

Protect 40% market share

Roll out national advertising campaign

Conduct new TV tie-in

Promote two new product uses

Expand product usage by 15%

Board of Directors Meeting

Fig. 4.15.

A simple list.

Unlike bullet lists, simple lists do not provide bullets before items or an automatic means to number items, but you can add bullets manually (see the "Adding Bullet Points to Simple List Items" section).

Starting a Simple List

Remember, before creating any chart you should check the settings of the current options by pressing F8 (Options) from the main menu.

To create a simple list, do the following procedure:

1. Select Create New Chart from the main menu.

2. Select Text from the Create New Chart menu.

3. Select Simple List from the Text Chart Styles menu.

The Simple List screen appears. (If you have not saved the last chart you created or your latest changes, a warning message appears. Press Esc so that you can return to the main menu and save your work. To abandon changes you have made, press Enter to continue.)

Note: If you have just saved another chart, that chart is still the current chart shown on the main menu screen. When you start a *new* chart, therefore, Harvard Graphics asks whether you want to keep the current data. If you select Yes, the program uses the preceding chart's data in the new chart. If you select No, the program presents you with a clear data screen, ready for new text. If you see this warning message now, respond by pressing the space bar to change the setting to No and then press Enter. A clear Simple List screen appears, as shown in figure 4.16.

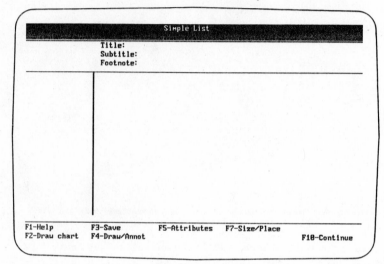

Fig. 4.16.

The Simple List screen.

Entering Simple List Text

If you want to label your chart with a title, subtitle, and footnote, type the appropriate text where prompted in the top three lines of the Simple List screen. Use the Tab or Enter keys to move from one line to another. You also can press Tab or Enter to move the cursor to the body of the page so that you can type the simple list text items.

For the second chart in the Superior Office Supplies presentation, create a simple list by following these steps:

1. Type *The Annihilator Pencil Eraser* as the title and press Enter.

2. Type *Identified Customer Needs* as the subtitle and press Enter.

3. Press Enter again to leave the footnote area blank and move the cursor to the main text entry area of the screen.

4. Type the following five text lines, pressing Enter twice after each line to double-space the lines:

Total erasure
Pointed end for precise erasures
Blunt end for broad erasures
No eraser flecking—eliminate pesky eraser bits
Long-lasting

Figure 4.17 shows the completed Simple List screen.

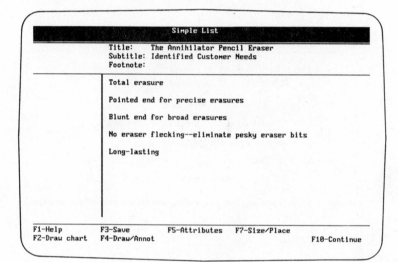

Fig. 4.17.

Entering a simple list.

To insert a new line between two items on a text chart screen, position the cursor where you want the new line to appear and press Ctrl-Ins. To delete a line, position the cursor on the line and press Ctrl-Del.

Adding Bullet Points to Simple List Items

If you want to place bullets on a simple list, you must enter the bullets manually. To enter a bullet before an item, position the cursor at the beginning of a new line and press Ctrl-B. Select one of the available bullet styles by using the space bar; then press Enter. Leave one space following the bullet and type the item.

You also can add a bullet point to the beginning of a line you already have typed. Position the cursor on the first character of the line and press Ins. The cursor changes from a blinking underline to a blinking block to indicate that anything you add will be inserted in the line. Press Ctrl-B, select a bullet style with the space bar, and press Enter. Think of a block cursor (Insert on) as an object that can push current text aside to make room for new text. An underline cursor (Insert off) undercuts current text so that anything you add replaces old text.

Previewing a Simple List

To preview your work, press F2 (Draw Chart). Figure 4.18 shows the chart you should see. Notice that Harvard Graphics has drawn a simple list. You can use the list as is or customize it. For example, you can make two changes to your simple list to make it more attractive: use a smaller text size for the list of items and underline the chart's subtitle.

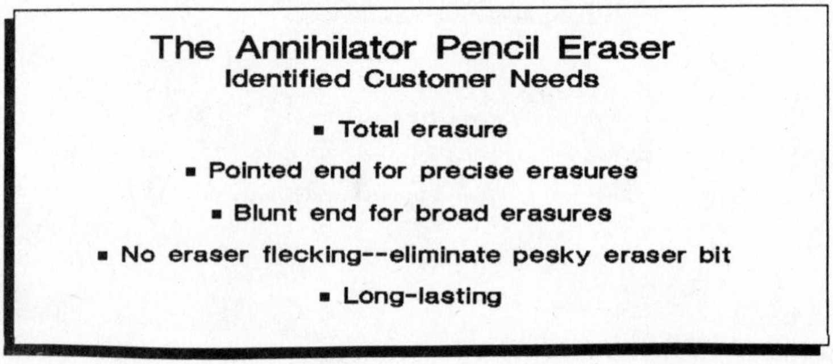

Fig. 4.18.

The Simple List with bullets added.

> ## The Annihilator Pencil Eraser
> ### Identified Customer Needs
>
> - Total erasure
> - Pointed end for precise erasures
> - Blunt end for broad erasures
> - No eraser flecking--eliminate pesky eraser bit
> - Long-lasting

To begin making changes, press Esc to return to the Simple List screen.

Changing a Simple List's Text Size and Placement

Press F7 (Size/Place) at the Simple List screen to modify the text's size and horizontal positioning. When the Size/Place overlay appears, notice that you can change the Size and Place settings for the title, subtitle, and footnote independently, but you can specify only one setting for all the list items. You also can choose to indent all the list items by making sure that the items' Place is set to L (left-aligned) and then typing over the current indent number with a new number. The number you use should be a percentage of the width of the screen; 50, for example, starts list items halfway across the screen. Because the current Indent setting is 0, items start at the left edge of the screen.

For the Superior Office Supplies simple list, alter the size of the list items from the default setting of 5.5 to 4, set Place to L, and set the Indent to 25. Press F10 (Continue) to accept the change and remove the Size/Place overlay. Then press F2 (Draw Chart) to preview the chart. Figure 4.19 shows the revised simple list. Notice the difference in appearance. Press Esc to return to the Simple List screen.

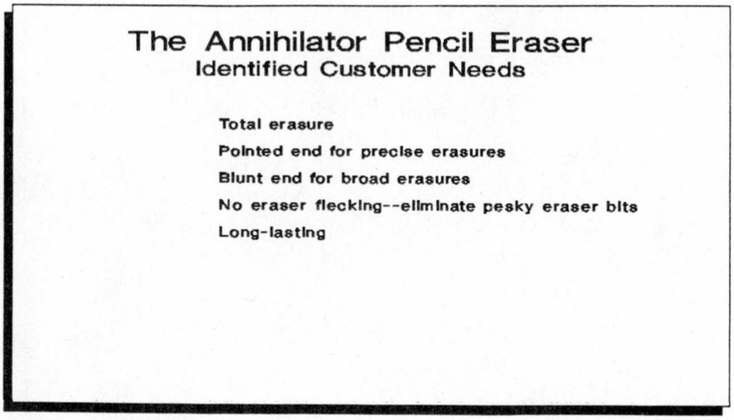

The Annihilator Pencil Eraser
Identified Customer Needs

Total erasure
Pointed end for precise erasures
Blunt end for broad erasures
No eraser flecking--eliminate pesky eraser bits
Long-lasting

Fig. 4.19.

Simple list previewed with items set to Size 4, Place L, and Indent 25.

Modifying Simple List Text Appearance

With simple lists, you can choose from the same set of possible text attributes available in title charts. For a description of each of these attributes, refer to "Modifying Title Chart Text Appearance" in this chapter.

To perfect your simple list chart and practice using the Attributes menu bar, underline the subtitle. Use the following procedure:

1. Position the cursor on the first character in the subtitle line.

2. Press Shift-F5 to highlight the entire line.

3. Press Tab to move the cursor next to the Underline option on the Attributes menu bar.

4. Press the space bar to turn on the Underline attribute and press Enter.

5. Press F2 (Draw Chart) to preview the changes.

Figure 4.20 shows the simple list after you have underlined the subtitle.

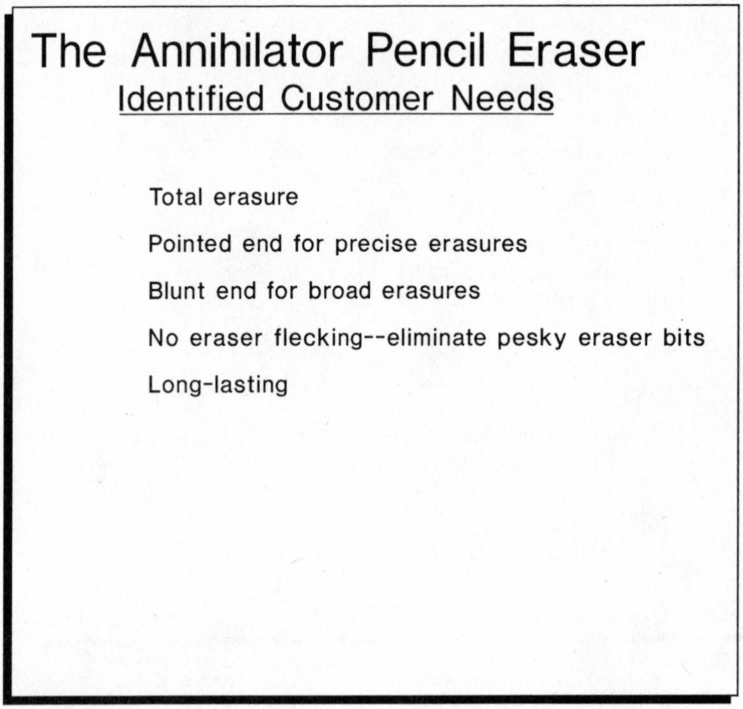

Fig. 4.20.

The simple list with the text attributes changed.

The Annihilator Pencil Eraser
Identified Customer Needs

Total erasure

Pointed end for precise erasures

Blunt end for broad erasures

No eraser flecking--eliminate pesky eraser bits

Long-lasting

Saving a Simple List

To save a simple list, press F10 (Continue) at the Simple List screen to return to the main menu. Choose Get/Save/Remove from the main menu and choose Save Chart from the Get/Save/Remove menu.

At the Chart Will Be Saved As line, type the name of the chart, such as *simplcht*, and press Enter. Notice that Harvard Graphics borrows the title of the chart as the description. Alter the description, if you want, by pressing Ctrl-Del in the Description field to erase the current entry and typing a new entry or press F-10 to save the chart with the name you have entered.

For more details on the process of saving a text chart, see "Saving a Title Chart" in this chapter.

Preparing a Bullet List

A *bullet list* serves the same purpose as a simple list: to communicate a series of ideas or to list a set of items. But bullet lists have several unique characteristics. Unlike simple list items, items in a bullet list are preceded by one of four bullet shapes and aligned so that the bullets line up under one another. A fifth option enables you to number items to designate a sequence.

Bullet lists have a title, subtitle, and footnote, like simple lists. You can add as many lines of text as you want to each bullet point, and you can group logically related items together as subitems under main bullet points, creating an outline format.

Figure 4.21 shows a sample bullet list, and figure 4.22 shows a bullet list with subitems.

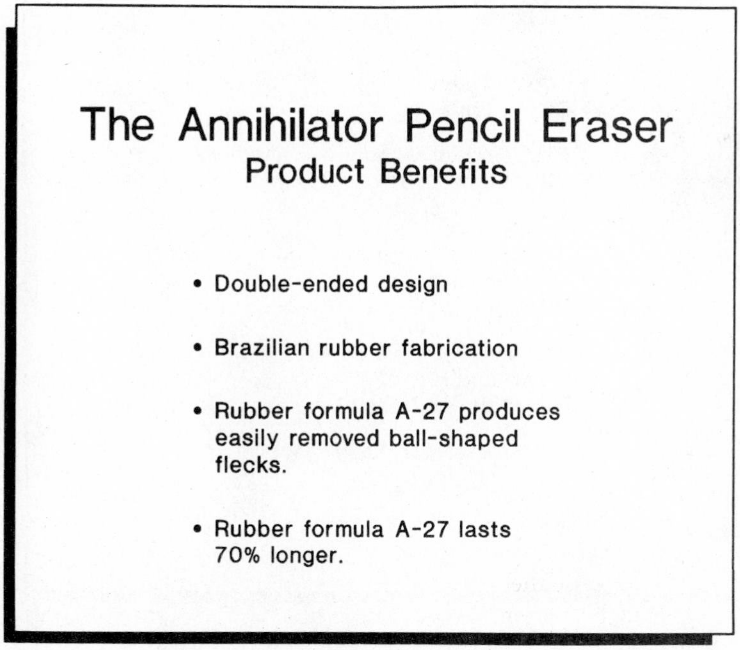

Fig. 4.21.

A bullet list.

The contents of the figure:

The Annihilator Pencil Eraser
Product Benefits

- Double-ended design
- Brazilian rubber fabrication
- Rubber formula A-27 produces easily removed ball-shaped flecks.
- Rubber formula A-27 lasts 70% longer.

Starting a Bullet List

To start a bullet list, follow these steps:

1. Select Create New Chart from the main menu.

2. Select Text from the Create New Chart menu.

3. Select Bullet List from the Text Chart Styles menu.

The Bullet List screen appears. (If you have not saved the last chart you created or saved your latest changes, a warning message appears. Press Esc so that you can return to the main menu and save the chart or press Enter to continue.) If the Change Chart Type overlay appears to ask whether you want to keep current data, reply No.

Fig. 4.22.

A bullet list in outline form.

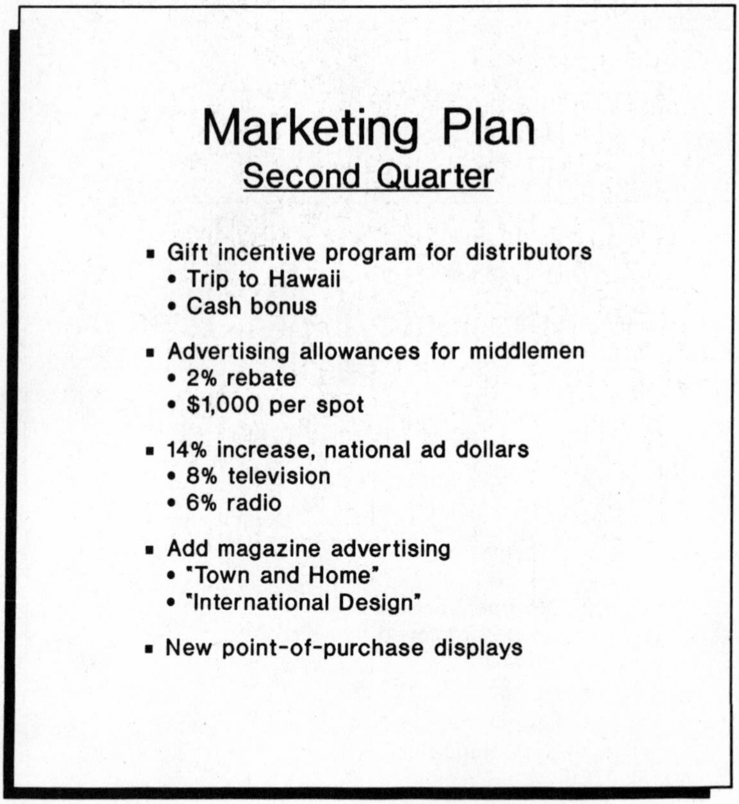

Marketing Plan
Second Quarter

- Gift incentive program for distributors
  - Trip to Hawaii
  - Cash bonus

- Advertising allowances for middlemen
  - 2% rebate
  - $1,000 per spot

- 14% increase, national ad dollars
  - 8% television
  - 6% radio

- Add magazine advertising
  - "Town and Home"
  - "International Design"

- New point-of-purchase displays

Entering Bullet List Text

When the Bullet List screen appears, the cursor is next to the Title prompt. Type a chart title, subtitle, and footnote in the appropriate fields, pressing Enter after each.

For the third chart in the sample Superior Office Supplies presentation, enter the title *The Annihilator Pencil Eraser*. For a subtitle, enter *Product Benefits*. Press Enter to skip the Footnote prompt.

Pressing Enter a third time creates the first bullet point and places the cursor to the right of the bullet. A new bullet appears each time you leave a blank line by pressing Enter or the down arrow twice. If you press Enter once at the end of a line, any new text you type continues as part of the current bullet item.

Type the first bullet item for the Superior Office Supplies chart, *Double-ended design*, and press Enter once. Notice that the cursor returns to the beginning of the next line, immediately under the first bullet's text. Press Enter again, and a new bullet appears. Bullet lists are always double-spaced.

By manually inserting a bullet with Ctrl-B at the beginning of the second line of a bulleted item, you can create the tiered effect shown in figure 4.23. Each new line starts under the first character of text after the bullet in the preceding line.

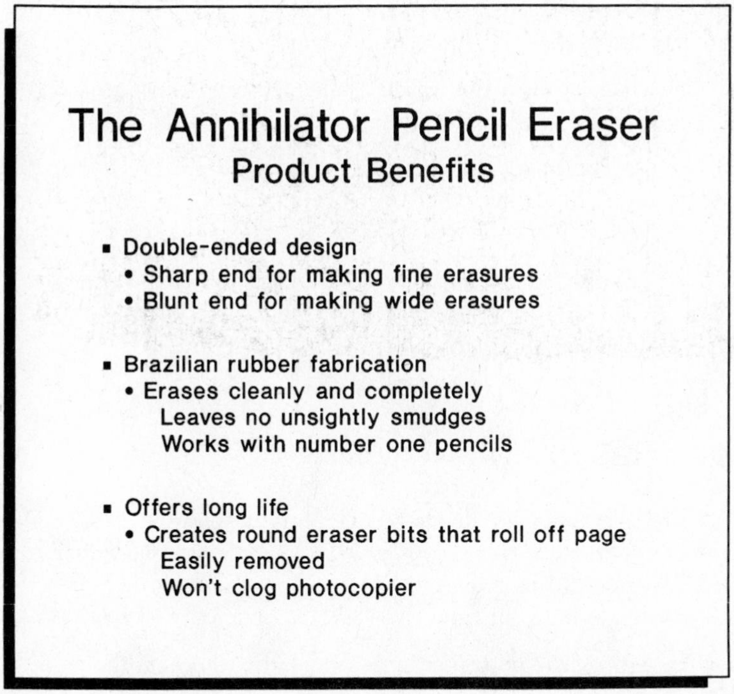

The Annihilator Pencil Eraser
Product Benefits

- Double-ended design
  - Sharp end for making fine erasures
  - Blunt end for making wide erasures

- Brazilian rubber fabrication
  - Erases cleanly and completely
    Leaves no unsightly smudges
    Works with number one pencils

- Offers long life
  - Creates round eraser bits that roll off page
    Easily removed
    Won't clog photocopier

Fig. 4.23.

Using subitems to create a tier of bullets.

Notice that the first two levels of the bullet list shown in figure 4.23 have consistent bullet styles. The third level is not bulleted. The rule of thumb for creating attractive bullet lists is to include no more than two bullet types per chart.

In general, to begin a new line with a bullet, press Ctrl-B before entering the line's text, use the space bar to select a bullet style from the Bullet Shape overlay, and press Enter. After the bullet appears, press the space bar and type your text.

To add a bullet to the beginning of an existing line, make sure that you are in insert mode by pressing Ins. (The cursor should be a flashing block rather than a flashing underline.) Position the cursor at the beginning of the line, press Ctrl-B, select the bullet style you want, and press Enter. Pressing Ctrl-B always adds a bullet at the current cursor position no matter what type of chart you are creating.

To match the bullet list shown in figure 4.23, add a second-tier bullet item by pressing the up arrow to move the cursor under the first bullet (double-ended design). Notice that the second bullet disappears. Press Ctrl-B and choose the round bullet from the Bullet Shape overlay by pressing Enter. Then press the space bar and type *Sharp end for making fine erasures*. Press Enter at the end of the line and add another second-tier bullet item preceded by a round bullet: *Blunt end for making wide erasures*. Press Enter twice to create a new first-level bullet item. Complete the bullet list to match the items in figure 4.23.

To insert a new blank line between two existing lines, position the cursor anywhere on the second line and press Ctrl-Ins.

To delete a line, position the cursor anywhere on the line and press Ctrl-Del. If the line has a bullet point, the bullet point does not disappear. To remove the bullet point, press the up-arrow key once.

Press F2 (Draw Chart) to preview the appearance of your bullet list. Then press Esc to return to the Bullet List screen to make changes.

Changing a Bullet List's Text Size and Placement

Changing the size and placement of lines of bullet lists by pressing F7 (Size/Place) is the same process you use when working with a simple list (see "Changing a Simple List's Text Size and Placement"). The effect of the Place settings on bullet list items, however, is different from the effect on simple list items.

With simple lists, the left, right, and center options align text lines on the page, as in figure 4.24.

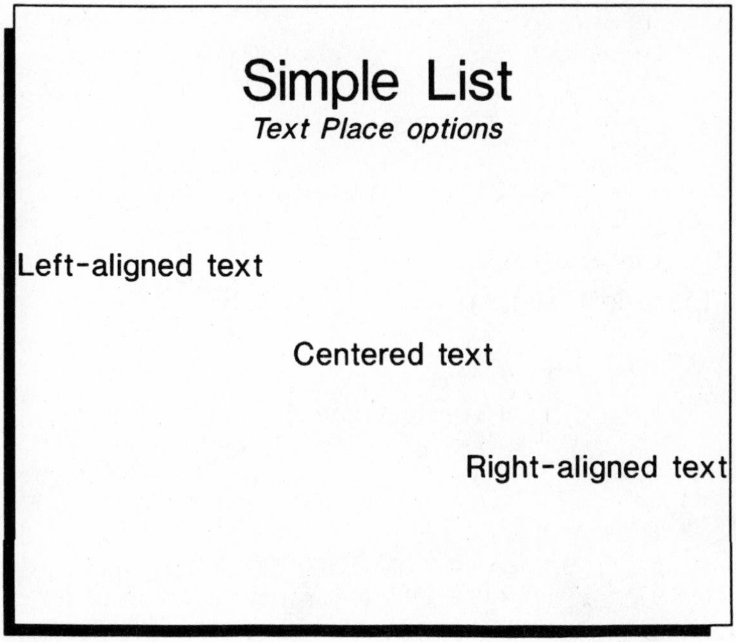

Simple List
Text Place options

Left-aligned text

Centered text

Right-aligned text

Fig. 4.24.

Changing the Place settings for a simple list.

Bullet list items always line up under one another so that the bullets line up vertically on the page. Choosing left or right alignment moves all bullet list items together so that the left or right edge of the group aligns with the left or right side of the page. The difference between the two actions is evident when bullet items are right-aligned and you have one bullet item longer than the others. The longest item is the only one aligned with the right edge of the page. The results of choosing left, center, and right alignment for bullet items are shown in figure 4.25.

Changing Bullet Types

The Size/Place overlay for bullet lists offers a new capability not seen with the charts discussed previously in this chapter. With the bullet list Size/Place command, you also can change the type of bullet used for main bullet points. Five bullet shapes are included on the Size/Place overlay. To change the bullet shape used, do the following:

1. With the Bullet List screen displayed, press F7 (Size/Place).

2. Use Tab to move the cursor to the bullet shape options.

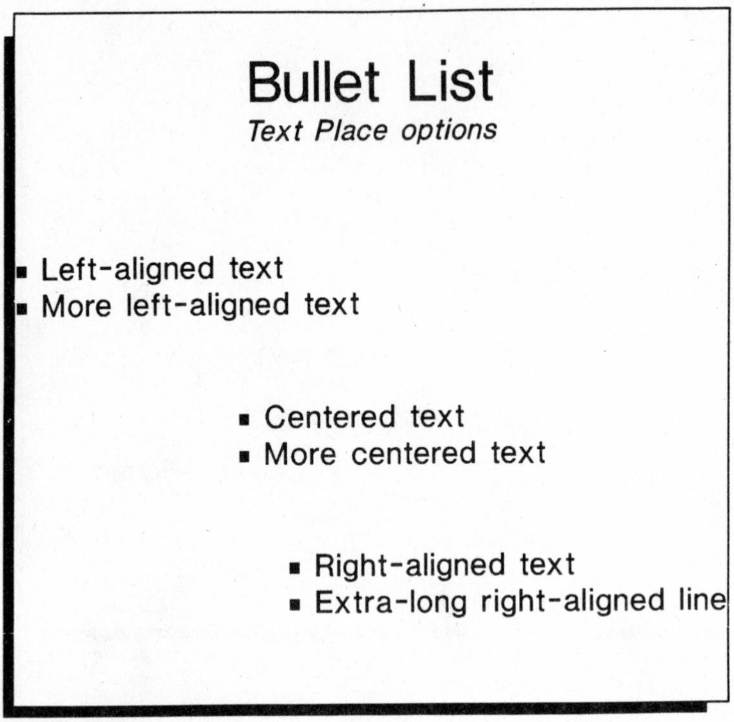

Fig. 4.25.

*Changing the Place
settings for a bullet
list.*

Bullet List
Text Place options

■ Left-aligned text
■ More left-aligned text

■ Centered text
■ More centered text

■ Right-aligned text
■ Extra-long right-aligned line

3. Use the space bar to select the bullet shape.

4. Press F10 (Continue) to return to the Bullet List screen.

5. Press F2 (Draw Chart) to preview the change.

To change the shape of bullets preceding second-tier bullet items, you must position the cursor on an existing bullet item, press Ctrl-B to bring up the Bullet Shape overlay, and then select a different bullet shape. Make sure that Insert mode is toggled off (press the Ins key until the cursor is an underline rather than a solid block), or the new bullet will appear in front of the old instead of replacing it.

Numbering Bullets

To number main bullets sequentially, choose the number sign (#) when you select a bullet shape. Subitems created when you press Ctrl-B do not have the # option and can be numbered only manually. Number signs appear on the Bullet List screen to indicate that numbers will appear on the final chart.

Modifying Bullet List Text Appearance

To modify text attributes, use F5 (Attributes) the same way you do for simple lists (see this chapter's section called "Modifying Simple List Text Appearance"). Bullets normally appear in the same color as the first character of the text that follows. If you want to alter the color of bullet points without changing the color of the text, follow this procedure:

1. Insert a blank space after the bullet point.

2. Modify the color attribute of only that space.

3. Preview the chart to see that the bullet has changed color.

You also can leave a space when you type the bullet item so that you can change the bullet's color attribute later.

Saving a Bullet List

To save a bullet list, follow these steps:

1. Press F10 (Continue) from the Bullet List screen to return to the main menu.

2. Choose Get/Save/Remove from the main menu.

3. Choose Save Chart from the Get/Save/Remove menu.

At the Chart Will Be Saved As line, type a file name for the chart, such as *buletcht*, and press Enter. Notice that Harvard Graphics uses the title of the chart as the description. Alter the description by typing over the current entry and pressing Enter or just press Enter or F10 to accept the description and save the chart.

For more details on the process of saving a text chart, see "Saving a Title Chart" in this chapter.

Building a Column Chart

A *column chart* displays related text items side by side in two or three columns. Some ideal uses for two-column charts are comparison lists with benefits and drawbacks. Column charts also are useful for comparing numeric information. Figure 4.26 is a typical three-column chart used for illustrating financial information. This chart compares revenues for the first quarter.

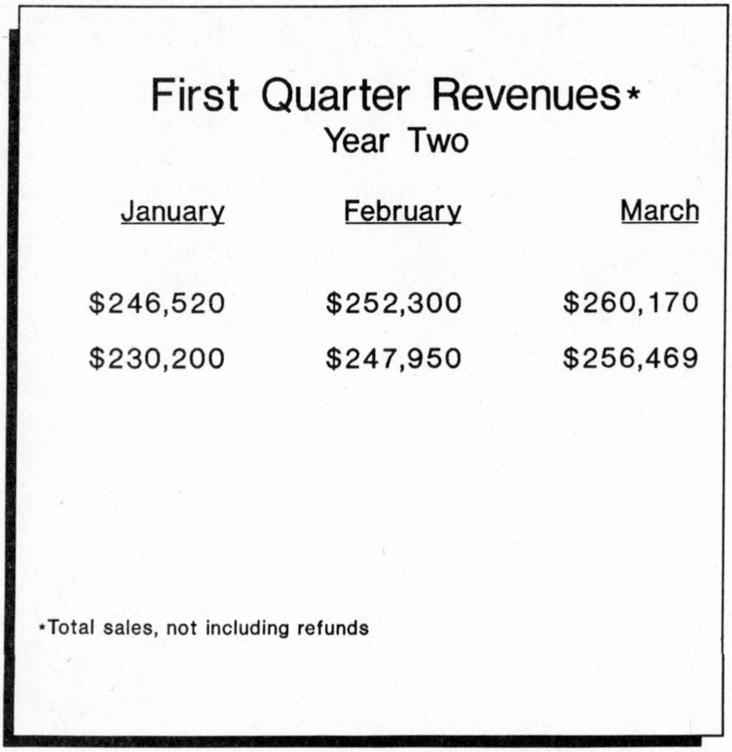

First Quarter Revenues*
Year Two
January
February
March
$246,520
$252,300
$260,170
$230,200
$247,950
$256,469
*Total sales, not including refunds

Fig. 4.26.

A column chart with three columns.

Starting a Two- or Three-Column Chart

Start a column chart as you do any other text chart but choose Two Columns or Three Columns from the Text Chart Styles menu. For the sample Superior Office Supplies presentation, choose Two Columns to create the chart shown in figure 4.27. If the Keep Current Data prompt appears, reply No so that you can enter new data. The Two Columns screen appears, providing areas in which you can type a title, subtitle, and footnote and areas for column headings and column items.

Entering Column Chart Text

To practice creating a two-column chart, enter data for the Superior Office Supplies column chart. Follow these steps:

1. Type *The Annihilator Pencil Eraser* in the Title field and press Enter.

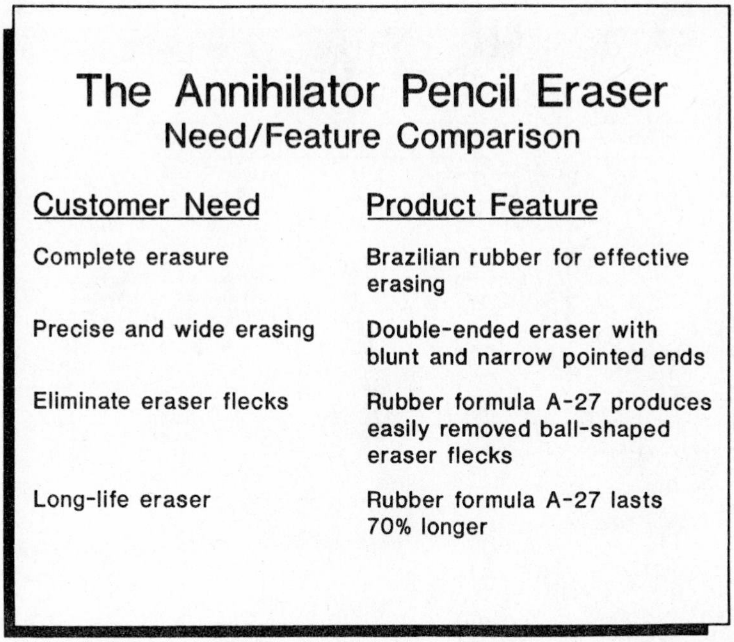

The Annihilator Pencil Eraser
Need/Feature Comparison

<u>Customer Need</u>   **<u>Product Feature</u>**

Complete erasure   Brazilian rubber for effective
                        erasing

Precise and wide erasing   Double-ended eraser with
                        blunt and narrow pointed ends

Eliminate eraser flecks   Rubber formula A-27 produces
                        easily removed ball-shaped
                        eraser flecks

Long-life eraser   Rubber formula A-27 lasts
                        70% longer

Fig. 4.27.

A two-column chart for Superior Office Supplies.

2. For the subtitle, type *Need/Feature Comparison* and press Enter.

3. Press Tab or Enter to leave the footnote area blank and move to the space for the first column heading.

4. Type *Customer Need* for the first heading and press Tab (not Enter) to move the cursor to the second column heading.

5. Type *Product Feature* for the second heading and press Enter.

6. Press Shift-Tab to begin entering text items in the first column.

7. Enter the items shown on the Two Columns screen in figure 4.28, pressing Tab to jump between columns. Pressing Enter moves the cursor down one line without moving to the next column. To double-space items, press Tab when you complete the right-hand column item and press Enter to skip a line before typing the next item. Harvard Graphics text chart screens do not have wordwrap. You must press Enter at the end of each line to continue typing on the next line.

8. Press F2 (Draw Chart) to preview your work.

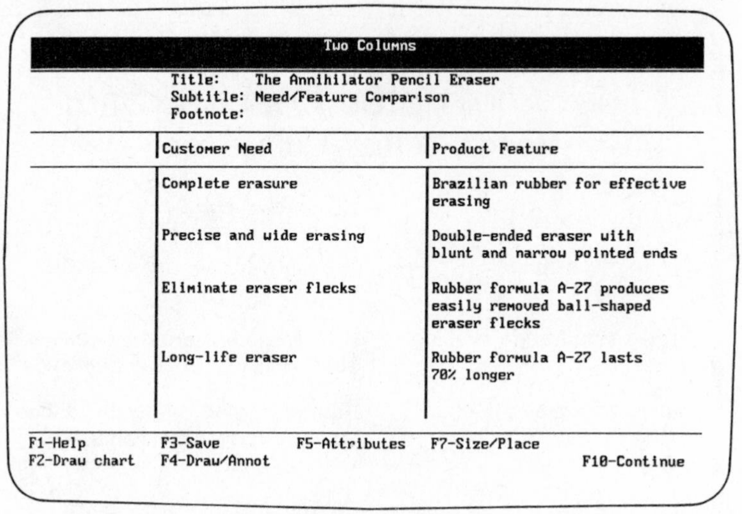

Fig. 4.28.

Completing the Two Columns screen.

```
┌─────────────────────────────────────────────────────────────┐
│                        Two Columns                          │
├─────────────────────────────────────────────────────────────┤
│     Title:    The Annihilator Pencil Eraser                 │
│     Subtitle: Need/Feature Comparison                       │
│     Footnote:                                               │
│     ─────────────────────────────────────────────          │
│     Customer Need            │ Product Feature              │
│                              │                              │
│     Complete erasure         │ Brazilian rubber for effective│
│                              │ erasing                      │
│                              │                              │
│     Precise and wide erasing │ Double-ended eraser with     │
│                              │ blunt and narrow pointed ends │
│                              │                              │
│     Eliminate eraser flecks  │ Rubber formula A-27 produces │
│                              │ easily removed ball-shaped   │
│                              │ eraser flecks                │
│                              │                              │
│     Long-life eraser         │ Rubber formula A-27 lasts    │
│                              │ 70% longer                   │
│                              │                              │
│     ─────────────────────────────────────────────          │
│  F1-Help      F3-Save      F5-Attributes  F7-Size/Place     │
│  F2-Draw chart F4-Draw/Annot                    F10-Continue │
└─────────────────────────────────────────────────────────────┘
```

Examining Special Size/Place Options

The F7 (Size/Place) feature works with text in column charts just as it works with text in other text charts. But you should be aware of a few Size/Place uses that are specific to column charts.

On the Size/Place overlay, Harvard Graphics presents four options, much like clothes sizes, for column spacing: S, M, L, and XL. S leaves the smallest spacing between consecutive columns. XL leaves the largest spacing. The best way to select the proper column spacing for your chart is to try one setting, preview the chart, and try the next setting. You may find that the default column width is the best. In the case of this two-column chart, the default is M.

In a column chart, all text items are placed against the left edge of a column, and all numeric items align with the right edge of a column so that the decimal points align. Numeric items can include dollar signs, commas, and decimal points. You cannot modify the place settings for the items in a column chart.

Modifying Column Chart Text Appearance

The F5 (Attributes) command used with column charts presents the same formatting commands described for other text charts. You highlight the text to format and use Tab and the space bar to choose attribute settings from the Attributes menu bar. Use Shift-F5 to set attributes for an entire line. When you preview the column chart, notice that the two column headings are underlined automatically. Column headings are always underlined in column charts.

Saving a Column Chart

After you have created and viewed your column chart, press Esc to return to the Two Columns screen. Press F10 (Continue) to return to the main menu. Notice that the chart type listed near the bottom of the screen is 2 COLUMN. Choose Get/Save/Remove from the main menu and then choose Save Chart from the Get/Save/Remove menu.

Follow the same procedure described earlier for entering the chart's name and revising the description. Enter the name TWOCOL after the Chart Will Be Saved As prompt and press Enter. Press F10 to save the chart with the current description. After the chart is saved, notice that the current chart name appears to the right of the chart type on the main menu screen.

For more details on the process of saving a text chart, see "Saving a Title Chart" in this chapter.

Adding a Third Column to a Two-Column Chart

You can add a third column to an existing two-column chart by using the Get Chart command under the Get/Save/Remove main menu option to retrieve the two-column chart and then returning to the main menu.

If you have not started a new chart and you have been following along with this chapter, you still have the two-column chart in the computer's memory. Choose Create New Chart from the main menu and then select Three Columns after you choose Text from the Create New Chart menu.

If you last created a different chart from the two-column chart described previously in this chapter, you need to retrieve the two-column chart first by following these steps:

1. Select Get/Save/Remove from the main menu.

2. Select Get Chart from the Get/Save/Remove menu.

3. Use the up- and down-arrow keys to move the highlight so that it is on the chart called TWOCOL.

4. Press Enter to get TWOCOL.

Next, press Esc twice to return to the main menu. To start the three-column chart, select Create New Chart from the main menu, select Text from the Create New Chart menu, and then select Three Columns from the Text Chart Styles menu.

If you choose Yes when the Keep Current Data prompt appears, Harvard Graphics uses the two-column chart's existing columns as the left two columns in the new Three Columns screen. You need to fill in only the third column to complete the chart.

If you have set the two-column chart to portrait orientation, you may need to change the chart to landscape orientation to accommodate a third column. To change the orientation of a chart, return to the main menu by pressing F10 (Continue) at the Three Columns screen, press F8 (Options) to call up the Current Chart Options overlay, and choose Landscape for the Orientation setting.

Creating Free-Form Charts

A *free-form chart* enables you to create a text chart design of your own. Because of this flexibility, free-form charts are ideal for text presentations that do not fit any of the predefined text chart molds. Among charts appropriate for the free-form chart style are charts with unusually wide columns and charts that include large areas of text. Free-form charts also are perfect for invitations, directions, and certificates, none of which fall neatly into Harvard Graphics' existing text chart categories. Figure 4.29 shows one example of a free-form chart. Figure 4.30 shows the free-form chart Superior Office Supplies uses to introduce promotional plans.

Start a free-form chart by choosing Create New Chart from the main menu and then Text from the Create New Chart menu. When the Text Chart Styles menu appears, choose Free Form. If the Keep Current Data query appears, reply No to start a new chart.

The Free Form Text screen that appears next includes areas for a title, subtitle, footnote, and text. You usually should type entries into the title, subtitle, and footnote areas so that Harvard Graphics can position the key elements of your chart on the page. You can place text for the chart anywhere within the text entry area on the Free Form Text screen. Text appears on the page in the same position as it appears on-screen. For example, text centered in the text entry area is centered on the page, and so on.

To set up columns in a free-form chart, line up the first characters of items under one another on-screen and be sure to leave at least two spaces between the end of an item in one column and the beginning of an item in the next column.

Travel Directions
Smith Wedding

From I-48

Turn right at end of Clovesdale exit ramp. Follow
signs to Route 46. Turn right onto Charles St.
House is large white Victorian on left. #140 on
mailbox.

From Davis Parkway

Exit at Forest Lake Road. Turn left off exit onto
Route 117. Go through two intersections to stop
light. Turn right onto Woodland Manor. Turn
left onto Charles St. Look for large white
Victorian on right. #140 on mailbox.

Fig. 4.29.

A free-form chart.

The Annihilator Pencil Eraser
Promotion Plan

PROMOTIONS

Free sample erasers	Stationery dealers
Eraser coupons	College bookstore managers

MTV TIE-IN

"Rub It Out" music video

ADVERTISING

National	2-page spread: major newsweeklies
Local	Co-op program with local dealers

Fig. 4.30.

*The free-form chart
for Superior Office
Supplies.*

Try creating the free-form chart shown in figure 4.30 by filling out a Free Form Text screen, as shown in figure 4.31. Notice that the centered headings on the chart are created from headings centered in the text entry area. Figure 4.31 does not show the two lines under the ADVERTISING head, but the Free Form Text screen scrolls as you enter text.

Fig. 4.31.

Completing the Free Form Text screen.

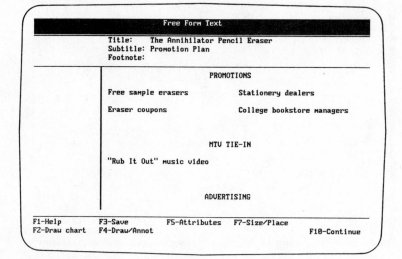

Save a free-form chart as you save other charts, with the following steps:

1. When you finish the chart, press F10 (Continue) to return to the main menu.

2. From the main menu, choose Get/Save/Remove.

3. From the Get/Save/Remove menu, choose Save Chart.

4. Type the name of the chart, such as *freeform*, and accept the chart's current description by pressing F10. Remember that Harvard Graphics derives the description from the title of the chart.

Starting a Chart from the Gallery

Harvard Graphics 2.3 provides a new, vastly improved method of starting new charts. Instead of selecting a chart style name from the Harvard Graphics menus, you can select From Gallery after you choose Create New Chart. Harvard Graphics then displays a representative sample of each of the chart styles available, including a text chart (see fig. 4.32). If you select the text chart, the Gallery then shows you a sample of each available text chart style (see fig. 4.33). You can choose a text chart style and a color palette (a predefined combination of colors) and then start with a blank text screen or a text screen completed with sample text. After you add new text or replace the text already on the text screen, you can press F2 (Draw Chart) and make any modifications you want to the chart's formatting.

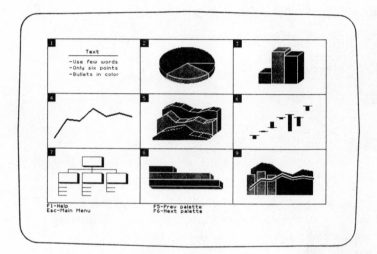

Fig. 4.32.

The first Gallery screen.

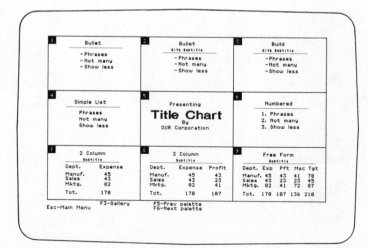

Fig. 4.33.

The sample text chart styles shown in the Gallery.

After reading this chapter, you are already familiar with all the text chart styles shown in the Gallery except for build. A *build chart* is a step in a presentation that includes a series of text charts. Each successive chart adds a new line of highlighted text until the final chart shows all the text. Build charts are helpful for highlighting each new topic as a speaker proceeds through a presentation. You can use build charts effectively in screenshows, which are discussed in Chapter 16 of this book.

To practice creating a new bullet list from the Gallery, follow these steps:

1. Select Create New Chart from the Harvard Graphics main menu.

2. Select From Gallery from the Create New Chart menu. In a moment, Harvard Graphics 2.3 shows you nine chart styles (see fig. 4.32).

3. Press 1 to select a text chart. Harvard Graphics shows you nine sample text charts from which to choose (see fig. 4.33).

4. Press 2 to choose the bullet list with a subtitle.

5. Press F6 (Next Palette) to cycle through the available color palettes and select a color combination you like.

   At this point, you can press F3 (Gallery) to return to the first Gallery screen if you decide to create a different type of chart. You also can press Esc to leave the Gallery and return to the Harvard Graphics main menu. If you press F10 (Edit + Clear), a blank text screen for a bullet list appears. You can enter your own text and have a completed chart. If you press F9 (Edit) instead, the text screen with the text for the sample bullet list appears. You must replace the text already there with your own text to create a chart.

6. Press F10 (Edit + Clear) to get to a blank bullet list text screen.

7. Enter text for the bullet list and press F2 (Draw Chart) to see your work.

You can use F7 (Size/Place) and F5 (Attributes) as you normally do to make changes to the formatting of your chart before you save it with F3 (Save).

Setting Up an Organization Chart

Because organization charts are so popular for representing the structure of an organization, Harvard Graphics includes a special menu option for constructing that kind of chart. Although organization charts are not on the list of text charts that Harvard Graphics creates, a discussion of organization charts is in this chapter because of their similarity to text charts and because organization charts concern text information rather than numeric data.

An *organization chart* diagrams the reporting structure of a multilevel organization, such as a corporation, club, or service. With this type of chart, you can illustrate the interrelationships of managers and subordinates: who reports to whom. Harvard Graphics can create organization charts depicting up to 8 levels of hierarchy and showing up to 80 members or components. Rarely, if ever, do you need to create a chart with that much detail. Figure 4.34 shows a typical organization chart produced by Harvard Graphics.

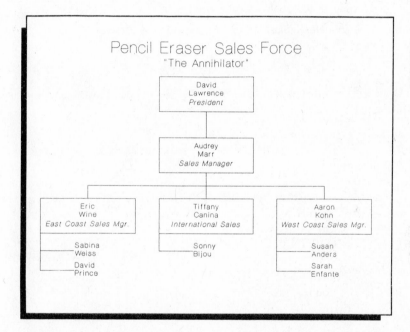

Fig. 4.34.

A sample organization chart.

To help you create an organization chart, Harvard Graphics takes you through a process that involves identifying the members of a hierarchical level and identifying all subordinates to that level. You can choose to print the entire organization or only the members of any one division or section of the organization.

Remember, before you create any chart, check the current option settings by pressing F8 (Options) at the main menu. Organization charts are best suited to a landscape orientation with a plain typeface.

Starting an Organization Chart

To start an organization chart, use the following procedure:

1. Select Create New Chart from the main menu.

2. Select Organization from the Create New Chart menu.

The Organization Chart screen appears. (If you have not saved the last chart you created or your latest changes, a warning message appears. To save the previous chart, press Esc so that you can return to the main menu and save the chart. Otherwise, press Enter to continue.)

Entering Names, Titles, Comments, and Abbreviations

Before typing the names of the individuals you want to depict in an organization chart, you may want to take a moment to sketch the chart on paper. Although you can preview your chart as you build it, you do not see the chart on-screen as you go. A drawing on paper in front of you, therefore, can serve as a map to the organization chart level by level.

In addition to the standard areas for title, subtitle, and footnote, the Organization Chart screen has areas for six items of information about each manager (name, title, comment, and abbreviations for name, title, and comment) and an area at the right side of the screen for a list of subordinates. Managers are the members of the current level you are creating, and subordinates are members of the level below. When you move down a level, individuals who were subordinates become managers, and you can type a new lower layer of subordinates. The Organization Chart screen provides spaces to fill in full and abbreviated information so that you can choose later which version to display.

To begin creating an organization chart that Superior Office Supplies can use to depict the structure of the sales force, type *Pencil Eraser Sales Force* as the title and *"The Annihilator"* as the subtitle, pressing Enter after each. Then type the managers' information as shown in figure 4.35. You may need to use a combination of the arrow keys, Tab, and Shift-Tab to move the cursor to the proper location on-screen.

With the manager's information in place, you are ready to enter the subordinates. Suppose that the sales manager is the only subordinate to the president in the sales organization depicted by this chart. Position the cursor at the first line in the Subordinates column and type the sales manager's name, *Audrey Marr*.

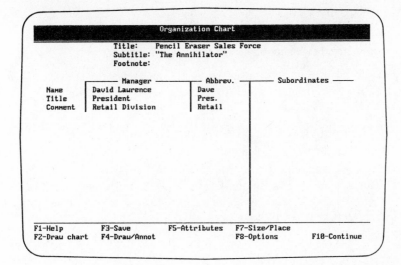

Fig. 4.35.

Entering the managerial information for Superior Office Supplies.

Using Ctrl-PgDn To Start a Lower Level

To add subordinates to any of the subordinates showing on-screen, position the cursor on the appropriate subordinate's name and press Ctrl-PgDn. This instant promotion changes the currently highlighted subordinate to a manager and opens spaces for a lower level of subordinates. You can add a title, comment, or abbreviation for the new individual in the Manager slot, and you can type a list of that manager's subordinates. To return to the higher level, press Ctrl-PgUp.

Follow these steps to complete the Superior Office Supplies organization chart:

1. Position the cursor on Audrey Marr's name in the Subordinates column and press Ctrl-PgDn.

2. Enter the list of subordinates under Audrey Marr, who is now the manager. In the Subordinates column, type three names: *Eric Wine, Tiffany Canina,* and *Aaron Kohn.*

3. You also may want to enter a title for Audrey Marr at this point. Position the cursor in the Manager column next to Title, using the arrow keys, Tab, or Shift-Tab, and type *Sales Manager.*

4. To enter the subordinates for Eric Wine, position the cursor on Eric's name, and press Ctrl-PgDn.

5. In the Subordinates column, type the subordinates shown in figure 4.34.

6. Press Ctrl-PgUp to move back to the higher level.

7. Position the cursor on Tiffany Canina's name, press Ctrl-PgDn, and enter the subordinates for Tiffany Canina.

8. Continue with this process until the entire organization's structure is depicted, as shown in figure 4.34.

Rearranging the Order of Subordinates

To move an existing subordinate up or down the list of subordinates, position the cursor on the subordinate's name on the Organization Chart screen and press Ctrl-up arrow or Ctrl-down arrow. Rearranging the order of subordinates also rearranges the order of items on all lower levels.

Adding a Staff Position

To enter an employee as staff rather than line (outside the hierarchical reporting structure), enter the employee as a subordinate but precede the employee's name with an asterisk. You can have only one staff position in a chart. Staff employees can have no subordinates. If you already have entered subordinates for an employee that you want to make staff, you must delete the subordinates before inserting an asterisk before the staff employee's name.

Changing Text Size, Placement, and Attributes

You have seen that pressing F7 (Size/Place) and F5 (Attributes) enables you to modify the appearance of any text in a chart. With organization charts, the function of these two commands is a little different. Size/Place and Attributes operate on the title, subtitle, and footnote only. To change the appearance of text in the body of a chart, you must use F8 (Options).

Fine-Tuning the Chart Layout with Options

With the Organization Chart screen displayed, press F8 (Options) several times. Notice how the screen changes. Pressing F8 toggles Harvard Graphics between the Organization Chart screen and the Org Chart Options screen shown in figure 4.36. Making changes on the Organization Chart screen changes the *contents* of the current chart. Changing options on the Org Chart Options screen modifies the *appearance* of the current chart. The menu at the bottom of the screen shows where you will go if you press F8 (either Options or Data), and the title at the top of the screen indicates whether you are working on the appearance (Options) or the content (Data) of the chart.

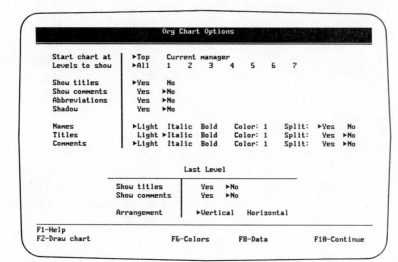

```
                        Org Chart Options

Start chart at        ▶Top    Current manager
Levels to show        ▶All    1    2    3    4    5    6    7

Show titles           ▶Yes    No
Show comments          Yes   ▶No
Abbreviations          Yes   ▶No
Shadow                 Yes   ▶No

Names                 ▶Light  Italic  Bold    Color: 1    Split: ▶Yes   No
Titles                 Light ▶Italic  Bold    Color: 1    Split:  Yes  ▶No
Comments              ▶Light  Italic  Bold    Color: 1    Split:  Yes  ▶No

                             Last Level

            Show titles         Yes   ▶No
            Show comments       Yes   ▶No

            Arrangement       ▶Vertical   Horizontal

F1-Help
F2-Draw chart              F6-Colors      F8-Data          F10-Continue
```

Fig. 4.36.

The Org Chart Options screen.

Press F8 until you see the Org Chart Options screen and examine the list of options shown. The options at the top of the screen affect the body of the chart, and the options at the bottom of the screen affect the lowest level. To change options, press Tab to move the cursor to the option you want to change and press the space bar to change the setting.

If you select Top for the Start Chart At option on the Org Chart Options screen, Harvard Graphics displays the entire chart. If you choose Current Manager, the program displays only the portion of the organization that falls under the current manager. You can check which manager is current by pressing F8 (Data) to return to the chart's data screen. With this option, you can create more than one chart to illustrate your organization's structure. A main chart can show the entire organization, and secondary charts can offer a breakdown of employees by manager.

Use the Levels To Show option with Start Chart At to display a specific number of organizational levels. To show all levels, select All. To show only the president and vice presidents of an organization, for example, set Levels To Show to 2.

Setting the Show Titles or Show Comments option to Yes displays the titles or comments you supplied for each manager. A manager's title and comments appear below the manager's name.

Harvard Graphics also enables you to display a chart showing only the abbreviations you supplied for each manager. Setting Abbreviations to Yes is helpful when you have many people and a limited amount of space. Unless you show abbreviations, Harvard Graphics produces small boxes with tiny text in an attempt to fit all employees in the chart. If the people you include in your chart have long names, you may see an error message indicating that you should break the names into two lines.

When you set Shadow to Yes, Harvard Graphics creates an appealing shadow effect behind each manager's box. The shadow is the same color as the one set as number 16 on the color palette. Depending on the output device you use, turning Shadow on may slow printing.

With the Names, Titles, and Comments lines on the Org Chart Options screen, you can assign most of the text attributes you are accustomed to setting with F5 (Attributes).

Light is normal text. Italic and Bold are self-explanatory. By default, names and comments are light, and titles are italicized. To change the color of text, position the cursor on the current Color number (the default setting is 1) and press F6 to choose another color from the color palette.

If you set the Split option to Yes, you are telling Harvard Graphics to split names, titles, or comments that include two words. The program splits these items between words so that they appear one under another. Harvard Graphics splits items between the first and second words by default. To indicate another position where words should be split, place a vertical bar (|) between words as you type.

You can decide whether to show titles or comments for items at the last level of the chart with the Show Titles and Show Comments options. You also can determine a vertical or horizontal arrangement for the last level. Figures 4.37 and 4.38 show the difference between arranging the last line vertically and horizontally.

When all options are set as you want, press F8 (Data) to return to the Organizational Chart screen or press F10 (Continue) to return to the main menu.

Saving an Organization Chart

After you complete an organization chart, return to the main menu by pressing F10 (Continue). Notice that the current chart type is specified as Org and that no current chart name exists. Select the Save Chart option from the Get/Save/Remove menu. Enter the chart name, such as *org*, and then press F10.

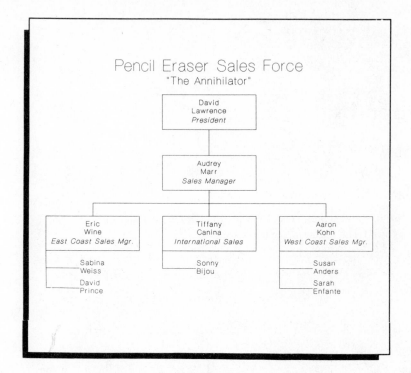

Fig. 4.37.

Using a vertical arrangement for the last level.

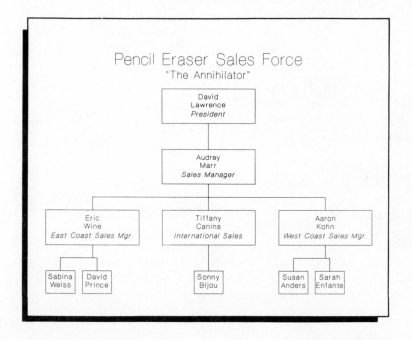

Fig. 4.38.

Changing to a horizontal arrangement.

Modifying Existing Text Charts

You can return to a chart after saving it, to make minor or major alterations.

Retrieving an Existing Chart

To retrieve a chart for editing, follow these steps:

1. Select Get/Save/Remove from the main menu.

2. Select Get Chart from the Get/Save/Remove menu.

3. Use the up- and down-arrow keys to highlight the chart from the list of files with a CHT extension and press Enter.

Harvard Graphics uses the three-letter file extension CHT to mark those files created as chart files. Only files with a CHT extension appear on the list.

As you highlight a file name with the cursor, the name appears at the top of the screen next to the Filename prompt. If you know the name of the file you want to retrieve, type the file name at the prompt to avoid having to search through the list.

If the file you want to edit is not in the current directory shown at the top of the screen, press F3 to view a list of directories above and below the current directory. The parent directory (signified by two periods) is the directory above the current directory. Subdirectories are below the current directory. Highlight the directory you want to examine, press Enter, and press F3 to view the contents of that directory.

When you get a chart from disk, the chart appears on-screen and becomes the current chart. If you have not saved the last chart you were editing, Harvard Graphics prompts you to press Enter to continue without saving the old chart or to press Esc to cancel the Get Chart command.

Changing Chart Orientation

Orientation is one of the options you should set before beginning a chart. But you can change a completed chart's orientation if you keep in mind that Harvard Graphics uses the same Size/Place settings even after you make the change. You need to update the text size settings to accommodate your new chart layout.

To change a chart's orientation, follow this procedure:

1. Make the chart you want to modify the current chart by using Get Chart from the Get/Save/Remove menu, highlighting the correct chart, and then pressing Enter.

2. Press Esc to return to the chart's data screen and press F10 (Continue) from the chart's screen to return to the main menu.

3. Press F8 (Options), tab to the Orientation option, and use the space bar to select the Orientation setting you want.

4. Press Enter several times until the Current Chart Options overlay disappears.

5. Press F2 (Draw Chart) to see the results of your change or select Enter/ Edit Chart from the main menu to begin editing the chart.

Checking the Spelling of a Chart

The most carefully thought-out and expressive presentation. can be undermined by a glaring typographical error or misspelling. To avoid such an embarrassment, you can use the Harvard Graphics spell-checking feature, which checks the words in your chart against the words in the program's dictionary. The spell checker also finds most incorrect punctuation and capitalization and words that you have inadvertently repeated (like like this).

To check the spelling of the chart you just completed, return to the main menu and press F4 (Spell Check). To check the spelling of a chart on disk, make that chart the current chart by choosing Get Chart from the Get/Save/Remove menu. Then return to the main menu so that you can use the F4 (Spell Check) command.

When you press F4, the spell checker scans through your chart, stopping at punctuation errors, repeated words, or words not found in the dictionary. The spell checker displays an overlay showing the error made and recommending possible corrections. If the word is correct, choose the Word Ok, Continue option from the overlay. If you want to add the word to your personal dictionary, choose Add to Dictionary. Harvard Graphics checks for a match against its dictionary and your personal dictionary so that the word is not flagged as incorrect. To type a correction manually, choose Type Correction from the overlay.

Spell checking is finished when you see the message Spelling check complete. At that point, press any key to continue with your work. To stop an in-progress spell-checking, press Esc.

Double-Spacing a Text Chart

To double-space an existing text chart, place the cursor at the beginning of each of the existing lines of text and press Ctrl-Ins to add a blank line. To delete extra blank lines, press Ctrl-Del.

Chapter Summary

Text charts are only one of two types of basic charts you can create with Harvard Graphics. In this chapter, you learned how to create a variety of text charts, set their appearance, and save the charts on disk. You use these charts in later chapters when you learn how to use Draw/Annotate to embellish charts and how to create animated desktop presentations called screenshows.

Without any further changes, the text charts you have created are satisfactory for most presentations. Using Draw/Annotate, covered in Chapter 9, however, you can embellish the text charts by adding text, lines, and other graphic shapes, such as arrows, boxes, and circles. You can draw on charts by hand or add symbols chosen from the extensive library provided by Harvard Graphics.

In the next two chapters, you learn about the second major Harvard Graphics chart type, graph charts.

5

Creating Graph Charts: Bar and Line

Text charts, covered in Chapter 4, are ideal when you need to convey topics, concepts, issues, arguments, or conclusions. But text charts nearly always serve as the accompaniment to a verbal presentation. In contrast, graph charts stand on their own as vivid illustrations of numbers, results, and totals, and as the most dynamic and compelling charts that Harvard Graphics produces.

In this chapter and in Chapters 6, 7, and 8, you learn about the varied types of graph charts available with Harvard Graphics and how to create and use them. You also learn how to enter data or import data from other programs, such as 1-2-3 or Excel, into your bar, line, area, or pie charts; how to display your data as a graph; and how to adjust the resulting chart's appearance by using the Titles & Options pages.

Defining the Types of Graph Charts

Harvard Graphics offers a huge variety of graph chart types—nearly two dozen, in fact. The most common are line, bar, and pie charts.

Line charts are especially useful when you want to show trends in data over time. Harvard Graphics can display three different line chart types representing three forms of data analysis: plain line charts, best fit trend charts, and curve charts.

143

The *plain line* chart connects each of the points on the chart with a straight line. *Trend* and *curve* lines are based on calculations that analyze the data and depict the line that most closely represents the general trend of the data. Figure 5.1 shows the three different types of charts for one set of data.

Fig. 5.1.

Three different chart types for one set of data.

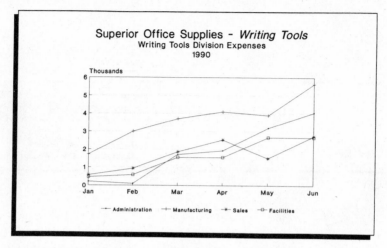

Plain line chart

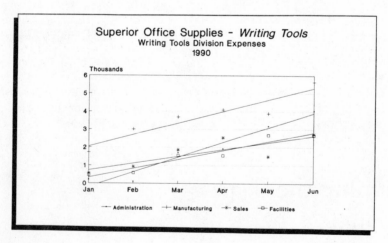

Trend chart

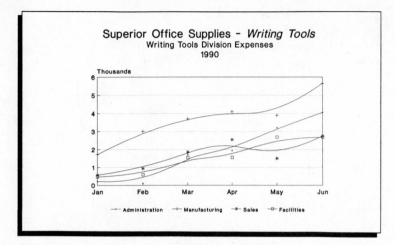

Fig. 5.1. *cont.*

Curve chart

Rather than analyze the progress of data over time, *bar* charts compare discrete data points at intervals. Bar charts are one of the most common business charts, and they are the starting point for this chapter. Understanding the bar chart options is fundamental to understanding the options for all the available chart types.

You use a *pie* chart to show how each value contributes to the overall "pie" or whole. Then, if you prefer, you can go one step further by analyzing a slice of the pie and showing the component parts with a link to a *column* chart, as shown in figure 5.2. A column chart is a special form of pie chart that shows the whole as a rectangle rather than a circle. The chart in figure 5.2 shows clearly that in the second half of the year, the December revenues were greatest and that mechanical pencils were the largest contributor to those revenues.

To show the relationship between two totals and analyze each of their components at the same time, you can pair two pie charts to create a set of proportional pies. Proportional pies compare two totals by reflecting them in the relative sizes of the two pies.

Harvard Graphics also offers a variety of other less common graph charts:

100% charts, a variation of bar charts, are similar to column charts in that values are expressed as a percentage of a whole (100 percent). 100% charts are well suited for examining the relative contribution of each factor in a financial picture, for example.

Bar/line combination charts display changes in data over time while emphasizing a factor or series.

Fig. 5.2.

A linked pie to
column chart.

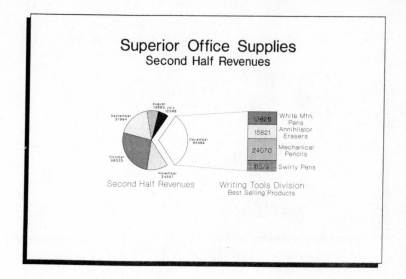

Area charts highlight volume. Figure 5.3 shows an area chart illustrating the
increase in the first half sales volume in the Writing Tools division of Superior
Office Supplies over three years.

Fig. 5.3.

An area chart.

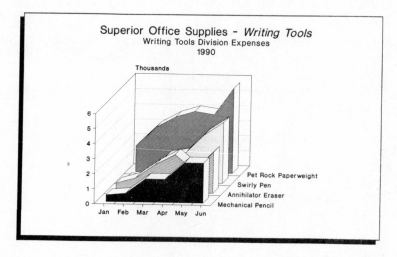

Point charts, or scattergrams, are composed of a series of points unconnected by a
line. Each point represents the intersection of the values of two variables, one on
the chart's x-axis and one on the chart's y-axis.

Paired bar charts compare two series that represent independent events. Each
series is charted against its own y-axis so that the observer can compare "apples
to apples" rather than "apples to oranges."

Dual y-axis charts compare two series that use different units of measure or that differ greatly in magnitude. Each series is measured and charted against its own y-axis.

High/low/close charts are a favorite among stockbrokers and financial professionals. Each item of data is composed of a high point, low point, and closing point, shown in comparison. High/low/close charts also are helpful for depicting any other varying numeric amount that has regular highs and lows, such as temperature or barometric pressure. Figure 5.4 shows one such example—the price fluctuations for Swirly pens in the Writing Tools division for the second half of 1990.

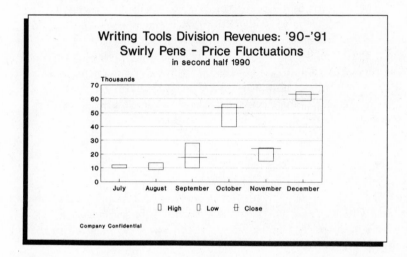

Fig. 5.4.

A high/low/close chart of price fluctuations.

This chapter covers bar and line charts and their variations. For information on area, high/low/close, and pie charts, see Chapter 6.

Using Galleries

A special feature in Harvard Graphics Version 2.3, called Gallery, makes the process of choosing a color scheme and setting options simple. The Gallery is a series of charts that have been preset with attractive combinations of colors and options so that you do not have to select them yourself. When creating text or graph charts, you can use Harvard Graphics' Gallery to pick a chart with the look you want your end product to have and then replace the existing data or type in your own. All your options are set, and the chart looks like the displayed chart from the Gallery.

One way to think of Harvard Graphics charts and the relationship of the Gallery is that all charts are a combination of data (content) and options (appearance). A chart from the Gallery provides a complete set of options so that you only need to provide the data to have a complete chart.

Before you create an original bar or line chart, you may want to view the Gallery of bar charts. Viewing the Gallery can give you ideas about how your chart should look. The Gallery provides a sampling of attractive charts to choose from, saving you the time and energy of trying to produce pleasing graphic effects on your own. Using the Gallery to create a chart from scratch, you can change palettes to provide an array of interesting color arrangements for your charts.

For versions of Harvard Graphics earlier than 2.3, two available accessory packages, Quick Charts and Designer Galleries, provide galleries. Both accessory products are made to speed up the chart design process. Both accessories are still available from Software Publishing Corporation, because the galleries included in the accessories are supplemental to the galleries included in Version 2.3. Like Version 2.3, Designer Galleries also provides a variety of palettes from which to choose. Palettes are sets of complementary colors that can be used in a chart. The procedure for changing palettes is described in this section.

Viewing the Gallery

To view the Gallery, first choose Create New Chart from the main menu. Then select From Gallery from the Create New Chart menu. Figure 5.5 shows the Gallery of chart types from which you can choose. The chart types included in the Gallery follow:

- ❏ Text charts
- ❏ Pie charts
- ❏ Bar charts
- ❏ Line charts
- ❏ Area charts
- ❏ High/low/close charts
- ❏ Organization charts
- ❏ Horizontal charts
- ❏ Bar/line combination charts

Select one of these chart types by pressing the number listed for the chart type, and another Gallery menu screen appears, displaying variations of your choice.

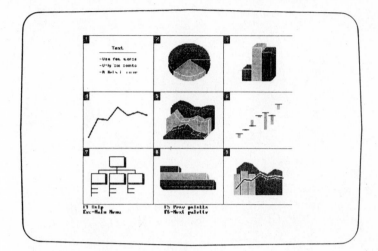

Fig. 5.5.

The Gallery of charts.

Five of the charts on the Gallery display are bar or line charts: choices 3, 4, 5, 8, and 9. Take a look at some of the bar chart variations by pressing 3 at the Gallery menu. Figure 5.6 shows the resulting screen.

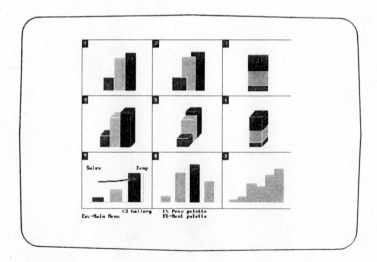

Fig. 5.6.

The bar chart Gallery.

From this screen, you can choose the bar chart style you want. The choices, described in detail later in this chapter, include the following types of bar charts (which you select by pressing the number for the chart style):

1. Cluster
2. Overlap
3. Stacked bar

4. 3-D cluster
5. 3-D overlap
6. 3-D stacked
7. Dual y-axis
8. Highlighted bars
9. Stepped

To get a close-up view of a chart, type the number of the chart you want to view. For example, press 4 at the first Gallery display menu to see how a 3-D cluster chart looks.

Select 8 at the main Gallery display menu to see the variety of horizontal bar chart types. A horizontal bar chart has the x- and y-axis switched. The x-axis appears on the vertical, and the y-axis appears on the horizontal in a horizontal bar chart. The types of horizontal bar charts shown in this choice follow (to select a type, press the number for that type):

1. 3-D cluster
2. 3-D stacked
3. Stacked
4. Overlap
5. Combination overlap
6. Overlap
7. Paired
8. Overlap
9. Logarithmic

Figure 5.7 shows the horizontal bar charts display menu. The chart types are described later in this chapter.

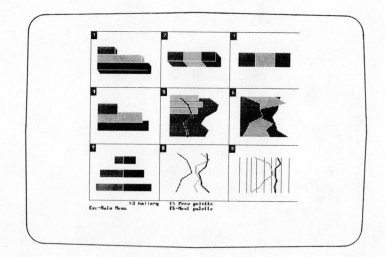

Fig. 5.7.

The horizontal bar chart Gallery.

Four Gallery charts mix bars with lines. You can view the charts by pressing 9 at the Gallery display menu. These charts include a bar and line chart, a combination overlap chart, a combination overlap chart with a data table, and a bar chart with numeric data.

Press F3 to return to the Gallery after you view it. Then press Esc to return to the main menu and create one of these charts from scratch.

Setting Color Palettes

You can adjust the colors in the chart by pressing F5 (Prev Palette) and F6 (Next Palette) repeatedly. Harvard Graphics cycles through each of the palette files available. When you find a combination you like, stop pressing F5 or F6, and you can make a chart.

Using the Chart

After you set the colors and select a chart type, you can press F9 (Edit) to use the chart and view the actual data that makes up the Gallery chart. Or you can press F10 (Edit + Clear) to select the chart's options without selecting the Gallery chart's data. If you press F10, the X Data Type Menu overlay appears, ready for fresh data that you can supply. Pressing F9 or F10, you still can alter the options to suit your aesthetic sense just as you can for any chart created from scratch.

Creating a Bar or Line Chart

Before you start a bar chart, you should check the current orientation setting. The current setting reflects the setup default you established earlier, and the setting may not match what you have in mind for your next chart. Bar charts are best suited to a landscape (horizontal) orientation, because these charts convey large amounts of information, and landscape orientation is more easily read. Press F8 (Options) at the main menu and be sure that Orientation is set to Landscape.

To start a bar or line chart, first choose Create New Chart from the main menu. Then select Bar/Line from the Create New Chart menu.

Setting the X-Axis

The X Data Type Menu overlay is the first screen to appear after you have chosen Bar/Line (see fig. 5.8). Use this menu to tell Harvard Graphics the range of values that the horizontal axis of your chart (the x-axis) represents and the unit of measure for those values. The program uses this information to create and label the chart's x-axis.

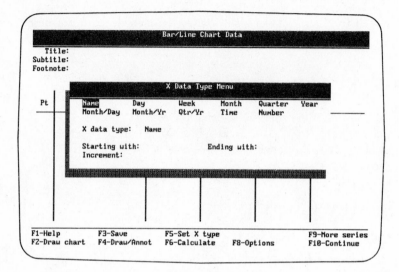

Fig. 5.8.

The X Data Type Menu overlay.

To complete the X Data Type Menu overlay for bar/line charts, follow these steps:

1. Use the space bar to highlight one of the X Data Type selections listed in the top two lines of the menu. Then press Enter. You also can press Tab to select the X Data Type option currently highlighted and move to the Starting With field. (For descriptions of the 11 data types available and their values, see the next section, "Understanding the X Data Types.")

2. Enter a Starting With value and press Enter or Tab to move the cursor to the Ending With option.

3. Enter an Ending With value and press Enter or Tab to move the cursor to the Increment field. You can press Enter at the Increment field if you want to use the default increment of 1.

   The Increment field tells Harvard Graphics how many units to increase each new point on the x-axis. After you select the Starting With and Ending With settings, Harvard Graphics supplies the appropriate values in between. If you set the starting and ending values to *Jan* and *Dec* and set the increment to 2, for example, the resulting X values are *Jan, Mar, May, Jul, Sep,* and *Nov* (every other month).

Understanding the X Data Types

This section gives you a summary of all the data types available on the X Data Type Menu overlay.

Name

Name enables you to name your own x-axis data values. If your media rating company wants to show the popularity of three TV shows in four regions, for example, you can use Name as the X Data Type option; then, on the next screen that appears, you can enter the name of each show for the chart's x-axis data. Figure 5.9 shows such a chart.

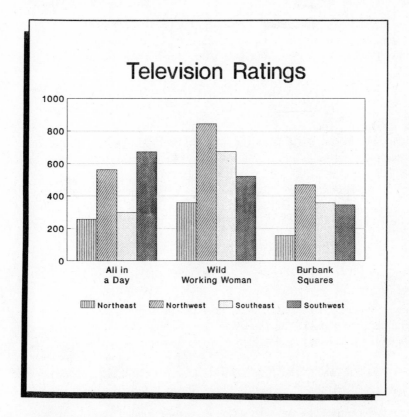

Fig. 5.9.

A TV *ratings chart with Name as the X data type.*

X-axis data that is name based can include any combination of letters, numbers, and special characters—even a space. You can add up to 60 values for your x-axis when the data type is Name. If you want to split a name into two lines, place a vertical bar (|) at the position where the label should split.

For example, typing *TV|Sales* produces

TV
Sales

on the chart.

Number

Number is the data type to use when the information you want to represent on the x-axis can be classified numerically. For example, if your graph represents the top four television shows for age categories in 5-year increments (15, 20, 25, 30, and so on), you can select Number for the X Data Type option, press 5 at the Starting With prompt, and press 5 at the Increment option. Harvard Graphics then enters the ages 5, 10, 15, 20, and so forth, on the x-axis.

Numeric X data can be a negative number and can include a decimal. Harvard Graphics also recognizes scientific notation in the Number data type.

Time

Time as an x-axis data type is expressed in hours and minutes. Use a colon in the time, following the format *10:15 AM*. Use the *AM* and *PM* abbreviations if you want to avoid using 24-hour time, which is how your computer keeps track of time (*00:00* is midnight, *23:00* is 11 p.m., and *11:00* is 11 a.m.). Suppose, for example, that you want to chart performance over a 10-hour period from midnight until 10 a.m. Type *00:00* at the Starting With field and *10:00* at the Ending With field. Then specify the increment in 10-minute segments by typing *00:10* at the Increment field.

Calendar-Based Data Types

The remainder of the X data types are calendar based. When you choose Day, Harvard Graphics enters days of the week on the x-axis. Acceptable options for the Starting With and Ending With fields are Sunday, Monday, Tuesday, Wednesday, Thursday, Friday, and Saturday. If you type a three-letter abbreviation for a day of the week, Harvard Graphics follows your lead and supplies three-letter abbreviations for the other days that are included on your x-axis.

Week is a numeric entry. The only difference from the Number type is that the program labels the x-axis *Week*. This data type is ideal for graphs relating to the management of a project or the weekly sales figures of a product. Acceptable entries for this field are numbers between 1 and 240. If you want to show every other week, press 2 at the Increment field. Note, also, that Harvard Graphics does not roll over to a new year after 52 weeks.

Month, Month/Day, and Month/Yr have similar acceptable entries. You can use the formats *Feb*, *FEB*, or *2* for Month. You can type such entries as *Feb 1*, *FEB 1*, or *2/1* for Month/Day. And you can type *Feb 91*, *Feb 1991*, *FEB 91*, *FEB 1991*, or *2/91* for Month/Yr.

When you use a named date such as *January* or *FEB*, use a space in the date (such as *January 91*) to separate its parts. If the date is numeric, be sure to separate its parts with a slash. You don't have to type a period after abbreviations. Harvard Graphics knows how many days are in each month and supplies the correct number of days in the months that are included when the x-axis spans more than one month.

Quarter and Qtr/Yr represent the four business quarters of a year. Harvard Graphics expects entries like *1*, *1/91*, *first*, *First 91*, *Q1*, or *Q1 '91*. When you choose *First*, Harvard Graphics completes the entries with *First*, *Second*, *Third*, and *Fourth*.

Year is a four-digit number, such as *1990*, or a two-digit number, such as *90* or *'90* (with or without the apostrophe).

As mentioned, Harvard Graphics accepts three-letter abbreviations for the calendar-based data types. When you type *Jan* for January, for example, Harvard Graphics accepts your entry and follows your lead, supplying the abbreviations *Feb* for February, *Mar* for March, and so on. If you type *JAN* in all uppercase letters, Harvard Graphics completes the remaining months in uppercase letters. If you type *jan* in lowercase letters, Harvard Graphics corrects your error and puts all the months in leading caps. You always can make the same months all caps or even all small letters afterward.

When you specify an x-axis data type, the completed chart shows the appropriate data names on the horizontal x-axis. Based on other decisions you make (such as the legend's position), however, Harvard Graphics may abbreviate the x-axis data values when you modify the appearance of the chart. If you place the legend to the left of the chart, for example, you reduce the horizontal space available for the graph and, therefore, for the labels along the x-axis. Instead of placing x-axis data labels on top of one another, Harvard Graphics abbreviates the labels to fit the available horizontal space. In an extreme case, for example, x-axis labels showing months may be abbreviated J, F, M, A, M, J, J, A, S, O, N, and D. To prevent such abbreviation, you can move the legend under or above the chart. As an alternative, you can change the chart orientation so that its x-axis is vertical and its y-axis is horizontal. You also can alter other aspects on the Titles & Options pages to cause the chart to use the full names or abbreviations you entered originally.

If you select Month/Yr as the X Axis Data Type, Harvard Graphics indicates which months belong to each year by adding text below the month names. Each year's months are delineated by vertical separating lines, and the year number appears between the vertical lines.

Now that you are familiar with X data types, create a graph chart showing a summary of the first six months of expenses at Superior Office Supplies. The X Data Type option for this chart is Month; the Starting With entry is *Jan*; and the Ending With entry is *Jun*. Leave the Increment entry blank to accept the default of 1.

After you have completed the X Data Type Menu overlay, the Bar/Line Chart Data screen appears. Figure 5.10 shows the Bar/Line Chart Data screen after Month has been chosen as the data type. At this point, Harvard Graphics is ready for you to enter data.

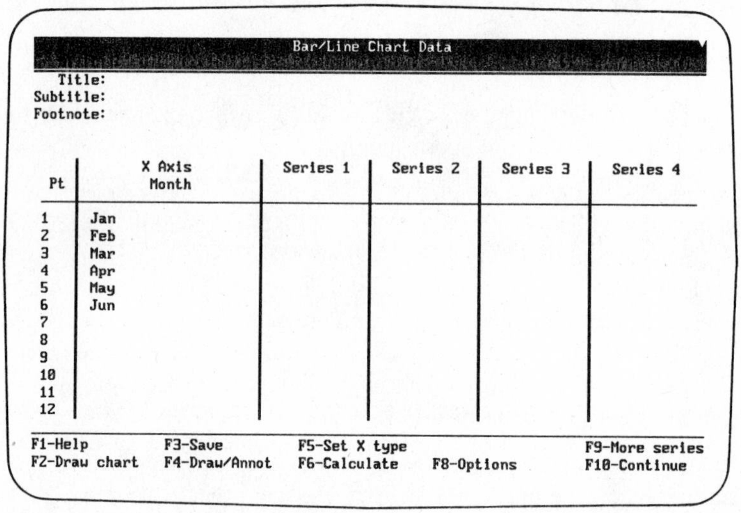

Fig. 5.10.

The Bar/Line Chart Data screen after you have completed the X Data Type Menu overlay.

Entering Data on the Data Page

In the preceding chapter, you entered data onto the data screen of an organization chart and then altered the resulting chart's appearance by using Titles & Options pages. You follow the same procedure with graph charts. You first enter the content of the chart onto a data page; then you press F8 (Options) to change the appearance of the chart.

In addition to supplying x-axis values when you complete the X Data Type Menu overlay, Harvard Graphics checks to ensure that any x-axis values you manually enter on the Bar/Line Chart Data screen match the data type you selected. If you select Month as the data type, for example, starting with *Jan* and ending with *Jun*, Harvard Graphics enters the months between January and June in the first six lines of the data-entry screen. The program prevents you from entering *Mon* for Monday on the seventh line, because Harvard Graphics recognizes that Monday is not a month (see fig. 5.11).

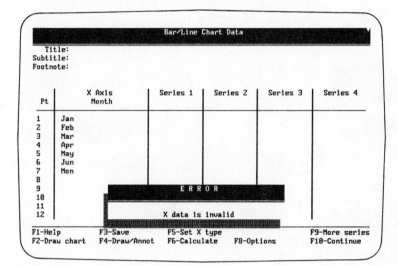

Fig. 5.11.

The results of entering invalid data.

Entering Titles

The first three lines on the Bar/Line Chart Data screen are available for you to supply a chart title, subtitle, and footnote. Typically, the title is a description of the chart or a headline about the chart's message; the subtitle supplies additional information about the chart; and the footnote appears at the bottom of the chart to provide such information as the date or a confidentiality statement. You can enter text on these three lines now or complete them when you are working with the Titles & Options pages. You must be on page 1 of 4 to enter the second line of the subtitle.

Entering Data

To create a bar/line chart, type your existing data on the Bar/Line Chart Data screen. You may want to assemble the data on paper first.

In Harvard Graphics, each bar or line on a chart represents one *series*, a set of related data. For example, the bar chart in figure 5.12 showing the expenses of Superior Office Supplies for half of a year is composed of four series. Series 1 is the administration budget; Series 2 is the manufacturing budget; Series 3 is the sales budget; and Series 4 is the facilities budget.

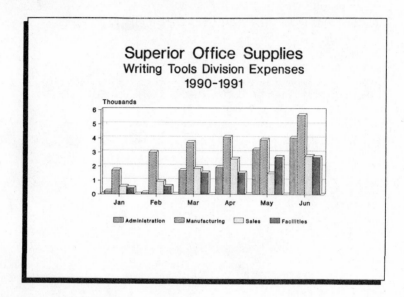

Fig. 5.12.

A bar chart comparing four series of data.

The first six months of expenses in the Superior Office Supplies Writing Tools Division look like the following:

	Administrative	Manufacturing	Sales	Facilities
Jan	215	1725	570	465
Feb	102	2993	932	578
Mar	1701	3706	1852	1545
Apr	1926	4096	2532	1545
May	3192	3896	1496	2665
Jun	4050	5653	2741	2665

To enter a chart's numeric data, you use the Tab key to move across the Bar/Line Chart Data screen and use the Enter key to move down line by line. You may find the easiest method to be typing all the values for one series, pressing Enter between each, and then proceeding to the next series.

To enter negative numbers, use a minus sign before the number. To enter decimals, type a period (decimal point) at the decimal place. Of course, Harvard Graphics also accepts extremely large numbers in scientific notation. To enter such a number, use an E and an exponent of 10 (for example, the number 560,000 is expressed as 5.6E5). Figure 5.13 shows a Bar/Line Chart Data screen complete with the four series of data entered. Even if you enter the data in different formats, Harvard Graphics converts the data into a single format after you preview the chart.

```
┌─────────────────────────────────────────────────────────────────────┐
│                        Bar/Line Chart Data                          ╲│
│                                                                      │
│     Title: Superior Office Supplies                                  │
│  Subtitle: Writing Tools Division Expenses                           │
│  Footnote:                                                           │
│                                                                      │
│             X Axis     │ Series 1 │ Series 2 │ Series 3 │ Series 4   │
│      Pt     Month      │          │          │          │           │
│                        │          │          │          │           │
│      1    Jan          │   215    │   1725   │   570    │   465     │
│      2    Feb          │   102    │   2993   │   932    │   578     │
│      3    Mar          │   1701   │   3706   │   1852   │   1545    │
│      4    Apr          │   1926   │   4096   │   2532   │   1545    │
│      5    May          │   3192   │   3896   │   1496   │   2665    │
│      6    Jun          │   4050   │   5653   │   2741   │   2665    │
│      7                 │          │          │          │           │
│      8                 │          │          │          │           │
│      9                 │          │          │          │           │
│     10                 │          │          │          │           │
│     11                 │          │          │          │           │
│     12                 │          │          │          │           │
│                                                                      │
│  F1-Help        F3-Save       F5-Set X type            F9-More series│
│  F2-Draw chart  F4-Draw/Annot F6-Calculate  F8-Options F10-Continue  │
└─────────────────────────────────────────────────────────────────────┘
```

Fig. 5.13.

The Bar/Line Chart Data screen with the data entered.

Note: Even after you enter the chart's data, you can go back and modify the x-axis data type by pressing F5 (Set X Type) to recall the X Data Type Menu overlay.

Previewing the Chart

After entering the title, subtitle, and all the data into the Bar/Line Chart Data screen, you should press F2 (Draw Chart) to preview the chart before you make any adjustments to its appearance. The first time you see your chart, all of the default options are in effect.

If you haven't done so already, type the data shown in figure 5.13 and compare your chart preview with the chart preview shown in figure 5.14. Press Esc to return to the Bar/Line Chart Data screen.

Saving the Chart

Save this first completed bar chart with the name SOSEXPEN. To save the chart, follow this procedure:

1. Press F10 (Continue) to return to the main menu.

2. Select Get/Save/Remove from the main menu.

3. Select Save Chart from the Get/Save/Remove menu. The cursor should be at the Chart Will Be Saved As option.

4. Type the chart name, *sosexpen.*

5. Press Enter.

6. The current description is derived from the title line. Press Enter to keep the current description. Or, if you want to change it, type a new description over the current one and press Enter.

7. Press Esc to return to the main menu and then select Enter/Edit Chart to continue working on the chart.

Fig. 5.14.

Preview of an unaltered bar/line chart.

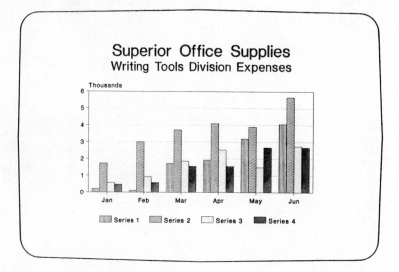

Editing the Chart

Harvard Graphics enables you to include up to eight series of data with as many as 240 items in each series, depending on the x-axis data type you select. On the Bar/Line Chart Data screen, you can see only four series displayed at one time. To view or enter data into the next four series, press F9 (More Series). To return to the first four series, press F9 again. Pressing PgDn enables you to see the next 12 lines of data. Pressing PgUp moves the display up a screenful of data. The Home and End keys move the cursor to the first and last values on the screen, respectively.

Changing the order of data on the page to show your results in a different sequence is easy with Harvard Graphics. Position the cursor on the line you want to move and press Ctrl-up arrow or Ctrl-down arrow. The line of data moves up or down correspondingly. This flexibility is important when you have five years of data entered, for example, and management decides to change the fiscal year from January through December to April through March. To change fiscal years, you can move the cursor to the line holding January's data and use the Ctrl-down arrow combination to move the line to the bottom of the list. Repeat the same procedure for February's and March's data, and your chart reflects the new fiscal year.

To insert or delete a full line of data, use the Ctrl-Ins and Ctrl-Del key combinations. Move the cursor to the line of data you want to delete and press the Del key while holding down the Ctrl key. Harvard Graphics provides no means to "undelete" a line, though, so be certain of the line you want to delete before proceeding. To insert a blank line at the same position, press the Ins key while holding down the Ctrl key.

Usually, a bar/line chart is more visually appealing if you use four or fewer series. The more series you place in a chart, the more cluttered the chart becomes. You may want to enter multiple series, however, and display only two or three series in each chart. With this approach, you can enter the data only once and show several variations. If your four series are 1987, 1988, 1989, and 1990, for example, you may want to show 1987 compared with 1988 and then compare 1989 with 1990 in another chart. In a third chart based on the same data, you can show the full four-year span. To suppress or display series, you can use the Titles & Options pages, described in the next section.

You can use an additional series to perform calculations on existing series. For example, you can use a series to sum all or selected series, calculate an increase in a series over the previous series, or average several series. These calculations work much like the @ functions in 1-2-3. These calculation functions are described in detail in Chapter 7.

Using the Titles & Options Pages

After you complete the data screen and preview your chart in progress, Harvard Graphics generates a standard chart based on the information you entered on the data screen. The program probably has already done much of the work in labeling the chart. The y-axis may have a label describing the units of the data in your chart, for example. If you enter numbers in thousands, the y-axis is labeled Thousands. Harvard Graphics makes other adjustments, too. The bars in your graph probably fit neatly across the width of the x-axis, and a legend appears on the chart. All of these adjustments are a result of the default options on the Titles & Options pages.

To refine your chart any further, you need to modify the selections on the Titles & Options pages. Each chart type has its own Titles & Options pages, with entries corresponding to the attributes of the chart. For example, bar charts have Titles & Options page entries that set the width, spacing, and other attributes of a chart's bars. In the next several sections, you learn about the four Titles & Options pages specific to bar and line charts.

Using the First Titles & Options Page

Pressing F8 (Options) at the Bar/Line Chart Data screen calls up the first of the four Titles & Options pages for bar/line charts (see fig. 5.15). You use the first Titles & Options page to tell Harvard Graphics your choices about the overall appearance of the chart. On this page, you can specify whether to represent each series with bars or lines, and you can give series names that are a little more descriptive than Series 1, Series 2, and so on.

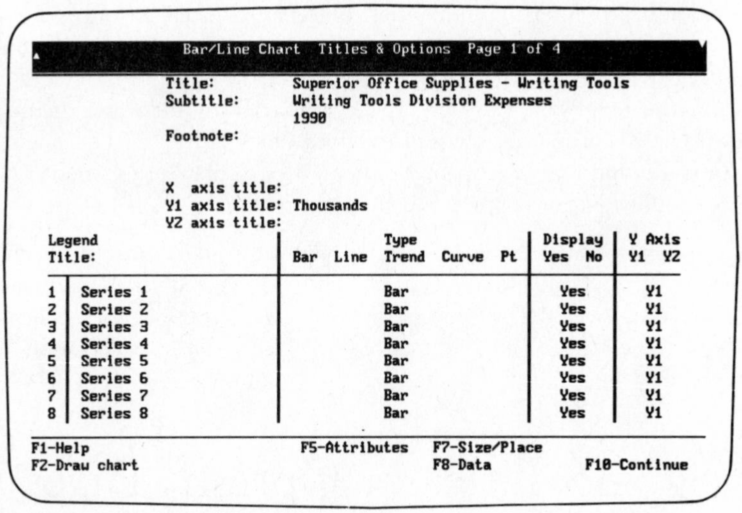

Fig. 5.15.

*The first Titles &
Options page.*

```
 ▲        Bar/Line Chart  Titles & Options  Page 1 of 4

          Title:      Superior Office Supplies - Writing Tools
          Subtitle:   Writing Tools Division Expenses
                      1990
          Footnote:

          X  axis title:
          Y1 axis title: Thousands
          Y2 axis title:
   Legend                          Type              Display │ Y Axis
   Title:              Bar  Line  Trend  Curve  Pt  Yes  No │ Y1  Y2

   1 │ Series 1                    Bar                Yes    │ Y1
   2 │ Series 2                    Bar                Yes    │ Y1
   3 │ Series 3                    Bar                Yes    │ Y1
   4 │ Series 4                    Bar                Yes    │ Y1
   5 │ Series 5                    Bar                Yes    │ Y1
   6 │ Series 6                    Bar                Yes    │ Y1
   7 │ Series 7                    Bar                Yes    │ Y1
   8 │ Series 8                    Bar                Yes    │ Y1

   F1-Help                F5-Attributes   F7-Size/Place
   F2-Draw chart                          F8-Data          F10-Continue
```

At the top of the first Titles & Options page is a pair of arrows, one pointing up and another pointing down. These arrows indicate that other Titles & Options pages are available above and below the current page. If you press PgDn, the next Titles & Options page appears (page 2 of 4). If you press PgUp to return to page 1 of 4 and press PgUp again, Harvard Graphics loops back to Titles & Options page 4 of 4.

Adding Titles

If you did not enter a title, subtitle, and footnote on the data screen, these items are blank on the first Titles & Options page. You now can use the Tab key to move the cursor to these lines and enter a title, subtitle, and footnote. In figure 5.15, the title line reads Superior Office Supplies-Writing Tools. If you are practicing by using the procedures in this chapter, add *Writing Tools* to the end of the first title line on the Titles & Options page. Then add *1990* under the subtitle on the first Titles & Options page. *1990* is the second line of the subtitle. When you first enter data, there is no place for a second subtitle line. That line instead becomes available as you set titles and options. Use this Titles & Options page also to set or change the titles for the x-axis, y1-axis, and y2-axis. Notice that Harvard Graphics sets the y1-axis title when you initially enter the data. Using the first Titles & Options page, you are free to overwrite the y1-axis title that was set.

Changing Text Appearance

After the title and subtitle lines are in place, you should preview the chart by pressing F2 (Draw Chart). When you do, notice that the title you just lengthened does not fit within the width of the page (see fig. 5.16). With Harvard Graphics, you can alter the size of the title text, however, by using the F7-Size/Place feature on the first Titles & Options page.

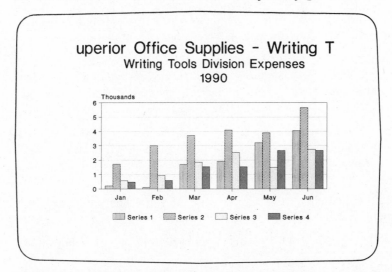

Fig. 5.16.

Preview of the chart with a long title.

In Harvard Graphics, *size* is a measure of the height of the text characters used in a line. You can change a line's size on both the first and fourth Titles & Options pages. The size of a character can be any number from 1 to 99.9, representing a percentage of the length of the shorter side of the page. For example, a character with a size of 99.9 fills the entire height of the shorter side of the page.

If you set the text in a graph chart's title to a size of 99.9, the title is too big and overwrites the graph. If you change the size of the title to 0, however, the title is removed altogether, and the remaining lines of text and the graph fill the left-over space. Figure 5.17 shows the same chart with the size of the first line set at 99. The first two letters of text take up the entire page and overwrite the graph, leaving no room for additional lines of text or detail in the bar chart.

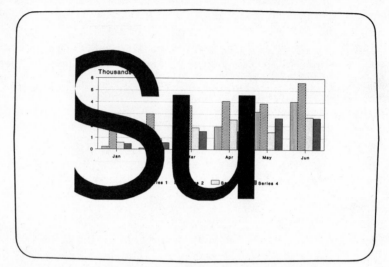

Fig. 5.17.

The chart with a large first line of text.

Size determines the height of lines of text. *Place* refers to their positioning. Text can be right-aligned (pushed against the right side of the page), left-aligned (pushed against the left side of the page), or centered.

Standard alignment and text sizes are set by Harvard Graphics when you create a chart and are part of the default options settings each chart type has. You may find the defaults satisfactory and choose to make no changes. But if you prefer to adjust text size and place, you can make these changes easily as you build a chart.

To modify the size and place of a line of text, press F7 (Size/Place) with the first Titles & Options page on-screen. An overlay appears, as shown in figure 5.18. You can use this overlay to change the size and placement of the title, subtitle, and footnote.

To reduce the size and alter the place setting of the title line on your chart, follow these steps:

1. Type over the Size number next to the title; change the value from 8 to 5.5.

2. Press the Tab or Enter key to move the cursor to the Size number next to the first subtitle line. Change the value from 6 to 4. Reducing the size of a line of text increases the space available for the graph.

3. Press the Tab or Enter key to move to the second line of the subtitle and replace the number 6 with 4. If you do not have text in the footnote line, repeat this procedure for the footnote, making the size of all three lines of the footnote 0. To clear the current entry so that you can type a new number, position the cursor on the current entry and press Ctrl-Del. You are thus assured of having the maximum amount of space for your graph.

```
 Size   Place       Bar/Line Chart  Titles & Options   Page 1 of 4

 8       L ►C  R Title:        Superior Office Supplies - Writing Tools
 6       L ►C  R Subtitle:     Writing Tools Division Expenses
 6       L ►C  R               1990
 2.5    ►L  C  R Footnote:
 2.5    ►L  C  R
 2.5    ►L  C  R
 4         ►C    X  axis title:
 3       ►→  ↓   Y1 axis title: Thousands
 3       ►→  ↓   Y2 axis title:
         X labels                                    Display   Y Axis
         Y labels           Bar  Line Trend Curve Pt Yes  No   Y1 Y2

 1     | Series 1                      Bar            Yes       Y1
 2     | Series 2                      Bar            Yes       Y1
 3     | Series 3                      Bar            Yes       Y1
 4     | Series 4                      Bar            Yes       Y1
 5     | Series 5                      Bar            Yes       Y1
 6     | Series 6                      Bar            Yes       Y1
 7     | Series 7                      Bar            Yes       Y1
 8     | Series 8                      Bar            Yes       Y1

 F1-Help                 F5-Attributes   F7-Size/Place
 F2-Draw chart                           F8-Data        F10-Continue
```

Fig. 5.18.

*The first Titles &
Options page with
the Size/Place
overlay.*

(Two lines are available for the subtitle, and three lines are available for the footnote. If you do not have a second line in your subtitle, or second and third lines in your footnote, make the values for these lines 0. The graphic portion of your chart will be larger as a result.)

4. Press F10 (Continue).

5. Press F2 (Draw Chart) to see the results of your actions. The result is shown in figure 5.19.

To change a Place setting on the Size/Place overlay, tab to the Place column for the line you want to reposition (left, center, or right) and press the space bar to highlight your choice. Press Enter or Tab to move to the next field and repeat the procedure.

To return to the Titles & Options page, press Esc. If you need to move the cursor back through the Size and Place fields to try other choices, hold down the Shift key and press Tab after pressing F7 to summon the Size/Place overlay.

The Size/Place overlay on the first Titles & Options page also enables you to decide the size and placement of the chart's x- axis and y-axis titles. You see two arrows next to each axis title in the overlay. Highlighting the arrow pointing to the right causes the axis title to start at the top of the axis and run across the screen to the right. Highlighting the arrow pointing down causes the title to start at the left of the axis and run down the page vertically. Try both of these options and preview the chart to see their effects. Note that you can label both Y1 and Y2 axes. The second axis, Y2, is used for dual y-axis charts, which are discussed later in this chapter (see "Creating Dual Y-Axis Charts").

Fig. 5.19.

The bar/line chart after size and place adjustments have been made.

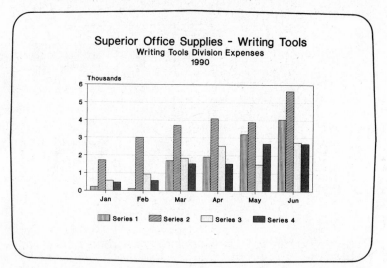

You can use the last two lines on the Size/Place overlay to set the size of X labels and Y labels. The X and Y labels are the numbers or words that appear on the horizontal and vertical axes of the chart. You can include labels on the bars themselves by using a setting on the second Titles & Options page, described later in this chapter (see "Displaying Value Labels"). Harvard Graphics calculates a size for the X and Y labels if you leave these two lines blank. The two settings also affect the size of data shown in a data table. (Data tables are an option on the third Titles & Options page.) To accept the changes you have made and remove the Size/Place overlay, press F10 (Continue).

Changing Text Attributes

Not only can you change the size and placement of text, but you also can change the formatting of text on-screen by changing its attributes. *Attributes* determine the appearance of text: whether the text is italicized, bold, or underlined, or whether the characters are filled or outlined. If you have a color output device, you also can change the color of text with the F5-Attributes feature.

To italicize "Writing Tools" after the hyphen in the chart's title, for example, follow these steps:

1. Position the cursor on the first letter of the word you want to change (on the W in the word Writing).

2. Press F5 (Attributes) to display the Attributes menu bar on the bottom line of the screen.

3. Use the right arrow to highlight all words that should be changed. You can use the down arrow to highlight an entire line.

4. Tab to the Italic menu option and press the space bar to turn on the italic attribute for those words. You can tab between attributes and press the space bar to turn on or off the small pointers that are to the left of the attribute names. When an attribute's pointer is displayed, the attribute is on.

5. You can tab to the Color option and press F6 (Choices) to see a list of the available colors for the highlighted text. Figure 5.20 shows the Attributes bar with the Color Selection overlay displayed.

Because you selected the palette you prefer earlier in this chapter, the colors listed on your screen may not match the colors listed in figure 5.20. In figure 5.20, the 11.PAL colors are displayed. This palette file is one of 37 available palette files that come with Harvard Graphics 2.3. Each palette file is a group of related colors that works well together when selected. You can see that Harvard Graphics makes recommendations about which color to use for Titles, Series, and Text.

Use the down-arrow key to highlight the color of your choice and then press Enter. If you know the number of the color you want to use, you can type the number before pressing F6. Try selecting 12 Red -Symbol if you have the same palette shown in figure 5.20. If not, select any other color you may like to see.

6. Press F10 (Continue) to confirm your choice.

7. Press F2 (Draw Chart) to see the results of your changes. Figure 5.21 shows how the chart appears on-screen after italicizing part of the title.

After you have set the title line of your chart, you may want to use other features on the first Titles & Options page to make additional changes to the graph.

Adding a Legend Title

The *legend* is the key that correlates series with their bars. You can supply your own description of the series legend by pressing the Tab key until the cursor is at Legend Title on the first Titles & Options page. Then type the title you want to display. To change the placement of the legend, you can use the four legend

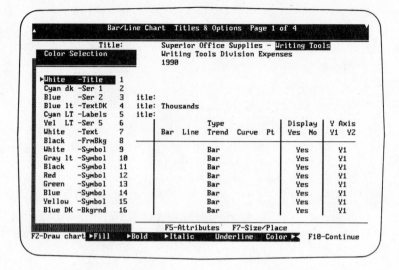

Fig. 5.20.

The Attributes bar with the Color Selection overlay.

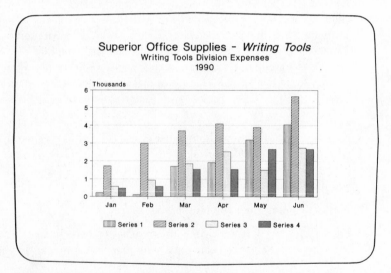

Fig. 5.21.

Preview of the bar/line chart with part of the title italicized.

options that appear on the second Titles & Options page, described in the section on "Using the Second Titles & Options Page."

Naming Series

Another helpful change is to alter the names of the series. The series names appear in the chart's legend. Try typing *Administration* in place of Series 1 in the first column, *Manufacturing* in place of Series 2, *Sales* in place of Series 3, and *Facilities* in place of Series 4. To move through the columns, use the Tab key.

You can use the Ctrl-Del key to delete the existing series name and then type in the empty space. To move the cursor to the next line, press Enter. Figure 5.22 shows the first Titles & Options page with the series names included.

```
  ▲        Bar/Line Chart  Titles & Options  Page 1 of 4        ▼
           Title:        Superior Office Supplies - Writing Tools
           Subtitle:     Writing Tools Division Expenses
                         1990
           Footnote:

       X  axis title:
       Y1 axis title:  Thousands
       Y2 axis title:
 Legend                          Type          | Display |  Y Axis
 Title:                  Bar  Line Trend Curve Pt| Yes  No | Y1  Y2

   1 │ Administration              Bar          |   Yes   |  Y1
   2 │ Manufacturing               Bar          |   Yes   |  Y1
   3 │ Sales                       Bar          |   Yes   |  Y1
   4 │ Facilities                  Bar          |   Yes   |  Y1
   5 │ Series 5                    Bar          |   Yes   |  Y1
   6 │ Series 6                    Bar          |   Yes   |  Y1
   7 │ Series 7                    Bar          |   Yes   |  Y1
   8 │ Series 8                    Bar          |   Yes   |  Y1

 F1-Help                F5-Attributes   F7-Size/Place
 F2-Draw chart                          F8-Data          F10-Continue
```

Fig. 5.22.

The first Titles & Options page with series names added.

Remember that the Ins key works as a two-position toggle switch whenever you are entering data. Pressing the Ins key toggles the cursor from one position to the other. In one position, the cursor appears as a box and new text typed on a line pushes existing text to the right. Pressing Ins once more changes the cursor to a small blinking underline that causes new text to be typed over the old.

Selecting a Bar or Line Type for Series

Use the Type column on the first Titles & Options page to tell Harvard Graphics whether to represent each series as a bar, line, trend line, curve, or point. When you first display a chart, Harvard Graphics uses bars for all the series. But you can choose another bar or line type to represent a series.

As mentioned at the beginning of the chapter, bar charts are the most common chart type and are especially effective when your data compares figures relative to one another instead of trends over time. If you want to compare series over a few time periods (division revenues over four quarters, for example), a bar chart is your best choice.

Line charts are best for displaying results over time. Three types of line charts are available in Harvard Graphics: plain, trend, and curve.

Plain line charts are graphs that use straight lines to connect data points in a series. Figure 5.23 shows a plain line chart. To produce this type of chart, choose the Line option in the Type column of the first Titles & Options page.

Fig. 5.23.

A plain line chart.

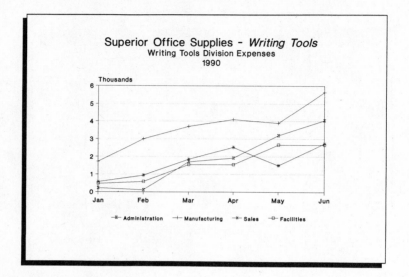

Trend line charts are useful if your data shows periodic variations but a tendency in one direction over a longer stretch of time. Statistical trends are usually shown as trend charts. When you select Trend as the graph type for a series, Harvard Graphics calculates the line that best fits through the data points. The line itself does not connect the data points but rather runs through the chart on a path that is least distant to all points. Figure 5.24 shows an example of a trend line chart in which Trend is chosen as the type for all series. Because this is a chart of expenses and not profits, you probably would not want to use the trend chart.

The *curve* line chart is a variation of the trend chart, but the curve chart uses a line that curves through the chart instead of remaining straight. Curve charts highlight periodic fluctuations as well as the general trend in data. Look at figure 5.25 for an example.

Point charts are not as easily interpreted as line and bar charts. Also called scattergrams and scatterplots, point charts are composed of unconnected dots (see fig. 5.26). Each point on the chart represents the intersection of the values of two variables. Commonly, statisticians use these charts to show correlation between variables. Use point charts with caution because they require an eye trained in statistics for full understanding. In most business environments, point charts are not the most easily understood method to display data. To create a point type chart, choose Pt in the Type column.

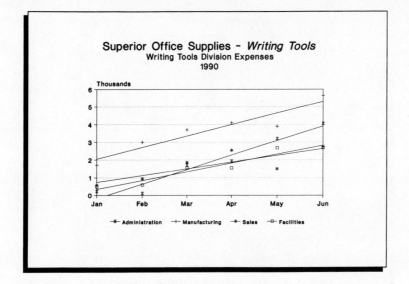

Fig. 5.24.

Trend type selected for all series.

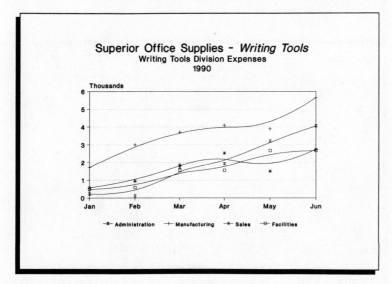

Fig. 5.25.

Curve type selected for all series.

Select a chart type by following these steps:

1. Press Tab until the cursor is next to the series you want to change and in the Type column of the first Titles & Options page.

2. Press the space bar to highlight the graph type you want to select.

3. Press F2 (Draw Chart) to view the chart with the new graph type.

A mixed bar/line chart, such as the chart shown in figure 5.27, can persuasively demonstrate a large difference among series. In the example in figure 5.27, the manufacturing budget is unusually high compared with other corporate expenses. The chart shows a line for manufacturing expenses well above the highest points of bars representing the other series in the chart.

Fig. 5.26.

An example of a point chart.

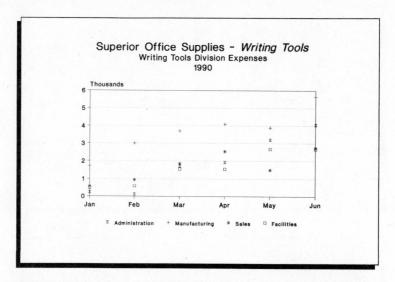

Fig. 5.27.

A mixed bar/line chart.

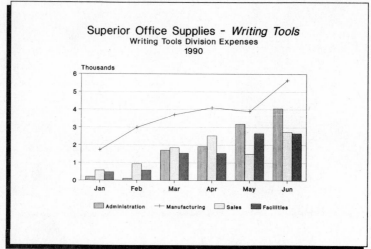

Displaying a Series

The third column on the first Titles & Options page controls the display of series. Use this column to specify whether Harvard Graphics should display or hide a specific series. With this feature, you can create two versions of a chart: one for management and one for staff. For the staff, you can choose not to display certain sensitive series data.

To change the display of a series, move the cursor to the Display column and press the space bar to change the setting from Yes to No. After you have set the display, press F2 (Draw Chart) to confirm that the bar is displayed in neither the graph nor the legend.

Try turning off the display for the manufacturing expenses on the SOSEXPEN chart. While you still are looking at the Titles & Options page 1 of 4, tab to the Display column opposite the manufacturing series and press the space bar. Press F10 (Continue) and F2 (Draw Chart) to see the results. Your screen should look like the chart shown in figure 5.28.

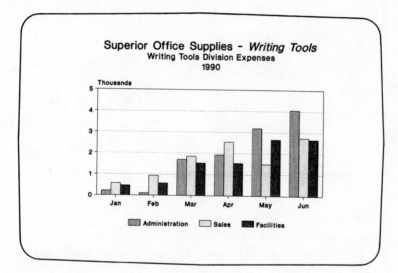

Fig. 5.28.

SOSEXPEN *chart with the manufacturing series display suppressed.*

Creating Dual Y-Axis Charts

When the range of data in two series is measured based on two different units of measurement, you can use a second y-axis to plot both series on the same chart. Figure 5.29 shows a line chart that plots the cost of Annihilator eraser production to the number of cartons shipped. The two products must be compared against their own axes because they use different units, dollars, and numbers, respectively.

To set up two y-axes, you can use Y1 at the left side of the chart and Y2 at the right side of the chart. Tab to the Y Axis column in the first Title & Options page, use the down-arrow key to position the cursor opposite the series you want to change, and press the space bar to toggle that series to Y2. Press F2 (Draw Chart) to see the results. Figure 5.30 shows the first Titles & Options page with settings for the dual y-axis chart.

Fig. 5.29.

A dual y-axis chart.

Bar/Line Chart Titles & Options Page 1 of 4

Title: Annihilator Erasers
Subtitle: Production Costs vs. Sales

Footnote:

X axis title:
Y1 axis title: Production Costs|(Dollars per carton)
Y2 axis title: Sales in Number of Cartons|(Thousands)

	Legend Title:	Type: Bar Line Trend Curve Pt	Display: Yes No	Y Axis: Y1 Y2
1	Production Costs	Line	Yes	Y1
2	Cartons Sold	Line	Yes	Y2
3	Series 3	Bar	Yes	Y1
4	Series 4	Bar	Yes	Y1
5	Series 5	Bar	Yes	Y1
6	Series 6	Bar	Yes	Y1
7	Series 7	Bar	Yes	Y1
8	Series 8	Bar	Yes	Y1

F1-Help F5-Attributes F7-Size/Place
F2-Draw chart F8-Data F10-Continue

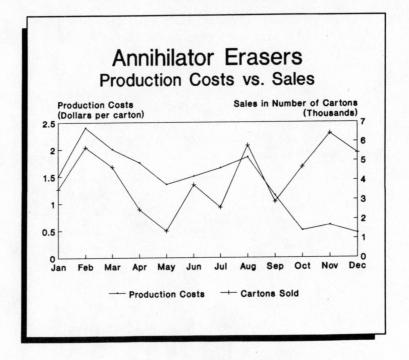

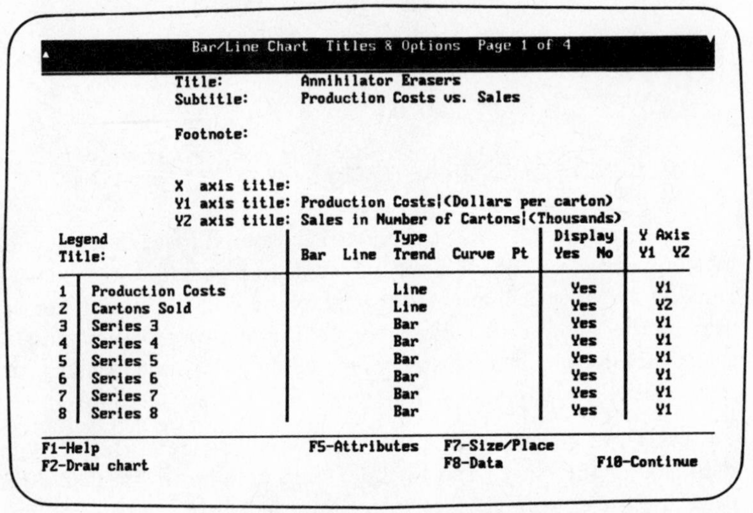

Fig. 5.30.

The first Titles & Options page with settings for the dual y-axis chart.

Keep the following suggestions in mind as you create dual y-axis charts:

❏ When two series have different units of measure, such as cost and volume sold, a dual y-axis chart is most appropriate.

❏ Dual y-axis charts cannot be three-dimensional.

❏ To avoid confusion, be sure to label your y-axes clearly and show which series belongs to which y-axis.

❏ Use line charts for dual y-axis charts that are oriented vertically and bar charts for charts set to a horizontal orientation. (You change orientation on the second Titles & Options page.)

❏ Use the Format option on the third Titles & Options page (described later in this chapter) to format the y-axis scales for the data you are describing.

❏ To show identical left and right y-axes so that the same axis appears on both sides of the graph, select Y2 as the axis on a blank series.

❏ Dual y-axis charts are easier to read if you remove grid lines behind the graph.

Using the Second Titles & Options Page

After you have completed the first Titles & Options page, you can press PgDn to move to the second Titles & Options page (see fig. 5.31). Use this page to set the characteristics of the elements of the current chart, such as the frame around the graph or the labels placed next to the bars. Also use this page to set the appearance and positioning of the legend.

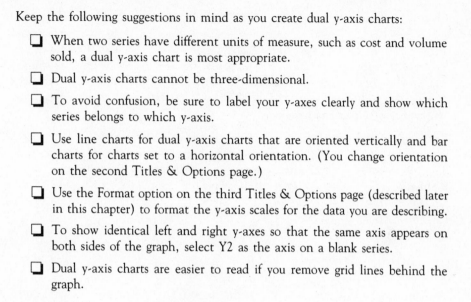

Fig. 5.31.

The second Titles & Options page.

To make adjustments on the second Titles & Options page, use the Tab key to move between options and press the space bar to highlight your selection. Always press F2 (Draw Chart) after each change, because some of the options on this page interact with options on other pages. If you wait to view the chart until you have made a number of changes, you may have trouble isolating the change that caused a glitch. If you press F2 (Draw Chart) after each change, you can find and resolve problems quickly.

For example, the Horizontal chart option on the second Titles & Options page, which trades x- and y-axes, does not work with charts that use both Overlap and 3D. You discover this fact when you press F2. You have to decide between trading the x- and y-axes and displaying the three-dimensional effect with the Overlap bar style.

Changing the Bar Style

You can use the first three options on the second Titles & Options page to give Harvard Graphics specific information about the appearance of the bars or lines in your chart. The Bar style option provides six mutually exclusive types of bars. When combined with Bar enhancement, these types create 16 distinct representations of the same data. With the additional option changes available on this page and other Titles & Options pages, you can produce hundreds of variations on every bar chart. As you become more familiar with these options, you will find ways to make your bar and line charts more expressive.

Descriptions of the six bar styles follow:

❏ *Cluster.* This is the default style when you first set up the bar chart. Selecting this style groups bars into sets of series with one set for each x-axis data value. Figure 5.32 shows the SOSEXPEN chart as a standard cluster style bar chart, with Pattern chosen as the fill style. (Bar fill style is discussed in detail in the section "Setting the Fill Style.")

❏ *Overlap.* When you have two or more series in a bar chart, selecting Overlap can make an interesting visual effect. This style causes the bars at each x-axis data point to overlap each other. Overlap bars are especially expressive when the data values for Series 1 are smaller than the data values for Series 2, and so on. Figure 5.33 shows an overlap style bar chart.

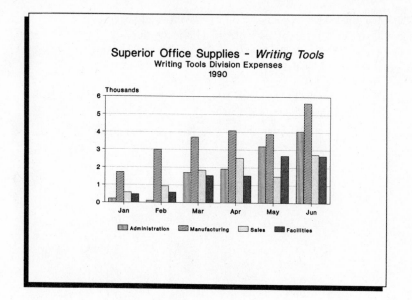

Fig. 5.32.

A cluster style bar chart.

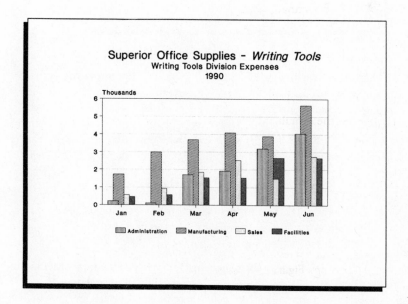

Fig. 5.33.

An overlap style bar chart.

❑ *Stack.* In a stack style bar chart, series are grouped together for each X value and stacked on top of each other. The values for Series 1 are closest to the x-axis, the values for Series 2 are above that, and so on. Figure 5.34 features a stack style bar chart.

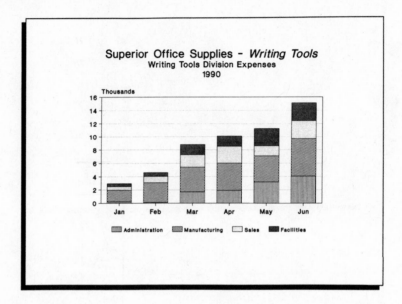

❑ *100%.* These bars are similar to stacked bars but do not show the actual values of each series. Instead, the relative percentages of the series in the bars represent their relative percentage contributions to the total. The total of all series represented by components of this style of bar chart is 100 percent. The bars in this style bar chart are all the same height because each of their totals is 100 percent. Figure 5.35 shows a 100% style bar chart.

To make a 100% bar chart or any stacked bar communicate with more meaning, use darker colors for the first series and progressively lighter colors for subsequent series. You can change the colors of a series on Titles & Options page 4, described later in this chapter.

❑ *Step.* Stepped bar charts also are called histograms or frequency distribution charts. Typically, histograms show the frequency of observations for a given category. For example, a histogram may be appropriate for showing the number of Mechanical pencils sold per district. The y-axis represents sales volume, and the bars show the proportion of the total sales each district contributed. Histograms can be effective particularly when one X value (a single district) accounts for a significantly larger proportion of the whole. Step charts require a trained eye for interpretation, however. Figure 5.36 shows a step style chart.

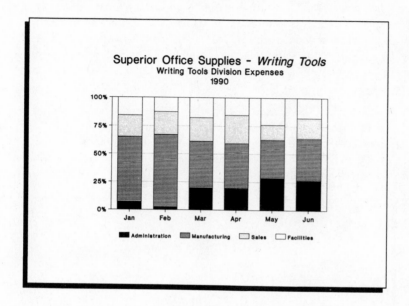

Fig. 5.35.

A sample 100% bar chart.

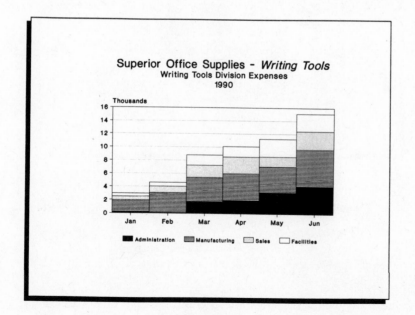

Fig. 5.36.

A step style bar chart (a histogram).

❏ *Paired.* A paired bar chart is appropriate to show the relationship between two or more series that have the same x-axis data but different y-axis data. Paired bar charts are always horizontal charts so that the x-axis is the vertical axis and the y-axis is horizontal. The Y1 axis is on the left and Y2 is on the right. The line down the middle is the y-axis zero point. If your chart has more than two series, Harvard Graphics stacks Series 1 closest to the x-axis zero point, Series 2 farther to the right or left, Series 3 even farther out, and so on.

Understanding a horizontal chart is easiest when the chart has the fewest series. Figure 5.37 shows a paired bar chart comparing the manufacturing and facilities costs to those of administration and sales. You can see that the chart represents two different measures based on the larger amounts spent on manufacturing and sales.

Fig. 5.37.

A paired style bar chart.

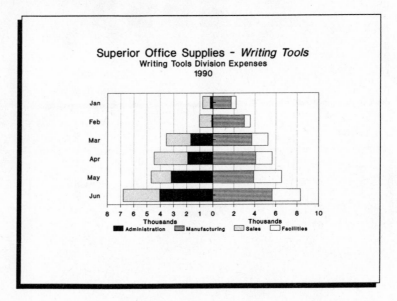

Try making your SOSEXPEN graph into a paired bar chart by following these steps:

1. Press F8 (Options) at the Bar/Line Chart Data screen to call up the first Titles & Options page and check to see that Display is on for all four series.

2. Tab to the Y Axis column opposite Manufacturing and press the space bar to set Manufacturing to Y2.

3. Tab to the Y Axis column opposite Facilities and press the space bar to flip Facilities to Y2.

4. Press PgDn to bring up the second Titles & Options page.

5. Press the space bar to highlight Paired.

6. Press F10 (Continue) and then press F2 (Draw Chart) to see your changes on-screen.

7. Press Esc to return to the main menu. Save your paired bar chart as SOSEXPR by selecting Get/Save/Remove from the main menu and then Save Chart from the Get/Save/Remove menu. Press Ctrl-Del to remove the old chart name, SOSEXPEN, and type the name *sosexpr* (for "SOS expenses, paired").

Using Bar Enhancements

You can use the second set of options on the second Titles & Options page to add substance to your chart by enhancing the appearance of its bars. The four enhancement styles available are 3D, Shadow, Link, and None. Selecting 3D yields a three-dimensional chart. (Remember, this option does not work on a paired chart.) Selecting Shadow produces a shadow effect on cluster, stack, and 100% bars. Choosing Link creates a dotted line, linking series across multiple X values in stack and 100% bar charts. To display a plain chart with flat bars and no enhancements, select None for the Bar enhancement option. Figure 5.38 shows several variations of the Bar styles and enhancements.

Combining the 3D option with an overlap style chart results in an eye-catching display for both bar charts and line charts, as you can see in figure 5.39. This chart works especially well because Series 3 (1990) has the largest figures. This type of chart works best when you order the series from lowest to highest. Try creating the 3-D and Overlap bar chart shown in figure 5.39 by entering the data shown in figure 5.40. Follow these steps:

1. Create a bar chart.

2. Press the space bar to highlight Month for the data type option; use *Jan* for Starting With and *Dec* for Ending With. Use an increment of 1 or leave the Increment option blank.

Fig. 5.38.

Several types of bar enhancement combinations.

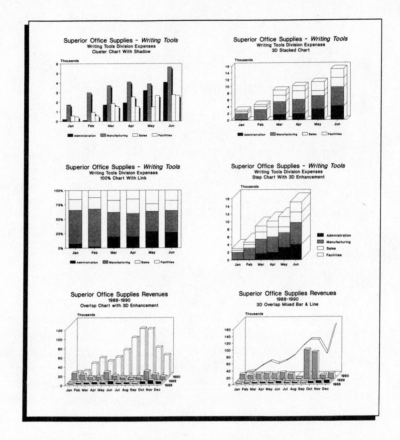

3. Enter the titles and data shown on the Bar/Line Chart Data screen.

4. Change the first three series names on the first Titles & Options page to *1988, 1989,* and *1990.*

5. Set Bar Style to Overlap and Bar Enhancement to 3D on the second Titles & Options page.

6. Press F2 (Draw Chart) to preview your choices.

When you use a chart that combines the Overlap and 3D effects, note that the values of individual bars are extremely hard to pinpoint. Use this type of chart

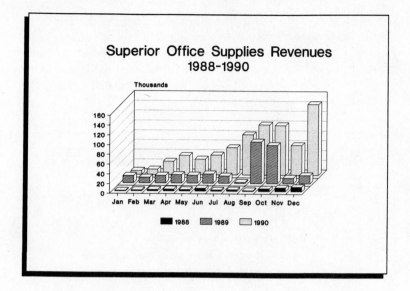

Fig. 5.39.

A bar chart with 3D enhancement and Overlap style.

Fig. 5.40.

The Bar/Line Chart Data screen for the combined three-dimensional and overlap chart.

```
                        Bar/Line Chart Data

      Title: Superior Office Supplies Revenues
   Subtitle: 1988-1990
   Footnote:


              X Axis
   Pt         Month          Series 1    Series 2    Series 3    Series 4

   1      Jan                 1356        14953        8215
   2      Feb                 2567        11449       11021
   3      Mar                 3577        15559       27028
   4      Apr                 4588        16978       39268
   5      May                 3452        16252       31921
   6      Jun                 6544        18938       40507
   7      Jul                 2788         2050       56132
   8      Aug                 3455         2050       82787
   9      Sep                 1517        84880      102834
   10     Oct                 5623        77991      101722
   11     Nov                 7866        11290       61407
   12     Dec                 9345        16745      145000

   F1-Help          F3-Save         F5-Set X type              F9-More series
   F2-Draw chart    F4-Draw/Annot   F6-Calculate    F8-Options  F10-Continue
```

only when you want to demonstrate the general variations in data, not the specific data values. If you want to add specific data to an Overlap and 3D chart, you can add a data table, described later.

Save this chart as SOSREVS by pressing F8 (Data) to return to the Bar/Line Chart Data screen, then press F3 (Save) to summon the Save Chart window. Figure 5.41 shows the Save Chart window, a feature that is new with Harvard Graphics Version 2.3. In previous versions, you had to return to the main menu to save a chart. Give this chart the name SOSREVS by typing that name after the prompt Chart will be saved as.

Fig. 5.41.
___

The Save Chart window.

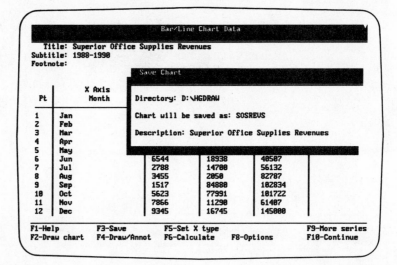

As you work with bar styles and enhancements, you develop your own personal favorites. Keep in mind that not all enhancements work with certain bar styles. Using a link enhancement with cluster style doesn't make sense, for example, and it doesn't work. When you try to use a conflicting style and enhancement combination, the style takes precedence, and Harvard Graphics omits the enhancement.

If you use three-dimensional enhancement with overlap style and your output device is a plotter, the resulting chart is plotted with overlap but without the three-dimensional enhancement. Standard plotters are incapable of plotting three-dimensional graphics.

Setting the Fill Style

You can fill the bars or lines in a chart with colors, patterns, or both. If you have set Harvard Graphics to use a monochrome monitor only, the program places patterns in the bars even if the Bar fill style option on the second Titles & Options page appears as Color. With a monochrome display and a noncolor printer, however, you still should select Pattern for your fill style choice.

Although Graphics places patterns in the bars, those patterns (which are used for colors) are not as vivid as the patterns that appear when you select Pattern.

Setting Bar Width, Overlap, and Depth

You can set the width, percentage of overlap, and depth of the bars in a chart by using the Bar Width, Bar Overlap, and Bar Depth options on the second Titles & Options page.

When you first create a bar chart, Harvard Graphics determines the optimum width of the bars so that they fit evenly across the page. You can change these options easily, however, by assigning them a number from 1 to 100. The number you use for Bar Width represents the width of bars measured relative to the overall number of bars in the chart. This option is not valid in step style charts.

The Bar Overlap option dictates the percentage amount that one bar overlaps another. When your bar chart is a three-dimensional overlap chart, this field determines the space between each x-axis grouping.

The Bar Width and Bar Overlap fields interact with each other. If you type a value of *30* in the Bar Overlap field, for example, the bars in your chart overlap by 30 percent of their widths. If you type *40* in the Bar Width field, the bars are 40 percent of the widest possible bar width in the chart, affected by the bar overlap. If you make both Bar Width and Bar Overlap 100, the resulting graph looks like a stacked chart, but on closer inspection you see that the graph is not a stacked chart because the back bars (like those for 1990) are hidden behind 1989's bars in the months of January and February. In August 1989, revenues were so small that they seem to disappear.

In a stacked chart, you usually can see all of the series in each line. Figure 5.42 shows SOSREVS with a bar width of 100 and a bar overlap of 100. You can see that the four bars take 100 percent of the available space so that one cluster is right against the next. Figure 5.43 shows the same chart as a Step chart with the same width and overlap settings. You can see that a step chart adds each series to the other (1988 is added to 1989 and so on), but a cluster chart does not.

You can examine the effect of changing overlap and width on SOSREVS by following this procedure:

1. Select Overlap for the Bar Style option on the second Titles & Options page by tabbing to the Bar Style field and pressing the space bar to highlight your choice.

2. Select a Bar Enhancement of None.

3. Select a Bar Fill Style of Pattern.

Fig. 5.42.

Overlap bar chart with bar width set at 100 percent and overlap set at 100 percent.

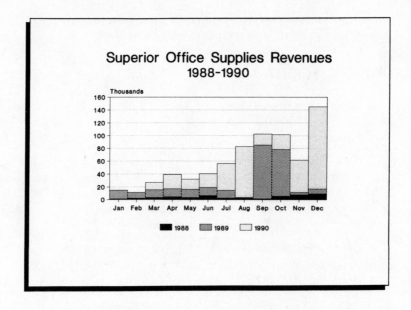

Fig. 5.43.

Same bar chart shown as a stacked chart.

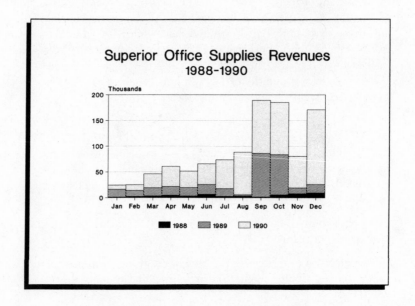

4. Tab to Bar Width, type *70*, and press Enter to move the cursor to Bar Overlap.

5. Type *35* in the Bar Overlap field.

6. Press F2 (Draw Chart) to preview your changed chart. Figure 5.44 shows the results of these changes.

7. Save this chart as SOSREVO (for "SOS Revenue chart, overlap").

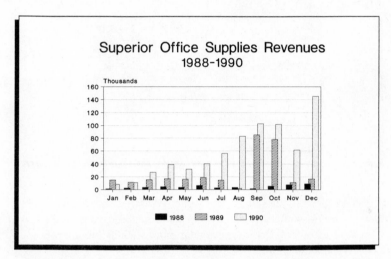

Fig. 5.44.

Overlap bar chart with bar width set at 75 percent and overlap set at 35 percent.

You use the Bar Depth option, with three-dimensional bars only, to determine the apparent depth of the bars caused by the three-dimensional effect. Figure 5.45 shows the same chart—SOSREVO—with the 3D enhancement, Bar Width set at 75, Bar Overlap set at 35, and Bar Depth set at 100. You can see that the bars now appear to have more depth.

Using Horizontally Displayed Bars

While still viewing the second Titles and Options page, set Bar Enhancement back to None, set Bar Width at 75, and toggle the Horizontal Chart option to Yes (by pressing the space bar) to switch the x- and y-axis of your chart. Selecting Yes displays the x-axis along the vertical axis and the y-axis along the horizontal plane of the graph. Using a horizontal chart is an effective way to handle a large number of x-axis values. Horizontal charts are most commonly used with

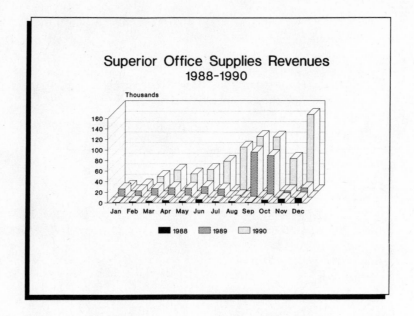

Fig. 5.45.

Bar width of 75, overlap at 35, and depth set at 100 to display bars.

bars, but they also work with lines and other chart types. If your x-axis values have a label type of Name, you may want to consider alphabetizing the labels so that the chart is easier to read. Of course, calendar data, such as the data shown in figure 5.46, is best left unalphabetized.

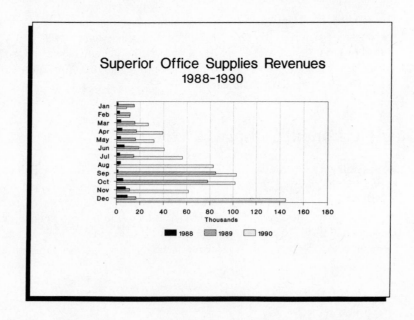

Fig. 5.46.

A horizontal bar/line chart.

With Horizontal Chart set to Yes and Bar Enhancement set at 3D, the chart appears as three-dimensional but not horizontal. To create a horizontal chart, you first must set the Bar Enhancement style to None, because none of the possible bar enhancement types works with horizontal graphs.

Displaying Value Labels

By setting the Value Labels option to All, you instruct Harvard Graphics to display on the chart the values represented by each of the bars or by each of the data points joined by line charts. Value labels do not appear in 100% types of charts. Figure 5.47 shows a chart with all value labels displayed. Notice that value labels appear on top of each bar. (If the chart has the Horizontal chart option still set to Yes, the value labels appear to the right of each bar.) The chart looks cluttered because the chart contains too many series to accommodate all value labels. In the section "Controlling the Interaction of Value Labels," you learn how to select only specific series to display, clearing up the clutter and driving home only those figures you want to emphasize.

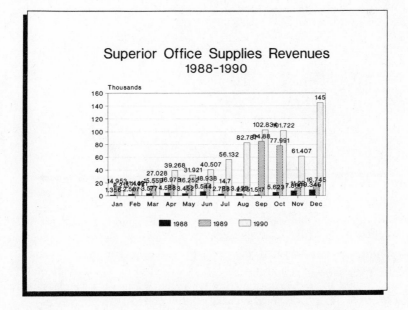

Fig. 5.47.

A bar/line chart with Value Labels set to All.

Setting the Value Labels option to Select enables you to choose (on the fourth Titles & Options page) which value labels you want to display. Harvard Graphics always sets Value Labels to None initially. This choice places no value labels on the points within a chart.

Adding a Chart Frame

You can change the frame around a graph by using the frame options on the second Titles & Options page. The Frame Style field includes these options: Full, Half, Quarter, and None. A full frame is a box surrounding a graph on all four sides. A half frame places a vertical line at the left side of the graph and a horizontal line along the graph's bottom. A quarter frame yields a single line along the bottom of the graph. You also can choose to use no frame at all. Figure 5.48 shows the SOSREVS chart with each of the frame styles.

Fig. 5.48.

The four frame styles (Full, Half, Quarter, and None).

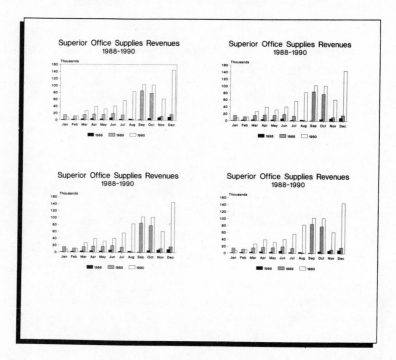

The second and third frame fields refer to the color of the frame and the color of the background. In both cases, you can press F6 (Colors) to see your choices, highlight a color, and press Enter. If you make the frame background the same color as one of your bars, the bar seems to disappear. Selecting a soothing color for a chart background and a contrasting color for a chart's frame can be pleasing visually. For example, select gray for the background with red as the frame color.

Including and Placing the Legend

Harvard Graphics offers 25 positions for the key to a graph—its legend. Using a combination of Legend Location, Legend Justify, and Legend Placement, you can position the legend or even decide not to display a legend at all. If you prefer, you can use Legend Frame to place a single line around the legend, a shadow along the bottom and to the right of the legend, or no line at all around the legend.

Different legend descriptions have an effect on the appearance of your chart. For example, you must decide whether the legend is on the top, bottom, left, or right of the chart by using the Legend Location option.

Use Legend Justify to determine whether the legend is justified to the left or as a line along the top (select the left arrow and up arrow choice) or whether you want to center the legend items. The last choice in Legend Justify places the legend along the bottom or justified right, depending on the decision you made for the location.

The third option, Legend Placement, tells Harvard Graphics to place the legend inside or outside the graph. A placement inside the graph can be effective only when the legend does not write over the bars.

The final legend option determines whether the legend frame is a single line or a shadow. You also can choose not to use a frame around the legend.

Adding a legend to the top or bottom of the chart reduces the height of the graphic portion of the chart. Reducing the overall height of the bars in a bar chart, for example, can decrease the apparent magnitude of change. If you want to emphasize the apparent degree of change in your data, you should place the legend to the left or right of the graph. Figure 5.49 shows several of the available legend option placements. All these legends have the Shadow option turned on.

When you are working on a 3-D chart, an effective Legend placement is Right for Location, with the down arrow/right arrow choice for Legend Justify. This combination of choices places the series names right next to the series, as shown in figure 5.50.

Fig. 5.49.

Legend variations.

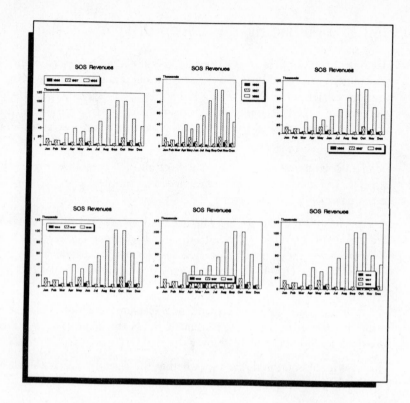

Fig. 5.50.

The chart with the legend next to the series.

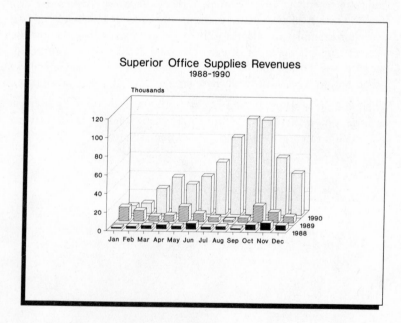

Using the Third Titles & Options Page

You use the third Titles & Options page (see fig. 5.51) to change the elements underlying the structure of the chart. For example, you can use options on this page to set grid lines behind a chart's bars or to scale and format a chart's x- and y-axis values. To set options on the third Titles & Options page, you use the same methods you used on the first two pages. Press the Tab key to move from field to field and the space bar to highlight your choice for an option. Then press F2 (Draw Chart) to view the result of your changes.

```
            Bar/Line Chart  Titles & Options  Page 3 of 4
   Data Table         | Normal    Framed   ▶None

   X  Axis Labels     | ▶Normal   Vertical  %        None
   Y1 Axis Labels     | ▶Value    Currency  %        None
   Y2 Axis Labels     | ▶Value    Currency  %        None

   X  Grid Lines      |  ....      ——      ▶None
   Y1 Grid Lines      | ▶....      ——       None
   Y2 Grid Lines      | ▶....      ——       None

   X Tick Mark Style  |  In      ▶Out      Both      None
   Y Tick Mark Style  |  In      ▶Out      Both      None
                      |    X Axis      |    Y1 Axis    |    Y2 Axis
   Scale Type         | ▶Linear   Log   | ▶Linear  Log | ▶Linear   Log
   Format             |
   Minimum Value      |
   Maximum Value      |
   Increment          |

   F1-Help
   F2-Draw chart                       F8-Data        F10-Continue
```

Fig. 5.51.

The third Titles & Options page.

Adding a Data Table

Data tables, new to Harvard Graphics in Version 2.1, list outside the chart the raw values for each of the points in the chart, series by series. The numbers in the data table add precision to the overall impression that the chart's bars or lines provide. They also eliminate the guesswork of trying to figure out the exact data by judging the height of the bars in a chart.

Harvard Graphics does not supply a data table automatically. Instead, you must turn on the data table by using the third Titles & Options page. The first line on that page lists the data table styles: Normal, Framed, and None. A normal data table is a list that appears directly below the graph's x-axis. A framed data table provides the same list but with framing lines surrounding the data. Figure 5.52 shows a framed data table on the SOSREVS chart.

Fig. 5.52.

*SOSREVS chart
with a framed data
table.*

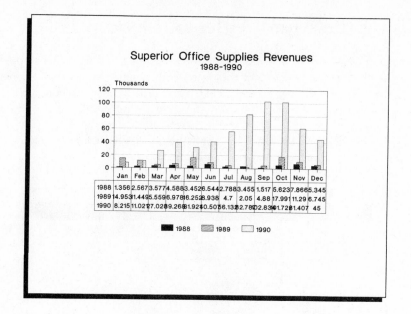

Try putting a framed data table on your SOSREVS chart, following this procedure:

1. Select Get/Save/Remove from the main menu.

2. Use the down-arrow key to highlight SOSREVS and press Enter.

3. Press Esc to bring up the Bar/Line Chart Data screen.

4. Press F8 (Options) at the Bar/Line Chart Data screen to bring up the Titles & Options pages. Make sure that Horiz. is set to No on the second Titles & Options page.

5. Press PgDn twice to summon the third Titles & Options page.

6. Press the space bar to highlight Framed at the Data Table option.

7. Press F2 (Draw Chart) to preview your chart with a data table.

Previewing Your Data Table

If the raw data in your data table is composed of long numbers, you may find that they do not seem to fit properly in the data table when you preview the chart. Check to see how the chart prints out by previewing the printed output on-screen. To preview the chart just as the output will be sent to your output device, follow these steps:

1. Press Esc to return to the main menu.

2. Select Produce Output from the main menu.

3. Press F2 (Draw Chart) to view the chart as the chart appears when printed.

Changing the Size of Data Table and X-Axis Values

If your data doesn't fit when you look at the print view, you need to reduce the size of the numbers in the data table. You can accomplish this by using F7-Size/Place on the first Titles & Options page. With the Size/Place overlay on-screen (see fig. 5.53), tab to the X Labels field and press 1. The size of the x-axis labels affect the size of the text and numbers in the data table. To complement the X labels, set the Y labels to 1 also. After you press F10 (Continue), press F2 (Draw Chart) and view the data table with its new size (see fig. 5.54).

```
Size    Place      Bar/Line Chart  Titles & Options   Page 1 of 4

5.5     L ►C   R  Title:          Superior Office Supplies Revenues
4       L ►C   R  Subtitle:       1988-1990
4       L ►C   R
2.5     ►L  C  R  Footnote:
2.5     ►L  C  R
2.5     ►L  C  R
4          ►C     X  axis title:
3       ►→  ↓     Y1 axis title:  Thousands
3       ►→  ↓     Y2 axis title:
1       X labels                                        Display │ Y Axis
1       Y labels                       Type             Yes  No │ Y1  Y2
                              Bar  Line Trend  Curve  Pt

1  │ 1988                          Bar                   Yes      Y1
2  │ 1989                          Bar                   Yes      Y1
3  │ 1990                          Bar                   Yes      Y1
4  │ Series 4                      Bar                   Yes      Y1
5  │ Series 5                      Bar                   Yes      Y1
6  │ Series 6                      Bar                   Yes      Y1
7  │ Series 7                      Bar                   Yes      Y1
8  │ Series 8                      Bar                   Yes      Y1

F1-Help                    F5-Attributes   F7-Size/Place
F2-Draw chart                              F8-Data          F10-Continue
```

Fig. 5.53.

The Size/Place overlay on the first Titles & Options page.

Data tables display data for all series, even if you set Display for a series to No on the first Titles & Options page. Eliminating series from a data table is discussed later in this chapter (see "Controlling the Interaction of Value Labels"). To change the size of the numbers in a data table, you change the size of the X labels. Normally, the X Labels and Y Labels options on the Size/Place overlay enable you to change the sizes of the labels that run along the horizontal and vertical axes of the chart. If you want to leave the Y labels large while changing the X labels, press Enter to move past the Y Labels line. Harvard Graphics treats each of these labels independently. In figure 5.55, the Y labels have been set to 5.5.

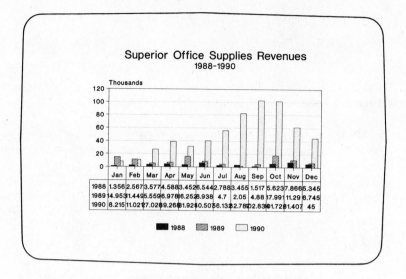

Fig. 5.54.

Viewing the chart as it will print.

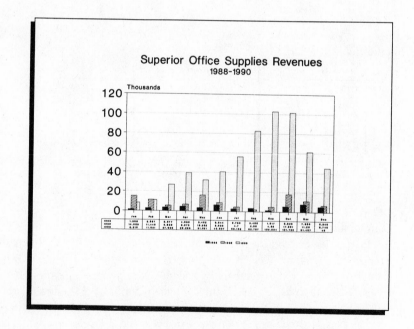

Fig. 5.55.

Preview of SOSREVS x-axis labels set at 1 and y-axis labels set at 5.5.

Altering X- and Y-Axis Labels

The X Axis Labels, Y1 Axis Labels, and Y2 Axis Labels options on the third Titles & Options page enable you to describe and format the numbers on the x- and y-axis. X-axis labels can appear in three different formats: Normal, Vertical, and %. Normal x-axis labels are displayed horizontally across the page below the axis. Vertical labels are displayed down the page, one letter under another. Figure 5.56 shows an example of vertical x-axis labels. To see this effect, be sure to switch the Data Table option to None.

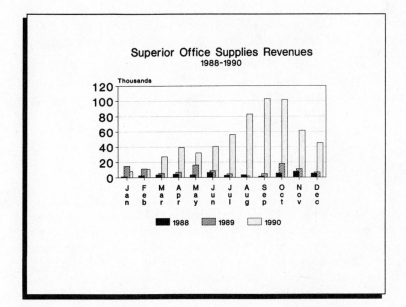

Fig. 5.56.

Vertical x-axis labels.

If you want to keep long x-axis labels horizontal, you can break the labels into two lines of text by typing a vertical bar (|) at the position at which you want to split the label.

Selecting the % format for the X Axis Labels option instructs Harvard Graphics to divide the value by 100 and add a percent sign. This method works only when X Data Type is Number. If you select None for X Axis Labels, no labels are on the finished chart.

Y1 and Y2 axis labels normally are placed on the left and right vertical sides, respectively, of the graph. Using the Y1 Axis Labels and Y2 Axis Labels options on the third Titles & Options page, you also can format the y-axis label values according to one of three formats: Value, $, and %. In addition, you can choose None to remove the y-axis labels. If you choose None, you may want to include value labels above the bars or lines and eliminate the chart's grid marks. To place the values on top of the bars, read the section in this chapter called "Controlling the Interaction of Value Labels." A clean chart, both informative and specific, is the result.

Altering Grid Lines and Tick Marks

If you have added grid lines behind the bars of the graph, you can change their style with the Grid Lines options on the third Titles & Options page. Grid lines can be dotted or solid. Because grid lines can be distracting, especially in line charts, you should use them cautiously. The presence of grid lines on your graph emphasizes values rather than trends. On a three-dimensional cluster chart, adding grid lines can clarify your data.

With the X Tick Mark Style and Y Tick Mark Style options, you can specify whether your graph should include tick marks. Tick marks are notches along the x- and y-axis. You can choose to display tick marks inside the graph by choosing In, outside the graph by choosing Out, or inside and outside the graph by choosing Both. As an alternative, you can select None to eliminate tick marks.

Scaling X- and Y-Axes

Harvard Graphics provides two methods for scaling the x- and y-axes. Scaling an axis sets the distance between its points. Most business graphics use linear scaling in which the distances between axis points are equal. When the change being described by the chart is geometric, a logarithmic scale type can better portray the data. A logarithmic scale in base 10 has distances between each unit on the axes that increase logarithmically. Each increment increases the preceding increment by a power of 10. For example, the first point is 10 to the first power, or 10; the second point is 10 to the second power, or 100; the third point is 10 to the third power, or 1,000; and so on.

Logarithmic scaling is fairly uncommon but can be effective when the data in a chart is diverse, when you have extraordinarily large changes between points, or when the high and low points of data in a series are of a different scope than data in other series in the chart. Large variations within a series are lessened in a logarithmic chart.

When you set the minimum and maximum values for a logarithmic scale axis, the maximum value should be a power of 10 over the minimum value. For example, a typical logarithmic scale may range from 1 to 10,000.

Using the third Titles & Options page, you may choose Log (logarithmic) for one axis and Linear for the other. This setup produces a semilogarithmic chart. Figure 5.57 shows a revenue chart with large variations between series displayed as a linear chart. Figure 5.58 shows the same chart with a logarithmic scale. You can see the visual difference the logarithmic scale makes when based on multiples of 10.

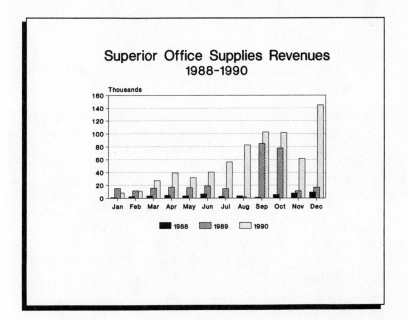

Fig. 5.57.

Chart with large variations between series displayed as a linear chart.

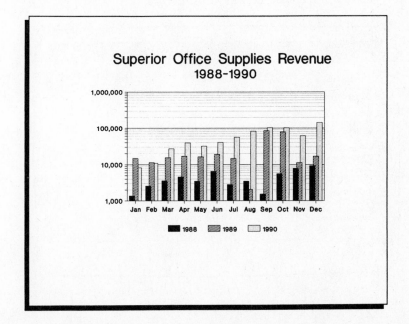

Fig. 5.58.

The same chart with a logarithmic scale.

When you set the x-axis on the X Data Type Menu overlay, you tell Harvard Graphics the appropriate starting and ending points for the data you are entering. The x-axis Minimum Value and Maximum Value fields on the third Titles & Options page affect the final Starting With and Ending With points you see when you preview the chart.

Formatting the Axis Labels

You can use the features on the bottom of the third Titles & Options page to add meaning to the x- and y-axis labels. For example, look at the SOSREVS chart in figure 5.57. The numbers that appear along the y-axis are in increments of 20 and range from 0 to 160. The Thousands label above the y-axis tells the viewer to mentally add three zeros to the figure. Suppose you wanted the numbers to appear with the zeros, instead. To make this change, you can use formatting commands with Minimum and Maximum values. For example, if you type a comma in the format line for the Y1 axis, set the Minimum value at 0, the Maximum value at 15, and set the increment to 50, the SOSREVS chart looks more detailed. Minimum and Maximum values and Increments are described in the next section of this chapter.

Figure 5.59 shows the third Titles & Options page with the formatting command added. Figure 5.60 shows the results. You can see that the Thousands label is no longer on the chart, but the numbers appear with three zeros.

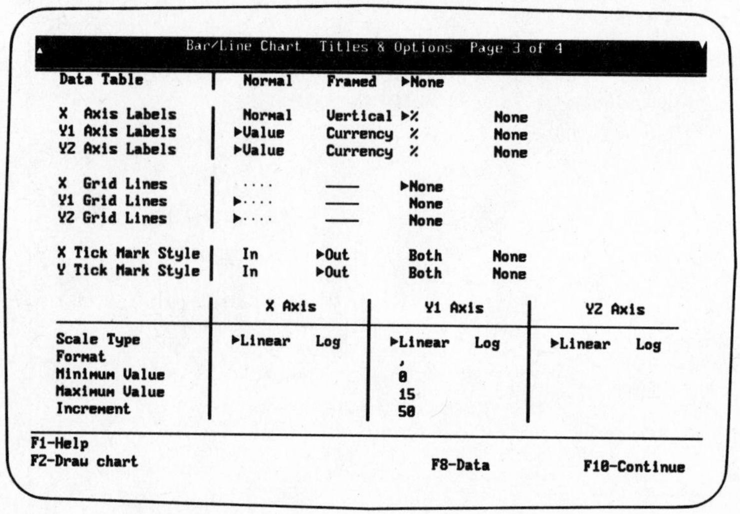

Fig. 5.59.

The third Titles & Options page with scaling and formatting commands included.

```
         ████    Bar/Line Chart  Titles & Options  Page 3 of 4    ▼

         Data Table      | Normal    Framed   ▶None

         X  Axis Labels  | Normal    Vertical ▶%       None
         Y1 Axis Labels  | ▶Value    Currency %        None
         Y2 Axis Labels  | ▶Value    Currency %        None

         X  Grid Lines   | · · · ·   ———      ▶None
         Y1 Grid Lines   | ▶· · · ·  ———       None
         Y2 Grid Lines   | ▶· · · ·  ———       None

         X Tick Mark Style | In     ▶Out      Both     None
         Y Tick Mark Style | In     ▶Out      Both     None

                         |   X Axis          Y1 Axis          Y2 Axis

         Scale Type      | ▶Linear   Log   ▶Linear   Log   ▶Linear   Log
         Format          |                   ,
         Minimum Value   |                   0
         Maximum Value   |                   15
         Increment       |                   50

         F1-Help
         F2-Draw chart                        F8-Data        F10-Continue
```

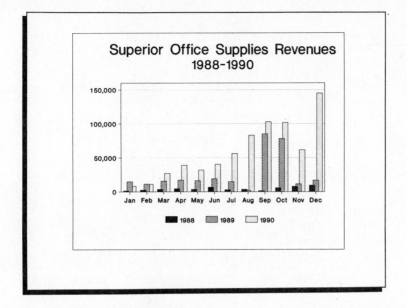

Fig. 5.60.

Three years of revenues with no scaling adjustments on the x-axis.

Use these figures and the format commands in table 5.1 to determine the appropriate scaling for your chart. You can include commas and measurement characters such as $, ft., and ″ (inches). In addition, you can set the number of decimal places for chart labels or display the labels in scientific notation. The scaling options interact with the Format option near the top of the third Titles & Options page. When you select $ or % in the Format option at the top of the page, Harvard Graphics formats the labels on the x- or y-axis in your chart but not on the Bar/Line Chart Data screen. In figure 5.61, the Y1 Axis Labels are set to Currency.

Formatting the y-axis labels also formats the y data values shown on your chart in Harvard Graphics. The four special Harvard Graphics formatting commands are simple to use. You need only type the format instruction on the Format line after you have selected the scale type for the x- and y-axis. Table 5.1 provides a summary, some examples, and descriptions of the formatting commands.

If all the numbers in your data are large, you can use the Format field to reduce the number of digits in the values by dividing all the numbers in your data by a constant. The result is fewer digits and numbers that are easier to read. Scaling formats are identical to standard formats.

Table 5.1
Format Commands for the X- and Y-Axis

To display	Enter on the Format line	Description
4,000	,	Inserts a comma in the number, if necessary
19.68	2	Displays two decimal places
2,590.6	,1	Displays a comma and a specific number of decimal places
12.2 mm	|1 mm	Vertical bar (|) adds preceding or trailing text (like mm) to the formatted value, and 1 tells Harvard Graphics to include one decimal place after the decimal point.
9,899.50 Yen	,2| Yen	Adds Yen as trailing text, places a comma in the number, and displays the number to two decimal places
£456.25	£,2	Displays a UK pound sign (£). To create a pound sign, type 156 on the keypad while holding down the Alt key.
9.55E+02	!	Displays numbers in scientific notation
2000	1|	Displays entire number with three zeros

Fig. 5.61.

Y1 Axis labels set to Currency.

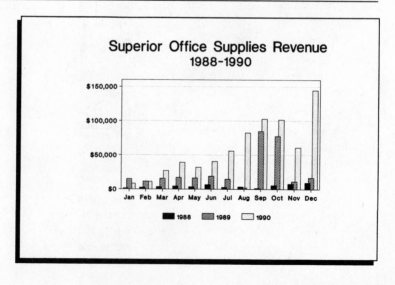

To display two cartons using scaling formats, use this command:

15| cartons

If you have the numbers of actual mechanical pencil sets sold (30 in this example), but you want to list the values in the chart by the number of cartons sold, you can use this scaling format to specify that each carton contains 15 sets of pencils.

To display 40 thousand, use this command:

1000| thousand

This formatting instruction divides the entered value by 1,000 and places "thousand" after the number.

If you place a $| formatting command in front of the formatting command already in the Y1 Axis, the resulting chart would have two dollar signs in front of the Y1 axis labels. The first dollar sign is a result of the Y1 Axis Label setting at the top of Options page 3, and the second dollar sign is from the Format command. Figure 5.62 shows the SOSREVS chart with both dollar sign commands.

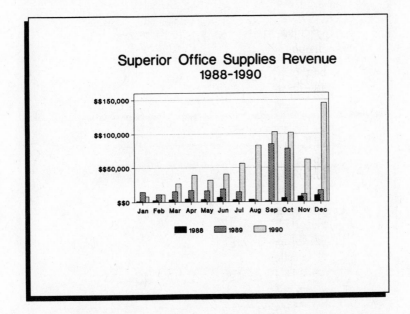

Fig. 5.62.

The chart with two currency formatting commands.

You can find another example in an earlier section of this chapter. When you set the data table (on Titles & Options page 2), you had to adjust the numbers to an appropriate size. If you place a data table on SOSREVS, the numbers are too large to fit in the frames of the data table. In fact, the data table looks cluttered and unreadable, as shown in figure 5.63. To solve this problem earlier, you changed the size of the x-axis labels. Suppose, however, that you want to keep the x-axis labels the same size but reduce the number of characters in the number. To do this, type a zero in the Y1 Format field on Titles & Options page 3, and Harvard Graphics does not show numbers that normally would be to the right of the comma. Figure 5.63 shows the original chart, and figure 5.64 shows the third Titles & Options screen with formatting commands. Figure 5.65 shows the resulting chart SOSREVS with the cleaner, readable data table.

Fig. 5.63.

The SOSREVS chart with a data table and no formatting.

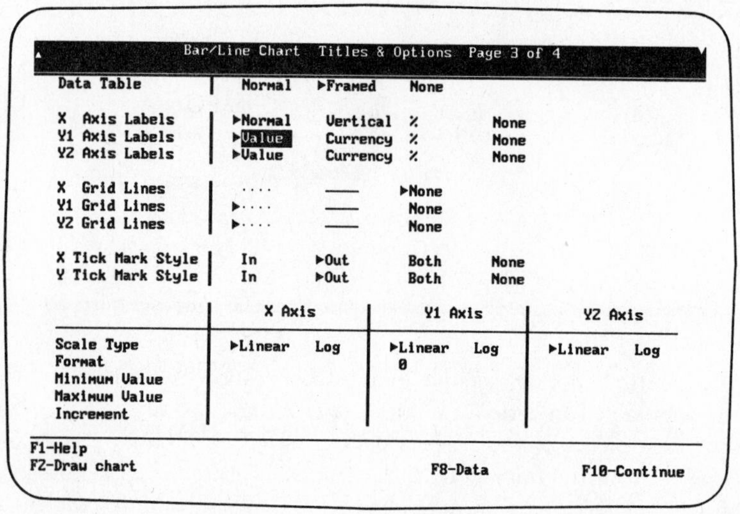

Fig. 5.64.

The third Title & Options page with formatting options.

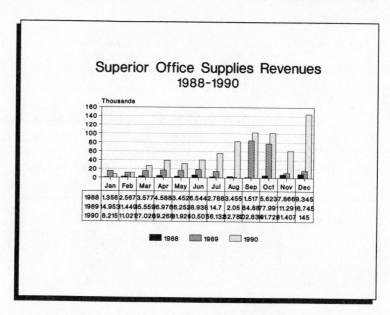

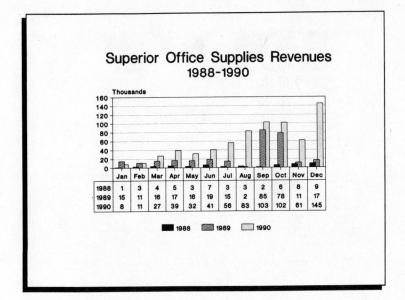

Fig. 5.65.

The chart with formatted data table values.

Setting Minimum and Maximum Values

Use the Minimum Value, Maximum Value, and Increment fields on the third Titles & Options page to override the scale that Harvard Graphics automatically uses for the axes of your chart. By specifying minimum and maximum values and increments in the X Axis column, you can limit the number of data points in a chart. If your chart includes data for the last 20 years of growth, for example, you can show data at 5-year intervals by using 1 as the Minimum Value, 20 as the Maximum Value, and 5 as the Increment. To show only the first 5 years, you can use 1 as the Minimum Value and 5 as the Maximum Value and leave Increment blank. If you omit an increment, Harvard Graphics assumes that you want an Increment setting of 1.

Figure 5.66 shows the third Titles & Options page set to show only the first six months of data. Figure 5.67 shows the same bar chart with the adjusted scaling. Note that if the X Data Type option is set to Number, you cannot use this technique to reduce the number of X values.

You can scale the Y1 and Y2 axes in a similar fashion. When you change minimum and maximum Y values, however, be sure that the minimum is smaller than the smallest value on the data screen and that the maximum is larger than the largest value on the data screen. Otherwise, Harvard Graphics overrides your values so that the program can chart every value in your data.

Fig. 5.66.

*The third Titles &
Options page with
x-axis scaling.*

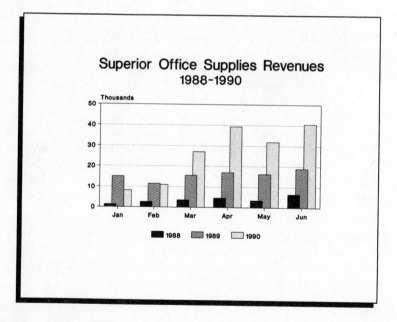

```
┌─────────────────────────────────────────────────────────────┐
│ ▲           Bar/Line Chart  Titles & Options  Page 3 of 4    │
├─────────────────────────────────────────────────────────────┤
│   Data Table          │ Normal   ▶Framed    None             │
│                       │                                      │
│   X  Axis Labels      │ ▶Normal   Vertical   %        None   │
│   Y1 Axis Labels      │ ▶Value    Currency   %        None   │
│   Y2 Axis Labels      │ ▶Value    Currency   %        None   │
│                       │                                      │
│   X  Grid Lines       │  ····      ——       ▶None            │
│   Y1 Grid Lines       │ ▶····      ——        None            │
│   Y2 Grid Lines       │ ▶····      ——        None            │
│                       │                                      │
│   X Tick Mark Style   │ In       ▶Out       Both      None   │
│   Y Tick Mark Style   │ In       ▶Out       Both      None   │
│                       ├──────────────────────────────────────│
│                       │  X Axis      │  Y1 Axis   │  Y2 Axis  │
│   Scale Type          │ ▶Linear  Log │ ▶Linear Log│ ▶Linear Log│
│   Format              │              │            │           │
│   Minimum Value       │ 1            │            │           │
│   Maximum Value       │ 6            │            │           │
│   Increment           │              │            │           │
├─────────────────────────────────────────────────────────────┤
│ F1-Help                                                      │
│ F2-Draw chart                        F8-Data      F10-Continue│
└─────────────────────────────────────────────────────────────┘
```

Fig. 5.67.

*The x-axis adjusted
to show only the
first six months.*

Sometimes the smallest value in your chart is considerably larger than 0. But
Harvard Graphics still starts the y-axis in a line chart at 0. (Harvard Graphics
always starts the y-axis values of bar charts at 0 to avoid distorting the chart.)
Suppose that your smallest value is 45, and your largest value is 200. To magnify
the results shown on this chart, make its minimum Y value 30 and its maximum

Y value 225. You may want to use a larger increment to reduce the chart clutter, too. If you decide that you want to return to the Harvard Graphics defaults, remove the minimum, maximum, and increment values you entered.

You can try setting new minimum, maximum, and increment values, using SOSREVS with only the first six months displayed, as set in the last example. Notice that with only six months, the y-axis labels range from 0 to 50 (thousand) in increments of 10 (thousand). To magnify the chart, try setting the Minimum Value at 0, with a Maximum Value set at 45,000. Try to zoom the chart out by setting the Minimum Value at 0 with a Maximum Value of 145,000. Figure 5.68 shows the results of these two changes.

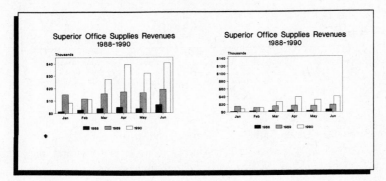

Fig. 5.68.

Scaling the Y1 axis.

Using the Fourth Titles & Options Page

Press PgDn at the third Titles & Options page to summon the fourth Titles & Options page (see fig. 5.69). The fourth page is the last of the Titles & Options pages for bar/line charts. Use this page to place the finishing touches on the appearance of your chart's titles and bars or lines. (Titles are the names you give to series, axes, and the overall chart.)

You can use the fourth Titles & Options page, for example, to set any series to display as a cumulative set of values, with each successive value representing its own value added to the sum total of all values before it. You also can change the style of marker used to indicate each point on a line chart. On the fourth Titles & Options page, you can type x- and y-axis titles, alter their size/place characteristics and their attributes, and change the line style of a line chart series. The fourth Titles & Options page also enables you to select which Y labels to display on the completed graph. This feature interacts with the third Titles & Options page when you tell Harvard Graphics to display only select Y values, described later in this section.

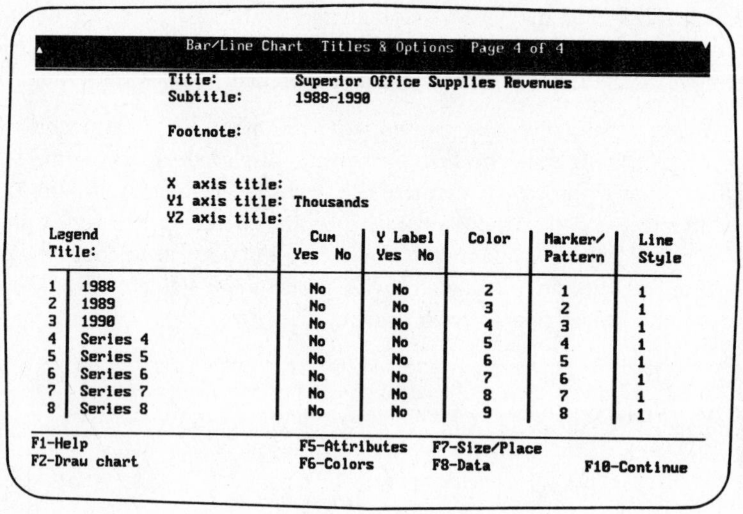

Fig. 5.69.

The fourth Titles &
Options page.

```
┌─────────────────────────────────────────────────────────────────────┐
│    ▲       Bar/Line Chart   Titles & Options   Page 4 of 4        ▼   │
│                                                                       │
│              Title:       Superior Office Supplies Revenues           │
│              Subtitle:    1988-1990                                   │
│                                                                       │
│              Footnote:                                                │
│                                                                       │
│                                                                       │
│              X  axis title:                                           │
│              Y1 axis title: Thousands                                 │
│              Y2 axis title:                                           │
│     Legend                Cum       Y Label   Color   Marker/   Line  │
│     Title:                Yes No    Yes No             Pattern  Style │
│                                                                       │
│     1 │ 1988              No        No        2        1         1    │
│     2 │ 1989              No        No        3        2         1    │
│     3 │ 1990              No        No        4        3         1    │
│     4 │ Series 4          No        No        5        4         1    │
│     5 │ Series 5          No        No        6        5         1    │
│     6 │ Series 6          No        No        7        6         1    │
│     7 │ Series 7          No        No        8        7         1    │
│     8 │ Series 8          No        No        9        8         1    │
│                                                                       │
│   F1-Help                 F5-Attributes  F7-Size/Place                │
│   F2-Draw chart           F6-Colors      F8-Data         F10-Continue │
└─────────────────────────────────────────────────────────────────────┘
```

You already are familiar with the first several lines on this screen, and you almost certainly have entered a title, subtitle, and footnote before you get to this page. Harvard Graphics gives you yet another opportunity to make changes and alterations, however, using the F7-Size/Place and F5-Attributes options.

Building a Cumulative Chart

The second column of the fourth Titles & Options page, Cum, enables you to set a series to be calculated and displayed as a *cumulative* set of values. In a cumulative series, the data from the first Y value in the first bar is added to the data of the second Y value in the second bar. The data from the first and second Y values then are added to the third Y value in the third bar, and so on. A cumulative chart, with Cum set to Yes for all series, is shown in figure 5.70.

Setting the Cum column to No results in a display of actual values rather than cumulative totals. Cumulative charts are effective for showing running totals but can be deceiving if not labeled properly. These charts can make a series of equal data values look like phenomenal growth.

A dual y-axis cumulative chart with a horizontal orientation can be particularly impressive. To see this effect, recall the dual y-axis chart (SOSEXPR) you made previously in this chapter and set all the series to cumulative. Figure 5.71 shows the resulting chart.

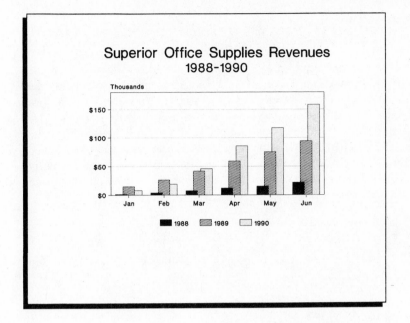

Fig. 5.70.

A cumulative chart.

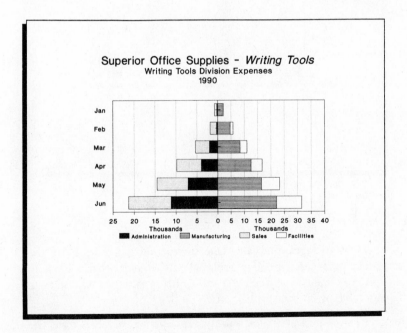

Fig. 5.71.

A paired bar chart
with Cum selected
for all series.

Displaying Y Labels

The Y Label column on the fourth Titles & Options page is tied directly to the Value Labels option on the second Titles & Options page. When you choose Select at the Value Labels option on page 2, Harvard Graphics displays only the Y values set to Yes in the Y Label column on page 4. You can use these two options to label only the most significant series in a chart with four series, for example. Figure 5.72 shows a bar chart with just one series labeled. This figure uses the SOSREVS chart, emphasizing only the last year. Its Y values formatted with the third Titles & Options page (a 0 in the Y1 Axis Format line). If you try to reproduce this chart, be sure that you set Value Labels to Select on the second Titles & Options page.

Fig. 5.72.

A bar chart with just one series labeled.

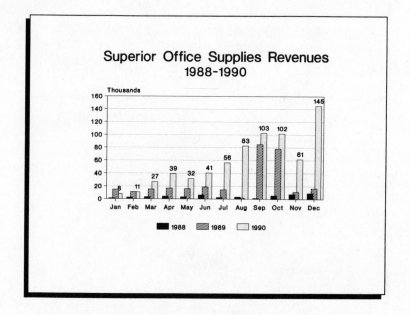

Controlling the Interaction of Value Labels

When you display a value label, the value label appears on the chart above the point for that value. But when a value is displayed on the graph, that value does not appear in a data table. Therefore, you must choose whether to display Y labels in the data table or on the graph itself.

Harvard Graphics leaves no option for omitting specific series values from the graph and the data table if you are using a data table. If you suppress the display of a bar on the graph, you do not want the data to show on the table. To keep the data from showing on the table, you must take advantage of a complex interaction between options on all four Titles & Options pages.

You can understand this complex interaction by trying to rid the SOSREVS chart of any numbers related to 1988, without altering the data page.

You begin by following this procedure using the SOSREVS chart:

1. On the first Titles & Options page, set the first series (1988) to Yes in the Display column.

2. Set the Value Labels option on the second Titles & Options page to Select.

3. Set Data Table to Normal or Framed on the third Titles & Options page.

4. On the fourth Titles & Options page, choose the 1988 series by toggling to Yes for that series in the Y Label column. Be sure that all other series are set on No.

The resulting chart is shown in figure 5.73. You can see that the Y labels are included above the bar for 1988, and the numbers in the data table include 1989 and 1990.

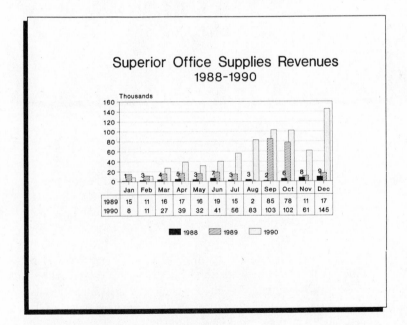

Fig. 5.73.

The bar chart with data table and y value selected for 1988.

To turn off the display of the values of a specific series in the data table and on the graph, follow this procedure:

1. Set Display to No on the first Titles & Options page for the series you want to affect.

2. For that same series, set Y Label to Yes on the fourth Titles & Options page.

Figure 5.74 shows the resulting chart, in which 1988 is not shown in the data table or the graph.

Fig. 5.74.

The chart with 1988 not displayed in data table or above bars.

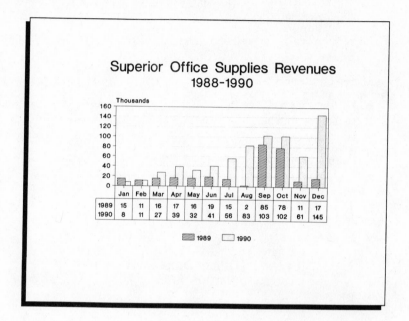

Controlling Color, Markers, Patterns, and Line Styles

The remaining columns on the fourth Titles & Options page describe the physical attributes of the markers, bars, and lines available for a chart. (*Markers* are the dots, circles, asterisks, and other figures used to mark each point in a line chart.) Harvard Graphics selects a different line style, color, and marker style for each series when you create a graph. The program provides four line styles and eight marker styles. Line Style 1 produces a thin, solid line; Line Style 2, a thick, solid line; Line Style 3, a dotted line; and Line Style 4, a dashed line. Markers are varied: asterisks, plus signs, Xs, circles, and other markers are available. Figure 5.75 shows the full range of line styles and all 12 marker styles available to you. (Unfortunately, in these black-and-white illustrations, you cannot see the phenomenal rainbow of colors chosen.)

To make changes in color, markers, and line styles, press Tab to move the cursor to the appropriate column and line on the fourth Titles & Options page. Press the space bar to highlight your choice. When the cursor is in the Color column, you can press F6 (Colors) to see your choices. If you want your lines to have no markers, press 0 in the Marker/Pattern column.

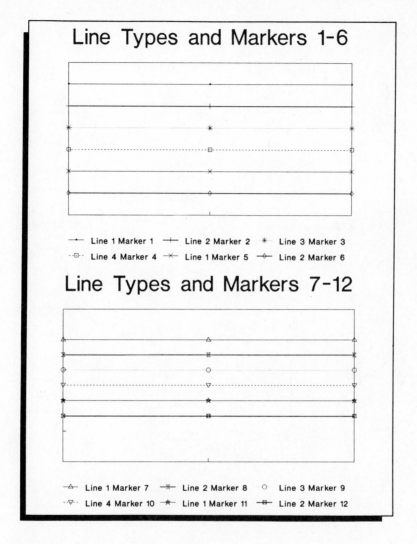

Fig. 5.75.

The available line and marker styles.

Chapter Summary

In this chapter, you learned how to make bar and line charts and how to use the Titles & Options pages to change the appearance of those charts. In the next chapter, you learn how to create and alter the other types of graph charts available in Harvard Graphics.

6

Creating Graph Charts: Area, High/Low/Close, and Pie

This chapter takes up where Chapter 5 leaves off and continues the discussion of Harvard Graphics graph charts. In this chapter, you learn how to create and modify area, high/low/close, and pie charts.

Creating Area Charts

Area charts dramatically illustrate large increases in volume. The SOSREVS bar chart shown in figure 6.1, for example, displays a minor increase in revenues in 1988 and 1989, and a major increase in 1990. The area chart shown in figure 6.2 shows the magnitude of this significant increase far more effectively than the SOSREVS bar chart does.

An area chart is a variation of one type of bar/line chart, the trend chart. Not surprisingly, the procedure for creating an area chart is nearly identical to the procedure used to create a standard bar/line chart (see Chapter 5). In addition, the four Titles & Options pages for area charts are almost identical to the four Titles & Options pages for bar and line charts.

Changing from a Bar/Line to an Area Chart Type

You may want to try different chart types with the same data, to determine which chart best suits your purposes. For example, you may want to convert the data from the SOSREVS bar chart into an area chart. By convert-

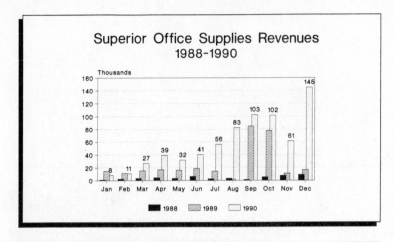

Fig. 6.1.

The SOSREVS bar chart.

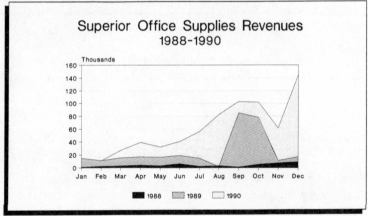

Fig. 6.2.

An area chart showing the SOSREVS data.

ing the data, you avoid having to reenter it in an Area Chart Data screen. To use the data from SOSREVS for your area chart, follow this procedure:

1. Select Get/Save/Remove from the main menu.

2. Select Get Chart from the Get/Save/Remove menu.

3. Use the down-arrow key to highlight the file SOSREVS, or type the name *sosrevs*, and press Enter.

4. When the SOSREVS chart is displayed, press Esc twice—once to return to the Bar/Line Chart Data screen and a second time to return to the main menu.

5. Select Create New Chart from the main menu.

6. Select Area from the Create New Chart menu and press Enter.

7. In the Change Chart Type overlay, press Enter to select Yes and keep the current data (see fig. 6.3).

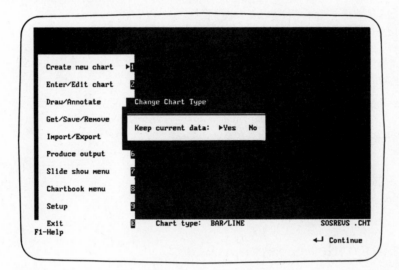

Fig. 6.3.

The Change Chart Type overlay.

When you borrow data directly from another chart type, the first screen you see is the Area Chart Data screen. If you answer No in the Keep Current Data field of the Change Chart Type overlay, however, Harvard Graphics displays the X Data Type Menu overlay first, in the customary procedure for starting a new chart. You must choose a setting for the X Data Type option, as usual, if that overlay appears. (For more information, see "Setting the X-Axis" in Chapter 5.)

Press F2 (Draw Chart) to review the area chart you converted from a bar style and save it with the name SOSREVA (for "SOS revenues, area chart").

Entering Data in an Area Chart

When you start a chart, the procedure for entering data on the Area Chart Data screen is the same as entering data on a Bar/Line Chart Data screen. As you enter data, you should be aware that Harvard Graphics arranges it in the chart in series order. Series 1 is shown at the bottom, Series 2 is above that, and so on. After entering your data and previewing the default area chart, press F8 (Options) at the Area Chart Data screen to summon the first Titles & Options page.

Using the Titles & Options Pages

The four Titles & Options pages (which are accessed by pressing F8 (Options) from the Area Chart Data screen) for area charts are so similar to the Titles & Options pages for bar/line charts, which are described in detail in Chapter 5, that this section highlights only the differences between the two sets of pages. To learn about options not described in this chapter, refer to "Using the Titles & Options Pages" in Chapter 5.

When you convert from a bar or line chart to an area chart, the area chart acquires the option settings of the bar or line chart. All series are converted initially to area style representations. To make changes to options on the Titles & Options pages, follow the same procedures you're accustomed to using with bar/line charts. Use the Tab key to move from option to option, the space bar to highlight a choice, and the Enter key to move to the next option. Press F2 (Draw Chart) after you have changed a chart option so that you can see how each incremental change affects the chart.

Using the First Titles & Options Page

Use the first Area Chart Titles & Options page, shown in figure 6.4, to inform Harvard Graphics about your choices for the overall appearance of an area chart. On this page, you can give the series names that are more descriptive than Series 1, Series 2, and so on. In figure 6.4, the first three series have been renamed 1988, 1989, and 1990. By pressing F7 (Size/Place) and F5 (Attributes) on the first Titles & Options page, you can change the appearance of the text in the titles and series names. In the Type column, you can specify whether to represent each series as an area, line, trend, or bar type. You can mix these different area types on a chart to emphasize a specific series. The resulting mixed chart can be useful when large differences exist among series values. The bar, trend, and line chart types are the same in area charts as they are in bar/line charts (described in Chapter 5). You also can choose whether to display the series or whether to display dual y-axes.

Press PgDn to view the second Titles & Options page.

Using the Second Titles & Options Page

Use the second Area Chart Titles & Options page, shown in figure 6.5, to set the characteristics of several elements of the current chart, such as the chart style, the style of the frame around the chart, and the location and appearance of the legend. This Titles & Options page is identical to the second Titles & Options page for bar/line charts, with the following exceptions:

```
┌─────────────────────────────────────────────────────────────┐
│  ▲        Area Chart   Titles & Options   Page 1 of 4      ▼  │
│                                                               │
│              Title:        Superior Office Supplies Revenues  │
│              Subtitle:     1988-1990                          │
│                                                               │
│              Footnote:                                        │
│                                                               │
│                                                               │
│              X  axis title:                                   │
│              Y1 axis title: Thousands                         │
│              Y2 axis title:                                   │
│     Legend                        Type          Display  Y Axis │
│     Title:              Area Line Trend Bar     Yes No   Y1 Y2 │
│                                                               │
│     1  1988                       Area           Yes      Y1  │
│     2  1989                       Area           Yes      Y1  │
│     3  1990                       Area           Yes      Y1  │
│     4  Series 4                   Area           Yes      Y1  │
│     5  Series 5                   Area           Yes      Y1  │
│     6  Series 6                   Area           Yes      Y1  │
│     7  Series 7                   Area           Yes      Y1  │
│     8  Series 8                   Area           Yes      Y1  │
│                                                               │
│   F1-Help              F5-Attributes    F7-Size/Place         │
│   F2-Draw chart                         F8-Data     F10-Continue │
└─────────────────────────────────────────────────────────────┘
```

Fig. 6.4.

The first Area Chart Titles & Options page.

❑ Area charts provide only six combinations of styles and enhancements.

❑ The Overlap setting in the Chart Style field refers to the overlap of one area on another.

❑ If you select Stack at the Chart Style field, Harvard Graphics displays the series one on top of another, adding the values of the first series to the second, and so on.

❑ Harvard Graphics displays all series in a 100% chart as an area chart, regardless of the choice made on the first Titles & Options page in the Type column.

Figure 6.6 shows the SOSREVS chart displayed with Chart Style settings of Stack, Overlap, and 100%. Notice the difference in appearance of these three chart styles for an area chart.

❑ If you mix series types (bar with area), Harvard Graphics does not display a three-dimensional enhancement. The three-dimensional enhancement does work with Trend and Line series types (even when they are combined with area enhancements).

❑ The 3D option (for the Chart Enhancement field) does not work with Horizontal Chart set to Yes or with dual y-axis charts. Figure 6.7 shows the SOSREVS chart displayed as an overlap chart with the Horizontal Chart option set to Yes. You can see that the horizontal chart creates an interesting effect.

Fig. 6.5.

The second Area Chart Titles & Options page.

```
┌─────────────────────────────────────────────────────────────┐
│ ▲        Area Chart   Titles & Options   Page 2 of 4      ▼  │
├─────────────────────────────────────────────────────────────┤
│   Chart style        │ Stack    ▶Overlap   100%             │
│   Chart enhancement  │ 3D       ▶None                       │
│   Chart fill style   │ Color    ▶Pattern   Both             │
│                      │                                      │
│   Bar width          │ 75                                   │
│   3D overlap         │ 35                                   │
│   3D depth           │                                      │
│                      │                                      │
│   Horizontal chart   │ Yes      ▶No                         │
│   Value labels       │ All      ▶Select    None             │
│                      │                                      │
│   Frame style        │ ▶Full    Half       Quarter   None   │
│   Frame color        │ 1                                    │
│   Frame background   │ 0                                    │
│                      │                                      │
│   Legend location    │ Top      ▶Bottom    Left    Right  None │
│   Legend justify     │ ← or ↑   ▶Center    ↓ or →           │
│   Legend placement   │ In       ▶Out                        │
│   Legend frame       │ Single   Shadow     ▶None            │
├─────────────────────────────────────────────────────────────┤
│ F1-Help                                                     │
│ F2-Draw chart              F6-Colors     F8-Data   F10-Continue │
└─────────────────────────────────────────────────────────────┘
```

Fig. 6.6.

Stack, Overlap, and 100% chart styles for an area chart.

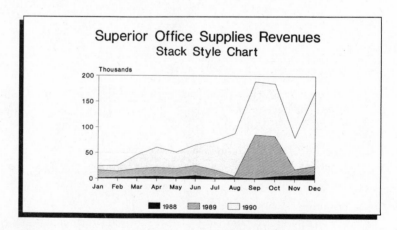

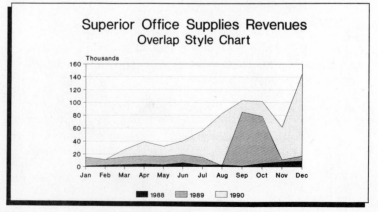

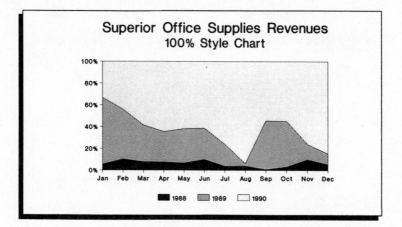

Fig. 6.6. cont.

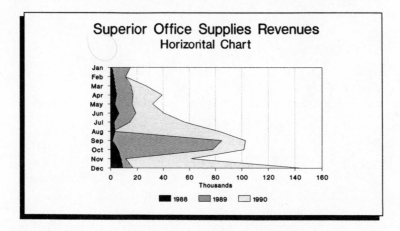

Fig. 6.7.

A horizontal area chart.

Press PgDn to move to the third Titles & Options page.

Using the Third Titles & Options Page

Use the third Area Chart Titles & Options page, shown in figure 6.8, to change the underlying structure of the chart's appearance. This Titles & Options page, like the same page for bar/line charts, enables you to include grid lines and tick marks and revise the scaling and formatting provided by Harvard Graphics.

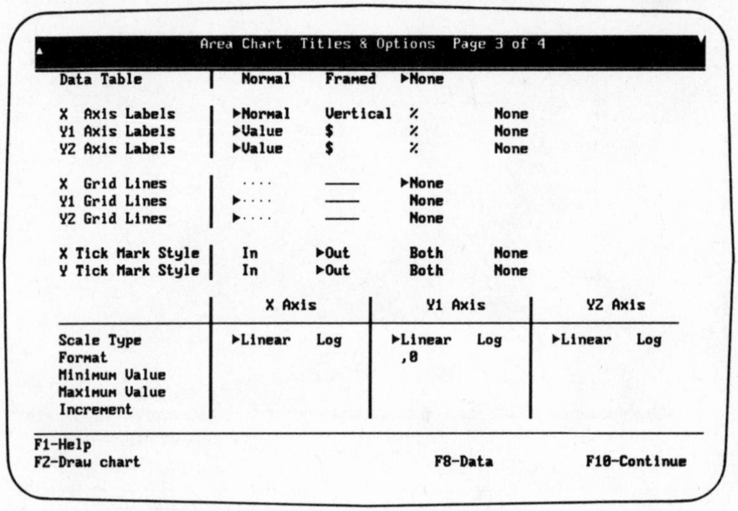

Fig. 6.8.

The third Area Chart Titles & Options page.

```
┌─────────────────────────────────────────────────────────────────────┐
│            Area Chart  Titles & Options   Page 3 of 4                 │
│  Data Table        │  Normal    Framed   ▶None                        │
│                    │                                                  │
│  X  Axis Labels    │ ▶Normal    Vertical   %          None            │
│  Y1 Axis Labels    │ ▶Value     $          %          None            │
│  Y2 Axis Labels    │ ▶Value     $          %          None            │
│                                                                       │
│  X  Grid Lines     │   ....      ─────    ▶None                       │
│  Y1 Grid Lines     │ ▶....       ─────     None                       │
│  Y2 Grid Lines     │ ▶....       ─────     None                       │
│                                                                       │
│  X Tick Mark Style │  In        ▶Out       Both       None            │
│  Y Tick Mark Style │  In        ▶Out       Both       None            │
│                    ├──────────────┬──────────────┬──────────────      │
│                    │   X Axis     │   Y1 Axis    │   Y2 Axis          │
│  Scale Type        │ ▶Linear  Log │ ▶Linear  Log │ ▶Linear  Log       │
│  Format            │              │ ,0           │                    │
│  Minimum Value     │              │              │                    │
│  Maximum Value     │              │              │                    │
│  Increment         │              │              │                    │
│  ───────────────────────────────────────────────────────────────     │
│  F1-Help                                                              │
│  F2-Draw chart                          F8-Data        F10-Continue   │
└─────────────────────────────────────────────────────────────────────┘
```

If you set the Scale Type for the x- or y-axis to Log (logarithmic), you cannot use the 3D option on the second Titles & Options page. (This limitation also applies to bar/line charts.) Three-dimensional and logarithmic are conflicting options.

Press PgDn to work on the fourth Titles & Options page.

Using the Fourth Titles & Options Page

On the last Area Chart Titles & Options page, shown in figure 6.9, you can place the finishing touches on your chart's titles, areas, bars, and lines. To make your chart easy to understand, select colors or patterns that make the layers of the chart vary from dark to light, with the darkest pattern on the bottom of the chart, and the lightest pattern on top of the chart. You can accomplish this by changing colors using Titles & Options page 4 or by changing the order of the series.

You can use the calculation features from the Data screen in Harvard Graphics to re-sort the data and change the order of the series, if necessary. For more information, see Chapter 7.

Unlike with bar/line charts, when you use calendar-based data in area charts and a gap exists between dates, you cannot set a single series to Yes in the Cum field on the fourth Titles & Options page. All of the series or none of them should be set to Yes in this field.

```
┌─────────────────────────────────────────────────────────────────┐
│  ▲        Area Chart  Titles & Options  Page 4 of 4              │
│           Title:        Superior Office Supplies Revenues        │
│           Subtitle:     1988-1990                                │
│                                                                  │
│           Footnote:                                              │
│                                                                  │
│           X  axis title:                                         │
│           Y1 axis title: Thousands                               │
│           Y2 axis title:                                         │
│    Legend               Cum      Y Label   Color   Marker/  Line │
│    Title:               Yes  No  Yes  No            Pattern Style│
│                                                                  │
│   1 │ 1988              No       No        2        1       1    │
│   2 │ 1989              No       No        3        2       1    │
│   3 │ 1990              No       Yes       4        3       1    │
│   4 │ Series 4          No       No        5        4       1    │
│   5 │ Series 5          No       No        6        5       1    │
│   6 │ Series 6          No       No        7        6       1    │
│   7 │ Series 7          No       No        8        7       1    │
│   8 │ Series 8          No       No        9        8       1    │
│                                                                  │
│  F1-Help              F5-Attributes   F7-Size/Place              │
│  F2-Draw chart        F6-Colors       F8-Data        F10-Continue│
└─────────────────────────────────────────────────────────────────┘
```

Fig. 6.9.

The fourth Area Chart Titles & Options page.

Using the Area Chart Gallery

When you are creating an area chart, you have a gallery of styles and enhancements from which to select, just as you do when creating a bar/line chart. To select an area chart from the gallery, follow this procedure:

1. Select Create New Chart from the main menu.

2. Select From Gallery from the Create New Chart menu.

3. Select the area chart graphic (choice 5) from the gallery by pressing 5.

4. Select an area chart type from the gallery of area charts by pressing the number of that chart (see fig. 6.10).

5. Press F9 to edit the data in the displayed chart or F10 to retain only the titles and options settings but not the data from the displayed chart.

Creating High/Low/Close Charts

Another variation of the bar/line chart format is the high/low/close chart. Typically, high/low/close charts show the opening, closing, high, and low values at specific intervals for a single stock, bond, or other financial instrument.

To see how high/low/close charts work, try creating a chart that shows the stock prices for Superior Office Supplies during the month of December. Suppose that the stock prices during the month varied as follows:

Fig. 6.10.

The gallery of area chart types.

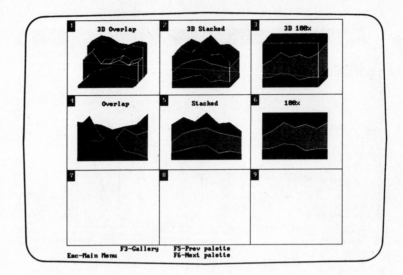

Week	High	Low	Close	Open
1	19.0	17.5	18.5	17.75
2	18.75	.17.75	18.5	18.5
3	18.5	17.5	17.75	18.0
4	18.75	17.25	17.75	17.5

Entering Data in a High/Low/Close Chart

To create and enter data in a high/low/close chart, follow this procedure:

1. Select Create New Chart from the main menu.

2. Select High/Low/Close from the Create New Chart menu.

3. Press the space bar to highlight Week on the X Data Type Menu overlay and press Enter.

4. Press 1 at the Starting With field and press Enter to move to the Ending With field.

5. Press 4 at the Ending With field and press Enter to move to Increment. Press Enter again because the default increment of 1 is correct. Just like the X Data Type overlay in bar/line charts, the increment is assumed to be 1 if you press Enter here. Figure 6.11 shows how the X Data Type Menu overlay should appear at this point.

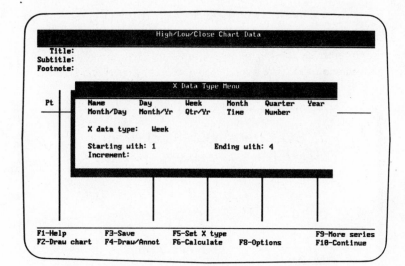

Fig. 6.11.

The X Data Type Menu overlay.

6. Type the following chart title in the Title field of the High/Low/Close Chart Data screen:

    SOS December Stock Prices

    Press Enter three times to move the cursor to the X Axis column at point 1.

7. Press Tab to move the cursor to the High column and type the high value for week 1. Then press Tab to move from column to column and Enter to move from line to line, typing the remainder of the data. Figure 6.12 shows the completed data screen.

```
                      High/Low/Close Chart Data
   Title: SOS December Stock Prices
Subtitle:
Footnote:

          X Axis       High      Lou      Close     Open
   Pt     Week

   1    1               19       17.5     18.5      17.75
   2    2               18.75    17.75    18.5      18.5
   3    3               18.5     17.5     17.75     18
   4    4               18.75    17.25    17.75     17.5
   5
   6
   7
   8
   9
  10
  11
  12

F1-Help        F3-Save      F5-Set X type              F9-More series
F2-Draw chart  F4-Draw/Annot F6-Calculate   F8-Options  F10-Continue
```

Fig. 6.12.

The completed High/Low/Close Chart Data screen.

8. Press F2 (Draw Chart) to view the chart with the data entered. Figure 6.13 shows the results.

9. Press Esc to return to the High/Low/Close Chart Data screen and press F3 (Save) to summon the Save overlay. Save the chart as SOSSTOCK.

Fig. 6.13.

The high/low/close chart.

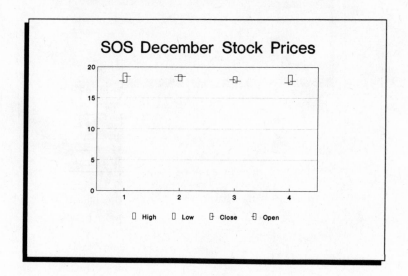

Using the Titles & Options Pages

To modify the appearance of a high/low/close chart, press F8 (Options) at the data screen to display the first High/Low/Close Chart Titles & Options page.

Using the First Titles & Options Page

Notice that the information in the Type column on the first High/Low/Close Chart Titles & Options page has been set by Harvard Graphics (see fig. 6.14).

If you try to move the cursor to Type, Harvard Graphics prevents you from changing the type of the first four series, which are set as High, Low, Close, and Open, respectively. You can change the legend entries, however, and the size, placement, and attributes of the titles by using F7 (Size/Place) and F5 (Attributes).

Connecting a second y-axis (Y2) with one of the first four series in a high/low/close chart is effective if you want to make the chart more clear by showing the same y-axis measure on both sides of the chart. The Y2 axis has no effect on the

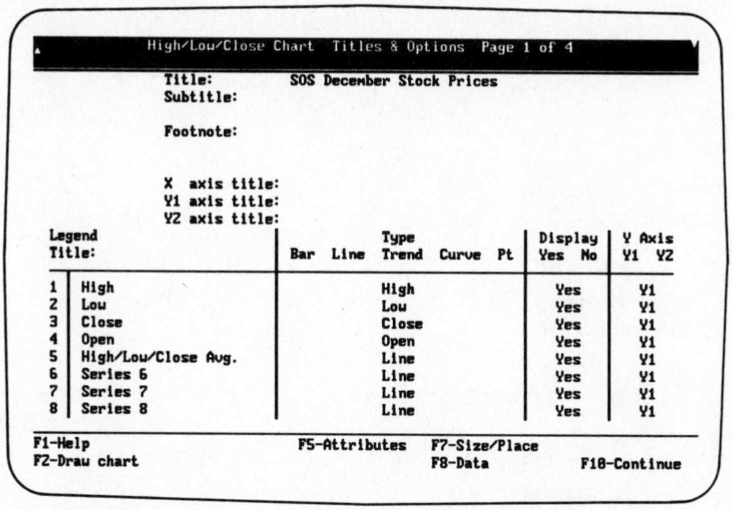

Fig. 6.14.

The first High/Low/Close Chart Titles & Options page.

chart, however, unless you apply the axis to data added to the chart in Series 5 through 8.

Press PgDn to see the second Titles & Options page.

Using the Second Titles & Options Page

Use the second High/Low/Close Chart Titles & Options page, shown in figure 6.15, to change the style of any bars in the chart. These style options (Cluster, Overlap, and Stack) apply only to series that are not part of the high/low/close series.

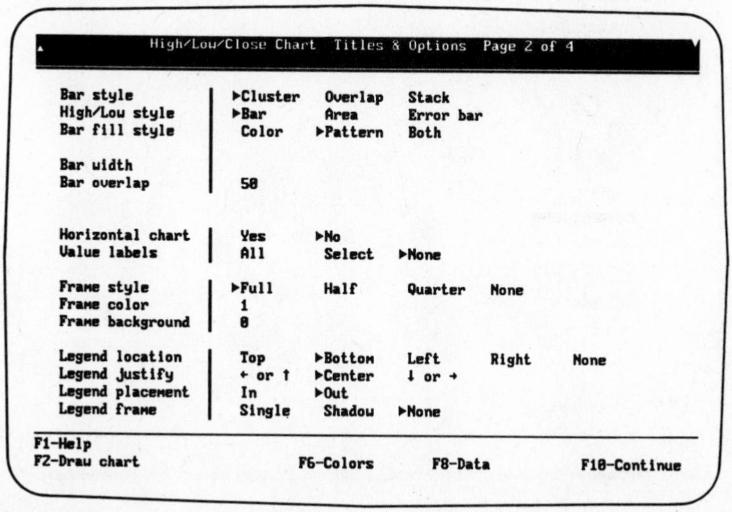

Fig. 6.15.

The second High/Low/Close Chart Titles & Options page.

The three available high/low styles are Bar, Area, and Error Bar. An error bar is a straight line that connects the high and low points of each value. Figure 6.16 shows a high/low/close chart that uses error bars to show clearly which bar correlates to which week. Error bars are even more effective when you have a larger amount of data.

Figure 6.17 shows a high/low/close chart with Area selected as the High/Low Style option. This type of chart, when shown with both x- and y-axis grid lines, can be an informative display of stock data.

You also can use the second Titles & Options page to specify bar widths for the bars in the chart's series. Setting the SOSSTOCK Bar Width option to 100

Fig. 6.16.

A high/low/close chart with Error Bar chosen for the High/Low Style option.

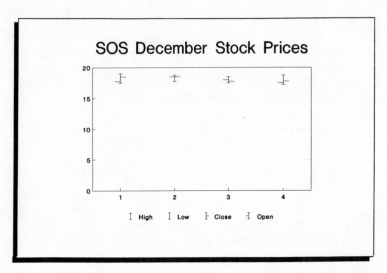

Fig. 6.17.

A high/low/close chart with High/Low Style set to Area.

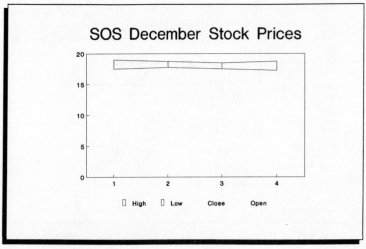

(when High/Low Style is set to Bar) yields the chart shown in figure 6.18. If you chart only the high/low/close and open series, the default bar width is usually best. Harvard Graphics sets the optimum default for you if you leave the Bar Width option blank. When you are working on high/low/close charts, notice that no 3D enhancement is available because no 3D high/low/close chart exists in Harvard Graphics. Likewise, the second Titles & Options page does not include a Bar Depth field, which only relates to 3D charts.

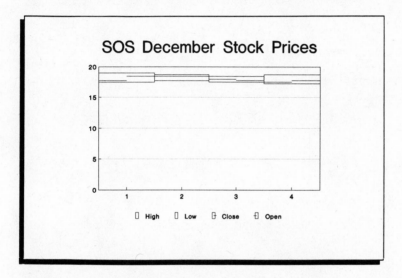

Fig. 6.18.

SOSSTOCK with the Bar Width option set to 100.

Figure 6.19 shows SOSSTOCK with the Bar Width option returned to the Harvard Graphics default and Horizontal Chart set to Yes.

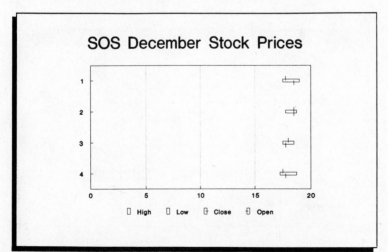

Fig. 6.19.

SOSSTOCK with Horizontal Chart set to Yes.

Press PgDn to work on the third Titles & Options page.

Using the Third Titles & Options Page

You can use this High/Low/Close Chart Titles & Options page to zoom in on the active portion of your high/low/close chart by modifying the minimum and maximum numbers on the y-axis (see fig. 6.20). You also can use this page to clarify the chart with grid lines and tick marks or to format the y-axis labels.

Try following this procedure to modify the y-axis range of SOSSTOCK and make the chart more readable:

1. On the third Titles & Options page, tab to the Y1 Axis Labels option. Press the space bar to highlight the Currency option.

2. Tab to the Y1 Axis column near the bottom of the page and move the cursor to the Format line.

3. Press 2 (for two digits after the decimal) opposite the Format field, and press Enter.

4. Type *17* for the Minimum Value option and press Enter to move the cursor to the Maximum Value line.

5. Type *19* for the Maximum Value option.

6. Press PgUp to return to the second Titles & Options page and tab to the Bar Width option.

7. Type *25* for the bar width.

8. Press F2 (Draw Chart) to view the chart. Figure 6.21 shows the results.

Fig. 6.20.

The High/Low/ Close Chart Titles & Options page 3.

High/Low/Close Chart Titles & Options Page 3 of 4				
Data Table	Normal	Framed	▶None	
X Axis Labels	▶Normal	Vertical	%	None
Y1 Axis Labels	▶Value	Currency	%	None
Y2 Axis Labels	▶Value	Currency	%	None
X Grid Lines	. . . .	——	▶None	
Y1 Grid Lines	▶. . . .	——	None	
Y2 Grid Lines	▶. . . .	——	None	
X Tick Mark Style	▶In	Out	Both	None
Y Tick Mark Style	▶In	Out	Both	None

	X Axis		Y1 Axis		Y2 Axis	
Scale Type	▶Linear	Log	▶Linear	Log	▶Linear	Log
Format						
Minimum Value						
Maximum Value						
Increment						

F1-Help
F2-Draw chart   F8-Data   F10-Continue

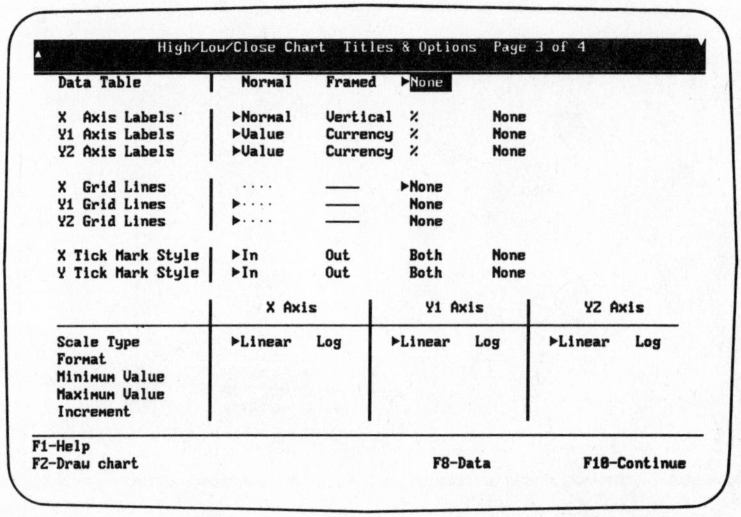

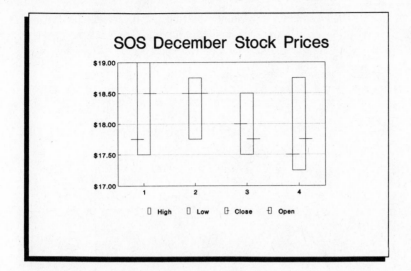

Fig. 6.21.

Preview of the high/low/close chart with a modified y-axis.

Press Esc to return to the second Titles & Options page and press PgDn twice to use the options on the fourth Titles & Options page.

Using the Fourth Titles & Options Page

The fourth High/Low/Close Titles & Options page, shown in figure 6.22, enables you to modify the physical qualities of the bars: their fill patterns, labels, colors, and attributes. With this page, you also can make the chart cumulative and choose which Y labels to display.

```
▲        High/Low/Close Chart   Titles & Options   Page 4 of 4        ▼

          Title:        SOS December Stock Prices
          Subtitle:

          Footnote:


          X  axis title:
          Y1 axis title:
          Y2 axis title:
 Legend                      Cum     Y Label   Color    Marker/   Line
 Title:                     Yes No   Yes  No             Pattern  Style

  1   High                   No       No        2        11        1
  2   Low                    No       No        3        2         1
  3   Close                  No       No        4        3         1
  4   Open                   No       No        5        4         1
  5   Series 5               No       No        6        5         1
  6   Series 6               No       No        7        6         1
  7   Series 7               No       No        8        7         1
  8   Series 8               No       No        9        8         1

 F1-Help                    F5-Attributes   F7-Size/Place
 F2-Draw chart              F6-Colors       F8-Data           F10-Continue
```

Fig. 6.22.

The fourth High/Low/Close Chart Titles & Options page.

To see the effect of the cumulative option, try setting the option to Yes for all four series. The resulting chart shows stock fluctuations adding each successive stock price to the total of the previous prices (see fig. 6.23). Obviously, the resulting chart is highly misleading.

Fig. 6.23.

Setting all series to Yes in the Cum field.

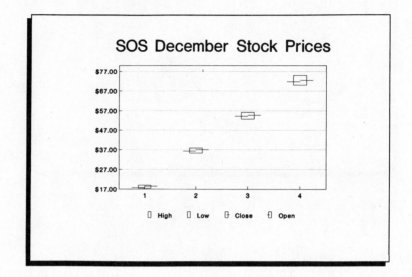

Viewing the High/Low/Close Chart Gallery Choices

As always, if you are using Version 2.3 of Harvard Graphics, you can select from a series of predesigned high/low/close charts. Figure 6.24 shows the gallery of high/low/close charts available when you choose to create a new high/low/close chart from the gallery.

Creating Pie Charts

Pie charts are the ideal Harvard Graphics chart type for representing the relative contributions of parts to a whole. To illustrate the month-by-month breakdown of a year's revenues, for example, you can represent each month with one pie slice. By adding a second special pie chart format, called a column chart, you also can show the breakdown of one month's revenues.

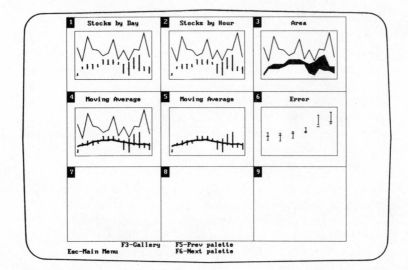

Fig. 6.24.

The gallery of high/ low/close charts.

To begin a pie chart, select Create New Chart from the main menu and Pie from the Create New Chart menu. Harvard Graphics displays the Pie Chart 1 Data screen shown in figure 6.25.

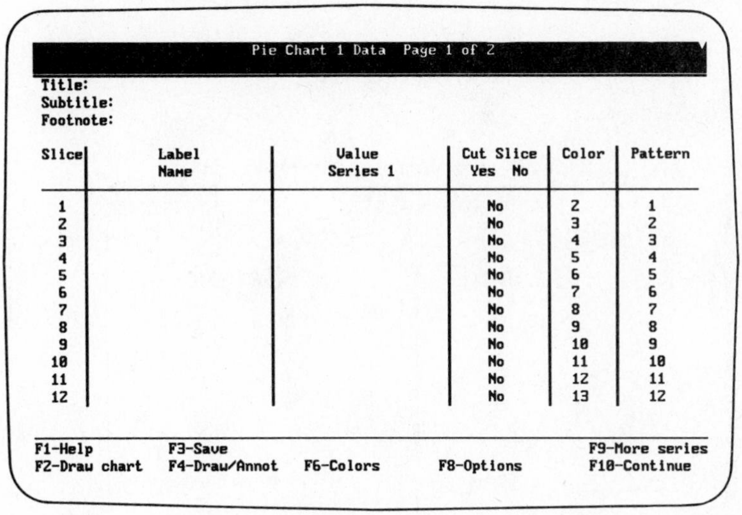

```
              Pie Chart 1 Data   Page 1 of 2

Title:
Subtitle:
Footnote:

Slice    Label           Value        Cut Slice   Color   Pattern
         Name            Series 1     Yes  No

  1                                      No         2       1
  2                                      No         3       2
  3                                      No         4       3
  4                                      No         5       4
  5                                      No         6       5
  6                                      No         7       6
  7                                      No         8       7
  8                                      No         9       8
  9                                      No        10       9
 10                                      No        11      10
 11                                      No        12      11
 12                                      No        13      12


F1-Help        F3-Save                              F9-More series
F2-Draw chart  F4-Draw/Annot   F6-Colors   F8-Options   F10-Continue
```

Fig. 6.25.

The Pie Chart 1 Data screen.

Entering Data on the Pie Chart Data Screens

Entering pie chart data is a little different from entering data in a bar/line, area, or high/low/close chart. Because Harvard Graphics can display two pies side-by-side, you enter pie chart data onto two "pages" corresponding to the sides of the chart. The pie on the left side represents data you enter on the Pie Chart 1 Data screen, and the right-side pie represents data you enter on the Pie Chart 2 Data screen. If you enter data on the first data page only, Harvard Graphics displays only one chart. To move between pages, press the PgDn or PgUp key. The top line of the screen indicates the current page.

You can enter up to eight series of data on the data pages and decide later which pie (right or left) should represent which series. To enter more than two series, press F9 (More Series) from page 1 or page 2. Notice the series number increments in the Value column. Unless you specify otherwise, the left pie (page 1) corresponds to Series 1 and the right pie (page 2) corresponds to Series 2. To change the series attached to the left or right pie, press PgDn or PgUp until the correct page is in view. Then press F9 (More Series) until the correct series number appears. (Pressing F9 repeatedly cycles through the eight available series.)

Confusing pages in pie charts with series is an easy thing to do. Figure 6.26 clarifies the distinction by showing the relationship between series and pages in pie charts.

Fig. 6.26.

The relationship between series and pages in pie charts.

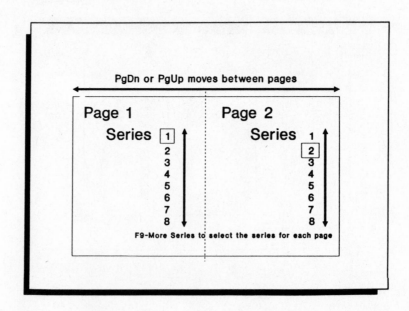

Many of the features available in bar/line charts also are available in pie charts. To reorder the data, for example, you can press and hold down Ctrl while pressing the up- or down-arrow key. To insert or delete a line, you can use the Ctrl key with Ins or Del.

Using the Tab and Enter keys to move through the chart, enter the Superior Office Supplies Writing Tools Division revenues for the second half of the year. Enter the month names in the Label column and the revenue figures in the Value column. Use the Tab key to move the cursor from column to column and press Enter to move the cursor down one line at a time. The figures line up like this:

Month	Revenue
July	12,098
August	13,663
September	37,994
October	56,323
November	24,557
December	65,389

Unlike bar charts, which use an X Data Type Menu overlay to set label data, pie charts have no x-axis. Series labels can be of mixed types. When you originate data on a bar chart and set an X Data Type option, that data type remains the same when you bring the data into a pie chart; you cannot change the X Data Type option for a different series in the pie.

Figure 6.27 illustrates how to complete the remainder of the columns on the page. The patterns selected in figure 6.27 contrast clearly when adjacent to each other, highlighting the differences between slices on a printed illustration.

```
                    Pie Chart 1 Data   Page 1 of 2
  Title:      Superior Office Supplies
  Subtitle: Second Half Revenues
  Footnote:

  Slice|      Label         |  Value    | Cut Slice | Color | Pattern
       |      Name          |  Series 1 | Yes  No   |       |

    1    July                 12098        No          2       1
    2    August               13663        No          3       2
    3    September            37994        No          4       3
    4    October              56323        No          5       4
    5    November             24557        No          6       5
    6    December             65389        No          7       6
    7                                       No          8       7
    8                                       No          9       8
    9                                       No         10       9
   10                                       No         11      10
   11                                       No         12      11
   12                                       No         13      12

  F1-Help          F3-Save                          F9-More series
  F2-Draw chart    F4-Draw/Annot   F6-Colors   F8-Options   F10-Continue
```

Fig. 6.27.

The completed Pie Chart 1 Data screen.

Press F2 (Draw Chart) to see how the pie chart looks before you add the data for the second pie. Figure 6.28 shows the results.

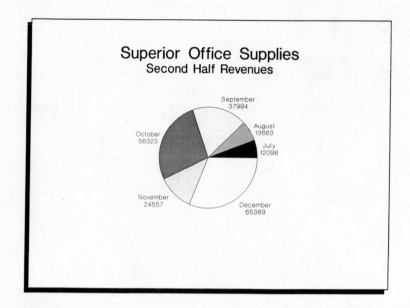

Use the second page of data on this chart to represent the components of December's revenue, the Writing Tools Division's biggest month. The revenue breaks down as follows:

Swirly Pens	$11,672
Mechanical Pencils	24,070
Annihilator Erasers	15,821
White Mountain Pens	13,826

Press PgDn to summon the second Pie Chart Data screen. Then, with the Pie Chart 2 Data screen (and Series 2) on-screen, enter the data for the right pie. Press Tab to move to the first line and press Enter to move down line-by-line. Typing a vertical bar (|) between words in the label splits the label onto two lines at the location of the vertical bar. Figure 6.29 shows the completed second data screen. Be sure to enter vertical bars where shown.

Press F2 (Draw Chart) to preview the chart with two pies. Figure 6.30 shows the chart as it appears with two pies, unaltered.

```
┌──────────────────────────────────────────────────────────────┐
│              Pie Chart 2 Data   Page 2 of 2                    │
│ ▲                                                              │
│ Title:     Superior Office Supplies                           │
│ Subtitle:  Second Half Revenues                               │
│ Footnote:                                                      │
│                                                                │
│ Slice│      Label        │    Value    │ Cut Slice │Color│Pattern│
│      │      Name         │   Series 2  │  Yes  No  │     │       │
│                                                                │
│   1  │ Swirly Pens       │   11672     │     No    │  2  │   1   │
│   2  │ Mechanical│Pencils │   24070     │     No    │  3  │   2   │
│   3  │ Annihilator│Erasers│   15821     │     No    │  4  │   3   │
│   4  │ White Mtn.│Pens    │   13826     │     No    │  5  │   4   │
│   5  │                   │             │     No    │  6  │   5   │
│   6  │                   │             │     No    │  7  │   6   │
│   7  │                   │             │     No    │  8  │   7   │
│   8  │                   │             │     No    │  9  │   8   │
│   9  │                   │             │     No    │ 10  │   9   │
│  10  │                   │             │     No    │ 11  │  10   │
│  11  │                   │             │     No    │ 12  │  11   │
│  12  │                   │             │     No    │ 13  │  12   │
│                                                                │
│ F1-Help       F3-Save                          F9-More series │
│ F2-Draw chart F4-Draw/Annot  F6-Colors  F8-Options F10-Continue│
└──────────────────────────────────────────────────────────────┘
```

Fig. 6.29.

The Pie Chart 2 Data screen with Series 2 data.

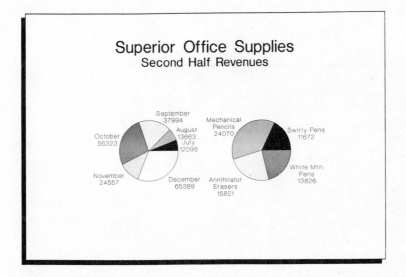

Fig. 6.30.

Preview of the two pies, unaltered.

Cutting Slices and Changing Colors and Patterns

Press Esc to return to the second data screen. Press PgUp to return to the Pie Chart 1 Data screen so that you can modify the left pie. Move the cursor to December, tab to the Cut Slice column, and press the space bar to highlight Yes.

Selecting Yes cuts the selected slice out of the pie. You also can use the Color and Pattern columns on page 1 to change the patterns and colors of individual slices of the pie. Press F2 (Draw Chart) to see the results, which are shown in figure 6.31.

Fig. 6.31.

Preview of the pie chart with the December slice cut out.

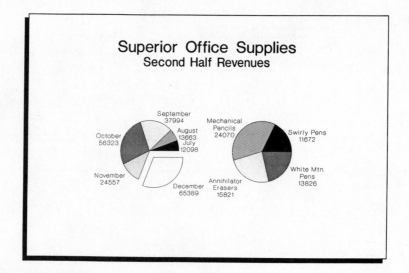

Superior Office Supplies
Second Half Revenues

Creating Effects with Titles & Options Pages

Press F8 (Options) to use the two Titles & Options pages Harvard Graphics provides for pie charts. The options on these pages are much like those for bar/line, area, and high/low/close charts.

Using the First Titles & Options Page

Figure 6.32 shows the first Pie Chart Titles & Options page. Use this page to set the titles and special effects of the chart. Enter the titles for the two pies as shown in the figure. To change an option, tab to that option and press the space bar to highlight a new choice. Pressing Enter moves you to the next line.

Notice that F7 (Size/Place) and F5 (Attributes) are available on the function key menu at the bottom of the screen. You can use these features to adjust the titles in your chart.

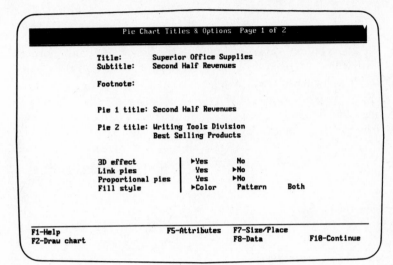

Fig. 6.32.

The first Pie Chart Titles & Options page.

Making Three-Dimensional Pies

You can make any pie three-dimensional by setting the 3D Effect option to Yes. When the three-dimensional effect is turned on, however, no slices are cut. If you cut a slice and then set 3D Effect to Yes, the three-dimensional effect overrides the option to cut a slice. Try turning on the three-dimensional effect in the current chart. Figure 6.33 shows how the chart looks.

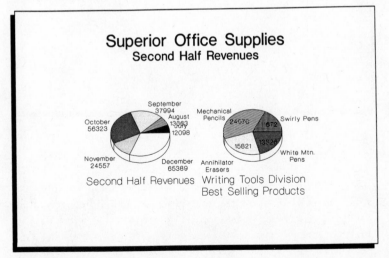

Fig. 6.33.

Three-dimensional pie charts.

Save this pie chart with the name SOS2HP3D (for "SOS second-half pie, three-dimensional").

Linking Pies

Now set the 3D Effect option to No, and turn on the Link Pies option by high-lighting Yes in that line. Harvard Graphics links the cutout slice to the second pie. When used in combination with a column chart (which is set on the second Titles & Options page), the Link Pies option can be especially effective. Figure 6.34 shows a pie linked to a column chart. (To produce this chart, you set Chart Style for the right pie to Column on the second Pie Chart Titles & Options page. You also set the label slice sizes on the second Pie Chart Titles & Options page. Using that feature, you can change the pie 1 labels to a size of 2 and set the pie 2 label size to 3. Use F7 (Size/place) to change the size of the headings under the pies from a size of 5 (default) to 4 on Titles & Options page one. Figure 6.35 shows the second Titles & Options page with the label size change made. See "Using the Second Titles & Options Page" for more information.)

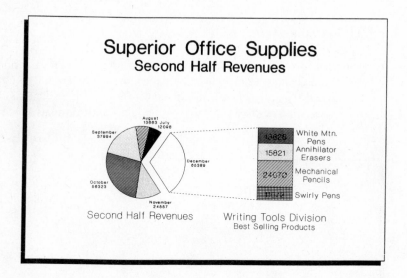

Fig. 6.34.

Linked pie and column charts.

Making Proportional Pies

Selecting Yes for the Proportional Pies option tells Harvard Graphics to display the right and left pies so that their relative sizes reflect their relative totals. Selecting No for this option bases the size of each pie on the Pie Size option on the second Titles & Options page. When you select No for Proportional Pies, Harvard Graphics makes each pie 50 percent of the page. The default setting for pie size is 50.

```
┌─────────────────────────────────────────────────────────────┐
│            Pie Chart Titles & Options   Page 2 of 2           │
│ ▲                                                             │
│                                                               │
│                  Pie 1                      Pie 2             │
│  Chart style      ▶Pie    Column        Pie  ▶Column   None   │
│  Sort slices       Yes   ▶No            Yes  ▶No              │
│  Starting angle  _ 0                    0                     │
│  Pie size          50                   50                    │
│                                                               │
│  Show label       ▶Yes    No           ▶Yes    No            │
│  Label size        2                    3                     │
│                                                               │
│  Show value       ▶Yes    No           ▶Yes    No            │
│  Place value      ▶Below  Adjacent  Inside  Below  Adjacent ▶Inside │
│  Value format                                                 │
│  Currency          Yes   ▶No            Yes  ▶No              │
│                                                               │
│  Show percent      Yes   ▶No            Yes  ▶No             │
│  Place percent    ▶Below  Adjacent  Inside  ▶Below  Adjacent  Inside │
│  Percent format                                               │
│                                                               │
│ F1-Help                                                       │
│ F2-Draw chart                    F8-Data         F10-Continue │
└─────────────────────────────────────────────────────────────┘
```

Fig. 6.35.

The completed Pie Chart Title & Options page 2.

Turn on the Proportional Pies option for the current chart. The results should look like figure 6.36 (if you set the second pie back from Column to Pie on Titles & Options page 2).

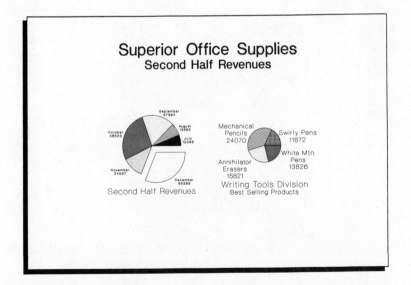

Fig. 6.36.

Drawing the chart with the Proportional Pies option set to Yes.

Selecting a Fill Style

As you can see in the Fill Style option, you can choose to fill the slices of pies with colors, patterns, or colors and patterns. You select the patterns used to fill the slices on the Pie Chart 1 Data and Pie Chart 2 Data screens. Try different combinations of patterns for the clearest marking of pie slices.

Using the Second Titles & Options Page

The second Pie Chart Titles & Options page includes options that enable you to change the style of the chart, control the labels, and format and scale the chart (see fig. 6.37). The settings you establish on this page control the overall appearance and readability of the chart. On the left side of the second Titles & Options page are the options that control the left pie (pie 1). The options on the right side of this Titles & Options page control the right pie (pie 2).

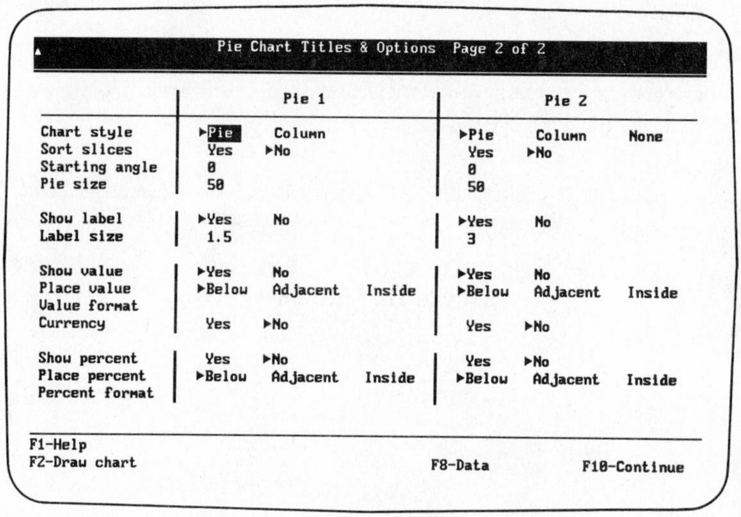

Fig. 6.37.

The second Pie Chart Titles & Options page.

```
                    Pie Chart Titles & Options   Page 2 of 2

                              Pie 1                        Pie 2

Chart style         ►Pie     Column          ►Pie     Column      None
Sort slices         Yes      ►No             Yes      ►No
Starting angle      8                        8
Pie size            58                       58

Show label          ►Yes     No             ►Yes     No
Label size          1.5                      3

Show value          ►Yes     No             ►Yes     No
Place value         ►Below   Adjacent  Inside  ►Below  Adjacent  Inside
Value format
Currency            Yes      ►No             Yes      ►No

Show percent        Yes      ►No             Yes      ►No
Place percent       ►Below   Adjacent  Inside  ►Below  Adjacent  Inside
Percent format


F1-Help
F2-Draw chart                        F8-Data          F10-Continue
```

Selecting a Chart Style

Harvard Graphics provides two pie chart styles: columns and pies. A column chart displays percentages of a whole just as the pie chart does, but the column chart is rectangular rather than circular. To set a pie to column style, position the cursor at the Chart Style field on the second Titles & Options page and press the space bar to highlight Column. You can opt to suppress the display of the right pie by selecting None for Chart Style on that side of the page. For this example, change the right pie on the current chart to Column style. Figure 6.38 shows the results of this change. (To change the month that is selected, you can cut a different slice on the Pie Chart 1 Data screen.)

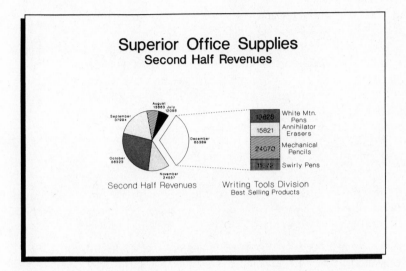

Fig. 6.38.

Setting the right pie style to Column.

Save this chart as SOS2HLK (for "SOS second-half, linked pie").

Sorting Pie Chart Slices

The second option on the second Titles & Options page is Sort Slices. If you turn Sort Slices on by selecting Yes for that option, Harvard Graphics sorts the slices in the pie in the order of their individual contributions to the whole. The largest slice appears on the right side of the pie or on the top of a column-style pie. The remaining slices run clockwise around the pie (or down a column chart) from largest to smallest.

Selecting No for Sort Slices leaves the pie slices in the order in which they appear on the data page. The Sort Slices option works dependably unless you have Link Pies set to Yes on the first Titles & Options page. In that case, the cutout slice is at the right side of the left pie, and that slice is the one that links to the second pie. Because this slice must be on the right side, the slices cannot be sorted.

Changing the Starting Angle

To rotate a pie that is not linked to another pie, use the Starting Angle option on the second Titles & Options page. Setting a starting angle of 180 degrees, for example, rotates the pie exactly one-half of the circle. Slices previously on the right side of the pie appear on the left. The pie rotates counterclockwise. Rotating a pie can help fix overlapping labels and titles.

Changing the Pie Size

The Pie Size option enables you to modify the pie size to make the chart more visually appealing. You can supply a number from 1 to 100. This option conflicts with the Proportional Pies option on the first Titles & Options page. If Proportional Pies is set to Yes, Harvard Graphics does not acknowledge a specified pie size for the second pie. The default pie size is 50. Try increasing or decreasing the Pie Size option until you are pleased with the result.

Adjusting Labels

You can control the appearance of labels on the chart with the Show Label and Label Size options on the second Titles & Options page. Set Show Label to No to suppress the display of labels or series names on the finished chart.

Type a number from 0 to 20 at the Label Size option to modify the size of the labels in your chart. As with size in text charts, Harvard Graphics increases or decreases the size of the letters in your chart based on the number you enter. Try experimenting with different sizes to find the best size for your chart. (The values and percentages described in the next section are the same size as the labels you set.)

Setting Value and Percentage Placement and Formats

Use the last seven options on the second Titles & Options page to alter the appearance of the values that display in your chart. As in bar/line charts, showing values (with the Show Value option) places the data numbers on-screen. Showing percentages (with the Show Percent option) places percentage numbers on-screen instead. To emphasize dramatic contributions to the whole, use percentages rather than values. Although you can use both, your chart looks cluttered if you do.

Formatting pie chart percentages and values is identical to formatting bar/line chart values. Do so to show less data or to modify the appearance of the values shown in your chart. For example, you may want to show data up to two decimals, or you may want to reduce the size of the numbers used by dividing them by 10. The scaling and formatting options enable you to modify your chart's values manually. Refer to "Using the Third Titles & Options Page" in Chapter 5 for complete information.

Viewing the Pie Chart Gallery Choices

When you are creating a pie chart, you can select from the gallery, just as you can with all other chart types in Harvard Graphics Version 2.3. Figure 6.39 shows the gallery of available pie charts.

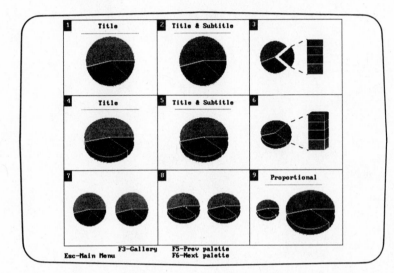

Fig. 6.39.

The gallery of pie chart choices.

Chapter Summary

This chapter explained how you create several types of graph charts with Harvard Graphics: area, high/low/close, and pie. Many of the screens for these different charts are similar, and you can use the same general procedures to create many charts.

In the next two chapters, you learn how to create calculations and graph calculated series, how to import data, and how to export charts.

7

Calculating Data

A helpful Harvard Graphics feature is the program's capacity to calculate new data based on the data you supply and then graphically display those results. In Chapter 5, you learn how to create bar/line charts. Chapter 6 detail the process of creating area, pie, and high/low/close charts. This chapter describes how you can use calculations in the charts you create in Chapters 5 and 6.

If you supply sets of sales data for different items over six months, for example, Harvard Graphics can calculate and graph six-month sales totals and six-month sales averages.

The calculation features resemble the calculation functions in 1-2-3 or Excel. You type a calculation referring to a group of values, and Harvard Graphics performs the calculation and creates a series of data based on that calculation. To specify the calculations to perform, you use keywords that instruct Harvard Graphics to average, sum, divide, calculate a moving average, or execute a host of statistical functions on your data.

To work with the calculation features in Harvard Graphics, you must have the current chart's data screen displayed. You can return to this screen from any of the Titles & Options pages by pressing F8 (Data). Press F6 (Calculate) with the cursor on an unused series to display the Calculate overlay.

Calculations at a Glance

To practice some simple calculations, you can use the chart called SOSREVS to project the growth of Superior Office Supplies during the following year. The calculation feature can be used with any type of graph chart, including bar/line charts, area charts, high/low/close charts, and pie charts. For this next example, however, a combination of a bar/line chart with an area chart is particularly effective because the chart already has three bars. Adding more bars also can add visual confusion to the chart. As a mixed bar/line and area chart, the growth series are displayed as areas, while the remaining series (with actual revenue figures) are shown as bars. Mixing bar/line charts with area charts is an effective technique for helping the viewer differentiate among series when you have multiple series in your charts.

To start, get the SOSREVS chart you created in Chapter 5 by selecting Get/ Save/Remove from the main menu and then selecting SOSREVS from the list of charts that appears. Figure 7.1 shows the SOSREVS Bar/Line Chart Data screen, and figure 7.2 shows the chart.

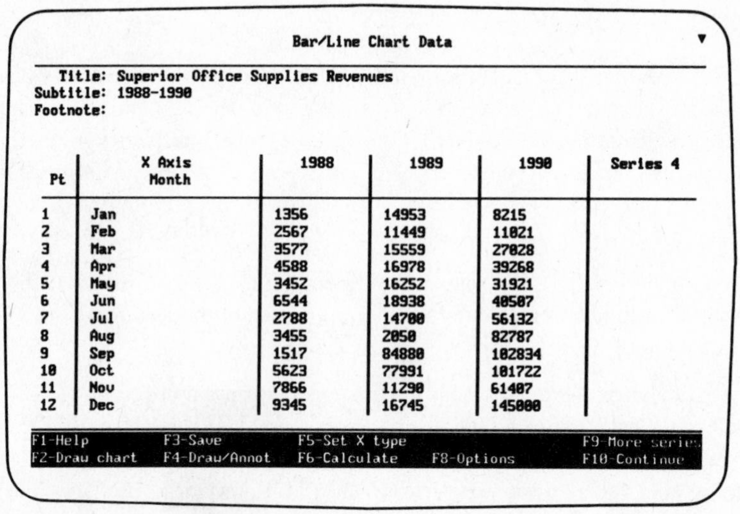

Fig. 7.1.

The SOSREVS Bar/Line chart data screen.

```
                              Bar/Line Chart Data                          ▼

        Title: Superior Office Supplies Revenues
     Subtitle: 1988-1990
     Footnote:


              X Axis        1988        1989        1990      Series 4
    Pt        Month

    1     Jan             1356        14953       8215
    2     Feb             2567        11449       11021
    3     Mar             3577        15559       27028
    4     Apr             4588        16978       39268
    5     May             3452        16252       31921
    6     Jun             6544        18938       40507
    7     Jul             2788        14700       56132
    8     Aug             3455        2050        82787
    9     Sep             1517        84880       102834
    10    Oct             5623        77991       101722
    11    Nov             7866        11290       61407
    12    Dec             9345        16745       145000

   F1-Help          F3-Save        F5-Set X type              F9-More series
   F2-Draw chart    F4-Draw/Annot  F6-Calculate    F8-Options  F10-Continue
```

Now, create a chart that is an area chart with the same data by following this procedure.

1. Press Esc to return to the main menu.

2. Select Create New Chart from the main menu and Area Chart from the Create New Chart menu. The Change Chart Type overlay appears. Notice that the bottom line of the screen indicates that the chart type is a Bar/Line chart. After you answer Yes to the next prompt, the chart type changes to Area chart. Because you are transporting data between chart types, the chart type line on the screen refers to the current chart.

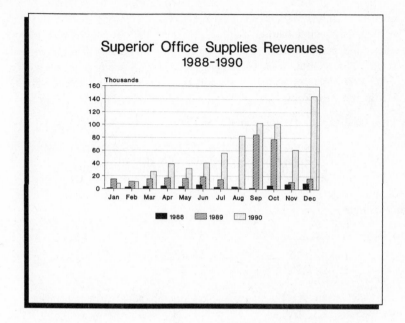

Fig. 7.2.

The SOSREVS chart.

3. Select Yes at the Change Chart Type overlay. Figure 7.3 shows the Change Chart Type overlay. Press F2 (Draw Chart) to see the SOSREVS chart as an area chart.

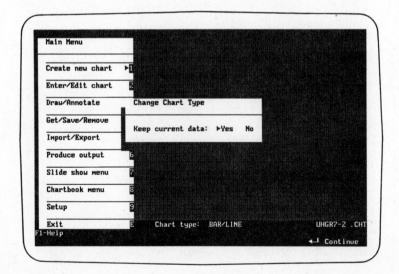

Fig. 7.3.

The Change Chart Type overlay.

Press F8 (Options) to summon the first area chart Titles & Options page so that you can change the first three series, 1988, 1989, and 1990, into bars. Tab to the Type column and press the space bar three times at each series to highlight Bar. The resulting chart should look like figure 7.2. Press F8 again to return to the data screen. Now, you can try a calculation that shows a conservative 15-percent growth in the next year.

Follow this procedure to perform the calculation:

1. Position the cursor at the top data line of the Series 4 column and press F6 (Calculate). The Calculate overlay appears with the cursor on Legend. Harvard Graphics overwrites any existing values in a column when filling the column with calculated data, you must be certain that the cursor is in a blank column.

2. Press Ctrl-Del to delete the words Series 4 in the Legend prompt.

3. Type *15% Growth in 1991* over Series 4, which appears after the Legend prompt. Press Enter.

4. Type the calculation *#3*1.15* (see fig. 7.4). This calculation multiplies the data in Series 3 (1990) by 1.15.

5. Press F10 (Continue) to calculate the series. Harvard Graphics indicates that it has calculated the series by showing a diamond in front of the series name on the Bar/Line Chart Data screen.

6. Press F2 (Draw Chart) to view the calculated series. See figure 7.5 for the results.

Fig. 7.4.

The Calculate overlay.

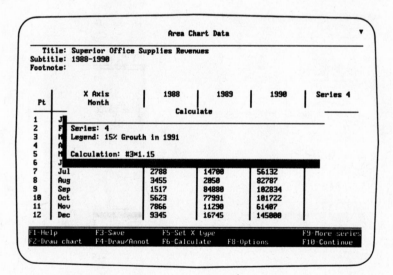

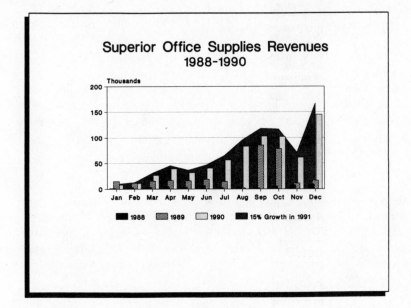

Fig. 7.5.

*The SOSREVS
chart with calculated
series.*

Save the new revenue chart as SOSRPROJ (for "SOS revenues, projected"). To
save the chart, press F3 (Save) or Ctrl-S with the Area Chart Data screen displayed. Type the new name of the chart, *sosrproj*. Press Enter to move the cursor
to the Description line. Delete the current description by pressing Ctrl-Del and
enter a new description, *Revenue Projections*. Press Enter to save the chart. Figure
7.6 shows the Save Chart overlay.

Fig. 7.6.

*The Save Chart
overlay.*

Following Calculation Syntax Rules

Straightforward arithmetic, such as adding two sets of data, is the most simple Harvard Graphics calculation. Suppose that you want to add the total manufacturing expenses to the total of all equipment expenses and then display only that result. You can instruct Harvard Graphics to perform the summation and then display only the sum line on your line chart, suppressing the equipment and manufacturing lines. If equipment is Series 1 and manufacturing is Series 2, the syntax for the calculation is as follows:

#1 + #2

The pound sign (#) represents the word Series in Harvard Graphics. Even though you may have renamed each of the series so that the series numbers no longer appear at the top of the series columns, Harvard Graphics remembers them: Series 1, Series 2, Series 3, and so on. In this example, Harvard Graphics adds all the numbers in Series 1 to the numbers in Series 2 and produces a third series with the results.

The four primary arithmetic calculations that you can instruct Harvard Graphics to perform are addition (+), subtraction (−), multiplication (*), and division (/). In addition to using series values in simple arithmetic calculations, you can include actual numeric values. The following are some sample arithmetic calculations with both series names and numeric values:

#4*#1/2   (Multiply Series 4 by Series 1 and divide by 2)
#3*6.7   (Multiply Series 3 by the number 6.7)

Caution: In Harvard Graphics, the order of precedence for arithmetic calculations is left to right. In the preceding example, Series 4 is multiplied by Series 1 before the result is divided by 2. Although you usually can change the order of calculation in a standard formula by enclosing certain parts of the formula in parentheses, you cannot use this method to change the order of precedence in Harvard Graphics. Instead, you must arrange the order carefully.

When calculations include series that have been calculated from other series, you can press F10 at the Calculate overlay to update all the calculations in a chart. Because calculations always are performed from left to right on the data screen, Harvard Graphics starts by updating Series 1, then Series 2, and so on.

Try adding the four series in SOSRPROJ to each other, creating a total revenue figure for the three years. To add a Sum series to your chart, perform the following procedure:

1. Press F9 (More Series) from the first Area Chart Data screen to summon the fifth through the eighth series.

2. Tab to the Series 5 column and press F6 (Calculate) to evoke the Calculate overlay.

3. Press Ctrl-Del to delete the words Series 5, and type *Total Revenues* in the Legend field. Press Enter to move the cursor to the Calculation field.

4. Type the calculation *#1 + #2 + #3* and press Enter. Figure 7.7 shows the Calculate overlay, and figure 7.8 shows the resulting chart.

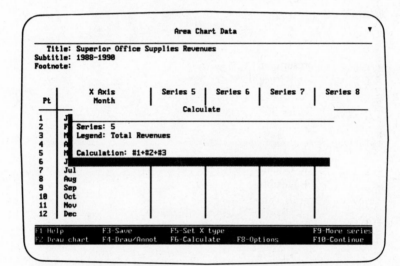

Fig. 7.7.

The Calculate overlay showing the calculation for Series 5.

The information shown in the two series in the area chart is not related because Series 4 (15% growth in 1991) has nothing to do with Series 5 (Total Revenues). You can suppress the display of Series 4 by pressing F8 (Options) to summon the first Titles & Options page and selecting No in the Display column for Series 4. Figure 7.9 shows the resulting chart. Save that chart as SOSRVTOT for "SOS Revenue chart with totals."

Using Keywords To Perform Calculations

You can type a calculation that includes data from several series by referring to all the series in a formula. For example, *#1 + #2 + #3* adds data in Series 1, 2, and 3. As an alternative, you can use one of the four Harvard Graphics row keywords listed in table 7.1.

Fig. 7.8.

The SOSRPROJ chart with the sum calculated.

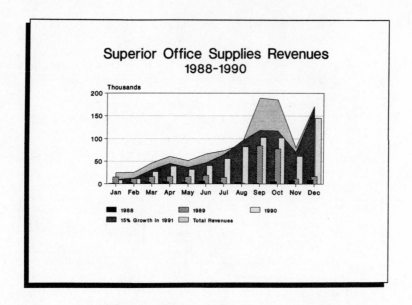

Fig. 7.9.

The SOSRPROJ chart with the calculated projections removed.

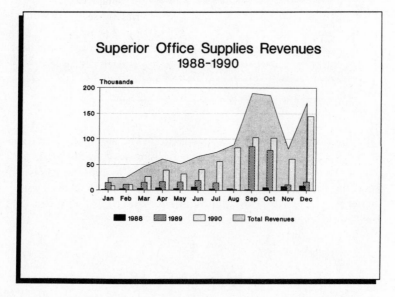

Row keywords can calculate up to seven series. You always must type an @ sign in front of a keyword, precede a series name by a pound sign (#), and enclose the series references in parentheses. To list several series, separate them with commas. An example of a valid row keyword formula is

@SUM(#1,#2,#3)

Table 7.1
Row Keywords

Keyword	Result
@AVG	Calculates the average of a row of values
@MAX	Extracts the maximum value from a row of numbers
@MIN	Extracts the minimum value from a row of numbers
@SUM	Sums or totals a row of numbers

Figure 7.10 shows an @AVG calculation used to average 1988, 1989, and 1990 values in the chart, using the six series for the results. Notice that no spaces are included between the series numbers and the commas. Figure 7.11 shows the resulting chart. Unfortunately, you cannot see the averages because the total revenues area is before the average area. Of course, the average area also is smaller than the total revenues area. To correct this problem, you can use the series keywords described in the next section of this chapter, or you can suppress the display of the calculated Total Revenue series by selecting No in the Display column of the first Titles & Options page for that series. Another way to display the average series is to change the series from an area display to a line display using the first Titles & Options page. Figure 7.12 shows the calculated average series shown as a line instead of an area. Save this chart as SOSRVAVG for "SOS revenues with a calculated average."

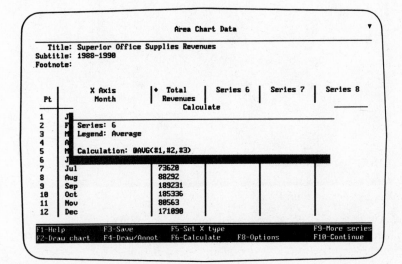

Fig. 7.10.

The Calculate overlay with an average.

Fig. 7.11.

*The SOSRPROJ
chart with an
additional average
calculation.*

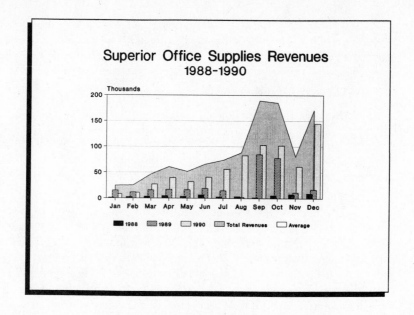

Fig. 7.12.

*The SOSRPROJ
chart with Average
shown as a line.*

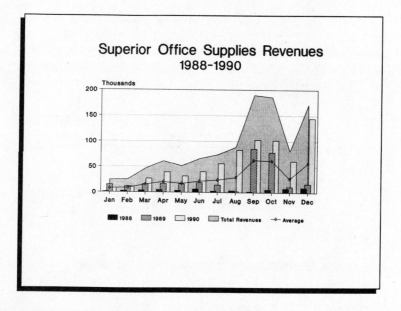

All the calculations described so far calculate series across rows. With one of these calculations, for example, you can add data from Series 1, Series 2, and Series 3 for a particular month. A second form of calculation, series calculation, calculates all the data in one series column. Series calculations enable you to manage individual series—deleting a series you don't need, copying a series to another series, or exchanging two series. Series calculations also enable you to perform a few specific mathematical calculations on all the data in series, such as calculating a value's percentage of the series total, calculating the net change from one series value to the next, calculating a moving average for the values in the series, and calculating one of four regression curves that describe the series visually.

When you calculate across rows, you can use specific numbers in your calculation formulas. For example, you can use #3*1.6 to multiply Series 3 by 1.6. When you calculate down a series column, however, the calculation can include only the actual series data. The pound sign (#) represents the word Series in series calculations just as the pound sign does in row calculations.

Harvard Graphics provides 15 keywords for calculations on series. Each keyword performs a different statistical calculation. Table 7.2 lists the available series keywords and provides an example of each.

Table 7.2
Series Keywords

Keyword	Example	Results
@CLR	@CLR	Clears the contents of a series. Use this keyword only when you want to erase a series. A series erasure cannot be undone. (Note: The program erases the @CLR keyword after clearing the series.)
@COPY	@COPY(#3)	Copies the contents of Series 3 to the current series. The program then erases the keyword.
@CUM	@CUM(#2)	Creates a cumulative series in which each value is added to the total of all previous values in the series. Using the @CUM keyword is the same as selecting Cum on the fourth Titles & Options page.
@DIFF	@DIFF(#4)	Subtracts the value of each value in the series from its predecessor and calculates the net change in each new value.
@DUP	@DUP(#2)	Duplicates Series 2 in the current series. Each time you press F10 at the Calculate overlay, @DUP updates values again. The @DUP keyword is different from

Table 7.2—*continued*

Keyword	Example	Results
		the @COPY keyword because of the continual updating of values that @DUP performs. Use @DUP when you want to look at the behavior of a calculated series in another series column.
@EXCH	@EXCH(#5)	Trades series or exchanges the values and series legend between Series 5 and the series in which you call up the Calculate overlay. The program erases the @EXCH keyword after performing the calculation.
@MAVG	@MAVG(#5,3,5)	Calculates the statistical moving average of Series 5 with 3 points before and 5 points after each value. Valid "points before" and "points after" values are between 1 and 120. If you omit the points before and points after values, Harvard Graphics assumes that you want 1 for each value.
@MOVE	@MOVE(#2)	Moves the values from the series in which the cursor rests to Series 2 and clears the series in which the cursor is located.
@PCT	@PCT(#4)	Calculates the percentage of the total of Series 4 that each value in Series 4 represents and places the results in the current series.
@REDUC	@REDUC	Reorders all series and X data on the Bar/Line Chart Data screen. This calculation is described in detail in the next section. The program erases the @REDUC keyword after performing the calculation.
@RECALC	@RECALC	Recalculates all the calculated values in the current chart. You can invoke the @RECALC keyword from any series column or even from the X Axis

Keyword	Example	Results
		column. Your cursor can be almost anywhere in the data screen when you perform this function. After the calculations are performed, the @RECALC keyword disappears.
@REXP	@REXP(#4)	Calculates the exponential regression curve for Series 4. Don't use this calculation with a trend type of line series. The results of an exponential regression curve are not linear. The trend line in Harvard Graphics is the result of another internal calculation, which is linear.
@RLIN	@RLIN(#2)	Calculates the linear regression for Series 2. Linear regression can be calculated for any bar/line style series.
@RLOG	@RLOG(#1)	Calculates the logarithmic regression curve for Series 1 and places the results in the current series. Do not use a trend line with this keyword calculation.
@RPWR	@RPWR(#5)	Calculates the power regression curve for Series 5. Don't use this calculation with a trend line.

Be careful to position the cursor where you want the series to appear before you summon the Calculate overlay. If you position the cursor on the wrong series when you perform a calculation, the calculated results can overwrite the existing data in a series.

You can try using the Series keywords with the SOSRVAVG chart that you just saved. If the SOSRVAVG chart is not on your screen, retrieve the chart by selecting Get/Save/Remove from the main menu and SOSRVAVG from the Select Chart list. Change the calculated average series (Series 6) back to an area chart by pressing F8 (Options) from the Area Chart Data screen and selecting Area in the Type column for that series.

To display the averages, you can use the @EXCH keyword. To do this procedure, follow these steps:

1. Press F8 (Data) to return to the Area Chart Data screen and press F9 (More Series) to summon Series 4-8.

2. Position the cursor in Series 6 (Average) and press F6 (Calculate).

3. Press Enter to move the cursor down to the Calculation field.

4. Press Ctrl-Del to delete the average calculation and type the instruction @EXCH(#5).

5. Press Enter to confirm the instruction and press F2 (Draw Chart) to see the chart. Figure 7.13 shows the data screen with the exchanged series. The series names no longer appear with diamonds in front. After you change the position of a series, the series no longer is treated by Harvard Graphics as a calculated series. Figure 7.14 shows the completed chart with averages and total revenues displayed as areas. Save this chart with the name SOSRAREA for "SOS revenues as an area chart."

Fig. 7.13.

The second Area Chart Data screen after the @EXCH calculation.

```
                         Area Chart Data                              ▼

        Title: Superior Office Supplies Revenues
     Subtitle: 1988-1990
     Footnote:


               X Axis        Average        Total      Series 7    Series 8
       Pt      Month                         Revenues

       1    Jan             8174.667       24524
       2    Feb             8345.667       25037
       3    Mar             15388          46164
       4    Apr             20278          60834
       5    May             17288.334      51625
       6    Jun             21996.334      65989
       7    Jul             24540          73620
       8    Aug             29430.666      88292
       9    Sep             63077          189231
       10   Oct             61778.668      185336
       11   Nov             26854.334      80563
       12   Dec             57030          171090

    F1-Help           F3-Save        F5-Set X type              F9-More series
    F2-Draw chart     F4-Draw/Annot  F6-Calculate   F8-Options  F10-Continue
```

Using the @REDUC Keyword

Data reduction is a method of consolidating and reordering the data in a chart. When you instruct Harvard Graphics to perform an @REDUC calculation, the program eliminates any duplicate x-axis labels or values, reorders imported data, removes spaces in the X data that cause gaps in the graph, and sorts x-axis labels or values. The x-axis data is set in sequence from smallest to largest or earliest to latest for all x-axis types, except Name.

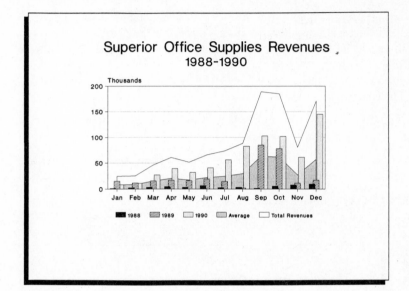

Fig. 7.14.

The completed chart after the @EXCH calculation.

You normally check data as you enter it, and you do not need to perform data reduction. When you import data from 1-2-3, however, the layout of the data in the spreadsheet may not be appropriate for Harvard Graphics. For example, the data in your 1-2-3 spreadsheet may have blank lines between lines of data. You can remove those blank lines with the @REDUC keyword. When you use @REDUC, Harvard Graphics performs the following processes:

❏ *An X and Y value check:* The program checks all X and Y values to ensure that they are valid entries. If the selected X data type is Month, for example, every X data point in the chart is checked against valid month entries. If an entry is invalid, Harvard Graphics displays the message Invalid X data type.

❏ *Value consolidation:* The program checks each X value to make sure that you don't have duplicate entries with the same X value. If the program finds two Y values for the same X value, Harvard Graphics adds the Y values to produce only one entry for each X value. If the X data type is Number, however, Harvard Graphics does not sum the Y values.

❏ *Data sort:* Harvard Graphics sorts the data. When the X data type is Name, the program does not sort the data but removes blank lines that do not contain X data. Harvard Graphics places Y values that do not have corresponding X values after the sorted data. Blank lines are moved to the end of the chart.

Try modifying the chart you just made by first moving one month out of sequence and then adding some lines in the middle of the chart. You then can practice using the @REDUC keyword to correct the changes. If you do not have SOSRAREA on-screen, retrieve SOSRAREA now by selecting Get/Save/ Remove from the main menu and SOSRAREA from the Select Chart list. Follow this procedure to make these changes:

1. Position the cursor on Jul and press Ctrl-Ins four times to separate the first half of the year from the second.

2. Position the cursor on Jan and press Ctrl-down arrow twice to alter the sequence of the months.

3. Press F2 (Draw Chart) to view the chart. Figure 7.15 shows the altered chart.

Fig. 7.15.

The altered SOSRAREA chart.

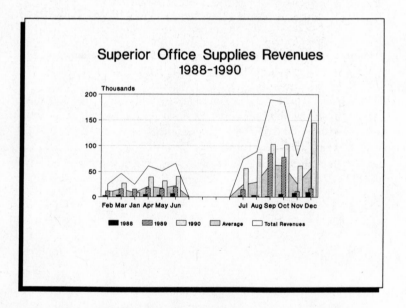

4. Press F6 (Calculate) with the cursor positioned anywhere on the data portion of the Area Chart Data screen. Because the @REDUC calculation is general and acts on all series, the placement of the cursor is not significant for this calculation.

5. Press Enter to move the cursor past the Legend field and to the Calculation field.

6. Type @REDUC in the Calculation field and press Enter. Figure 7.16 shows the Calculate overlay with the @REDUC keyword. Notice that the cursor was in the X Axis month when F6 was pressed, so that the series name is listed as X on the Calculate overlay.

You can see that the data has been reordered and consolidated. The @REDUC keyword does not appear on-screen, nor is there a new series. Seven out of the 15 available keywords do not show calculated series, but rather perform some general operation on all of the series or on one series. The seven keywords that do not add a calculation diamond include @CLR, @COPY, @DUP, @EXCH, @MOVE, @REDUC, and @RECALC.

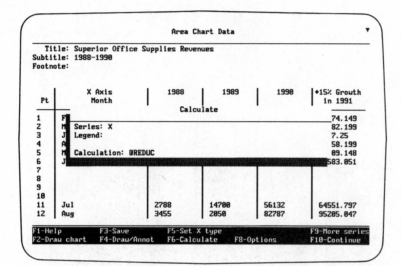

Fig. 7.16.

The Calculate overlay with the @REDUC keyword.

Chapter Summary

In this chapter, you learned how to use Harvard Graphics' calculation features to perform calculations on individual series and on a group of series. In Chapter 8, you use the import and export features available in Harvard Graphics.

8

Importing and Exporting Data

Harvard Graphics' capability to move data and graphs from other software into a chart is one of its most impressive features. Using the Import/Export option from the main menu, you can transform a series of numbers into a graphically pleasing presentation in minutes. Instead of asking your viewers to look at a 1-2-3 spreadsheet and evaluate raw numbers, you can import that spreadsheet and present an expressive chart. Using Harvard Graphics' import feature, you can transform worksheets from 1-2-3, Symphony, or Excel. You also can add flair to a graph made in a spreadsheet package by importing the graph directly into Harvard Graphics. Additionally, you can import data from an ASCII file into Harvard Graphics, fashioning appealing text or graph charts.

Using the Export features, you can convert your original charts into a format that can be read by other software, such as Ventura Publisher, PageMaker, or PC Paintbrush. If you want to combine text documents with graphics on the same page using the export features, you can create a file format that is recognized by a variety of publishing and graphics packages.

Importing Spreadsheet Graphs and Data

Using the Harvard Graphics import features, you can import spreadsheet graphs or data from other software packages, such as 1-2-3, Symphony, Excel, or Quattro Pro, quickly and easily. This section describes the process of importing graphs and data from spreadsheets into Harvard Graphics. After the data or graph is in Harvard Graphics, you can manipulate and modify the data or graph like any other Harvard Graphics chart.

265

Importing Lotus Graphs into Charts

Harvard Graphics can spruce up any of the dull and boring graphs that come out of 1-2-3 or Symphony, as long as you save them as named graphs before you save the 1-2-3 or Symphony worksheet file. When you import a Lotus graph, Harvard Graphics reads in all its graph settings and sets the options on the chart Titles & Options pages to match. The result in Harvard Graphics is a very close approximation of the 1-2-3 graph. After you have imported the graph, you can make any changes you want to the graph's options settings as though you had created the graph in Harvard Graphics.

To import a Lotus graph, follow these steps:

1. Select Import/Export from the main menu.

2. Select Import Lotus Graph from the Import/Export menu.

3. Choose the WKS, WK1, WRK, or WR1 file you want from the list that appears by moving the highlight to the file with the arrow keys and then pressing F10. Harvard Graphics shows you all of the Lotus worksheet files in the default Import directory. For information about changing the default Import directory, refer to the instructions in Chapter 2.

4. Select the named Lotus graph from the list of named charts in the worksheet file.

5. Press Tab to move the cursor to the Import Data Only settings. Press the space bar to move the cursor to No if you want to import the chart's data and settings (the settings that determine its appearance). Press the space bar to move the cursor to Yes if you want to import only the chart's data into a blank chart data screen and use the default Harvard Graphics options settings.

When you import a Lotus graph successfully, Harvard Graphics draws the resulting chart on-screen. You can immediately make any changes you want on the chart's Titles & Options pages. You also can edit the chart's data on the chart data screen.

You may notice a few minor changes between your original Lotus graph and the Harvard Graphics version. The Harvard Graphics chart does not show a Lotus graph's data labels, and the y-axis title in a Harvard Graphics chart appears at the top of the y-axis. More importantly, you should check the scaling of the Harvard Graphics chart y-axis. Harvard Graphics uses a slightly different scaling method, and you may need to make a minor adjustment on the chart's scaling option.

Importing Lotus Data into Charts

Many Harvard Graphics users maintain data in a 1-2-3 file or a program that generates 1-2-3 worksheets. Harvard Graphics, therefore, provides a smoothly integrated mechanism for pulling data from a 1-2-3 spreadsheet directly into a chart data screen. Users no longer have to manually duplicate numbers in a spreadsheet on a chart data screen.

Combining 1-2-3 number crunching and Harvard Graphics chart building is a financial analyst's dream come true. With a few keystrokes, you can create a detailed pictorial view of the data you need to analyze. Figure 8.1 shows the SOSREVS spreadsheet.

```
A3: [W15]                                                    READY


         A           B        C        D       E       F       G
 1  Superior Office Supplies
 2  Revenues  (1988-1990)
 3
 4      Month        1988     1989     1990
 5
 6  Jan             1,356   14,953    8,215
 7  Feb             2,567   11,449   11,021
 8  Mar             3,577   15,559   27,028
 9  Apr             4,588   16,978   39,268
10  May             3,452   16,252   31,921
11  Jun             6,544   18,938   40,507
12  Jul             2,788   14,700   56,132
13  Aug             3,455    2,050   82,787
14  Sep             1,517   84,880  102,834
15  Oct             5,623   77,991  101,722
16  Nov             7,866   11,290   61,407
17  Dec             9,345   16,745  145,008
18
19
20
```

Fig. 8.1.

The SOSREVS spreadsheet.

Setting the Default Import Directory

Before you begin importing spreadsheet data, select Setup from the main menu and Defaults from the Setup menu so that you can enter the default import directory. By specifying an import directory, you can instruct Harvard Graphics to look in a specific directory on your hard disk for 1-2-3 spreadsheets. If you keep your spreadsheets in C:\LOTUS, for example, you can specify C:\LOTUS as the default import directory. You also can specify a default import file. Harvard Graphics imports from the default file unless you specify otherwise. Figure 8.2 shows the default settings with the import directory specified.

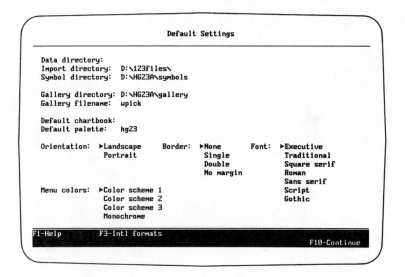

Loading the Import File into the Chart

To try the Lotus data-import process, copy the spreadsheet data shown in figure 8.1 into a 1-2-3 spreadsheet. Use the Range Name Create command to name the data ranges for each year in the spreadsheet. Give the data in the 1988 column the range name 1988. Give the data in the 1989 column the range name 1989, and so on. Name the range that contains the x-axis titles, as well. Try naming the range with the month names Jan through Dec as XAXIS. Importing Lotus data is easiest when you name the ranges in your spreadsheet. When you instruct Harvard Graphics which spreadsheet data to import, you can use range names such as 1988 rather than range addresses such as C6..C17.

Save the spreadsheet as SOSREVS.WK1. Harvard Graphics accepts files from 1-2-3 Versions 1A, 2, or 3 (WKS or WK1 files) and Symphony spreadsheet data (WRK or WK1 files). After you save the spreadsheet, start Harvard Graphics and create a graph chart (bar/line, area, high/low/close, or pie). Select an appropriate X data type to match the spreadsheet data and press Enter to reach a blank data screen.

After you see the blank data screen, follow this procedure:

1. Press Ctrl-L at the data screen.

2. Select Import Lotus Data from the Import/Export menu.

3. Select the file SOSREVS.WK1.

4. At the Import Lotus Data screen, if you want to import the title in the spreadsheet, type a backslash (\) followed by the Lotus cell address of the title. In this case, type \A1.

5. If you want to import the subtitle in the spreadsheet, type a backslash followed by the Lotus cell address of the subtitle. In this case, type \A2.

   Follow the same procedure if you want to import a spreadsheet's footnote.

6. Position the cursor at the entry for Data Range for the x-axis data and type the range name *XAXIS*.

7. Position the cursor on Series 1 and press Ctrl-Del to erase Series 1. Type the series name *1988* and tab to the Data Range column. Type the range name *1989* and press Enter to move the cursor to the next line.

8. Continue filling in the second and third series lines as you did in step 7.

9. Press Enter to move the cursor to Append Data and select No. Press F10 to continue. If you select Yes for Append Data, Harvard Graphics adds the spreadsheet data to the end of any data already present on the Bar/Line Chart Data screen. Selecting No instructs Harvard Graphics to write over any existing data with the newly imported Lotus data. Figure 8.3 shows the completed Import Lotus Data screen.

10. Press F2 (Draw Chart) to view the chart with imported data.

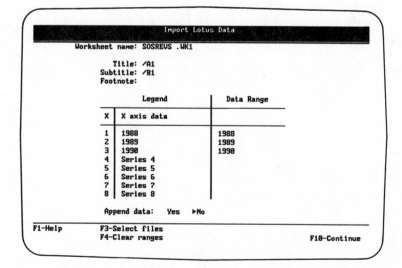

Fig. 8.3.

The completed Import Lotus Data screen.

You can start the Lotus import process by pressing Ctrl-L (for Lotus) at a blank chart data screen, or you can return to the Harvard Graphics main menu and select Import/Export. Pressing Ctrl-L is much faster than returning to the main menu and using the Import/Export menu.

After you import titles from a spreadsheet, you can format the files using the Size/Place overlay, as you would any chart title.

If you have not named the ranges in your spreadsheet, you can type cell addresses when Harvard Graphics asks for data ranges on the Import Lotus Data screen. In the preceding spreadsheet, for example, you could have specified the 1988 data as B6..B17.

When you import Lotus data into a pie chart, do not type pie slice names because Harvard Graphics imports pie labels.

After you import Lotus spreadsheet data into a Harvard Graphics chart, you can save the chart as a template to create a data link that imports Lotus data into a new chart. Instructions for creating a template are in Chapter 13.

Importing Excel Charts

Just as you can import Lotus charts or worksheet data, you can import a completed Microsoft Excel chart or a set of Excel data to chart in Harvard Graphics.

To import an Excel chart, follow these steps:

1. Select Import/Export from the main menu.

2. Select Import Excel Chart from the Import/Export menu.

3. Select the Excel chart you want from the list of XLC charts that appears by moving the highlight to the chart name with the arrow keys and then pressing F10. This list shows all the XLC charts in the default Import directory.

4. Press the space bar to move the cursor to Yes or No, depending on whether you want to import only the data and use the Harvard Graphics default options settings or whether you want Harvard Graphics to import the data and match the options settings to the settings of the Excel chart.

When you import an Excel chart successfully, Harvard Graphics displays the chart on-screen. You can immediately begin changing the options on the chart's Titles & Options pages to make any modifications you want to the chart. You also can edit the chart's data on the data screen.

You should be aware of a few restrictions in importing Excel charts. Harvard Graphics does not graph data referred to in linked Excel spreadsheets. Harvard Graphics also does not graph more than eight data series or 240 data points.

Some minor differences in the appearances of Excel charts and Harvard Graphics charts include: Harvard Graphics may place x- and y-axis labels differently; text attributes in titles and axis labels are not imported; data is displayed in a different order in pie and area charts; and extremely long Excel titles may be truncated to fit the Harvard Graphics 40-character maximum.

Importing Excel Data

Importing Excel data is like importing Lotus data. Use the same procedures you use to import Lotus data but select Import Excel Data rather than Import Lotus Data from the Import/Export menu. Fill out the Import Excel Data screen by entering Excel data range addresses or range names.

You also can press Ctrl-E (for Excel) from a blank chart data screen to start the Excel data import process. Harvard Graphics displays the Select Excel Worksheet screen so that you can choose an Excel spreadsheet and then complete the process as you would if you were importing Lotus data.

Importing ASCII Files

If the text you want to use in a text chart exists already in a file in your computer, you can import selected text from the file into your text chart. The file, however, must be in ASCII format (plain text). If you created the file with a word processor, you may need to use a special command in the word processor to save the text in ASCII format first.

From an ASCII file, you can import selected text into a Harvard Graphics free-form chart. Then, to use the same text in another text chart type, you can choose to create a chart. When Harvard Graphics asks whether you want to keep the current data, respond with Yes.

Figure 8.4 shows a memo that includes data about pencil eraser sales. To get some practice importing text data into a chart, re-create this memo with a word processor and save the resulting file in ASCII format. Your word processor user's manual probably provides specific steps you can follow to save text as an ASCII file. Use spaces or tabs to align the three numbers. Don't worry about positioning the text exactly. Just be sure that you leave at least three spaces between each of the sales figures and between each of their headings.

Next, start Harvard Graphics and create a text chart of any type. (No matter which type you choose, Harvard Graphics imports ASCII text into a free-form chart.) Before entering any text into the new chart, return to the main menu by pressing F10 (Continue). Then select Import/Export from the main menu and Import ASCII Data from the Import/Export menu.

Fig. 8.4.

*The ASCII file
ready for import.*

```
                    M E M O R A N D U M


    To: John Bartlett
    From: Marion Clarke
    Re: Eraser sales


    John, here are the Annihilator sales figures for three regions:

            Annihilator Sales

        East    West    Midwest

        364     256      259


    Please pass them on to all concerned.

    Best,

    Marion
```

If you already have imported text from an ASCII file during the current Harvard
Graphics session, that file appears on the Import ASCII Data screen. To choose
a new file, press F3 (Select Files). If you have not yet chosen an ASCII file,
select the ASCII memo file you created earlier and press Enter. The file then
appears on the Import ASCII Data screen, as shown in figure 8.5.

Fig. 8.5.

*The Import ASCII
Data screen.*

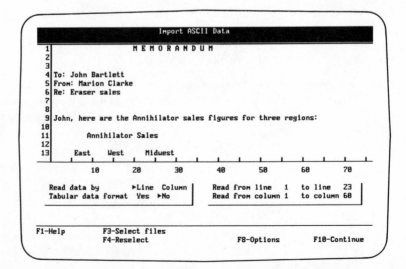

```
                            Import ASCII Data
    1              M E M O R A N D U M
    2
    3
    4 To: John Bartlett
    5 From: Marion Clarke
    6 Re: Eraser sales
    7
    8
    9 John, here are the Annihilator sales figures for three regions:
   10
   11         Annihilator Sales
   12
   13     East    West    Midwest
        ┴───────┴───────┴───────┴───────┴───────┴───────┴───────┴
           10      20      30      40      50      60      70

    Read data by        ▶Line  Column    Read from line   1  to line    23
    Tabular data format  Yes ▶No          Read from column 1  to column 68


 F1-Help        F3-Select files
                F4-Reselect                     F8-Options       F10-Continue
```

You can press Ctrl-up arrow and Ctrl-down arrow to scroll through the file. The Import ASCII Data screen includes four options near the bottom. You must set these options to inform Harvard Graphics which data to import and how to import the data. The options on the Import ASCII Data screen include the following:

- ❏ *Read Data by*. Set this prompt to Line to read the selected lines of the file line by line. Set this prompt to Column to read the text column by column.

- ❏ *Read from Line* and *to Line*. Enter the first and last lines of the text to import. To import one line, enter the same number for the Read from Line and to Line Fields.

- ❏ *Tabular Data Format*. If the text to be read is tabular (arranged in columns separated by spaces or tabs), set this prompt to Yes. If the text is not tabular (a paragraph for a free-form chart, for instance), set this prompt to No.

- ❏ *Read from Column* and *to Column*. To read text from only one horizontal position to another, set beginning and ending columns at these fields.

Follow this procedure to set the options for importing the sample memo:

1. Press Tab to leave the Read Data by field set at Line.

2. At the Read from Line field, enter the line number of the memo's title, Annihilator Sales. In the preceding example, the title is on line 11. By making the title the first line to be read, you tell Harvard Graphics that the title in the file should become the title on the Free Form Text screen.

3. Press Ctrl-down arrow, if necessary, to find the line number of the line containing the sales figures. In the preceding example, that line number is 15.

4. At the Read to Line field, enter the last line to be read.

5. Because the text you want to import is tabular, press Tab to move the cursor to the Tabular Data Format option and use the space bar to highlight Yes. (If the text is not tabular, choose No for this option. Harvard Graphics then displays column numbers below the text so that you can fill out the Read from Column and to Column options.)

6. Press Tab to move the cursor to the Read from Column and to Column fields.

7. The text in this example is columnar; therefore, press Enter to accept each of the default settings and import the text. (If the text is not columnar, specify a beginning and ending horizontal position for text import at the Read from Column and to Column fields, using the column numbers displayed immediately below the text.)

Figure 8.6 shows the Free Form Text screen with imported ASCII text.

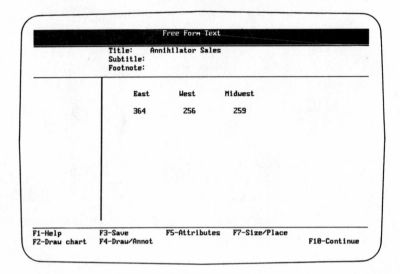

Fig. 8.6.

The Free Form Text screen with imported ASCII data.

When you import ASCII text, the first line of text imported becomes the text chart title. The next and remaining lines become text items. When you import ASCII text, the subtitle and footnote lines are left blank. You can enter these titles later if you want.

Importing ASCII Data into a Graph Chart

1-2-3 spreadsheets are not the only ASCII files you can import with Harvard Graphics. You also can import data arranged in columns in standard ASCII files.

Figure 8.7 shows the SOSREVS data as the data appears in an ASCII file. To follow along with this example, type the data shown in the figure into an ASCII file with any word processor capable of creating ASCII files. Make sure that you use three or more spaces between columns of data so that Harvard Graphics recognizes each column as a series. Follow this procedure:

1. Create a bar/line chart and complete the X Data Type Menu overlay by pressing Enter to accept Name at the X Data Type prompt; leave the Starting With, Ending With, and Increment fields blank. You must use Name as the X data type when importing ASCII data.

2. Press F10 (Continue) to return to the main menu.

3. Select Import/Export from the main menu and Import ASCII Data from the Import/Export menu.

4. Select the ASCII file on the Select File screen that appears and press Enter.

5. Press Enter to accept all the selections at the bottom of the screen. These selections are described following this procedure. The Import Titles and Legends overlay appears as shown in figure 8.8.

6. Press Enter twice to select Yes in answer to both prompts on the Import Titles and Legends overlay. Your Bar/Line Chart Data screen should look like the one in figure 8.9.

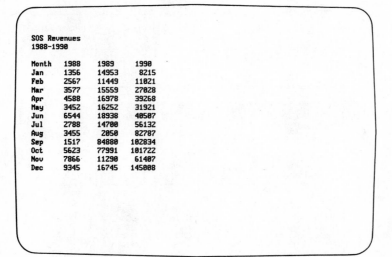

```
SOS Revenues
1988-1990

Month   1988    1989    1990
Jan     1356    14953   8215
Feb     2567    11449   11021
Mar     3577    15559   27028
Apr     4588    16978   39268
May     3452    16252   31921
Jun     6544    18938   40507
Jul     2788    14700   56132
Aug     3455    2050    82787
Sep     1517    84880   102834
Oct     5623    77991   101722
Nov     7866    11290   61407
Dec     9345    16745   145008
```

Fig. 8.7.

The SOSREVS figures in an ASCII file.

The four options near the bottom of the Import ASCII Data screen perform the following functions:

❑ *Read Data by.* Select Column if the first value in each column is the X data or pie slice label.

Select Line if the first value of each line is the X data or pie slice label.

❑ *Read from Line.* Type the number of the first line of the file to include in the chart as data. To include only one line of data, enter the same number for Read from Line as you enter for to Line.

❑ *Tabular Data Format.* Select Yes for this prompt if your ASCII data is in columns or set by tabs, such as the data shown in figure 8.4. If your data is

Fig. 8.8.

The Import Titles and Legends overlay.

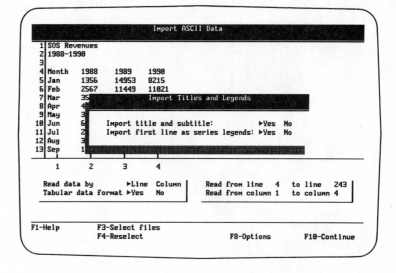

```
                          Import ASCII Data
  1│SOS Revenues
  2│1988-1990
  3│
  4│Month    1988     1989     1990
  5│Jan      1356     14953    8215
  6│Feb      2567     11449    11021
  7│Mar      35│          Import Titles and Legends
  8│Apr       4│
  9│May       3│
 10│Jun       6│   Import title and subtitle:          ▶Yes  No
 11│Jul       2│   Import first line as series legends: ▶Yes  No
 12│Aug       3│
 13│Sep       1│

          1       2       3       4

     Read data by          ▶Line  Column    Read from line   4   to line   243
     Tabular data format ▶Yes   No          Read from column 1   to column 4

  F1-Help        F3-Select files
                 F4-Reselect                        F8-Options       F10-Continue
```

Fig. 8.9.

The Bar/Line Chart Data screen.

```
                          Bar/Line Chart Data
       Title: SOS Revenues
    Subtitle: 1988-1990
    Footnote:

         │  X Axis    │  1988  │  1989  │  1990  │ Series 4
      Pt │  Name      │        │        │        │
      ───┼────────────┼────────┼────────┼────────┼─────────
       1 │  Jan       │  1356  │  14953 │  8215  │
       2 │  Feb       │  2567  │  11449 │  11021 │
       3 │  Mar       │  3577  │  15559 │  27028 │
       4 │  Apr       │  4588  │  16978 │  39268 │
       5 │  May       │  3452  │  16252 │  31921 │
       6 │  Jun       │  6544  │  18938 │  40507 │
       7 │  Jul       │  2788  │  14700 │  56132 │
       8 │  Aug       │  3455  │  2050  │  82787 │
       9 │  Sep       │  1517  │  84880 │  102834│
      10 │  Oct       │  5623  │  77991 │  101722│
      11 │  Nov       │  7866  │  11290 │  61407 │
      12 │  Dec       │  9345  │  16745 │  145008│

   F1-Help        F3-Set X type                        F9-More series
   F2-Draw chart  F4-Calculate           F8-Options    F10-Continue
```

not tabular, select No. Harvard Graphics displays column numbers under the data on-screen so that you can judge the position of the characters in the file to fill out the field labeled Read from Line.

❏ *Read from Column.* Use this prompt and the to Column prompt to enter the starting and ending column numbers that mark the limits of the data you want to include.

When you read data from an ASCII file by line, the data in the first column becomes the x-axis labels on the Bar/Line Chart Data screen or the pie slice labels on the pie chart screen (covered in the next chapter). The second column fills Series 1. The third column fills Series 2, and so on. However, when you read data from an ASCII file by column, the data in the first line becomes the x-axis labels (or the pie slice labels). The second line fills the first series of data; the third line fills the second series of data; and so on.

The Import Titles and Legends overlay enables you to import the first three lines with any data in an ASCII file as the title and subtitle by setting Import Title and Subtitle to Yes. If you set this field to No, Harvard Graphics uses the title and subtitle you enter. The Import First Line as Series Legends field entry instructs Harvard Graphics to use the first line included at the Read from Line setting as series legends. If you set Read Data by to Column, the prompt Import First Column as Series Legend appears instead.

Importing Mixed ASCII Data

Suppose that you receive from a colleague a report with mixed ASCII text and columnar information, and you want to take selective portions of the file to analyze. You can use a special feature when importing this ASCII file to a graph chart. In figure 8.10, the same ASCII file used in the preceding section is shown, but some text is added to the file. You can extract just the columnar data from this memo.

```
TO:   Carol Pettit, Carol Sullivan, & Donna Ambrosi
FROM:  Janet Kingston & Linda Bittman
RE:   SOS Revenues        1988-1990

As you can see from these figures 1990 was a winning year.   We think our success
this year can be attributed to:
          -The addition of the Annihilator Eraser to our line.
          -The increase of sales of mechanical pencils.
          -The addition of Swirly Pens to our line of products.

Month    1988      1989      1990
Jan      1356     14953      8215
Feb      2567     11449     11021
Mar      3577     15559     27028
Apr      4588     16978     39268
May      3452     16252     31921
Jun      6544     18938     40507
Jul      2788     14700     56132
Aug      3455      2050     82787
Sep      1517     84880    102834
Oct      5623     77991    101722
Nov      7866     11290     61407
Dec      9345     16745    145008
```

Fig. 8.10.

The ASCII file with
3 columns showing.

To display and import the columnar data from the memo, do the following:

1. Create a bar/line chart. At the X Data Type Menu overlay, select Name at the X Data Type field. Press Enter to move through the rest of the options and to return to the Bar/Line Chart Data screen. Then press Esc at the Bar/Line Chart Data screen to return to the main menu.

2. Select Import/Export from the main menu and select Import ASCII Data from the Import/Export menu.

3. From the Select File screen that appears, choose the ASCII file that you are importing. Press Enter, and the Import ASCII Data screen appears. You can see only the text portion of the memo; the columnar data is not in view.

4. Press Ctrl-PgDn to position and view the columnar data on-screen.

5. Tab to the Read from Line field and type *17* if you are following the example presented at the beginning of this section.

6. Tab to the Read to Line field and type *29*.

7. Press Enter and then select Yes at the Tabular Data Format prompt.

8. Press F4 (Reselect) to view the available columns. Harvard Graphics displays column numbers under each column of data. Press F10 to confirm that you want four columns imported.

9. The Import Titles and Legends overlay appears. Select No at the Import Title and Subtitle field. Select Yes at the Import First Line as Series Legend field.

10. Press Enter to import your data.

Selecting ASCII Data Columns To Include in Your Chart

You can customize your data to select only specific columns rather than all the columns in an ASCII file. Using the same ASCII data shown in figure 8.7, you can show just the 1988 and 1990 columns by following this procedure:

1. Create a bar/line chart. At the X Data Type Menu overlay, select Name at the X Data Type field. Press Enter to move through the rest of the options and to return to the Bar/Line Chart Data screen. Press Esc to return to the main menu.

2. Select Import/Export from the main menu and select Import ASCII Data from the Import/Export menu.

3. Select the file to import and press Enter. When you are viewing the memo at the Import ASCII Data screen, press Ctrl-PgDn to view the columnar data.

4. Position the cursor at the Tabular Data Format option and select Yes. Press F4 (Reselect) to display the data column numbers on the bottom of the columns.

5. Press F8 (Options) to select and adjust your columns. The first column should be highlighted.

6. Press the right-arrow key twice to expand the width of the column by two spaces and include the entire word Month. Press Enter.

7. Press Tab to highlight the second column, 1988, and press Enter to include Column 2 in your chart data.

8. Press Tab to highlight the third column, 1989. This column is omitted from your chart data; therefore, press Ctrl-Del to remove the column from the highlighted columnar data. The fourth ASCII column is now highlighted. Its label is now 3. Just as you press Ctrl-Del to omit a column of data, you can press Ctrl-Ins to add a column or series between two other series.

9. Press Enter to confirm your choices and press F10 to continue.

10. The Import Titles and Legends overlay appears as shown in figure 8.11. Select No at Import Title and Subtitle and select Yes at Import First Line as Series Legends. Press Enter to accept your data and return to the Bar/Line Chart Data screen.

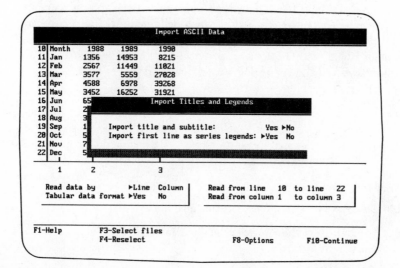

Fig. 8.11.

The Import Titles and Legends overlay.

When you complete the preceding procedure, your Bar/Line Chart Data screen should look like the one shown in figure 8.12.

Fig. 8.12.

The completed Bar/Line Chart Data screen with only two series.

```
                              Bar/Line Chart Data
       Title: SOS Revenues
    Subtitle: 1988-1990
    Footnote:

              X Axis          1988      1990    Series 3   Series 4
     Pt       Name

     1     Jan              1356      8215
     2     Feb              2567     11021
     3     Mar              3577     27028
     4     Apr              4588     39268
     5     May              3452     31921
     6     Jun              6544     40507
     7     Jul              2788     56132
     8     Aug              3455     82787
     9     Sep              1517    102834
    10     Oct              5623    101722
    11     Nov              7866     61407
    12     Dec              9345    145000

    F1-Help        F3-Set X type                              F9-More series
    F2-Draw chart  F4-Calculate                 F8-Options    F10-Continue
```

Importing Delimited ASCII Files

If your data is in a database like dBASE IV instead of a spreadsheet package, you still can import the data into Harvard Graphics. Database packages like dBASE IV produce delimited ASCII files. In addition, some mainframe and minicomputer programs produce delimited ASCII files. In a delimited ASCII file, special characters set the boundaries of a field. For example, a quotation often appears at the beginning of a field, with a comma marking the end of the field. Figure 8.13 shows a delimited ASCII file comparing second quarter revenues for three products at Superior Office Supplies.

If you are not certain about the delimiters in the file, you can look at the file in a standard word processor. To import a delimited ASCII file, you first create a chart and then return to the main menu to import a file. Harvard Graphics then prompts you for the delimiter characters, and the data is imported.

You can try importing a delimited ASCII file by following this procedure:

1. Select Create New Chart from the main menu.

2. Select Pie chart from the Create New Chart menu.

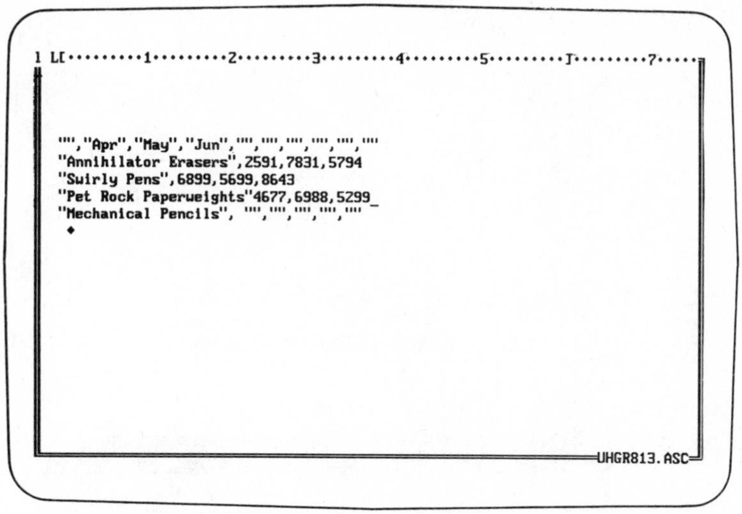

```
1 L[ · · · · · · · · · 1 · · · · · · · · 2 · · · · · · · · 3 · · · · · · · · 4 · · · · · · · · 5 · · · · · · · · I · · · · · · · · 7 · · · · · · · ·

     "","Apr","May","Jun","","","","","","",""
     "Annihilator Erasers",2591,7831,5794
     "Swirly Pens",6899,5699,8643
     "Pet Rock Paperweights"4677,6988,5299
     "Mechanical Pencils", "","","","","",""
       ◆
```

UHGR813.ASC

Fig. 8.13.

A delimited ASCII file.

3. Press Esc to return to the main menu and select Import/Export. Figure 8.14 shows the Import/Export menu.

4. Select Import Delimited ASCII by highlighting this option and pressing Enter.

5. Select the delimited ASCII file on the Select File screen by highlighting the file and pressing Enter. The ASCII Delimiters overlay shown in figure 8.15 appears. A description of the delimiters follows this procedure.

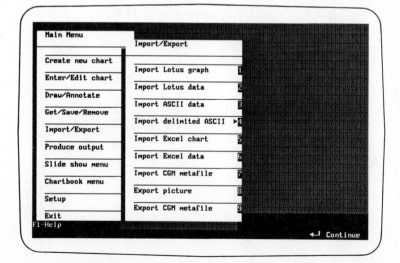

Fig. 8.14.

The Import/Export menu.

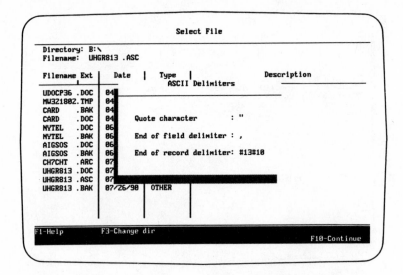

Fig. 8.15.

*The ASCII
Delimiters overlay.*

6. Press Enter three times to accept the default ASCII delimiters that Harvard Graphics has provided. Another overlay prompts you to decide whether you want to import the first record as the series legend.

7. Select Yes if the first record in your ASCII files contains the headings for the chart. Select No if the first record in your ASCII file does not contain headings for the chart. If you are creating a text file instead of a pie chart, the prompt line does not appear.

8. Press F10 to import the data.

The ASCII Delimiters overlay requires you to type the delimiters for that file. For the most part, the default Harvard Graphics delimiters are fine. But any printable character can be a delimiter. For example, you can use colons (:), semicolons (;), exclamation points (!), or even a tilde (~) as delimiters to set the boundaries of the file. You also can use up to two characters for each delimiter.

To use nonprinting delimiters like a tab or space, type a pound sign (#) followed by the ASCII value for that character.

Following is a description of the delimiter fields on the ASCII Delimiter overlay:

❏ *Quote Character.* This character marks the beginning and end of text in the file. The Harvard Graphics default character is a quotation mark, which is the most common delimiter for the beginning and end of text in a delimited ASCII file.

❏ *End of Field Delimiter.* The End of Field Delimiter tells Harvard Graphics when the contents of one field ends and another begins. Be careful to make your End of Field Delimiter a unique character. If you are using commas as decimal place markers (9,999), for example, then you cannot use commas as End of Field markers. In that case, change the delimiter for the end of a field to another printable character.

❏ *End of Record Delimiter.* This field is used to define the end of a record. Harvard Graphics places the last record on the last row of the Chart Data screen. The Harvard Graphics default delimiter for this field is #13#10, which is the same as a carriage return. This delimiter is correct for most PC programs, but may not be the correct delimiter for any mainframe and minicomputer programs you may be using.

Importing CGM Metafiles

You can add symbols to your collection with clip-art files you purchase from third-party vendors. Harvard Graphics provides a utility for converting Computer Graphics Metafiles (CGM files) to symbol files. One company that produces excellent CGM files is Marketing Graphics, Inc., of Richmond, Virginia. They have over 2,000 predrawn symbols available, in six different categories (grouped by type of symbol). You can purchase a variety of predrawn files, convert them into symbols, and incorporate the files into Harvard Graphics symbol libraries. In addition, if you save as CGM files graphics in other packages such as Freelance Plus, you also can import those graphics.

To import from a CGM metafile, you can use the Import metafile feature in Harvard Graphics Version 2.3. To use the Import metafile feature, you must have installed the VDI tables in the Installation process. Then copy the CGM file you want to convert into the directory holding the Harvard Graphics symbol files.

To import a CGM metafile, follow this procedure:

1. Select Import/Export from the main menu.

2. Select CGM Metafile from the Import/Export menu.

3. Select the file name on the Select File screen of the metafile you want to import. The metafile appears on-screen. You can save the metafile as a symbol, or chart, and use the graphic in your presentation.

If you are working with an earlier version of Harvard Graphics, you can use a special utility on the utility disk called META2HG. Copy the META2HG program into your Harvard Graphics program directory, with the CGM files that you want to import.

From your Harvard Graphics program directory, type the following command:

META2HG *filename1*.cgm *filename2*.sym.

Filename1 is the name of the CGM file you want to convert, and *filename2* is the name of the symbol library in which you want to place the symbol. Do not use the name of an existing symbol library, because the metafile symbol writes over and replaces the existing library.

When you import metafiles, the graphic may appear different from the original. The text appears in a standard Harvard Graphics font, which may not be the original font. Colors in text and in objects may be different. Fill patterns, line styles, and line widths also may appear different. If the imported graphic has complex polylines with more than 200 line segments, part of the graphic may be missing. You may have to simplify the CGM file before importing the file.

After you have imported the metafile, some parts may not appear because some objects or text may be the same color as the background of your screen. You can change the screen background to view the imported graphic.

Exporting to a File

If your goal is to incorporate a Harvard Graphics chart within a document or graphic produced by another program, you can export the chart to a file in one of three formats: Computer Graphics Metafile (CGM), Encapsulated PostScript (EPS), or Hewlett-Packard Graphics Language (HPGL). With another program, you can import that CGM, EPS, or HPGL file.

Exporting a Computer Graphics Metafile

To export a file in CGM (metafile) format, you need to install VDI device drivers in your computer's CONFIG.SYS file (see Chapter 2). The VDI device drivers are special utilities that Harvard Graphics needs to communicate with output devices that use the VDI (Virtual Device Interface) standard. Harvard Graphics also requires the VDI to output CGM files. The easiest way to install the VDI device drivers is to allow the Harvard Graphics Install program to do the job for you. The Install program adds two VDI device drivers to your CONFIG.SYS file—META.SYS and GSSCGI.SYS. After the drivers are installed and you have rebooted your computer, follow this procedure to export a CGM file:

1. Select Import/Export from the main menu.

2. Select Export Metafile from the Import/Export menu.

3. Enter a name for the export file on the Export Metafile overlay. Harvard Graphics adds a file-name extension of CGM. You may enter a different extension.

4. Select Yes or No at the Use Harvard Graphics Font field. Yes causes the program to use a Harvard Graphics font in the CGM file. Because the resulting CGM file is larger, it takes longer to create. No causes Harvard Graphics to use the standard Metafile font when the program creates the CGM file. The Metafile font depends on the program used to import the Metafile later.

When you import a CGM file into another program, colors, patterns, and line styles may vary from your choices in the Harvard Graphics original file. You may need to use that program's capabilities to adjust those aspects of the image.

Exporting an Encapsulated PostScript File

To export a file in Encapsulated PostScript (EPS) format, you must have either of two files in the directory in which you installed Harvard Graphics: HGPROLOG.PSC for black-and-white PostScript printers or HGPROLOG.CPS for color PostScript printers. These two files are provided with Harvard Graphics and are copied to your program directory when you use the INSTALL program. Exporting to an EPS file works best with a PostScript printer, although other programs can use EPS files to create graphics for non-PostScript printers.

To export an EPS file, follow this procedure:

1. Select Import/Export from the main menu.

2. Select Export Picture from the Import/Export menu.

3. Enter a file name and an extension for the exported file. The typical file-name extension for EPS files is EPS.

4. Select Standard or High for Picture Quality. Standard uses PostScript fonts in the EPS file. High uses Harvard Graphics fonts and creates a larger EPS file that takes longer to convert and print.

5. Select Encapsulated PostScript as the format and press F10 to create the EPS file.

Exporting a Hewlett-Packard Graphics Language File

The Hewlett-Packard Graphics Language (HPGL) is the standard for communications between software packages and plotters. To export a file in HPGL format, follow this procedure:

1. Select Import/Export from the main menu.

2. Select Export Picture from the Import/Export menu.

3. Enter a file name and file-name extension for the HPGL file. (Recommended extensions are PLT or HPG.)

4. Select Standard or High at the Picture Quality prompt. Standard picture quality uses built-in plotter fonts. High picture quality causes the plotter to reproduce the fonts used in Harvard Graphics.

5. Select HPGL at the Format prompt and press F10 to create an HPGL file.

If you plan to export an HPGL file, use any Harvard Graphics font, except Executive or Square Serif, when you create the chart. When you use High picture quality, Harvard Graphics creates these two fonts in the HPGL file by generating filled polygons. This process creates a large HPGL file that takes a long time to print.

Chapter Summary

In this chapter, you learned how to import and export files to and from Harvard Graphics. The Import/Export feature gives Harvard Graphics tremendous flexibility. You can maintain your data on 1-2-3, Excel, or just about any other spreadsheet or word processor and use the data in your Harvard Graphics chart. Likewise, you can create charts in Harvard Graphics that can be exported to just about any popular desktop publishing program or word processor that accepts graphic files.

In the next chapter, you learn about how to enhance your charts with Draw/Annotate.

Part III

Adding Pizzazz

Includes

Drawing with Harvard Graphics:
Draw/Annotate

Quick Start: Using Draw Partner

Adding Graphic Objects
in Draw Partner

Modifying Graphic Objects
in Draw Partner

9

Drawing with Harvard Graphics: Draw/Annotate

In Chapter 4, you learn how to create text charts to express concepts and relate information. In Chapters 5, 6, and 7, you learn how to create graph charts that make numeric data clear and easily understood. In Chapter 8, you learn to import and export those charts to and from other software packages. This chapter introduces Draw/Annotate, a feature you can use to enhance and embellish the text and graph charts you have created.

Defining Draw/Annotate

Even without Draw/Annotate, you can be confident that the text and graph charts that emerge from Harvard Graphics are colorful, clear, and attractive; the program's built-in chart designs ensure that. But you may want to add elements to charts that Harvard Graphics does not add on its own, such as boxes, lines, arrows, and circles. In addition, you may want to add freehand drawings, symbols, and an assortment of other effects to spice up your charts and make them even more presentable.

With Draw/Annotate, Harvard Graphics provides a special drawing board that you can use to add distinctive adornments to either text or graph charts after they are otherwise complete. If you're a good artist, you can draw freehand on the drawing board. If your imagination is better than your drawing hand, you can select from Draw/Annotate's symbol libraries and add predrawn figures to your charts. Just as the possibilities with a standard drawing program are unlimited, the possibilities with Draw/Annotate, Harvard Graphics' drawing program within a program, are endless.

Software Publishing has added several new features to the tools in Draw/Annotate of Harvard Graphics 2.3. Using Version 2.3, you can use a different font for each line of text added in Draw/Annotate. Also, you can add an invisible "button" to your charts with the newest Draw/Annotate. You later can use these buttons to connect several charts in a slide show. The charts you connect become a hypershow. A *hypershow* displays connected charts in a variety of sequences, which you preset.

Hypershows encourage viewer participation/interaction. For example, suppose that you have made several related text charts. The first chart is a statement of objectives, and the other charts present details of each objective. Using buttons, you can connect the charts so that from the initial chart viewers can select the next chart they want to view. Viewers can position the cursor on a specific object that you draw to indicate to the viewer where to place the cursor to see the next screen; then the viewer can press Enter to see the related detail chart. Buttons are invisible boxes. Buttons can be made as large or small as you like, to match the size of the object you display on-screen.

Harvard Graphics Version 2.3 also includes more than 500 new, vastly improved symbols. If you upgraded Version 2.13 to Version 2.3, you have the earlier libraries plus the new symbols. However, if Version 2.3 is your first Harvard Graphics purchase, you will find a complete assortment of symbol libraries, including the most-used symbols from the preceding version of the software.

You also can use Draw Partner to add graphics to an existing chart. Draw Partner, which originally was sold as an add-on package for Versions 2.0 and 2.1, is a standard application in Harvard Graphics Version 2.3. Use Draw Partner to add more sophisticated illustrations to a chart and use Draw/Annotate for basic enhancements to a chart. Draw Partner is described in the next three chapters of this book.

Understanding the Draw/Annotate Main Menu

With Draw/Annotate, you can start with a current chart made in the Graph or Text mode, or you can begin with a blank drawing board. If you have just finished a chart or have retrieved one off your disk, Harvard Graphics displays that chart in the drawing board when you enter Draw/Annotate. If no chart is in memory, the drawing board is empty when you start Draw/Annotate.

To start Draw/Annotate, select Draw/Annotate from the Harvard Graphics main menu. The Draw/Annotate screen, shown in figure 9.1, looks different from other screens in Harvard Graphics. Usually the Harvard Graphics menus disappear after you begin working with a chart. The Draw/Annotate menus on the left, however, share the screen with the drawing board and provide quick access to Draw/Annotate commands.

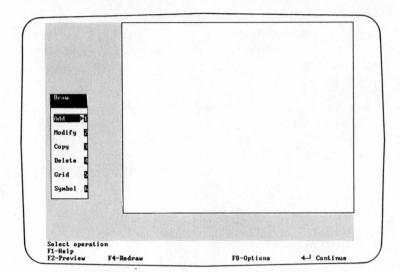

Fig. 9.1.

The blank Draw/ Annotate screen.

Examine the Draw menu. Choosing from its options, you can do the following:

❑ Add boxes, text, lines, circles, polygons, and a special type of line (called a *polyline*) used for making curved figures.

❑ Modify the objects you add in Draw/Annotate by moving them, resizing them, changing their characteristics, or placing objects in front of or behind them.

❑ Copy objects to other parts of the drawing board.

❑ Delete one or more objects added to your chart using Draw/Annotate.

❑ Set a grid to align objects with others or with specific locations on the drawing board.

❑ Use the Harvard Graphics symbol libraries to add predrawn pictures to a chart or save your own drawn objects as symbols to use again.

The process of enhancing charts with Draw/Annotate is similar for graph and text charts. First, you select a Draw/Annotate command such as Add or Copy. Next, you select an object to add or edit. Then, press F8 (Options) to change the appearance of the object you are adding or editing.

In Draw/Annotate, the F8 key works differently than elsewhere in Harvard Graphics. Usually, pressing F8 calls up a series of Options pages that enable you to set formatting characteristics for the current chart. In Draw/Annotate, pressing F8 displays the options for the current command. To move the cursor back to the drawing board, press F8 again, and you can draw the text or shape on-screen.

When an options panel is visible to the left of the screen, F8 is labeled F8 (Draw), indicating that pressing F8 moves the cursor back to the drawing board. Likewise, when the crosshairs are on the drawing board, F8 is labeled F8 (Options), indicating that you can change the options for the object you are drawing. To return to the options panel, press F8.

When the options for the current object are set and the cursor is back on the drawing board, you can draw the remainder of the object. Press Enter to set the first corner of the object and press Enter again to complete the drawing. After you set the options for an object, they remain in effect for any other objects you draw of the same type. For example, if you set a circle's color to red, all new circles you draw also are red until you stop drawing circles or until you change the options.

Using the Draw/Annotate Screen

The Draw/Annotate screen has several other features worth noting. The bottom two lines of the screen display the function key commands available. These lines change as you work with different Draw/Annotate features. F2 (Preview) in Draw/Annotate works just like F2 (Draw Chart) from the Harvard Graphics main menu.

When you work with Draw/Annotate, Harvard Graphics prompts you every step of the way by describing the current action or the next step you should perform. The prompts appear in a special prompt line under the Draw/Annotate menus. Each operation in Draw/Annotate involves a sequence of prompted steps. By reading the prompts and checking the menu at the left of the screen, you always can determine your next step.

Sizing and Placing a Chart at the Main Menu

Before starting Draw/Annotate, you should be familiar with F7 (Size/Place) on the main menu. This selection enables you to reduce proportionally the size of an entire chart. Reducing a chart's size may be necessary because Harvard Graphics fills as much of the page as possible when creating a chart. Therefore, you may need to add some space around the chart for your graphics. After the chart is made smaller on the page, you can add drawings and annotations with Draw/Annotate in the white space remaining around the chart.

To practice using Draw/Annotate, suppose that you are the marketing manager of the Superior Office Supplies Writing Tools Division. You have just attended a presentation given by the company vice president in which a Harvard Graphics bar chart was used for depicting the company's phenomenal growth. Now, you want to share this news with your staff by adapting the chart for your own presentation. For your purposes, you decide to reduce the size of the bar chart and add text describing some of the division's successes. Because, the vice president used the bar chart SOSREVS for the presentation, you borrow a copy of the file, copy SOSREVS into your data directory, and use the file for your chart. You create SOSREVS in Chapter 5.

You can reduce the size of the chart by outlining a box that represents the new size. To outline a box in Draw/Annotate, you must define two diagonally opposite corners of that box by pressing Enter at each corner.

If the Draw menu is on the screen now, press Esc to return to the Harvard Graphics main menu. Retrieve SOSREVS with the Get Chart command. After the SOSREVS chart is displayed, press Esc twice to return to the main menu and then press F7 (Size/Place). The chart appears on a screen that looks like the Draw/Annotate screen. The prompt Select first box corner appears near the bottom of the screen. Harvard Graphics expects you to draw a box on the screen and fits a smaller version of the bar chart in the box you draw.

To draw the box, press and hold down the Home key to position the cursor at the top left corner of the drawing board area. Press Enter to set the top left corner of the box. The prompt Select opposite box corner appears. Press F3 (XY Position) to set the lower right corner of the resized chart. Following Horiz=, type *19456* and press Enter. Then type *7680* in the Vert= space and press Enter again to set the bottom right corner of the box. The chart is redrawn in the confines of the box. Figure 9.2 shows the reduced chart.

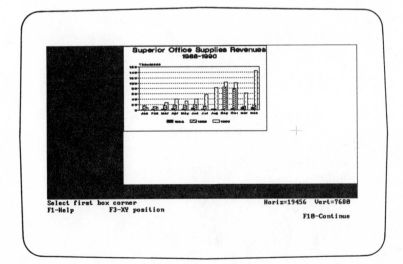

Fig. 9.2.

The reduced chart after using F7 (Size/Place) at the main menu.

After you add objects in Draw/Annotate, you find one inconsistency with the F7 (Size/Place) selection from the main menu worth noting: F7 (Size/Place) does not reduce the size of objects added to a chart with Draw/Annotate. Be sure to use the Size/Place command to reduce charts before you enhance them with Draw/Annotate.

You also can save the chart as a symbol, reduce its size after clearing the screen, and place the saved symbol back on the screen in its smaller size. Saving a chart as a symbol is discussed later in this chapter. You should use this technique only when you are sure the data in the chart will not change. After you have saved a chart as a symbol, the chart is interpreted as a group of objects rather than a series of numbers. You no longer can change the data that is graphed. However, if you change the size of a chart using F7 (Size/Place) from the main menu, you can edit the chart's data on the Bar/Line (or other chart type) Chart Data screen.

Adding Elements to a Chart

In the next sections, you learn how to add text, boxes, lines, polygons, and polylines to enhance the base graphs you already have created. A polyline is a special type of line that can have curves. Polylines usually have multiple line segments connected by points that you define. Some of the segments can be curved. Using a polyline, you can sign your name in script.

Adding Text

Text is just one of the "objects" you can add to a chart when you use Draw/Annotate. After you add a line of text to your chart, that line of text can be modified like any other object created in Draw/Annotate.

To explain the dramatic growth in the company's revenues, you can add a few lines of text to the SOSREVS revenue chart. In this example, you try adding the following bullet items:

- ❏ White Mountain Pens - introduced in August
- ❏ Swirly Pens - a huge success in October
- ❏ Annihilator Erasers - a winner in September
- ❏ Mechanical Pencils - doubled in December

Press F10 (Continue) to return to the main menu and select Draw/Annotate. To add the text, select Add from the Draw menu and select Text from the Add menu. Figure 9.3 shows the Draw/Annotate screen as it appears when the screen is ready for you to add text.

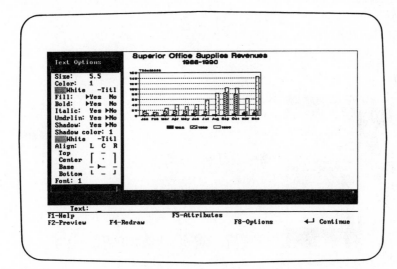

Fig. 9.3.

The Draw/Annotate screen ready for you to add text.

Adding text is not a straight typing task because you must place each line. Harvard Graphics enables you to enter the text, and then you can change the options and attributes of that text. Finally, you position a box (which outlines the perimeter of the text) on-screen and press Enter to draw the text on the page.

Follow this procedure to add the lines of text:

1. Press Ctrl-B to enter a bullet on the Text line under the drawing board. Press the space bar twice to select the checkmark bullet type from the Bullet Shapes overlay superimposed on the menu. Highlight the correct bullet type and press Enter.

2. Enter a space after the bullet character and then type *White Mountain Pens - introduced in August.*

3. Position the cursor on the "i" of the word "introduced" and press F5 (Attributes). The Attributes bar appears on the bottom of the screen.

4. Press the right-arrow key repeatedly to highlight the entire phrase "introduced in August" and press Tab to move the cursor on the Attributes bar to Italic.

5. Press the space bar to turn italic on for that phrase and then press F10 (Continue) to confirm that the italic attribute is on.

Figure 9.4 shows the attributes being set on the Attributes bar. The Tab key moves the cursor from one option on the attributes bar to the next. The Home key moves the cursor to the first option, and the End key moves the cursor to the last option. Pressing Shift-Tab moves the cursor to the preceding option.

Fig. 9.4.

Adding text with attributes.

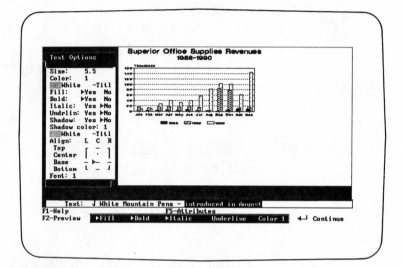

6. Press Enter. A long horizontal box representing the line of text you typed appears on the drawing board.

7. Before positioning the text properly, press F8 (Options) to move the cursor to the Text Options menu to select attributes for the new line of text.

8. Press Enter to move the cursor to the Size option and type 4.5. Size in Draw/Annotate is equivalent to the Size option used with text and graph charts on the Size/Place overlay. The Harvard Graphics default text size is 5.5. Press Enter to highlight Color on the Add Text options menu.

9. Press F6 (Choices) to view the available color choices. These choices are available in the current color palette you have selected. Select any color for the text by highlighting the color and pressing Enter. You also can type the first letter of any color name to quickly select a color. If two color names have the same first letter, press the letter again to select the second color. The color palette was selected when you set the defaults for this chart. You can change the color palette by pressing F8 (Options) at the main menu.

10. Press Enter again to move the cursor to Fill; leave the selection at Yes by pressing Enter. Detailed descriptions of Fill and the remaining options on the Text Options menu appear after this procedure.

11. Press Enter to move the cursor past Bold to Italic; set Italic to No.

12. Press Enter to move the cursor to Undrlin.

13. Press Enter to leave the Undrlin choice No.

14. Press Enter three more times to move the cursor past Shadow and Shadow Color to Align.

15. At Align, press the space bar repeatedly until the bottom left corner of the Align box is highlighted and then press Enter to move the cursor to Font.

16. Press F6 to see the font choices and select Executive by highlighting this option.

    Figure 9.5 shows the font choices now available in Harvard Graphics Version 2.3. Previous Harvard Graphics versions allow only one font within a chart.

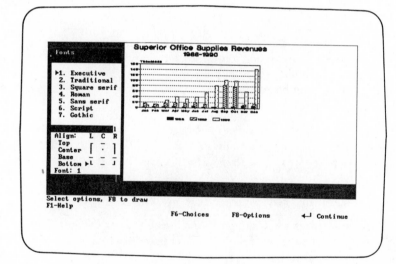

Fig. 9.5.

The font choices when adding text.

17. Press F8 (Draw) to move the cursor back to the drawing board. The horizontal box representing the line of text reappears in the color you have chosen. (Because Font is the last option on the Text Options menu, you also can press Enter after setting the Font option to return the cursor to the drawing board.)

18. Use the arrow keys to position the box under the graph where you want the text to appear. Press Enter. The text replaces the horizontal box. Figure 9.6 shows the screen with the text in its proper position before you press Enter.

Fig. 9.6.

Adding text to the chart.

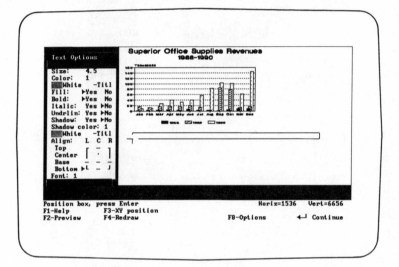

Now Draw/Annotate is ready for you to add another line of text. Each time you finish adding an object, Draw/Annotate offers you the chance to add another object of the same type. If you want to return to the menu instead, press Esc. Follow these steps to create the second bullet:

1. Press Ctrl-B to make a bullet for the second line of text. Press Enter to select another checkmark bullet. Enter a space after the bullet and then type the next line of text: *Swirly Pens - a huge success in October.*

2. Position the cursor under the word "a" and follow the preceding steps 3-5 to italicize the phrase "a huge success in October."

3. Press Enter twice to position the line directly under the first line of text. The text options have not changed, and the new text line takes on the same characteristics as the first line of text.

4. Press Ctrl-B again and select the bullet type for the third line of text. Enter a space and type the third line of text: *Annihilator Erasers - a winner in September.* Position the cursor under the word "a" and follow the preceding steps 3-5 again to italicize the entire phrase.

5. Press Enter twice to position this line under the first two lines of text.

6. Make another bullet and type the final line of text: *Mechanical Pencils - doubled in December*. Press Enter twice to position this line of text under the first three lines. Press Esc three times to return to the main menu. Figure 9.7 shows the chart with the text added.

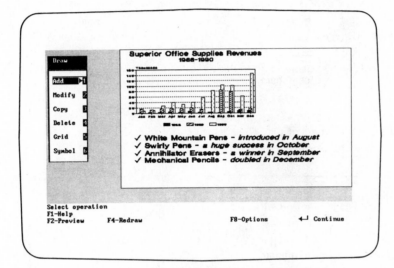

Fig. 9.7.

The SOSREVS chart with new lines of text.

When you use the Text Options menu to set the characteristics of the text you add, you may notice several options not explained in the preceding steps. Following is a list of the options available on the Text Options menu with an explanation for each option:

Size in Draw/Annotate is identical to the Size option used with the F7 (Size/Place) feature on text or graph charts. Size can be a number from 1 to 99.9 and represents a percentage of the shorter of the two sides of the page.

Color fills the current object with the selected color. Press F6 (Choices) to see the available colors. Use the space bar to move the highlight from color to color; to choose the highlighted color, press Enter or type the first letter of the color name. If you are using a plotter to print, the numbers next to the colors correspond with the plotter pen numbers on your plotter.

Fill tells Harvard Graphics whether to color in or outline letters. Select Yes if you want the letters to be solid or No if you want to show the outline only of each letter.

Bold, Italic, and *Undrlin* change the characteristics of added text to boldface, italic, or underline. These options affect an entire line. To format selected words, you must use the Attributes feature as described in the preceding for the additional phrases.

Shadow enables you to add a shadow effect to text characters. If you set Shadow to Yes, you can select a color for the shadow at the Shadow Color option. Draw/Annotate is the only mode in Harvard Graphics that enables you to write text with shadows.

Align determines the placement of the text in relation to the position of the cursor. The Align option shows a picture of the text box and enables you to pick one of 10 cursor positions around the edge of the box or one of two cursor positions inside the box. Harvard Graphics places the text box on the drawing board in the selected position relative to the cursor. If you select one of the three Base positions, Harvard Graphics aligns the baseline of the text (the line on which most characters rest) with the cursor position. The Align option stays constant when you type multiple lines of text, so that text lines align under one another. Figure 9.8 shows how the text aligns relative to the cursor based on the alignment selection you make.

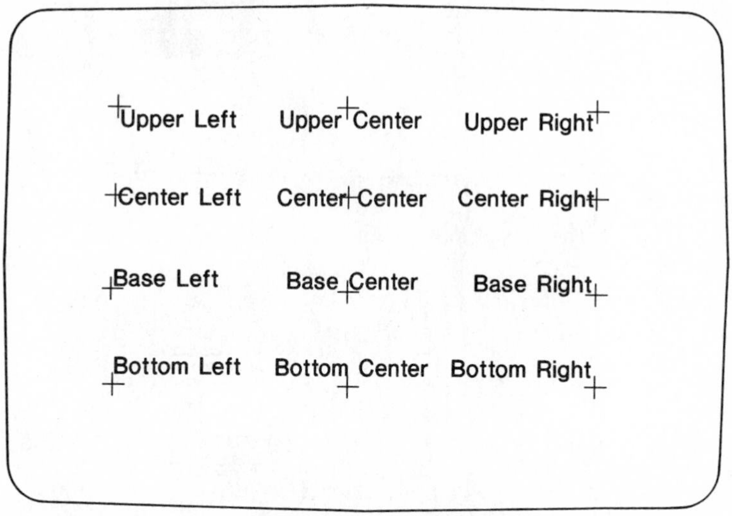

Fig. 9.8.

The align box locations.

Upper Left   Upper Center   Upper Right

Center Left   Center Center   Center Right

Base Left   Base Center   Base Right

Bottom Left   Bottom Center   Bottom Right

Font establishes the typeface for that line of text. A new feature in Harvard Graphics 2.3 is its capacity to set typefaces line by line. Also, a new font named Traditional has been added to the fonts available in Harvard Graphics. Traditional is a standard serif typeface that is appropriate in text and graph chart types.

Adding Boxes

To highlight an aspect of a chart, you can add a box to enclose and call attention to that aspect. Placing a box around a group of objects can show that they are related or that together they form a set. Placing a box around a line of text also can emphasize a specific point on your chart. A box in Draw/Annotate has two parts—an outline and fill. The box can be drawn with or without an outline, creating an unusual effect. If you create a box with an outline but no fill, the box can be placed on an object and the object shows through.

Adding boxes is similar to the process of adding text. You start drawing a box by selecting its upper left corner. Then you change any of the box options you want. Finally, you finish adding the box by selecting its opposite corner.

Try placing a box around the text you just added by following this procedure:

1. Select Draw/Annotate from the main menu and Add from the Draw menu.

2. Select Box from the Add menu. The cursor appears on the drawing board.

3. Position the cursor at the upper left corner of the lines of bullet text as shown in figure 9.9 and press Enter.

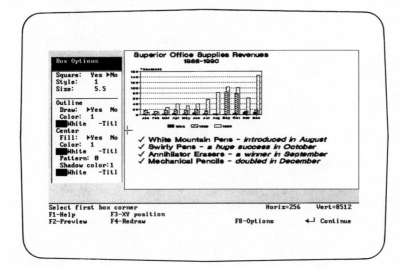

Fig. 9.9.

The upper left corner of the box.

4. Use the PgDn and right-arrow keys to open the box until the box surrounds the text completely. Do not press Enter yet. You can press the gray minus key (−) on the numeric keypad to make cursor-movement increments smaller, or you can press the gray plus key (+) to make them larger. Pressing an asterisk resets the movement increment to the default.

5. Press F8 (Options) to move the cursor to the Box Options panel so that you can make selections regarding the box you are drawing. A description of the options available for the box appears after this procedure.

6. Set the Square option to No (if Yes is highlighted).

7. With the cursor on the Style option, press F6 (Choices) to view the available box types. Select Oct Frame (octagonal frame) by pressing the space bar twice and pressing Enter. Box types are described in detail later in this chapter.

8. Press Enter again to move the cursor to Size. Type 7.5.

   Notice that the next several options on the Box Options menu are divided into two groups. The first group sets the attributes of the outline of the box you are drawing; the second group defines the center of the box. When you set the center of a framed octagon, the fill color affects the area between the octagon and its outside frame.

9. Press Enter to move the cursor to Draw. Select Yes to indicate that you want to draw the outline of the box.

10. Press Enter to move the cursor to Color. Press F6 (Choices) so that you can select a color for the outline of the box. Highlight a color and press Enter to move to the Center options.

11. With the cursor at the Fill option, press the space bar to select Yes to fill the box. Press Enter to move the cursor to Color.

12. Press F6 (Choices) and select a color for the inside of the box you are drawing. Press Enter to move to Pattern.

13. Press F6 (Choices) to select a pattern for the center of the box. Select pattern 3. Figure 9.10 shows the screen with the patterns available.

Fig. 9.10.

The box pattern choices.

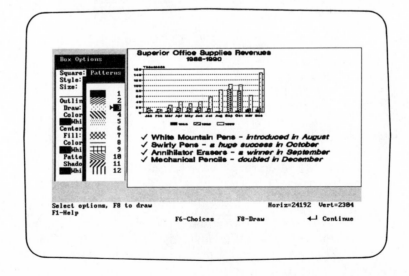

14. You can skip over Shadow and return the cursor to the drawing by pressing Enter twice. Position the cursor below and to the right of the last line of text and press Enter to draw the box.

Figure 9.11 shows the completed chart with the new box. In octagonal boxes, the fill pattern or color fills in the frame between the inside and outside box. In boxes that do not have inside frames, the fill is placed in the whole box.

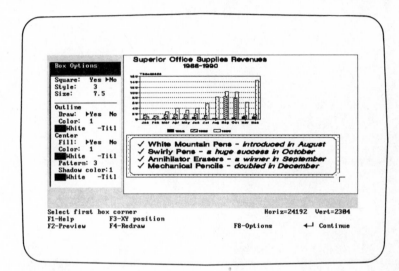

Fig. 9.11.

The chart with a box around bulleted items.

Press Esc until you return to the main menu. Save the finished chart with the name SOSRVBX (for "SOSREVS with a box around the text").

The box options available on the Box Options menu are described in the following sections.

Square

Set Square to Yes if you want the box to be a perfect square with four equal sides. Even if you set Square to No, you can hold down the Shift key as you draw a box to make it square.

Style

Harvard Graphics has 21 different box styles. Figure 9.12 shows these styles. When the cursor is on the Style option, you can press F6 (Choices) to see the different box options. Press the space bar to cycle through all 21 box types. When you have highlighted the desired box style, press Enter to select that style.

Fig. 9.12.

The 21 available box types in Draw/Annotate.

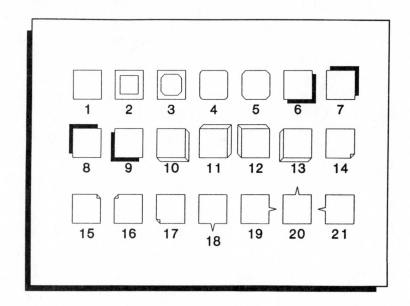

Size

The Size setting of a box almost always interacts with the Style setting for the box. If you draw a box in style 1, Size has no effect. If you draw a box in style 2 or 3, Size dictates the width of the space between the inner box and the outer box. If you draw a box in style 4, Size determines how round the corners of the box are. Size on box style 5 specifies how deep Draw/Annotate is to cut the diagonals into the sides of the box. A Size setting of 100 with a square box of style 5 creates a diamond. The Size option affects the depth of the shadow or of the third dimension in box styles 6 through 13. Box styles 14 through 17 have a turned corner, much like a dog-eared page corner. Size with styles 14 through 17 determines how wide the page corner is. Size on box styles 18 through 21 sets the size of the caption box in relation to the pointer. A Size setting of 100 with box type 18 makes the caption arrow very large with a small caption box. Figure 9.13 shows the effect of the Size option on the different box styles.

Outline Options

A box in Draw/Annotate is composed of two parts: its outline and center. You can choose whether to draw the outline and fill the center. If the center of the box is filled, you may want to omit the box outline for a varied effect. Pressing F6 (Choices) when the cursor is on the Color option displays the available options for the outline color.

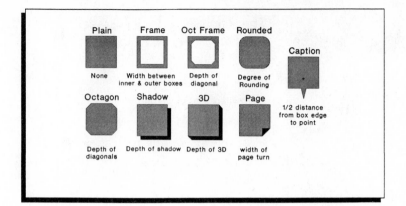

Fig. 9.13.

Box styles affected by Size option with two different sizes.

Center Options

To draw a box outline only, set Fill to No. To fill a box with a color or pattern, set Fill to Yes. With box types 2 or 3, the Fill option fills only the space between the two boxes but does not fill the inside of the box.

After you set Fill to Yes, you can select the color or pattern for the fill by positioning the cursor next to each option and pressing F6 to see the choices available. You can choose both color and pattern.

Adding Lines

Describe lines to Harvard Graphics by pressing Enter at each endpoint (the start and end of the line). Like with boxes and text, pressing F8 enables you to set the options for that line first.

To experiment with adding lines to a chart, try annotating some of the facts in the chart called SIMPLCHT, which you created in Chapter 4. Use Get Chart to retrieve SIMPLCHT. Figure 9.14 shows the chart on the drawing board, ready for enhancements.

In this example, you can highlight the most important entries on the list of customer needs with arrows. Then you can use an annotation to remind your viewers that Superior Office Supplies' A-27 formula for eraser rubber was a major breakthrough in satisfying customer needs. Figure 9.15 shows the completed chart.

Fig. 9.14.

*The SIMPLCHT
list ready for
enhancement in
Draw/Annotate.*

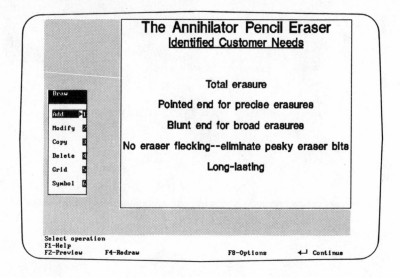

Fig. 9.15.

*The SIMPLCHT
list with arrows,
circles, and text
added.*

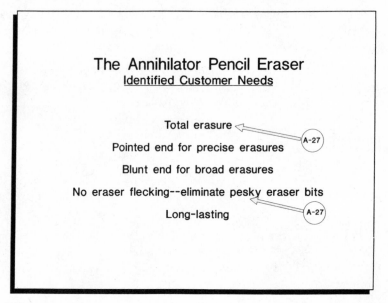

To add the arrows, follow this procedure:

1. Retrieve SIMPLCHT if you have not already done so and return to the main menu. Select Draw/Annotate from the main menu.

2. Select Add from the Draw menu; select Line from the Add menu. The cursor appears on the drawing board.

3. Position the cursor just to the right of the last "e" in the word "erasure" in the first line and press Enter to set the first point of your line.

4. Use the PgDn and right-arrow keys to move the line diagonally down and away from the starting point so that the line looks like the arrow in figure 9.15.

5. Press F8 (Options) to move the cursor to the Line Options panel.

6. At the Arrows option, select the arrow with the arrowhead on the left.

7. Press Enter to move to the Width option. Press Enter to leave the width at 5.5 and move the cursor to Outline.

8. At the Draw option, select Yes. Press Enter to move to Color.

9. Press F6 (Choices) to view the available colors for the outline of the arrow. Press B twice to move the highlight past Blue and on to Blue Lt and press Enter.

10. Press Enter again to move to the Center option.

11. Set Fill to Yes and press Enter to move the cursor to Color.

12. Press F6 (Choices) to view the colors available for the center of the arrow. Press G to highlight Gray Lt-10 and press Enter.

13. Press Enter again to move the cursor to Pattern.

14. Press F6 (Choices) to view the pattern choices. Use the down-arrow key to highlight pattern 3 and press Enter.

15. Press Enter to return the cursor to the drawing board. Press Enter again to anchor the other end of the arrow and set the length and endpoint. Figure 9.16 shows the chart with the first arrow added.

16. With the cursor still on the drawing board, position the crosshair under the word "pesky" in the fourth line of text and press Enter to anchor the first point of a new arrow.

17. Use the PgDn and arrow keys to draw the arrow. Press Enter when the arrow is positioned properly.

18. Press Esc twice to return to the Draw menu. Press F2 (Preview) to view the chart. Figure 9.17 shows the chart with arrows.

Fig. 9.16.

Adding an arrow.

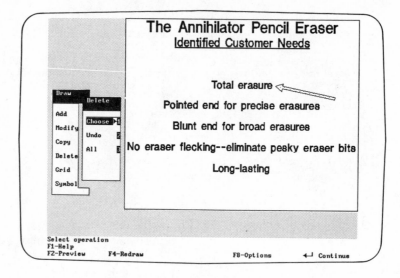

Fig. 9.17.

Previewing the chart with arrows.

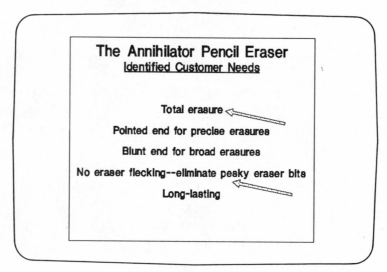

Save this chart as SLARRO (for "simple list with arrows"). When you used the Line Options menu to set the characteristics for the arrows, you may have noticed several unfamiliar options. The following sections describe the options available on the Line Options menu shown in figure 9.18.

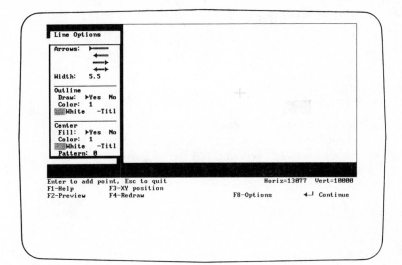

Fig. 9.18.

The Line Options menu.

Arrows

You can draw four types of lines, depicted by the four lines shown next to the Arrows prompt on the Line Options menu. The first choice is a line, and the remaining three choices are arrows. To draw a line or arrow, position the cursor at one end of the line you want to draw and press Enter. Use the arrow keys to move the cursor to the other end of the line and press Enter again. Press F8 (Options) to move the cursor to the Line Options panel.

To draw a plain line, select the first line at the Arrows prompt. To draw a line with the arrowhead at the first point where you pressed Enter, select the second line. To draw a line with the arrowhead at the second point where you press Enter, pick the third line. The fourth line draws an arrowhead at both ends of the line. To select a line type, use the space bar to highlight that choice and press Enter.

Width

Width determines the width of the line and arrowhead. Line width can be a number from 1 to 100. To determine the best width, experiment with several different settings.

Outline and Center Options

The Outline and Center options for lines are identical to the Outline and Center options for boxes. To select colors or patterns, press F6 (Choices) to view your choices.

Now that you have used arrows to point to the principal product benefits in the list, try adding text annotations to the other ends of the arrows. For these annotations, use the characters *A-27*, the name of the formula referred to in an earlier chart as the source of these product benefits. You can add two circles to the ends of the arrows to contain the text.

Using the add text procedure you learned earlier in the chapter, add the text *A-27* to the ends of the arrows. Use a text size of 3.5. Figure 9.19 shows the chart with the *A-27* text added.

Fig. 9.19.

The chart with added text ready for circles.

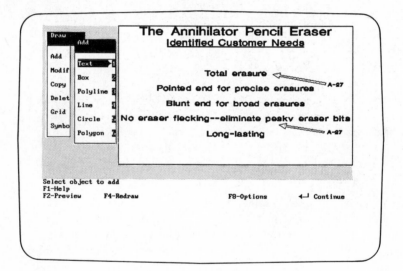

Adding Circles

The process of adding circles is similar to the process of adding boxes. The first point you locate on the screen is the center of the circle; the second point is a corner of a box surrounding the circle. After you set an anchor by locating the center point of the circle on the screen, use the PgUp, PgDn, Home, and End keys to open the box. If necessary, you can use the Backspace key to break the anchor and move the cursor to a new position and try again. After the center point is set and the perimeter is defined, press Enter again to draw the circle on-screen.

Follow this procedure to add a pair of circles to contain the text annotations:

1. Select Add from the Draw menu; select Circle from the Add menu.

2. Position the crosshairs in the middle of the circle you want to draw. In this example, position the crosshair directly over the hyphen in A-27. Press Enter to set the anchor. Figure 9.20 shows the middle of the first circle on SLARRO.CHT.

3. Use PgDn to open the circle box until the box closely surrounds the text. PgDn closes the circle box again. Do not press Enter yet.

4. Press F8 (Options) to view and change the Circle Options menu. The cursor is on Shape: Circle.

5. Press Enter to leave Shape set to Circle and move to Draw in the set of options for the circle's outline.

6. Set Draw to Yes to draw the outline of the circle and press Enter to move to Color for the outline.

7. Enter a color number for the outline of the circle or press F6 (Choices) to view the available colors; then highlight your choice and press Enter. (For this example, select Red, 12.)

8. Press Enter to move the cursor to the Center options.

9. Set Fill to No and press Enter three times to return the cursor to the drawing board.

10. Press Enter again to draw the circle.

11. Position the cursor at the exact position of the center of the second circle. Figure 9.21 shows the proper positioning for the second circle center on SLARRO.

12. Use the PgDn, PgUp, Home, and End keys to open up the box around the text.

13. Press Enter when the box is the correct size. Notice that the second circle has the same characteristics as the first.

Save the revised chart as SLDRAW (for "simple list with drawing") by returning to the main menu and using Save Chart.

The options for circles are virtually identical to those for boxes and arrows. Only the Shape option is different. Setting Shape to Ellipse instead of Circle produces an elongated circle.

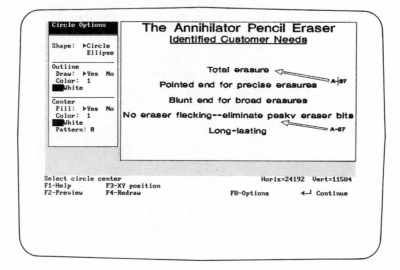

Fig. 9.20.

The first circle center.

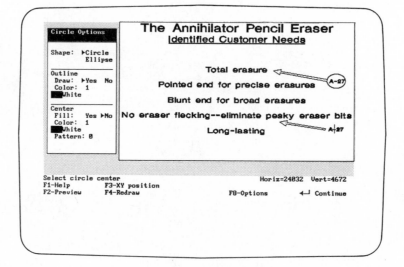

Fig. 9.21.

The center of the second circle on SLARRO.

Adding Polygons

A *polygon* is a figure with multiple sides. To draw a polygon, you must position the cursor at each of the polygon's corners and press Enter. Each time you press Enter, Draw/Annotate adds another polygon segment. Press Backspace to remove segments in reverse order. Press Esc at any point to complete the polygon.

Figure 9.22 shows the Polygon Options panel and two stars drawn with the use of Add Polygon. On the left star, the fill is set at Yes. On the right star, the fill is set to No. After you have created a star once, you can save the star to use on charts later. The section of this chapter describing symbols teaches you how to save a figure for use with other charts.

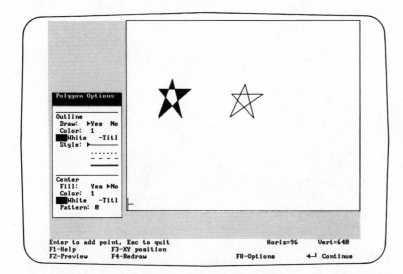

Fig. 9.22.

Making a star using Add Polygon.

To draw a star, start with a clean drawing board. Use the Create New Chart command from the main menu to create any type of new text chart. Then press Esc to return to the main menu and select Draw/Annotate.

From the Draw menu, select Add. Then select Polygon (not Polyline) from the Add menu. Draw the star, pressing Enter at each corner of the figure and using the arrow keys to draw lines between each corner. Try pressing Backspace to erase segments of the polygon. Before you press Esc to complete the star, press F8 (Options) to adjust the polygon's characteristics. When you have set the options on the Polygon Options menu, press F8 (Draw) to return the cursor to the drawing board and press Esc to complete the star.

When you press F8 (Options) to open the Polygon Options menu, the options are split into two groups (just like the options in boxes): options for the outline of the polygon and options for its center. The following sections describe these options.

Outline Options

To draw the outline of the polygon, set Draw to Yes. If the polygon has fill, you may want to consider omitting the outline.

You can use four line styles when drawing polygons: solid, dotted, dashed, and bold. To select a line style, highlight its representation at the Style option and press Enter.

Center Options

You can fill the center of a polygon with a color, a pattern, or both. Position the cursor on the Color or Pattern option and press F6 (Choices) to reveal the roster of available choices. Select the desired color or pattern and press Enter to return to the Polygon Options menu.

Adding Polylines

Polylines are lines composed of multiple straight or curved segments. To draw a polyline, follow the same procedure used for drawing a polygon. Press Enter for each segment endpoint and press Esc to complete the polyline. If you choose a curved shape for the segments from the Polyline Options menu, you may notice that all the segments of that polyline curve between the starting and ending points and may not touch all the points you set. To cause the polyline to follow your points more closely, press Enter more often as you draw the segments. To force the polyline to touch a point, press Enter three times when you position the point.

Figure 9.23 shows three versions of the same star made with curved polylines. You make the left star by pressing Enter three times at each point of the star; you make the middle star by pressing Enter three times at the top and bottom points of the star but only once at the side points of the star. You make the right star by pressing Enter once at each point.

Figure 9.24 shows three curved polylines and the number of times Enter was pressed at each point.

The options in the Polyline Options menu are similar to the polygon options with two additions: Shape and Close. These options are described in the following sections.

Shape

Shape tells Harvard Graphics whether you want the segments of the line to be sharp or curved. Selecting Sharp draws straight lines between points. Selecting Curved draws curved lines between points.

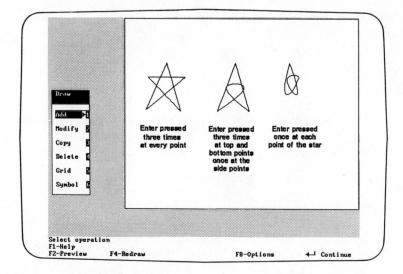

Fig. 9.23.

The star figure as a polyline instead of a polygon.

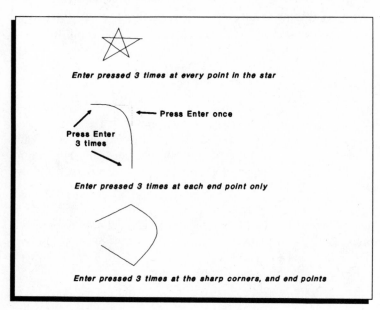

Fig. 9.24.

Polylines in Draw/ Annotate.

Close

Setting Close to Yes instructs Harvard Graphics to connect the first and last points on the polyline when you press Esc. Creating a polyline with Close to Yes and Shape to Sharp is the same as creating a polygon. If you set Close to No, the polyline remains open-ended when you press Esc to complete the figure. (A polygon is always closed.)

Adding Buttons

A button feature is now available in Harvard Graphics Version 2.3. A *button* is a box used in a slide show that enables the viewer to select the next logical slide to be displayed. This type of slide show is called a *hypershow*.

Using Draw/Annotate, you can place a button in any location on a chart. In fact, you can place up to 20 buttons on any one chart. If you display a chart in a slide show, buttons appear on the screen as boxes with dotted outlines. On the chart with a button, you can instruct viewers to position the cursor on that button and press Enter. When the viewer places the cursor on the button and presses Enter, the next appropriate slide appears. When you display the slide show as a screenshow rather than a hypershow, the buttons do not appear.

Two button symbol libraries have been added to Harvard Graphics Version 2.3. These libraries contain an array of button symbols that you can use on the charts themselves. You can retrieve these symbols and place them over the dotted outline of the button box so that the viewer of the show knows where to press Enter when viewing the screenshow.

Harvard Graphics comes equipped with seven preset buttons that perform specific actions in a hypershow. For example, one preset button is 213. Pressing this button when you are viewing the show returns you to the first slide and is the equivalent of pressing the Home key. Press F1 (Help) while you are adding a button to view a list of the preset buttons. Figure 9.25 shows the help screen with the list of reserved buttons.

A good example of the use of buttons is the screenshow called SPCINFO, installed on your disk when you first loaded Harvard Graphics 2.3. Software Publishing Corporation used the hypershow concept to create that tutorial. To view the hypershow, call up the SPCINFO slide show from the main menu and select Display ScreenShow from the Slide Show menu.

When you create a slide show in Chapter 16, you see the full benefit of the button feature. For now, you can practice adding a button in Draw/Annotate by following this procedure:

1. Select Add from the Draw/Annotate main menu and Button from the Add menu. The Button Options overlay prompts for a button number, from 1 to 10.

2. Press 1.

3. Position the cursor where you want the button to appear in the chart and press Enter to anchor the first corner of the button box. Position the button at the location where your viewer positions the cursor to press Enter.

4. Use the arrow keys to open the button box to the size of the object that the viewer sees on the chart and press Enter to set the far corner of the box.

5. Press Esc to return to the Add menu.

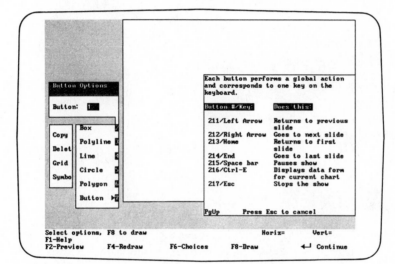

Fig. 9.25.

The reserved buttons list.

In the next section of this chapter, you modify the text and objects you added to your chart earlier. Buttons can be modified just like any other element on a chart.

Modifying, Deleting, and Copying Elements

If you inadvertently press Enter before pressing F8 (Options) as you draw any of the objects in this chapter, the results on the screen may not be exactly as you want. Fortunately, Draw/Annotate enables you to easily delete, copy, or move any object or text created in Draw/Annotate. Delete and Copy are commands from the Draw menu; the Modify command enables you to move an object, change the size or options of that object, and place the object in front of or behind other objects.

To modify, copy, or delete an object, first select the object by following this general sequence:

1. Tell Harvard Graphics which function to perform (Delete, Copy, Move, or Modify) by selecting that function from the Draw menu.

2. Select the second-level command from the function menu. For example, decide whether you want to use the Delete menu to choose, undo, or delete all. Highlight your choice and press Enter.

3. Select the object to delete or modify by positioning the cursor on that object and pressing Enter. Four small boxes surround the object, and the following prompt appears:

    Choose this   Select next   Retry

    If the four small boxes surround the correct object, highlight Choose this and press Enter. If the four small boxes do not surround the object you want to modify, highlight Select next. The four small boxes will surround the next closest object.

The following sections explain the Modify commands in greater detail.

Selecting and Deleting an Object

To practice modifying an object, retrieve the chart you saved earlier with the name SLDRAW. This chart has three different types of objects: text, circles, and arrows. Suppose that you want to remove the circles and leave only the text. To remove the circles, follow this procedure after entering Draw/Annotate:

1. Select Delete from the Draw menu; select Choose from the Delete menu.

2. Highlight the object you want to modify by placing the crosshairs on the object and pressing Enter. You see the following prompt at the bottom of the screen.

    Choose this   Select next   Retry

3. Harvard Graphics surrounds the object with four small circles. If the correct object is highlighted, press Enter to confirm your choice. If the small circles surround the wrong object, use the right-arrow key to highlight Select next at the bottom of the screen and then press Enter. Figure 9.26 shows SLDRAW with the first circle selected. (Retry enables you to try again to select the object you want.)

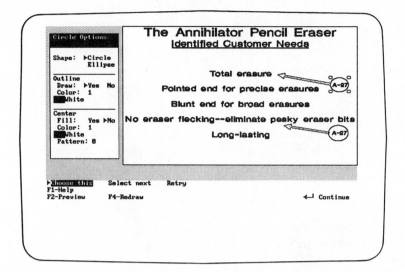

Fig. 9.26.

SLDRAW with the first circle selected for deletion.

If you want to delete the circle and the text the circle encloses, you can select both for simultaneous deletion by enclosing them in a box. To do so, first select Delete from the Draw menu and Choose from the Delete menu. Then position the cursor above and to the left of the objects you want to delete. The prompt Select first box corner appears at the bottom of the screen. Press Enter to anchor the box and PgDn to open the box to enclose the entire circle. Press Enter again, and the same prompt appears at the bottom of the screen:

Leave the cursor on Choose this and press Enter to confirm that the correct object is selected. Any object entirely within the box is deleted.

If you change your mind immediately and want to restore an object that you have just deleted, you can select Undo from the Delete menu. Undo "undeletes" only the last object you deleted. If you leave Draw/Annotate and then return to Delete, Undo does not undo your last deletion. Undo works only when used immediately. However, if you choose All from the Delete menu to delete all the Draw/Annotate additions to your chart, Undo does not restore the objects. Undo may restore some of the objects that you drew last.

Copying an Object

If you regret having removed the first circle from SLDRAW, you easily can copy the remaining circle to the first circle's place. To copy the second circle, follow these steps:

1. Select Copy from the Draw menu. At the bottom of the screen, you see a prompt to select an object.

2. Position the cursor anywhere on the circle you want to copy and press Enter. Harvard Graphics places four small circles around the circle to indicate that the circle is the chosen object. Notice that the prompt now reads

Choose this   Select next   Retry

Figure 9.27 shows SLDRAW with the remaining circle selected.

3. Press Enter with Choose this highlighted. A box surrounds the circle marked for copy. Use the arrow keys to position the box for the destination of the duplicate and press Enter. A circle surrounding the text appears.

Fig. 9.27.

SLDRAW with the second circle selected for copying.

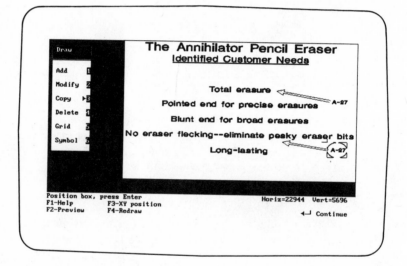

After you successfully copy an object, you can continue pressing Enter to copy the object again and again. The second time you press Enter, a duplicate of the object appears. The object is the same distance from the first copy as the first copy was from the original. Each time you press Enter, the object is copied at the same distance, moving in the same direction. With this technique, you can make evenly spaced, repetitive patterns on a page. Figure 9.28 shows a diagonal pattern made with a circle and star symbol.

Modifying Objects

You can use Draw/Annotate's Modify command to move and resize an object or group of objects. You also can use the Modify command to change the Options settings of an object. For example, you can change an object's color, change the attributes of text, or even change the text itself. The Modify command also enables you to place one object in front of or behind another object.

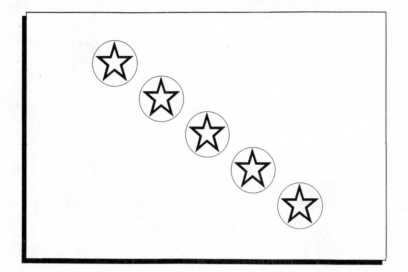

Fig. 9.28.

A circle and star pattern.

Moving and Resizing Objects

To move an object, select Modify from the Draw menu and select Move from the Modify menu. Choose the object you want to move by pointing to the object with the cursor and pressing Enter. Check to see that you have selected the correct object and that four small boxes surround the object. Then position the box where you want to move the object. Complete the move by pressing Enter to confirm your positioning choice.

When you use the Move command and select an object to move, it appears as though you are moving an empty box around the screen. After you press Enter to confirm the Move command, however, the object moves to the new position and may even appear to take pieces of surrounding objects with it. Press F4 (Redraw) to refresh the screen and see an accurate view of the chart.

To change the size of an object without changing its position, select Size from the Modify menu. Select the object to resize. After you select an object, Harvard Graphics draws a box around the object and the prompt Select opposite box corner appears. Reposition the bottom right corner of the box with the cursor to resize the box and the object in the box. Then press Enter.

With the Size command, you can change the size and position of an object (or group of objects) simultaneously. Select the object or group of objects as described in the preceding paragraph. Press the Backspace key to release the cursor and enable the cursor to move freely around the screen. Position the cursor at the upper left corner of the new location of the object. Press Enter to anchor this corner. Use PgDn, PgUp, Home, or End to open and size the box to its new proportions. When the lower right corner of the box is in the correct position, press Enter. Then press F4 (Redraw) to see the true appearance of your changes.

Modifying the Options of a Group

Normally, you modify the options of one object at a time. With Draw/Annotate, you can modify the options of a group of objects simultaneously.

To practice modifying the options of a group of objects, retrieve SOSRVBX, the chart you made earlier in this chapter. Select Modify from the main menu; select Options from the Modify menu. For this exercise, you change all the text in the chart and make the added text smaller. To make the changes, follow these steps:

1. Position the cursor just above and to the left of the first line of text and press Enter.

2. Press PgDn and the right-arrow key several times until all the lines of text are enclosed in the box and press Enter.

3. Select Choose this from the bottom of the screen by pressing Enter. Figure 9.29 shows the chart with all lines of text selected.

Fig. 9.29.

SOSRVBX with lines of text selected for change.

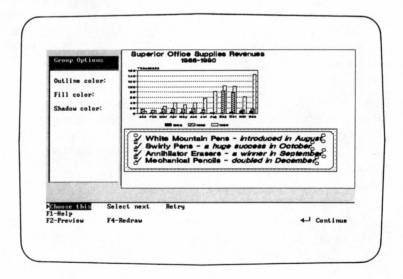

4. Harvard Graphics recognizes that the currently selected object is text. When the Text Options menu appears, change Size to 3.5 and set Font to 2 Traditional. Then press F10 (Continue) to return the cursor to the drawing board.

Figure 9.30 shows SOSRVBX with the modified text.

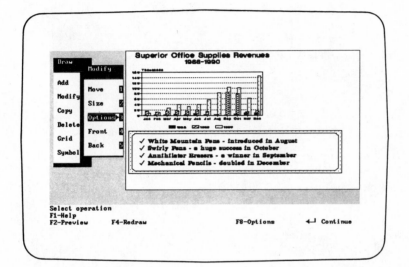

Fig. 9.30.

SOSRVBX *with lines in new font.*

The italics in each line no longer show because you changed the font. If you want to restore the italics, modify the options of each line and use F5 (Attributes) to reset the attributes. Figure 9.31 shows the chart with the text in the Traditional font and the phrases in italics.

Using Harvard Graphics Symbols

Symbols are predrawn collections of individual objects. A symbol can include circles, boxes, lines, polylines, and text—all grouped together as one image. A symbol also may be a group of one type of object, such as a series of names.

Typical symbols are pictures of buildings, people, cities, and figures such as arrows, stars, and currency signs. These images are stored in special Harvard Graphics files called symbol files. Each symbol file, distinguished by the SYM extension, has as many as 20 different symbols from which you can choose.

Fig. 9.31.

SOSRVBX *with lines in new font, with italics.*

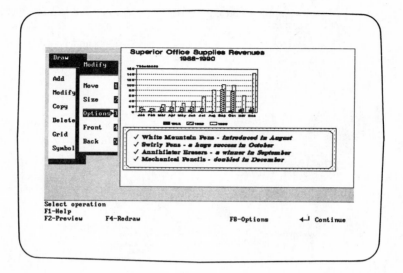

You can assemble your own symbol libraries by saving the objects you draw in existing symbol libraries. You also can continue collecting new symbols to build your own customized set of symbol libraries, ready for use in new charts. You even can save an entire chart as a symbol and then modify the chart just as you would modify a single symbol. You can change the size of a symbol, stretch its shape, or make any of a variety of other alterations. Later, you can separate or *ungroup* the elements in a chart saved as a symbol and change the appearance of any element individually. This feature is one of the most powerful and unique features in Harvard Graphics.

Symbols can be remarkably useful. For example, you can convert your company logo into a symbol to save for use again and again in a variety of charts and sizes.

Although you can save virtually anything you create as a symbol to use in future charts, you may want to start with the predrawn symbols provided by Harvard Graphics in its symbol libraries.

To spruce up the Superior Office Supplies Writing Tools Division presentation you have been creating throughout this book, you can use Draw/Annotate to create a logo for your division and save the logo as a symbol. Then you can add the symbol to all the charts in your presentation.

To make a simple logo, start by creating a new free-form text chart. (Free-form charts are described in Chapter 4.) Press Esc to return to the main menu and select Draw/Annotate.

Getting and Placing Symbols

To get a symbol, select Symbol from the Draw menu and Get from the Symbol menu. Then select the library from which you want to get the symbol and retrieve the symbol from that library. The Draw/Annotate screen appears, and the symbol is positioned on the screen as an empty box. To position the box, press the Backspace key, press Enter at the first corner of the box, open the box by using the arrow keys, and press Enter at the second corner of the box. The symbol is drawn on-screen where you positioned the box.

To add symbols and customize the chart for the Writing Tools Division, follow this procedure:

1. Select Symbol from the Draw menu.

2. Select Get from the Symbol menu. Harvard Graphics displays a list of the available symbol files.

3. Use the down-arrow key to highlight PRESENT2.SYM and press Enter. Figure 9.32 shows the Presentation symbol library as displayed on-screen.

4. Position the cursor on the clipboard symbol in the top right corner of the library and press Enter.

5. Press the Backspace key to release the cursor to move freely about the screen.

6. Use the arrow keys to position the left corner of the clipboard. When the crosshairs are at Horiz = 7232 and Vert = 15744, press Enter to set the upper left corner of the symbol.

7. Press F3 to set the lower right corner of the symbol. Set Horiz = to 16800 and Vert = to 4096. Press Enter to draw the picture.

The colors that appear on the clipboard on-screen look clear in print if you are using Harvard Graphics Version 2.3 on a black-and-white printer. In Version 2.3, Software Publishing has added a feature that replaces on-screen colors with varying gray tones when the image is printed on a black-and-white printer.

To add a yellow pencil to the clipboard, the clipboard illustration must be changed to a contrasting color. The following procedure modifies the symbol to show a gray fill:

1. Press Esc to return to the Draw menu and select Modify.

2. Select Options from the Modify menu. Position the crosshair on the clipboard symbol and press Enter to select the symbol. Select the Choose this prompt and press Enter.

3. Set the Outline Color to 1 (White) and press Enter to move to the Fill Color option.

4. Set Fill Color to 10 (Gray Lt). Press Enter twice to pass Shadow Color and redraw the symbol with gray fill.

Figure 9.33 shows the logo with the gray clipboard.

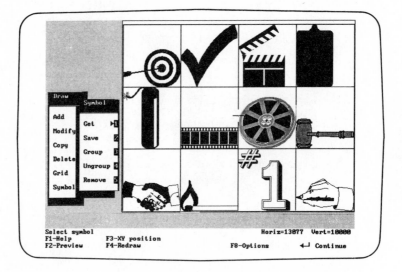

Fig. 9.32.

The PRESENT2.SYM symbol library.

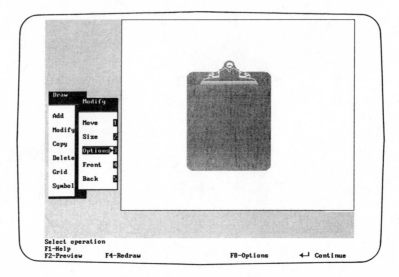

Fig. 9.33.

The gray filled clipboard.

To get another symbol for your logo, follow this procedure:

1. Select Get from the Symbol menu and choose the COMNOBJ2.SYM library. Figure 9.34 shows the COMNOBJ2 symbol library.

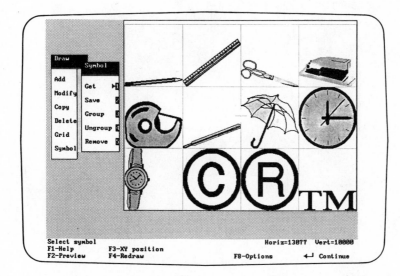

Fig. 9.34.

The COMNOBJ2.SYM library.

2. Select the pencil symbol by positioning the crosshairs on the box in the upper left corner of the library. Press Enter to confirm your choice. The Draw/Annotate screen appears again.

3. Press the Backspace key to break the anchor so that you can set the upper left corner of the pencil. Position the cursor under the left edge of the clip on the clipboard and press Enter to set the left edge of the pencil symbol.

4. Press the right-arrow key and PgDn key to open up the box that surrounds the pencil symbol and press Enter when the lower right corner is below the right edge of the clip on the clipboard.

Figure 9.35 shows the logo with the clipboard and pencil symbols in place.

To complete the logo, add the name of the company and division on the clipboard. To add text to your symbol, use the following procedure:

1. Press Esc to return to the Draw menu. Select Add and then select Text from the Add menu.

2. Type *Superior* in the prompt line and press F8 (Options) to set the options for this and the remaining text.

3. Press Enter to leave the Text Size at 5.5. Set Color to 15 to set the color to Yellow. Press the down-arrow key to highlight Fill and set Fill to Yes.

Fig. 9.35.

The logo with two symbols.

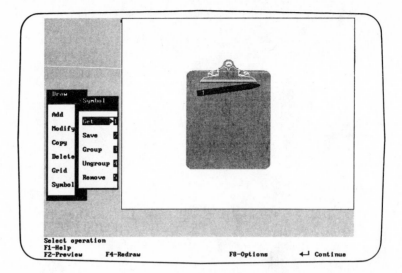

4. Press the down-arrow key to highlight Bold and set Bold to Yes. Set Italic, Undrlin, and Shadow to No.

5. Press the down-arrow key to pass Shadow Color and highlight the Align option. Position the Align highlight at the center base position, using the space bar. Press Enter to move the cursor to Font.

6. Select the Executive font and press Enter to position the text box.

7. Use the arrow keys to position the text box so that the crosshairs are under the pencil symbol and centered on the clipboard. Press Enter to draw the text.

8. Type *Office* and press Enter twice to position the second word under the first.

9. Type *Supplies* and press Enter twice to position the third word under the first two.

10. Type *Writing Tools Division* and press F8 (Options) to modify options for the division's name.

11. Change Size to 3.5, set Color to Red 12, set Italic to Yes, and change Font to Traditional. Press Enter to summon the text box containing the words *Writing Tools Division*.

12. Use the arrow keys to position the text box at the bottom of the clipboard and press Enter to draw the words.

Figure 9.36 shows the finished logo.

Fig. 9.36.

The completed logo.

Grouping and Ungrouping Symbols

Using the Group command, you can gather together all the individual objects within a drawing so that they can be modified as one object. After you group the objects in your logo, save the objects as a symbol in the OFFICE4.SYM file. To group the objects in your logo, follow this procedure:

1. Select Symbol from the Draw menu.

2. Select Group from the Symbol menu.

3. Move the cursor to above the top left corner of the logo and press Enter to anchor the first corner of the selection box.

4. Press PgDn to position the box around all the items in the logo and press Enter. Harvard Graphics places four small boxes around each object in the picture (see fig. 9.37).

5. Press Enter to select Choose this from the bottom of the screen. Press Esc to group the selected objects. When you press Esc, the small boxes surrounding the objects disappear. Harvard Graphics now treats all the items as one object.

To verify that the objects are one group, select Modify Options, position the cursor in the middle of the logo, and press Enter. Notice that small boxes surround the entire group of objects as shown in figure 9.38.

Fig. 9.37.

Boxes surrounding all items in a group.

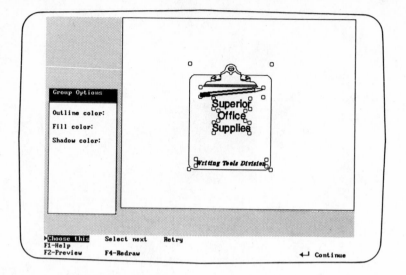

Fig. 9.38.

Four small boxes surrounding the grouped logo.

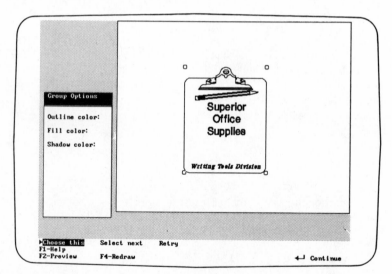

If you want to change only one object in the group, you first must ungroup the objects. To ungroup the objects, select Symbol from the Draw menu and select Ungroup from the Symbol menu. Highlight the group you want to separate and press Enter. Each object in the group is treated as an individual object again. In the next section, you save the logo as a symbol. If you have ungrouped the objects, take a minute to regroup the objects before continuing.

Saving a Group of Objects as a Symbol

To save the logo as a symbol into an existing library, follow this procedure:

1. Select Symbol from the Draw menu.

2. Select Save from the Symbol menu.

3. Highlight the group so that the four small boxes surround it.

4. Press Enter to select Choose this.

5. To highlight a symbol library file name, use the down-arrow key. In this case, highlight OFFICE4.SYM and press Enter to save the object in the symbol library.

Check to see that the symbol was saved in OFFICE4.SYM by selecting Get from the Symbol menu; then select the OFFICE4.SYM library. When the library is drawn on-screen, your logo symbol is positioned in the third box of the top row of the symbol library. Figure 9.39 shows the OFFICE4.SYM library with the added logo symbol.

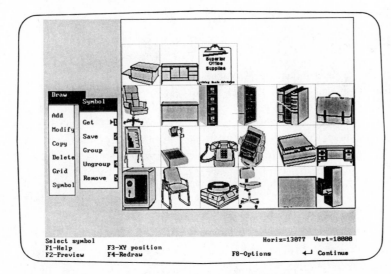

Fig. 9.39.

The OFFICE4 symbol library with the logo.

You can use the logo symbol just as you would use any other symbol on an existing chart. Try adding your logo symbol to your text and graph sales chart, SOSRVBX, which you created earlier in this chapter. The results look like figure 9.40.

Fig. 9.40.

The logo symbol on SOSRVBX.

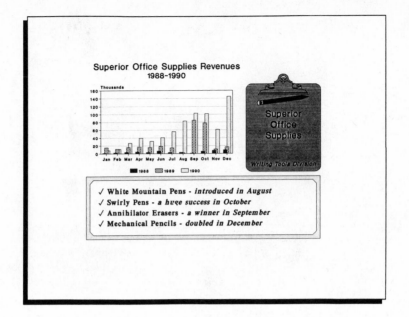

Saving and Modifying a Chart as a Symbol

You also can save an entire chart as a symbol. When you save a chart as a symbol, each element in that chart is treated as an object made in Draw/Annotate. For example, when a bar chart is converted to a symbol, the bars are treated as boxes. In a pie chart, the slices of the pie become polygons. The text of the chart—the title, subtitle, footnote, and labels—is interpreted in Draw/Annotate as text, and so on. For charts that do not change, saving as a symbol is a useful tool. If the data or elements of a chart are expected to go through a lot of change, however, then saving as a symbol is not a wise choice.

Retrieve the linked pie chart named SOS2HLK that you created in Chapter 6 to show second-half revenues. To save this chart as a symbol, follow these steps:

1. Press Esc at the chart display and Esc again at the Pie Chart 1 Data screen to return to the main menu.

2. Select Get/Save/Remove from the main menu and Save As Symbol from the Get/Save/Remove menu.

3. The cursor is on Symbol Will Be Saved As on the Save Chart As Symbol overlay. Type the name *sos2hpic* (for "second-half picture") and press Enter to move the cursor to For Device.

4. Select the output device you want to use (printer or plotter), press the space bar to highlight the device, and press Enter to confirm your choice.

Because you typed a new symbol library name, another overlay appears for you to type a description. If you type the name of an existing symbol library, the chart is added to the library directly. Figure 9.41 shows the sequence of overlays.

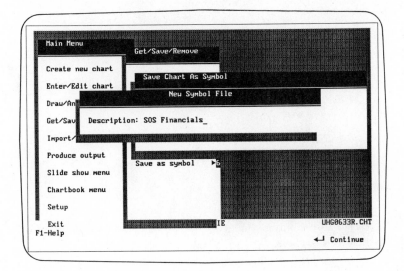

Fig. 9.41.

Overlays when saving as a symbol.

After you save a chart as a symbol, you can retrieve and ungroup the symbol as described earlier in this chapter. Then using Modify from the Draw menu, you can change the appearance of a bar chart by moving individual bars or by changing the size or placement of text. You also may want to delete certain bars or text on the chart. To modify the pie chart symbol, follow this procedure:

1. Create a free-form text chart by selecting Create New Chart from the main menu, Text from the Create New Chart menu, and Free Form from the Text menu.

2. Press F4 (Draw/Annotate) from the Free Form Text data screen to summon Draw/Annotate.

3. Select Symbol from the Draw menu and Get from the Symbol menu. Retrieve the symbol library you just made: SOS2HPIC. Figure 9.42 shows the SOS2HPIC library as it appears on the screen.

4. Position the cursor on the pie chart symbol and press Enter. The Draw/Annotate screen appears again. Notice that a symbol does not appear to be on the screen. Because the pie chart is the size of the entire screen, the box surrounding the symbol also fills the entire screen, and you cannot see that a symbol is in memory.

Fig. 9.42.

*The SOS2HPIC
symbol library.*

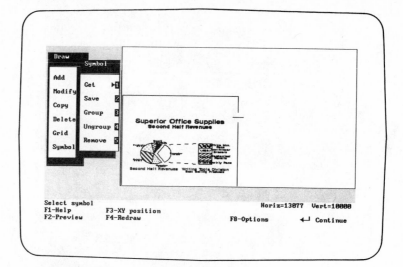

5. Press Backspace to break the symbol anchor. Press F3 (XY Position), type *1000* at the Horiz= space, type *19000* at Vert=, and press Enter. Press Enter again to set the first corner of the box surrounding the symbol.

6. Press PgDn several times to open the box surrounding your symbol and press Enter when you see Horiz=20000 and Horiz=3000. Press Enter again. The symbol is drawn on-screen. Figure 9.43 shows the repositioned symbol.

7. Select Ungroup from the Symbol menu, position the cursor on the symbol, and press Enter. Four small boxes surround the symbol. Press Enter again to ungroup the symbol.

8. Press Esc to return to the Draw menu and select Modify.

9. Select Move from the Modify menu and position the cursor on the September slice.

10. Use the arrow keys to move the September slice to cut it from the pie. Figure 9.44 shows the September slice cut from the pie symbol.

You can see that when a pie chart is saved as a symbol, you can "ungroup" the symbol and change its appearance by altering individual components. In the next section of this chapter, you learn how to use the special drawing tools that Harvard Graphics offers.

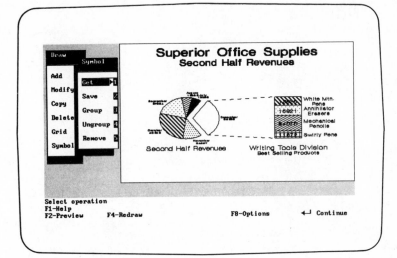

Fig. 9.43.

The repositioned symbol.

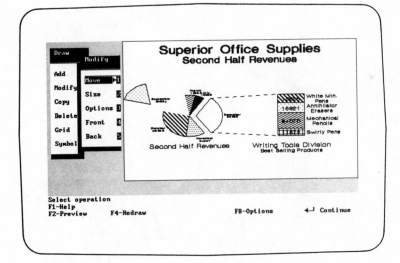

Fig. 9.44.

The cut September slice.

Using Special Drawing Tools

Harvard Graphics offers two helpful drawing tools that you can use to "line up"
and position the objects you are drawing: the Grid feature and the cursor position
indicators. You can turn these tools on and off as you draw in Draw/Annotate to
reduce the chance of producing a crooked chart.

Using the Grid Feature

With Harvard Graphics' Grid feature, you can display a grid made up of dots arranged in a regular pattern behind any objects or text you place on the page. When Snap is turned on, each dot on the grid acts like a magnet, pulling objects and aligning them with the horizontal and vertical grid lines.

To use a grid, select Grid from the Draw menu and complete the Grid Options panel:

Size   The size of the intervals between grid points is a number between 1 and 25 that is a percentage of the shorter side of the drawing board. A good grid size to work with is 4, the default grid setting. With a setting of 4, the grid has 25 rows of dots.

Show   If you want to show the grid, select Yes. If you prefer not to look at the grid, select No. When you remove a grid by turning off Show, you should press F4 (Redraw) to clean up the screen.

Snap   Use Snap to turn on the magnet effect for each dot in the grid. Use Snap with Show set to Yes. Turning on Snap doesn't affect the objects you already have drawn.

Figure 9.45 shows the Draw/Annotate screen with the grid set at 4.

Fig. 9.45.

A grid where Size = 4.

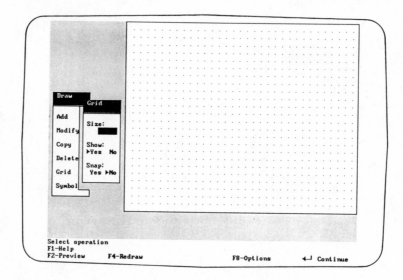

Using Cursor Position Indicators

As you have seen in the procedures in this chapter, you can use Draw/Annotate's cursor position indicators to set the points of your objects with precision. Press F3 to set manually the position of the cursor in any Draw/Annotate operation. When the cursor is at the lower left corner of the screen, Horiz= and Vert= should be at 1. As you move the cursor up the screen, the Vert= number increases. As you move the cursor to the right, the Horiz= number increases.

Setting Draw/Annotate's Defaults

If you are accustomed to adding text with a size of 3 and box type 4 when you use Draw/Annotate, you will appreciate the default settings feature in Draw/Annotate. When you set Draw/Annotate defaults, Harvard Graphics uses those settings when first displaying each options panel. To summon the Draw/Annotate Default Options menu, press F8 (Options) at the main Draw menu (see fig. 9.46).

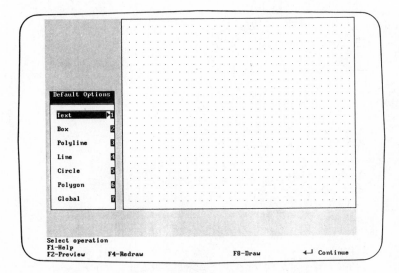

Fig. 9.46.

The Default Options panel.

When you choose to set defaults for one of the options, the options panel shown is exactly the same as the options panel you use when adding or modifying the object you selected. Of course, you always can change the setting for an object as you are drawing by pressing F8 before pressing Enter the second time to confirm your choice.

To set defaults, tab through the options, highlight the default you want to set, and press Enter to make your choice and move to the next option. Press F10 to return to the Draw menu to continue with your drawing.

You also can choose global options, which are unique in Draw/Annotate. When you select Global from the Default Options menu, the Global Options panel appears (see fig. 9.47). After you set the global options, all objects you create are preset to those options.

Fig. 9.47.

The Global Options panel.

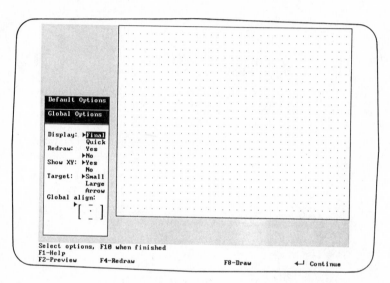

The Global Options panel includes the following options:

Display	Set Display to Final to view the most accurate picture of the finished work, including all the details in your graphic. Setting Display to Quick displays the chart faster, but bold text does not display.
Redraw	Selecting Yes at this prompt directs Harvard Graphics to redraw the graphic each time you make a change. If you select No at Redraw, the chart is redrawn only when you press F4. As a result, you may see blank spaces when you move, resize, or delete objects; and when you use the Back or Front feature, the results do not appear until you press F4.
Show XY	Select Yes at this prompt to display the Vert = and Horiz = numbers under the right side of the drawing board. These numbers are useful when you are lining up objects.

Target   The crosshairs on the drawing board are called a *target*. If
                you select Small, the target is the plus sign that you are
                accustomed to. If you select Large at this option, the
                crosshairs extend to the edges of the screen, making a
                large cross the entire size of the screen. If you select
                Arrow, the target appears as a diagonal arrow like the
                one shown in figure 9.48. You can use the arrow as you
                use the crosshairs.

Global Align   You can set the alignment point of the rectangle you use
                to position an object. The *alignment point* is the corner of
                the rectangle referred to by the XY position indicators.
                You always can reset the alignment of the target while
                you are drawing an individual object.

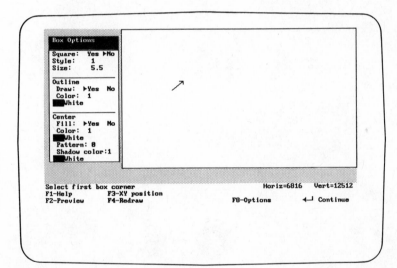

Fig. 9.48.

The target as an arrow.

Chapter Summary

In this chapter, you learned how to enhance charts by using Draw/Annotate. In
Draw/Annotate, you can add lines, circles, boxes, polylines, polygons, and symbols. You also learned how to create symbols from a group of objects and how to
create a symbol library from a graph or text chart. In the next chapter, you learn
about the newest addition to Harvard Graphics—Draw Partner.

10

Quick Start: Using Draw Partner

Whether you have wanted to draw pictures or enhance charts, Harvard Graphics has always offered you the features of Draw/Annotate. Now the newest addition to Harvard Graphics, Draw Partner, offers you far more.

When you need only to add a quick line or two to a chart, getting into and out of Draw/Annotate is quick and easy. For more complex tasks, however, use the new Draw Partner. Draw Partner, has all the features you learned about in Chapter 9, "Drawing with Harvard Graphics: Draw/Annotate." Just as with Draw/Annotate, with Draw Partner, you can enhance existing charts or start with a blank screen and create graphic illustrations from scratch.

But Draw Partner offers more than Draw/Annotate. Draw Partner's extensive features give you the ability to add perspective—rotate text or objects, flip objects so that they face in another direction, add shadows, or create text in a circle. With Draw Partner, you can create several objects—such as arcs and wedges— that are not available in Draw/Annotate, and you can even draw freehand with a mouse!

In the next few chapters, you learn in detail how to use Draw Partner. In this quick start, you examine features in Draw Partner that aren't available in Draw/Annotate. If you are familiar with Draw/Annotate, you see just how similar, but better, Draw Partner is.

Suppose that your company's president wants you to create a logo for Superior Office Supplies. In the past, you made a simple logo by using Draw/Annotate, but now you want to make a more sophisticated logo. You wisely decide to use the advanced features offered to you by Draw Partner.

Starting Draw Partner

To start Draw Partner, press F3 (Applications) at the Harvard Graphics main menu. The Applications menu appears (see fig. 10.1). When you install Harvard Graphics Version 2.3, two applications are added to the Applications menu: Draw Partner and AGX Slide Service.

Select Draw Partner by moving the highlight to the Draw Partner option and pressing Enter, or by just pressing 1. The message `Please wait...Loading Application` appears, and then the Draw Partner main menu appears.

You also can start Draw Partner by pressing Ctrl-D from most places within Harvard Graphics. Often, this method is quicker.

Fig. 10.1.

The Applications menu from the main menu.

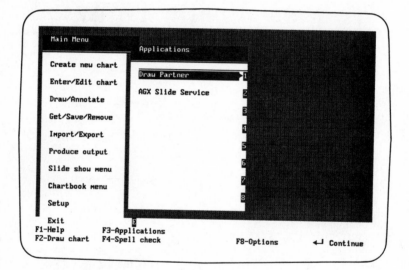

Reviewing the Draw Partner Main Menu

The Draw Partner main menu looks similar to the Draw/Annotate menu, but many more choices are available. Notice, for example, that Move and Size are choices on the Draw Partner main menu. In Draw/Annotate, Move and Size are options on the Modify menu. Also notice the availability of several new features: Point Edit, Align, Group, View, and File. These features are some of the highlights of Draw Partner's enhanced capabilities. If you have worked with Draw/Annotate, you will find the transition to Draw Partner simple, because most sequences of steps are the same.

The lower left corner of the screen always displays an instruction about the selection you are making. In figure 10.2, for example, the Add option is selected, and the instruction on the lower left corner of the screen is Add objects to the drawing. This is the first place to look if you are uncertain about what to do next or what a menu selection does.

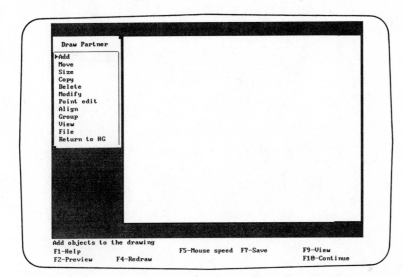

Fig. 10.2.

The Draw Partner main menu.

Two ways are available for you to use your keyboard to make Draw Partner main menu selections. You can highlight your choice by using the up- and down-arrow keys and then pressing Enter. You also can press the first letter of the choice. For example, if you press S at the main menu, Draw Partner interprets your choice as Size, and the instruction Select an object to size, Esc-menu is displayed in the lower left corner. If you press D at the main menu, a Delete menu appears in the upper left corner, and the message Select object to erase appears in the lower left corner. If two options start with the same letter (like Move and Modify, or Add and Align), Draw Partner starts at the top of the list and selects the first option that starts with that letter, and then the program cycles down to the next option when you press the first letter again.

Pressing the first letter of an option is the most efficient way to make a menu selection.

Creating Your Logo

Suppose that you're having lunch with the vice president of sales for Superior Office Supplies. You ask the vice president to sketch out what he or she would like to see for a new logo. The vice president roughs out a drawing on a cocktail napkin and suggests that the logo be made to look like a desk calendar sent to clients (see fig. 10.3).

Fig. 10.3.

The rough sketch of the logo.

Planning the Drawing

As you work with Draw Partner, you learn to plan out your drawing before starting. By planning each section of the logo in advance, you can concentrate on the details of each object without having to worry about the interaction among different parts of the finished picture. A little prior planning can make a big difference when you are working with Draw Partner.

For this quick start, you create the logo in three parts. In the first part, you turn on the grid and create the circular text with the file cabinet symbol. Then you can save that portion of the logo and clear the screen. The calendar portion of the logo is created next and saved as a second file. For the third part, you put it all together—circular text with the calendar—to finish the picture!

At the end of the chapter, you save the entire logo as a symbol so that the logo can be placed on any Harvard Graphics chart.

Setting a Grid

Because you are creating a company logo to be reproduced in a variety of methods, precision is critically important. After all, the logo will be printed on correspondence, business cards, and even boxes sent to clients with office supplies. The logo needs to be clean, and the placement of letters and objects within the logo must be exact.

A *grid* is one tool that Draw Partner provides to help place text and objects on the screen. Placing a grid on the screen is analagous to using graph paper for drawing. The grid can be set with large or small squares (large or small spaces between grid points). For the logo, you can set the squares small, but not so small that you cannot see the spaces between grid points. If you set the grid with large squares, the grid provides less precision in lining up objects.

To turn on the grid, follow this procedure:

1. Select View from the Draw Partner main menu. The View menu appears in the upper left corner of the screen.

2. Select Grid from the View menu (see fig. 10.4). The Grid menu appears in the upper left corner.

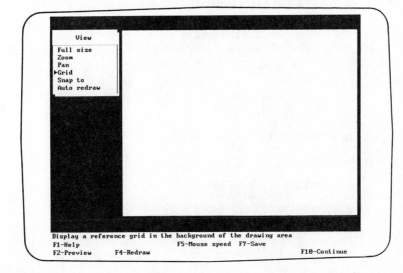

Fig. 10.4.

The View menu with Grid selected.

3. Toggle Grid On. The instruction Enter new grid size (Small=1, Large=25) appears at the bottom left corner. Press 4 and then Enter. The grid appears on the drawing portion of the screen.

4. Press Esc to return to the Draw Partner main menu.

The dots in a grid are only a drawing aid. The dots are displayed on the screen but do not print on your finished chart. In Chapters 9 and 11, the grid feature and the associated snap feature are described in more detail. The snap feature makes each point in the grid act like a magnet, attracting the corner of an object to a point on the grid. Snap is a powerful way to line up objects when you are using Draw Partner. For the purposes of this quick start, however, turning on the snap feature is not necessary. By looking at the grid, you can easily line up the objects you add.

Checking the Palette

In this example, you use the standard Harvard Graphics palette. Harvard Graphics Version 2.3 offers numerous color palettes, which are groups of related colors. When you first install Harvard Graphics, the default palette is HG23.PAL. You can verify that you are using the HG23 palette by selecting File from the Draw Partner main menu and then Palette from the File menu. All the available palettes are displayed. Use the arrow keys to highlight HG23 and press Enter to confirm your choice.

Creating the Text Portion of the Logo

To start the logo, you can use circular text and create the company name that will be on the left side of calendar. *Circular text* follows the perimeter of an invisible circle. With Draw Partner, you can place the text around the top or bottom of the circle. For this logo, place the text around the top of the circle. First, you should set the Circular Text options so that the created text is exactly the right size. To set the options and create the circular text, follow this procedure:

1. Select Add from the Draw Partner main menu.

2. Select Circular Text from the Add menu (see fig. 10.5).

Fig. 10.5.

The Circular Text Add menu.

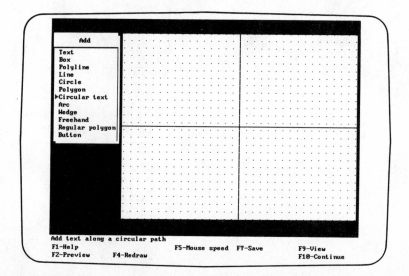

3. Press F8 (Options) to invoke the Circular Text options menu.

4. Highlight the Size option and press Enter. You see the prompt `Enter new text size (Small=0.01, Large=100.00, Current=8)`. (**Note:** The Current size setting is based on the last size setting used for circular text. This setting may vary.) Type *15* to indicate your desired text size and press Enter. Text size in Draw Partner is the same as text size in the rest of Harvard Graphics. Text size is equal to a set percentage of the short side of the page. (See Chapter 4 for more information about text size.)

5. Use the down-arrow key to highlight the Color option and press Enter. The color selection menu appears.

6. Use the arrow keys to highlight White-Sy and press Enter. Because you are creating a symbol that can be printed again and again in black and white, use the white color that can be saved as a symbol (White-Sy) rather than the white color listed as White-Ti. The White-Ti option is for titles in charts—not symbols. Figure 10.6 shows the color choices with the correct white selected.

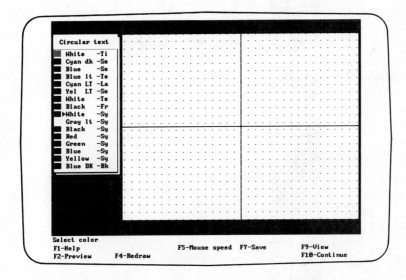

Fig. 10.6.

The Circular Text color options menu.

7. Use the down-arrow key to highlight Weight and press Enter to see the available choices.

8. Use the arrow keys to highlight Solid Bold and press Enter.

9. Press the down-arrow key twice to highlight Drop Shadow and press Enter. The shadow selection menu shown in figure 10.7 appears.

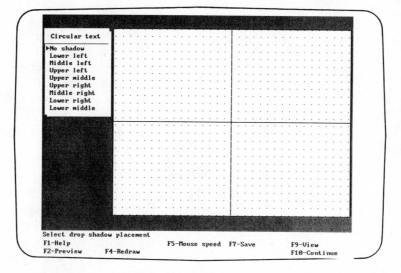

Fig. 10.7.

The Circular Text drop shadow menu.

10. Use the arrow keys to highlight No Shadow and press Enter to confirm your choice.

11. Press the down-arrow key twice to highlight Font and press Enter to see your choices.

12. Use the arrow keys to highlight Executive and press Enter to confirm your choice. The completed Circular Text options menu should look like the one shown in figure 10.8.

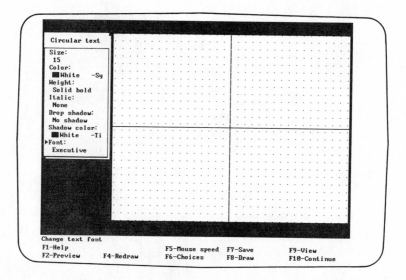

Fig. 10.8.

The Circular Text options.

13. Press F8 (Draw) to select the placement of your circular text. The choices you make are reflected in the options box in the top left corner of the screen. The drawing portion of the screen has crosshairs that you can use to outline the circle for your text.

14. Position the crosshairs at the exact middle of the screen and press Enter.

15. Press the PgDn key six or seven times to create a circle in which text will be placed and then press Enter. The top and bottom of the circle should be one grid point from the top and bottom of the screen. To move the crosshairs a greater distance between keystrokes, press the plus (+) key on the numeric keypad. Press the minus (−) key to decrease movement and set crosshair movement back to its original default. The Circular Text placement prompt box appears (see fig. 10.9).

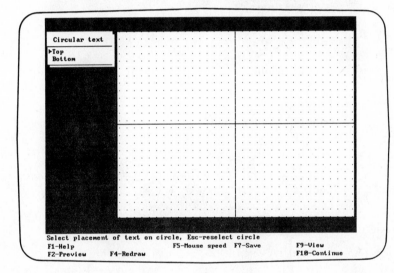

Fig. 10.9.

The Circular Text prompt box.

16. Use the arrow keys to highlight Top and press Enter.

17. Type *Superior Office Supplies*. Notice that on the drawing board, two thin delineating lines show the edges of the circular text as you type the words. Press Enter to draw the words. The resulting text should look like figure 10.10.

Later in this quick start, you save the circular text as a symbol. After it is saved as a symbol, the text can be easily resized or positioned on any other chart you create. Note that after you save circular text in Draw Partner, the text becomes a group of polygons. You cannot change the font or any of the other text features. You cannot change the typeface or use italics or shadows. You can change the outline color, line style, fill color, and pattern only by changing polygon options in Draw/Annotate.

Fig. 10.10.

The Circular Text logo.

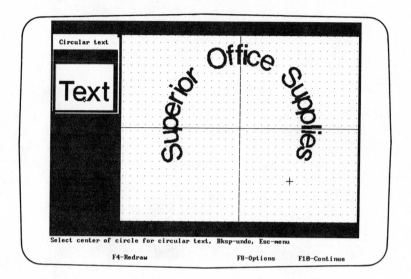

Drawing Arcs

To highlight the words in the logo, you can place outlines around the inside and outside of the words, using the Arc feature in Draw Partner. An arc is part of a circle.

The Add menu should still be displayed, so start from that menu and follow these steps to create the outlines (arcs) around the text:

1. Press Esc to return to the Add menu from the Circular Text menu and then select Arc.

2. Highlight Arc on the Draw Partner Add menu and press Enter. The current arc options are displayed in the options box at the upper left corner of the screen, and crosshairs appear on the drawing portion of the screen. The prompt Select center point of arc, Esc-menu is displayed in the lower left corner of the screen.

3. Press F8 (Options) to determine how you want the arc to appear. The Arc options overlay appears (see fig. 10.11).

4. Highlight the Color option and press Enter. Then use the arrow keys to select White-Sy on the color selection screen and press Enter to confirm your choice.

5. Press the down-arrow key to highlight Style and press Enter for the arc style choices.

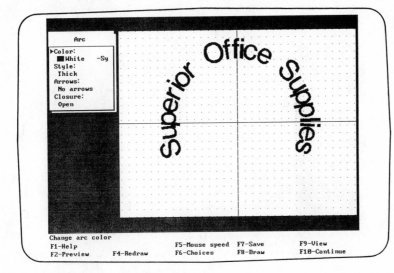

Fig. 10.11.

The Arc options menu.

6. Use the arrow keys to highlight Thick and press Enter to confirm your choice.

7. Use the down-arrow key to highlight Arrows and press Enter. Then highlight No Arrows and press Enter.

8. Use the down-arrow key to highlight Closure and press Enter to display the choices. Highlight Open and press Enter to confirm your choice.

9. Press F8 (Draw) to draw the arc. You see the prompt Select center point of arc, Esc-menu. Position the crosshairs at the exact middle of the grid and press Enter.

10. Position the crosshairs at the grid point that is six points in from the right of the screen and eight points up from the bottom of the screen. Press Enter to indicate where the arc should begin. Figure 10.12 shows the first point of the outside arc.

11. Use the PgUp and Home keys to move the arc around the circular text until the endpoint is positioned six points from the left edge of the drawing screen and eight points up from the bottom of the screen. Press Enter to confirm the endpoint. The arc is drawn around the outside of the circular text, as shown in figure 10.13.

12. Position the crosshairs at the exact center of the grid and press Enter to set the center of the inside arc.

13. Use the PgDn and arrow keys to position the first point of the arc at the grid point that is 10 points in from the right of the screen and 9 points up from the bottom of the screen and press Enter.

Fig. 10.12.

The first point of the outside arc.

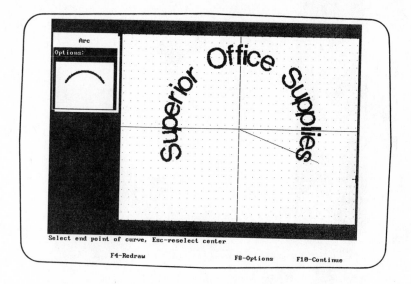

Fig. 10.13.

The completed outside arc.

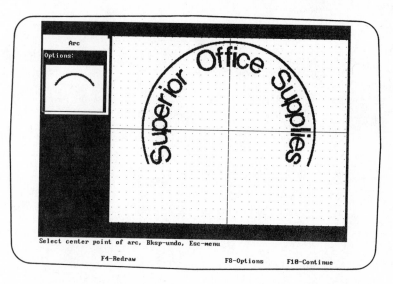

14. Use the arrow and Home keys to draw the arc and position the endpoint so that it's 10 points in from the left edge of the screen and 9 points up from the bottom of the screen. Press Enter to draw the inside arc. Figure 10.14 displays the circular text with both arcs drawn.

15. Press Esc twice to return to the Draw Partner main menu.

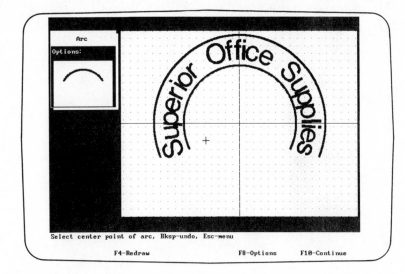

Fig. 10.14.

The circular text with top and bottom arcs.

Placing a Symbol

Now you're going to place a symbol inside the circular text. You can use the extensive symbol libraries of Harvard Graphics to highlight the concept of office supplies. A file cabinet is perfect. Fortunately, several file cabinets are available in the predrawn symbol libraries that come with the software. The symbol libraries (shown in Appendix A) are a good place to check when you want to draw a familiar object. Artists at Software Publishing Corporation already may have drawn the object for you and stored the object in the symbol libraries.

Pictures that you draw and want to use again also can be saved as symbols. You can use these symbols in any chart.

A symbol also can be a group of objects that Draw Partner interprets as one object. The benefit of having several objects appear as one object is that you can modify all the objects included in the group together. Grouping of objects is described more fully in Chapter 9.

To retrieve a file cabinet symbol from the symbol libraries, follow this procedure:

1. Highlight File on the Draw Partner main menu and press Enter. The File menu appears in the upper left corner of the screen (see fig. 10.15). Select Get Symbol.

   Note: If you have installed Harvard Graphics Version 2.3, the install program created a directory called SYMBOLS, which is a subdirectory of your main Harvard Graphics directory. If that directory is not listed on the top

Fig. 10.15.

The File menu before pressing Enter.

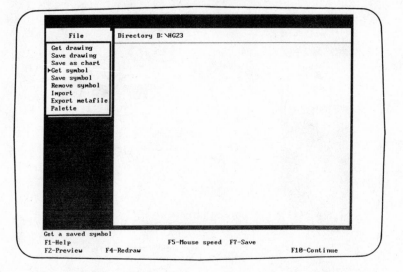

line of your screen, press F3 (Change Dir), highlight the directory line by using the arrow keys, and press Enter. The prompt line instructs Enter the name of another directory. Type the name of the SYMBOLS subdirectory and press Enter. For example, the symbol directory illustrated in figure 10.16 is D:\HG23\SYMBOLS.

Fig. 10.16.

The symbols directory.

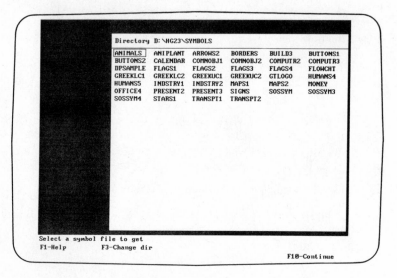

2. Use the arrow keys to position the box around the OFFICE4 symbol library and press Enter. The OFFICE4 symbol library is drawn on the screen (see fig. 10.17).

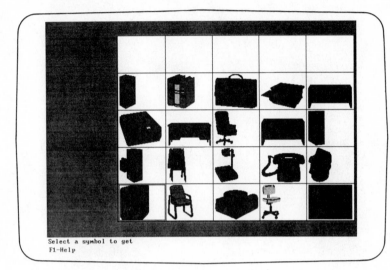

```
Select a symbol to get
F1-Help
```

Fig. 10.17.

The OFFICE4.SYM library.

3. Select the open file cabinet symbol by moving the arrow keys until a box surrounds that symbol. Press Enter to confirm your choice. The Directory screen appears.

4. Press Esc to return to the drawing board. The original drawing is constructed on the screen, with the open file cabinet in the middle.

Flipping the Symbol

You can improve your logo's appearance by "flipping" (rotating) the file cabinet to the right and positioning it correctly within the circular text. Fortunately, Draw Partner has a feature for flipping an object.

To turn the file cabinet so that it faces to the right, follow this procedure:

1. Select Modify from the Draw Partner main menu. The Modify menu appears (see fig. 10.18).

2. Use the arrow keys to highlight Flip and press Enter to confirm your choice. The Flip overlay appears in the upper left corner.

3. Select Horizontal. The prompt line in the lower left corner displays Select an object to flip, Esc-menu.

Fig. 10.18.

The Modify menu.

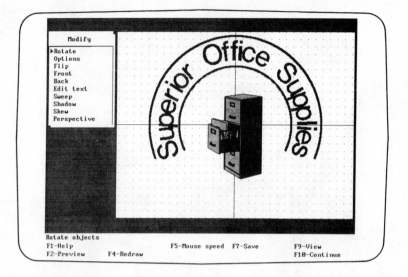

4. Position the crosshairs in the middle of the file cabinet and press Enter. The prompt box in the upper left corner of the screen displays

   ```
   This object
   Next object
   ```

   Select Next Object until four small boxes surround the file cabinet, as shown in figure 10.19.

Fig. 10.19.

Selecting the object to flip.

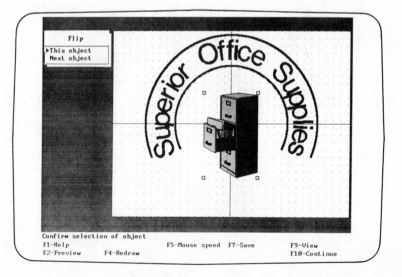

5. When the four small boxes surround the file cabinet, highlight This Object and press Enter. The symbol flips to face the other direction.

6. Press Esc twice to return to the Draw Partner main menu.

Moving the Symbol

Using the Move command from the Draw Partner main menu, you can position the flipped file cabinet in the middle of the circular text.

Moving is an easy operation in Draw Partner. To move the file cabinet, follow these steps:

1. Select Move from the Draw Partner main menu.

2. Highlight the file cabinet by selecting Next Object until the four small boxes surround the file cabinet. Then highlight This Object and press Enter.

3. Use the arrow keys to position the move box so that its lower left corner is 14 grid points from the left side of the screen and its lower right corner is 13 grid points in from the right side of the screen. The bottom line should be 8 grid points from the bottom of the screen.

4. Press Enter to confirm the position of the file cabinet.

Figure 10.20 shows the finished drawing with the flipped file cabinet moved into position.

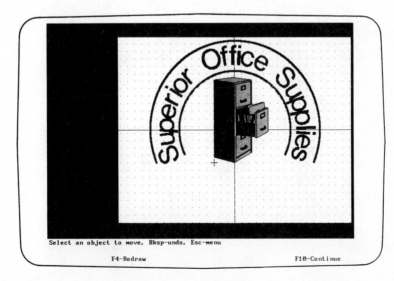

Fig. 10.20.

The finished drawing.

Saving a Drawing as a Symbol

Later, you will want to use the circular text and file cabinet logo in your desk calendar. Therefore, you should save what you have created thus far as a symbol. Then you can use this symbol in any other chart you make. If you save this picture as a chart rather than a symbol, you cannot bring the picture into another chart type.

To save the circular text and file cabinet logo as a symbol, follow this procedure:

1. Press Esc to return to the Draw Partner main menu.

2. Select File, and the File menu appears.

3. Select Save Symbol. The directory of files is displayed, and New File has a box around it.

4. While the box is around New File, press Enter to create a symbol file. The instruction line at the bottom of the screen displays Enter new filename.

5. Type *sossym* and press Enter. WAIT appears in the lower right corner of the screen. The file SOSSYM is saved as a symbol.

6. Press Esc to return to the Draw Partner main menu.

Clearing the Screen

Next, you clear the screen and create the desk calendar. (Later, you place the circular text and file cabinet logo on this calendar. Because you previously saved the circular text and file cabinet as a symbol, you easily can retrieve them later.)

Whenever you want to start with a clear screen, follow this procedure:

1. Select Delete from the Draw Partner main menu.

2. Select the Everything option from the Delete menu.

3. Select Clear Drawing from the second Delete menu. The drawing screen becomes blank, and the main menu appears.

Making the Desk Calendar

You now are ready to make the desk calendar. You can construct the calendar by creating and modifying two basic boxes: one for the base and another for the pages of the calendar. To make the page box look like numerous pages, you can use a Draw Partner feature called Sweep, which redraws an object multiple times. After the pages have been swept on one side, they can be swept again on the other side so that the page boxes appear on both sides of the calendar box.

Then, to complete the desk calendar, you add arcs to represent the rings on the calendar and add address text to the calendar base.

Making the Calendar Base Box

To make the desk calendar in which you will place the circular text symbol, follow these steps:

1. Select Add from the Draw Partner main menu and select Box from the Add menu. The box that was made last appears in the upper left corner.

2. Press F8 (Options) to summon the Box options menu.

3. Select the Shape option to determine whether the box is square or rectangular. Highlight Rectangular and press Enter.

4. Press the down-arrow key once to highlight Box Style and press Enter to summon the Box styles overlay (see fig. 10.21). Select 3-D, and the 3-D Box menu appears.

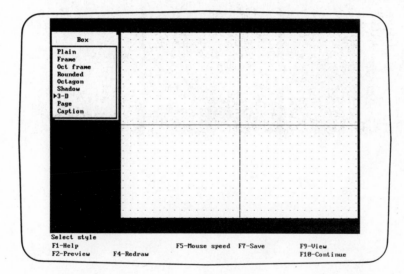

Fig. 10.21.

The Box styles overlay.

5. Highlight Bottom Left and press Enter to confirm your choice.

6. Press the down-arrow key to highlight Size and press Enter to determine the size (depth) of your 3-D box. The Size option for a three-dimensional

box determines the depth of the third dimension. In this case, an appropriate depth is 35. Type *35* and press Enter.

7. Press the down-arrow key to highlight Outline Color and press Enter to view the outline color choices. Select White-Sy.

8. Press the down-arrow key to highlight Outline Style and press Enter to summon the outline style options. Select Solid.

9. Press the down-arrow key to highlight Fill Color. Press Enter to see the color options. Highlight Background and press Enter to confirm your choice.

10. Press the down-arrow key to highlight Pattern and press Enter to view the pattern options. Highlight Hollow (so that there is no pattern) and press Enter to confirm your choice. Figure 10.22 shows the completed Box options panel.

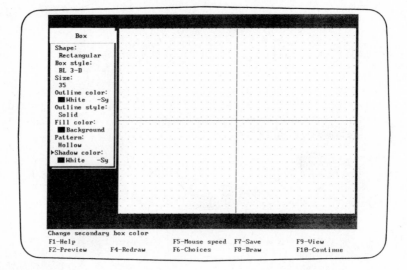

Fig. 10.22.

The completed Box options panel for the base box.

11. Press F8 (Draw) to move to the drawing board. The crosshairs appear on the drawing board, and the prompt Select corner of box, Esc-menu appears at the lower left corner.

12. Position the crosshairs so that they are five grid points down and four grid points in from the upper left corner of the drawing board. Press Enter to anchor the upper left corner of the box.

13. Use the PgDn key to open the box so that the lower right corner is four grid points up and four grid points in from the right edge of the screen. Press Enter to draw the box. Figure 10.23 shows the completed box.

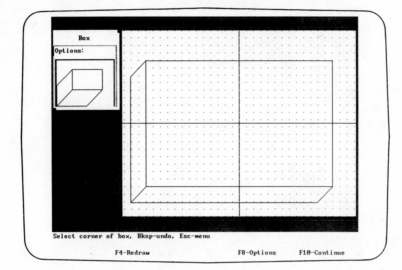

Fig. 10.23.

The completed base box.

Making the Calendar Page Box

While you are still in the Box Add feature of Draw Partner, make the box that forms a page of the calendar. You can make the page on the right side of the calendar and then copy the page over to the left side of the calendar later. To make the page, follow this procedure:

1. Press F8 (Options) to change the Box options. A single page is not a three-dimensional box, but a simple box.

2. Press the down-arrow key to highlight Box Style and press Enter. The Box Styles overlay appears.

3. Use the up-arrow key to highlight Plain and press Enter.

4. Press the down-arrow key five times to highlight Pattern and press Enter.

5. Select Solid from the pattern menu and press Enter. Because all the other Box options should be the same as they were for the first box, you are ready to draw. Figure 10.24 shows the completed Box options panel for the page box.

6. Press F8 (Draw) to return to the drawing board. Position the crosshairs one-half of a grid point in from the center and one grid point down from the top of the base box and press Enter to set the first point of the page.

7. Press PgDn and the down-arrow key several times to open the box until the lower right corner is one-half of a grid point up and one-half of a grid point in from the bottom right corner of the base box. Press Enter to draw the box. Figure 10.25 shows the completed page box.

Fig. 10.24.

*The completed Box
options panel for the
page box.*

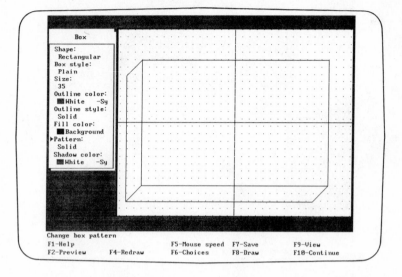

Fig. 10.25.

*The completed page
box.*

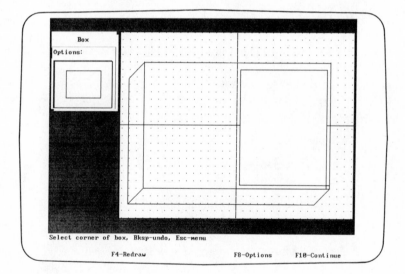

Sweeping the Page Box

To make the on-screen calendar look as if it has many pages (as many pages as
the days of the year), you can copy the page box by using the Draw Partner
Sweep tool. When you use the Sweep feature, an object is copied repeatedly within the parameters you define. In this case, you draw the page
repeatedly toward the screen's midline shown on the grid.

You can combine the sweep of the box with other tools in Draw Partner as well. For example, you can have the object move from a start position to an end position, getting smaller at the end position, which creates the appearance of a stack of cards swept across a table.

To sweep the initial page box, follow these steps:

1. Select Modify from the Draw Partner main menu.

2. Select Sweep from the Modify menu. The crosshairs appear on the drawing board, and the prompt line reads Select an object to sweep, Esc-menu.

3. Position the crosshairs on the page box and press Enter. Four small boxes surround the page box, and the prompt Select location for final object of sweep, Esc-no sweep appears.

If the four small boxes surround the base box rather than the page box, select Next Object in the prompt box in the upper left corner of the screen until the four small boxes surround the page box. Then highlight This Object in the prompt box and press Enter to confirm your choice.

To define the end object of the sweep, follow these steps:

1. Use the arrow keys to position the highlighted box in the right side of the base box so that the lower left corner of the sweep box is one grid point up from the bottom and one-half of a grid point to the left of the midline of the screen. Press Enter to confirm your choice. Figure 10.26 shows the position of the end sweep box at this point in the procedure.

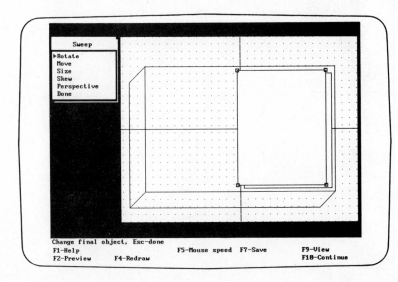

Fig. 10.26.

The initial placement of the end sweep box.

2. Select Move from the Sweep menu.

3. Use the left-arrow key to move the sweep box against the left edge of the underlying page box, while in the same position vertically on the screen (up one grid point from the bottom of the base box), and press Enter.

4. Select Size from the Sweep menu, position the right side of the page box one-half of a grid point in from the right edge of the original page box, and press Enter.

5. Press Esc to continue the sweep action, without altering the end object any further. The prompt line displays Enter number of intermediate objects (1..50). In other words, how many pages do you want to show between the first page and the last? Press 5 and then press Enter to complete the sweep. Figure 10.27 shows the completed sweep pages.

Fig. 10.27.

The completed sweep.

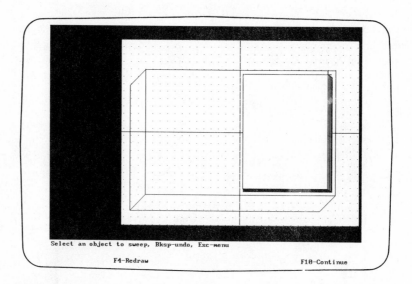

6. Press Esc twice to return to the Draw Partner main menu.

Copying and Flipping the Page

You now can copy the pages created on the right side of the base and flip them over so that the sweep is to the left rather than the right. The following procedure creates the effect of pages on both sides of the base box:

1. Select Copy from the Draw Partner main menu. The prompt Select an object to copy, Esc-menu appears.

2. Position the crosshairs in the middle of the swept page box and press Enter. Four small boxes should surround the page box. If the four boxes don't surround the page box, select Next Object in the Copy prompt box until they do. Then select This Object in the Copy prompt box. The prompt line displays Select location for copied object, Esc-no change.

3. Position the page box on the left side of the base box so that the right edge of the box is one-half of a grid point in from the left of the midline, and the top and bottom are at the same position of the top and bottom lines of the original page box. Press Enter to copy. Figure 10.28 shows the copied page box.

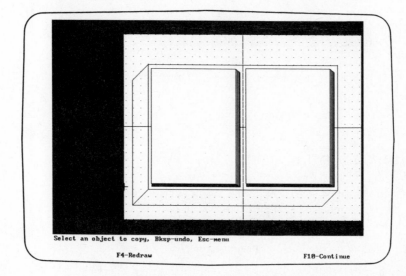

Fig. 10.28.

The copied pages.

4. Press Esc to return to the Draw Partner main menu and select Modify.

5. Select Flip from the Modify menu. The Flip prompt box appears in the upper left corner, and the prompt line displays Select copy method.

6. Highlight Horizontal in the Flip prompt box and press Enter. The prompt line displays Select an object to flip, Esc-menu.

7. Position the crosshairs on the left page box and press Enter. The four small boxes should surround that box. The Flip prompt box appears in the upper left corner, and the prompt line displays Confirm selection of object. Highlight This Object in the Flip prompt box and press Enter. The pages are drawn on the left side of the calendar base. Figure 10.29 shows the completed picture at this point.

Fig. 10.29.

The flipped calendar
pages.

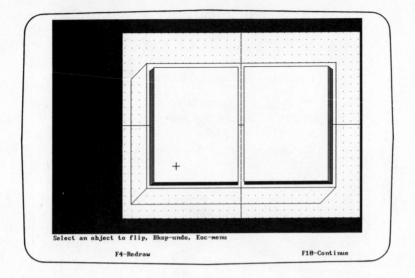

Select an object to flip, Bksp-undo, Esc-menu

F4-Redraw   F10-Continue

8. Press Esc twice to return to the Draw Partner main menu.

Adding the Calendar Symbol

At this point in the quick start, you have a base box with pages on the left and right side, but the graphic still doesn't look like a desk calendar. Fortunately, Harvard Graphics Version 2.3 has some terrific calendar symbols you can use.

Follow this procedure to retrieve and place the calendar on the right page:

1. Select File from the Draw Partner main menu and then select Get Symbol from the Draw Partner File menu.

2. Select the CALENDAR symbol library from the directory of symbols by positioning the highlight box around the word CALENDAR and pressing Enter. The symbol library is drawn on the screen, and the prompt Select a symbol to get appears.

3. Select the daily calendar, which is the second symbol from the left in the top row of the symbol library. To select that calendar, press the up-arrow key twice and the right-arrow key once and then press Enter.

4. Press Esc to return to the original drawing. The calendar is drawn on top of the midline of your original drawing. Figure 10.30 shows the drawing with the retrieved calendar symbol.

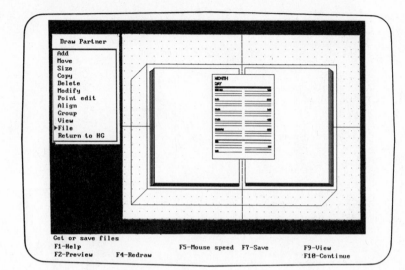

Fig. 10.30.

The drawing with the calendar symbol.

Positioning the Calendar

The next step is to position the calendar on the right pages of the base box. Then you must resize the calendar to fit the right pages of the base box.

Follow this procedure to position and resize the calendar:

1. Select Move from the Draw Partner main menu and highlight the calendar symbol by positioning the crosshairs on it. Then select Next Object in the Move prompt box until the four small boxes surround the symbol. Highlight This Object in the prompt box and press Enter.

2. Position the lower left corner of the calendar symbol move box on top of the lower left corner of the right page box and press Enter to confirm your choice. Figure 10.31 shows the moved calendar at this point in the quick start.

3. Press Esc to return to the Draw Partner main menu, highlight Size, and press Enter. The prompt line displays Select an object to size, Esc-menu.

4. Position the crosshairs on the calendar symbol. When the four small boxes surround the symbol, make sure that This Object is highlighted in the Size prompt box and press Enter.

5. Press the right-arrow key three times and the up-arrow key four times so that the upper right corner of the calendar is directly on top of the upper right corner of the right page box. Press Enter to draw the resized calendar. Figure 10.32 shows the resized calendar.

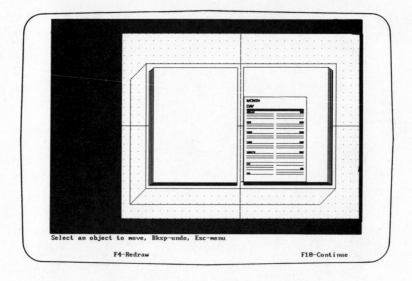

Fig. 10.31.

The initially moved calendar symbol.

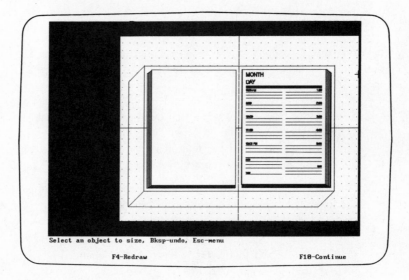

Fig. 10.32.

The resized calendar.

6. Press Esc to return to the Draw Partner main menu.

Adding the Rings to the Calendar

Now the only things missing from your desk calendar are the rings. You can create rings by adding arcs to your calendar. Most desk calendars have three or six rings. For this quick start, add six rings by following these steps:

1. Select Add from the Draw Partner main menu and select Arc from the Add menu. If you have followed this quick start from the beginning, the arc that appears in the options box should be the same as the one you made earlier, and you do not need to modify the options.

   Note: If you have changed the arc options since you started, press F8 (Options) to change them back. Take a look back at figure 10.11 to check the option settings.

2. Position the crosshairs at the center line, one grid point down from the top of the base box. Press Enter to set the first arc center point. The prompt line `Select start point of curve, Esc-reselect center` appears.

3. Press the left-arrow key to set the start point of the curve and press Enter. The left side start point of the arc should be one grid point to the left of the center line. The prompt line `Select endpoint of curve, Esc-reselect center` appears.

4. Press the up-arrow key once and the right-arrow key three times to position the endpoint of the arc on the right side of the calendar. Press Enter to draw the arc. Figure 10.33 shows the first arc drawn on the calendar.

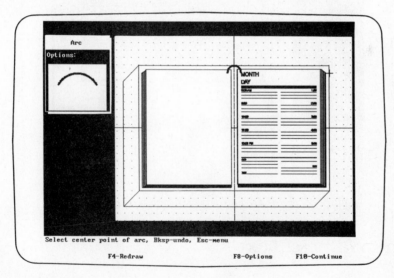

Fig. 10.33.

The arc-ring on the calendar.

5. Press Esc twice to return to the Draw Partner main menu and select Copy. The prompt line `Select an object to copy, Esc-menu` appears.

6. When the four small boxes surround the arc, position the crosshairs on the arc and press Enter with This Object highlighted in the prompt box.

7. Press the down-arrow key once and press Enter to position the second arc one grid point below the first.

8. Press Enter to draw the third arc one grid point below the second.

9. Press the down-arrow key 10 times and press Enter to position the top of the lower set of rings (the ring that is the farthest from the base of the calendar).

10. Use the down-arrow key to position the second bottom ring just below the first bottom ring. Press Enter to draw the second bottom ring.

11. Press Enter again to draw the third bottom ring. Figure 10.34 shows the drawing with the completed rings.

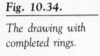

Fig. 10.34.

The drawing with completed rings.

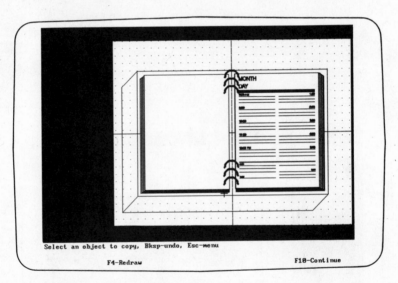

12. Press Esc to return to the Draw Partner main menu.

Adding the Address Text

To complete your calendar, you need to add your company's address and phone number. To add text to your calendar picture, follow this procedure:

1. Select Add from the Draw Partner main menu.

2. Select Text from the Add menu.

3. Press F8 (Options) to select the text options for the address text. The Text options panel appears in the upper left corner of the screen.

4. Select the Size option. Then press 2 at the prompt line and Enter to confirm your choice.

5. Press the down-arrow key to highlight Color and press Enter to view the color choices. Select White-Sy.

6. Press the down-arrow key to highlight Weight and press Enter. Select Solid Bold.

   All other options should be just as you set them for the circular text earlier in this chapter, so you should not need to alter them. Figure 10.35 shows the completed Text options menu. However, if you have produced text in another chart and altered these options, you should change them back to those shown in figure 10.35.

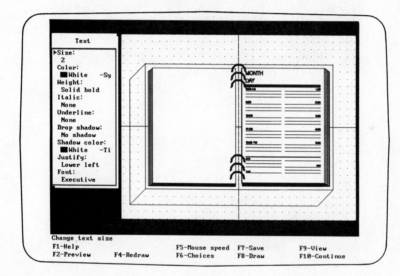

Fig. 10.35.

The Text options panel.

7. Press F8 (Draw) to type the text. The prompt line `Select location for text, Esc-menu` appears.

8. Position the crosshairs under the lower left edge of the calendar base (in the third dimension) and press Enter to set the location of the text. The prompt line `Enter a line of text, F8-character options, Esc-no text entered` appears.

9. Type *10 Holden Street Suite J Tinton Falls, N.J. 07724* and press Enter. The outline of the words appears on the drawing board as you type the text. When you press Enter, the words appear on the drawing board, and the crosshairs are positioned for a second line of text.

10. Type the second line of text, *201-530-8566*, and press Enter. Figure 10.36 shows the completed address text lines.

Fig. 10.36.

The completed address text lines.

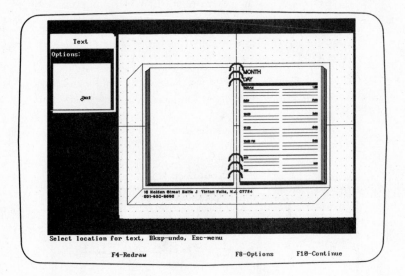

11. Press Esc twice to return to the Draw Partner main menu.

Saving the Calendar Drawing

Just as you saved the circular text drawing as a symbol in the first half of this chapter, you should save the calendar drawing as a symbol before adding the circular text. Then when you combine the circular text symbol with the calendar, you have to work with only two objects instead of the multiple objects included in each part. Currently, the calendar consists of 12 objects: the base box, the right and left page boxes, the calendar symbol, the six rings, and two lines of text. Saving all these objects as one symbol reduces them to just one object.

The next part of this chapter involves putting the two symbols (the calendar and the circular text) together. To make that job easier, do some planning now. For example, you know that the circular text symbol will be placed on the left calendar page and that the symbol has to be resized to fit properly. To take the guesswork out of resizing, count the grid points horizontally and vertically on the left page. Then when you bring the circular text part of the logo onto the screen, you know what size to make the logo. If you have been following along with this quick start, the left page should be 11 grid points across and 14 grid points tall. Note this before you save your calendar as a symbol.

To save the desk calendar as a symbol, follow these steps:

1. Select File from the Draw Partner main menu and Save Symbol from the File menu.

2. Highlight SOSSYM, the symbol library you made previously, and press Enter to confirm your choice.

Before clearing the screen, you may want to check that the calendar symbol has been saved. To do so, select Get Symbol from the File menu and select the SOSSYM file. If you do not see your symbol in the library, try saving it again by repeating steps 1 and 2.

You can clear the screen by following this procedure:

1. Press Esc to return to the Draw Partner main menu.

2. Select Delete from the main menu, and the Delete prompt box appears.

3. In the prompt box, highlight the Everything option and press Enter to confirm that you want to clear the screen. A second prompt box appears.

4. Highlight Clear Drawing and press Enter to clear the screen.

Putting the Logo Together

Now you are ready to put the calendar and your company logo together! In this section, you retrieve and resize the circular text symbol you made. Then you retrieve the calendar symbol and place the circular text symbol on the left page. Finally, you add perspective to the drawing and make it appear as if the calendar really is sitting on a desk. Finally, you save the calendar and logo together as a symbol or chart that can be printed in Harvard Graphics.

You can see that even for a simple project, planning in advance makes sense. By splitting the drawing into its component parts, you can perfect each part before adding new elements. This planning process is helpful when you are working with Draw Partner.

Retrieving the Circular Text Symbol

To retrieve the first symbol (the circular text with the file cabinet), follow this procedure:

1. Select File from the Draw Partner main menu.

2. Select Get Symbol from the File menu.

3. Position the highlight box around the SOSSYM file name and press Enter to summon the SOSSYM library of symbols. Because you created this symbol file earlier in the quick start, SOSSYM should contain just two symbols. Figure 10.37 shows the SOSSYM file. The selection box should be on the circular text symbol.

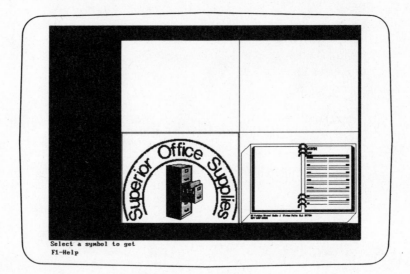

Fig. 10.37.

The SOSSYM library.

4. Press Enter to select the circular text symbol.

Sizing the Symbol

The circular text is displayed on the screen exactly as you created it. Because the text is going to be placed on the left page of the calendar base, you need to make the text smaller so that it will fit. Earlier, you made a note of the size (11 grid points across and 14 grid points tall). Now you can use that measurement to resize the circular text. To reduce and place correctly the circular text symbol's size, follow this procedure:

1. Select Size from the Draw Partner main menu. The prompt line `Select an object to size, Esc-menu` appears.

2. Position the crosshairs on the circular text symbol and press Enter.

3. Press the left-arrow key 13 times and the down-arrow key 2 times to adjust the size of the symbol. The box around the symbol reduces accordingly.

4. Press Enter, and the logo is reduced in size.

Figure 10.38 shows the reduced circular text symbol.

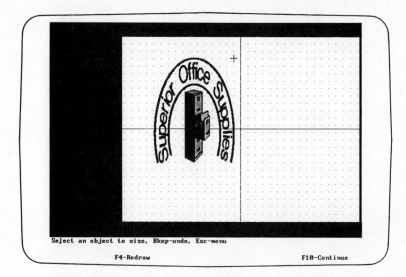

Select an object to size, Bksp-undo, Esc-menu

F4-Redraw   F10-Continue

Fig. 10.38.

The reduced circular text symbol.

Adding the Calendar Symbol

To add the calendar symbol, follow these steps:

1. From the preceding step, press Esc to return to the Draw Partner main menu and select File.

2. Select Get Symbol from the File menu and select the SOSSYM library.

3. Position the highlight box on the calendar symbol and press Enter.

   Note: At this point, the following message flashes on the bottom of the screen: Warning: The picture may be too complex to return to HG. Esc continues.

   Usually, this would be a good time to check whether your chart is too large to return to HG or to save as a chart or symbol. However, for the purposes of this quick start, we checked the chart for you and no problem exists.

4. Press Esc to continue with the quick start.

Positioning the Symbols

The next step is to place the calendar symbol behind the circular text symbol. Then you must reposition the logo. As the drawing appears now, you cannot see the circular text logo because the desk calendar drawing is on top of the circular text. To place the calendar behind the circular text symbol, follow these steps:

1. Select Modify from the main menu and select Back from the Modify menu.

2. Highlight the calendar symbol by positioning the crosshairs on it. Press Enter until the four small boxes surround the calendar symbol and press F4 (Redraw) to see the redrawn logo.

3. Press Esc twice to return to the Draw Partner main menu.

To complete the picture, move the circular text logo into position by selecting the Move command from the Draw Partner main menu. Highlight the circular text symbol and press the down-arrow key five times to position the logo on the left page. Press F4 (Redraw) to redraw the screen.

Adding Perspective

Draw Partner has a special feature that enables you to add perspective to an object. An actual desk calendar appears wider at the top and narrower toward the bottom. Adding perspective in Draw Partner creates this effect.

To add perspective to the desk calendar, you first must group the two symbols so that they are interpreted as one object. You then can use the Modify Perspective command to add perspective to the grouped object.

To group the two symbols so that they are interpreted as one object, follow this procedure:

1. Select Group from the Draw Partner main menu.

2. Select Everything from the Group prompt box.

3. Press Esc twice to return to the Draw Partner main menu.

Follow these steps to add perspective to the grouped symbol:

1. Select Modify from the Draw Partner main menu.

2. Select Perspective from the Modify menu. The prompt line Select an object for which to change perspective, Esc-menu appears.

3. Position the crosshairs in the middle of the desk calendar and press Enter. Four small boxes surround the entire picture. The prompt line Select new location, Esc-no change appears.

4. Press the right-arrow key once (to add perspective) and press Enter. When you press the right-arrow key, the outline of the right top edge of the desk calendar appears one grid point out from the original location. The graphic is redrawn on the screen with subtle perspective. Figure 10.39 shows the calendar with perspective.

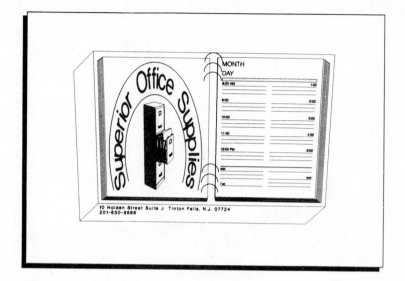

5. Press Esc twice to return to the Draw Partner main menu.

Saving the Finished Logo

Save the logo by following this procedure:

1. Select File from the Draw Partner main menu.

2. Select Save Symbol.

Now you easily can return to Harvard Graphics and print the symbol, or you can put the symbol on other charts as you work on the software.

Chapter Summary

In this quick start, you learned how to draw boxes, circular text, and straight text. You learned how to retrieve symbols, flip objects, save your drawing as a symbol, add a sweep to a symbol, and put perspective on a symbol.

You have learned about many features available in Draw Partner that are not available in Draw/Annotate. However, this quick look into the features of Draw Partner is only a beginning. Many more features are available to you with this unique and powerful drawing tool. How you use Draw Partner from here is limited only by your imagination. The next two chapters explain how to use Draw Partner in more detail.

11

Adding Graphic Objects
in Draw Partner

Before Harvard Graphics 2.3, Draw Partner was a separate program you could buy if you wanted to add more advanced drawing capabilities to those already included in the Draw/Annotate module of Harvard Graphics. In the new release, Draw Partner is integrated with Harvard Graphics. The new combination does everything that the individual Draw/Annotate module and the previous version of Draw Partner could do and adds even more features to the Harvard Graphics repertoire.

Draw Partner's capacity to manipulate objects on-screen gives Harvard Graphics many of the capabilities of a good drawing program. You not only can add simple geometric figures and text to your drawings, but you can rotate and slant them, change their perspective, and create across the screen a sweep of many copies of an object that change from one appearance to another.

Draw/Annotate is available almost instantly at a single keystroke from the edit screen of any chart and has only a portion of the commands and capabilities of Draw Partner. But that makes Draw/Annotate readily accessible for a quick modification to a chart and easy to learn. Accessing Draw Partner takes longer because Harvard Graphics puts itself away and loads the second program. Draw Partner's menus also list many additional commands. Draw Partner's power comes at the slight expense of convenience and the more considerable expense of time invested to learn the program.

379

If you already know how to use Draw/Annotate, learning Draw Partner is easier, because the two include many of the same techniques. Draw Partner pulls in the current chart you have loaded in Harvard Graphics and places the chart on the drawing board as a background, just as Draw/Annotate does. On top of this background, you can add a variety of text and graphic objects. Then you can modify the objects, move them, change their sizes, or combine them into larger, more complicated objects.

The key to using both Draw/Annotate and Draw Partner is to remember that you can add objects on top of an existing chart and make changes to the objects, but you cannot modify the existing chart unless you return to the Edit Chart module of Harvard Graphics.

Keep in mind that each object you add in Draw Partner has a set of options that determine the object's appearance. If you want, you can modify these options *before* you place the object on the chart. If you don't, the object appears with whatever options were last used to draw that family of objects in Draw Partner. If the last object within the family had a red fill color, for example, the new object also is filled with red. One family of objects is text objects (text and circular text), and another family is lines (lines, polylines, and freehand lines). Other geometric shapes form the third family. This carryover effect is unlike Draw/Annotate, which always draws new objects with the original default options. After you have added an object to a drawing, you must use the Modify Options command to make any changes to the object's options.

To get an overview of Draw Partner's capabilities, follow the quick start in Chapter 10. This chapter moves on to teach you more details about using Draw Partner. In the process, you add several types of text and objects to create the design shown in figure 11.1.

Fig. 11.1.

The catalog cover design.

Starting Draw Partner

Before starting Draw Partner, make sure that you have a blank chart on-screen. That way, you have a blank Draw Partner screen so that you can begin creating a design. To make sure that you have a blank chart loaded, save any chart on which you are working and then select Create New Chart from the main menu, Text from the Create New Chart menu, and any type from the Text Chart Styles menu. If the Keep Current Data overlay appears, make sure that you set the Keep Current Data option to No and then press Enter. When you see the blank text chart data screen, press Esc to return to the main menu.

You also should check to be sure that the current screen palette is HG23.PAL, the default palette used by Harvard Graphics and Draw Partner. You then have available the same combination of screen colors described in the following pages. To check the palette setting within Harvard Graphics, take this brief detour:

1. Select Setup from the Harvard Graphics main menu.

2. Select Color Palette from the Setup menu.

3. Choose Select Palette from the Color Palette menu.

4. Select HG23 from the list of palettes that appears.

5. Press Esc to return to the main menu.

If you already have started Draw Partner, you can check the palette within Draw Partner by following these steps:

1. Select File from the Draw Partner main menu.

2. Select Palette from the File menu.

3. Use the arrow keys to position the highlight box on HG23 on the list of palettes that appears.

4. Press Enter to return to the File menu.

5. Press Esc to return to the main menu.

You can start Draw Partner in one of several ways. From the DOS prompt, you can change to the directory in which you have installed the Harvard Graphics program files, type *hgdp*, and then press Enter. This method starts Draw Partner as a separate application but does not enable you to jump back quickly to Harvard Graphics, as you can if you start Draw Partner within Harvard Graphics.

By far, the easiest way to start Draw Partner within Harvard Graphics is to press Ctrl-D. If you forget about this shortcut key combination, you always can press F3 (Applications) and select Draw Partner or press 1 when you see the Applications menu. Refer to Chapter 2 to review the steps for modifying the Applications list.

When you start Draw Partner, the program's opening screen appears, as shown in figure 11.2.

Fig. 11.2.

The Draw Partner opening screen.

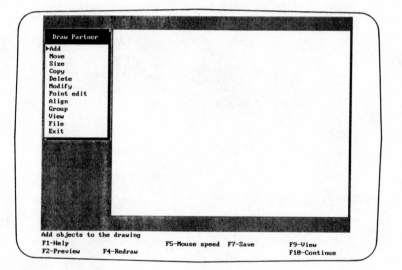

On the left side of the screen is the Draw Partner menu. You can use the arrow keys or the mouse to move the highlight up and down the menu and then press Enter to select an option. You also can press the first letter of the menu choice to select the option. You cannot press the space bar to move from one option to the next, as you can with most Harvard Graphics menus. To back up through the menu choices, you can press Esc or click the right mouse button (the middle button if your mouse has three buttons).

On the right side of the screen is the drawing board. Here is where your ravishing works of art appear. Any chart that is loaded when you start Draw Partner shows up here, too. At the bottom of the screen are your current function key choices. The available function key options change depending on where you are and what you are doing in the program. Table 11.1 lists the key functions available in Draw Partner.

Table 11.1
Key Functions in Draw Partner

General Key	Function
Enter	Selects a highlighted menu item, an object, or a position on the screen; completes some actions
Esc	Returns to the menu, backs up within menus, or ends the current action
Backspace	Undoes the last action while drawing
Space bar	Stops the redrawing of the drawing
Text-Editing Key	*Function*
Left or right arrow	Moves the cursor left or right in a text line
Home	Moves the cursor to the beginning of a text line
End	Moves the cursor to the end of a text line
Backspace	Deletes the character to the left of the cursor
Del	Deletes the character at the cursor location
Function Key	*Function*
F1	Summons context-sensitive help or a help topics list
F2	Previews the current drawing or a file saved on disk
F3	Changes the current directory or drive
F4	Redraws the drawing on-screen
F5	Changes mouse movement speed
F6	Chooses new settings from the options list
F7	Saves the current drawing as a Draw Partner drawing file
F8	Changes options while creating an object or editing text

Table 11.1—*continued*

Function Key	Function
F9	Changes the View or Redraw options
F10	Continues the current action

Crosshair Cursor-Movement Key	Function
Up, down, left, or right arrow	Moves the crosshair cursor up, down, left, or right
Home, End, PgUp, or PgDn	Moves the crosshair cursor diagonally
Minus key (on numeric keypad)	Moves the crosshair cursor in smaller steps
Plus key (on numeric keypad)	Moves the crosshair cursor in larger steps
Shift	Retains an object's original proportions when resizing or maintains square boxes and buttons or round circles

Help Menu Key	Function
F1	Summons context-sensitive help for the cursor location
F1 twice	Summons a list of help topics
PgDn	Moves to the next help screen
PgUp	Moves to the preceding help screen
Esc	Leaves Help and returns to Draw Partner

Setting a Grid

Before you begin drawing, you should add a grid to the screen so that you can follow the directions in this chapter with greater accuracy. A grid is a regular pattern of dots that appear on the background of the drawing area. You can determine the distance between the dots. A grid can be helpful in lining up objects precisely. If you turn on Snap To, the points of an object you are placing on the drawing are pulled to the nearest grid points. Snap To does not affect objects already placed on the drawing.

To set a grid, follow these steps:

1. Select View from the Draw Partner menu.

2. Select Grid from the View menu.

3. Select Grid On from the Grid menu.

4. Press 5 for the new grid size and then press Enter.

5. Press Esc to return to the main Draw Partner menu.

A grid of dots appears on-screen.

Adding Boxes and Circles

Adding boxes and circles in Draw Partner is just like adding them in Draw/
Annotate. First, you select Add from the Draw Partner menu and then you select
Box or Circle from the Add menu. You can use the current options shown in the
Options window in the upper left corner of the screen, or you can press F8
(Options) to modify the current options.

Drawing a Box

Draw Partner offers 21 different box styles. These box styles and the other
options for boxes are covered in detail in Chapter 9. The only box option that
differs is the box outline, the line that is the outside edge of the box. With
Draw/Annotate, you can include or omit an outline for most graphic shapes.
Draw Partner offers four outline styles for boxes (in addition to None), including
Solid, Dotted, Dashed, and Thick.

To learn how to use this feature of Draw Partner, start the Superior Office Supplies catalog cover design by adding the large background box in the center of
the logo. To add the box, follow this procedure:

1. Select Add from the Draw Partner menu.

2. Select Box from the Add menu.

Notice that the prompt above the function keys tells you to begin drawing the
box by selecting a corner of it. In this example, you first should modify the box
options. Follow these steps:

1. Press F8 (Options) to display a menu listing box options, similar to the
   one shown in figure 11.3.

   The options showing on your screen may be different if you or someone
   else used Draw Perfect before and changed them.

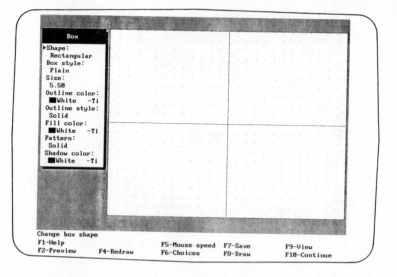

Fig. 11.3.

The Box menu.

2. With the small triangle pointer next to Shape, press Enter or click the mouse to select a shape for the box. Because you do not need the box to remain square for this example, highlight Rectangular on the Box menu and press Enter or click the left mouse button. A second menu listing further options usually appears when you select one of the Box menu options.

3. Select Box Style from the Box menu. Figure 11.4 shows you all the available box styles. Select Shadow from the list of choices on the menu that appears and press Enter.

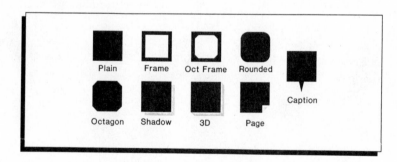

Fig. 11.4.

The available box styles.

4. From the list of choices that now appears on the Box menu, select Bottom Right and press Enter to specify the location of the shadow.

5. Move the highlight to Size and press Enter or click the left mouse button. Then type 5.5 and press Enter. On a shadow box, the Size option determines the depth of the shadow. Size has a different effect on each box style, as described in table 11.2.

6. Skip over the Outline Color option, because this box has no outline.

   To see the available choices for outline color, highlight Outline Color and then press Enter or click the left mouse button. The colors of the currently selected palette appear. Press Esc to return to the Box menu.

7. Set Outline Style to None to omit the outline. You also can place a solid, dotted, dashed, or thick line around an object as an outline.

8. Set Fill Color to Blue (the fourth choice from the bottom) by selecting Fill Color, highlighting Blue on the menu that appears, and then pressing Enter or clicking the left mouse button. Draw Partner recommends that you use this color for symbols (hence the -Sy to the right of the color name).

9. Set Pattern to Solid if it is not already set. The pattern options are shown in figure 11.5.

10. Set Shadow Color to Blue Lt (a light blue normally recommended for text).

Table 11.2
Using the Size Option for Different Box Styles

Box Style Option	Element Affected by Size Option
Plain	None
Frame	Width between inner and outer boxes
Oct Frame	Depth of diagonal
Rounded	Degree of rounding
Octagon	Depth of diagonals
Shadow	Depth of shadow
3D	Depth of 3-D
Page	Width of page turn
Caption	1/2 distance from box edge to point

When you finish changing the box options, press F8 (Draw) to draw the box with your new options. When you press F8, a small sample box appears in the corner, showing what your drawn box will look like. If you don't see what you expected, return to modify the options by pressing F8 (Options) again. Then press F8 (Draw) when you're ready to redraw.

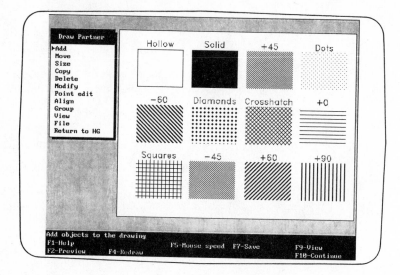

Fig. 11.5.

The pattern options.

Draw Partner now prompts Select corner of box. Move the cursor to a starting point and then press Enter or click the left mouse button. For this example, select a point that is 5 grid points from the top of the screen and 7 grid points from the left of the screen. Next, pick the opposite corner of the box. For this example, count 10 grid points across to the right and 8 grid points down and then press Enter again. The box shown in figure 11.6 appears. If the box is in the wrong place, press the Backspace key to remove the box and then try again. Press Esc or click the right mouse button to return to the Add menu when you're satisfied with the box's location.

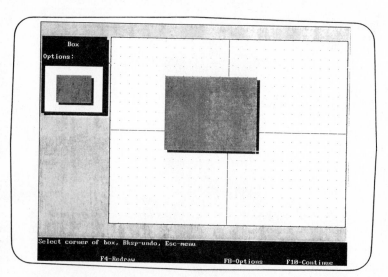

Fig. 11.6.

The completed shadow box.

Drawing a Circle

Next, you should add a small circle that you can use as an alignment point for several other objects you will be adding. An *alignment point* is an object with which you can line up other objects. You learn later that the Align command can help you align objects already drawn, and you already know that you can use the Snap To grid option to place objects precisely. But this technique can help you align several objects of different types, such as arcs and wedges. To add the circle, follow these steps:

1. Select Circle from the Add menu. Note the appearance of the sample circle that shows up in the upper left corner. This circle has the same options as the box you just drew, except for the Shadow feature (circles are not available with a shadow). You need to change one of these options so that the circle has a contrasting color and shows up on the box.

2. Press F8 (Options) to change the circle options. For the example, leave the first option, Shape, set to Circular. Shape for circles is much like the Shape option for boxes. When Shape is set to Circular, a perfect circle appears, in the largest possible size that can fit within the square or rectangle you have drawn. If Shape is set to Elliptical instead, a circle or oval appears that has the same width and height as the square or rectangle.

3. Move the cursor to the Fill Color option and set it to Yellow-Sy so that the circle stands out.

4. Press F8 (Draw) to go on. Note the Draw Partner message in the lower left corner of the screen: Select center of circle.

5. Position the cursor in the middle of the bottom line of the box and press Enter or click the left mouse button.

6. Move the cursor diagonally down and to the right just a tiny bit and click the left mouse button. If you prefer to use the keyboard, press the minus (−) key on the numeric keypad three or four times to diminish the distance the cursor moves each time you press an arrow key, press the down- and right-arrow keys to move the cursor, and press Enter.

7. Press Esc to return to the Add menu after the small circle appears, as shown in figure 11.7.

Fig. 11.7.

The box with a small reference circle added at the bottom edge.

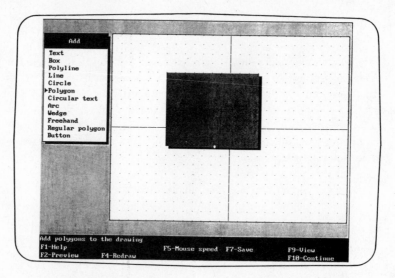

Adding Circular Text

Circular text is a new feature that Draw Partner brings to Harvard Graphics. With this feature, you can place text on-screen that follows the path of a circle. You should be aware, however, that when you return to Harvard Graphics, the program interprets the circular text in your drawing as polylines or polygons. Thus, you cannot edit the text—delete or add characters or words—in Harvard Graphics. To edit the text, you must save your work as a Draw Partner file in addition to saving it as a Harvard Graphics chart. You find detailed information about saving your work in Chapter 12.

Circular text can follow the top or the bottom of a circle, as shown in figure 11.8. If all the text you type does not fit on the circumference of the circle you draw, Draw Partner switches to a smaller text size.

To add circular text, follow these steps:

1. Select Circular Text from the Add menu.

2. Press F8 (Options) to modify the appearance of the circular text.

3. For the catalog cover example, set the Size option to 6. (You become accustomed to working with different size settings the more you use Draw Partner.)

4. Set Color to Yel Lt (a light yellow).

5. Set Weight to Solid Bold. You also can choose Light or Hollow Bold. These choices are shown in figure 11.9.

6. Set Italic to None.

7. Set Drop Shadow to Lower Right. Other choices for drop shadow are Lower, Middle, and Upper Left; Lower, Middle, and Upper Right; Upper Middle; Lower Middle; and No Shadow.

8. Set Shadow Color to Black. You can use Black-Fr (recommended for the frame of a chart) or Black-Sy (recommended for symbols).

9. Set Font to Executive. Draw Partner offers you the chance to use a different font for each text object you add to a drawing. All the available Draw Partner fonts are shown in figure 11.10.

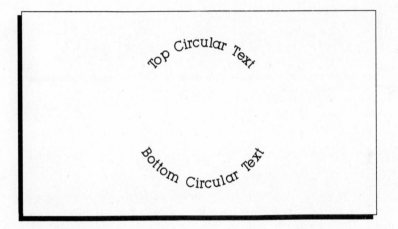

Fig. 11.8.

Examples of top and bottom circular text.

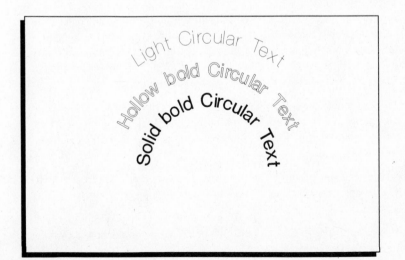

Fig. 11.9.

Choices for circular text weights.

Fig. 11.10.

*The Draw Partner
text fonts.*

Executive
Traditional
Square Serif
Roman
Sans Serif
Script
Gothic

After setting the options for the circular text, you can place the text on your current drawing by following these steps:

1. Press F8 (Draw) and then notice the sample text in the upper left corner of the screen.

2. Position the cursor on the small yellow reference circle you drew previously, and click the left mouse button or press Enter. This action positions the center of the circle for circular text. Draw Partner prompts Select radius of circle for circular text.

3. Move the cursor in any direction away from the point until the edge of the circle that appears reaches the spot through which you want the circular text to pass. Then click the left mouse button or press Enter. For this example, move the cursor until the top of the circle touches the top edge of the box, and click the left mouse button or press Enter.

4. From the Circular Text menu, choose which way you want the text to curve. Top causes text to flow around the top of the circle. Bottom causes text to flow around the circle's bottom, instead. For this example, choose Top.

5. When Draw Partner prompts Enter a line of text, type the circular text. For this example, type *Superior Office Supplies*. Then press Enter to add the circular text.

6. Press Esc to return to the Add menu. Your drawing should now look like the one shown in figure 11.11.

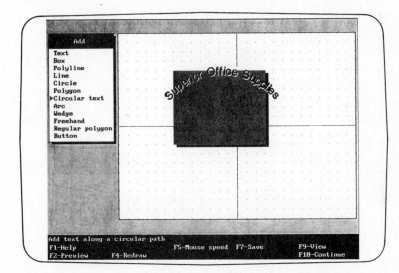

Fig. 11.11.

After adding the circular text.

Adding Arcs and Wedges

Draw Partner enables you to add two types of objects, both based on the circle, that are new to Harvard Graphics. An *arc* is a portion of the circumference of a circle. A *wedge* is a slice from the interior of the circle. After you add an arc to a drawing, Draw Partner treats the arc as a polyline. After you add a wedge, Draw Partner treats the wedge as a polygon.

Drawing Arcs

To add an arc, first select a point for the center of an imaginary circle. Then select starting and ending points along the circle's circumference. Draw Partner draws an arc between these two points. To draw a wedge, follow the same steps, but Draw Partner connects the starting and ending points of the arc to the center of the imaginary circle with straight lines to form an object shaped like a pie slice.

To practice adding arcs, add one arc above and one arc below the circular text you already have added. These two arcs frame the text and enhance its appearance. To begin working on the first arc, follow these steps:

1. Select Arc from the Add menu.

2. Press F8 (Options) to modify the appearance of the arc.

3. For this example, select Cyan Lt for Color.

4. For the Style option, select Thick. The other choices (Solid, Dotted, and Dashed) are shown on the Arc menu.

5. Make sure that the Arrows option is set to No Arrows. Otherwise, arrow-heads appear at one or both ends of the arc. If you choose Start Arrow instead, an arrowhead appears at the beginning of the line. If you choose End Arrow, an arrowhead appears at the end of the line. Both arrows puts an arrowhead at both ends of the line.

6. Make sure that the Closure option is set to Open. If you select Closed instead, Draw Partner joins the starting and ending points of the arc with a straight line.

Now that you have set the options for the arc, continue with these steps to draw the arc:

1. Press F8 (Draw).

2. Position the cursor on the small yellow reference circle you drew previously. This circle marks the center of the arc.

3. Click the left mouse button or press Enter to select the center of the arc.

4. Move the cursor up and to the left just beyond the top of the uppercase S in the word *Superior*. Then click the left mouse button or press Enter to select the beginning point of the arc.

5. Move the cursor to the right, just beyond the lowercase *s* at the end of the word *Supplies*. Then click the left mouse button or press Enter to select the ending point of the arc.

Your first arc should look like the one shown in figure 11.12.

If the arc is not properly positioned, you can press the Backspace key immediately so that you can try again. The Backspace key is labeled Undo in the key menu at the bottom of the screen.

After you successfully add one arc, you are ready to add another object of the same type and with the same options. Draw Partner always offers you the chance to add another object of the same type. In this case, you want to add a second arc below the circular text, so follow these steps:

1. Position the cursor on the yellow reference circle again and click the left mouse button or press Enter.

2. Move the cursor just below the uppercase S in *Superior* and click the left mouse button or press Enter.

3. Move the cursor just below the lowercase *s* at the end of *Supplies* and click the left mouse button or press Enter.

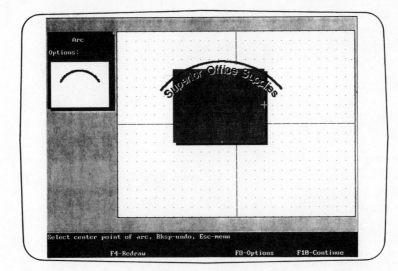

Fig. 11.12.

An arc added to the drawing.

A second arc appears below the circular text, looking just like the first arc. To return to the Add menu, press Esc.

Drawing Wedges

To experiment with adding wedges, follow these steps:

1. Select Wedge from the Add menu.

2. Press F8 (Options) to modify the appearance of the wedge you are about to draw. Notice that the wedge has the same options as the circle you drew previously.

3. For this example, skip over the Outline Color and Outline Style options. The wedge in the catalog cover does not have an outline (a line that surrounds the center filled area).

4. Make sure that Yellow is selected as the Fill Color.

5. Make sure that Solid is selected as the pattern.

After setting these options, draw the wedge by following these steps:

1. Press F8 (Draw).

2. Move the cursor to a point that is four visible grid points below the bottom edge of the box and halfway between the left and right edges and click the left mouse button or press Enter. This point is the center of an imaginary circle.

3. Move the cursor to a point halfway up the height of the box and toward the left side of the box; click the left mouse button or press Enter. This action selects a starting point for the wedge on the circumference of the imaginary circle.

4. Move the cursor to the right and select a point on the right side of the box that is the ending point of the wedge. Make sure that the wedge is even on both sides. The wedge that appears should look like the one shown in figure 11.13.

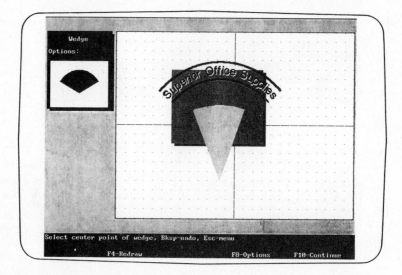

Fig. 11.13.

A wedge added to the drawing.

If you are unhappy with the wedge that appears, press Backspace to try again.

Now, rather than press Esc to return to the Add menu, press F8 (Options) and change Fill Color to Red. Then press F8 (Draw) so that you can add a second wedge just above and to the left of the first wedge. The second wedge should overlay the first, as shown in figure 11.14. This design gives your drawing a three-dimensional appearance.

Adding Text

You easily can add extra text to any drawing in Draw Partner, with even more flexibility than you find in Draw/Annotate. To add text in Draw Partner, select Text from the Add menu and then press F8 (Options) to select a particular combination of text options before you enter the text. After you type the text, you can modify the options for individual words or characters by pressing F8 again. Then you can add the final text to your drawing.

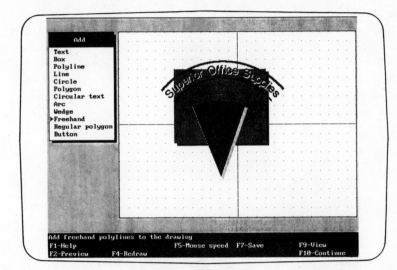

Fig. 11.14.

Adding a second wedge.

To experiment with adding text, add the text line *Fall Catalog* to the catalog cover. First select Text from the Add menu. Notice that a few characters of text appear in the upper left corner, formatted with the current text options, as shown in figure 11.15. Then follow these steps to modify the options for the line of text you are about to enter:

1. Press F8 (Options).

2. For this example, set Size to 6. Size here is a relative number just as it is within Harvard Graphics. The best way to use the Size option is to take a look at the current setting and then change the Size number up or down until the text appears just right.

   After you modify size, press F8 (Draw) to examine the sample text showing on the Text menu. To try another size or change other options, press F8 (Options).

3. Set Color to Yel Lt (a light yellow that Software Publishing recommends for series in graph charts).

4. Set Weight to Solid Bold. The other options for Weight are the same as the options for circular text shown earlier.

5. Set Italic to None, Underline to None, and Drop Shadow to No Shadow.

6. Because this text has no shadow, skip over the Shadow Color option by pressing the down-arrow key twice.

7. For this example, set Justify to Base Center. The Justify options determine the position of the text relative to the current cursor position. Base Left, for example, places the left end of the text baseline (a line that passes just under the capital letters of text) at the cursor position. Refer to figure 11.16 for an illustration of the various Justify options. With these options, you easily can line up text relative to an object on-screen by positioning the cursor precisely on the object.

8. Set Font to Executive.

Fig. 11.15.

The sample text showing on the Text menu.

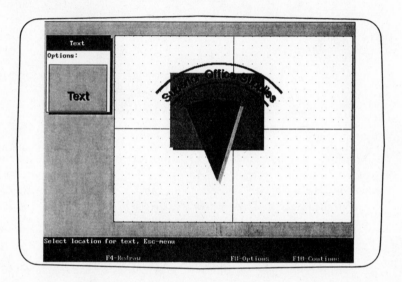

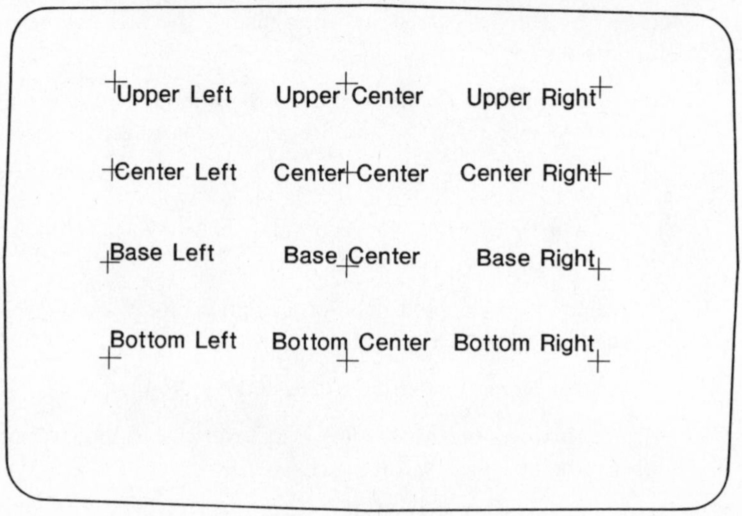

Fig. 11.16.

Understanding the Text Justify options.

Upper Left   Upper Center   Upper Right

Center Left   Center Center   Center Right

Base Left   Base Center   Base Right

Bottom Left   Bottom Center   Bottom Right

After setting the options for the text, you're ready to enter the text itself. Follow these steps:

1. Press F8 (Draw). Notice that Draw Partner prompts you to select a location for the text.

2. For this example, position the cursor just above the bottom point of the red wedge and then click the left mouse button or press Enter.

3. Type *Fall Catalog* but do not press Enter. These words appear in the text edit line at the bottom of the screen, and a box appears on-screen showing where the text appears when you press Enter or click the left mouse button.

At this point, you can add the text to the drawing or modify the options of individual text characters if you prefer. For this example, you do not need to modify individual characters. But you should see how the process works, so follow this brief detour:

1. Press the Home key to move the cursor to the beginning of the line of text. (The End key moves the cursor to the end of the line.)

2. Press F8 (Character Options) to modify the options of individual characters.

3. Select the characters you want to modify. For this example, press the right-arrow key three times to highlight the word *Fall*.

4. Press Enter to indicate to Draw Partner that you have selected the text to be modified.

5. Examine the text options available for you to change. Notice that you easily can change certain options for the selected text, including Color, Weight, Italic, and Underline, by selecting them from a menu just as you did when you first set the options.

6. Press F8 (Enter Text) to return to the text you have typed without changing any options.

7. Press Enter to add the text with the current options. As always, you can press the Backspace key immediately to remove the text you have added so that you can try again. You also can press Esc twice to return to the Add menu.

Figure 11.17 shows how the drawing should look at this point.

Fig. 11.17.

The drawing with text added.

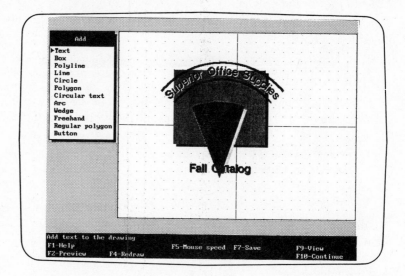

In the next chapter, you learn that in Draw Partner you can make various types of modifications to any text you have entered. You can use the Modify Options command to change the appearance of an entire line of text. You can use the Modify Edit Text command to change the wording of your text and to add, delete, or change the appearance of individual characters. You also can use the Rotate command to rotate the entire line of text to a new angle.

Adding Lines and Polylines

Lines and polylines are related objects that you can add to a Draw Partner drawing. *Lines* can be any available color or thickness and can have arrows at one or both ends. *Polylines* are lines that have two or more segments. Each segment ends and a new segment begins at points you specify when you draw the polyline. In fact, polylines can have up to 200 points each. If you prefer, you can set the options so that your polyline is a smoothly curving line that passes near rather than through each of the points you draw.

Adding a Line

To examine the options for lines, try adding a line under the words *Fall Catalog* on your drawing. Follow these steps:

1. Select Line from the Add menu.

2. Press F8 (Options) so that you can set the options for the line you are about to draw.

3. Set the Size option, which determines the thickness of the line, to 3. You can press F8 to examine the current thickness and then press F8 again to continue modifying other options.

4. Leave the Outline Color option set as is because this line should not have an outline.

5. Make sure that the Outline Style option is set to None so that the line outline is turned off.

6. Set Fill Color to Cyan Dk.

7. Set Pattern to Solid. If on other occasions your line is particularly thick, you can fill it with any of the available patterns. These patterns are the same as those used for filling all objects. You can see the available patterns in figure 11.5.

8. Set the Arrows option to No Arrows. The Start Arrow and End Arrow options put an arrow at the beginning and end of the line, respectively. The Both Arrows option puts an arrow at both ends of the line.

9. Press F8 (Draw) so that you can add the line.

10. Move the cursor to a starting point under the first letter of *Fall Catalog* and press Enter or click the left mouse button.

11. Move the cursor to another point under the last letter of *Fall Catalog*, the ending point, and press Enter or click the left mouse button.

The line that appears has all the options settings you specified. If you want to modify any of these and try again, press Backspace. The drawing with the added line is shown in figure 11.18.

Adding a Polyline

The options for polylines are slightly more involved. To examine the available options, follow these steps:

1. Select Polyline from the Add menu. (Make sure that you don't inadvertently select Polygon instead.)

2. Press F8 (Options) to change the polyline options.

3. Set Color to any color of your choice other than Black because black does not show up against the black background of the screen.

4. Set Style to Thick. The other choices (Solid, Dotted, Dashed, and None) are illustrated on the menu.

5. Set Arrows to No Arrows. The Arrows options for polylines are the same as the Arrows options for lines (Start Arrow, End Arrow, and Both Arrows).

6. For now, set the Smoothing option to Straight Line. This choice instructs Draw Partner to draw a straight line from one point to the next. (The other option, Curved Line, creates a line that curves toward but doesn't pass through each point.)

7. Set Closure to Open. The Closed option draws a line that connects the first and last points you select.

Fig. 11.18.

The catalog design with a line added.

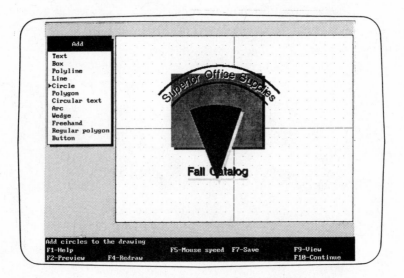

Now, with the polyline's options set, you are ready to select the points for the polyline. Follow these steps:

1. Press F8 (Draw).

2. Select a starting point in the blank area in the lower right corner of the screen.

3. Select four other points so that the lines that connect them are in the shape of the letter W.

4. Press Esc to finish the polyline. Figure 11.19 shows how your polyline should look.

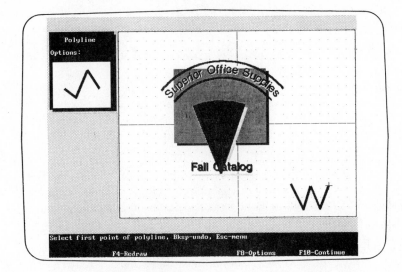

Fig. 11.19.

A straight polyline added.

Notice that the lines connecting the points are straight. Now try using Curved Line for the Smoothing option. To draw the same polyline again but with a new option setting, press Backspace once to undo the first polyline. Then press F8 (Options) to return to the Polyline options menu. Set the Smoothing option to Curved Line and then press F8 (Draw) to return to the drawing board. Finally, press Esc to finish the polyline. The polyline becomes a single curving line that curves toward each point but hits only the first and last points (see fig. 11.20). To return to the Add menu, press Esc again.

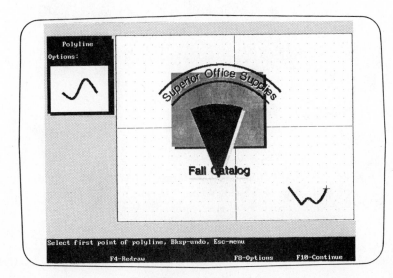

Fig. 11.20.

Changing to a curved polyline.

Adding Polygons and Regular Polygons

A *polygon* is a closed figure with more than two sides (a figure with only two sides is a *line*, and a figure with one side is a *point*). Draw Partner offers you two different ways to add polygons to a drawing. If all the sides of the polygon you want to draw have equal lengths (for example, a perfect triangle, square, hexagon, or octagon), you can use Add and then the Regular Polygon option. You use the Polygon option to draw an object that has sides of different lengths.

As with polylines, you draw polygons by selecting points that define the sides of the polygon. The first side of the polygon (a straight line) forms between the first two points you draw. As you continue to add points, additional sides form, up to a limit of 200 points. Therefore, polygons can have as many as 199 sides before Draw Partner stops you with a warning.

Try adding a polygon by selecting Add from the Draw Partner menu and then choosing Polygon from the Add menu. If you press F8 (Options), you see only four options listed for polygons: Outline Color, Outline Style, Fill Color, and Pattern. Choose a combination that pleases you and then press F8 (Draw) so that you can draw the polygon.

Notice that Draw Partner prompts Select first point of polygon. Select a point in an unused area of the screen, and click the mouse or press Enter. Draw Partner then prompts you to select point 2. Keep adding points until you have formed the outline of an object. If you decide that you don't like a point's position, you can press the Backspace key to remove the last point added.

When all the points are in place, press Esc to complete the polygon. Even with the polygon fully drawn, you can undo it step by step by pressing the Backspace key.

Adding Freehand Objects

Freehand objects are shapes you draw on-screen with the cursor. After you begin adding a freehand object, each time you move the cursor you add another point. A freehand object is thus a collection of up to 200 points. As you move the cursor, a counter at the bottom of the screen changes. Before you can draw the 201st point, the counter stops, and your freehand object seems to freeze in place. Press Esc at any point while you are drawing when you want to finish the object. To remove the freehand object and try another, press Backspace.

Note: As always, if you are using the keyboard, you can press the plus (+) key on the numeric keypad to increase the distance the cursor moves each time you press an arrow key. Conversely, the minus (−) key decreases the cursor movement.

You set options for freehand objects after you select Freehand from the Add menu. Freehand objects have options similar to those of polylines. You can select color and style and whether to have an arrowhead at the first end, the last end, or both. You also can determine whether freehand objects have straight or curved smoothing. Curved smoothing causes Draw Partner to draw a curving line from one point to the next when you press Esc. Straight smoothing causes Draw Partner to draw straight lines between the points instead. Also, the two Closure options, Open and Closed, tell Draw Partner whether to join the first and last points of the freehand object with a straight line.

Figure 11.21 shows an example of using a freehand object to form a signature.

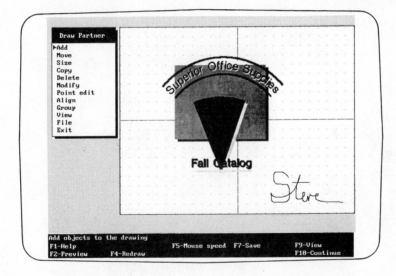

Fig. 11.21.

The completed drawing with a freehand signature.

Adding a Button

A *button* is an area of the screen a viewer can click with the mouse while watching a hypershow to jump quickly to another portion of the show. Hypershows are covered in depth in Chapter 16.

To add a button in Draw Partner, follow these steps:

1. Select Button from the Add menu.

2. Move the cursor to the upper left corner where you want the button and press Enter or click the left mouse button.

3. Move the cursor to the lower right corner where you want the button and press Enter or click the left mouse button.

4. Type a number from 1 to 10 to assign the button a reference number. The hypershow uses the reference number to determine where in the show to move next.

Certain special numbers are reserved for particular movements in a hypershow, such as jumping to the first or last screen. These special numbers are covered in the section on hypershows in Chapter 16.

Saving the Completed Drawing

To save your completed work as a Draw Partner drawing file, follow these steps:

1. Select File from the Draw Partner menu.

2. Select Save Drawing from the File menu.

3. Highlight New File on the list of available drawing files and press Enter.

4. Type a new file name of up to eight characters and then press Enter.

In a moment, your drawing is saved so that you can retrieve the drawing later within Draw Partner and make changes. In the next chapter, you find information about other steps you can take with your completed work.

If you have other Draw Partner drawings already saved on disk, you see their names when you save the new drawing. You can take a look at any of these files by positioning the highlight on the file name and then pressing F2 (Preview).

You also can save a drawing as a Harvard Graphics chart file by selecting Save As Chart. When you select Save As Chart, Draw Partner saves all the objects you added in Draw Partner in a file with the extension CHT. You can retrieve this chart later in Harvard Graphics and print or incorporate the chart in a slide show.

If you have a Harvard Graphics chart in the background (you started Draw Partner from within Harvard Graphics while you had a chart in memory), that chart is not saved along with the Draw Partner drawings. The chart file contains only the objects you have added in Draw Partner. To save the chart and the Draw Partner drawings you have placed on top of it, return to Harvard Graphics and use the Save Chart command.

You also can save your work as a symbol. Then, later, you can get the symbol to add to any chart or other drawing, resizing and positioning the symbol the way you want.

You also can use Save As Symbol to get around the size limitation of the Draw Partner files that you can pull back into Harvard Graphics. Draw Partner files may be no more than 32K in size. When you create a drawing greater than 32K, you see the message Warning: picture may be too complex to return to HG, Esc continues. To save such a drawing, follow this procedure:

1. Save the drawing by using the Save Drawing command on the File menu.

2. Delete half the objects and save the drawing as a symbol.

3. Retrieve the full drawing.

4. Delete the other half of the objects and save the drawing as a second symbol.

5. Combine the two symbols in Draw/Annotate or add each symbol to a chart and then combine the two charts into a multiple chart.

Returning to Harvard Graphics with a Drawing

Even without saving your work in Draw Partner, you can return to Harvard Graphics, print, and then save your work as a chart file. You may want to save your work as a Draw Partner drawing before you return to Harvard Graphics, however, so that you can edit your annotations in Draw Partner in the future.

To bring your Draw Partner drawing back to Harvard Graphics, select Return to HG from the Draw Partner menu. Draw Partner ends, and Harvard Graphics returns to the screen in a few moments. If you press F2 (Draw Chart), you see your Draw Partner work on-screen. If you enter Draw/Annotate, you can make changes to some objects you added in Draw Partner, but others you can edit only if you get the Draw Partner drawing file you saved.

Importing and Exporting Files

You can pull into Draw Partner graphic files from other applications in two formats: CGM (Computer Graphics Metafiles) and PIC (Lotus 1-2-3 picture files). CGM is a widely used file format that enables different programs to exchange graphics images. If you created a CGM file in another graphics program, you can import it into Draw Partner by following these steps:

1. Select File from the Draw Partner menu.

2. Select Import from the File menu.

3. Select Metafile if you want to import a CGM file, or select Lotus if you want to import a Lotus PIC file.

   Draw Partner shows a list of all the CGM files or the PIC files in the default Import directory you specified on the Setup Defaults screen.

4. Select a file name from the list that appears.

If you have a drawing on-screen, Draw Partner asks whether you want to save it before proceeding, because the file you import replaces the existing drawing. You may want to highlight a file name on the list and press F2 to take a look at the image before you import the image. When the CGM or PIC file is on the screen, you can edit the screen just as though it were a drawing you created in Draw Partner. You learn about ways to modify objects in the next chapter.

You can export a completed Draw Partner file to any other program that imports CGM files. When you select Export from the File menu, Draw Partner asks whether you want to use Polygon fonts or Hardware fonts. If you use Polygon fonts, the text in your drawing is transformed into polygons that look exactly like the text character shapes in Draw Partner. The disadvantage to polygon fonts, however, is that you cannot edit them as text in the other graphics application. To provide that capability, you should select Hardware fonts. Your fonts may not look the same when you import the CGM file into another graphics program, but you can edit the text and then select a similar font format or a font that is completely different in the second graphics application.

When you select a name for the file to export, Draw Partner appends a CGM file extension.

Chapter Summary

This chapter introduced you to the basic steps in adding objects within Draw Partner to a blank screen or an existing Harvard Graphics chart. Remember, in Draw Partner, you add objects on top of an existing chart, which serves as a background.

Each of the shapes you can add offers its own set of options that determine the appearance of the object. Before you add the object, you can modify its options by pressing F8 (Options). When you have set the combination of options you want, you can examine their effect by pressing F8 (Draw). A sample object with all your options settings appears in a window at the upper left corner of the screen. If everything looks right, go ahead and add the object. If you need to make other options changes, press F8 (Options) again.

The next chapter describes the great variety of Draw Partner commands you can use to modify the objects you already have added.

12

Modifying Graphic Objects in Draw Partner

After you have added objects to a drawing using the techniques you learn in Chapter 11, you can go back and make changes to the drawing's appearance. The easiest changes are those you can make by modifying the options of objects. Draw Partner, however, provides far more sophisticated techniques to modify the appearance of objects—well beyond anything offered in Draw/Annotate. In Draw Partner, for example, you can flip and rotate objects or add shadows and perspective. You can skew objects to make them lean to one side or sweep objects to create a series of objects on-screen that gradually mutate to a new shape. These commands provide far greater flexibility and power when you create drawings or enhance charts. You learn about these techniques and more later in this chapter. First you begin by reviewing the easier ways to modify objects in Draw Partner.

Selecting Objects To Modify

To modify any object in Draw Partner, you first select the modify command you want and then select the object. Unlike Draw/Annotate, which enables you to draw a box around one or several objects, you must point to an object to select it in Draw Partner. You move the cursor on top of the object, click the left button of the mouse, or press Enter.

After you select an object, Draw Partner displays a window containing the choices This Object and Next Object. If the correct object is highlighted (a small square appears at each corner of an imaginary box containing the object), select This Object. If not, select Next Object, and Draw Partner highlights another object and presents the same choice. If the object you want is on top of another object, Draw Partner may seem to always highlight the wrong object first because the program selects the object at the bottom first. Then, each time you select Next Object, Draw Partner moves up one and tries again until you select This Object.

Knowing how to select objects in Draw Partner is critical to your success with the program. You may want to add a few objects to a blank Draw Partner screen, therefore, before continuing to practice selecting them. Make sure that two of the objects overlap so that you can see how Draw Partner first suggests the object underneath. Then select Move from the Draw Partner menu and practice selecting an object to move. The Move command is described later in this chapter.

To finish the drawing and add another object to practice modifying, try adding a symbol by following the directions in the next section.

Adding a Symbol to a Drawing

In Draw Partner, you can add one of the predrawn figures from the Harvard Graphics symbol libraries just as you can in Draw/Annotate. Use Appendix A to help you select a symbol from one of the symbol libraries. The following is the general procedure for adding a symbol:

1. Select File from the Draw Partner menu.

2. Select Get Symbol from the File menu.

3. Highlight the symbol file name you want to pull a symbol from and click the left mouse button or press Enter.

4. Move the box so that the box surrounds the symbol you want to use and click the left mouse button or press Enter.

5. To see the symbol, return to the Draw Partner File menu by pressing Esc or clicking the right mouse button.

You probably need to use the Move and Size commands to position the symbol in your drawing.

To get the drawing you created in the preceding chapter, follow these steps:

1. Select File from the Draw Partner menu.

2. Select Get Drawing from the File menu.

3. Highlight the file you saved earlier and press Enter or click the left mouse button.

4. Press Esc to return to the main menu.

In a moment, the catalog cover logo appears on-screen, as shown in figure 12.1.

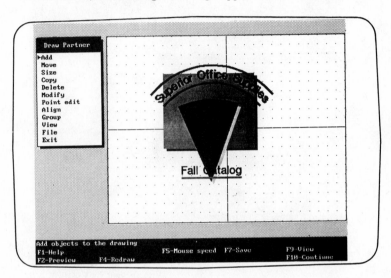

Fig. 12.1.

The logo created in Chapter 11.

Then get the file cabinet symbol from the OFFICE4 symbol library by following these steps:

1. Select File from the Draw Partner menu.

2. Select Get Symbol from the File menu.

3. Highlight the OFFICE4 symbol library and press Enter or click the left mouse button.

4. Move the rectangle so that the rectangle surrounds the symbol of the file cabinet (second from the bottom in the leftmost column) and then press Enter or click the left mouse button.

5. Press the right mouse button or Esc to return to the main menu.

You should see the file cabinet in the middle of your drawing, as shown in figure 12.2. In the next section of this chapter, you learn to move and resize the file cabinet symbol so that the symbol fits neatly in the middle of the logo.

Fig. 12.2.

The file cabinet symbol as it appears in the drawing.

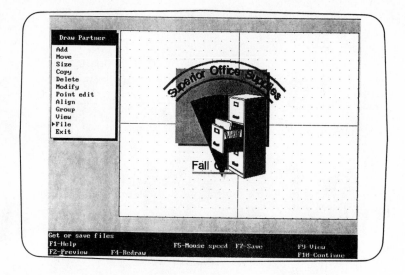

Modifying Objects Directly

Some of the commands on the Draw Partner main menu modify objects directly. These commands include the Move, Size, Copy, Delete, Group, and Align commands. The Modify menu holds another set of commands that perform more sophisticated alterations on objects. This section covers the commands that modify objects directly. The next section covers the Modify menu commands.

Moving and Sizing Objects

To move an object, you first must select the Move command from the Draw Partner menu and then select the object. Then you can move the box that surrounds the object to any other location on the screen. Using a mouse is the easiest way to move an object, but if you use the keyboard, press the minus key on the keypad at the right of your keyboard several times to reduce the amount the box moves each time you press an arrow key. Later, the plus key on the numeric keypad can increase the cursor movement again.

To size an object, select the Size command from the Draw Partner menu and then select the object to resize. When you select the object, a box surrounds it. Move the cursor to change the size of the box.

Before you proceed, make sure that the grid is still on and visible. If the grid is off, follow these steps:

1. Select View from the Draw Partner menu.

2. Select Grid from the View menu.

3. Select Grid On from the Grid menu.

4. Press 5 for the grid size and press Enter.

At the View menu, select Auto redraw and then select At All Changes from the Auto Redraw menu. This process makes Draw Partner update the screen after you make each change. If you select the other option, When Requested, the screen is updated only when you press F4 (Redraw). Press Esc to return to the Draw Partner menu.

Use the Size command to reduce the size of the file cabinet symbol by following these steps:

1. Select Size from the Draw Partner menu.

2. Select the file cabinet symbol.

3. Move the cursor down and to the left to reduce the size of the symbol until the symbol is approximately five grid points tall and three grid points wide.

4. Click the left mouse button or press Enter.

5. Press Esc to return to the Draw Partner menu. The smaller file cabinet appears as in figure 12.3.

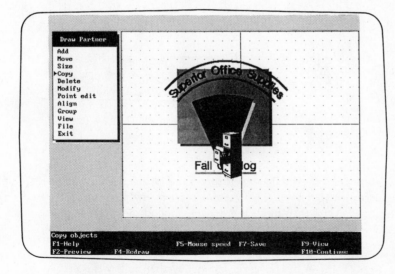

Fig. 12.3.

The smaller file cabinet.

Now use the Move command to properly position the symbol by following these steps:

1. Select Move from the Draw Partner menu.

2. Select the file cabinet symbol.

3. Move the box surrounding the file cabinet so that the box is slightly to the left of the center of the blue background box and extends above the top of the two wedges.

4. Press Enter or click the left mouse button.

5. Press Esc or the right mouse button to return to the main menu.

The symbol now should appear as shown in figure 12.4.

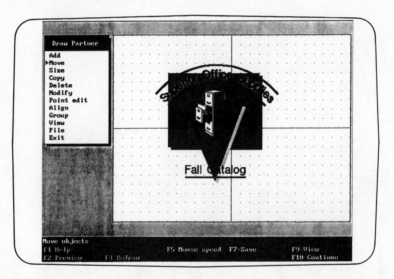

Fig. 12.4.

The symbol positioned properly.

Using the View Commands

Before you select an object, you may want to use one of the View commands so that you can better see your work. The View commands enable you to zoom into an area of the drawing and then move the drawing around the screen so that you can view just the area you want.

You can try using the View commands with the file cabinet you just placed on your catalog cover. To zoom in on the file cabinet symbol, follow this procedure:

1. Select View from the Draw Partner menu.

2. Select Zoom from the View menu.

3. Position the cursor above and to the left of the file cabinet symbol and then click the left mouse button or press Enter.

4. Move the cursor below and to the right of the file cabinet symbol so that the entire file cabinet is enclosed in a box.

5. Click the left mouse button or press Enter.

The area of the drawing you enclosed in a box, the file cabinet symbol, now fills the screen (see fig. 12.5).

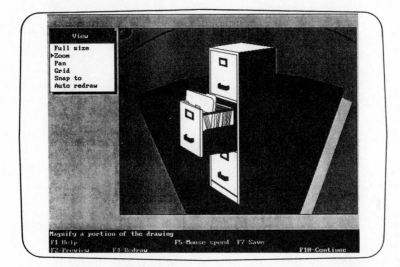

Fig. 12.5.

Zoom magnifies a portion of the drawing.

By using the Zoom command, you now see a smaller portion of the drawing in greater detail on-screen. The screen has become a window onto the drawing, which you can move to see other parts of your work. To move a zoomed-in window, use the Pan command.

When you select Pan from the View menu, a box appears on the screen that shows which part of the drawing you are viewing. At first, the box completely surrounds the screen. But if you move the cursor left or right, the box moves to cover a different part of the drawing, including some of the drawing that is off the edge of the screen. When you click the left mouse button or press Enter, the portion of the drawing enclosed on the box moves over and fills the screen. To use the Pan command, follow these steps:

1. Select Pan from the View menu.

2. Move the box up so that the box covers only the top half of the drawing.

3. Click the left mouse button or press Enter.

Now you can see the top half of the file cabinet and the area directly above the file cabinet (see fig. 12.6). To move back down so that you can see the entire file cabinet symbol again, select Pan, move the top edge of the box down so that it is just above the top edge of the file cabinet, and then press Enter or click the left mouse button.

Fig. 12.6.

Pan used to move the view of the drawing up.

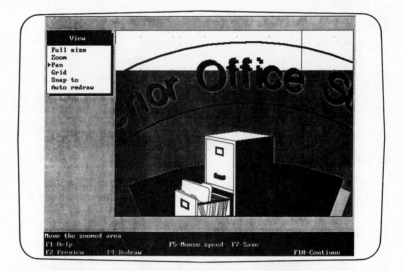

Another procedure you may find helpful is to select Full Size from the View menu and then use the zoom command again to see just the area you want. This procedure may be more helpful when you want to move quickly to another part of a drawing that is far away or you want to change the magnification factor.

To use this procedure, select Full Size from the View menu. Then, zoom in on the bottom half of the logo, being sure to include the words "Fall Catalog" at the bottom. Draw Partner now should be zoomed in on the bottom half of the logo, as shown in figure 12.7.

Grouping Objects

Rather than make changes to one object at a time, you can combine two or more objects into a group. Then you can make a change to the group, such as moving all of the objects together. You also can use the Group command to combine objects that are not meant to be separated, such as several different geometric shapes that form part of a company logo. You also can make more sophisticated changes to a group, such as flipping, sweeping, skewing, or changing the group's perspective. You learn about these modifications later in this chapter.

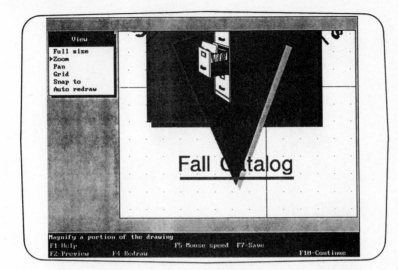

Fig. 12.7.

Zoom used to magnify the bottom half of the logo.

If you group objects and then include the group in another group, any modify command that you use to change the last group created also affects the objects in earlier groups. If you have several groups on-screen, you can group all of your groups into one object and then use one modify command to alter all of the groups simultaneously.

To group two objects, follow these steps:

1. Select Group from the Draw Partner menu. Draw Partner offers you the following choices:

    Everything. Groups everything in the drawing.

    In Box. Groups only those items that are surrounded completely by a box that you draw.

    Object. Groups only one object you select.

    Ungroup. Ungroups an existing group and returns its objects to independence.

2. Select In Box so that you can draw a box around two objects.

3. Select a point above and to the left of "Fall Catalog" and press Enter or click the left mouse button.

4. Select a second point below and to the right of "Fall Catalog" and the line that serves as an underline, as shown in figure 12.8.

5. Press Enter or click the left mouse button.

Fig. 12.8.

Selecting two objects to group by drawing a box around them.

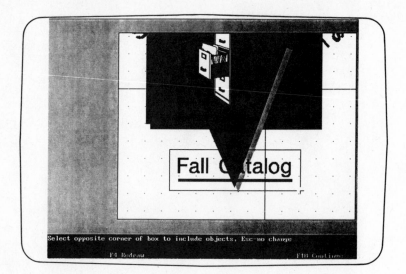

Four small circles appear at the corners of an imaginary box that contains the text and the line to show you which objects are included in the group. Note that the box also contains a portion of the two wedges you drew earlier. Because the wedges are not completely enclosed in the box, however, they are not included in the group.

6. Select Choose This from the In Box window that appears at the upper left corner of your screen to confirm your selection.

   You now can group other objects into a second group. If you select the wrong objects inadvertently, you can select Retry. Retry gives you a chance to select the correct objects.

7. Press Esc twice to return to the Draw Partner menu.

Now, try moving only the line without moving the text. You cannot make a change to only one of the objects in a group.

To ungroup the objects, select Group from the Draw Partner menu, then select Ungroup, and finally select the group you want to break up. If you have included a group as one of the objects in your group, the one created last is ungrouped first.

Copying and Deleting Objects

To copy an object, select the Copy command from the Draw Partner menu, select the object, and then identify a location for the copy.

Try adding and then copying an object by following these steps:

1. Add to the drawing a small box about one quarter the size of one of the squares marked by grid points.

2. Position the box just under the left end of the line under the text on your screen, as shown in figure 12.9. Use the following options:

   Shape: Square
   Box Style: Plain
   Size: 5.5
   Outline color: Doesn't matter
   Outline style: None
   Fill color: Cyan dk
   Pattern: Solid
   Shadow color: Doesn't matter

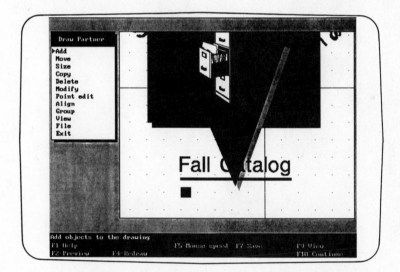

Fig. 12.9.

A box added to the drawing.

Now, you can copy the box you just added so that you have two identical boxes, one under each end of the line. To copy the box, follow these steps:

1. Select Copy from the Draw Partner menu.

2. Select the box you just created (make sure that the four small squares surround the box).

3. Move the cursor to the right until the small box is under the right end of the line.

The four small squares remain around the original item you are copying. You must position a hollow box to hold the copy.

4. Press Enter or click the left mouse button to copy the box to the new position. The drawing now should look like figure 12.10.

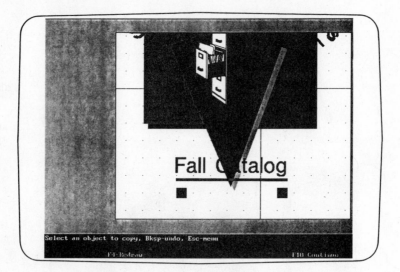

Draw Partner then tries to position another box the same distance away in the same direction so that you can continue to make copies of the box at even distances. The next copy box bumps against the right edge of the screen, however, so press Esc to stop the copying process. As with most Draw Partner operations, you can press Backspace immediately after a copy to undo the operation and try again.

Try another copy operation so that you can see the Delete command in action. Copy the leftmost box to the right just a bit, between the two boxes already on-screen. Then try pressing Enter or clicking the mouse button a few more times. Draw Partner copies the same box across the screen at equal distances. With the Copy command, therefore, you can make repeating patterns of objects.

To delete the extraneous boxes (and leave only the two original boxes), follow these steps:

1. Select Delete from the Draw Partner menu.

2. Select Object from the Delete menu.

3. Select the box copies to delete one by one.

If an object you want to delete is on top of another object, you must select Choose This or Retry to confirm the deletion. If the object is in the clear, the object is deleted immediately. To restore an object you have just deleted, press Backspace.

Aligning Objects

The Align command on the Draw Partner main menu enables you to line up two objects with one another. You can align two objects so that their tops, bottoms, left sides, right sides, or horizontal or vertical centers correspond. You also can align two objects so that their center points are over one another. This places one object on top of the center of another.

To align two objects, select the object that remains stationary, select an alignment type (left, right, top, bottom, and so on), and then select the object to align with the stationary object.

Figure 12.11 shows you all of the Align options.

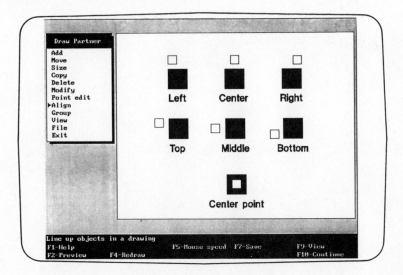

Fig. 12.11.

The Align options.

Use the Align command to modify the text, line, boxes, and the bottom of the logo. Begin by ungrouping the line and text so that you can align them separately. To ungroup these two objects, select Group from the Draw Partner menu, then select Ungroup from the Group menu, and finally select the group to ungroup. Then follow this procedure to align the text and line:

1. Select Align from the Draw Partner menu.

2. Select the line object on the drawing (make sure that the four small squares surround the line). You may need to ungroup the group composed of the text and line first.

3. Select This Object from the Align menu.

4. Select Left from the Align menu (to align the left edges of the text and the line).

5. Select the text (make sure that the four small squares surround the text).

6. Select This Object from the Align menu.

   You see the text redraw on-screen, aligned with the line. Use a similar procedure to align the box with the left edge of the line.

   While Align is still active, you can align the leftmost box with the line by selecting the box.

7. Press Esc twice to return to the Draw Partner menu. The first time you press Esc, you can choose another object to line up. The second time you press Esc, you return to the Draw Partner main menu.

Follow these steps to align the second box:

1. Select Align from the Draw Partner menu.

2. Select the line object on the drawing (make sure that the four small squares surround the line).

3. Select This Object from the Align menu.

4. Select Right from the Align menu (to align the left edges of the box and the line).

5. Select the rightmost box (make sure that the four small squares surround the box).

6. Press Esc to return to the Draw Partner menu.

   The box moves so that its right edge aligns with the right end of the line.

7. Select Choose This from the Align menu. Table 12.1 describes the align options.

Table 12.1
Options from the Align Menu

Option	Function
Center Point	Aligns the exact center of two objects so that one is on top of the second
Top	Aligns the top edges of two objects
Middle	Aligns the vertical center of two objects
Bottom	Aligns the bottom edges of two objects
Left	Aligns the left edges of two objects
Center	Aligns the horizontal center of two objects
Right	Aligns the right edges of two objects

Using the Modify Commands

The commands under the Modify menu make more sophisticated changes to the objects in your drawing. These commands enable you to flip and rotate objects, edit text, add shadows and perspective to objects, and perform other changes. Most of the capabilities these commands provide are unique to Draw Partner and do not appear in Draw/Annotate. This section covers each of these commands.

Positioning Objects in the Front or Back

Because the principle behind Draw Partner is that you add new objects until you have formed a completed drawing, each new object goes on top of the existing pile of objects. As you work, you may want to bring one of the objects from the pile to the top. You also may want to send an object in the pile to the bottom. Draw Partner offers two commands, Front and Back, that enable you to change how objects overlap.

To understand how Draw Partner works, imagine that your drawing is actually a painting on a canvas. The paint for each new object covers an object already painted on the canvas. When you paint, you are stuck with the layers of paint as you have added them. But when you use Draw Partner, you can move any layer of paint to the front or to the back of other layers. This capability is part of the power of Draw Partner and offers something you cannot do when you paint on canvas or when you use a paint-type software program.

Before you try the Front and Back commands, make one additional change to the drawing that will help you later. Group the two wedges into one object. The second wedge provides the three-dimensional effect for the first wedge, and the two should remain together, even if one is moved. To group the wedges, select Group from the Draw Partner menu, select Object from the Group menu, select the first wedge, and then select the second wedge. When both wedges are selected, press Esc and then select Choose This to join the two wedges into a group.

Notice that the group now moves to the front of the drawing, covering the words Fall Catalog and the file cabinet symbol, as in figure 12.12. (Use the Full Size command under the View menu to see the entire drawing again.) To fix this problem, you can move the wedges to the bottom of the pile using the Back command, but that action places the wedges behind the blue box. Instead, use the Front command to bring the file cabinet and text to the front.

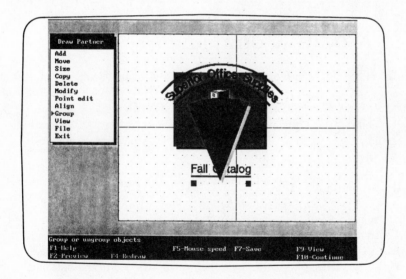

Fig. 12.12.

Grouping the wedges brings them to the front.

To use the Front command on these two objects, follow these steps:

1. Select Modify from the Draw Partner menu.

2. Select Front from the Modify menu.

3. Select the file cabinet symbol and press Enter or click the left mouse button.

   While the Front command is still active, you also can bring the text and line to the front.

4. Select the text and then select the line ("Fall Catalog" and the underline).

5. Press Esc to return to the Modify menu.

Changing Object Options

Just as in Draw/Annotate, you can change the options of objects you added earlier to a drawing. To do so, you must select the object and use the Modify Options command. Draw Partner then presents you with an options panel that shows all the current options settings for the object.

To change an option of an existing object, follow these steps:

1. Select Modify from the Draw Partner menu.

2. Select Options from the Modify menu.

3. Select one of the two small boxes.

4. Select This Object from the Options menu.

   Notice that all of the original options for the box appear in the Options panel at the left side of the screen.

5. Make whatever changes you want to the options. (In this case, change the fill color from Cyan to Yellow.)

6. Press F8 (Draw) to make the change.

Now you can make the same options change to another object, or you can press Esc to return to the menu. You also can press Backspace to undo your change. Press Backspace now to return the box to its original fill color.

If you choose a group of objects after you select Modify Options, the options panel for the objects shows the options that all of the objects share. By changing any or all of those options, you can change the appearance of the entire group simultaneously.

Flipping Objects

Draw Partner enables you to *flip* objects horizontally or vertically as though you were to pick the objects up, turn them over, and then place them back down again. A horizontally flipped object previously facing right now faces left. A vertically flipped object previously facing up now faces down. You can use this command to flip the file cabinet horizontally to face in the opposite direction and match the file cabinet in the logo you created in the guided tour of Draw Partner.

To flip the file cabinet horizontally, follow these steps:

1. Select Flip from the Modify menu.

2. Select Horizontal from the Flip menu (the other choice is vertical).

3. Select the file cabinet symbol.

When you confirm your choice by selecting Choose This, the file cabinet flips horizontally, facing to the right rather than to the left, as shown in figure 12.13. You can press Backspace to undo your last change. You must press F4 (Redraw) to fill in the space left by the repositioned file cabinet. Use the Move command from the Draw Partner main menu to move the file cabinet slightly to the right so that the file cabinet is centered again in the logo.

Fig. 12.13.

The file cabinet symbol flipped horizontally.

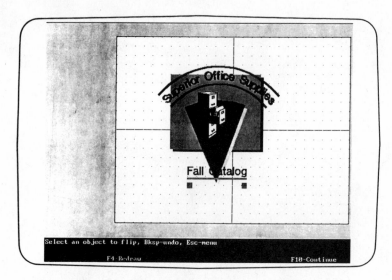

If you had chosen to flip the file cabinet vertically, the file cabinet now would be standing on its head with your papers all over the floor.

You cannot flip text as easily as you can flip other objects. The Flip command does not work with text objects. Instead, you must convert text into polygons or polylines, using the Point Edit Convert command. You then can use the Flip command on the polygons or polylines.

To convert text into polygons, select Point Edit from the Draw Partner menu and then select Convert. Select the text object and press Esc. Whether your text is converted to polygons or polylines depends on the weight of the text and whether the text has shadow (both options you set when you first add the text). After you convert the text, you can flip the group of polygons or polylines and achieve the effect of text reading backwards or upside down. You find more information about the Point Edit Convert command in the last section of this chapter.

Rotating Objects

Flipping objects changes the direction an object faces by 180 degrees. *Rotating* objects enables you to twist them by as little as a one-degree increment. You can use the mouse or the keyboard to visually rotate the object on-screen, or you can type a rotation angle between 1 and 359 after you press F6 (Type Angle). Zero degrees is at the 3 o'clock position, and the rotation angle increments counter-clockwise (90 degrees is at 12 o'clock).

To rotate one of the boxes under the text 45 degrees (to make a diamond), follow these steps:

1. Select Rotate from the Modify menu.

2. Select one of the two boxes.

3. Select This Object from the Rotate menu.

   A box appears around the object with an arrow pointing from its center to the right, as shown in figure 12.14.

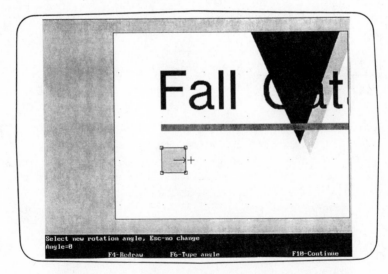

Fig. 12.14.

The box ready to be rotated.

4. Move the cursor around the box with the mouse or by using the arrow keys.

As you move the cursor, the box rotates and the Angle = number at the lower left corner of the screen changes to show the current rotation angle. By pressing the minus key on the numeric keypad, you can reduce the amount the cursor moves each time you press an arrow key. This procedure helps you rotate the object in smaller increments when you use a keyboard.

5. Press F6 (Type Angle) and then type 45 as the new rotation angle.

6. Press Enter or click the left mouse button.

7. Press Esc to return to the Modify menu.

Figure 12.15 shows the box rotated 45 degrees. You have made a diamond.

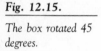

Fig. 12.15.

The box rotated 45 degrees.

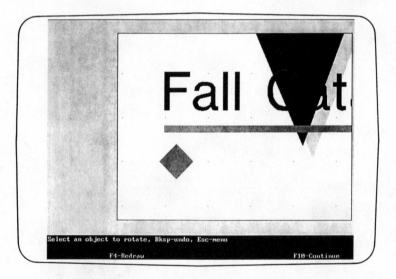

Unfortunately, you cannot easily restore most objects to their upright position unless you keep track of the angle to which you rotate the objects. If not, you have to use the Rotate command repeatedly, until the square looks level. If you keep track of the angle, you can type a complementary rotation angle that brings the object to a full 360-degree rotation and returns the object to its starting position. In this case, rotate the box by another 45 degrees to stand the box upright.

Modifying Text Using Edit Text

Using Modify Options to change a text object enables you to change any of the options that affect the appearance of the entire line of text. Edit Text under the Modify menu enables you to change the appearance of individual characters or words.

To use Edit Text, follow these steps:

1. Select Edit Text from the Modify menu.

2. Select the text object Fall Catalog.

The text returns to the bottom of the screen along with a text editing cursor. You can move the cursor and add new text or delete existing text. You also can press F8 (character options), highlight a portion of the text by using the left- or right-arrow keys or the mouse, and change options for those characters, including their color, weight, and whether they are italic or underlined. The Home key moves the cursor to the beginning of the line, and the End key moves the cursor to the end of the line.

To change character options, follow these steps:

1. Move the cursor before the word "Catalog" and type *1991* and a space.

2. Move the cursor back to the first character of 1991.

3. Press F8 (character options) and then move the cursor to the right with the right-arrow key to highlight the year number 1991.

4. Press Enter to accept your selection. A set of options for the text appears, as shown in figure 12.16. Notice that you can change four of the options that affect text (Color, Weight, Italic, and Underline).

5. When you finish making changes, press F8 (Enter Text) to continue.

6. If you have further changes, repeat the process. If not, press Enter to redraw the revised text.

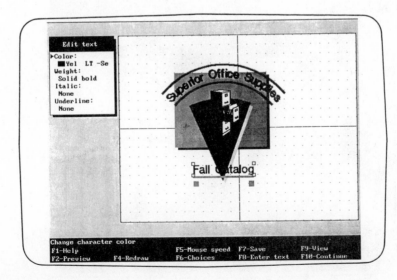

Fig. 12.16.

Options available for the selected text.

Notice that the text with the changes you made appears on-screen. Before continuing, press Backspace to undo these temporary changes.

Shadowing Objects

The Shadow command inserts an identical copy behind the original of any object in any color and position you choose. The result is the appearance of a shadow in one direction behind the object. You can use Shadow to create the yellow wedge, which adds a three-dimensional appearance to the red wedge. The advantage of the Shadow command is that the command adds an identical copy of the original and then groups the original and the copy into one object. The disadvantage is that you must ungroup the group to change or delete the shadow.

Use Modify Shadow to add a shadow to the two small boxes at the bottom of the logo. First, use the View Zoom command to zoom in on that area of the logo. Then follow these steps:

1. Select Shadow from the Modify menu.

2. Select the small box on the left.

3. Select Cyan as the color for the shadow and then press Enter.

4. Move the outline box that appears over the original box down and slightly to the right.

   You can press the Backspace key to return to the color selection menu.

5. Press Enter or click the left mouse button to place the shadow, as shown in figure 12.17.

Fig. 12.17.

A shadow added to the left box.

To delete a shadow, you must ungroup the object and its shadow and then delete the shadow object.

For balance, you should add the same shadow to the box at the right. You can try the Shadow command again, but you may have trouble creating the identical shadow. Instead, you may choose to delete the box at the right and copy the box with the shadow from the left to the right.

Skewing Objects

Skewing an object makes the object lean to the left or right. Just as your feet remain stationary when you lean while standing, the bottom points of an object remain stationary when you skew it. Only the top points move to the side. You can skew any object except text.

To use Skew, follow this procedure:

1. Select Skew from the Modify menu.

2. Select the box on the right at the bottom of the logo to skew.

3. Move the cursor to the left and right and watch the outline shape of the object change, as shown in figure 12.18.

4. Move the cursor to the right and press Enter or click the left mouse button.

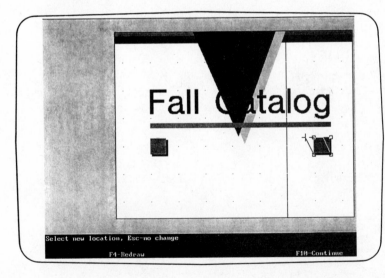

Fig. 12.18.

Moving the cursor to the left while using Skew.

Notice how the top two corners of the box are moved to the right, but the bottom two corners are in their original position. Skew looks particularly effective when used on an object with a shadow. In this case, skew actually is affecting a group of objects (the box and its shadow). You can skew one object as easily as you can a group, however. The skewed box and shadow appear in figure 12.19.

Before you proceed, press Backspace to return the box to its normal position.

Fig. 12.19.

The skewed box and shadow.

Sweeping Objects

When you *sweep* an object across the screen, Draw Partner creates multiple copies and places them along a line from the starting to the ending points you select. You can even instruct Draw Partner to gradually modify each new copy incrementally toward a particular effect such as a change in size, rotation, or skew.

To use Sweep, select an object to sweep. Then select an ending point and ending appearance for the object by executing a modification to the ending object. Finally, instruct Draw Partner how many intermediate objects to draw.

To sweep an object, follow these steps:

1. Select Sweep from the Modify menu.

2. Select the leftmost box as the object to sweep.

3. Select an ending position for the box near the lower right corner of the screen and press Enter (see fig. 12.20).

Fig. 12.20.

The location for the final object in the sweep.

Next, decide whether you want to modify the appearance of the final object so that there is a gradual transition from the original to the modified object. If you do not want to change the object, select Done from the menu at the left of the screen. In this case, however, try skewing the ending object and changing its size so that you can see the effect.

4. Select Skew and skew the box to the right.

5. Select Size and increase the size of the box.

6. Press Esc or click the right mouse button to indicate that you have finished making modifications.

7. Type 5 as the number of intermediate objects and press Enter. (You can enter up to 50 intermediate copies.)

Figure 12.21 shows you the seven objects you should see on-screen (the first, last, and five intermediate objects). Notice how the objects change gradually from the first to the last. All seven objects are grouped together as one object. To change any of the objects, you must ungroup them.

To return to the Modify menu, press Esc.

Although the Sweep command does work with text, you cannot use the skew and perspective options to modify the text gradually, unless you use Point Edit Convert to convert the text into a group of polygons or polylines. Then you can sweep the group to achieve either or both effects. Figure 12.22 shows an example of Sweep used on text converted to polygons.

Fig. 12.21.

Sweep used to copy and modify the square.

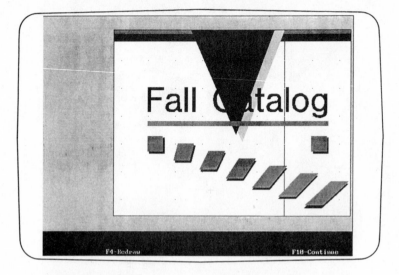

Fig. 12.22.

Sweep used on text converted to polygons.

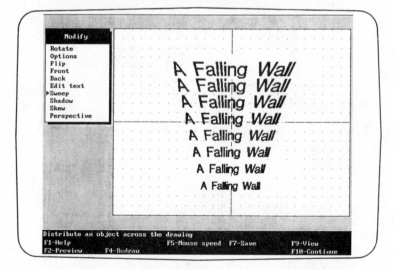

Putting Objects into Perspective

Draw Partner's Perspective command makes an object appear to recede into the distance by moving the top points of an object farther apart or closer together. Move the points closer together, and the object appears to lean back. Move the points farther apart, and the object leans forward. Modifying the perspective of an object that has been rotated causes a particularly dramatic effect.

To add perspective to an object, add a box with a three-dimensional effect to the lower left corner of your illustration. The box should have these options:

Shape: Square
Box style: 3D (with the 3D effect to the bottom right)
Size: 3
Outline color: Doesn't matter
Outline style: None
Fill color: Cyan dk
Pattern: Solid
Shadow: Yellow

Next, rotate the box 20 degrees, as shown in figure 12.23. Then follow these steps to add perspective to the box:

1. Select Perspective from the Modify menu.

2. Select the box you just added.

3. Move the cursor slightly to the right with the mouse or the right-arrow key so that the two sides of the outline box move together slightly at the top. You don't need too much perspective to see a dramatic change in the box. In fact, adding too much perspective can look silly—far worse than not adding enough. If you need to, press the minus key on the numeric keypad a few times to reduce the amount the cursor moves with each keypress.

4. Press Enter or click the left mouse button.

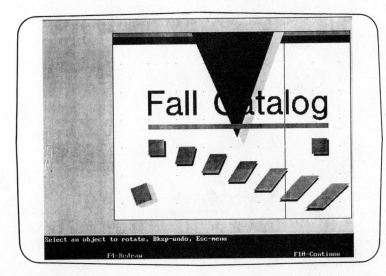

Fig. 12.23.

The box rotated 20 degrees.

The box redraws with perspective, as shown in figure 12.24. To return the box to its original configuration, you can press Backspace before you make any further changes, or you can follow the same procedure again, but move the top edges of the vertical sides farther apart by the same amount.

Fig. 12.24.

The rotated box with perspective added.

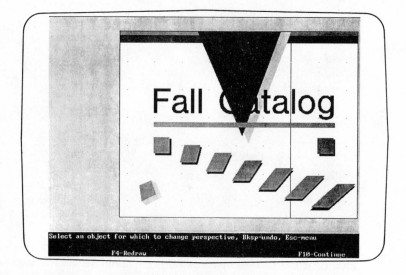

You cannot add perspective to text objects. You can convert a text object to polygons and polylines, however, and then add perspective to these objects.

Using Point Edit

As you have learned Draw Partner, you may have noticed that you specify the shape of most objects by selecting points. Two points are enough to describe the location and size of a line or circle. Three points are enough for a wedge. Polylines and polygons can require as many as 200 points.

The Point Edit commands enable you to control these points. You can add new points to existing objects, delete points, and move points to increase or decrease the number of sides in an object or to change the position of certain sides. The Break command adds two more endpoints to a line, splitting the line into two independent lines. The Join command deletes line endpoints and brings two separate lines or polylines together. The Break command also breaks the starting and ending points of polygons, converting them to polylines. The Close command does the reverse, joining the starting and ending points of polylines and forming polygons.

To see the various permutations of these commands, follow along with this example. You modify the line under the words Fall Catalog and change the line to a polygon with a rounded side. Then you break the polygon to form a polyline. After you are sure that you have a polyline, you can close the polyline to create a polygon once again. At the same time, you create a polyline so that you can see the effect of the Break and Join commands.

Before you proceed, ungroup the object composed of the seven boxes you made with the Sweep command. Then delete all of the boxes except for the original two (one under each end of the line).

Adding Points

Each time you choose to add a new point, Draw Partner suggests a new point on the edge of a polygon or on a polyline halfway between two existing points. A small diamond indicates the suggested point. If the polygon or polyline is composed of several sides, you can decide which side should get a new point halfway down its length. Then you can select a new position for the point.

To add a new point, follow these steps:

1. Select Point Edit from the Draw Partner menu.

2. Select Add from the Point Edit menu.

3. Select the thick line you added earlier under the text object "Fall Catalog."

   Draw Partner suggests the location for a new point halfway across the width of the line, along its top or bottom edge, by placing a small diamond on the line. If you move the cursor in a circle around the line, Draw Partner also suggests three other points (one in the middle of each end and one in the middle of the other side of the line).

4. Make sure that the point in the middle of the bottom of the line is selected and then press Enter or click the left mouse button. The drawing now should look like figure 12.25.

5. Move the cursor down so that the cursor is about even with the middle of the two small boxes. Press Enter or click the left mouse button.

The line is now a polygon with five sides (although the polygon looks roughly triangular). You now can add new points in the middle of any of the five sides of this polygon. Draw Partner is ready to add more points. To add two new points that pull the lower two sides of the polygon away from the center, follow this procedure:

Fig. 12.25.

A point added to the bottom middle of the line.

1. Move the cursor until the small diamond is in the middle of the lower right side of the polygon.

2. Click the left mouse button or press Enter and move the cursor slightly away from the center of the polygon to give the polygon a more rounded look (see fig. 12.26).

3. Click the left mouse button or press Enter to add the point.

4. Repeat this procedure for the lower left side.

5. Press Esc twice to return to the Point Edit menu.

Fig. 12.26.

Adding a point to the lower right side of the polygon.

Aligning Points

The Align command on the Point Edit menu enables you to align two points along an imaginary horizontal or vertical line. Align enables you to be sure that the new points you have added are even. To align the two latest points, follow this procedure:

1. Select Align from the Point Edit menu.

2. Select the polygon.

3. Move the diamond to the point in the middle of the lower right side.

   This point is the reference point against which you align the point on the opposite side.

4. Press Enter or click the left mouse button.

5. Select Horizontal on the menu that appears to indicate you want to align the points along an imaginary horizontal line.

6. Move the diamond to the opposite point on the left side and press Enter or click the left mouse button.

The left point moves to align with the right point. You can continue to align other points or press Esc to align points on another object. If you press Esc twice, you can return to the Point Edit menu to pick another command. Your drawing now should look similar to the drawing shown in figure 12.27.

Fig. 12.27.

The left bottom point aligned with the right bottom point.

Breaking a Polygon

The object you have created is a polygon, a polyline whose last point touches its first point. The Break command separates these two points and transforms a polygon into a polyline. If you use Break on a filled polygon, the only change you see is that the fill disappears. That makes sense, because you cannot fill a polyline that is not closed.

Break the polygon you have created by following these steps:

1. Select Break from the Point Edit menu.

2. Select the polygon.

3. Move the small diamond to a point along the polygon at which you want to break the polygon.

4. Press Enter or click the mouse button.

The fill disappears from the polygon, as shown in figure 12.28, but little else seems to change. If you try to modify the options of the object, you modify the options for a polyline.

Fig. 12.28.

The polygon after the Break command is used.

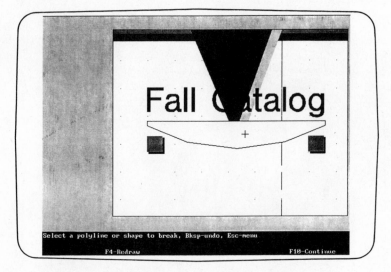

Breaking a Polyline

When you use the Break command on a polyline, the polyline becomes two polylines. You can think of the Break command as adding two endpoints to a polyline. After you break a polyline, you can modify its two pieces separately. To break a polyline, first add a polyline in the shape of a large letter W below the polygon, as shown in figure 12.29. Then follow this procedure:

1. Select Break from the Point Edit menu.

2. Select the polyline.

3. Move the cursor along the line until the small diamond is at the center of the object.

4. Press Enter or click the left mouse button.

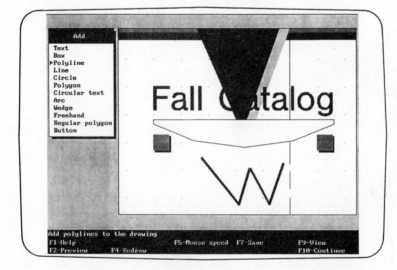

Fig. 12.29.

A polyline added to the drawing.

Now, the polyline is two polylines. You can select each polyline and make changes individually.

Closing a Polyline

The opposite of breaking a polygon is closing a polyline. A closed polyline is a polygon. To transform a polyline into a polygon, follow these steps:

1. Select Close from the Point Edit menu.

2. Select the polyline that was once a simple underline and press Enter or click the left mouse button.

3. Press Esc to return to the Point Edit menu.

Now you can use the Modify Options command to modify the polygon. To fill the polygon again, change its Pattern from Hollow to Solid.

Joining a Polyline

The opposite of breaking a polyline is joining two polylines, which removes one endpoint on each polyline and binds the two together into one object. Join the two polylines that form the letter W by following these steps:

1. Select Join from the Point Edit menu.

2. Select the polyline that is formed by the two left segments of the letter W.

   To join the two polylines into one object, which is the letter W, you select Endpoint from the menu that appears. This joins the endpoint of the left segment with a point on the right segment. To test all the options, select Start Point instead.

3. Select the polyline formed by the two right segments of the letter W.

A menu appears offering you two options: Nearest and Farthest. Move the highlight in this menu up and down so that you can see the effect of these two choices. Notice that Nearest joins the leftmost end of the first polyline with the nearest end of the second polyline, as shown in figure 12.30. The effect of Farthest point is shown in figure 12.31. But you don't need to join these lines now. Press Esc several times to return to the Point Edit menu.

Fig. 12.30.

Joining two polylines to the Nearest point.

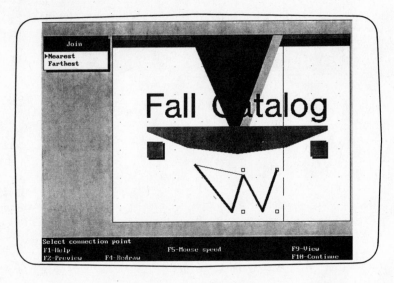

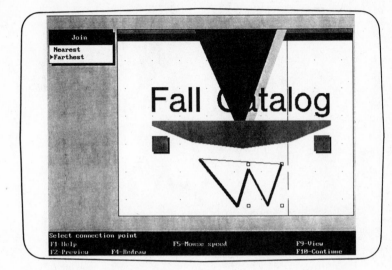

Fig. 12.31.

Joining two polylines to the Farthest point.

Moving a Point

You can move any of the points in an object by using the Move command under Point Edit. After you select Move, you select the object to edit and then the point to move. Select a new position for the point, and you are done.

To move a point, follow these steps:

1. Select Move from the Point Edit menu.

2. Select the polygon under "Fall Catalog."

3. Move the cursor until the small diamond appears on the bottommost point.

4. Click the left mouse button or press Enter to select the point.

5. Move the cursor down, as shown in figure 12.32, and press Enter.

The point moves down and the polygon changes shape. You can move another point immediately, or you can press Esc so that you can move a point on another object. Press Esc again to return to the Point Edit menu.

Deleting a Point

To delete a point, select Delete from the Point Edit menu, select the object that holds the point to delete, and move the small diamond to the point you want to delete.

Fig. 12.32.

Moving a point.

Fig. 12.32.

Moving a point.

To delete several points, follow these steps:

1. Select Delete from the Point Edit menu.

2. Select the polygon again.

3. Move the small diamond to the bottommost point and press Enter or click the left mouse button.

The bottommost point is deleted, as shown in figure 12.33.

Fig. 12.33.

The bottommost point deleted.

If you press Enter or click the left mouse button two more times, you remove the other two points you added to the original line, and the line is restored to the way the line was when you started. You can press Backspace at any time to restore the last point you deleted. To return to the Point Edit menu, press Esc twice.

Finally, delete the polyline forming the letter W to finish the logo. The catalog cover logo appears in figure 12.34.

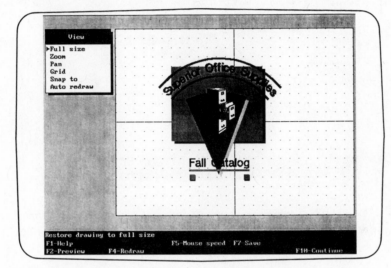

Fig. 12.34.

The completed catalog cover logo.

Converting Objects to Polygons or Polylines

The Convert command can transform three different types of objects into polygons or polylines: text, boxes, and lines. Whether the object is converted into a polygon or polyline or a group of polygons or polylines depends on which is closest to the original object. If an object is converted into a group of polygons (for example, a line of text may be converted into a group of polygons), you can ungroup the polygons and then edit the polygons individually. You no longer can use Edit Text to add or delete characters, but you can use other Modify commands you could not use before, such as Perspective. (Perspective does not affect text.)

To convert a line, box, or text object, select Point Edit from the Draw Partner menu and then select Convert from the Point Edit menu. Finally, select the object to convert and press Enter or click the left mouse button. Press Esc to return to the Point Edit menu.

Figure 12.35 shows several lines of text that first were converted and then reduced in size. Finally, their perspective was modified.

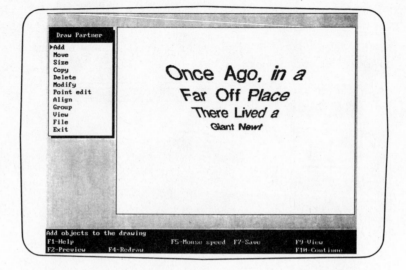

Fig. 12.35.

Text converted to polygons and then modified.

Now that you have finished your work, you should save your work as a Draw Partner drawing file and then return to Harvard Graphics and save the drawing file as a chart. You can print the chart to see your work.

Chapter Summary

In this chapter, you learned to modify the objects you add in Draw Partner. You can make some modifications by selecting from among commands on the Draw Partner main menu. You must select from among the Modify commands to make more sophisticated changes, however.

In the next section of this book, Part IV, you learn to use templates and macros to save time as you work in Harvard Graphics.

Part IV

Simplifying Your Work

Includes

Using Step-Savers: Templates

Using Step-Savers: Macros

13

Using Step-Savers: Templates

If you need to create charts and graphs regularly, the information in this chapter will help you a great deal. Especially if you update the same charts over and over, templates and macros are invaluable.

Templates are remarkable time- and effort-savers that store the basic blueprints for Harvard Graphics charts. With templates, you need to create a chart of a certain type from scratch only once. After that, you can load its template and let Harvard Graphics do all the work. The only embellishments you may want to add are annotations unique to that particular chart.

This chapter explains how to create and use templates and addresses their benefits and limitations. This chapter also covers how to manage groups of templates by storing them in a separate Harvard Graphics feature called a chartbook.

Macros, covered in the next chapter, can reduce your work further. After you have stored in a special macro file the keystrokes used to create a chart, you can reconstruct the chart with a single command. Harvard Graphics imitates the keystrokes you saved and constructs the same chart again. Using macros, you can automate virtually anything you find yourself doing repetitively in Harvard Graphics.

By combining templates and macros, you can reduce to almost nothing the amount of work required to create certain charts. For example, after you have updated the information in a 1-2-3 worksheet, you can run the macro you created earlier to import that data into a bar chart template. The template formats the chart, and then the macro saves the chart and prints it automatically. Users who need to graph data daily (or even more often) delight in the ability to use templates and macros in combination.

449

Templates are special Harvard Graphics files that store predefined charts. Templates provide a number of benefits:

- ❑ Eliminate creating frequently prepared charts from scratch
- ❑ Eliminate typing errors in recurring charts by including constant information
- ❑ Ensure that the formatting of all charts in a presentation is consistent
- ❑ Set the default features for new charts of each Harvard Graphics chart type
- ❑ Set up prefabricated charts for Harvard Graphics beginners

If you chart the same type of data regularly, you can use a template to store the characteristics that reappear time and time again. For example, a template for a bar chart can include your company's name as an underlined subtitle. Each week the company name appears as an underlined subtitle in the new bar chart. You need only to fill in the updated data.

If you need to prepare a presentation with a sequence of similar charts, you can create a single chart and then save it as a template. To record the sales volume of identical products at six regional sales offices, for example, you can create a single sales chart and then save it as a template. To create similar charts for the other sales offices, recall the same template for each office in succession, supply that office's data, and save the new chart.

Sometimes, the task of creating complex charts falls to people who are newcomers to computers and business graphics software. You can predefine charts for computer neophytes so that they can create full-fledged presentations with only minimal training.

Templates also come in handy as you prepare slide shows and screenshows (both covered in detail in Chapter 16). You can use templates to ensure that successive slides share certain characteristics, such as color schemes.

To create a template, you save a completed chart as a template file. To create a chart with the same features later, you call up the template instead of starting a chart from scratch.

By using special reserved names when you save templates, you can even have Harvard Graphics use template information when beginning any of its basic predefined chart types, such as line graphs. A special template for creating bullet lists, for example, may set all main bullets as checkmarks and their text sizes to 6. Any time you choose to create a bullet list, the new chart uses checkmarks and 6 as the text size. Another ideal use for templates is setting all charts created in a division so that they include the division's name as an italicized footnote.

Templates store the following characteristics of charts:

- ❑ Actual text and data
- ❑ Text size and placement
- ❑ Text attributes

❏ All Titles & Options page settings
❏ Draw/Annotate embellishments
❏ Import data links
❏ Titles and subtitles

Templates do not store the following:

❏ Print settings
❏ Setup Defaults settings

Creating a Template

To create a template, create a chart first with all its characteristics set. So that you can preview the chart and be sure that its settings are proper, use data similar to the data you use with the template. Real or dummy information does the trick. Return to the main menu, choose Get/Save/Remove, and then choose Save Template from the Get/Save/Remove menu. When Harvard Graphics prompts you for a name, enter up to eight characters. The program automatically supplies the template's TPL file extension and provides a description based on the title you supplied for the chart. To retrieve a template, choose Get Template from the Get/Save/Remove menu.

To learn how templates are made, create a template that Superior Office Supplies can use weekly to track sales of its two most popular products: pens and pencils. To display the sales results vividly, use a graph chart that combines both bars (for pencils) and a line (for pens).

To create the chart, follow these steps:

1. Start a bar chart by choosing Create New Chart from the Harvard Graphics main menu and then Bar/Line from the Create New Chart menu.

2. On the X Data Type Menu overlay, set the X Data Type option to Day and then type *Mon* at the Starting With option and *Fri* at the Ending With option. Leave the Increment option blank.

3. On the Bar/Line Chart Data screen, enter *Pen/Pencil Sales* as a title and *Stationery Division* as a subtitle. Leave the Footnote section blank.

4. Use the following two sets of sales results for Series 1 and Series 2:

Series 1	Series 2
21,000	32,000
26,300	21,700
27,500	29,800
28,200	21,700
34,000	20,000

5. After you have entered the data, pull up the Titles & Options pages by pressing F8 (Options). On the first Titles & Options page, set X Axis Title to Day and Y1 Axis Title to Units.

6. For the first Legend Title option, type *Pens*, and for the Type option, select Line. For the second Legend Title option, type *Pencils*, and for the Type option, select Bar.

7. Press PgDn to view the second Titles & Options page. On this page, set Bar Style to Overlap and Bar Enhancement to 3D.

8. Press PgDn to view the third Titles & Options page. On this page, include a data table by setting Data Table to Framed.

9. Press F2 to preview the chart. Figure 13.1 shows the completed pen/pencil weekly sales chart.

Fig. 13.1.

The Pen/Pencil Sales chart.

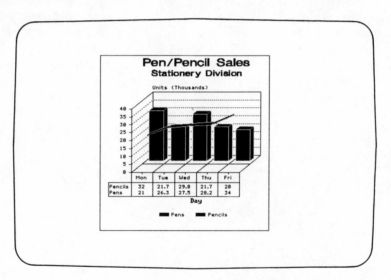

Because this chart is exactly what you have in mind for a weekly report, save it as a template to reuse from week to week. To save the chart as a template, press Esc two times to return to the main menu. Choose Get/Save/Remove from the main menu and then select Save Template from the Get/Save/Remove menu. Figure 13.2 shows the Save Template overlay that appears. When Harvard Graphics asks for a template name, enter *pen-pncl*, for "pen/pencil chart template." Harvard Graphics derives the template description it provides from the title of the chart. To accept the description already present, press Enter. To change the description, type new text over the present description and press Enter.

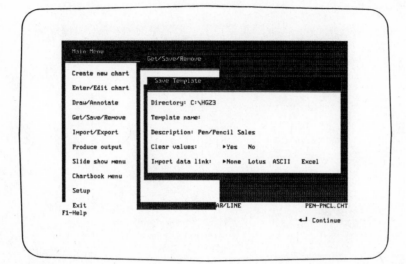

Fig. 13.2.

The Save Template overlay.

On the Save Template overlay still visible on your screen, Harvard Graphics asks whether you want to clear values. When you create a chart that will become a template, you need to use actual data so that you can format the chart properly. If you set Clear Values to Yes, Harvard Graphics deletes the chart's data before saving it as a template. To retain the current data so that it is included the next time the template is retrieved, set Clear Values to No. For this template, set Clear Values to Yes and press Enter so that Superior Office Supplies can start with a new, clear chart each week. That way, the company needs only to enter new data, and the chart is complete.

The last option on the overlay asks whether your chart includes a Lotus or ASCII data link. (Using templates with data links is covered in the following section.) For now, select None and press Enter. You see a warning message that reads Chart values are about to be cleared. Press Enter to continue and then press Esc to return to the main menu.

To use the template the following week, choose Get Template from the Get/Save/Remove menu (which you access from the main menu). Harvard Graphics displays a list of available templates and enables you to pick PEN-PNCL from the list.

When the template appears (see fig. 13.3), notice that it has retained its title and subtitle. In fact, all the settings on the Titles & Options pages are preset as well. The X data type already is set to Day, and Series 1 and Series 2 are properly renamed Pens and Pencils.

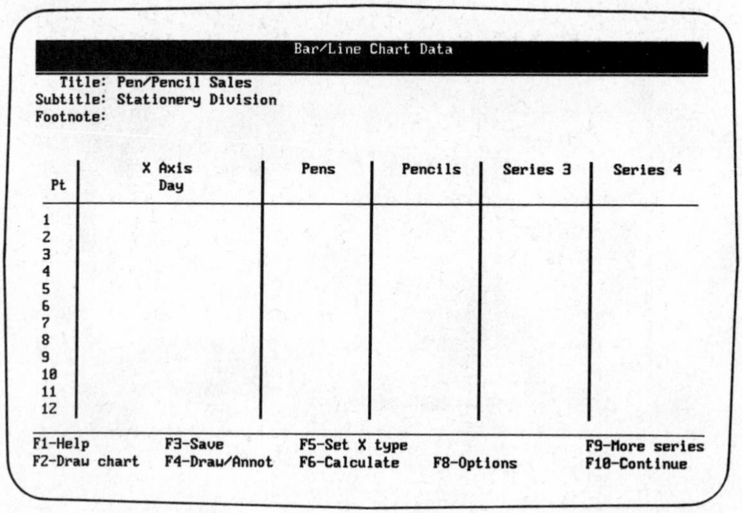

Fig. 13.3.

The PEN-PNCL
template.

```
┌─────────────────────────────────────────────────────────────────────┐
│                          Bar/Line Chart Data                        ▼ │
│                                                                       │
│        Title: Pen/Pencil Sales                                        │
│     Subtitle: Stationery Division                                     │
│     Footnote:                                                         │
│                                                                       │
│             X Axis          Pens        Pencils     Series 3   Series 4│
│     Pt      Day                                                       │
│     ────────────────────────────────────────────────────────────────│
│     1                                                                 │
│     2                                                                 │
│     3                                                                 │
│     4                                                                 │
│     5                                                                 │
│     6                                                                 │
│     7                                                                 │
│     8                                                                 │
│     9                                                                 │
│     10                                                                │
│     11                                                                │
│     12                                                                │
│                                                                       │
│  F1-Help        F3-Save      F5-Set X type              F9-More series │
│  F2-Draw chart  F4-Draw/Annot F6-Calculate  F8-Options  F10-Continue  │
└─────────────────────────────────────────────────────────────────────┘
```

To use the template, you need to reset the x-axis Starting With and Ending
With settings, but that takes only a moment. Press F5 (Set X Type) and reenter
Mon and *Fri* as the Starting With and Ending With options, respectively. Now
type imaginary data for the chart's values and then press F2 to preview the chart.
All the chart's formatting is in place. Save the chart as PEN-PCL1 so that you
can retrieve it later in this chapter as you learn how to create a chartbook.

Using Templates To Set
Default Chart Styles

Using templates, you can predefine the default formatting for each of the charts
in the Harvard Graphics repertoire. When you choose Create New Chart from
the main menu, Harvard Graphics scans the files on disk to see whether you
have created a template for that chart type. If you have, the program uses that
template to set the chart characteristics that are predefined.

By using templates to set default chart styles, you can ensure consistency in the
charts produced within a company, department, or division. For example, you
can decide that all pie charts will display a graphic of the company logo in the
top right corner, use the Roman font, and include the company name italicized
in the subtitle with a text size of 13.

To create a default template for a chart type, create one representative chart that
includes all the characteristics you want to include in all future charts of that

type and save the chart with the proper reserved template names. For example, to create the default template for all future area charts, name the template AREA when you save it. Here are the reserved names for default chart style templates:

Chart Style	Name
Title charts	TITLE
Simple lists	LIST
Bullet lists	BULLET
Two-column charts	2_COLUMN
Three-column charts	3_COLUMN
Free-form charts	FREEFORM
Pie charts	PIE
Bar or line charts	BARLINE
Area charts	AREA
High/low/close charts	HLC
Organization charts	ORG
Multiple charts	MULTIPLE

Importing Data into a Template-Based Chart

If you have established a data link with a Lotus or Excel worksheet or an ASCII data file by using an Import command, you can instruct Harvard Graphics to use the same data link when it creates a chart from a template. That way, you can update the data in the Lotus, Excel, or ASCII data file, for example, by changing your figures in a Lotus worksheet. When you retrieve the template, Harvard Graphics pulls in the revised data from the worksheet or data file and uses the template settings to format the chart. With just one step in Harvard Graphics, your chart is complete.

To create a template with a data link to an external data file, create a chart that uses a data link and save the chart as a template. When you save the template, the Import data link option on the Save Template overlay reflects that you used a Lotus, Excel, or ASCII data link. Leave the Import data Link setting as is and save the chart. Setting Import Data Link to None breaks the data link so that you can create a different data link.

Using Chartbooks
To Manage Templates

Templates are so useful that you probably will create dozens of them as you use Harvard Graphics. For you to manage groups of templates, Harvard Graphics provides a special type of file called a *chartbook*.

A chartbook contains a catalog of templates you assemble to manage related charting needs. A typical chartbook may hold, for example, all templates you have fashioned for bulleted lists. Another chartbook may hold all the charts you create as part of a quarterly presentation to the division vice president.

Creating a Chartbook

You can practice creating a chartbook with more than one template by using the chart you created earlier in this chapter to create a second template that is altered in several respects.

Follow this procedure to create a second template:

1. Get the chart entitled PEN-PCL1 by selecting Get Chart from the Get/ Save/Remove menu.

2. On the second Titles & Options page, set Bar Style to 100% so that you can compare the relative percentages of sales of pens and pencils.

3. Save the new chart as a template with the name PP-PRCNT. Set Clear Values to Yes and Import Data Link to None.

4. Press Esc to return to the main menu.

Now you have two related templates that you can store in a chartbook. To create the chartbook, follow these steps:

1. Select the Chartbook Menu option from the main menu.

2. Select Create Chartbook from the Chartbook menu. The Create Chartbook overlay appears (see fig. 13.4).

3. Enter *pen-pncl* as the name of the chartbook. (There is no problem with using the same name as one of the templates because Harvard Graphics supplies the chartbook file with an extension reserved for chartbooks—CBK.)

4. Type *Pen and Pencil Sales Comparison Charts* as a description for the chartbook and press Enter. The Create/Edit Chartbook screen appears (see fig. 13.5).

Main Menu
Chartbook Menu
Create new chart
Enter/Edit chart
Draw/Annotate
Get/Save/Remove
Import/Export
Produce output
Slide show menu
Chartbook menu
Setup
Exit
F1-Help
Create Chartbook
Directory: C:\HGZ3
Chartbook name:
Description:
AR/LINE
PEN-PNCL.CHT
Continue

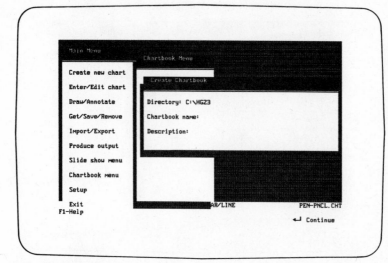

Fig. 13.4.

The Create Chartbook overlay.

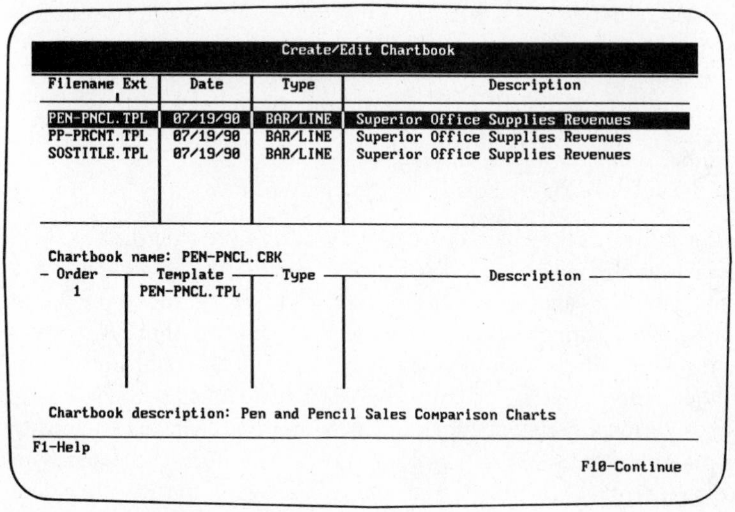

Create/Edit Chartbook
Filename Ext
Date
Type
Description
PEN-PNCL.TPL 07/19/90 BAR/LINE Superior Office Supplies Revenues
PP-PRCNT.TPL 07/19/90 BAR/LINE Superior Office Supplies Revenues
SOSTITLE.TPL 07/19/90 BAR/LINE Superior Office Supplies Revenues
Chartbook name: PEN-PNCL.CBK
Order
Template
Type
Description
1
PEN-PNCL.TPL
Chartbook description: Pen and Pencil Sales Comparison Charts
F1-Help
F10-Continue

Fig. 13.5.

The Create/Edit Chartbook screen.

At the top of the Create/Edit Chartbook screen is a list of templates in the current directory on your disk. Below that are the contents of the chartbook you are about to create. The chartbook is empty, but the currently highlighted template name on the list above appears to be the first entry. To choose the template called PEN-PNCL.TPL, use the arrow keys to highlight its name and press Enter. To add a second related template, PP-PRCNT.TPL, highlight its name and press Enter. Figure 13.6 shows the Create/Edit Chartbook screen with both templates added to the PEN-PNCL chartbook.

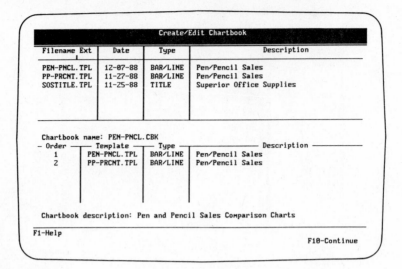

Now press Tab several times and notice three different results in the bottom half of the screen. Your three possible courses of action (other than saving the chartbook and continuing on) are to

- ❏ Edit the description of the chartbook
- ❏ Add another template to the chartbook's contents
- ❏ Change the order of the templates in the chartbook

When the cursor moves to the chartbook description, stop pressing the Tab key. Now you can change the chartbook's description by editing it or by typing in a new description. Press Tab and notice that you can now add another template to the chartbook by highlighting a template name with the up- and down-arrow keys and pressing Enter. Press Tab once again. Now one of the templates in the chartbook is highlighted. You can change the order of templates in the chartbook to suit your personal preference by positioning the highlight on a template name and pressing Ctrl-up arrow or Ctrl-down arrow. The highlighted template moves up or down in the list. When you are satisfied with the new template order, press F10 (Continue) to save the chartbook on disk and return to the Chartbook menu.

To delete a template from a chartbook, press Tab so that any one of the template names on the chartbook contents list is highlighted, move the highlight to the template you want to delete by using the up- and down-arrow keys, and press Ctrl-Del. The chartbook no longer includes the template in its catalog, but the template remains available on disk.

Choosing a Template from a Chartbook

To open a chartbook so that you can select from among its templates, follow these steps:

1. Select the Chartbook Menu option from the Harvard Graphics main menu.

2. Choose Select Chartbook from the Chartbook menu.

3. Highlight the chartbook you want to select and press Enter to open the chartbook and return to the Chartbook menu.

If you choose From Chartbook after selecting Create New Chart from the main menu, Harvard Graphics enables you to choose from among the templates in the currently open chartbook.

If you have specified a default chartbook on the Default Settings screen, you need only select a chartbook to open if it is different from the default chartbook. Otherwise, the default chartbook is open at all times. The From Chartbook option on the Create New Chart menu shows you the contents of the default chartbook.

Modifying an Existing Chartbook

You easily can modify the contents or order of templates in an existing chartbook. If the chartbook you want to modify is the default chartbook, choose Edit Chartbook from the Chartbook menu. If the chartbook you want to modify is not the default chartbook, you first must use Select Chartbook from the Chartbook menu and then select Edit Chartbook.

Chapter Summary

This chapter described how to use templates to automate the task of creating graphs and make repetitive chores easy. In the next chapter, you learn to use macros, another Harvard Graphics step-saver, to automate the process of working in Harvard Graphics. Macros can automate making, saving, and printing charts, among other tasks.

14

Using Step-Savers: Macros

Of all the work computers do, repetitive chores are the tasks for which computers are probably the most appreciated. Even though their human counterparts perform tasks more than once only begrudgingly, computers obey repetitive commands unquestioningly. If you need to perform a charting task regularly, such as creating a weekly pie chart for your office, why not put your computer on the case?

To automate repetitive procedures, you can use a feature common to most popular software programs called a *macro*. Harvard Graphics provides its own version of macros with a special add-on utility called MACRO. With macros, you can record all the keystrokes that go into performing a specific Harvard Graphics function. Later, when you need to carry out the exact same task, you can run the macro and watch as Harvard Graphics performs an instant replay of the same routine, step by step, just as you recorded it. Using a special feature of the Harvard Graphics MACRO utility, you can even have a macro depart from its script, pausing temporarily to enable whoever is sitting at the computer to enter revised data or make additional changes to the chart.

By using macros in combination with templates, you can speed your work even further. With a macro, you can load a preformatted chart, pull revised data from an external data file, save the file, and even print the chart with as little as a single keystroke combination. As the ultimate example of the power of macros, imagine a hypothetical 1-2-3 user employing a 1-2-3 macro to update the figures in a 1-2-3 worksheet by importing sales results from a Point-of-Sale system. Combined with that, the user takes advantage of a Harvard Graphics macro that retrieves a template including a data link to the Lotus worksheet and prints the chart. With just a few keystrokes, the hypothetical chart maker has fashioned a complete Harvard Graphics chart, with all the bells and whistles.

461

Harvard Graphics 2.3 includes the new Version 1.1 of MACRO. This version is compatible with DOS 4. Version 1.0 of MACRO, the version that shipped with earlier releases of Harvard Graphics, works only with DOS 3.3 and earlier.

Recording a Macro

To record macros, you must run a separate utility before actually starting Harvard Graphics. This utility, called MACRO, resides in the same DOS directory as Harvard Graphics. MACRO was installed in this directory when you installed Harvard Graphics.

To run MACRO, follow these steps:

1. Change to the directory in which Harvard Graphics is installed.

2. Before typing *hg* to start Harvard Graphics, type *macro* and press Enter.

You see an overlay indicating that the MACRO utility is now ready for action (see fig. 14.1).

Fig. 14.1.

MACRO loaded and ready.

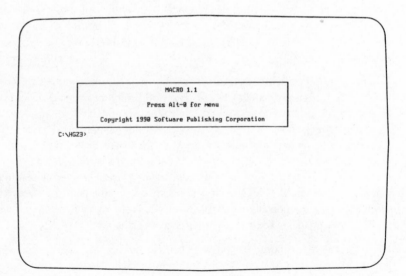

After MACRO is loaded, do the following:

1. Start Harvard Graphics by typing *hg* and pressing Enter.

2. Press Alt-0 (zero) when the Harvard Graphics main menu appears.

The main MACRO overlay appears (see fig. 14.2).

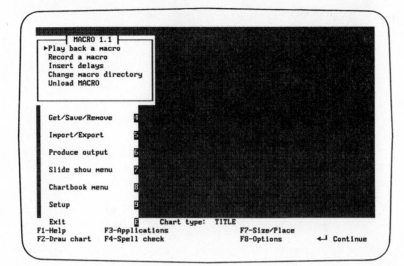

Fig. 14.2.

The main MACRO overlay.

Pressing Alt-0 any time you are viewing one of the Harvard Graphics menus summons the MACRO overlay, which offers a number of choices. To play back an existing prerecorded macro, choose Play Back a Macro. To create a macro, choose Record a Macro. The other choices on the MACRO menu provide additional commands covered later in this chapter.

To record a macro, choose Record a Macro on the MACRO overlay, carry out the exact same steps you want the computer to repeat later, and then press Alt-0 and choose Stop Recording Macro from the MACRO overlay. Stop Recording Macro is a new choice that appears after you start recording a macro. Suppose that you want to create a macro to retrieve and print PEN-PCL1, the chart you created earlier in this chapter. To start such a macro, select Record a Macro from the MACRO overlay (press R—the first letter of the option's name—or move the cursor-movement key to highlight the choice and press Enter). A second, smaller overlay appears to request a standard DOS file name of up to eight characters for the macro you want to record. The cursor is positioned next to a prompt showing the current directory. If you type the macro name at the current cursor position, Harvard Graphics saves the macro in your main Harvard Graphics directory.

Storing macros in the same directory as the Harvard Graphics program or data files works fine, but you also may want to keep all macros together in a separate directory so that the macros do not clog your main Harvard Graphics directory with too many additional files. To make this step easy, type the following at the DOS prompt before starting the MACRO utility:

SET MACROS = *path name*

(You may want to include this step in a batch file that starts Harvard Graphics.) For *path name*, substitute the full name of a directory you have created especially for storing macros—C:\HG23\MACROS, for example. Then, when Harvard Graphics prompts for a macro name, the program supplies the correct directory location for saving the macro.

For now, type *pp-print* (for "print the pen-pencil chart") at the Macro Name prompt and press Enter. Figure 14.3 shows how the Macro Name overlay looks before you type the macro name. Then the MACRO overlay disappears, and Harvard Graphics looks ready for business as usual. Record these steps by running through them once (be sure to use numbers rather than the space bar at this stage to select from Harvard Graphics menus):

1. Press 4 to select Get/Save/Remove from the main menu.

2. Press 1 to select Get Chart from the Get/Save/Remove menu.

3. Type *pen-pncl* and press Enter to select the chart named PEN-PNCL from the file list.

4. Press Esc to return to the Bar/Line Chart Data screen.

5. Press F10 (Continue) to return to the main menu.

6. Press 6 to select Produce Output from the main menu.

7. Press 1 to choose Printer from the Produce Output menu.

8. On the Print Chart Options overlay, choose the following:

   Quality: High
   Chart Size: 1/4
   Paper Size: Letter
   Printer: Printer 1
   Color: No
   Number of Copies: 1

9. Press Enter and watch as your output device produces the chart.

When you have run through all the steps you want to record successfully, press Alt-0 to call up the MACRO overlay again. Now select Stop Recording Macro from among the options by pressing S, the first letter of the command name, or by moving the highlight to the choice and pressing Enter. Figure 14.4 shows the MACRO overlay displayed when you press Alt-0 while recording a macro. Notice three new choices on the overlay: Stop Recording Macro, Insert Delays, and Type Macro Commands. The macro menus change as necessary to offer you the proper options for the current step in working with macros.

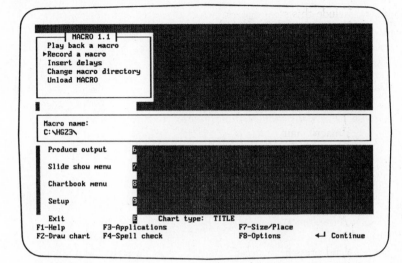

Fig. 14.3.

The Macro Name overlay.

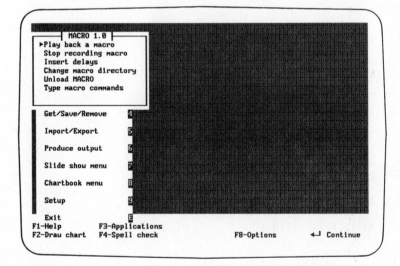

Fig. 14.4.

The MACRO overlay with three new choices.

Recording any macro always works the same way:

1. Summon the MACRO overlay by pressing Alt-0.

2. Select Record a Macro from the overlay.

3. Execute the procedures to be recorded.

4. Summon the MACRO overlay again by pressing Alt-0.

5. Select Stop Recording Macro from the overlay.

Here is one suggestion for recording macros: Always start recording a macro from the Harvard Graphics main menu and return to the main menu before stopping the macro recording. That way, you can be sure that the macro starts properly at the Harvard Graphics main menu.

By naming a macro with a letter or number, you can instruct MACRO that you want to play back the macro by pressing Alt and that key. To create a macro that runs when you press Alt-S, for example, name the macro S.

Playing Back a Macro

To play back a prerecorded macro, you must have the MACRO utility loaded in memory before you start Harvard Graphics. To load the MACRO utility, type *macro* before starting Harvard Graphics. You see an overlay indicating that MACRO is ready. After you start Harvard Graphics and its main menu appears, press Alt-0 to summon the MACRO overlay and select Play Back a Macro from the overlay options. You see a prompt for the name of the macro. Type the correct macro name and press Enter. Harvard Graphics runs through its paces automatically. If you ever need to interrupt a macro during execution, press Alt-End.

To play back the macro you recorded earlier in this chapter, press Alt-0 at the Harvard Graphics main menu to call up the MACRO overlay. Select Play Back a Macro by pressing P, type the file name *pp-print* when Harvard Graphics requests the name of the macro to play back, and press Enter. Unless you have taken special care when recording the macro to have the macro return to the main menu before proceeding, make a habit of starting macros from the main menu. That way, you can be sure that the macros always start at the same place you started when you recorded the macros.

Editing a Macro File

If you make a mistake while recording a macro, you can do one of two things: stop recording the macro and start over or edit the macro file to make your corrections. In fact, editing a macro file is the only way you can change the operation of a macro, after the macro is recorded, without creating a macro from scratch.

As you record a macro, you actually are writing abbreviations for each of the keystrokes you carry out into a standard DOS file. To change the macro, you can delete some abbreviations and add others with any word processor capable of reading and writing ASCII computer files (plain text file format). You also can add comments to the macro so that the macro is easier to understand, or you can include messages that the user sees as the macro runs.

To edit a macro file, call the file up with any standard word processor and make additions and deletions just as you would to any text document. If you edit the macro file PP-PRINT.MAC, which prints the PEN-PNCL chart you recorded earlier, the macro appears as shown in figure 14.5. Special macro commands are surrounded by <CMD>. If you press the space bar to choose from among menu options as you record the macro, actual spaces appear in the macro file. Keys other than the alphanumeric set are enclosed in greater-than and less-than symbols, and any alphanumeric characters you typed appear exactly as entered. Appendix H in the Harvard Graphics user's manual provides a list of actual keystroke combinations and their macro file representations. If you need to add keystrokes, the letters C, A, and S can replace Ctrl, Alt, and Shift in the macro keystroke representations. For example, you can type <CtrlM> as <CM>.

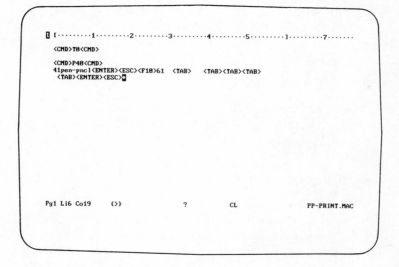

Fig. 14.5.

The PP-PRINT macro as it appears in a word processor.

Notice that the PP-PRINT.MAC macro shown in figure 14.5 begins with two special commands: T0 and P40. These two commands, which start every macro, set an initial timing delay and polling delay. A *timing delay* slows down the execution rate of a macro by adding time between each macro step. A *polling delay* also slows macro execution to prevent Harvard Graphics from dropping keystrokes as the program runs macros. The MACRO program records a default timing and polling delay in each macro file that you create. The next section of this chapter describes these two commands and a number of others that you encounter and use in Harvard Graphics macros.

Harvard Graphics macros have a variety of special features that you can set by calling up the MACRO overlay again as you record a macro. These features, discussed later in this chapter, carry out such tasks as waiting until a specific time before continuing the macro. Each of these features adds a special command to the macro file you are recording. When you examine such a file, therefore, you are likely to encounter these special entries:

<*comment>

You can embed comments in macro files as a reminder to you of how the macros work or to communicate that information to someone else examining the macro file later. Comments start with <* and end with >. Comments are completely transparent to the operation of the macro and do not affect how the macro works. An example is <*This next section prints the file>.

<AUTO>

If you want to send a macro into a repeating loop that returns to the beginning of the current macro, place <AUTO> at the end of the macro to be repeated. The MACRO utility repeats the current macro even if the macro is embedded within another macro. You can cancel a repeating macro by pressing Alt-End as the macro is playing back.

<CMD><*Message to be displayed on-screen><CMD>

When Harvard Graphics encounters the preceding command in a macro file, the program displays the message following the asterisk. This message can be up to 22 lines long. An example is <CMD><*Please enter a chart file name><CMD>.

<CMD>Pnnnn<CMD>

To introduce a polling delay in a macro, type a polling delay number from 1 to 9,999. Polling delays slow the execution of the macro so that the macro does not drop any of your keystrokes as it plays back (for technical reasons). If you find that your macros are skipping steps, increase the polling delay by 50 and try again. You may have to increase the delay several times until the macro works dependably. An example is <CMD>P1500<CMD>.

<CMD>Fmacro file name<CMD>

The preceding entry temporarily pauses the current macro and runs the second macro specified after the F by macro file name. This macro enables you to nest a second macro, such as a macro to print the current chart, within a macro. An example is <CMD>FPRNTR2.MAC<CMD>. You must be sure to include the extension of the macro file name (MAC).

<CMD>Rhh:mm:ss:nn<CMD>

The preceding entry pauses the execution of a macro for the time specified in hours (hh), minutes (mm), seconds (ss), and milliseconds (nn). You must specify each time unit, even if the time unit is zero, but you can drop leading zeros. To enter a minute-and-a-half pause in the execution of a macro, enter <CMD>R0:1:30:0<CMD>.

<CMD>T*nnn*<CMD>

The preceding entry enters a timing delay into a macro. The time unit *nnn* is a number from 0 to 999. A timing delay of 18 is equal to 1 second. Divide the timing delay by 18 to calculate the current delay between each macro step. An example is <CMD>T35<CMD> (35 divided by 18 is nearly 2 seconds).

<CMD>W*hh:mm*<CMD>

The preceding entry pauses the macro until a time specified in hours (hh) and minutes (mm). Be sure to use 24-hour time. As an example, to continue a macro that prints charts late in the evening when the printer is free, enter <CMD>W23:00<CMD>. Of course, if you forget to leave on the printer before leaving for the night, Harvard Graphics stops and displays the same message the program always displays when the printer is not ready (Output device is not ready) until you arrive the next morning.

<STOP>

The preceding entry stops the execution of a macro and unloads MACRO from memory if you have exited Harvard Graphics and returned to DOS.

<VFLD><VFLD>

This entry inserts a variable field in a macro. Variable fields are described in detail later in this chapter.

Using Special MACRO Features

The MACRO program provides a host of special commands for fine-tuning the execution of macros. You can use these features by selecting from the MACRO program's menu, summoned with Alt-0, or by entering commands as you edit a macro in a word processor.

Nesting Macros

When programmers write computer programs, the programmers make their work easier by writing and then joining separate modules, each designed to accomplish a specific task. You can emulate this method by writing individual macros to accomplish specific tasks, such as retrieving a chart from disk or printing the current chart. This approach also provides you with a set of macros you can use to automate specific Harvard Graphics steps, as well as larger macros that carry out full procedures. After each macro that accomplishes a specific step is recorded and saved on disk, you can call the macro from within another macro as you record the macro by using one of two approaches.

First, as you create a macro and reach the point where a second macro should run, press Alt-0 and select Play Back a Macro from the MACRO overlay. Enter the second macro name and press Enter. When the second macro finishes running, continue recording the first macro.

A second approach is to edit the macro file and enter the special command described earlier:

    <CMD>F*macro file name*<CMD>

Figure 14.6 shows how several lines of a macro may look with a second macro embedded. Notice that the embedded macro is named C:\HG\PP-PRINT.MAC.

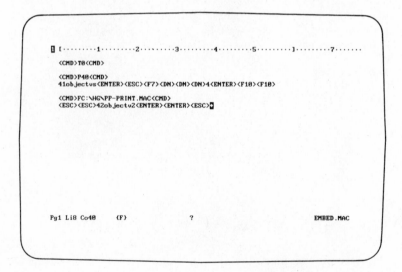

Fig. 14.6.

The PP-PRINT macro embedded within another macro.

When you run a second macro within a macro, you need to use the same care as when you record a single macro. You should play back every macro from the same place you started recording the macro. To ensure that you do, return to the main menu during a macro before calling up a second macro. In fact, because you always are returning to the main menu before starting a new macro, you can think of nesting macros as stringing a chain of macros together.

Pausing a Chart Display

Whenever a macro includes the command to preview a chart with the F2-Draw Chart selection, the macro pauses for 30 seconds while the chart is displayed. To cut short this pause as you record the macro, press the Ctrl key and the right Shift key at the same time (Ctrl-Right Shift).

You also can set a specific delay by pressing Alt-0 just before pressing F2 (Draw Chart) as you record a macro. Select Insert Delays from the MACRO overlay and Real-Time Delay from the Delays overlay that appears (see fig. 14.7). Type the number of seconds for the delay and press Enter. Then press Esc twice to return to recording the macro.

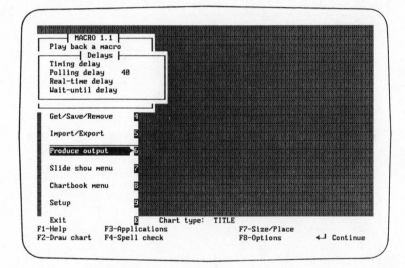

Fig. 14.7.

The Delays overlay.

You also can change a playback delay by editing the macro file and entering a <CMD>R*hh:mm:ss:nn*<CMD> command just before F2 in the macro file.

Including Variable Fields

By including a *variable field*, you can allow whoever is playing back the macro to supply certain information as the macro proceeds. If your macro prints a chart, for example, you can let the user enter the chart name to print. The macro pauses for your input during playback. Another good use for variable fields is to request that the user enter a new name for a saved chart so that the new chart's information does not overwrite the original.

To include a variable field in a macro, press Ctrl-- (hyphen) as you record the macro. Nothing appears any differently, but the macro recording pauses and enables you to enter anything you want without recording it. To continue recording actual macro commands, press Alt-0.

When the macro with the variable field plays back, the program stops at the variable field for your input, telling you to press F10 to begin typing. Figure 14.8 shows this prompt on-screen during macro playback. When you are finished, press Alt-0 to continue playing back the macro.

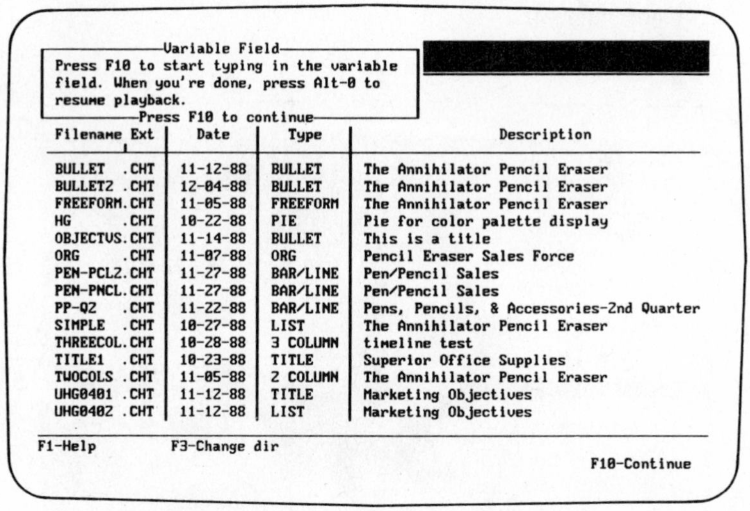

Fig. 14.8.

A variable field during macro playback.

```
┌─Variable Field────────────────┐ ████████████████████████
│ Press F10 to start typing in the variable │
│ field. When you're done, press Alt-0 to   │
│ resume playback.                          │
│ └─Press F10 to continue─┘                 │
 Filename Ext    Date      Type          Description

 BULLET   .CHT  11-12-88   BULLET        The Annihilator Pencil Eraser
 BULLET2  .CHT  12-04-88   BULLET        The Annihilator Pencil Eraser
 FREEFORM.CHT   11-05-88   FREEFORM      Pie for color palette display
 HG       .CHT  10-22-88   PIE           Pie for color palette display
 OBJECTVS.CHT   11-14-88   BULLET        This is a title
 ORG      .CHT  11-07-88   ORG           Pencil Eraser Sales Force
 PEN-PCL2.CHT   11-27-88   BAR/LINE      Pen/Pencil Sales
 PEN-PNCL.CHT   11-27-88   BAR/LINE      Pen/Pencil Sales
 PP-Q2    .CHT  11-22-88   BAR/LINE      Pens, Pencils, & Accessories-2nd Quarter
 SIMPLE   .CHT  10-27-88   LIST          The Annihilator Pencil Eraser
 THREECOL.CHT   10-28-88   3 COLUMN      timeline test
 TITLE1   .CHT  10-23-88   TITLE         Superior Office Supplies
 TWOCOLS  .CHT  11-05-88   2 COLUMN      The Annihilator Pencil Eraser
 UHG0401  .CHT  11-12-88   TITLE         Marketing Objectives
 UHG0402  .CHT  11-12-88   LIST          Marketing Objectives

 F1-Help        F3-Change dir                              F10-Continue
```

Starting a Macro at a Specific Time

To continue a macro's execution at a specific hour, you can enter a *wait-until delay*. As an example of the value of wait-until delays, suppose that the data in your 1-2-3 spreadsheet is updated with information from the company's mainframe at 2 a.m. each morning. You can have Harvard Graphics run a macro at 3 a.m. to create and print a chart that will be ready for your arrival later that morning based on the new data.

To enter a wait-until delay at the beginning of a macro, press Alt-0 after starting a macro recording, choose Insert Delays from the MACRO overlay, and choose Wait-Until Delay from the Delays overlay. Specify the time for the macro to continue in hours and minutes, using 24-hour time. To enter 1:15 p.m., for example, type *13:15*. After you enter the delay, press Esc twice to continue recording the macro that will execute at the specified time.

You also can enter a wait-until delay in a macro by using the <CMD> W*hh:mm*<CMD> command described earlier in this chapter.

Including On-Screen Messages to Users

As a macro proceeds, you may want the macro to display messages to the user about the macro's progress or to request the user's input at a variable field. To include an on-screen message to a user, press Ctrl-F10 at the point during recording a macro that you want to include a message. Type a message of up to 78 characters on the overlay that appears and press Enter to continue recording the macro (see fig. 14.9).

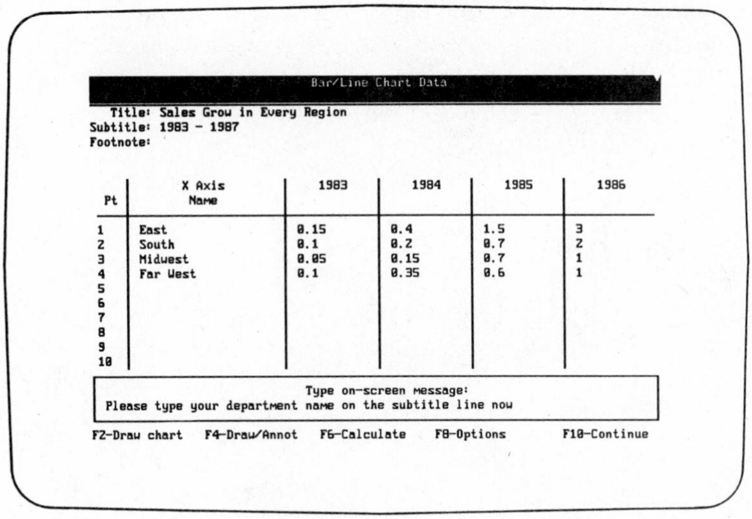

Fig. 14.9.

Entering an on-screen message in your macro.

To include a longer message of up to 22 lines, you must use the <CMD><*Message to appear on-screen*><CMD> command, described earlier in this chapter, when you edit the macro file in your word processor.

Debugging Macros

If your macro does not perform as you expected, or you need to examine someone else's macro to determine what steps that macro carries out, you can have a macro advance only one step at a time so that you can examine the macro carefully. To play back a macro one keystroke at a time, press Ctrl-Alt to pause the macro you are playing back as the macro begins and change Single-Step Playback on the Pause menu from No to Yes. Then press Esc to return to playing back the macro and press any key to advance the macro one step.

Unloading MACRO from Memory

If you loaded MACRO before starting Harvard Graphics, MACRO remains in your computer's memory even after you exit Harvard Graphics. To remove MACRO from memory to free that memory for the use of other programs, exit Harvard Graphics, press Alt-0 at the DOS prompt, and select Unload MACRO from the MACRO overlay. Press Enter to confirm your choice or any other key to leave MACRO in memory.

Examining Useful Macros

The macros you decide to create depend on the nature of the work you do. As you work, remember that any procedure you find yourself doing repeatedly deserves a macro. In the sections that follow, you examine three useful suggestions for taking advantage of the power of macros.

Macro To Print a Draft of the Current Chart

As you work, you may want to see how your chart is shaping up so far on paper. Normally, you would leave your work, return to the Harvard Graphics main menu, and print a 1/4-page copy of the chart in draft quality. The following macro, called DRAFT, prints a 1/4-page draft of the current chart for you.

To create the macro, follow these steps:

1. Load MACRO and then start Harvard Graphics.

2. Make sure that you are at the Harvard Graphics main menu.

3. Press Alt-0 to bring up the MACRO overlay.

4. Press R to select Record a Macro.

5. For a macro file name, type *draft*.

6. Press Esc seven or eight times so that Harvard Graphics returns to the main menu from wherever you are in the program.

7. Press 6 to select Produce Output from the main menu.

8. Press 1 to select Printer from the Produce Output menu.

9. Press D when the Print Chart Options overlay appears.

10. Press Tab once and press the space bar three times to set Chart Size to 1/4.

11. Press Tab three times to move the cursor past Paper Size and Printer to the Color option.

12. Press N to set Color to the No option.

13. Press Tab twice to move to Number of Copies and press Enter to print one copy of the chart. (Make sure that your printer is connected when you send the chart to the printer; otherwise, the machine hangs up when you are in the middle of recording a macro.)

14. After the chart finishes printing, press Alt-0 to bring up the MACRO overlay again.

15. Press S to select Stop Recording Macro.

To test the macro, try retrieving any of the charts you have on disk and viewing its data screen or bringing the chart into Draw/Annotate mode. Press Alt-0 and then press P to select Play Back a Macro. When MACRO prompts you for a macro name, type *draft* and press Enter. The current chart should be printed as a draft-quality, 1/4-page chart.

Figure 14.10 shows how the DRAFT macro looks when displayed in a word processor. Notice that the actual numbers you typed at the Harvard Graphics menus while you were recording the macro appear in the file. A different way to select from among Harvard Graphics menu choices is to use the space bar, but doing so places enigmatic spaces in the macro file instead of more easily understood numbers. Perhaps more importantly, if you select from among Harvard Graphics menus by using numbers when you record a macro, you can be sure that the macro plays back the same selections later, even if the macro is started with the cursor highlighting a different command on the menu.

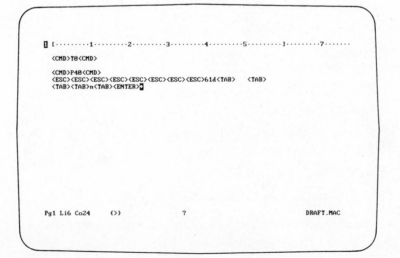

Fig. 14.10.

The DRAFT macro file in a word processor.

Macro To Save Your Work in Progress

Another useful macro is one that saves your work in progress to a temporary file on the disk with a keystroke combination: Alt-S (for Save). Regardless of the name or type of the current chart, this macro saves the chart to a temporary file named TEMP. By naming the macro S when asked for a macro file name, you can specify that you want to begin the macro by pressing Alt-S in the future.

Before you create this macro, you need to call up any chart on the disk and save the chart as TEMP. Because you will be saving every chart as TEMP, you always will see a warning message reminding you that TEMP already exists on disk. By saving a file as TEMP before you create the macro, you can cause this circumstance to occur the first time you create the macro. Therefore, the following macro includes the proper steps for dealing with this situation.

To record the temporary save macro, follow these steps:

1. Load MACRO before starting Harvard Graphics.

2. Retrieve any chart in Harvard Graphics and save the chart as TEMP.

3. Return to the Harvard Graphics main menu and press Alt-0 to summon the MACRO overlay.

4. Press R to select Record a Macro.

5. Name the macro S and press Enter.

6. Press Esc seven or eight times to be sure that Harvard Graphics returns to the main menu from wherever you are in the program when you start the macro.

7. Press 4 to select Get/Save/Remove from the main menu.

8. Press 2 to select Save Chart from the Get/Save/Remove menu.

9. Press Del seven or eight times so that any file name already present at the Chart Name prompt is deleted.

10. Type *temp* and press Enter, leave the description as is, and press Enter twice to save the chart.

11. Press Esc to return to the main menu and press Alt-0 to bring up the MACRO menu.

12. Press S to select Stop Recording Macro.

Figure 14.11 shows the resulting macro file called S.MAC.

Test the macro by retrieving any file and viewing its data screen or bringing the file into Draw/Annotate mode. Press Alt-S and watch as the file is saved on disk as TEMP. Now, if you need to leave your desk suddenly, you can press Alt-S to save your work temporarily.

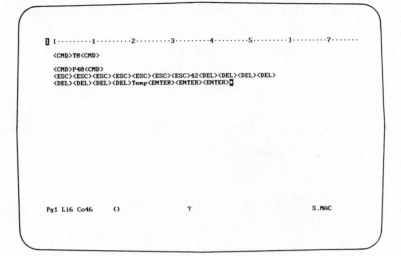

Fig. 14.11.

The S.MAC macro file.

Macro To Print a User-Specified Chart

A macro that prints a specific chart determined by whoever is operating the program must give the user the chance to enter the chart name, and the macro should contain a message to the user with instructions about how to proceed. To accomplish these objectives, you should use a variable field and an on-screen message. This macro prints using the options Chart Size: 1/2 and Quality: High. You may want to replace these two print settings for others, however, or create a set of macros to print at varying qualities and sizes.

To record the macro to print a user-specified chart, follow these steps:

1. Load MACRO before starting Harvard Graphics.

2. At the Harvard Graphics main menu, press Alt-0 to call up the MACRO overlay.

3. Press R to select Record a Macro.

4. Type *printhq* (*hq* for "high quality") as the macro file name and press Enter.

5. At the main menu, press 4 to select Get/Save/Remove.

6. Press 1 to select Get Chart from the Get/Save/Remove menu.

7. Press Ctrl-F10 after the Select Chart menu appears so that you can enter a message to the user.

8. Type the name of a chart in the variable field in the overlay that appears and press Enter.

9. Press Ctrl-- (hyphen) to insert a variable field.

10. Type the file name *pen-pcl1* to be sure that the macro works, but do not press Enter. The macro does not record PEN-PCL1 as the specific file name but stops for user input at this point.

11. Press Alt-0 to continue recording the macro.

12. Press Enter, press Esc, and then press F10 to return to the main menu.

13. Press 6 to select Produce Output from the main menu.

14. Press 1 to select Printer from the Produce Output menu.

15. Press H to select High at the Quality prompt on the Print Chart Options overlay.

16. Press Tab once to move to Chart Size and press the space bar once to select 1/2.

17. Press Tab several times to move the cursor past Paper Size and Printer to the Color option.

18. Press N to set Color to the No option.

19. Press Tab twice and press Enter to set Number of Copies to 1 and press Enter to print the chart.

20. When the printing is complete, press Alt-0 to call up the MACRO overlay again.

21. Press S to select Stop Recording Macro.

To test this macro, start Harvard Graphics with the MACRO program already loaded, press Alt-0, and choose P for Play Back a Macro from the MACRO overlay. Enter *printhq* as the name. Notice that a window appears during the macro's execution to remind the user how to fill out the variable field that follows.

Figure 14.12 shows how the PRINTHQ macro file appears in a word processor. Notice the embedded message to the user and the two <VFLD> references that cause a variable field.

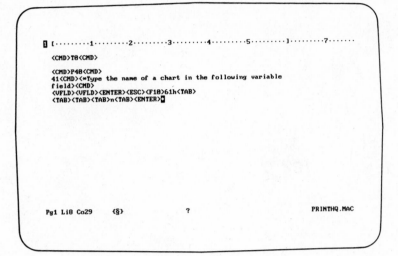

```
▌[·······1········2········3·······4·······5······]·······7······

  <CMD>T8<CMD>

  <CMD>P48<CMD>
  41<CMD><*Type the name of a chart in the following variable
  field><CMD>
  <VFLD><VFLD><ENTER><ESC><F18>61h<TAB>
  <TAB><TAB><TAB>n<TAB><ENTER>▌



  Pg1 Li8 Co29    {§}              ?              PRINTHQ.MAC
```

Fig. 14.12.

The PRINTHQ
macro file.

Using Macros with
Chartbook Templates

To automate chart building, you can set up a one-keystroke macro that first loads a template that pulls its data from an external data file and then prints the resulting chart. For example, a hypothetical macro named D enables you to press Alt-D to load a template with a data link to a 1-2-3 worksheet, pause because of a variable field so that you can make any minor adjustments to the chart, and then pause again to enable you to modify the print settings before printing the chart.

Chapter Summary

This chapter described how to use one of the most powerful tools of Harvard Graphics: macros. With templates and macros, you can automate the task of creating graphs and make repetitive chores easy. In the next several chapters, you learn how to produce output, set up slide shows and screenshows, print batches of charts, and make dazzling animated presentations.

Part V

Wrapping Up

Includes

Producing Stellar Output

Creating Slide Shows and Screenshows

15

Producing Stellar Output

Harvard Graphics makes getting output one of the smoothest steps in the process of creating graphics. In this chapter, you learn about how Harvard Graphics can send charts to a variety of output devices, accommodating just about any printer, plotter, or slide maker. You also learn how to export Harvard Graphics charts to files you can use in other software, and you learn how to mix charts on a page in a multiple chart.

Printing with Harvard Graphics

Before graphics software surged into popularity, getting printouts from word processors, spreadsheets, and other common business packages could be a struggle. Printing a page was easy, usually just a matter of choosing Print from the menu. But finding a compatible software-printer combination was maddening, unless you stuck with one of the market leaders.

To compound the difficulty, a wide array of printers, plotters, and slide makers has appeared on the market as a result of the popularity of graphics software. If support for these output devices exists in the software, each new piece of hardware promises to reproduce faithfully graphs and charts on paper, transparencies, or film, and in black and white or color.

Harvard Graphics supports a broad range of dot-matrix, inkjet, and laser printers. Other computer programs demand that you have one of the most popular printers, such as an Epson dot-matrix printer or a Hewlett-Packard LaserJet, or they expect you to use a printer that emulates one of these models. Harvard Graphics provides a host of printer drivers, special software that serves as an interpreter between Harvard Graphics and your printer. By using a printer driver written expressly for a certain model printer, Harvard Graphics can send the printer the proper commands to control its capabilities.

Harvard Graphics also supports a variety of plotters, devices that draw graphs on paper using pens. Plotters provide sharp, crisp drawings. Plotters used in architectural and engineering firms routinely produce large pages, 36 inches by 48 inches or more.

The advantage to using a plotter is its precision and capacity to draw graphs that look carefully hand-drawn. Formerly, plotters provided the only way to get charts with multiple colors. But new inkjet and thermal printers can create graphs in unlimited colors, instead of the limited number of colors provided by plotters. Another disadvantage to using plotters is their inability to produce three-dimensional images. Plotters cannot draw objects that overlap, the prime means of achieving a three-dimensional effect in a chart.

If you use a printer with Harvard Graphics, you probably are limited to a standard page size, but you enjoy relatively fast output speed. Color printers can produce full-color charts. Laser printers offer high-resolution black-and-white charts that look professional. Chapter 2 contains information about setting up a printer with Harvard Graphics.

Selecting an Orientation

Printing sideways used to be easy—nothing more than putting the paper in sideways. However, with some new printers, all laser printers, and plotters, you can feed paper only one way. To print sideways on a page, you must tell Harvard Graphics to rotate a chart 90 degrees. Sideways printing is called *landscape orientation*. Standard printing, with the paper vertical, is called *portrait orientation*. With Harvard Graphics, you can mix landscape and portrait charts by printing them in a slide show at half size. Later in this chapter, "Printing a Series of Charts" examines printing charts in a slide show.

By choosing landscape as the default for a chart, you inform Harvard Graphics that the paper or film area is horizontal. Harvard Graphics displays a horizontal page on-screen and creates a wide chart.

Landscape orientation is best for the following types of slides and charts:

❏ Charts showing data measured over extended time periods

❏ Organizational charts

❏ Two- and three-column charts

❏ Bar/line charts

Because landscape orientation is usually best for these charts, you may want to set landscape as the default orientation for your charts. You can, of course, still specify portrait orientation for particular charts. To set landscape as the default orientation, follow these steps:

1. Select Setup from the Harvard Graphics main menu.

2. Choose Defaults from the Setup menu.

3. Use the Tab key to move the cursor to the Orientation field. Portrait or Landscape already is chosen.

4. Press the space bar to change the current selection to Landscape, if necessary.

5. Press F10 (Continue) to return to the Setup menu.

6. Press Esc to return to the main menu.

All future charts are in landscape orientation unless you override landscape. To choose portrait orientation for a chart, follow this procedure before or during the creation of a chart:

1. Press F8 (Options) at the main menu. The cursor is positioned next to the Orientation prompt on the Current Chart Options overlay.

2. Use the space bar to select Portrait.

3. Press Enter three times to pass the Border and Font fields and return to the main menu.

Selecting the Chart

You can send a chart you have just completed to a printer, plotter, slide maker, or disk. You also can retrieve a chart from disk and then send it to an output device. Either way, the chart you print must be the current chart. The *current chart* is the chart you are presently working on or the chart you have just retrieved from disk with Get Chart. The name of the current chart appears near the bottom right side of the main menu screen. A chart remains current until you exit Harvard Graphics, start a new chart, or retrieve a different chart from disk.

To send the current chart to an output device, follow these steps:

1. Select Produce Output from the main menu.

2. Choose Printer, Plotter, or Film Recorder (slide maker) from the Produce Output menu depending on the output device you are using. The other options on this menu are discussed later in this chapter.

3. Complete the Print Chart Options, Plot Chart Options, or Record Chart Option overlay that appears.

Figure 15.1 shows the Produce Output menu.

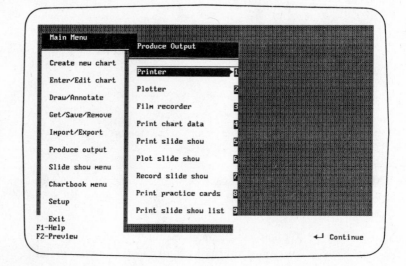

Fig. 15.1.

The Produce Output menu.

Printing with a Printer

If your output device is a printer, you see the Print Chart Options overlay (see fig. 15.2) when you select Printer from the Produce Output menu. The Print Chart Options overlay presents several options, discussed next.

Specifying the Quality

Quality is a measure of the resolution and clarity of your chart printing. You can choose from among Draft, Standard, or High quality output. The higher the quality, the sharper a chart looks. But the higher the quality, the longer charts take to print. Figures 15.3, 15.4, and 15.5 show the same chart printed in draft, standard, and high quality with a Hewlett-Packard LaserJet Series II. The difference in appearance you see with your charts depends on the type of printer you use.

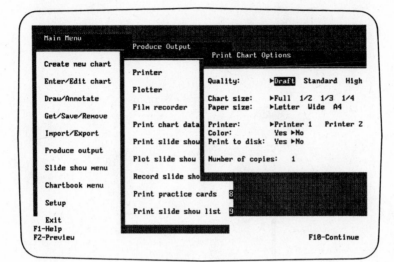

Fig. 15.2.

The Print Chart Options overlay.

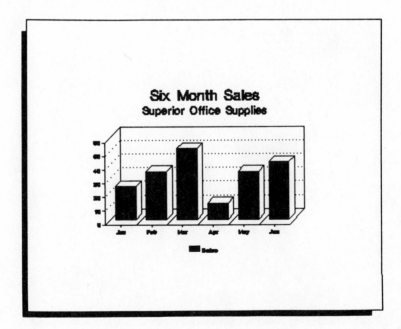

Fig. 15.3.

Draft quality.

Fig. 15.4.

Standard quality.

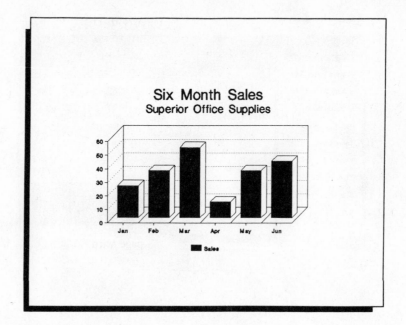

Fig. 15.5.

High quality.

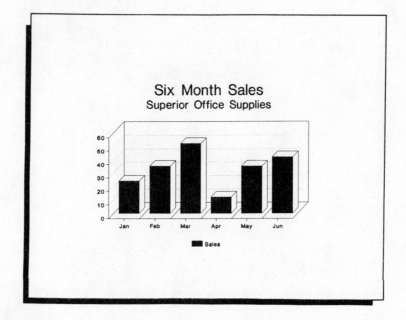

Generally, you should print draft-quality charts to check a chart's appearance quickly. You should print standard-quality charts to show others your charts, perhaps for their opinion or approval. Finally, you should take the time to print high-quality charts when you are certain your charts are ready for presentation.

If you have a laser printer with less than 1.5M of memory (such as the Hewlett-Packard LaserJet or LaserJet Series II without a memory expansion card), you may not be able to print a full page of high-quality graphics for complex charts, like a 3-D bar chart. Unless you add memory to your printer, you can get around this problem by printing a smaller chart size (discussed next) or using standard resolution.

Selecting the Size

You can print charts in four sizes. To fill a page with a chart, choose full size. The other options, 1/2, 1/3, and 1/4, print charts at the left of the page or, in the case of 1/4, at the top left of the page.

Selecting the Paper Size

You can choose among three paper sizes in Harvard Graphics 2.3: Letter, Wide, or A4. Earlier versions of the program supported the first two sizes. Letter size is 8 1/2 inches by 11 inches and wide is 11 inches by 14 inches. A4 is 29.7 centimeters by 21 centimeters.

Selecting the Printer

When you set Harvard Graphics defaults, you can set up two printers, Printer 1 and Printer 2. By selecting one of the printers in the Print Chart Options overlay, you tell the program which printer is connected.

Specifying Color and Gray-Scale Printing

Set Color to Yes if you have a color printer and you want to print the current chart in color. Set Color to No if you want to print in black and white. When you print a chart in black and white, Harvard Graphics uses patterns to fill colored series bars, pie slices, or areas in a graph chart. If your printer cannot print in color, Harvard Graphics ignores the color setting.

Harvard Graphics 2.3 supports gray-scale printing. If you use a black-and-white printer to print a chart that is filled with color, Harvard Graphics converts the colors to shades of gray. Harvard Graphics follows these rules when it converts a chart to gray-scales:

❑ Outlines become solid black.

❑ Background colors and colors identical to the background appear as white.

❑ Colored patterns become patterns in solid black lines.

The gray shades you see when you print depend on the resolution of your printer. Printers with higher resolution print darker grays.

Printing to Disk

The Print To Disk option enables you to send output to a file on a disk. Later, you can copy the file from disk to the printer using the standard DOS Copy command. Printing a file from disk can be handy when you need to print on a printer not physically connected to your computer. You can carry a copy of the printed chart on disk to the printer's location and then use DOS Copy to copy the file to PRN. To copy the file CHART1.PRN from the Harvard Graphics directory to the printer, for example, type the following:

COPY CHART1.PRN PRN:

Printing Multiple Copies

For the Number Of Copies option, the default is 1. To print more than one copy, your printer or plotter must have the capacity to feed sheets of paper or use continuous-form paper. Unlike most other graphics packages, Harvard Graphics constructs a chart only once before sending multiple copies to a printer. Other packages waste time by reconstructing a chart for each copy.

Printing with a Plotter

If your output device is a plotter, you see the Plot Chart Options overlay when you select Plotter from the Produce Output menu (see fig. 15.6). The Plot Chart Options Overlay options are discussed next.

Like the Quality setting when you print, the three possible Quality settings when you plot cause the plotter to operate at one of three levels, from quick-and-dirty to slow-and-presentation form. Unlike printer resolution, however, plotting resolution remains constant. What differs is the level of detail, the attention to your color and text attribute selections, and the fonts used.

Use table 15.1 to anticipate the results of the Quality setting when plotting.

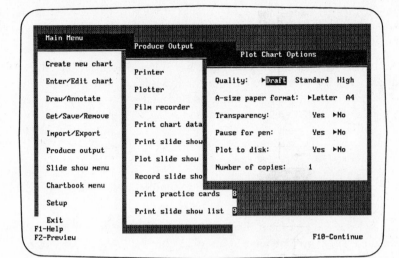

Fig. 15.6.

*The Plot Chart
Options overlay.*

Table 15.1
Quality Settings

	Draft Quality	Standard Quality	High Quality
Fonts	Built-in plotter fonts only	Built-in plotter fonts proportionally spaced	Harvard Graphics fonts
Fill	Bars and pie slices filled with patterns	Bars and pie slices filled in	Characters, bars, and pie slices filled in
Color	Line of text color determined by color of first character	Each character can be colored individually	Each character can be colored
Text Attributes	Do not appear	Do not appear	All appear

If you use the British A4 paper size, you should set A-size paper format to A4.

When you use transparency paper, Harvard Graphics plots more slowly and separates the slices of a pie chart to prevent colors from running together. Check your plotter's instructions for using transparencies to see whether any special considerations are necessary.

Harvard Graphics matches the pen it uses for a bar or pie slice to the color number you chose when you created the chart. For example, a color 4 bar is drawn with pen 4.

If your plotter has fewer pens than your chart has colors, you may want to set Pause For Pen to Yes. Then, if the color your chart uses is not one of the current pens in the plotter, Harvard Graphics pauses and enables you to replace the pen with an appropriately colored pen. To continue plotting with the new pen, press Enter. If you set Pause For Pen to No, Harvard Graphics uses the pens available in your plotter to draw the chart, even though the colors do not match.

You can send a copy of your chart to disk when plotting just as you can when printing. Later you can copy the disk file to a plotter using the DOS copy command.

As with printing, you can plot more than one copy of a chart. Harvard Graphics pauses between each copy so that you can insert another page, except for plotters that have a paper bin or support continuous-feed paper.

Printing with a Film Recorder

If your output device is a film recorder, you see the Record Chart Option overlay when you select Film Recorder from the Produce Output menu (see fig. 15.7). The only setting on the Record Chart Option overlay is Number Of Copies. Harvard Graphics advances the film between each of the copies (exposures) you request. When you use a Polaroid Palette or PalettePlus with 669 film, Harvard Graphics prompts you to remove the film after each exposure. When you are ready to record the next chart, press Enter.

Fig. 15.7.

The Record Chart Option overlay.

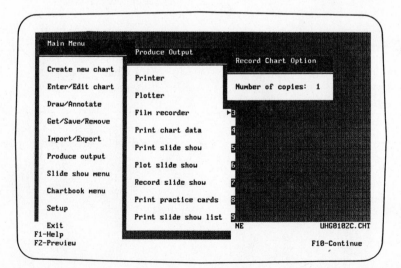

Sending a Chart to the Autographix Slide Service

Harvard Graphics comes with a utility program, called ToAGX, that can send charts via modem to the Autographix Overnight Slide Service. The utility also can prepare a disk that you can send to Autographix via normal mail. When you produce output for the ToAGX utility, make sure that you set Film Recorder to Slide service on the Film Recorder Setup screen.

Many other slide service bureaus can create stunning slide versions of your CHT files. Autographix is the only service, however, with support built into Harvard Graphics.

Printing Chart Data

Harvard Graphics can print a table of a graph chart's data—even if the data is not displayed in the chart. To print a chart's data, select Print Chart Data from the Produce Output menu. In the Chart Data Option overlay that appears, Harvard Graphics enables you to send the output to Printer 1 or Printer 2.

Printing a Series of Charts

Normally, you can print, plot, or record only one chart at a time. To send a series of charts to an output device, you should create a slide show that incorporates the charts and then choose Print Slide Show, Plot Slide Show, or Record Slide Show at the Produce Output menu. Complete information about creating slide shows is provided later in this chapter.

When you send a series of charts to an output device using this method, the Print Slide Show Options overlay appears. This overlay is much like the Print Chart Options, Plot Chart Options, or Record Chart Option overlay. The two following options on this overlay, however, are new:

From slide/ To slide   To print only part of the slide show of charts you have created, enter the beginning slide show chart number and the ending slide show chart number at these two prompts. To check the numbers of slides in a slide show, you can print a slide show list by choosing Print Slide Show List from the Produce Output menu.

Collate

By setting Collate to Yes when you have chosen to print more than one copy, you can produce the full set of charts and then a second full set of charts. Setting Collate to No produces more than one copy of each chart in succession. By not collating charts, producing multiple copies of slide show charts is much faster.

Mixing Charts on a Page

Harvard Graphics enables you to reproduce more than one chart on a page or screen. By displaying up to six charts side by side in a multiple chart, you can facilitate comparisons among charts. You also can pair a text chart describing information with a graph chart showing the information. Figure 15.8 shows a multiple chart.

Fig. 15.8.

A typical multiple chart.

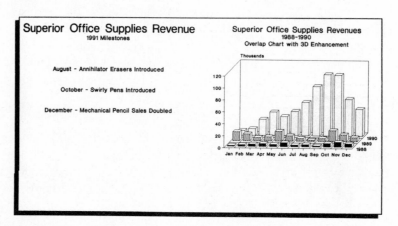

A multiple chart depends on the charts you already have created and saved on disk. You do not create a text or graphic chart as you work with a multiple chart. Instead, you combine pre-existing charts into a multiple chart. After you have created a multiple chart, however, you can bring it into Draw/Annotate mode and give it a life of its own by adding annotations and symbols. After you decide which charts to display together, you can arrange up to four charts by selecting from three preset layouts. You can arrange up to six charts if you create a custom layout.

After you complete a multiple chart, you can save or print the chart as a standard Harvard Graphics chart. You can even bring a multiple chart into Draw/Annotate to add annotations, which point out the differences among the charts on a page or screen.

Each time you recall a multiple chart from disk, the multiple chart gathers its component charts from disk. If you change one of the individual charts that constitute a multiple chart, the multiple chart also changes.

Making a Multiple Chart

Making a multiple chart requires a few simple steps. First, you must select the charts you want to display together. When you know how many charts you need to arrange, you may accept a standard layout or custom-design your own. Figure 15.9 shows the three Harvard Graphics standard layouts. If you have chosen a standard arrangement, the charts appear in their allotted positions. If you have chosen custom-design, you must position the charts manually.

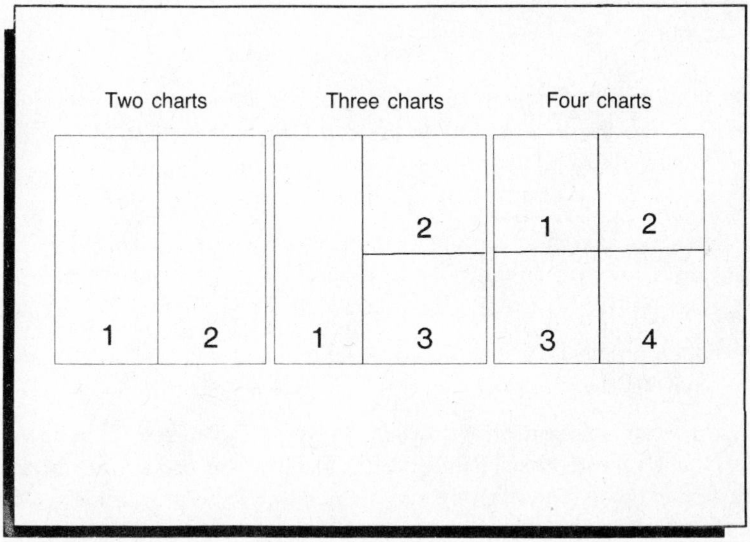

Fig. 15.9.

The three standard multiple chart layouts.

To create a standard multiple chart, combine three of the charts you created in earlier chapters, OBJECTVS, SOSREVS, and SOSREVO, onto one page. Follow these steps:

1. Select Create New Chart from the main menu.

2. Select Multiple Charts from the Create New Chart menu.

3. Select Three from the Multiple Charts Styles menu that appears.

The Edit Multiple Chart screen appears, as shown in figure 15.10.

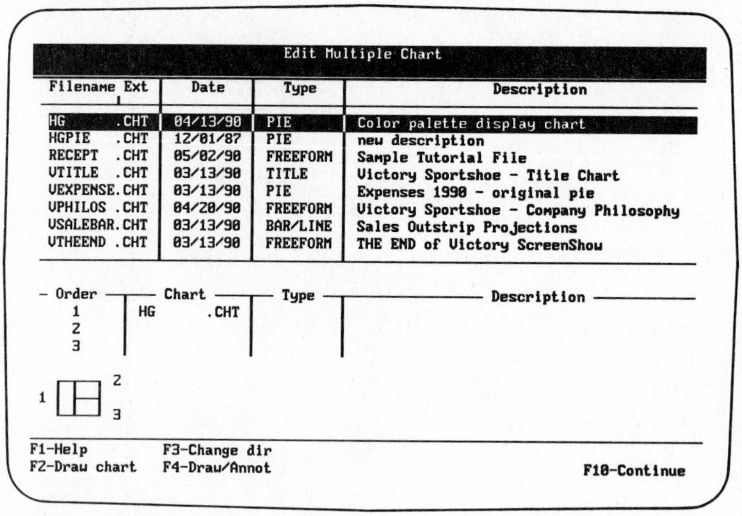

Fig. 15.10.

The Edit Multiple Chart screen.

The Edit Multiple Chart screen shows a list of the charts in your data directory and, below that, a list of the charts in the current multiple chart. At the bottom left of the screen is a small diagram representing the arrangement of the charts. If you choose a custom layout, the word custom appears.

All the charts included in a multiple chart must come from the same directory on your hard disk. Harvard Graphics keeps track of the names of the charts in a multiple chart, but not the directory from which they come.

Use the Edit Multiple Chart screen to select the three charts for the multiple chart by following these steps:

1. Use the up or down arrows or the PgUp or PgDn keys to position the highlight on the chart name OBJECTVS in the list at the top of the screen and press Enter or type the file name *objectvs*, press Enter, and press Tab to continue highlighting chart names.

2. Use the same method to pick the remaining two charts for the multiple chart (SOSREVS and SOSREVO). Figure 15.11 shows the completed Edit Multiple Chart screen.

3. Press F10 (Continue) to return to the main menu.

4. Save the multiple charts just as you save any other chart. Harvard Graphics gives the multiple chart a CHT file name extension. Press Esc to return to the main menu.

5. Press F2 (Draw Chart) to see the multiple chart, as shown in figure 15.12.

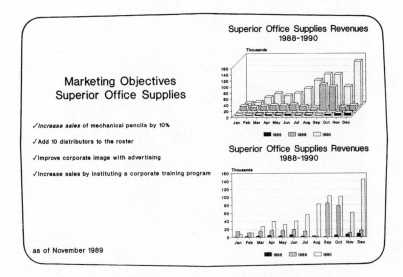

```
                        Edit Multiple Chart
   Filename Ext    Date       Type            Description

   UHGR567 .CHT   07/01/90   CHART
   UHGR568 .CHT   07/01/90   CHART
   UHGR572 .CHT   07/01/90   CHART
   UHGR573 .CHT   07/01/90   CHART
   UHGR574 .CHT   07/01/90   CHART
   OBJECTUS.CHT   07/02/90   BULLET     Marketing Objectives
   SOSREVS .CHT   07/02/90   BAR/LINE   Superior Office Supplies Revenues
   SOSREVO .CHT   07/02/90   BAR/LINE   Superior Office Supplies Revenues

  - Order ──── Chart ──── Type ──── Description ────
      1      OBJECTUS.CHT   BULLET     Marketing Objectives
      2      SOSREVS .CHT   BAR/LINE   Superior Office Supplies Revenues
      3      SOSREVO .CHT

  1  ┌─┬─┐  2
     │ ├─┤
     └─┴─┘  3

   F1-Help        F3-Change dir
   F2-Draw chart  F4-Draw/Annot                      F10-Continue
```

Fig. 15.11.

The completed Edit Multiple Chart screen.

Fig. 15.12.

Preview of the completed multiple chart.

Creating a custom chart layout is slightly more involved. To create a custom chart arrangement with the same three charts, follow these steps:

1. Select Create New Chart from the main menu.

2. Select Multiple Charts from the Create New Chart menu.

3. Select Custom from the Multiple Charts Styles menu.

If you are trying this procedure immediately after creating the preceding multiple chart, a Change Chart Type overlay appears with the query Keep current data: Yes No. To use the same three charts in the same order, press Enter to accept Yes as the response. To create a multiple chart composed of different charts, highlight No and press Enter. If you are beginning a new custom multiple chart from scratch, you must select the three charts to include in the custom chart by following the same procedure described previously.

When all three charts for the custom multiple chart are listed on the Edit Multiple Chart screen, press F2 (Draw Chart) to preview the multiple chart. Figure 15.13 shows how the multiple chart preview appears. Notice that the three charts are displayed left to right across the bottom of the screen. Above the three charts is space for three more charts because a custom multiple chart can hold up to six charts.

Fig. 15.13.

Preview of the custom multiple chart.

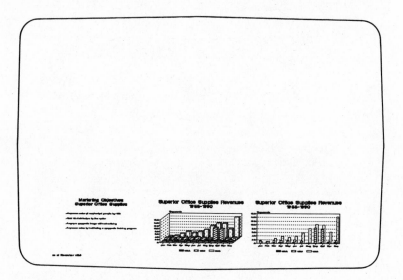

To vary the size and positioning of the charts in the custom multiple chart, use the F7-Size/Place feature at the Edit Multiple Chart screen. To try F7-Size/Place, follow these steps:

1. Press Esc to return to the Edit Multiple Chart screen.

2. Press F7 (Size/Place) to view the Custom Layout screen, as shown in figure 15.14.

The panel on the left lists the charts included in the multiple chart. The area to the right, which resembles the Draw/Annotate drawing board, displays the current size and positioning of the charts. You may find working in Quick mode faster than in Final mode. Press F8 (Quick Mode) to see its effect. Quick mode displays only the frame holding the chart and the chart's name. Quick mode operates much faster because it does not draw each chart on-screen. Figure 15.15 shows how the same custom layout shown in figure 15.14 is displayed in Quick mode.

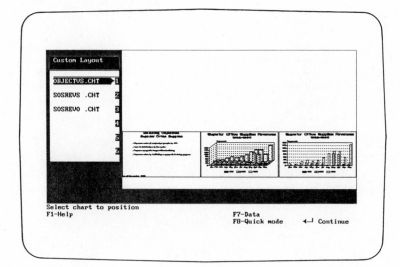

Fig. 15.14.

The custom layout screen.

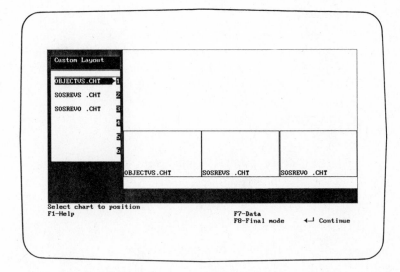

Fig. 15.15.

Custom layout displayed in Quick mode.

To vary the size and positioning of a chart, pick the chart to modify from the menu at the left and draw a new frame to contain the chart. Follow these steps to do so:

1. Position the cursor on the first chart name in the list, OBJECTVS, and press Enter. A small crosshair cursor appears in the drawing board area to the right.

2. Position the cursor at the top left of the rectangle that contains the chart and press Enter to anchor the first point.

3. Press PgDn repeatedly, use the arrow keys to position the bottom right corner of the rectangle, and then press Enter. The chart frame appears at the new position.

When you define the custom layout for a multiple chart, you can place one chart on top of another or superimpose an area of one chart on another chart. When you display the actual charts on the screen by pressing F8 (Final Mode), you may notice that the chart maintains its original proportion of length to width even though the rectangle containing the chart may have different proportions. Harvard Graphics maintains the chart's width to height ratio, called *aspect ratio*, so that the chart does not become distorted. To demonstrate this, try creating a tall, narrow rectangle for chart number 2 (SOSREVS).

To alter a chart's aspect ratio, you can save the chart as a symbol and then modify the symbol's shape. You find complete information about saving a chart as a symbol in Chapter 7.

To save the multiple chart or change which charts are included in the multiple chart, press F7 (Data) at the Custom Layout screen to return to the Edit Multiple Chart screen. To edit the multiple chart, follow the procedures in the next section. To save the chart, press F10 (Continue) to return to the main menu.

Editing a Multiple Chart

To change the charts in a multiple chart, you must return to the Edit Multiple Chart screen from the Custom Layout screen or select Enter/Edit Chart from the main menu. When the Edit Multiple Chart screen appears, one of the three charts in the lower portion of the screen is highlighted. You may delete any chart and replace it by following these steps:

1. Position the highlight on the chart to be replaced.

2. Press Tab to delete the chart name and replace it with the currently highlighted chart on the list above.

3. Position the cursor on a new chart name to replace the old and press Enter.

From the Harvard Graphics main menu, you also can change the current multiple chart's orientation and border by pressing F8 (Options) to summon the Current Chart Options overlay. These changes affect the multiple chart, not the individual charts constituting the multiple chart. The font setting on the Current Chart Options overlay has no effect on the individual charts in a multiple chart. If you change the chart's orientation, be sure to preview the chart afterwards. You probably need to modify the positioning of the charts in the multiple chart using the F7-Size/Place feature.

Chapter Summary

This chapter explained the many ways you can get output copies of your charts. Because producing output includes printing, plotting, and recording slides, the term "printing" is far too limiting. You also learned how to combine up to six charts on a page or slide by creating a multiple chart.

In the next chapter, you learn how to gather the charts you have into a slide show so that you can perform several tasks, such as printing the group of charts or adding screenshow effects so thatyou can create an animated desktop presentation.

16

Creating Slide Shows and Screenshows

For most of the output you need, sending individual charts one by one to a printer, plotter, or film recorder is satisfactory. Occasionally, a presentation requires an entire set of charts, and, from time to time, printed pages or projected slides are not enough. With slide shows, Harvard Graphics provides an answer to both of these needs.

Defining a Slide Show

A *slide show* is a collection of charts that you can instruct Harvard Graphics to display on-screen one after another, much like an actual slide presentation. A slide show also can send a series of charts to an output device rather than to the screen, saving you the tedium of manually printing, plotting, or recording charts one by one.

After you have assembled charts into a slide show in a specific sequence, you can print a list of the show's contents or create practice cards with notes for your speech about each of the show's charts. You also can add special transition effects between each of the charts in a slide show to create an animated presentation called a screenshow.

503

Assembling a Slide Show

To assemble a slide show, you must pick from among the charts you created and that now reside in your data directory and add the charts to the slide list one by one. After you have completed the list, save the slide show in the same data directory with your charts.

To practice creating a slide show, use six of the text charts created in Chapter 4 for a slide show designed to accompany your new product presentation. These charts are listed as follows:

TITLECHT: A title chart to start the presentation

SIMPLCHT: A simple list describing customer needs

BULETCHT: A bullet list describing the new product's benefits

TWOCOL: A two-column chart comparing customer need and product benefit

FREEFORM: A free-form chart detailing the new product promotional plan

ORG: An organization chart diagramming the sales force for the new product

To begin assembling a slide show, follow these steps:

1. Select the Slide Show Menu option from the main menu and press Enter. The Slide Show menu appears, as shown in figure 16.1.

2. Select Create Slide Show from the Slide Show menu and press Enter.

3. At the Slide Show name prompt, type a name of up to eight characters for the slide show and press Enter. For this example, enter *newprod* as the slide show name.

   Usually, when you create a Harvard Graphics file, you create the file first and save the file with a name. Here, you name the file first and then create its contents. As you add charts to the slide show, the revised show is saved on disk.

4. Type a description for the slide show after the Description prompt on the Create Slide Show overlay and press Enter. (Harvard Graphics supplies the SHW file name extension.) In this case, type *New Product Presentation* as the slide show's description and press Enter. The Create/Edit Slide Show screen appears, as shown in figure 16.2.

The Create/Edit Slide Show screen is much like the Create/Edit Chartbook screen discussed in Chapter 7. The top half of the screen lists the available charts in your data directory. The slide show name, with the three-letter file extension

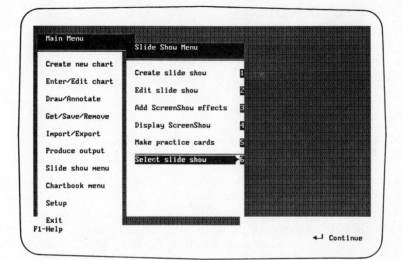

Fig. 16.1.

The Slide Show menu.

Main Menu

Create new chart
Enter/Edit chart
Draw/Annotate
Get/Save/Remove
Import/Export
Produce output
Slide show menu
Chartbook menu
Setup
Exit
F1-Help

Slide Show Menu

Create slide show   1
Edit slide show   2
Add ScreenShow effects   3
Display ScreenShow   4
Make practice cards   5
Select slide show   6

↵ Continue

Fig. 16.2.

The Create/Edit Slide Show screen for NEWPROD.

Create/Edit Slide Show

Filename Ext	Date	Type	Description
HG .CHT	04/13/90	PIE	Color palette display chart
HGPIE .CHT	12/01/87	PIE	new description
RECEPT .CHT	05/02/90	FREEFORM	Sample Tutorial File
VTITLE .CHT	03/13/90	TITLE	Victory Sportshoe - Title Chart
VEXPENSE.CHT	03/13/90	PIE	Expenses 1990 - original pie
VPHILOS .CHT	04/20/90	FREEFORM	Victory Sportshoe - Company Philosophy

Show name: NEWPROD .SHW

— Order —	— File —	— Type —	— Description —
1	HG .CHT		

Show description: New Product Presentation

F1-Help

F10-Continue

SHW, appears in the center of the screen, just below the data directory file list. Below that is the current slide show list as the list is built. The bottom of the screen displays the description of the slide show.

To modify the slide show description, press the Tab key. The cursor moves to the description so that you may edit the description as though you were editing a line of text in a word processor. To return to the slide show list, press the Tab key again.

When the cursor is back on the slide show list, you can press the up- and down-arrow keys and the PgUp and PgDn keys to select the next chart for the list. When the correct chart name appears on the list, press Enter to select that chart and continue building the slide show. A slide show can contain up to 90 charts. When the slide show list is complete, press F10 (Continue) to return to the Slide Show menu.

Select the six charts to include in the slide show by following these steps:

1. Use the up- or down-arrow and PgUp or PgDn keys to highlight TITLE.CHT on the chart list at the top of the screen and press Enter.

2. Highlight each chart to be included in the slide show one by one, pressing Enter to add each chart to the slide show. The Create/Edit Slide Show screen appears as shown in figure 16.3. If you accidentally add an incorrect file, you need to return to the Slide Show menu and choose Edit Slide Show. You find complete information about editing slide shows in the next section.

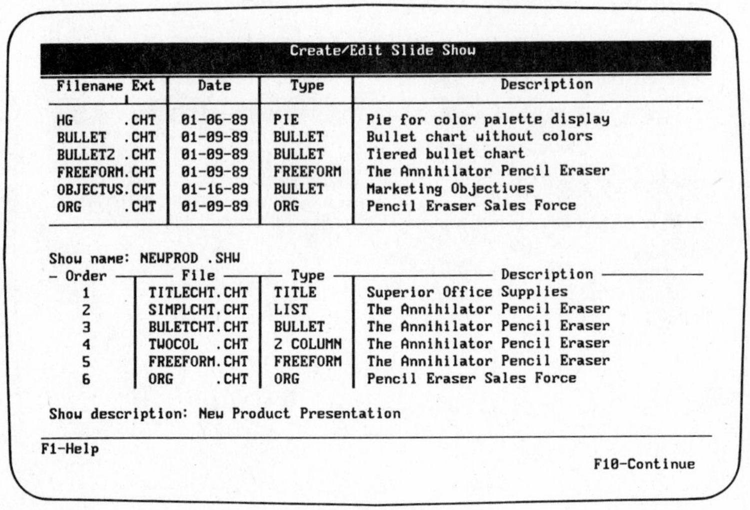

Fig. 16.3.

The Create/Edit Slide Show screen with six charts added.

```
                        Create/Edit Slide Show

    Filename Ext      Date      Type           Description

    HG      .CHT   01-06-89   PIE      Pie for color palette display
    BULLET  .CHT   01-09-89   BULLET   Bullet chart without colors
    BULLETZ .CHT   01-09-89   BULLET   Tiered bullet chart
    FREEFORM.CHT   01-09-89   FREEFORM The Annihilator Pencil Eraser
    OBJECTUS.CHT   01-16-89   BULLET   Marketing Objectives
    ORG     .CHT   01-09-89   ORG      Pencil Eraser Sales Force


    Show name: NEWPROD .SHW
    - Order -------- File -------- Type ---------- Description -------
        1      TITLECHT.CHT   TITLE      Superior Office Supplies
        2      SIMPLCHT.CHT   LIST       The Annihilator Pencil Eraser
        3      BULETCHT.CHT   BULLET     The Annihilator Pencil Eraser
        4      TWOCOL  .CHT   2 COLUMN   The Annihilator Pencil Eraser
        5      FREEFORM.CHT   FREEFORM   The Annihilator Pencil Eraser
        6      ORG     .CHT   ORG        Pencil Eraser Sales Force

    Show description: New Product Presentation

    F1-Help
                                                        F10-Continue
```

3. Press F10 (Continue) after you add all six charts to the slide show list.

The Slide Show menu reappears.

You now can press Esc to return to the main menu. The slide show you have created is saved on disk. Unlike Harvard Graphics charts, you need not specifically save a slide show after you finish assembling the slide show list. The new slide show is saved each time you add a new chart. The slide show you just created, NEWPROD, remains the current slide show until you select another slide show by retrieving it from disk. If you select Edit Slide Show from the Slide Show menu, the NEWPROD slide show list reappears.

Editing a Slide Show

After you complete a slide show, you can return to the slide show list and make several modifications. You can delete charts, add new charts, or rearrange the order of charts on the list.

To retrieve a slide show from disk, follow these steps:

1. Select the Slide Show Menu option from the main menu and press Enter.

2. Choose Select Slide Show from the Slide Show menu and press Enter. Harvard Graphics displays the slide shows stored in the current data directory, as shown in figure 16.4.

3. Highlight the slide show you want to retrieve by moving the cursor with the up- or down-arrow keys or type the slide show file name after the Filename prompt at the top of the screen and press Enter. In this case, highlight NEWPROD.SHW and press Enter.

```
┌──────────────────────────────────────────────────────────┐
│                    Select Slide Show                      │
│ ████████████████████████████████████████████████████████ │
│  Directory: C:\HG                                         │
│  Filename:  TEST    .SHW                                  │
│                                                           │
│  Filename Ext   │  Date   │  Type   │    Description      │
│ ─────────────────────────────────────────────────────────│
│  TEST    .SHW   │ 01-17-89│ SLD SHOW│                     │
│  BUILD   .SHW   │ 01-15-89│ SLD SHOW│ Demo of building text charts │
│  HGACCESS.SHW   │ 01-06-89│ SHOW    │                     │
│  LISA    .SHW   │ 01-13-89│ SHOW    │                     │
│  NEWYORK .SHW   │ 01-13-89│ SLD SHOW│ New York & Vancouver show │
│  SOFTSEL .SHW   │ 01-06-89│ SHOW    │                     │
│  TEMPLATE.SHW   │ 01-06-89│ SHOW    │                     │
│  FUNNGAME.SHW   │ 01-09-89│ SLD SHOW│ Fun and Games Slide Show │
│  NEWPROD .SHW   │ 01-17-89│ SLD SHOW│ New Product Presentation │
│  SOSRAP  .SHW   │ 01-13-89│ SLD SHOW│ SOS Revenues Area w/projected 1989 │
│  GROW    .SHW   │ 01-13-89│ SLD SHOW│                     │
│  GROWBARS.SHW   │ 01-13-89│ SLD SHOW│ SOS Expenses with Growing Bars │
│  RUNLINES.SHW   │ 01-13-89│ SLD SHOW│ SOS Expenses with Running Lines │
│  BITMAP  .SHW   │ 01-15-89│ SLD SHOW│                     │
│  MENUSHOW.SHW   │ 01-15-89│ SLD SHOW│ Screenshow with User Menu │
│ ─────────────────────────────────────────────────────────│
│  F1-Help        F3-Change dir                             │
│                                            F10-Continue   │
└──────────────────────────────────────────────────────────┘
```

Fig. 16.4.

The Select Slide Show screen.

The Slide Show menu reappears. NEWPROD, the slide show you selected, is the current slide show.

To edit a slide show, choose Edit Slide Show from the Slide Show menu. Harvard Graphics displays the Create/Edit Slide Show screen for the current slide show. When you choose to edit NEWPROD, notice that NEWPROD.SHW reappears in the middle of the screen (see fig. 16.5).

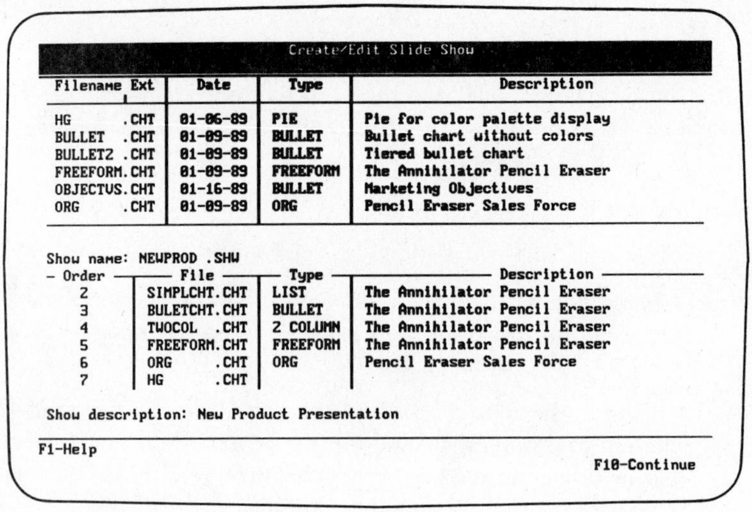

Fig. 16.5.

The Create/Edit
Slide Show screen
showing
NEWPROD.

```
┌──────────────────────────────────────────────────────────────────────┐
│                       Create/Edit Slide Show                           │
│ ┌──────────────────────────────────────────────────────────────────┐  │
│ │ Filename Ext │  Date  │   Type   │        Description              │  │
│ ├──────────────────────────────────────────────────────────────────┤  │
│ │ HG      .CHT │ 01-06-89 │ PIE      │ Pie for color palette display │  │
│ │ BULLET  .CHT │ 01-09-89 │ BULLET   │ Bullet chart without colors   │  │
│ │ BULLET2 .CHT │ 01-09-89 │ BULLET   │ Tiered bullet chart           │  │
│ │ FREEFORM.CHT │ 01-09-89 │ FREEFORM │ The Annihilator Pencil Eraser │  │
│ │ OBJECTUS.CHT │ 01-16-89 │ BULLET   │ Marketing Objectives          │  │
│ │ ORG     .CHT │ 01-09-89 │ ORG      │ Pencil Eraser Sales Force     │  │
│ └──────────────────────────────────────────────────────────────────┘  │
│                                                                        │
│  Show name: NEWPROD .SHW                                               │
│ ─ Order ──┬── File ──┬── Type ──┬──────── Description ────────         │
│      2    │ SIMPLCHT.CHT │ LIST     │ The Annihilator Pencil Eraser    │
│      3    │ BULETCHT.CHT │ BULLET   │ The Annihilator Pencil Eraser    │
│      4    │ TWOCOL  .CHT │ 2 COLUMN │ The Annihilator Pencil Eraser    │
│      5    │ FREEFORM.CHT │ FREEFORM │ The Annihilator Pencil Eraser    │
│      6    │ ORG     .CHT │ ORG      │ Pencil Eraser Sales Force        │
│      7    │ HG      .CHT │          │                                  │
│                                                                        │
│  Show description: New Product Presentation                            │
│ ──────────────────────────────────────────────────────────────────    │
│ F1-Help                                               F10-Continue     │
└──────────────────────────────────────────────────────────────────────┘
```

Adding a Chart

When you edit a slide show, you can cycle among three activities by pressing the Tab key. When the Create/Edit Slide Show screen first reappears, you can add new charts to the slide show list. When you press the up- or down-arrow keys, the highlight moves on the chart list at the top of the screen. Press Enter to add a highlighted chart to the list at the bottom of the screen. Press the Tab key again so that you can carry out a second activity, such as deleting charts or rearranging their order.

Editing the Description

Pressing the up- or down-arrow keys moves the cursor on the slide show list in the lower portion of the screen. Pressing the Tab key a third time enables you to edit the slide show description. The cursor rests on the description, awaiting your edits. To cycle among these three options, continue pressing the Tab key.

Deleting a Chart

To delete a chart, press the Tab key until the highlight appears in the slide show list in the lower portion of the screen only. Position the cursor on the chart name to delete and press Ctrl-Del. Delete the chart called ORG from the slide show list.

Rearranging Chart Order

Before you press Tab again, you can rearrange the order of the charts in your slide show list by positioning the cursor on the chart to move up or down the list and pressing Ctrl-↑ (up arrow) or Ctrl-↓ (down arrow). Highlight and move FREEFORM.CHT up the list and then back down to the bottom of the list. Figure 16.6 shows FREEFORM.CHT moved to the top of the list. The charts in the slide show are renumbered to reflect their new order.

```
╭──────────────────────────────────────────────────────────────╮
│                      Create/Edit Slide Show                    │
│  ┌──────────────────────────────────────────────────────────┐ │
│  │ Filename Ext      Date      Type         Description      │ │
│  ├──────────────────────────────────────────────────────────┤ │
│  │ HG      .CHT    01-06-89   PIE       Pie for color palette display │
│  │ BULLET  .CHT    01-09-89   BULLET    Bullet chart without colors   │
│  │ BULLET2 .CHT    01-09-89   BULLET    Tiered bullet chart           │
│  │ FREEFORM.CHT    01-09-89   FREEFORM  The Annihilator Pencil Eraser │
│  │ OBJECTUS.CHT    01-16-89   BULLET    Marketing Objectives          │
│  │ ORG     .CHT    01-09-89   ORG       Pencil Eraser Sales Force     │
│  └──────────────────────────────────────────────────────────┘ │
│                                                                │
│  Show name: NEWPROD .SHW                                       │
│  ─ Order ──────── File ──────── Type ──────── Description ──── │
│       1        FREEFORM.CHT    FREEFORM   The Annihilator Pencil Eraser │
│       2        TITLECHT.CHT    TITLE      Superior Office Supplies       │
│       3        SIMPLCHT.CHT    LIST       The Annihilator Pencil Eraser  │
│       4        BULETCHT.CHT    BULLET     The Annihilator Pencil Eraser  │
│       5        TWOCOL  .CHT    2 COLUMN   The Annihilator Pencil Eraser  │
│       6        ORG     .CHT    ORG        Pencil Eraser Sales Force      │
│                                                                │
│  Show description: New Product Presentation                    │
│  ────────────────────────────────────────────────────────────│
│  F1-Help                                           F10-Continue │
╰──────────────────────────────────────────────────────────────╯
```

Fig. 16.6.

FREEFORM.CHT moved to the top of the list.

To add a chart, press the Tab key until the highlight appears in the chart name list at the top of the screen. To add ORG back to the slide show list, highlight the chart name ORG and press Enter. Now press F10 (Continue) to return to the Slide Show menu.

Adding Other File Types

In addition to charts, you can add several other types of files to a slide show. If you add another slide show file name, the slide show branches to the second slide show and begins displaying its files. If you add a template name or a bit-mapped file, you can create certain special effects for screenshows. You read about these effects later in this chapter.

Displaying a Slide Show

To display a slide show, select Display Screenshow from the Slide Show menu. Later, you learn that screenshows are slide shows with transition effects. Even though the slide show you created has no transition effects added, Harvard Graphics still considers the slide show a screenshow if you choose to display the slide show on-screen. When you choose Display Screenshow, Harvard Graphics begins showing the current slide show (in this case, NEWPROD.SHW).

Just as you must press the advance button on a slide projector to view the next slide, you may press any key while displaying a screenshow to view the next chart on the list. After you have viewed all the charts in the slide show, Harvard Graphics returns to the Slide Show menu.

To display a series of charts in a presentation, you probably want to add a few interesting transition effects between charts. You can read detailed information about the variety of transitions available for screenshows later in this chapter.

Editing Chart Data in a Slide Show

As you view a screenshow, you may notice charts that need alterations. You can return quickly to the data screen of a chart for modifications by pressing Ctrl-E while the chart is in view on-screen. After you have completed modifying a chart's data or its options, you must return to the main menu, save the chart on disk, and select Display Screenshow from the Slide Show menu to restart the show.

Suppose, for example, that as you display NEWPROD, you realize that one of the entries on the second chart, the simple list, reads "Long-lasting" rather than "Longer lasting." To correct this error, display NEWPROD.SHW and press Ctrl-E when the simple list appears on-screen. The data screen for SIMPLCHT appears. Correct the word, save the chart, and return to the Slide Show menu to select and display NEWPROD.SHW again.

Printing a Slide Show List

While NEWPROD is still the current slide show, you can print a list of its contents. To print a slide show list, choose Produce Output from the main menu. Then choose Print Slide Show List from the Produce Output menu. The Slide Show List Option menu appears, enabling you to send the list to Printer 1 or Printer 2. Select the appropriate printer with the space bar and then press Enter. Figure 16.7 shows the printed slide show list for NEWPROD.SHW. Slide show lists can help you to keep track of the contents of slide shows.

```
SLIDE SHOW NAME: NEWPROD .SHW

ORDER      CHART        TYPE                      DESCRIPTION
-----   -------------   --------   ------------------------------------------
  1     TITLECHT.CHT    TITLE      Standard Office Supplies
  2     SIMPLCHT.CHT    LIST       The Annihilator Pencil Eraser
  3     BULETCHT.CHT    BULLET     The Annihilator Pencil Eraser
  4     TWOCOL  .CHT    2 COLUMN   The Annihilator Pencil Eraser
  5     FREEFORM.CHT    FREEFORM   The Annihilator Pencil Eraser
  6     ORG     .CHT    ORG        Pencil Eraser Sales Force
```

Fig. 16.7.

The printed Slide Show list for NEWPROD.SHW.

Printing Practice Cards

Another task made possible by slide shows is printing practice cards for a presentation. Practice cards hold notes about the charts in a slide show or screenshow and images of the charts themselves. You can create one practice card for each of the slides in a slide show. As you give a speech, you can refer to these cards as you describe the information conveyed by each chart. Each card holds your notes about the chart and a printed copy of the chart.

Now create a practice card for the first slide in NEWPROD.SHW by following these steps:

1. Retrieve from disk the slide show or screenshow for which you want to make practice cards, thus making it the current show. Make sure that NEWPROD.SHW is the current slide show. You may need to choose NEWPROD from the Select Slide Show screen (accessed from the Slide Show menu) to be certain.

2. Select Make Practice Cards from the Slide Show menu. The Practice Cards screen appears (see fig. 16.8). The cursor rests in an open area under the current slide number, chart name, and chart description.

3. Type your notes about the chart and then press PgDn or F10 (Continue) to create a practice card for the next chart in the show.

   When you type a practice card note, you can precede an item with a bullet by pressing Ctrl-B, selecting a bullet style from the Bullet Shape overlay that appears, and pressing Enter before typing the note text.

4. Press Ctrl-B to make a bullet, choose the round bullet shape by pressing the space bar to highlight it, and press Enter.

5. Type a space, type *Welcome*, and press Enter twice to skip a line.

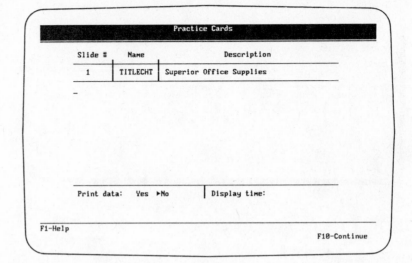

Fig. 16.8.

*The Practice Cards
screen.*

6. Press Ctrl-B again to enter another round bullet. For the note, type *Introduce myself* and press Enter twice to skip another line.

7. Enter another round bullet, type *Purpose of the presentation* as the next note item, and press Enter twice.

8. Press the space bar twice to indent, enter a hyphen bullet, and type *Introduce new product*.

9. Enter two more hyphen bullets with the following lines of text: *Describe marketing plans* and *Describe sales force organization*. (Figure 16.9 shows the completed practice card for slide number 1.)

10. Press PgDn to create a note for slide 2.

11. Complete the second practice card as shown in figure 16.10.

12. Press Esc to return to the Slide Show menu when you have created all the practice cards you need.

Moving to a Slide

After you enter a note for a practice card, you may want to go to a specific slide in a presentation to enter a new note or modify an existing note. To jump to a specific slide, press the Tab key until the cursor is on the slide number, enter a new slide number, and press Enter. You can determine slide numbers easily by printing a slide show list before making practice cards.

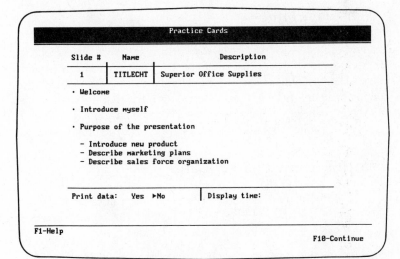

Fig. 16.9.

The Practice Cards screen for slide 1.

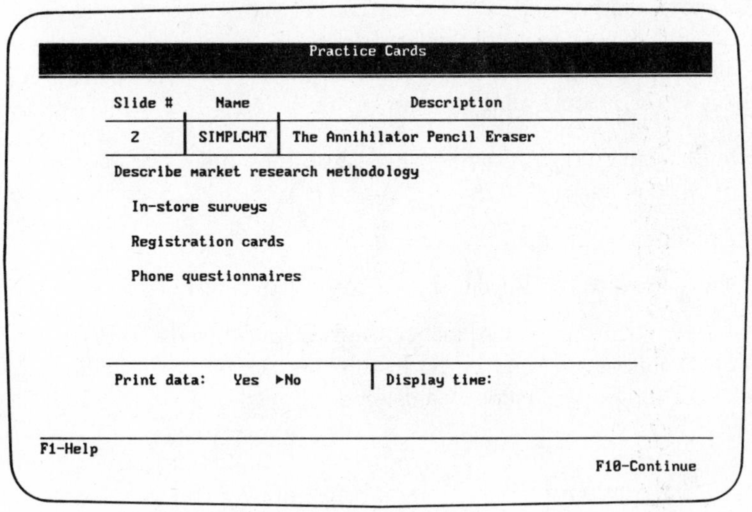

Fig. 16.10.

The Practice Cards screen for slide 2.

Printing Chart Data

To print a page with the chart data after each practice card, press the Tab key to move the cursor to the Print Data prompt at the bottom of the screen and change its setting to Yes. The default setting is No.

Changing the Display Time

To alter the amount of time the chart displays before the next slide appears, press Tab to move the cursor to the Display Time field. In this field, you can enter a number of minutes and seconds, such as *1:30* (1 minute and 30 seconds), to display the current chart during the show. Later, you learn that you can add a display time for a chart when you add screenshow effects. That display time and this display time are the same. Change one display time, and the other changes.

Saving and Printing the Practice Cards

Practice cards are saved with the slide show. The next time you select the same slide show, the practice cards also are retrieved. To edit the current practice cards, select Make Practice Cards from the Slide Show menu.

When you complete practice cards for the charts in a slide show, you can print the cards by choosing Print Practice Cards from the Produce Output menu. Harvard Graphics prints the practice cards for the current slide show. Practice cards display the slide number, chart name, chart description, note, and display time on the top half of the page and the actual chart on the bottom half of the page. Figure 16.11 shows the practice card for chart #1 of the NEWPROD slide show.

To print the practice cards you created for the first two slides in NEWPROD.SHW, follow these steps:

1. Select Produce Output from the main menu.

2. Select Print Practice Cards from the Produce Output menu.

3. Select a print quality from the Practice Cards Options overlay that appears by pressing the space bar and Enter. In this case, set Quality to Standard. Figure 16.12 shows the Practice Cards Options overlay.

4. Select Printer 1 and press Enter.

5. You can choose a range of practice cards to print by entering a starting slide number and ending slide number. Press 1 at the From Slide field and 2 at the To Slide field and press Enter.

Using Slide Shows for Batch Printing

To print, plot, or record a series of charts, you can assemble them into a slide show, even if you have no intention of displaying the charts on-screen. Make a slide show with all the charts you want to send to an output device and choose Print Slide Show, Plot Slide Show, or Record Slide Show from the Produce Output menu.

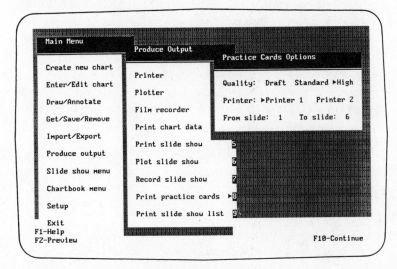

Fig. 16.11.

The practice card for NEWPROD slide 1.

Fig. 16.12.

The Practice Cards Options overlay.

For more information about producing output using this option, see "Printing a Series of Charts" earlier in this chapter.

Creating Screenshows

A *screenshow* is a slide show designed expressly for display on a PC screen. Of course, you also can project a screenshow in an auditorium or large room with a special computer screen projector that projects a computer monitor's image onto a large screen.

To create a simple screenshow, you add special transitions between the charts of a slide show. These effects are much like the transitions between scenes of a television program. Like the special effects available to the editor of a film, you have an entire arsenal of wipes, fades, and other transitions to liven up slide shows at your disposal.

But screenshows offer even more. By keeping in mind the transition effects available when you create the charts of a screenshow, you can use special techniques to build text charts line by line, make the bars of a bar chart grow, move the lines of a line chart across the screen, and add the slices of a pie one by one.

Adding Effects To Create a Screenshow

To create a screenshow, you first must assemble a slide show. While that slide show is the current slide show, you can add screenshow transition effects.

To add special transitions between the charts of the NEWPROD slide show you created earlier, choose Select Slide Show from the Slide Show menu and select NEWPROD. Select Add Screenshow Effects from the Slide Show menu. If you choose Add Screenshow Effects before you select a slide show, Harvard Graphics displays the slide show list so that you can select a slide show first. The Screenshow Effects screen appears, as shown in figure 16.13.

The Screenshow Effects screen contains eight columns. The first three display the numbers, names, and types of charts in the slide show. In the next five columns, you add transitions between charts. These five columns perform the following actions:

❏ *Draw* determines the effect used to display that chart.

❏ *Dir* determines the direction for the draw effect (up, down, left, right, and so on).

❏ *Time* determines the display time for the current chart.

❏ *Erase* determines the effect used to erase that chart. You can erase a chart with one effect and then draw the next chart with another effect to create a particularly dramatic transition.

❏ *Dir* determines the direction for the erase effect.

```
┌──────────────────────────────────────────────────────────────┐
│  ┌──────────────────────────────────────────────────────┐    │
│  │              Screenshow Effects                      │    │
│  ├──────────────────────────────────────────────────────┤    │
│  │   Filename      Type    Draw   Dir  Time  Erase  Dir │    │
│  ├──────────────────────────────────────────────────────┤    │
│  │   Default               Replace                      │    │
│  │ ──────────────────────────────────────────────────── │    │
│  │ 1 TITLECHT.CHT   TITLE                               │    │
│  │ 2 SIMPLCHT.CHT   LIST                                │    │
│  │ 3 BULETCHT.CHT   BULLET                              │    │
│  │ 4 TWOCOL  .CHT   2 COLUMN                            │    │
│  │ 5 FREEFORM.CHT   FREEFORM                            │    │
│  │ 6 ORG     .CHT   ORG                                 │    │
│  │                                                      │    │
│  │                                                      │    │
│  │ ──────────────────────────────────────────────────── │    │
│  │ F1-Help                                              │    │
│  │ F2-Preview show        F6-Choices   F8-HyperShow   F10-Continue │
│  └──────────────────────────────────────────────────────┘    │
└──────────────────────────────────────────────────────────────┘
```

Fig. 16.13.

The Screenshow Effects screen.

Under the column titles, near the top of the screen, is a row labeled Default. In this row, you can enter a choice to use for any blank entry in a column. At the moment, the default for the Draw column is Replace. If you leave an entry blank in the column, Harvard Graphics uses Replace as the Draw effect for that chart. Replace is the default for Harvard Graphics screenshows and cannot be changed. Replace produces a screenshow which looks much like a standard photographic slide presentation. Each successive picture replaces the previous picture.

To view the choices available for a column, position the cursor in the column and press F6 (Choices). If the cursor is in the Draw column, for example, pressing F6 displays the effects available for drawing the chart. Figure 16.14 shows the Transitions overlay for Draw. If the cursor is in the Dir column, pressing F6 displays an overlay showing the available directions for the direction effect.

The available Draw and Erase effects are as follows:

- ❑ *Replace* switches from one full-screen chart to the next.

- ❑ *Overlay* displays the next chart on top of the current chart. Both charts then are visible.

- ❑ *Wipe* sweeps up, down, left, or right across the chart. The default is Right.

- ❑ *Scroll* pushes the chart onto the screen to the right, left, up, or down. The default is Up.

- ❑ *Fade* fades the chart onto the screen all at once or gradually down the screen. The default is all at once. Use Down to have the new chart gradually fade down the screen.

Fig. 16.14.

The Transitions overlay for Draw.

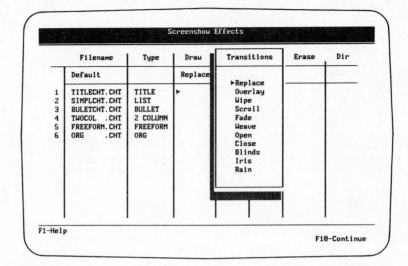

Fig. 16.14.

The Transitions overlay for Draw.

❑ *Weave* joins two halves of a chart swept in from the left and right sides of the screen. The direction setting has no effect.

❑ *Open* reveals the screen from the center out. The visible portion of the chart expands in a straight line vertically or horizontally. The default is Up. Setting Direction to Right opens the screen horizontally.

❑ *Close* closes the screen from the edge in. The visible portion of the chart contracts in a straight line vertically or horizontally. The default is Up. Setting Direction to Right closes the screen horizontally.

❑ *Blinds* brings the next chart into view in stripes that move down or across the screen. The default is Down. Set Direction to Right for stripes that roll across the screen.

❑ *Iris* reveals the chart from the center of the screen growing outward. The default is Out. To close the screen from the edge in toward the center, set Direction to In. Left and right are not valid directions with Iris.

❑ *Rain* paints the screen from the top down in small drips. The direction setting has no effect.

Position the cursor in each of the columns and press F6 to see the available choices for that column (F6 does not, however, work in the Time column. You must enter a time manually). Press Esc after pressing F6 to remove the Transitions overlay. To erase an effect in a column, position the cursor on the effect and press Ctrl-Del. You also can replace an effect by entering a new effect over the current effect.

Experiment with the available transition effects by moving the cursor down the Draw column and picking a transition from the Transitions overlay for each chart. You can start with the Replace choices shown in figure 16.15. Then press F2 (Preview Show) to display the screenshow. Because the Time column is blank, you must press a key or click the right mouse button to advance to the next chart in the show. Later, you can try entering a time (in minutes and seconds) to display the chart on-screen before advancing to the next chart.

```
┌───────────────────────────────────────────────────────────────┐
│                       Screenshow Effects                        │
│  ═══════════════════════════════════════════════════════════   │
│                                                                 │
│     Filename    │ Type    │ Draw    │ Dir │ Time │ Erase │ Dir  │
│   ──────────────┼─────────┼─────────┼─────┼──────┼───────┼───── │
│     Default     │         │ Replace │     │      │       │      │
│                 │         │         │     │      │       │      │
│   1 TITLECHT.CHT│ TITLE   │ Fade    │     │      │       │      │
│   2 SIMPLCHT.CHT│ LIST    │ Wipe    │     │      │       │      │
│   3 BULETCHT.CHT│ BULLET  │ Scroll  │     │      │       │      │
│   4 TWOCOL .CHT │ 2 COLUMN│ Weave   │     │      │       │      │
│   5 FREEFORM.CHT│ FREEFORM│ Open    │     │      │       │      │
│   6 ORG    .CHT │ ORG     │ Rain    │     │      │       │      │
│                 │         │         │     │      │       │      │
│                                                                 │
│  F1-Help                                                        │
│  F2-Preview show         F6-Choices    F8-HyperShow  F10-Continue│
└───────────────────────────────────────────────────────────────┘
```

Fig. 16.15.

Sample Draw transition choices.

When the screenshow is finished, Harvard Graphics returns to the Screenshow Effects screen. To interrupt a show while displaying and return immediately to the Screenshow Effects screen, press Esc. To start a show on a particular chart, position the cursor in the chart's row before pressing F2 (Preview Show).

If you know the name of the transition or the direction you want to use, you can type the first one or two letters and move to the next column to set. For example, you can type *wi* and Harvard Graphics fills in Wipe when you move to the next column.

The screenshow is already far more exciting than the simple slide show you created earlier. But you can fine-tune the show by adding complementary Erase effects to the Draw effects you used for certain charts. For example, erasing a chart with Iris Out leads well into drawing a chart with Iris In. If you omit an Erase effect, Harvard Graphics uses the default. If you have not supplied a default Erase effect, the program uses the Draw effect for the next chart to replace the current chart.

Try the effects shown in figure 16.16. Notice the use of Wipe Up, Wipe Down, Open Left, Close Left, Iris Out, and Iris In to erase and draw successive charts. In addition, notice that the default time is 1 second in figure 16.16. To advance to the next chart before the time you have chosen expires, press Enter or click the right mouse button. To move from chart to chart as quickly as possible, you can use a time of 0.

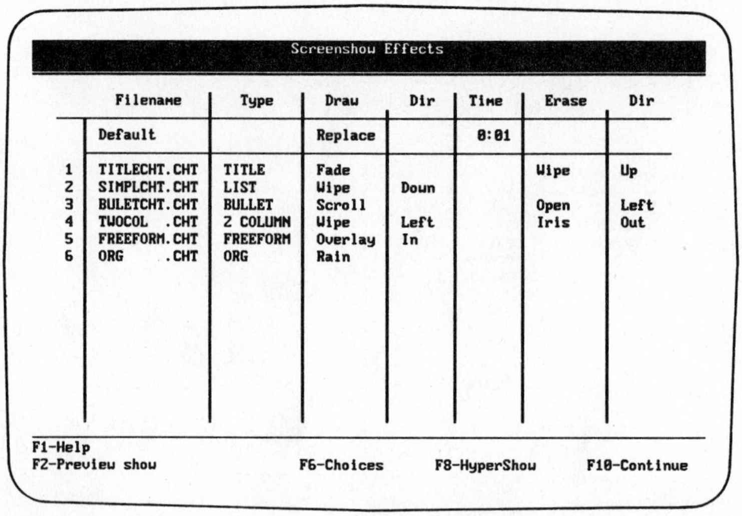

Fig. 16.16.

Various effects from the Screenshow Effects screen.

	Filename	Type	Draw	Dir	Time	Erase	Dir
	Default		Replace		0:01		
1	TITLECHT.CHT	TITLE	Fade			Wipe	Up
2	SIMPLCHT.CHT	LIST	Wipe	Down			
3	BULETCHT.CHT	BULLET	Scroll			Open	Left
4	TWOCOL .CHT	2 COLUMN	Wipe	Left		Iris	Out
5	FREEFORM.CHT	FREEFORM	Overlay	In			
6	ORG .CHT	ORG	Rain				

F1-Help
F2-Preview show   F6-Choices   F8-HyperShow   F10-Continue

When you complete the screenshow, press F10 (Continue). Harvard Graphics displays the Slide Show menu. To return to the main menu, press Esc. The screenshow transition effects are saved with the slide show as you build the show. You do not need to issue a specific command to save the show with its effects. Because the effects are saved with the slide show, you must assemble a second slide show with the same charts to display the charts with different transition effects.

Using Special Techniques for Animating Charts

Screenshows also enable you to animate the transitions between charts. But they provide even more appealing effects. Special techniques enable you to animate the actual charts in a slide show in addition to transitions between charts. The following sections describe some of the best of these techniques for making charts take shape right before your audience's eyes.

Adding Text Chart Items

A technique that provides an interesting alternative to presenting a fully composed list of text items on-screen is to add the items on a text chart one by one, highlighting each as the item appears and causing the items already present to recede into the background.

To build a text chart on-screen line by line, create the complete chart first. Remove items from the bottom up, one by one, saving each new slightly diminished chart as a separate file. When you build a slide show, add the individual text chart files in reverse order, using fade or overlay for a transition. Successive text items seem to appear one by one.

To make the newest addition to the chart stand out as the chart is built step by step, highlight the last item in each of the charts you save as you dismantle the original chart.

To try this effect, create a bullet list by filling out the Bullet List data screen and the Size/Place overlay so that they match the screen shown in figure 16.17.

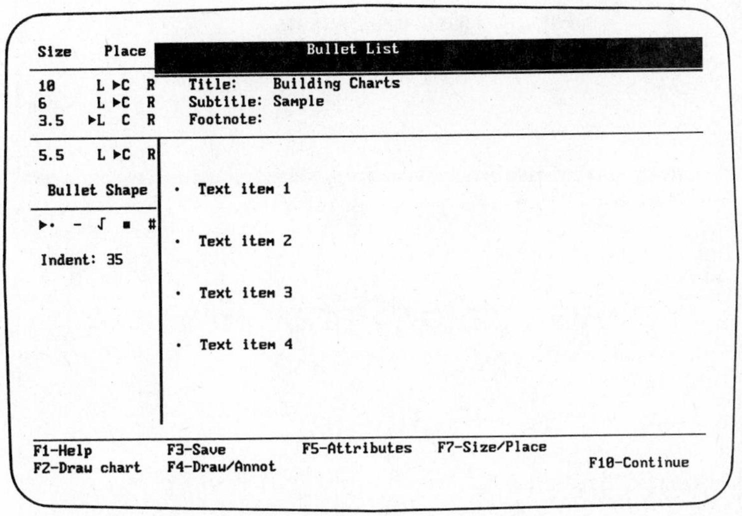

```
  Size    Place           Bullet List

  10    L ▶C  R    Title:    Building Charts
  6     L ▶C  R    Subtitle: Sample
  3.5   ▶L  C  R    Footnote:

  5.5   L ▶C  R

  Bullet Shape        ·  Text item 1

  ▶·  -  ∫  ▪  #      ·  Text item 2

  Indent: 35
                      ·  Text item 3

                      ·  Text item 4



 F1-Help         F3-Save       F5-Attributes   F7-Size/Place
 F2-Draw chart   F4-Draw/Annot                               F10-Continue
```

Fig. 16.17.

The Bullet List data screen showing the Size/Place overlay.

To ensure that the text aligns properly on successive charts, left justify the lines of text and use Indent to move the text to the center of the screen. In this case, a setting of 35 works perfectly. If you right align text, the text shifts horizontally based on the current, longest line on-screen. When you remove a long line from a text chart as you use this technique, the remaining text shifts to the right, ruining the consistency between charts. Figure 16.18 shows a right-aligned text chart before the last lines are removed. Figure 16.19 shows the same chart after two items are removed. Notice that the remaining lines are shifted horizontally in the second chart.

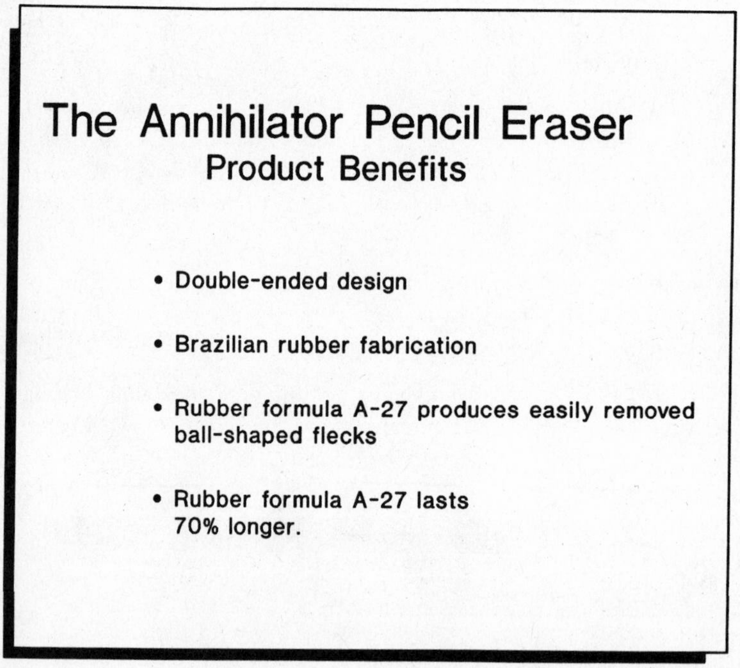

Fig. 16.18.

Before removing the last two items of right-aligned text.

The Annihilator Pencil Eraser
Product Benefits
• Double-ended design
• Brazilian rubber fabrication
• Rubber formula A-27 produces easily removed ball-shaped flecks
• Rubber formula A-27 lasts 70% longer.

Fig. 16.19.

After removing the last two items of right-aligned text.

The Annihilator Pencil Eraser
Product Benefits
• Double-ended design
• Brazilian rubber fabrication

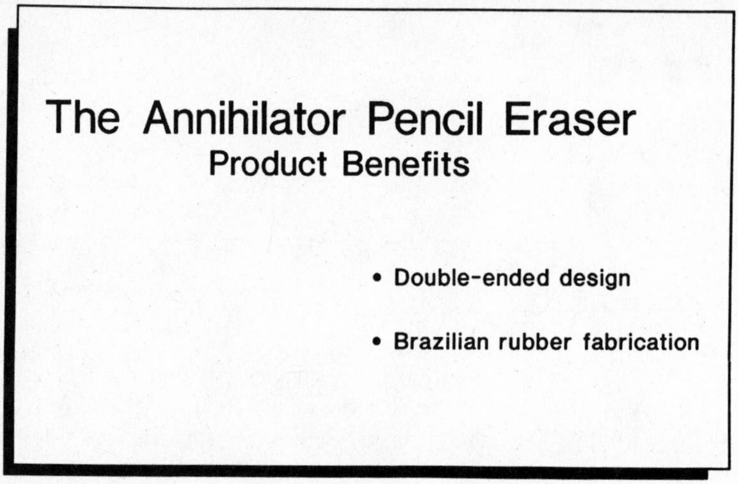

Using the F5-Attributes feature, set the last item of the chart in yellow and the earlier items in red. Color the title any way you want. Save the chart as BUILD5. Because BUILD5 is the current chart, select Enter/Edit Chart from the main menu to review the data screen. Delete the last item by pressing Ctrl-Del with the cursor on that line and color the new last item yellow. Save the revised chart as BUILD4. Repeat the same procedure, removing lines one by one, and creating BUILD3, BUILD2, and BUILD1 showing only the titles.

On the Slide Show menu, select Create Slide Show and add BUILD1, BUILD2, BUILD3, BUILD4, and BUILD5 to a slide show named BUILD, as shown in figure 16.20. Enter *Demo of building text charts* as the description. With all five charts included in a screenshow, press F10 (Continue) to return to the Slide Show menu.

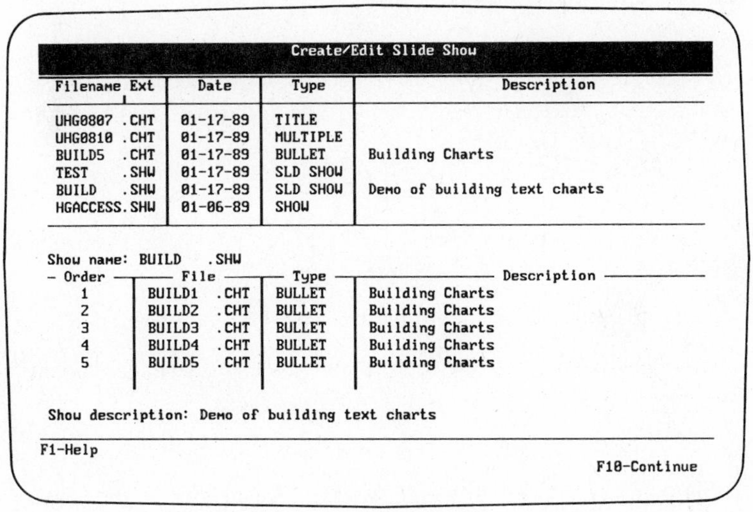

Fig. 16.20.

The BUILD slide show.

Select Display Screenshow from the Slide Show menu. The current screenshow, BUILD, appears. Because you have added no display time yet, you must press Enter repeatedly to cause each new screen to appear.

To place the finishing touches on your screenshow, select Add Screenshow Effects from the Slide Show menu. Replace the current default Draw transition (Replace) with Fade. Position the cursor at the top of the list of charts and press F2 (Preview Show) to view the screenshow with its effects.

For even more pizzazz, bring all five charts into Draw/Annotate and add additional highlighting to the last text item on each chart. Currently, the last items are yellow, and all the other items are red. You may want to try enclosing the last item in a box or highlighting the item with colorful arrows.

Adding Graph Chart Series

You can animate the appearance of graph charts as well. One of the easiest and most striking effects is to add series to a graph chart one by one. To add series, you follow much the same procedure as adding text items to a text chart one by one. First, create and save the completed chart with all series. Then remove a series and save the revised chart. To remove a series from view in a graph chart, you can set Display to No for that series on the first Titles & Options page, or you can use the @Clr calculation at that series as discussed in Chapter 5. @Clr removes the entire series of data so that the chart's data screen does not contain uncharted data. Continue until only one series remains. When you display the charts in reverse order in a screenshow, each new series seems to add to the series already in view.

Using the data from the Superior Office Supplies Revenue chart you created in Chapter 5, create an area chart to try this technique. Use the chart entitled SOSRPROJ because that chart has four series—three of actual data and the fourth projected by means of a calculation.

To animate an area chart, follow this procedure:

1. Select Get Chart from the Get/Save/Remove menu and retrieve SOSRPROJ.CHT. Figure 16.21 shows this chart.

2. Press Esc twice to return to the main menu.

3. Select Create New Chart from the main menu and Area from the Create New Chart menu.

4. Make sure that the Keep Current Data query is set to Yes.

5. Press F2 (Draw Chart) to preview the chart. Make a note of the y-axis minimum and maximum values. These values are 0 and 200,000, as shown in figure 16.21.

   The minimum and maximum y-axis values are important when you begin removing series. As you remove series, the maximum Y value of the data left on the chart may change. As a result, the y-axis may readjust to fit the remaining data. To avoid this adjustment, you must set the chart's minimum and maximum y-axis values manually. By making note of the y-axis minimum and maximum values when all the data is in place, you know what to enter for y-axis minimum and maximum values on the third Titles & Options page for the area chart, later in this procedure.

6. Press Esc to return to the Area Chart Data screen.

7. Modify the subtitle to reflect all four years of data (1986-1989 rather than 1986-1988).

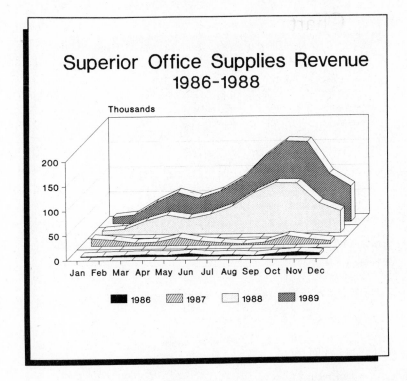

Fig. 16.21.

The SOSRPROJ chart.

8. Press F8 (Options) to view the first Titles & Options page. Notice that Display is set to Yes for Series 1 through Series 4.

9. Press PgDn to view the second Titles & Options page and set Chart enhancement to None. Animating the adding of series to a three-dimensional chart with this technique is not particularly effective. As you add new series in a three-dimensional chart, the depth of the chart increases, breaking the continuity between successive charts that makes the animation effect so impressive.

10. Press PgDn again to view the third Titles & Options page.

11. Set the Y1 Axis Minimum Value to 0 and the Maximum Value to 200,000, as shown in figure 16.22.

12. Press F10 (Continue) and F2 (Draw Chart) to preview the area chart.

Next, begin removing series and saving the incremental charts:

1. Save the current chart as SOSRAP4, for "Superior Office Supplies Revenue Area Projected, chart 4."

2. Select Enter/Edit Chart from the main menu to return to the Area Chart Data screen.

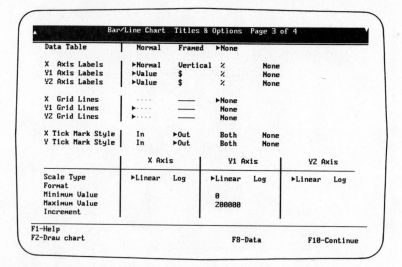

Fig. 16.22.

The third Titles &
Options page
showing y-axis
minimum and
maximum values.

3. Press F8 (Options) to display the first Titles & Options page.

4. Set Display for Series 4 (1989) to No.

5. Press F10 (Continue) to return to the main menu and save the chart as SOSRAP3.

6. Select Enter/Edit Chart from the main menu again to return to the Area Chart Data screen.

7. Press F8 (Options) to display the first Titles & Options page.

8. Set Display for Series 3 (1988) to No. Now set Display Series 3 and Series 4 to No.

9. Save the chart as SOSRAP2.

10. Return to the data screen and the first Titles & Options page.

11. This time, set Display for Series 2, 3, and 4 to No. Only Series 1 (1986) is displayed.

12. Save this chart as SOSRAP1.

Now you have created four charts that you can add to a slide show by following these steps:

1. Choose the Slide Show Menu option from the main menu.

2. Choose Create Slide Show from the Slide Show menu.

3. Enter *sosrap* as the slide show name and *SOS Revenues Area w/projected 1989* as the description and press Enter.

4. On the Create/Edit Slide Show screen, add the charts SOSRAP1, SOSRAP2, SOSRAP3, and SOSRAP4 to the SOSRAP slide show. Press F10 (Continue) to return to the Slide Show menu.

Finally, you should add screenshow effects to create the effect of adding a new series one by one:

1. Select Add Screenshow Effects from the Slide Show menu.

2. Use Wipe as the default for Draw effect and Up as the default for draw direction. Position the cursor in the Default row under Draw, choose Wipe from the overlay summoned with F6-Choices, position the cursor in the same row under Dir, and choose Up from the Transitions overlay.

3. Enter :02 as the default time so that the show proceeds automatically. Figure 16.23 shows the completed Screenshow Effects screen for SOSRAP.

	Filename	Type	Draw	Dir	Time	Erase	Dir
	Default		Wipe	Up	0:02		
1	SOSRAP1 .CHT	AREA					
2	SOSRAP2 .CHT	AREA					
3	SOSRAP3 .CHT	AREA					
4	SOSRAP4 .CHT	AREA					

Screenshow Effects

F1-Help
F2-Preview show   F6-Choices   F8-HyperShow   F10-Continue

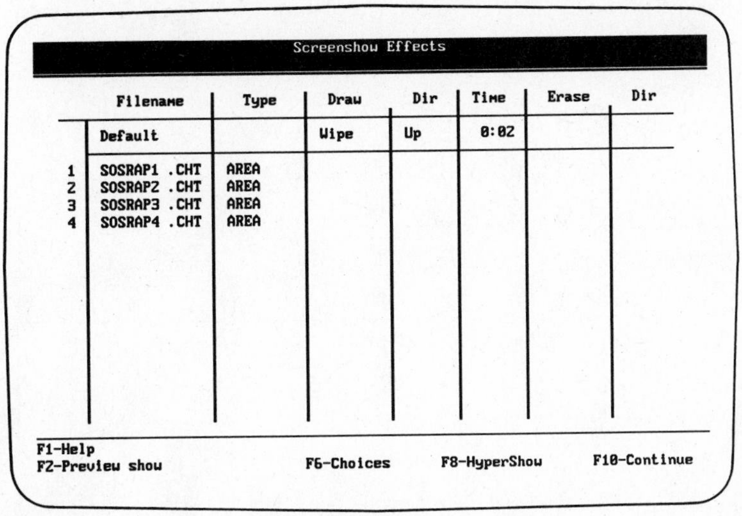

Fig. 16.23.

The completed Screenshow Effects screen for SOSRAP.

Now that the screenshow is complete, press F2 (Preview Show) to see the completed effect.

Try other Draw effects, but avoid Weave, Overlay, and Scroll. Weave and Scroll move the entire chart on-screen, ruining the illusion that the chart is changed only by the addition of a new series. Selecting Overlay as the Draw effect causes each new legend to overwrite the preceding legend. Because the legends change as each new series is added, the result is a blurred mess where a clean, clear legend should be.

Making Bars Grow

To make the bars of a bar chart grow, use Wipe Up as the screenshow transition effect between two slides. The first slide hides the bars by displaying the bars in black. The second slide shows the bars in full color. As the second slide wipes up across the first, the full-color bars seem to grow on-screen.

To try this technique, follow these steps:

1. Retrieve the chart entitled SOSEXPEN created in Chapter 5. Figure 16.24 shows the SOSEXPEN chart.

2. Press Esc to view the chart's data screen and F8 (Options) to view the first Titles & Options page.

3. Press PgDn twice to view the third Titles & Options page.

4. Set Y1 Grid Lines to None. When you set the bars to black, if Y1 Grid Lines are showing, the black bars hide portions of the grid lines on-screen, lessening the effect.

5. Press PgDn to view the fourth Titles & Options page.

6. Set Color for Series 1, 2, 3, and 4 to 16 (black).

7. Press F10 (Continue) to return to the main menu.

8. Save the chart as SOSEXP2.

Fig. 16.24.

The SOSEXPEN chart.

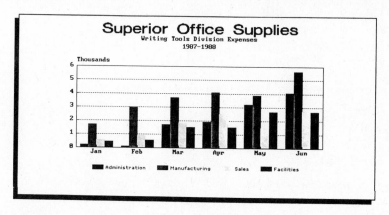

Now build the slide show and add the screenshow effects by following this procedure:

1. Select Create Slide Show from the Slide Show menu.

2. Name the slide show GROWBARS and enter *SOS Expenses with Growing Bars* as the description.

3. Add SOSEXP2 to the GROWBARS slide show.

4. Add SOSEXPEN to the GROWBARS slide show.

5. Press F10 (Continue) to return to the Slide Show menu.

6. Select Add Screenshow Effects from the Slide Show menu.

7. Enter *0:00* as the default time.

8. Select Wipe as the Draw effect for the second chart in the slide show, SOSEXPEN.

9. Select Up as the direction for the Draw effect for SOSEXPEN.

10. Enter *10:00* as the time for SOSEXPEN so that the last image remains on-screen until you press Enter.

11. Move the cursor to the top of the Screenshow Effects screen and press F2 (Preview Show) to view the screenshow. Figure 16.25 shows the completed Screenshow Effects screen for GROWBARS.

	Filename	Type	Draw	Dir	Time	Erase	Dir
	Default		Replace		0:00		
1	SOSEXP2 .CHT	BAR/LINE					
2	SOSEXPEN.CHT	BAR/LINE	Wipe	Up	10:00		

Screenshow Effects

F1-Help
F2-Preview show   F6-Choices   F8-HyperShow   F10-Continue

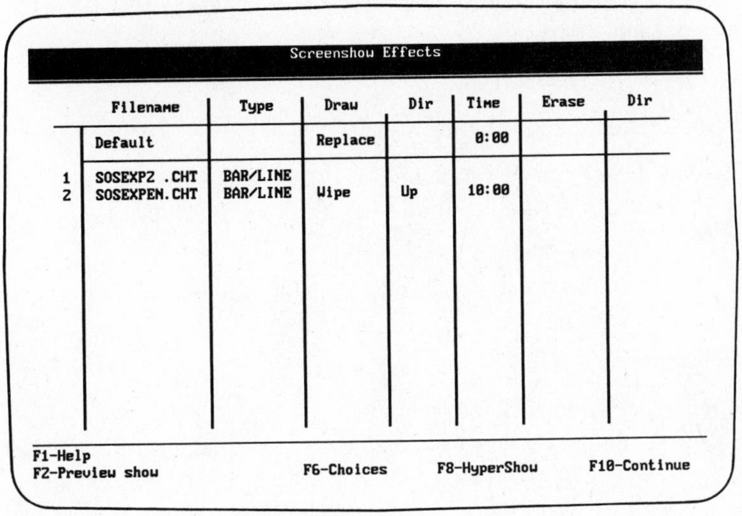

Fig. 16.25.

The completed Screenshow Effects screen for GROWBARS.

Making Lines Run

Just as you can make bars grow, you can make lines run across a line chart. To achieve this effect, display a succession of charts, each with an additional data point for each series. Use Wipe Right as the transition effect. The lines on your line chart appear to extend across the screen point by point from left to right.

To make a line run, follow these steps:

1. Retrieve the chart SOSEXPEN. Its y-axis minimum and maximum values are 0 and 6,000, respectively. You need to enter these values later on the component charts of the screenshow, as you did earlier when animating the area chart.

2. On the first Titles & Options page of SOSEXPEN, set Type for all four series to Line.

3. For a dramatic effect, set Bar style to Overlap and Bar enhancement to 3D on the second Titles & Options page.

4. Save the chart as SOSEXPL ("SOS Expenses Line").

5. Return to the SOSEXPL Bar/Line Chart Data screen by choosing Enter/Edit Chart from the main menu.

6. Delete the four series data for June, but leave the word Jun in the X Axis column.

7. Set the Y1 Axis Minimum Value to 0 and Maximum Value to 6000 on the third Titles & Options page.

8. Save the chart as SOSEXPL5.

9. Select Enter/Edit Chart from the main menu.

10. Delete the data for all four series for May, but leave the word May in the X Axis column. The X Axis column now has May and Jun with no data in the series columns.

11. Set the Y1 Axis Minimum Value to 0 and Maximum Value to 6000 on the third Titles & Options page.

12. Save the chart as SOSEXPL4.

13. Continue removing data for all four series month by month. Continue setting the Y1 Axis minimum and maximum values on the third Titles & Options page until you have saved SOSEXPL3, SOSEXPL2, and SOSEXPL1. SOSEXPL1 should have data for January only.

14. Return to the main menu and select the Slide Show Menu option.

15. Select Create Slide Show from the Slide Show menu.

16. Name the slide show RUNLINES and enter SOS Expenses w/ Running Lines as the description.

17. Add SOSEXPL1 to the slide show first.

18. Add SOSEXPL2 to the slide show second.

19. Continue until you have added SOSEXPL3, SOSEXPL4, and SOSEXPL5.

20. Complete the slide show by adding SOSEXPL.

21. Press F10 (Continue) to return to the Slide Show menu.

22. Select Add Screenshow Effects from the Slide Show menu.

23. Set the default time to 0:00.

24. Set the Draw effect to Wipe and the direction to Right for SOSEXPL2 through SOSEXPL5 and SOSEXPL.

25. Set Time for SOSEXPL to 10:00 to ensure that SOSEXPL remains on-screen until you press Enter.

26. Position the cursor at the top of the Screenshow Effects screen and press F2 (Preview Show) to watch RUNLINES in action. Figure 16.26 shows the completed Screenshow Effects screen for RUNLINES.

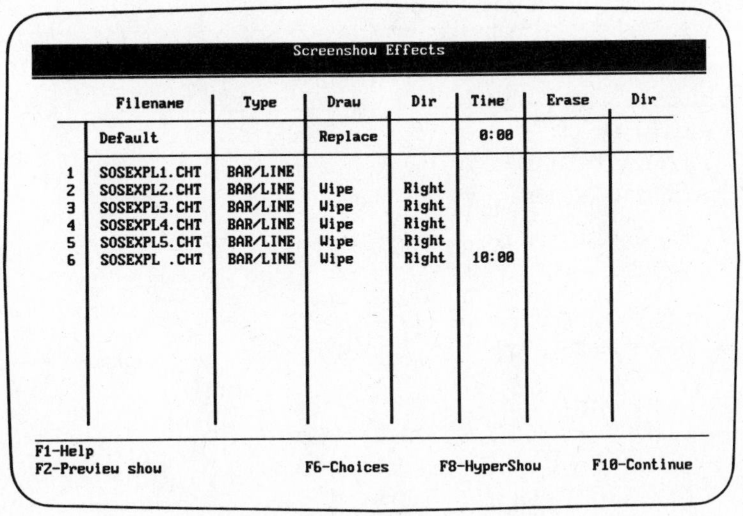

Fig. 16.26.

The completed Screenshow Effects screen for RUNLINES.

You may be surprised that the first chart in the screenshow has data for the month of January, but the screenshow seems to start without any visible lines. Because the chart uses lines, the first chart, with data for only one month, appears blank. The lines appear when they can connect data for at least two months.

Using the Animated Sequences in a Screenshow

Harvard Graphics 2.3 now includes 10 animated sequences you can incorporate into your own screenshows. To view these sequences, display the screenshow ANIMATOR.SHW in the \HG\SAMPLE directory.

To use one of these animated sequences in a screenshow, you must copy all of its component files to the directory in which you have the rest of the screenshow files. All files in a screenshow must be in the same directory. Then, you must include the file names of the screenshow in your screenshow and add the correct transition effects. Table 16.1 lists the 10 animated shows and tells you the component files you need to include and the transition effects you must set.

Table 16.1
Animated Sequences

Show Name	Files	Transition Effects			
		Draw	Dir	Time	Erase
Fireworks	CITY.PCX	Open	Right	0:00	
	FIREWRKZ.CHT	Overlay			Replace
	(Edit this chart in Draw/Annotate to use your own text)				
Hourglass	COLORSET.PCX			0:00	
	HOURGLAS2.CHT	Overlay			Replace
Rat in maze	COLORSET.PCX			0:00	
	RATMAZE1.CHT	Overlay			Replace
Shooting ducks	COLORSET.PCX			0:00	
	DUCKROW0.CHT	Scroll	Left	0:00	
	DUCKROW0.CHT	Scroll	Left	0:00	
	DUCKROW1.CHT	Overlay			Replace
William Tell	WILTEL01.PCX				
	WILTEL00.CHT	Overlay			
	WILTEL01.CHT	Overlay			Replace
Fish eating fish	COLORSET.PCX				
	FISHA.CHT	Overlay			
	FISHB.CHT	Overlay			
	FISHC.CHT	Overlay			Replace
Dartboard	COLORSET.PCX			0:00	
	DARTS.CHT	Overlay			Replace

Show Name	Files	Transition Effects			
		Draw	Dir	Time	Erase
Fish story	FISHTALE.PCX				
	FISHTAL0.CHT	Overlay			
	FISHTALE.CHT	Overlay			
	FISHTAL1.PCX				
	FISHTAL2.PCX				
	FISHTAL3.PCX				Replace
Birdman	COLORSET.PCX			0:00	
	BIRDMAN4.CHT	Overlay			
	BIRDMAN3.CHT	Overlay			Replace
Cash register	CASHREG1.PCX			0:05	
	CASHREG0.PCX	Overlay			Replace

Using a Template in a Screenshow

Ordinary templates, the same templates used to format charts, gain special powers when they are incorporated into screenshows. Any annotations, logos, and footnotes the templates carry appear on all subsequent screenshow slides. In addition, their title, subtitle, and footnote text attributes and color settings rub off on the settings for subsequent charts. By setting a template's title to underlined and italicized, for example, and placing the template as the first slide in the screenshow, you can underline and italicize all the titles in the following screenshow charts whether they are text or graph charts.

These settings stay in effect until the screenshow reaches another template with different settings, ensuring consistency in formatting among subsequent slides. Templates also affect slide shows because they are considered screenshows as soon as you display them on-screen.

To place the company logo at the top right corner of all slides in a screenshow, for example, create a chart with the company logo in the top right corner. Save the chart as a template and incorporate the template as the first slide when you create the slide show that becomes a screenshow. Because the logo is on a template preceding other charts, the logo remains on-screen as chart after chart appears. With this technique, you also can draw a border or add a footnote to appear on all charts in a screenshow. Even if some of the charts in a presentation are created for other occasions, you can use a template's footnote to add the same date to all charts to make the charts look custom-made for the current presentation.

If you adjusted the overall size and placement of the chart on the template by using the F7-Size/Place feature at the main menu, all subsequent charts in the screenshow appear in the same size and placement. Then you easily can leave a space to one side of all charts for a company logo or special text annotation.

To see the effect of a template on a preexisting screenshow, create a template that has three effects for NEWPROD.SHW, the screenshow you created earlier. The three effects of the template are as follows:

1. Format the titles of the charts.

2. Add the presentation date as a footnote.

3. Add a symbol that appears on all charts.

Begin by creating the template with the following steps:

1. Create a simple list.

2. Enter *Superior Office Supplies* as the title, *Presentation* as the subtitle, and *February 12, 1991* as the footnote.

3. Use the F5-Attributes selection to underline and set the subtitle to color number 9 (royal blue).

4. Use the F7-Size/Place selection to make sure that the title is set to size 8, the subtitle to size 6, and the footnote to size 3.5.

5. Press F10 (Continue) from the Simple List screen to return to the main menu.

6. Pull up the chart in Draw/Annotate mode and add the slide projector from the OFFICE4.SYM symbol library to the right and below the titles. The chart titles and the added symbol are shown in figure 16.27.

7. Save the chart as a template with the name NEWPROD. On the Save Template overlay, set Clear Values to No.

Next, include the chart in the NEWPROD slide show by following these steps:

1. On the Slide Show menu, choose Select Slide Show.

2. Select NEWPROD.SHW from the Select Slide Show screen.

3. Choose Edit Slide Show from the Slide Show menu.

4. Highlight the name of the template you created, NEWPROD.TPL, and press Enter to add the name to the end of the NEWPROD slide show.

5. Press Tab to move the cursor to the slide show chart list in the lower half of the screen.

Superior Office Supplies
Presentation

February 12, 1991

Fig. 16.27.

The NEWPROD template.

6. Highlight NEWPROD.TPL and press Ctrl-↑ (up arrow) to move NEWPROD.TPL to the top of the slide show.

7. Press F10 (Continue) to return to the Slide Show menu.

8. Select Display Screenshow from the Slide Show menu.

The templates you add to a screenshow do not actually appear on-screen when you display the screenshow, but their effects are certainly visible. As the screenshow displays, notice that all titles and subtitles are sized similarly; all subtitles are underlined and in blue; and the slide projector symbol appears on all charts. Notice also that the presentation date appears in the footnote of every chart. If the chart already had a footnote, the template's chart displaces the chart's footnote. However, the template has little effect on the first chart in the show, the title chart. The title chart displays the symbol added in the template, but because the title chart has no formal title, subtitle, and footnote, the template's title, subtitle, and footnote formatting has no effect on the title chart. In fact, because title charts lack titles, subtitles, and footnotes, a title chart template inserted into the middle of a screenshow interrupts the effect of an earlier template in the show, turning off the earlier template's formatting effect.

Incorporating Bit Maps into Screenshows

To add the finishing touches to a screenshow, you can use a file from a popular paint program, such as PC Paintbrush Plus, Publisher's Paintbrush, or Dr. Halo, as the background to a chart or group of charts. Paint programs produce bit-mapped files, and acceptable file formats have a file extension of PIC or PCX. You can purchase libraries of PCX format files from a number of companies. Marketing Graphics Incorporated (MGI) of Richmond, Virginia, offers an excellent collection of PCX images. Another source of superb CGM files is New Vision Technologies of Nepean, Ontario. Because many scanners produce graphic files with PC Paintbrush format (PCX), you can scan a photo or drawing to use as the background to a screenshow. What could be more effective than scanning a picture of a product and superimposing the picture on a graph chart showing sales figures?

To import a bit-mapped file into a screenshow, select the file when you create the slide show. If you use Overlay to draw the next chart in the show, the chart appears superimposed over the bit-mapped image. To display the next chart in the show, you need to use a transition effect other than Overlay to avoid seeing both charts on-screen at the same time. That effect removes the bit map, unless you replace the current chart with the same bit-mapped file again. To have a bit-mapped image display as the background to all the charts of a screenshow, you must include the bit-mapped image as every other file in the show. Figure 16.28 shows the Screenshow Effects screen for a screenshow that displays the file SUPERIOR.PCX as a constant background throughout the show.

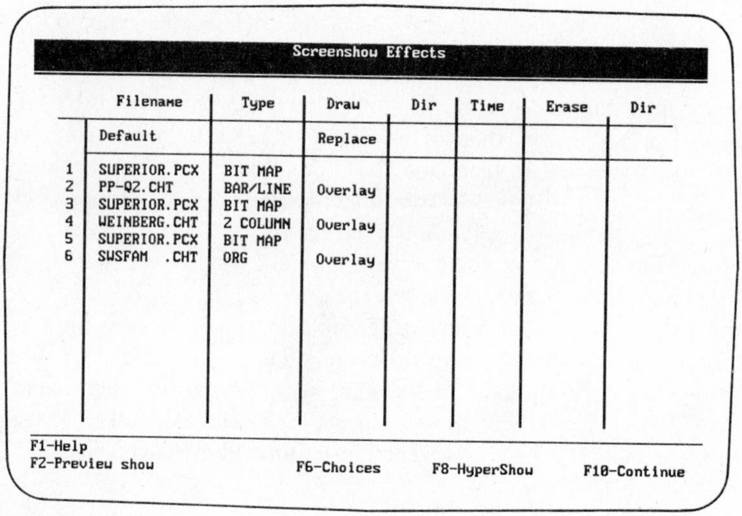

Fig. 16.28.

Screenshow Effects screen with SUPERIOR.PCX included.

	Filename	Type	Draw	Dir	Time	Erase	Dir
	Default		Replace				
1	SUPERIOR.PCX	BIT MAP					
2	PP-Q2.CHT	BAR/LINE	Overlay				
3	SUPERIOR.PCX	BIT MAP					
4	WEINBERG.CHT	2 COLUMN	Overlay				
5	SUPERIOR.PCX	BIT MAP					
6	SWSFAM .CHT	ORG	Overlay				

F1-Help
F2-Preview show   F6-Choices   F8-HyperShow   F10-Continue

For a bit-mapped image to be compatible with the current screenshow, you must have used the same type of graphics card to create both the bit-mapped image and the Harvard Graphics charts. For example, you can use two different machines to create the files as long as both have EGA cards installed, CGA cards installed, or VGA or monochrome graphics cards. IBM PS/2 computers have built-in VGA, so you should create both charts and bit-mapped files on another PS/2 or on a PC with a VGA card. The same rule applies if you use a clip-art PCX file or a scan-in image to create a bit-mapped file.

To display full-screen in the background of a chart, a bit-mapped file should be created in landscape orientation and should fill the screen.

When you incorporate bit-mapped images in screenshows, you may notice that the colors of your charts change when displayed following a bit-mapped image. Bit-mapped images almost invariably use a different color palette from the Harvard Graphics default color palette. When the bit-mapped image displays, the color palette in use changes. Harvard Graphics then displays the chart that follows in the altered color palette. To adjust the colors of the charts in your show to compensate for this effect, add a Harvard Graphics palette file (PAL) into the screenshow after the bit-mapped file to reset the Harvard Graphics color palette. Designer Galleries, a Harvard Graphics accessory available from Software Publishing Corporation, offers a number of professionally color-coordinated palette files.

Creating Circular or Continuous Screenshows

Just as you can embed template files in screenshows, you can include another screenshow in a screenshow list. When Harvard Graphics reaches a screenshow file name as the program works its way down the list, the program branches to and begins displaying that screenshow. You can combine smaller screenshows into one longer presentation by adding the name of each successive screenshow in the presentation to the end of the prior screenshow list. Combining individual screenshows to create a longer screenshow is necessary when you want to create a screenshow with more than 90 files or create an interactive screenshow, a presentation that the viewer can control. If you want to branch to another slide show, enter another slide show name as the last entry. When the first slide show reaches a second slide show name, the second slide show takes control. Remaining entries in the first slide show list are ignored.

By making two screenshows refer to each other, as shown in figure 16.29, you can create a circular or continuous screenshow. You also can create a continuous screenshow by including the name of the current screenshow file at the end of a screenshow. Harvard Graphics begins the same screenshow over again. To interrupt a continuous screenshow, press Esc.

Creating Hypershows

Hypershows are a new feature added to Harvard Graphics 2.3. Enabling the viewer to choose the portions of a screenshow he or she wants to see can be invaluable in a number of situations. Viewers may enjoy a presentation more if they feel the presentation is at their control. But more importantly, viewers can select the information they want presented to them, leaving other information

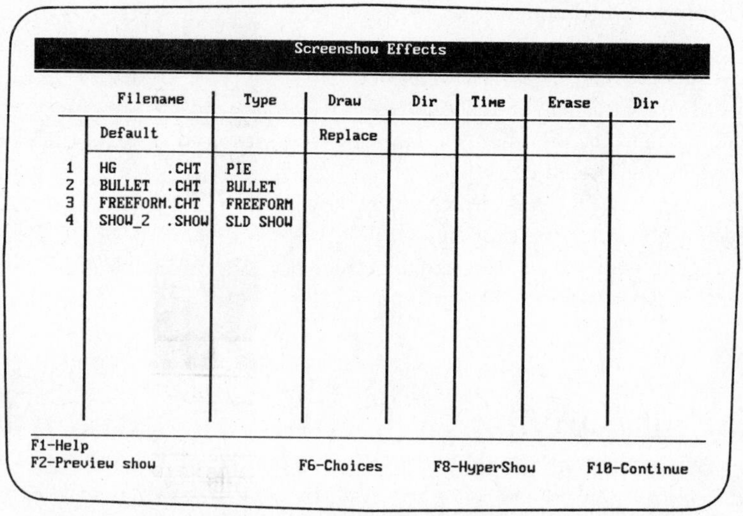

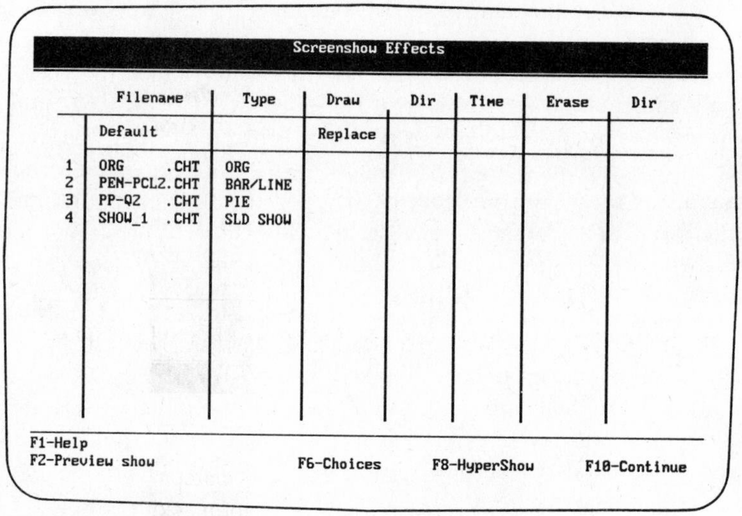

Fig. 16.29.

A continuous screenshow made from two screenshows.

```
                        Screenshow Effects

        Filename   | Type    | Draw    | Dir | Time | Erase | Dir
        Default    |         | Replace |     |      |       |
     1  HG     .CHT| PIE     |
     2  BULLET .CHT| BULLET  |
     3  FREEFORM.CHT| FREEFORM|
     4  SHOW_2 .SHOW| SLD SHOW|

   F1-Help
   F2-Preview show        F6-Choices    F8-HyperShow    F10-Continue
```

```
                        Screenshow Effects

        Filename   | Type    | Draw    | Dir | Time | Erase | Dir
        Default    |         | Replace |     |      |       |
     1  ORG    .CHT| ORG     |
     2  PEN-PCL2.CHT| BAR/LINE|
     3  PP-Q2  .CHT| PIE     |
     4  SHOW_1 .CHT| SLD SHOW|

   F1-Help
   F2-Preview show        F6-Choices    F8-HyperShow    F10-Continue
```

for later viewing. Viewer control even makes rudimentary computer-based training (CBT) possible within Harvard Graphics. Screenshows that give the viewer command over a presentation are called hypershows. An example of a hypershow is provided with Harvard Graphics. SPCINFO.SHW is installed in your program directory when you use the INSTALL program to install Harvard Graphics 2.3. To view SPCINFO.SHW, use Select Slide Show on the Slide Show menu to choose SPCINFO.SHW. Use Display Screenshow from the Slide Show menu to view the hypershow.

To create a hypershow, you include a number of smaller screenshows in one large screenshow by listing screenshow names rather than file names as the contents of a new slide show. Then you create a menu of choices and corresponding keystrokes and buttons to use to select different segments of the show. Next, you inform Harvard Graphics about which screenshow within a screenshow to display, based on viewer key presses or button pushes.

Try creating a hypershow composed of screenshows you created earlier in this chapter: GROWBARS, RUNLINES, and NEWPROD. To create the interactive screenshow, you need to carry out these steps:

1. Create a Text Chart menu, which appears on-screen first and lists viewing choices. This chart can instruct the viewer to press certain keys to proceed or press on-screen buttons. If you use buttons, you must add the buttons in Draw/Annotate or Draw Partner.

2. Create a master screenshow composed of the Text Chart menu file you created first and the three screenshows you want to offer as options.

3. Fill out the Hypershow overlay to match screenshows with viewer keypresses or button presses.

4. Add the master screenshow name to the end of each of the component screenshows so that the viewer returns to the Text Chart menu after viewing any screenshow.

To create the menu chart first, create a free-form text chart by completing the Free Form Text data screen so that the screen matches figure 16.30.

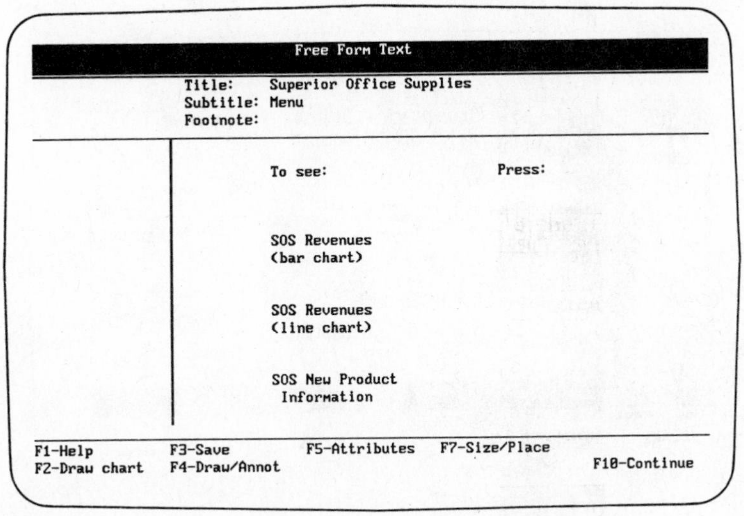

Fig. **16.30.**

The Free Form Text data screen.

You now are ready to add buttons viewers can push to select segments to view.

Adding Buttons for a Hypershow

While you are looking at the Free Form text screen, press F4 (Draw/Annot) to pull the text chart into Draw/Annotate. First, you add a button symbol to draw buttons on-screen, and then you add actual hypershow buttons that can control a screenshow.

To add button symbols, follow these steps:

1. Select Symbol from the Draw/Annotate menu.

2. Select Get Symbol from the Symbol menu.

3. Select the BUTTONS1.SYM symbol library.

4. Select the leftmost button in the middle row. (You can use any button symbol, but this particular button matches the illustrations in this book.)

5. Press Backspace so that you can draw a box to contain the symbol anywhere on the screen.

6. Draw a box for the button to the right of menu choice 1, as shown in figure 16.31.

7. Use Copy on the main Draw/Annotate menu to copy this button two times, once beside each menu choice. You should now have three buttons on-screen, as shown in figure 16.32.

Fig. 16.31.

The text chart with one button added.

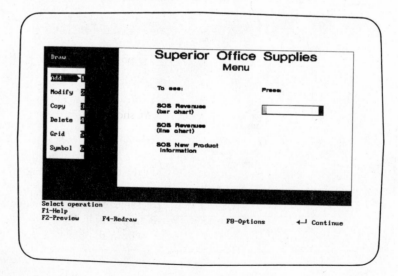

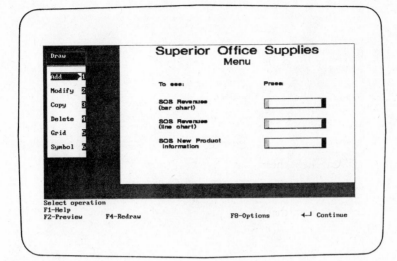

Fig. 16.32.

*The text chart with
three buttons added.*

You can leave the buttons as is, or you can place text on top of the buttons to label them. To label the buttons, follow this procedure:

1. Select Add from the Draw/Annotate menu.

2. Select Text from the Add menu.

3. Type *1 Bar Chart* and then press F8 (Options) to change the appearance of the text.

4. Set Size to 3.5, Color to 8 (black), and Font to 5 (sans serif). Press F8 to return to the text.

5. Press Enter so that you can position the text.

6. Move the cursor so that the text box is positioned on top of the button and press Enter.

Use the same procedure to label the other buttons *2 Line Chart* and *3 New Products*. The chart now should look like the chart shown in figure 16.33.

The final step is to add functional buttons to the chart. These buttons are invisible, but they can control a hypershow when clicked with the mouse. Each button gets a number from 1 to 10, which determines the action the button causes. You actually can have up to 20 buttons on one chart, so that more than one button can have the same number and lead to the same portion of the screenshow. When you add a button on the screen, you draw a box that marks the button area. Then when the viewer clicks the mouse within the box, the portion of the show linked to that button number appears.

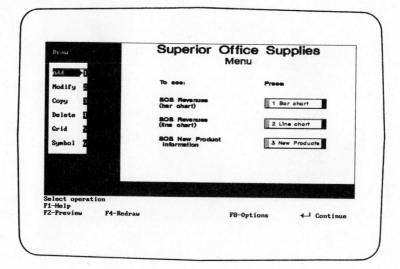

To add the buttons, follow these steps:

1. Select Add from the Draw/Annotate menu.

2. Select Button from the Add menu.

3. Make sure the number 1 appears in the Button window at the upper left corner of your screen.

4. Press Enter to accept the number 1 and begin drawing the button.

5. Draw a box that covers the first button on the screen and press Enter.

6. Change the button number to 2 and press Enter so that you can add a second button.

7. Draw a box over the second button on the screen and press Enter.

8. Change the button number to 3 and press Enter.

9. Draw a box over the third button and press Enter.

10. Press Esc to return to the Add menu.

Save the text chart you have created, shown in figure 16.34, as MENU1.CHT.

Figure 16.35 shows another configuration for the menu. This chart has only the three buttons. But, like the first chart, the buttons are numbered, so viewers without a mouse can press the correct key.

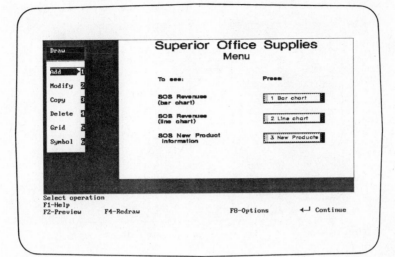

Fig. 16.34.

The completed Text Chart menu.

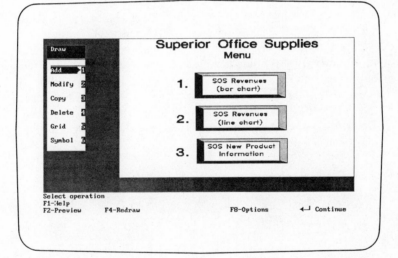

Fig. 16.35.

A menu chart with large buttons.

Creating and Running a Hypershow

You now have made the menu chart with three buttons numbered 1, 2, and 3. Next, create a slide show named MENUSHOW with four slides: MENU1.CHT, GROWBARS.SHW, RUNLINES.SHW, and NEWPROD.SHW. When the slide show is complete, choose Add Screenshow Effects from the Slide Show menu so that you can use the Hypershow menu to connect button numbers with screenshows. Figure 16.36 shows the Screenshow Effects screen.

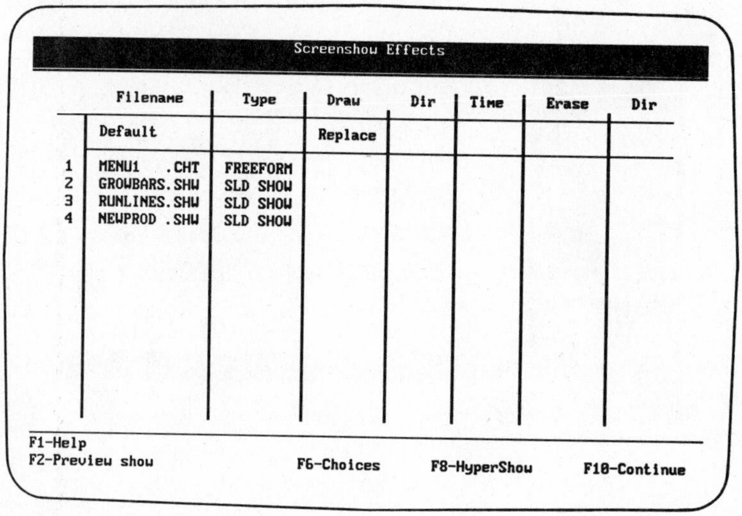

Fig. 16.36.

The Screenshow Effects screen showing four slides.

```
                        Screenshow Effects

           Filename      Type     Draw    Dir   Time   Erase    Dir

           Default                Replace

      1  MENU1   .CHT   FREEFORM
      2  GROWBARS.SHW   SLD SHOW
      3  RUNLINES.SHW   SLD SHOW
      4  NEWPROD .SHW   SLD SHOW




   F1-Help
   F2-Preview show         F6-Choices    F8-HyperShow    F10-Continue
```

Position the cursor anywhere in the line where the viewer choice should begin (on line 1, which has MENU1.CHT) and press F8 (Hypershow). A three-column Hypershow menu appears. The Button column holds the 10 button numbers. Your job is to enter corresponding keys and line numbers in the other two columns. In the Key column, enter the user keypress that corresponds with each button. Valid keys are any of the number or letter keys. In the right column, enter the line number on the Screenshow Effects screen to which the screenshow should jump. Fill in the Hypershow Menu overlay so that the overlay resembles the overlay shown in figure 16.37.

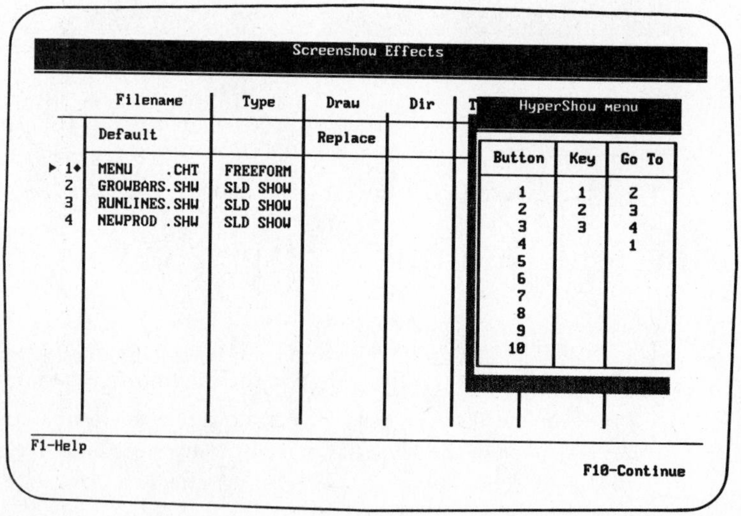

Fig. 16.37.

The Hypershow Menu overlay.

```
                        Screenshow Effects

           Filename      Type     Draw    Dir   T   HyperShow menu

           Default                Replace

    ▶ 1◆ MENU    .CHT   FREEFORM                 Button  Key  Go To
      2  GROWBARS.SHW   SLD SHOW
      3  RUNLINES.SHW   SLD SHOW                    1     1     2
      4  NEWPROD .SHW   SLD SHOW                    2     2     3
                                                    3     3     4
                                                    4           1
                                                    5
                                                    6
                                                    7
                                                    8
                                                    9
                                                   10

   F1-Help
                                                        F10-Continue
```

If a user clicks button 1 or presses 1 on the keyboard, the screenshow jumps to slide 2, the GROWBARS screenshow. If a user clicks button 2 or presses 2 on the keyboard, the screenshow jumps to slide 3, the RUNLINES screenshow, and so on. If slide 1 is entered in the right column next to a blank keypress, the screenshow jumps to the first slide, the menu, if the viewer clicks anywhere else on the screen or presses any other key.

Position the cursor at the top of the screenshow list and press F2 (Preview Show) to display the screenshow. Choose from the menu that appears. Notice that the master screenshow displays the screenshow you chose and then stops. To cause the screenshow to return to the menu after displaying each component screenshow, you must add the master screenshow's name at the end of each of the component screenshows. To do this, call up each of the individual screenshows with Edit Slide Show, add MENUSHOW.SHW to the end of each slide list, and press F10 (Continue).

Now, try the screenshow again and note that the menu reappears after each screenshow displays. If you press any key other than 1, 2, or 3 at the menu, nothing appears to happen. To display an ending slide when the viewer presses anywhere on the screen except a button or when the viewer presses any key other than the keys on the menu, enter the slide's number next to the blank keypress on the User Menu overlay. Harvard Graphics signals that slide 1 on the MENUSHOW screenshow has a Hypershow menu by placing a diamond next to the slide number on the Add Screenshow Effects screen.

Because buttons are invisible on-screen, you can use them in a variety of interesting ways. A screenshow can start with a bar chart, for example. Each group of bars can have its own invisible button superimposed. Later, while viewing the show, someone can click on a set of bars to see a screenshow segment that provides explanation or describes a breakdown of those numbers. Similarly, you can superimpose buttons over slices of a pie.

When a template in a screenshow has its own buttons, these buttons are added to the buttons on each chart that follows. Therefore, with a template, you can add a button to the bottom corner of each drawing, which takes you to a particular part of the screenshow (with instructions for using the screenshow, perhaps).

Using Reserved Button Numbers

Certain button numbers are reserved for special uses. These buttons perform the same actions as certain keys. Buttons given these numbers always cause actions according to the following table:

Button number	Corresponds to	Action
211	Left-arrow key	Shows preceding slide
212	Right-arrow key	Shows next slide
213	Home	Shows first slide
214	End	Shows last slide
215	Space bar	Pauses show
216	Ctrl-E	Displays the chart's data screen
217	Escape	Stops the show

Using ShowCopy

ShowCopy, a utility installed on your hard disk along with Harvard Graphics 2.3, can help you by copying all the files in a screenshow from one disk to another or from one directory on a hard disk to another. ShowCopy also can ensure that all the files you need to run a screenshow are present. ShowCopy can even create a screenshow using all the files in a particular directory. The alternative to using ShowCopy is to manually copy all of the screenshow files. Show-Copy can help you copy all of the files in a screenshow to a disk (so that you can distribute the screenshow). ShowCopy is available to users of Harvard Graphics 2.13 or earlier in the ScreenShow Utilities accessory product.

To run ShowCopy, you must return to the DOS prompt by exiting Harvard Graphics. Then make sure that you are in the same directory in which Harvard Graphics is installed and type:

SHOWCOPY *source,destination*

In place of *source*, type the file name of the screenshow you want to copy, including its path. If the screenshow you want to copy is called SLIDES.SHW and is located in the HG23 directory, for example, *source* is C:\HG23\SLIDES (you can omit the SHW file extension).

In place of *destination*, type the location for the copy of the screenshow. To copy the screenshow and all its files to a floppy disk in the A: drive, for example, type A: in place of *destination*.

To see the file names of the files being copied, type /s at the end of the SHOWCOPY command. To update the file description information for the files you are copying, type /u at the end of the SHOWCOPY command (which you may always want to use). To make a slide show compatible with the ScreenShow Projector accessory product for Harvard Graphics, type /a at the end of the SHOWCOPY command. (ScreenShow Projector enables you to show your screenshows without running Harvard Graphics.)

A SHOWCOPY command that uses all three additions looks like the following:

SHOWCOPY SLIDES A: /a /u /s

SHOWCOPY checks the destination you have entered for the slide show copy to ensure that enough disk space is available. If not, you see a warning message on-screen.

Before you run a slide show, perhaps before an important sales presentation, you should have SHOWCOPY verify that all of the files you need are present. To do so, type the following:

SHOWCOPY VERIFY *directory name*

Replace *directory name* with the directory in which your slide shows are stored. SHOWCOPY checks each slide show in the directory and verifies that all files necessary are present. You see a message confirming the presence of all the files you need or a message indicating which files are missing. If you type a /s after the SHOWCOPY VERIFY command, SHOWCOPY displays each file name as the program checks for /s.

To create a slide show that contains all the charts in a directory, type the following:

SHOWCOPY CREATE *directory name, slide show name*

Replace *directory name* with the name of the directory in which the charts are located. Replace *slide show name* with the name of the slide show that holds all the CHT files in the directory. If you omit a slide show name, SHOWCOPY uses NEWSHOW.SHW. You can see each file name being added to the slide show if you type /s at the end of the command. You can use SHOWCOPY CREATE to quickly peruse all the charts in your working directories. You also can use Print Slide Show on the Produce Output menu to print the contents of a slide show you create with SHOWCOPY CREATE. This technique enables you to print all the charts in a directory.

Chapter Summary

In this chapter, you learned several ways to present your work to others. Slide shows and screenshows also provide methods to easily print a group of files.

The next chapter is up to you. You can learn to use a program by reading a book such as this, but you can only master it with experience.

Adding Flair with Symbols

As mentioned in Chapter 9, symbols in Harvard Graphics are collections of individual objects that form predrawn images. Some examples include collections of people, countries, cities, buildings, currency signs, vehicles, and figures such as arrows and stars.

These images are stored in symbol files, with the extension SYM, and each symbol file has many different symbols from which you can choose. After you choose symbols, you can work with them—change their sizes, stretch their shapes, move them, copy them, and so on.

This appendix contains an alphabetical listing of all the symbols included with Harvard Graphics. The fill from many of these symbols has been removed so that the symbols are more viewable. To make the symbols on your screen appear exactly the same as those presented here, you also can remove the fill.

In addition to the Harvard Graphics symbols, two special utilities—Business Symbols and Military Symbols—are available as accessories that come with the Harvard Graphics software. The contents of these two accessories also are shown in this appendix.

For more information about symbols and how to use them, turn to Chapter 9, "Drawing with Harvard Graphics: Draw/Annotate."

Harvard Graphics Symbols

Fig. A.1.

The ANIMALS symbol library.

Fig. A.2.

The ANIPLANT symbol library.

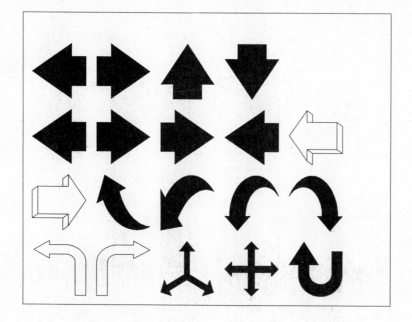

Fig. A.3.

The ARROWS2
symbol library.

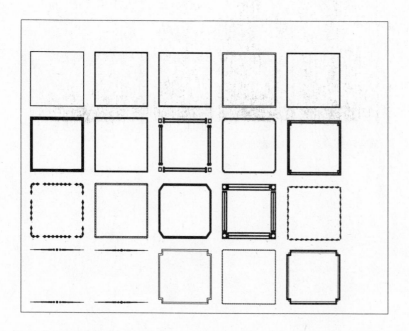

Fig. A.4.

The BORDERS
symbol library.

Fig. A.5.

The BUILD3 symbol library.

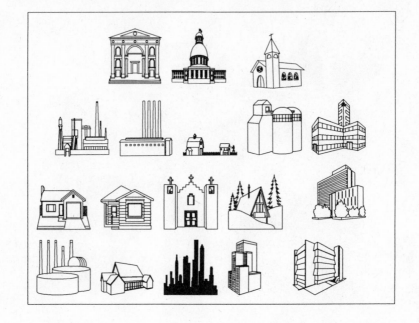

Fig. A.6.

The BUTTONS1 symbol library.

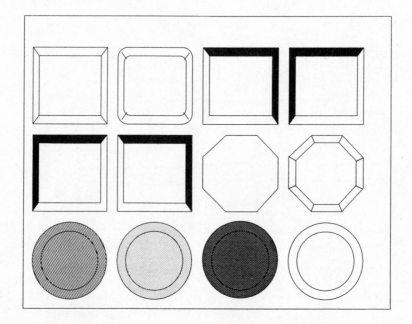

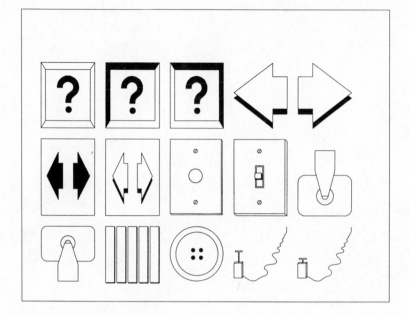

Fig. A.7.

The BUTTONS2 symbol library.

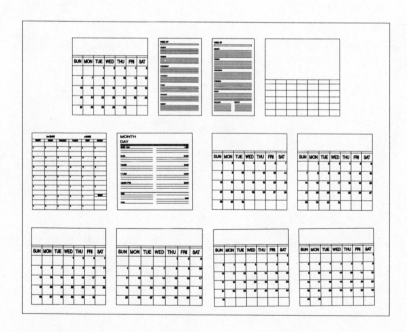

Fig. A.8.

The CALENDAR symbol library.

Fig. A.9.

The COMNOBJ1
symbol library.

Fig. A.10.

The COMNOBJ2
symbol library.

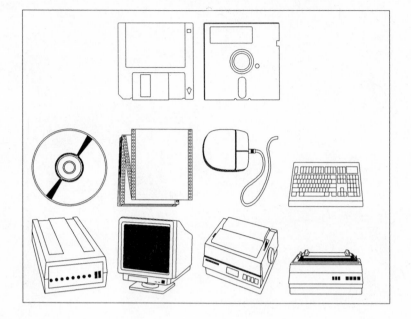

Fig. A.11.

The COMPUTR2 symbol library.

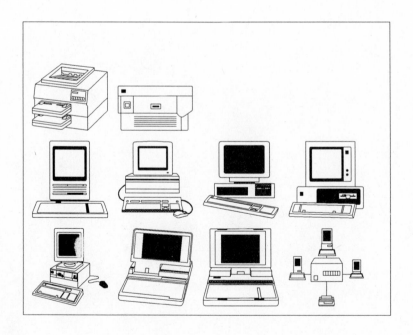

Fig. A.12.

The COMPUTR3 symbol library.

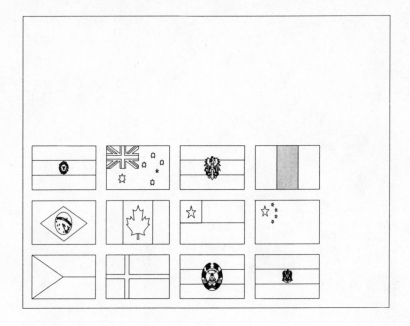

Fig. A.13.

The FLAGS1 symbol library.

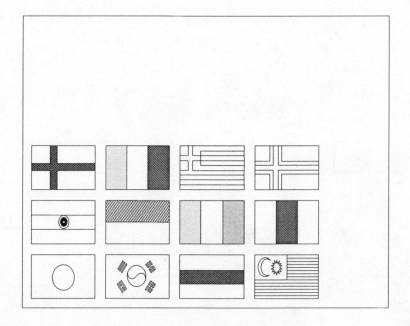

Fig. A.14.

The FLAGS2 symbol library.

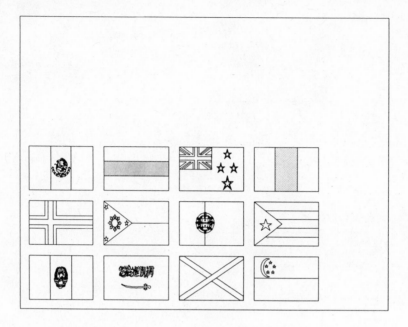

Fig. A.15.

The FLAGS3 symbol library.

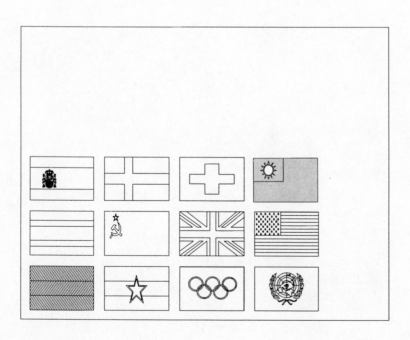

Fig. A.16.

The FLAGS4 symbol library.

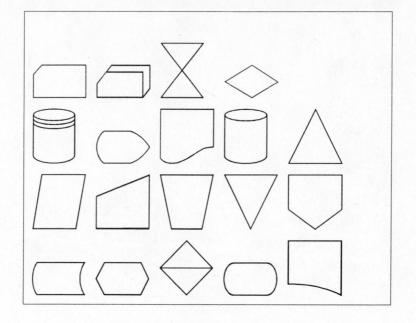

Fig. A.19.
The GREEKLC2
symbol library.

Fig. A.20.
The GREEKUC1
symbol library.

Fig. A.21.

The GREEKUC2 symbol library.

Fig. A.22.

The HUMANS4 symbol library.

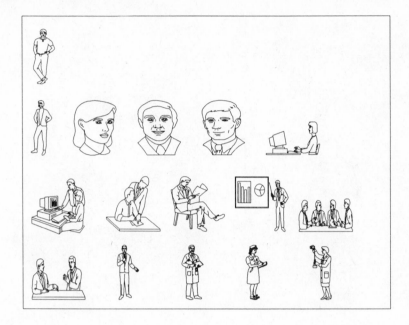

Fig. A.23.

The HUMANS5 symbol library.

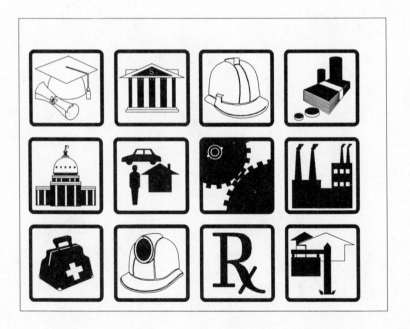

Fig. A.24.

The INDSTRY1 symbol library.

Fig. A.25.

*The INDSTRY2
symbol library.*

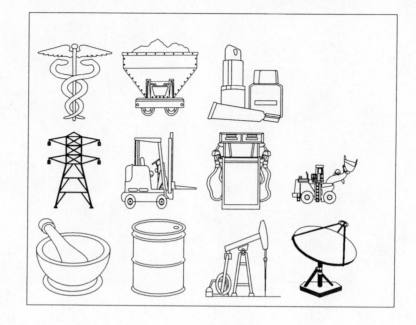

Fig. A.26.

*The MAPS1
symbol library.*

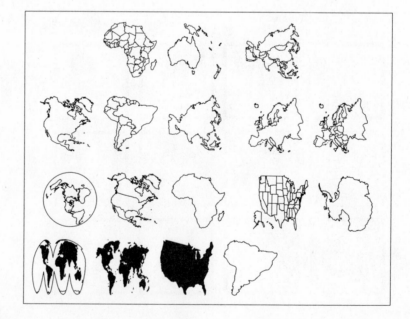

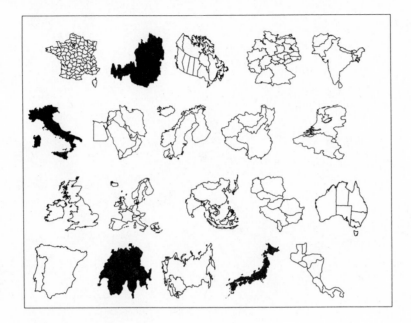

Fig. A.27.

The MAPS2 symbol library.

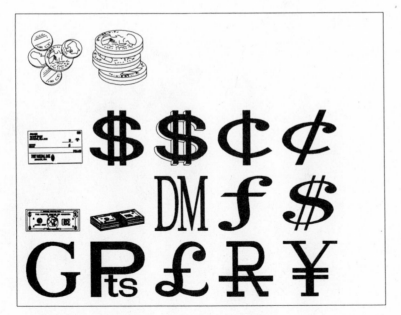

Fig. A.28.

The MONEY symbol library.

Fig. A.31.

The PRESENT3 symbol library.

Fig. A.32.

The SIGNS symbol library.

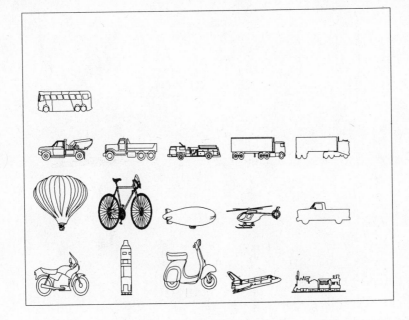

Fig. A.35.

The TRANSPT2 symbol library.

Business Symbols

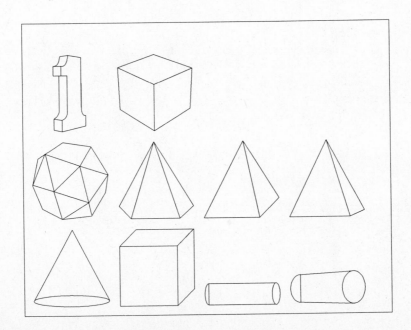

Fig. A.36.

The 3DOBJECT symbol library.

Fig. A.37.

The BUILD2 symbol library.

Fig. A.38.

The CHEMICAL symbol library.

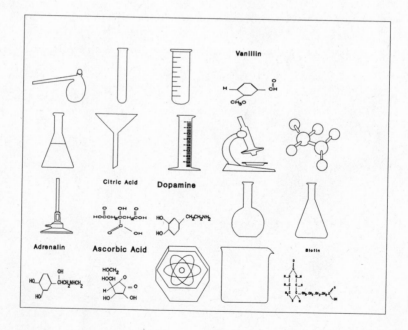

Fig. A.39.

The COMMUNIC
symbol library.

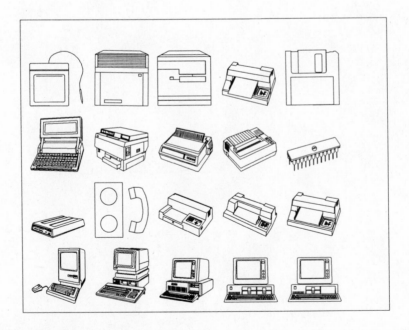

Fig. A.40.

The COMPUTER
symbol library.

Fig. A.41.

The ELEMENT symbol library.

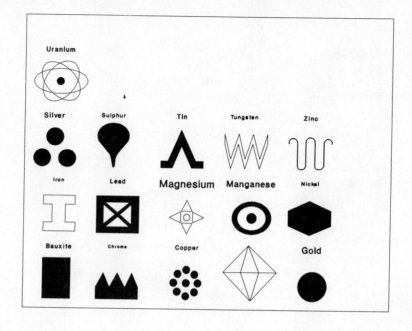

Fig. A.42.

The HUMANS2 symbol library.

Fig. A.43.

The HUMANS3 symbol library.

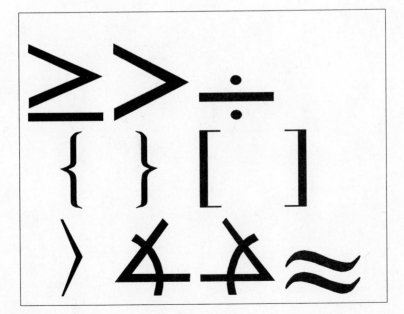

Fig. A.44.

The MATH1 symbol library.

Fig. A.45.

The MATH2 symbol library.

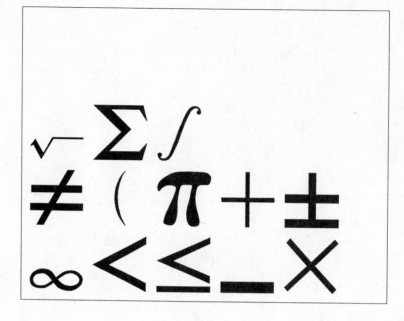

Fig. A.46.

The MISC2 symbol library.

Fig. A.47.

The MISC3 symbol library.

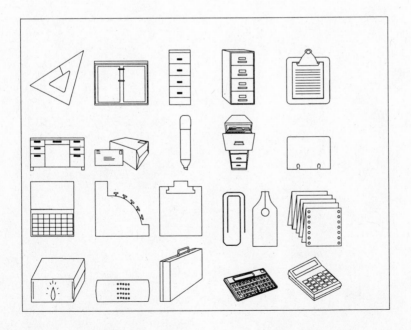

Fig. A.48.

The OFFICE2 symbol library.

Fig. A.49.

The OFFICE3 symbol library.

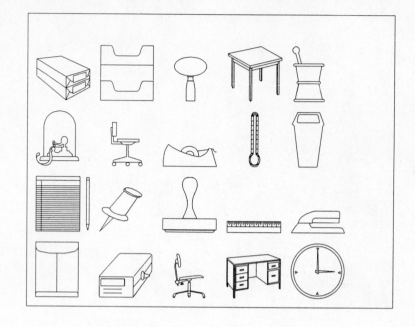

Fig. A.50.

The PACKAGE symbol library.

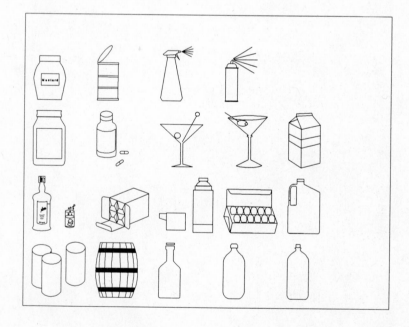

Fig. A.51.

The TRAFFIC1 symbol library.

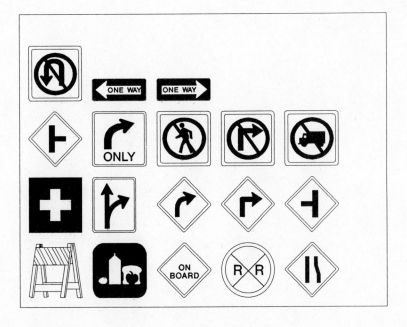

Fig. A.52.

The TRAFFIC2 symbol library.

Fig. A.53.

The TRAFFIC3 symbol library.

Fig. A.54.

The WEATHER symbol library.

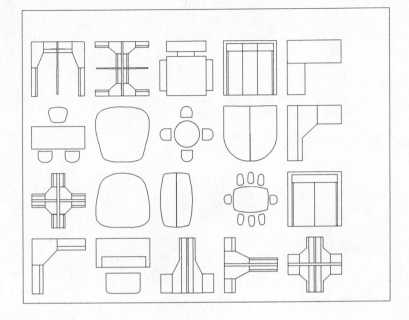

Fig. A.55.

The WORKSTAT symbol library.

Military Symbols

Fig. A.56.

The BOMBREC symbol library.

Fig. A.57.

The ELECTRON
symbol library.

Fig. A.58.

The FIGHTER
symbol library.

Fig. A.59.

The FVEHICLE symbol library.

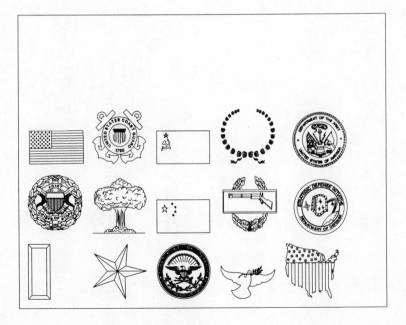

Fig. A.60.

The ICONS symbol library.

Fig. A.61.

*The SHIP symbol
library.*

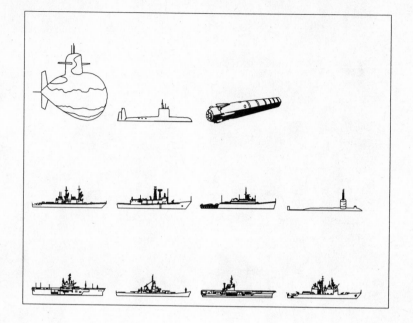

Fig. A.62.

*The SOLDIER
symbol library.*

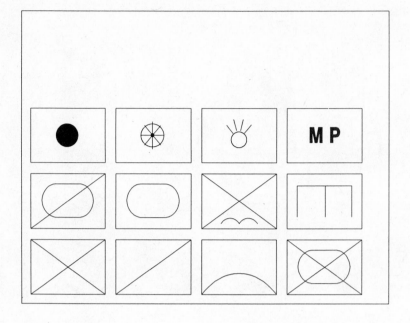

Fig. A.63.

*The TACTICAL
symbol library.*

Fig. A.64.

*The TRANSAIR
symbol library.*

Fig. A.65.

The USAF symbol library.

Fig. A.66.

The USARMY symbol library.

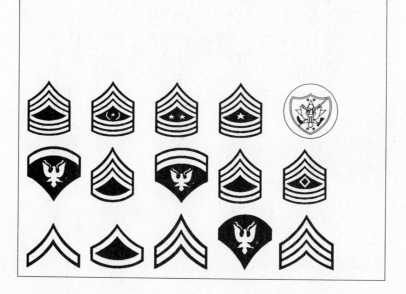

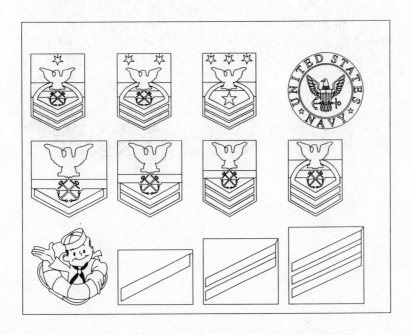

Fig. A.69.

The VEHICLE symbol library.

Fig. A.70.

The WEAPON symbol library.

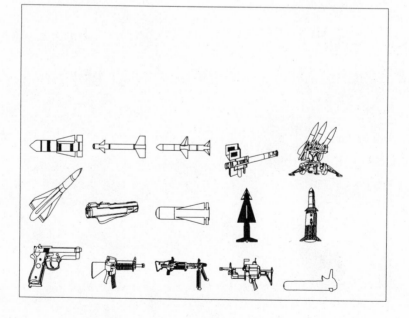

Harvard Graphics
Quick Reference

This appendix provides quick reference information you may need as you use Harvard Graphics. This appendix is divided into reference information about text charts, graph charts, Draw/Annotate, Draw Partner, and templates.

Mouse and Keyboard Equivalents

Your mouse buttons have the same effect as certain keyboard keys:

Mouse Operation	Keyboard Equivalent
Left button	Enter key
Right button	Esc key
Both buttons	Function keys that toggle to and from the function-key menu

Text Charts

Figure B.1 shows the seven fonts available in Harvard Graphics for you to use in creating your charts.

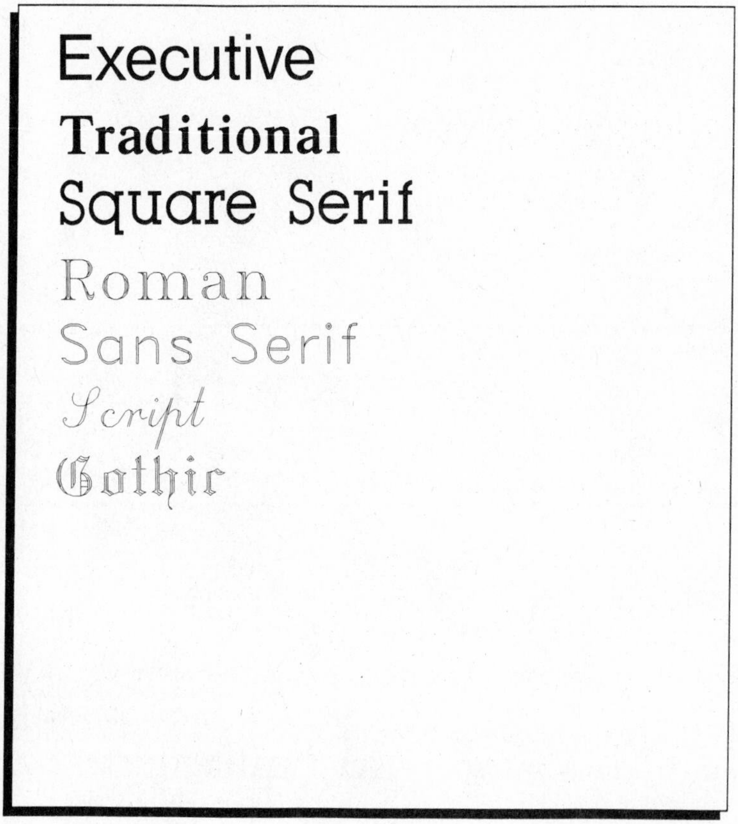

Fig. B.1.

The seven Harvard Graphics fonts.

Executive

Traditional

Square Serif

Roman

Sans Serif

Script

Gothic

You also have the choice of using fill in your text. Figure B.2 shows the difference between characters with the Fill option toggled on and off.

Graph Charts

Table B.1 provides a summary, some examples, and descriptions of the formatting commands available for your graph charts.

Superior Office Supplies
Superior Office Supplies

Fig. B.2.

Fill on (above) versus Fill off (below).

Table B.1
Format Commands for the X- and Y-Axis

To Display	Enter on the Format Line	Description
4,000	,	Inserts a comma in the number, if necessary
19.68	2	Displays two decimal places
2,590.6	,1	Displays a comma and a specific number of decimal places
12.2 mm	|1 mm	Vertical bar (|) adds preceding or trailing text (like mm) to the formatted value, and 1 tells Harvard Graphics to include one decimal place after the decimal point
9,899.50 Yen	,2| Yen	Adds Yen as trailing text, places a comma in the number, and displays the number to two decimal places
£456.25	£,2	Displays a UK pound sign (£). To create a pound sign, type 156 on the keypad while holding down the Alt key.
9.55E+02	!	Displays numbers in scientific notation
2000	1|	Displays entire number with three zeros

Figure B.3 shows the full range of line styles and all 12 marker styles available to you.

You can type a calculation that includes data from several series by referring to all the series in a formula. You also can use one of the four Harvard Graphics row keywords, listed in table B.2.

Fig. B.3.

The available line and marker styles.

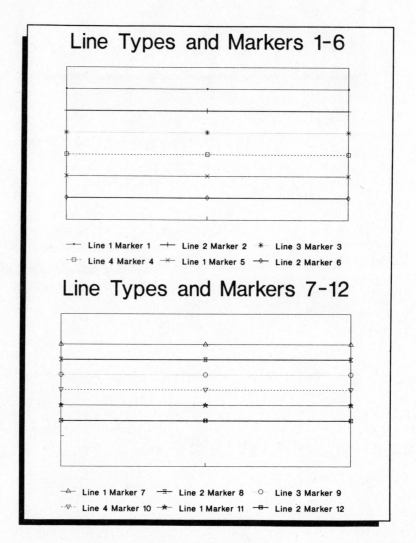

Table B.2
Row Keywords

Keyword	Result
@AVG	Calculates the average of a row of values
@MAX	Extracts the maximum value from a row of numbers
@MIN	Extracts the minimum value from a row of numbers
@SUM	Sums or totals a row of numbers

Table B.3 lists the available series keywords and provides an example of each.

Table B.3
Series Keywords

Keyword	Example	Results
@CLR	@CLR	Clears the contents of a series. Use this keyword only when you want to erase a series. A series erasure cannot be undone. (**Note:** The program erases the @CLR keyword after clearing the series.)
@COPY	@COPY(#3)	Copies the contents of Series 3 to the current series. The program then erases the keyword.
@CUM	@CUM(#2)	Creates a cumulative series in which each value is added to the total of all previous values in the series. Using the @CUM keyword is the same as selecting Cum on the fourth Titles & Options page.
@DIFF	@DIFF(#4)	Subtracts the value of each value in the series from its predecessor and calculates the net change in each new value
@DUP	@DUP(#2)	Series 2 is duplicated in the current series. Each time you press F10 at the Calculate overlay, @DUP updates values again. The @DUP keyword is different from the @COPY keyword because of the

Table B.3—*continued*

Keyword	Example	Results
		continual updating of values that @DUP performs. Use @DUP when you want to look at the behavior of a calculated series in another series column.
@EXCH	@EXCH(#5)	Trades series or exchanges the values and series legend between Series 5 and the series in which you call up the Calculate overlay. The program erases the @EXCH keyword after performing the calculation.
@MAVG	@MAVG(#5,3,5)	Calculates the statistical moving average of Series 5 with 3 points before and 5 points after each value. Valid "points before" and "points after" values are between 1 and 120. If you omit the points before and points after values, Harvard Graphics assumes that you want 1 for each value.
@MOVE	@MOVE(#2)	Moves the values from the series in which the cursor rests to Series 2 and clears the series in which the cursor is located
@PCT	@PCT(#4)	Calculates the percentage of the total of Series 4 that each value in Series 4 represents and places the results in the current series
@REDUC	@REDUC	Reorders all series and X data on the Bar/Line Chart Data screen. This calculation is described in detail in the next section. The program erases the @REDUC keyword after performing the calculation.
@RECALC	@RECALC	Recalculates all the calculated values in the current chart. You can invoke the @RECALC keyword from any series column or even from the

Table B.3—*continued*

Keyword	Example	Results
		X-Axis column. Your cursor can be almost anywhere on the data screen when you perform this function. After the calculations are performed, the @RECALC keyword disappears.
@REXP	@REXP(#4)	Calculates the exponential regression curve for Series 4. Don't use this calculation with a trend type of line series. The results of an exponential regression curve are not linear. The trend line in Harvard Graphics is the result of another internal calculation, which is linear.
@RLIN	@RLIN(#2)	Calculates the linear regression for Series 2. Linear regression can be calculated for any bar/line style series.
@RLOG	@RLOG(#1)	Calculates the logarithmic regression curve for Series 1 and places the results in the current series. Do not use a trend line with this keyword calculation.
@RPWR	@RPWR(#5)	Calculates the power regression curve for Series 5. Don't use this calculation with a trend line.

Figure B.4 shows the fill patterns available for you to use in your graph charts.

Draw/Annotate

Figure B.5 shows the 21 different box styles available in Harvard Graphics.

Fig. B.4.

Graph chart fill patterns.

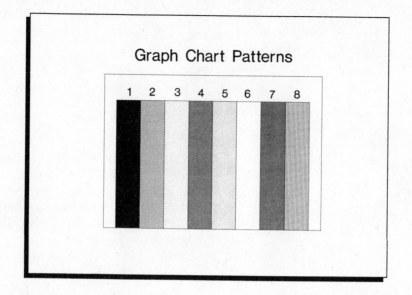

Fig. B.5.

The 21 available box types.

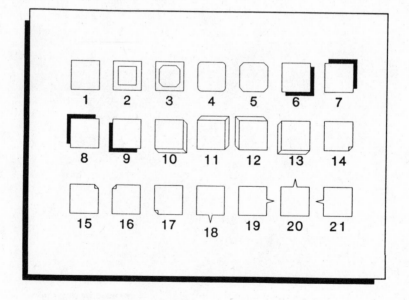

Figure B.6 shows how the text aligns relative to the cursor based on the alignment selection you make.

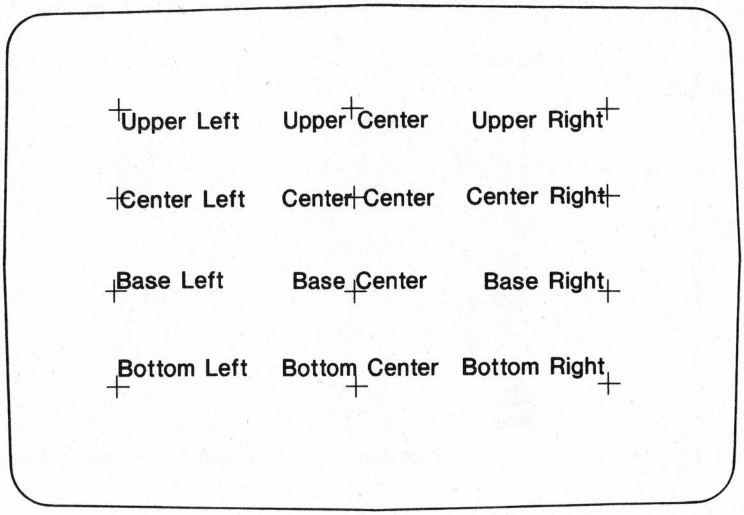

Upper Left   Upper Center   Upper Right

Center Left   Center Center   Center Right

Base Left   Base Center   Base Right

Bottom Left   Bottom Center   Bottom Right

Fig. B.6.

The align options.

Figure B.7 shows the effect of the Size option on the different box styles.

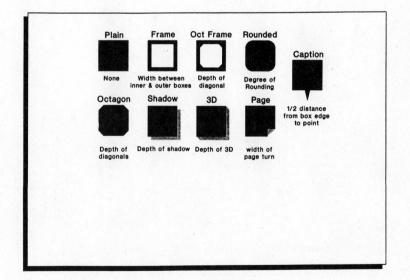

Fig. B.7.

The effect of Size on boxes.

Figure B.8 shows the object fill patterns available in Draw/Annotate.

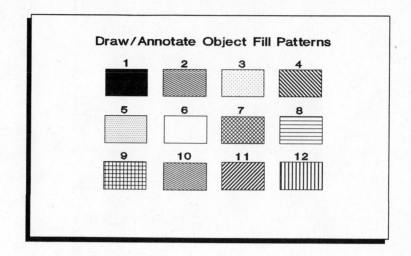

Fig. B.8.

The object fill patterns for Draw/Annotate.

Draw Partner

Figure B.9 shows the object fill patterns available in Draw Partner.

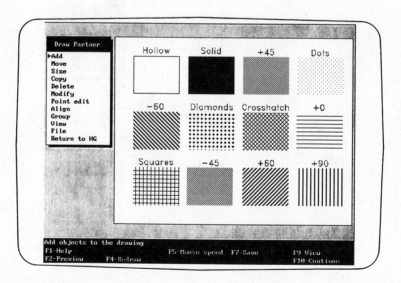

Fig. B.9.

The object fill patterns for Draw Partner.

Figure B.10 shows the Text Weight options available in Draw Partner.

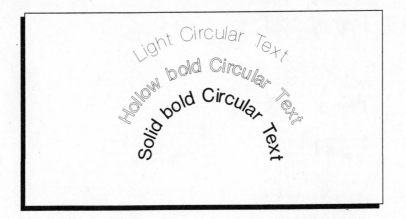

Fig. B.10.

The Text Weight options.

Figure B.11 shows the Object Align options available in Draw Partner.

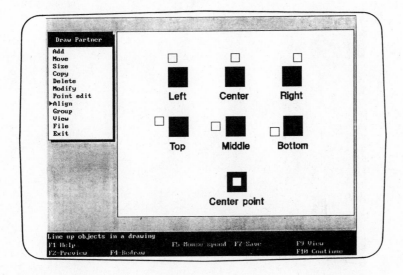

Fig. B.11.

The Object Align options.

Templates

Following is a listing of the default chart style template names:

Chart Style	Default Template Name
Title charts	TITLE
Simple lists	LIST

Chart Style	*Default Template Name*
Bullet lists	BULLET
Two-column charts	2-COLUMN
Three-column charts	3-COLUMN
Free-form charts	FREEFORM
Pie charts	PIE
Bar or line charts	BARLINE
Area charts	AREA
High/low/close charts	HLC
Organization charts	ORG
Multiple charts	MULTIPLE

C

What's New in Harvard Graphics 2.3

Harvard Graphics 2.3 is a revision of the prior release of Harvard Graphics, Version 2.13. Software Publishing Corporation made several substantial improvements. These improvements are discussed in summary fashion in this appendix.

Changes to Draw Partner

Draw Partner used to be an add-on to the basic Harvard Graphics package. In earlier versions, you had to exit Harvard Graphics to start up Draw Partner. Now you can get to Draw Partner from within Harvard Graphics by pressing Ctrl-D or by selecting Draw Partner from the new Applications menu (F3 at the main menu).

Even after you make enhancements to a chart with the capabilities of Draw Partner, you still can edit the chart's data in Harvard Graphics. Draw Partner has been enhanced with several advanced drawing features, including freehand drawing, the capability to add arcs, wedges, and regular polygons, and the addition of the Skew command, which makes objects appear to lean dramatically to the left or right.

Chart Gallery

Version 2.3 of Harvard Graphics introduces a new feature called a Chart Gallery. Instead of selecting from a menu of chart names, you can select a new chart style from an on-screen display of charts. These miniature pictures show how each chart looks when completed. You can use the gallery to inspect the preset color schemes provided by the Harvard Graphics color palettes. You can cycle among all the available color palettes and choose one to your liking. After you have started a chart from the gallery, you supply the data to have a finished, attractive chart.

New Color Palettes

The new Harvard Graphics comes with 12 predefined color palettes. You can view the color schemes these palettes provide when you create a chart from the gallery. You also can select a color palette by name from a new menu option, Select Palette. Harvard Graphics 2.3 saves information about the palette used with each chart, so that you can include a variety of charts in a screenshow and know that each chart uses the correct palette.

Hypershows

A new feature in Harvard Graphics screenshows is the hypershow. Now, a viewer can use a mouse to push up to 10 buttons on the screen and select the portion of a presentation to watch next. A similar capability was available in prior versions of Harvard Graphics, but viewers were limited to selecting segments of a presentation by typing at the keyboard. The on-screen buttons are far more friendly. Hypershows make possible interactive presentations and rudimentary computer-based training.

Applications Menu

A new function-key choice at the Harvard Graphics main menu brings up a menu of up to seven software applications. With this menu, you can launch different applications without quitting Harvard Graphics. Draw Partner is the default first selection on the Applications menu. You may want to put other programs you use often on the menu. You can put spreadsheets, word processors, database programs, utilities, and just about any other applications software on this menu.

After you start an application from the Applications Menu, Harvard Graphics puts itself away, using expanded memory if possible. The put-away Harvard Graphics requires only 15K of memory. While Harvard Graphics is put away, you can run other programs, such as a word processor or a spreadsheet. When you exit the second program, Harvard Graphics returns to the same screen.

Multiple Text Fonts in Charts

Each character or line of text you add with Draw/Annotate or Draw Partner can have its own text font. In prior versions of Harvard Graphics, all the text in a chart used the same font. A new font, Traditional, provides a Times Roman-style font to the available font selection.

Microsoft Excel Graph and Data Import

Harvard Graphics 2.3 now imports completed Excel graphs and data, in addition to importing Lotus 1-2-3 and Symphony graphs and data.

Speed Keys

The new version of Harvard Graphics offers seven speed keys—the most frequent actions are one keystroke away. For example, you can print charts by pressing Ctrl-P.

More than 500 New Symbols

More than 500 new symbols expand the symbol libraries in Harvard Graphics with greatly enhanced images. The new symbols are more complex, colorful, and attractive. New symbol libraries include: computer equipment, animals, humans, flags, and signs.

Animated Sequences

You now can use one of 10 animated sequences in your Harvard Graphics screen-shows. The sequences that come with Harvard Graphics 2.3 are installed when you install the Harvard Graphics program.

ShowCopy

ShowCopy, a utility that was available separately, is now built into Harvard Graphics. ShowCopy copies all the charts in a slide show from one directory on a hard disk to another or from a hard disk to a floppy or vice versa. ShowCopy also can accumulate all the charts in a directory into a slide show.

New No Margin Option

A new option for a chart's border, No Margin, enables you to fill an entire page with a chart. The normal margin for the border does not appear. The only margin you see on the page is the margin the printer causes.

Additional Improvements

Harvard Graphics 2.3 now offers better international support, including country setting options, Norwegian characters, the German paragraph symbol, and an option for A4 paper. Finally, the new version of Harvard Graphics has the following miscellaneous additions:

❑ An on-line tutorial

❑ Support for a greater selection of printers

❑ Easier CGM import

❑ An option for importing metafiles appears on the Import/Export menu

❑ A reduced memory requirement for running Harvard Graphics—420K

D

Harvard Graphics
Accessory Programs

Software Publishing Corporation offers five accessories that work with Harvard Graphics to help you produce attractive charts quickly. The accessories include

Quick Charts. A series of common predefined charts and templates that can be used just like the gallery of charts in Harvard Graphics 2.3 for selecting a chart type and editing the data accordingly. To view the gallery of quick charts, select the Slide Show menu and select the file QCHARTS.SHW. Then choose the chart type and chart subtype you want by pressing the number of each. Pressing Ctrl-E enables you to start editing the chart.

Designer Galleries. Another series of professionally designed preset charts and templates and a dozen color palettes for use with your charts. Designer galleries also offers a preview gallery that can be accessed exactly like the gallery of quick charts.

Business Symbols. A series of symbol libraries that adds to the libraries provided in Harvard Graphics. Appendix A shows all the business symbols available in this accessory.

Military Symbols. A series of symbol libraries that can be used for military presentations. Appendix A shows the available military symbols in this accessory.

U.S. MapMaker. This accessory can be used for creating United States maps in detail—even color coding the maps based on data about the states.

Two additional accessory products, Draw Partner and Screenshow Utilities, are now included in Harvard Graphics 2.3 and are no longer sold as separate utilities. If you have an earlier version of Harvard Graphics, you can find directions for these two accessories in Chapters 10 through 12 for Draw Partner and Chapter 16 for screenshows.

On the following pages, you can find the entire assortment of Quick Charts and Designer Galleries charts available to you with these two accessories. The last section of this appendix covers the U.S. MapMaker accessory.

Quick Charts CHT Files

This section presents all the Quick Charts available for you to use.

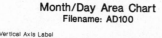

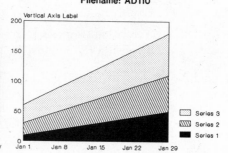

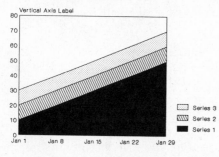

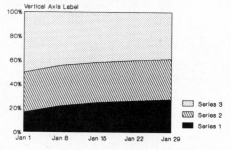

Labeled Area Chart
Filename: AL100

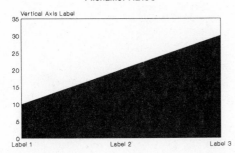

Stacked Labeled Area Chart
Filename: AL110

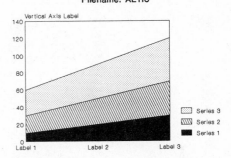

Overlapped Labeled Area Chart
Filename: AL120

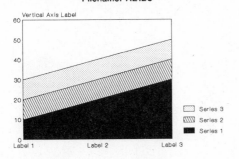

100% Labeled Area Chart
Filename: AL130

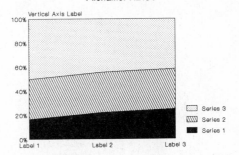

Monthly Area Chart
Filename: AM100

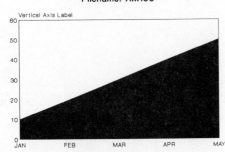

Stacked Monthly Area Chart
Filename: AM110

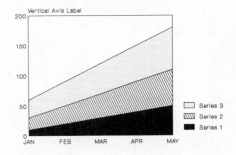

Overlapped Monthly Area Chart
Filename: AM120

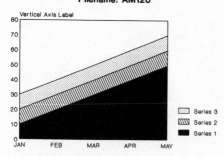

100% Monthly Area Chart
Filename: AM130

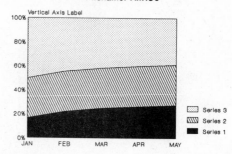

No Data Labels

 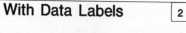

With Data Labels

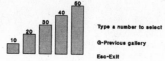

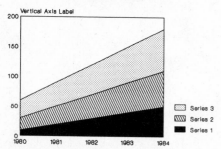

Yearly Area Chart
Filename: AY100

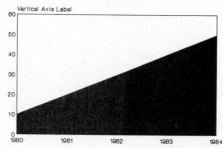

Stacked Yearly Area Chart
Filename: AY110

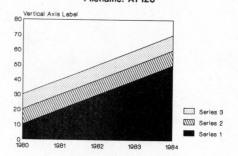

Overlapped Yearly Area Chart
Filename: AY120

100% Yearly Area Chart
Filename: AY130

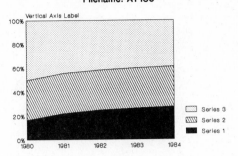

Horizontal Bar Chart
Filename: BC100

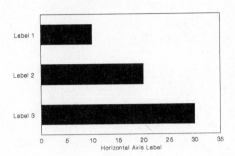

Horizontal Clustered Bar Chart
Filename: BC110

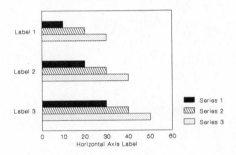

Horizontal Overlapping Bar Chart
Filename: BC120

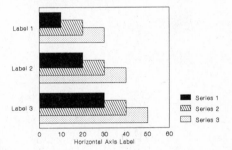

Horizontal 100% Overlapped Bar Chart
Filename: BC130

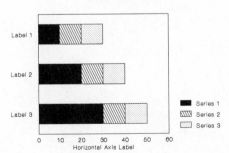

Horizontal Stacked Bar Chart
Filename: BC140

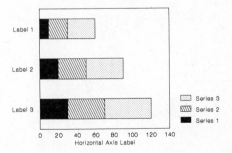

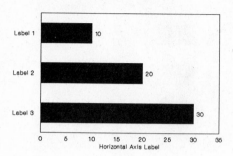

Horizontal Bar Chart
Filename: BC200

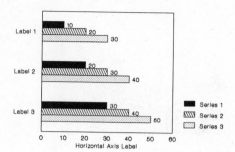

Horizontal Clustered Bar Chart
Filename: BC210

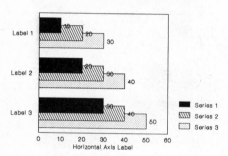

Horizontal Overlapping Bar Chart
Filename: BC220

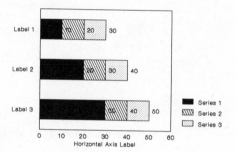

Horizontal 100% Overlapped Bar Chart
Filename: BC230

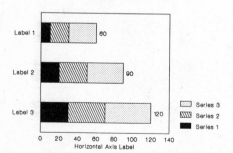

Horizontal Stacked Bar Chart
Filename: BC240

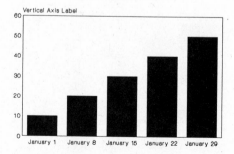

Month/Day Bar Chart
Filename: BD100

Clustered Month/Day Bar Chart
Filename: BD110

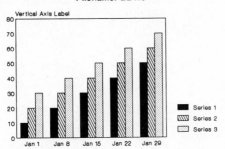

Overlapping Month/Day Bar Chart
Filename: BD120

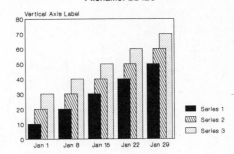

100% Overlapped Month/Day Bar Chart
Filename: BD130

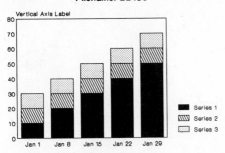

Stacked Month/Day Bar Chart
Filename: BD140

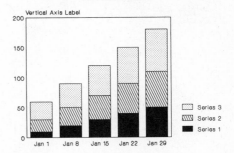

Month/Day Bar Chart
Filename: BD200

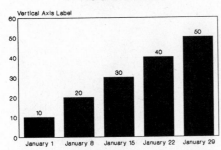

Clustered Month/Day Bar Chart
Filename: BD210

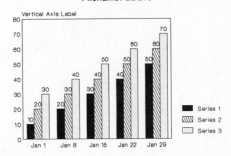

Overlapping Month/Day Bar Chart
Filename: BD220

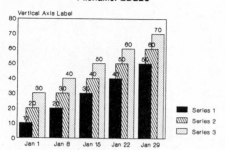

100% Overlapped Month/Day Bar Chart
Filename: BD230

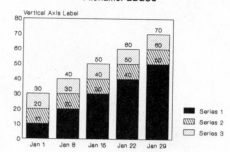

Stacked Month/Day Bar Chart
Filename: BD240

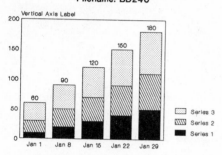

Labeled Bar Chart
Filename: BL100

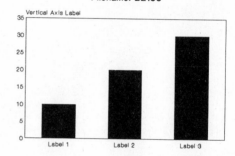

Clustered Labeled Bar Chart
Filename: BL110

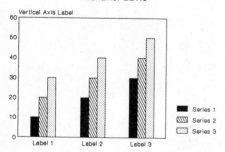

Overlapping Labeled Bar Chart
Filename: BL120

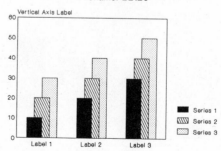

100% Overlapped Labeled Bar Chart
Filename: BL130

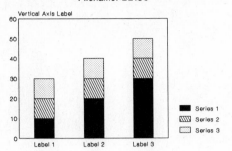

Stacked Labeled Bar Chart
Filename: BL140

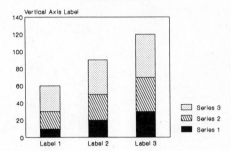

Labeled Bar Chart
Filename: BL200

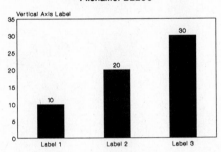

Clustered Labeled Bar Chart
Filename: BL210

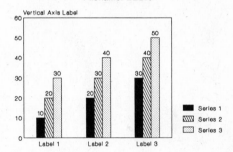

Overlapping Labeled Bar Chart
Filename: BL220

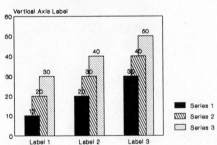

100% Overlapped Labeled Bar Chart
Filename: BL230

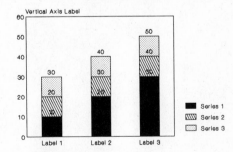

Stacked Labeled Bar Chart
Filename: BL240

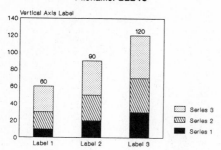

Monthly Bar Chart
Filename: BM100

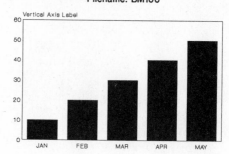

Clustered Monthly Bar Chart
Filename: BM110

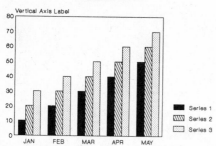

Overlapping Monthly Bar Chart
Filename: BM120

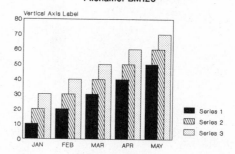

100% Overlapped Monthly Bar Chart
Filename: BM130

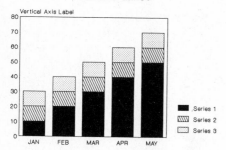

Stacked Monthly Bar Chart
Filename: BM140

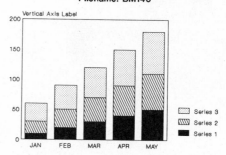

Monthly Bar Chart
Filename: BM200

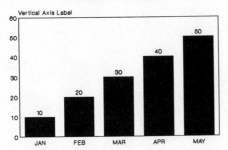

Clustered Monthly Bar Chart
Filename: BM210

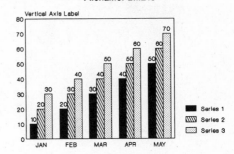

Overlapping Monthly Bar Chart
Filename: BM220

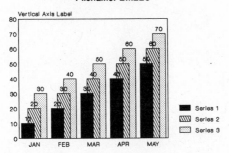

100% Overlapped Monthly Bar Chart
Filename: BM230

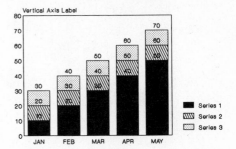

Stacked Monthly Bar Chart
Filename: BM240

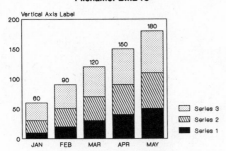

Yearly Bar Chart
Filename: BY100

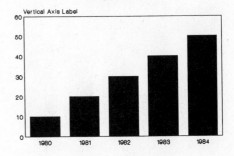

Clustered Yearly Bar Chart
Filename: BY110

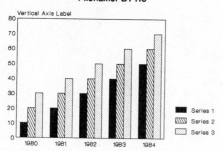

Overlapping Yearly Bar Chart
Filename: BY120

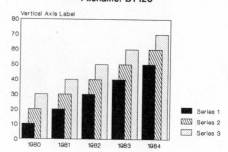

100% Overlapped Yearly Bar Chart
Filename: BY130

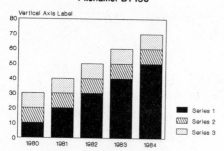

Stacked Yearly Bar Chart
Filename: BY140

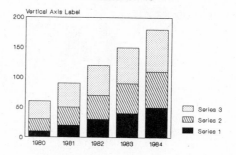

Yearly Bar Chart
Filename: BY200

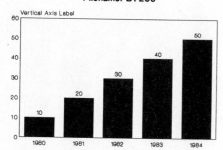

Clustered Yearly Bar Chart
Filename: BY210

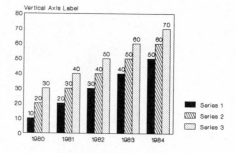

Overlapping Yearly Bar Chart
Filename: BY220

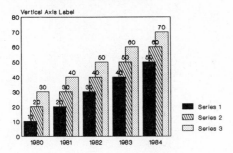

100% Overlapped Yearly Bar Chart
Filename: BY230

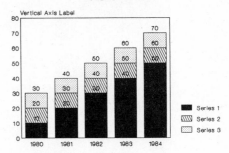

Stacked Yearly Bar Chart
Filename: BY240

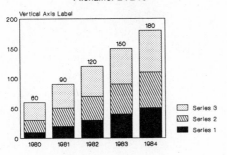

Month/Day Straight Line Chart
Filename: LD100

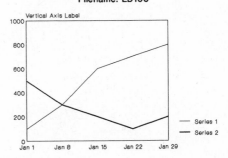

Month/Day Curved Line Chart
Filename: LD200

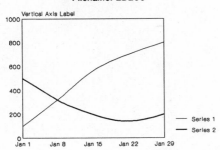

Month/Day Scattered Point Chart
Filename: LD300

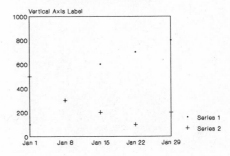

Month/Day Trend Line Chart
Filename: LD400

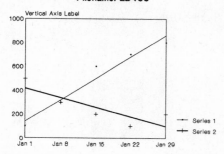

Labeled Straight Line Chart
Filename: LL100

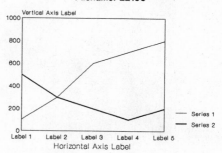

Labeled Curved Line Chart
Filename: LL200

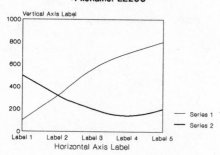

Labeled Scattered Point Chart
Filename: LL300

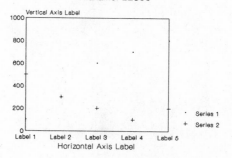

Labeled Trend Line Chart
Filename: LL400

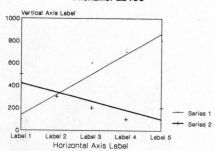

Month Straight Line Chart
Filename: LM100

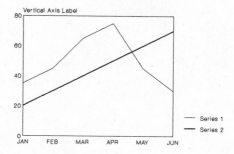

Month Curved Line Chart
Filename: LM200

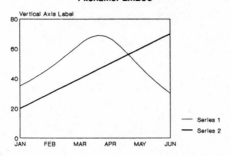

Month Scattered Point Chart
Filename: LM300

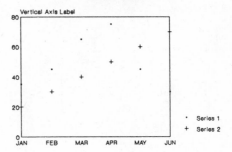

Month Trend Line Chart
Filename: LM400

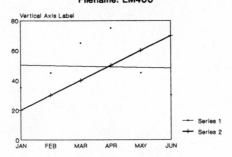

Numbered Straight Line Chart
Filename: LN100

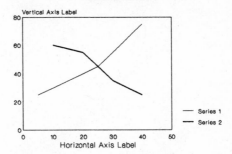

Numbered Curved Line Chart
Filename: LN200

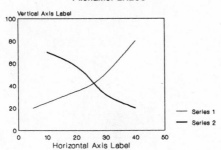

Numbered Scattered Point Chart
Filename: LN300

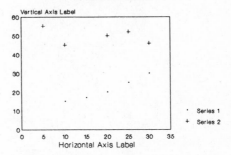

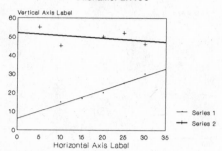

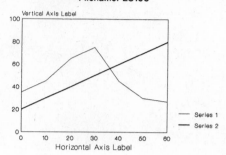

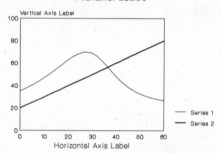

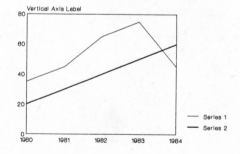

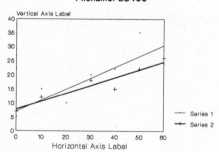

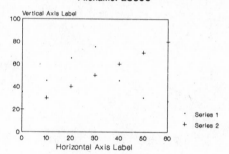

Year Curved Line Chart
Filename: LY200

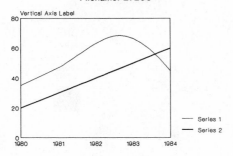

Year Scattered Point Chart
Filename: LY300

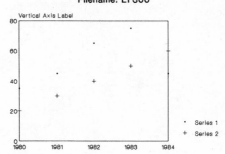

Year Trend Line Chart
Filename: LY400

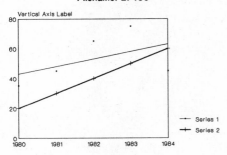

High/Low/Close Chart
Filename: HL100

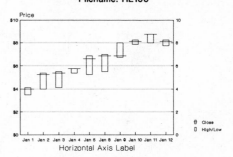

High/Low/Close Chart with Volume Data
Filename: HL110

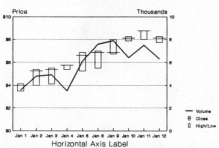

Pie and Bar with Internal Labels
Filename: PB201

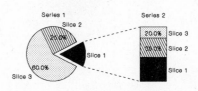

Pie and Bar
with External Labels
Filename: PB202

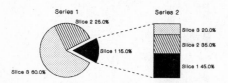

3D Pie and
Bar with Internal Labels
Filename: PB203

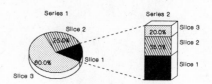

3D Pie and
Bar with External Labels
Filename: PB204

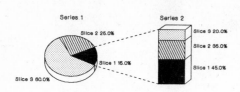

Pie Chart with
Internal Data Labels
Filename: PIE101

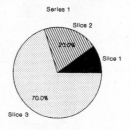

Pie Chart with
External Data Labels
Filename: PIE102

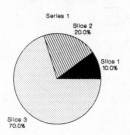

3D Pie Chart
with Internal Data Labels
Filename: PIE103

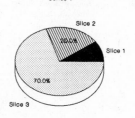

3D Pie Chart
with External Data Labels
Filename: PIE104

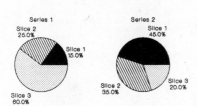

Two Pies with
Internal Data Labels
Filename: PIE201

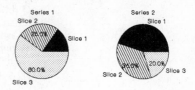

Two Pies with
External Data Labels
Filename: PIE202

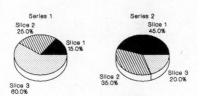

Two 3D Pies
with Internal Data Labels
Filename: PIE203

Two 3D Pies
with External Data Labels
Filename: PIE204

Proportional
Pies with Internal Labels
Filename: PIE205

Proportional Pies with External Labels
Filename: PIE206

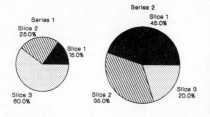

Bullet List with Two Items
Filename: WB120

- Item One:
  The second line of text.
  The number of lines depends
  on character size.
  The fifth line of text.
  The sixth line of text.

- Item Two:
  The second line of text.
  The third line of text.

Bullet List with Three Items
Filename: WB130

- Item One:
  The second line of text.
  The number of lines depends
  on character size.
  The fifth line of text.

- Item Two:
  The second line of text.
  The third line of text.

- Item Three:
  The second line of text.
  The third line of text.

Bullet List with Four Items
Filename: WB140

- Item One:
  The second line of text.
  The number of lines depends
  on character size.

- Item Two:
  The second line of text.
  The third line of text.

- Item Three:
  The second line of text.
  The third line of text.

- Item Four:
  The second line of text.
  The third line of text.

Bullet List with Five Items
Filename: WB150

- Item One:
  The second line of text.
  The number of lines depends
  on character size.

- Item Two:
  The second line of text.
  The third line of text.

- Item Three:
  The second line of text.
  The third line of text.

- Item Four:
  The second line of text.
  The third line of text.

- Item Five:
  The second line of text.
  The third line of text.

Bullet List with Six Items
Filename: WB160

- Item One:
  The second line of text.
  The number of lines depends
  on character size.

- Item Two:
  The second line of text.
  The third line of text.

- Item Three:
  The second line of text.
  The third line of text.

- Item Four:
  The second line of text.
  The third line of text.

- Item Five:
  The second line of text.
  The third line of text.

- Item Six:
  The second line of text.
  The third line of text.

Word Chart with Left Justification
Filename: WD100

Simple charts with few words
are the most effective. Limit
information to only what your
audience can absorb rapidly.

Word Chart with Centering
Filename: WD110

Although each line can hold
up to 60 characters,
avoid putting too many on a line.

The practical limit depends on
character size.
In general, try to keep each line
to about 25 characters.

Word Chart with Left Justification
Filename: WD120

Simple charts with few words are the most
effective. Limit information to only
what your audience can absorb rapidly.

Although each line can hold up to 60
characters, avoid putting too many on a
line. The practical limit depends on
character size. In general, try to keep
each line to about 25 characters.

Word Chart with Centering
File Name: WD130

Simple charts with few words are the most
effective. Limit information to only
what your audience can absorb rapidly.

Although each line can hold up to 60
characters, avoid putting too many on a
line. The practical limit depends on
character size. In general, try to keep
each line to about 25 characters.

Title Page
Presentation Title
Filename: WM110

Speaker's Name
Company Name
Affiliation

Occasion
Date

Miscellaneous Word Chart with Two Groups of Text
Filename: WM120
Simple charts with few words are the most
effective. Limit information to only
what your audience can absorb rapidly.

Although each line can hold up to 60
characters, avoid putting too many on a
line. The practical limit depends on
character size. In general, try to keep
each line to about 25 characters.

Miscellaneous Word Chart with Three Groups of Text
Filename: WM130

Simple charts with few words are the most
effective. Limit information to only
what your audience can absorb rapidly.

Although each line can hold up to 60
characters, avoid putting too many on a
line. The practical limit depends on
character size. In general try to keep
each line to about 25 characters.

Quotation Page
Filename: WM140

When you include a quotation from someone
in your presentation, consider using this
type of chart design. Center the quotation
on the page by inserting or deleting blank
lines above the beginning of the quote using
Ctrl-Ins and Ctrl-Del, respectively.

The Author
Reference

Question and Answer Page
Filename: WM150

The question goes here. The number of lines
depends on character size. Did you remember
to leave a blank line between the question
and the answer?

Yes! You should also center the question
and answer on the page by inserting or
deleting blank lines above the questions,
using Ctrl-Ins and Ctrl-Del, respectively.

Numbered List with Two Items
Filename: WN120

1. Item One:
   The second line of text.
   The number of lines depends
   on character size.
   The fifth line of text.
   The sixth line of text.

2. Item Two:
   The second line of text.
   The third line of text.

Numbered List with Three Items
Filename: WN130

1. Item One:
   The second line of text.
   The number of lines depends
   on character size.
   The fifth line of text.

2. Item Two:
   The second line of text.
   The third line of text.

3. Item Three:
   The second line of text.
   The third line of text.

Numbered List with Four Items
Filename: WN140

1. Item One:
   The second line of text.
   The number of lines depends
   on character size.

2. Item Two:
   The second line of text.
   The third line of text.

3. Item Three:
   The second line of text.
   The third line of text.

4. Item Four:
   The second line of text.
   The third line of text.

Numbered List with Five Items
Filename: WN150

1. **Item One:**
   The second line of text.
   The number of lines depends
   on character size.

2. **Item Two:**
   The second line of text.
   The third line of text.

3. **Item Three:**
   The second line of text.
   The third line of text.

4. **Item Four:**
   The second line of text.
   The third line of text.

5. **Item Five:**
   The second line of text.
   The third line of text.

Numbered List with Six Items
Filename: WN160

1. **Item One:**
   The second line of text.
   The number of lines depends
   on character size.

2. **Item Two:**
   The second line of text.
   The third line of text.

3. **Item Three:**
   The second line of text.
   The third line of text.

4. **Item Four:**
   The second line of text.
   The third line of text.

5. **Item Five:**
   The second line of text.
   The third line of text.

6. **Item Six:**
   The second line of text.
   The third line of text.

Designer Galleries CHT Files

This section presents all the Designer Galleries charts available for you to use.

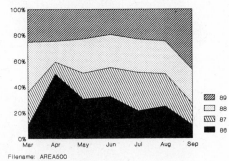

Filename: AREA500

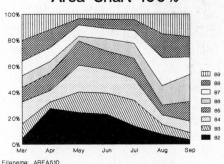

Filename: AREA510

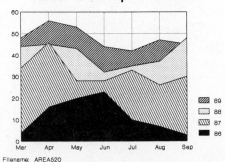

Filename: AREA520

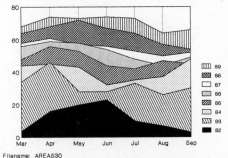

Filename: AREA530

Area Stacked 4 Series

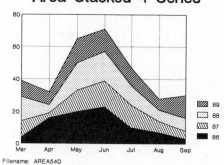

Filename: AREA540

Area Stacked 8 Series

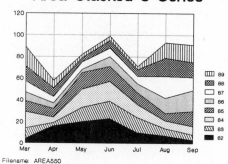

Filename: AREA550

Area Chart 100%

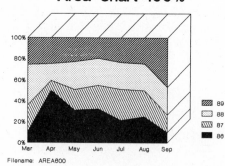

Filename: AREA600

Area Chart 100%

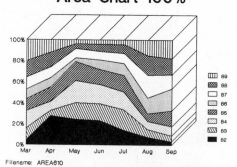

Filename: AREA610

Area Overlap 4 Series

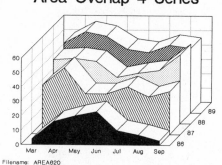

Filename: AREA620

Area Overlap 8 Series

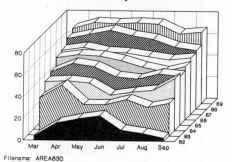

Filename: AREA630

Area Stacked 4 Series

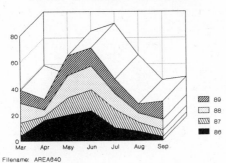

Filename: AREA640

Area Stacked 8 Series

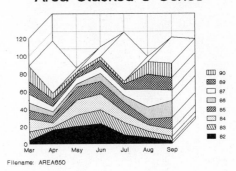

Filename: AREA650

Bar Chart 4 Series

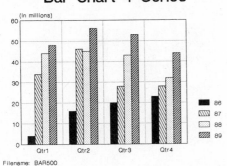

Filename: BAR500

Bar Chart 8 Series

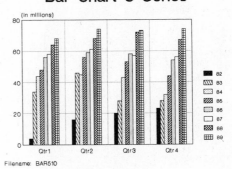

Filename: BAR510

Bar Chart 4 Series

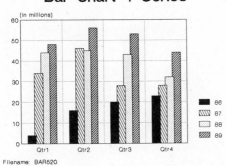

Filename: BAR520

Bar Chart 8 Series

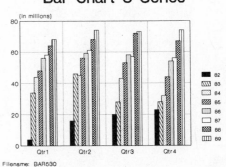

Filename: BAR530

Paired Bar Chart

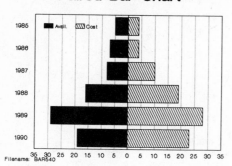

Filename: BAR540

Bar Chart 4 Series

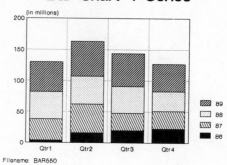

Filename: BAR550

Bar Chart 8 Series

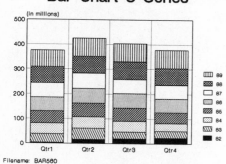

Filename: BAR560

Compare & Breakdown

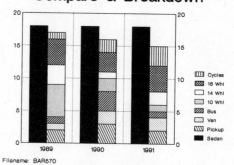

Filename: BAR570

Title Inside the Frame

Filename: BAR580

Seasonality

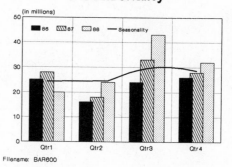

Filename: BAR600

Lemonade vs Temperature

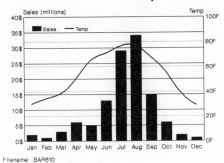

Filename: BAR610

Step Chart

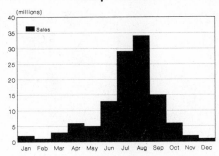

Filename: BAR620

Estimated MPG

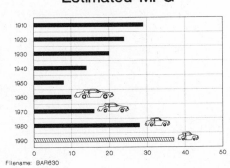

Filename: BAR630

Bar Chart 4 Series

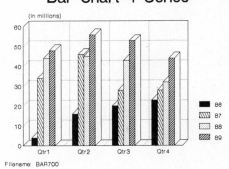

Filename: BAR700

Bar Chart 8 Series

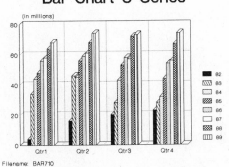

Filename: BAR710

Bar Chart 6 Series

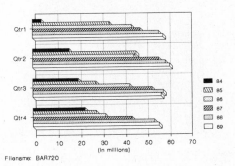

Filename: BAR720

Bar Chart 4 Series

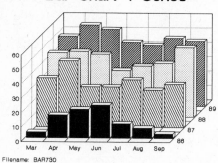

Filename: BAR730

Bar Chart 8 Series

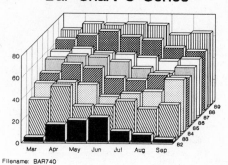

Filename: BAR740

Bar Chart 8 Series

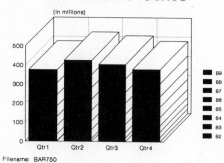

Filename: BAR750

Alternating Labels

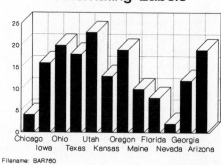

Filename: BAR760

Compare & Breakdown

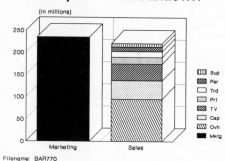

Filename: BAR770

Highlighted Bars

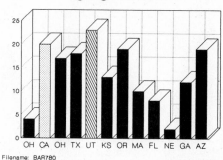

Filename: BAR780

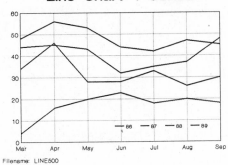

Line Chart 4 Series

Filename: LINE500

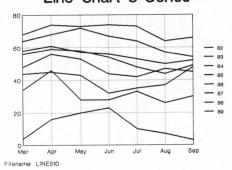

Line Chart 8 Series

Filename: LINE510

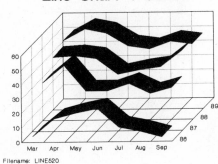

Line Chart 4 Series

Filename: LINE520

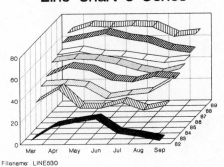

Line Chart 8 Series

Filename: LINE530

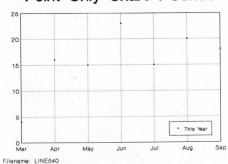

Point Only Chart 1 Series

Filename: LINE540

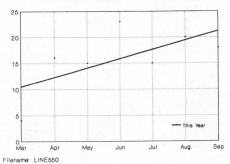

Trend Chart 1 Series

Filename: LINE550

Curve Chart 1 Series

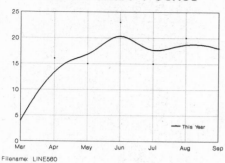

Filename: LINE560

Log Line Chart 1 Series

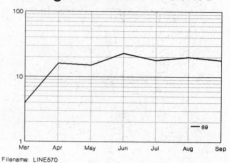

Filename: LINE570

Bar and Line Mix

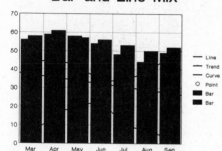

Filename: LINE580

Data Table Included

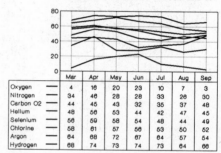

	Mar	Apr	May	Jun	Jul	Aug	Sep
Oxygen	4	16	20	23	10	7	3
Nitrogen	34	46	28	28	33	26	30
Carbon O2	44	45	43	32	35	37	48
Helium	48	56	53	44	42	47	45
Selenium	56	59	58	54	48	44	49
Chlorine	58	61	57	56	53	50	52
Argon	64	68	72	67	64	57	54
Hydrogen	68	74	73	74	73	64	66

Filename: LINE590

Stocks Qtr 1 by Day

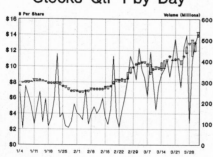

Filename: HLC500

65 Dow Jones 1 Day

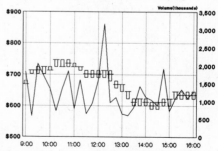

Filename: HLC610

Ridgeway Corporation

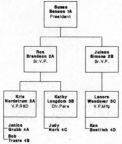

Filename: ORG500

Ridgeway Corporation

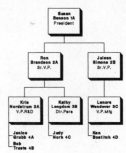

Filename: ORG510

Four Slice Pie Chart

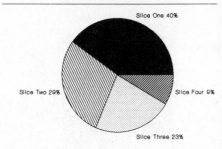

Filename: PIE500

Ten Slice Pie Chart

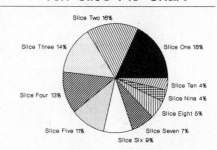

Filename: PIE510

Four Slice Pie Chart
Including a Subtitle

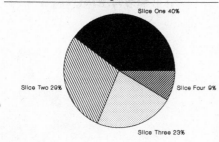

Filename: PIE520

Ten Slice Pie Chart
Including a Subtitle

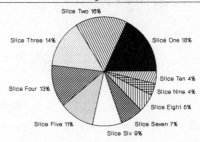

Filename: PIE530

Slice Breakdown

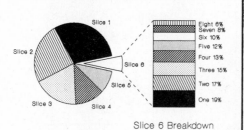

Slice 6 Breakdown

Filename: PIE540

Four Slice Pie Chart

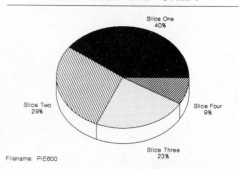

Filename: PIE600

Ten Slice Pie Chart

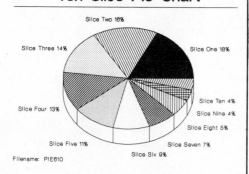

Filename: PIE610

Four Slice Pie Chart
Including a Subtitle

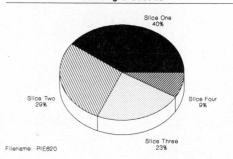

Filename: PIE620

Ten Slice Pie Chart
Including a Subtitle

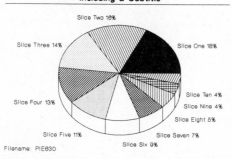

Filename: PIE630

Slice Breakdown

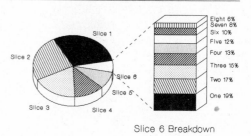

Slice 6 Breakdown

Filename: PIE640

Proportional Pies

Pie totals determine relative pie size

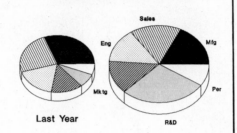

Last Year

Filename: PIE700

2 Column

Department	Expense
Manufacturing	1345
Sales	243
Marketing	182
Total	1770

Filename: TEXT500

2 Column

With Subtitle

Department	Expense
Manufacturing	1345
Sales	243
Marketing	182
Total	1770

Filename: TEXT510

3 Column

Department	Expense	Profit
Manufacturing	1,345	143
Sales	243	1,523
Marketing	182	2,341
Total	1,770	4,007

Filename: TEXT520

3 Column

Including Subtitle

Department	Expense	Profit
Manufacturing	1,345	143
Sales	243	1,523
Marketing	182	2,341
Total	1,770	4,007

Filename: TEXT530

Build Chart

- Use short phrases

Filename: TEXT600

Build Chart

- Use short phrases
- Not too many of them

Filename: TEXT610

Build Chart

- Use short phrases
- Not too many of them
- Break up into two slides

Filename: TEXT620

Build Chart

- Use short phrases
- Not too many of them
- Break up into two slides
- Talk more, show less

Filename: TEXT630

Build Chart
Including a Subtitle

- Use short phrases

Filename: TEXT640

Build Chart
Including a Subtitle

- Use short phrases
- Not too many of them

Filename: TEXT650

Build Chart
Including a Subtitle

- Use short phrases
- Not too many of them
- Break up into two slides

Filename: TEXT660

Build Chart
Including a Subtitle

- Use short phrases
- Not too many of them
- Break up into two slides
- Talk more, show less

Filename: TEXT670

Bullet Chart

- Use short phrases
- Not too many of them
- Break up into two slides
- Talk more, show less

Filename: TEXT680

Bullet Chart
Including a Subtitle

- Use short phrases
- Not too many of them
- Break up into two slides
- Talk more, show less

Filename: TEXT690

Freeform Chart, Build

Anything goes in a freeform chart

Many columns of numbers or data

Outlines with different indents

Talk more, show less, still best

Filename: TEXT700

Freeform Chart, Build
Including a Subtitle

Anything goes in a freeform chart

Many columns of numbers or data

Outlines with different indents

Talk more, show less, still best

Filename: TEXT710

List Chart

Use short phrases

Not too many of them

Break up into two slides

Talk more, show less

Filename: TEXT800

List Chart
Including a Subtitle

Use short phrases

Not too many of them

Break up into two slides

Talk more, show less

Filename: TEXT810

List Chart, Build

Use short phrases

Not too many of them

Break up into two slides

Talk more, show less

Filename: TEXT820

List Chart, Build
Including a Subtitle

Use short phrases

Not too many of them

Break up into two slides

Talk more, show less

Filename: TEXT830

Presenting

Title Chart

By
OUR Corporation

Filename: TEXT900

OUR Logo

Annotate your logo on a title chart

Place the logo template first in your
screen show and the logo will appear on
every chart automatically

Filename: TEXT910

Use the curved polylines
option in Annotate to
create a handwritten look

Filename: TEXT920

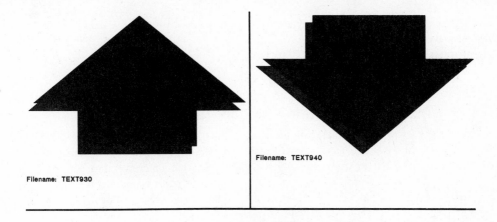

Filename: TEXT930

Filename: TEXT940

Illustrated

- Short phrases
- Not many of them
- Break into two slides
- Show less
- Symbols tell story

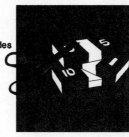

Filename: TEXT950

Your Current Palette

U.S. MapMaker

You can create customized maps of the United States by using U.S. MapMaker. You create the map with U.S. MapMaker, save the map as a symbol or a chart, and then return to Harvard Graphics where you can print the map, modify the map with Draw/Annotate, or incorporate the map into a slide show presentation.

If you need to display maps, U.S. MapMaker is a simple tool with an assortment of possibilities. You can customize maps to show the sales of your products by store or by state. You can create maps of two states that are not connected—like California and New York. U.S. MapMaker can show both states on-screen. California appears on the West Coast while New York appears on the East Coast in the same positions they would be in if all the other continental states also were included on the map.

States also can be given color codes based on numerical data. For example, you can make states with sales of more than 100,000 one color and use another color for states with less sales.

U.S. MapMaker also provides standard predefined geographical areas that you can access with one keystroke. To show only New England on your map, for example, you can select and display that region.

As you work with MapMaker, you also find that the most obscure cities are part of its large library of maps. With more than 32,000 towns listed, few cities or towns are unknown to the library. After you create your map, you can convert your map into a Harvard Graphics symbol or chart and add elements with Draw/ Annotate or Draw Partner. Then you can use Harvard Graphics to print or plot your map, or even record it on 35mm film.

Installing and Using MapMaker

MapMaker is an independent program that is not part of any version of Harvard Graphics. If you have Version 2.3 of Harvard Graphics, however, you can attach MapMaker as an application. Chapter 2 describes how to attach an application to Harvard Graphics.

Working in MapMaker is similar to working in other parts of Harvard Graphics. When you start MapMaker, a main menu appears. As you make selections from the main menu screen, press F2 (Preview) to view the map. After you have looked at the map, press Esc to make alterations using the main menu.

MapMaker is flexible in its design. You can create a map by adding cities first, or you can create a map by adding states first. You also can import data graphically interpreted by MapMaker.

Installing U.S. MapMaker

The U.S. MapMaker accessory comes on two 5 1/4-inch disks or one 3 1/2-inch disk. The installation process is simple and can be completed in minutes.

Install U.S. MapMaker in its own directory, not in the Harvard Graphics program directory. Then when you need to backup your files, the process is simplified. To create a separate directory for U.S. MapMaker and install it, follow these steps:

1. Make sure that the DOS prompt is on-screen.

2. Type *cd* and press Enter to make sure that you are at the hard disk's root directory.

3. Type *md\map* and press Enter to create a directory for U.S. MapMaker.

4. Type *cd\map* and press Enter to change to the U.S. MapMaker directory.

5. Insert the U.S. MapMaker Disk 1 into drive A.

6. Type *a:install* and press Enter.

7. Follow the instructions on-screen.

After you install U.S. MapMaker, you can start the program by changing to its directory and typing *USMAP*.

The Main Menu

Use the arrow keys to select an on-screen option or select from a menu by pressing the number corresponding to your choice. You cannot make a MapMaker menu selection using a mouse or typing the first letter of an option, and the space bar does not move between choices. Figure D.1 shows the MapMaker main menu.

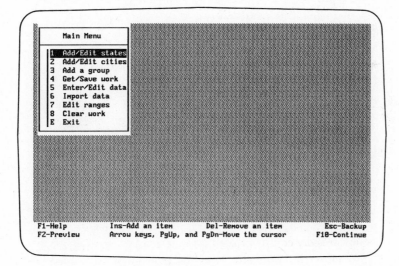

Fig. D.1.

The MapMaker main menu.

By examining the main menu, you can get a sense of how the utility is organized and how the task of creating maps flows logically. The main menu choices enable you to add and edit states or cities. Several function keys shown on the bottom of the screen are used to manipulate items on the map.

The Add/Edit States option from the main menu takes you to a list of all 50 states (and the District of Columbia) from which to choose. After you select a state, choosing the Add/Edit option brings you to a list of states you already have chosen for the current map, enabling you to add to, delete from, and edit the list.

Choosing the Add/Edit Cities option enables you to type the first few letters of a city name so that U.S. MapMaker can present a list of all the available cities whose names start with those letters. From that list, you may select to add a city to the map. After you select a city, choosing the Add/Edit option brings up a list of selected cities for the current map so that you can add, delete, or edit the cities in your map.

Choosing the Add a Group option enables you to select states or cities by group, such as New England States or Arizona Major Cities. Figure D.2 shows the first page of the list of groups from which to choose.

Fig. D.2.

The first page of the list of groups.

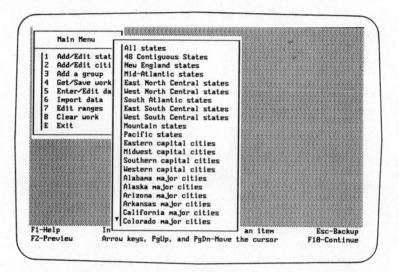

```
┌─ Main Menu ─────┬─────────────────────────────
│                 │ All states
│ 1  Add/Edit stat│ 48 Contiguous States
│ 2  Add/Edit citi│ New England states
│ 3  Add a group  │ Mid-Atlantic states
│ 4  Get/Save work│ East North Central states
│ 5  Enter/Edit da│ West North Central states
│ 6  Import data  │ South Atlantic states
│ 7  Edit ranges  │ East South Central states
│ 8  Clear work   │ West South Central states
│ E  Exit         │ Mountain states
│                 │ Pacific states
│                 │ Eastern capital cities
│                 │ Midwest capital cities
│                 │ Southern capital cities
│                 │ Western capital cities
│                 │ Alabama major cities
│                 │ Alaska major cities
│                 │ Arizona major cities
│                 │ Arkansas major cities
│                 │ California major cities
│                 ▼ Colorado major cities
│ F1-Help      In              an item      Esc-Backup
│ F2-Preview   Arrow keys, PgUp, and PgDn-Move the cursor   F10-Continue
```

After you create your map, you can save your map by choosing the Get/Save Work option. Later, you can add titles to the map and print the map in Harvard Graphics. You can color-code your map based on numeric data, such as number of employees by date or sales statistics for a specific product, or you can color-code based on descriptive data, such as major imports or major sources of energy. To color-code a map, choose the Enter/Edit Data, Import Data, and Edit Ranges options.

The Clear Work option erases all the current map information so that you can start a new map. The Exit option ends your session in U.S. MapMaker. Exit is the only option on the main menu that can be selected by pressing the first letter of the choice—E. In U.S. MapMaker, your selections of states and cities appear in lists that are placed on a form when you make a selection. If you select Add/

Edit States from the main menu, for example, you see a list of states available. Using the cursor, you can highlight the state you want to add. A second list appears, on which you can define the characteristics of that state. The second list is used to describe the inside and border colors of the selected state. After you complete the list of choices, the state or city is added to the form and to the map. To complete a form, you usually make your choices from lists, such as lists of colors, cities, or states. When a list appears, you can press F10 to retain the default color that appears highlighted on the list and move the cursor to the next list.

Creating a Map

Imagine that you want to add a map to your Superior Office Supplies presentation, showing locations of the corporate headquarters and major sales offices. This map then can be color-coded to reflect sales volume in each of the states.

Because the main corporate office is in Red Bank, New Jersey, you add Red Bank first. Then you can add the sales offices in Tinton Falls, New Jersey; Stamford, Connecticut; and West Hempstead, New York. You can add these sales offices to your map by selecting each city or state. In this example, you first select by state and then you can add the cities to the picture.

Adding a State

You should add states one at a time when you add just a few states, states that do not share a border, or states that are not in the same geographic group. For this example, New Jersey has two SOS offices, so you can add New Jersey—Superior Office Supplies corporate headquarters—first.

To add the state of New Jersey to your map, follow these steps:

1. Select Add/Edit States from the MapMaker main menu by pressing 1 to summon the States Form and a list of the states to the screen.

2. Press the down-arrow key to highlight New Jersey and press Enter. The state overlay appears. Use this overlay to select colors for the added state. Figure D.3 shows the list of states as it appears, with New Jersey highlighted. Figure D.4 shows the State overlay.

3. Press Enter to display a list of colors so that you can select a color for the inside of New Jersey. Highlight a color and press Enter to move to the Border Color option. Because this map will not be printed on a color printer, select Not Drawn from the list of colors to create the outline of the map only.

Fig. D.3.

The States list.

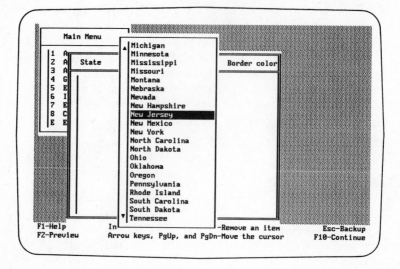

Fig. D.4.

The State overlay.

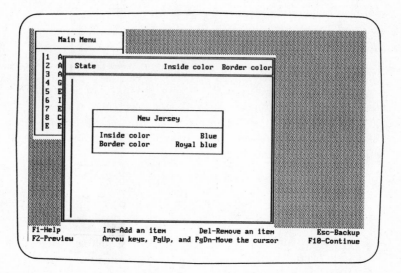

4. Press Enter so that you can select a color for the border of the state you have selected. Highlight a color and press Enter.

5. Press F10 (Continue) to complete your selection and to add the selected state and its options to the State Form.

6. Press F2 (Preview) to see the map. Figure D.5 shows the map with just New Jersey added.

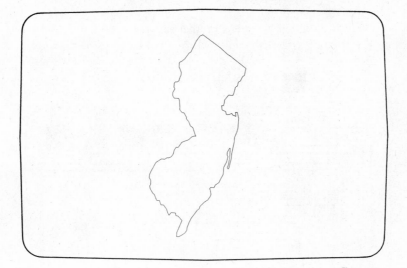

Fig. D.5.

The first state added to the map.

To add more states while you are already in the state form, press the Ins key (Add an item). You can remove states from the list by pressing the Del key (Remove an item). To delete a state on the list, press the Del key, highlight that state, and press Enter. To edit the colors of a state, highlight that state and press Enter.

When you finish adding and editing the states in your map, press Esc to return to the MapMaker main menu.

Adding a City

You can add cities to your map next. In this section, you add the three main cities for Superior Office Supplies sales: Tinton Falls, Stamford, and West Hempstead. You also add Red Bank as corporate headquarters.

U.S. MapMaker has a file of more than 32,000 cities and towns that you can choose from. After a city is selected from the file, its name and a map symbol (such as a dot or star) is added to the map. When you select a city, you can modify the name of the city as the name appears on the map, the type of symbol used to mark the city's location, and the colors of the name and symbol.

To add a city to your map, follow these steps:

1. Select Add/Edit Cities from the main menu. The City Name overlay appears.

2. Type the first two letters or more of the city name and press Enter. Because you want to add Red Bank, NJ, as the corporate headquarters, type *red* and press Enter. Figure D.6 shows the City Name overlay with red typed in. Figure D.7 shows the list of cities that start with red.

Fig. D.6.

The City overlay.

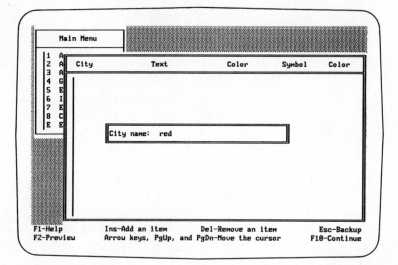

Fig. D.7.

*The list of cities
that start with red.*

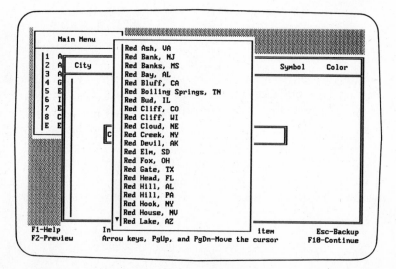

3. Press the down-arrow key to highlight Red Bank, NJ, and press Enter. The City overlay appears.

4. The options for that city appear. If you like the default choices, press F10 (Continue) to confirm your choices. To change a choice, use the down-arrow key to highlight it and press Enter to display the available choices. Highlight the color you want to use and press Enter to confirm your choice. For this map, you can change the symbol for Red Bank to a star.

5. Press the down-arrow key to highlight the city option you want to change—in this case, Symbol Type—and press Enter.

6. Press the down-arrow key to highlight Star and press Enter.

7. Press F10 (Continue) to complete your selection and to add the selected city and its options to the City Form.

8. Press F2 (Preview) to check the map. After you view the map, press Esc to return to the main menu.

9. Press Ins (Add an Item) to add another city. The City Name overlay appears.

10. Type *tin* and press Enter to add the Tinton Falls, NJ, sales office to your list.

11. Press the down-arrow key until Tinton Falls, NJ, is highlighted.

12. Press Enter to select the highlighted city.

13. Press F10 (Continue) to complete your selection and add Tinton Falls to the City Form.

Follow steps 9-13 again to add the remaining SOS sales offices: West Hempstead, NY; Philadelphia, PA; and Stamford, CT. Figure D.8 shows the map with all of the sales offices added. Tinton Falls and Red Bank are so close together that they overwrite each other. You can correct this problem by editing Red Bank to read "Superior Office Supplies" as the city name in the next section.

Adding a city to your map is done with the same process as adding a state. When you add a city to the Cities Form whose state has not yet been added to the States Form, MapMaker adds that state for you, using the default options. You may go back to the Add/Edit States option and change any of the options for any of the states that appear on the form (even those added automatically).

Fig. D.8.

The map with all sales offices added.

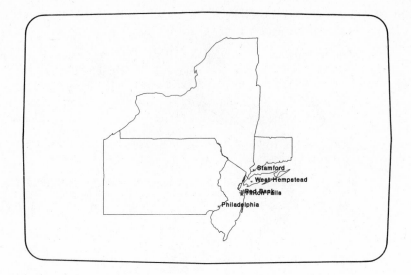

Editing a Map

Now that you see what the map looks like, you may decide to make a number of changes. For example, you may want to replace the name Red Bank on your map with the name of your company, Superior Office Supplies . Using MapMaker, this change is simple to make. Follow this procedure to change the name of the city:

1. Press 2 (Add/Edit Cities) from the MapMaker main menu to summon the Cities Form.

2. Press the down-arrow key to highlight the city you want to edit—in this case, Red Bank—and press Enter.

3. Press F9 (Insert On/Off) to turn Insert mode off and type *Superior Office Supplies, inc.*

4. Press F10 (Continue) to complete your changes to the city options and place the modified city options back into the City overlay.

Figure D.9 shows the completed map with the company name replacing the city name.

You can make changes to other cities now, as well. Highlight the city you want to modify and press Enter. Otherwise, you can leave the City overlay by pressing Esc.

Fig. D.9.

The map with Superior Office Supplies label added.

Deleting a City

You can change cities and add new ones, and you also can delete cities from the cities list (which deletes them from the map). Because Red Bank and Tinton Falls are so close to each other geographically, you can show them as just one sales office by deleting Tinton Falls.

To delete a city, follow these steps:

1. Select Add/Edit Cities on the main menu and press the down-arrow key to highlight the city you want to delete, Tinton Falls.

2. Press Del (Remove an Item) to delete the highlighted city from the list.

   A prompt appears, asking whether you want to remove the current city (see fig. D.10).

3. Highlight Yes and press Enter to complete the deletion process.

4. Press Esc to return to the main menu and press F2 (Preview) to see the map. Figure D.11 shows the resulting map.

Fig. D.10.

The Remove Current City overlay.

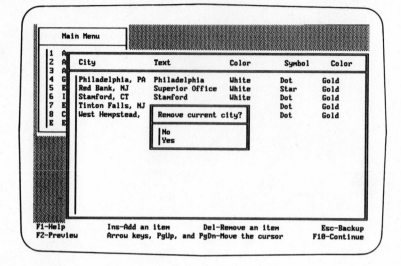

Fig. D.11.

The map with Tinton Falls deleted.

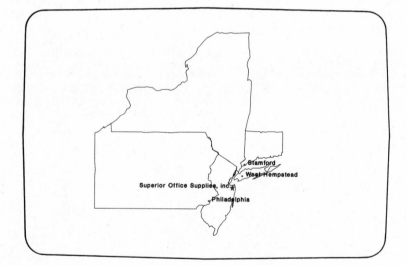

Deleting a State

You also can delete a state. When you delete a state from the states list, Map-Maker deletes that state's cities from the cities list. Deleting every city from a state, however, does not remove the state from the states list. Try deleting Connecticut from your map by following this procedure:

1. Press 1 (Add/Edit States) to summon the states list.

2. Press the down-arrow key to highlight the state you want to delete—Connecticut.

3. Press Del (Remove an Item) to delete the highlighted state from the list.

   The Remove Current State prompt appears. Highlight Yes and press Enter to complete the deletion process.

4. Press Esc to return to the main menu and F2 (Preview) to view the map without Connecticut (see fig. D.12).

Fig. D.12.

The map with Connecticut deleted.

Color-Coding a Map

You can color-code a map based on numeric data (such as per capita income) or descriptive data (such as major export). MapMaker assigns the colors of your choice to a state based on where it falls in a range. In MapMaker, the range is like a series and is displayed in a legend below the map.

To color-code a map, you must enter a value for each state. Values cannot be fractions. For example, try adding sales data for the past fiscal year to color-code your map based on sales revenues. To enter or edit state values, follow these steps:

1. Press 5 (Enter/Edit Data) to bring the Enter/Edit Data form to the screen (see fig. D.13).

   The states currently selected for the map are listed in alphabetical order.

Fig. D.13.

The States list for the current map.

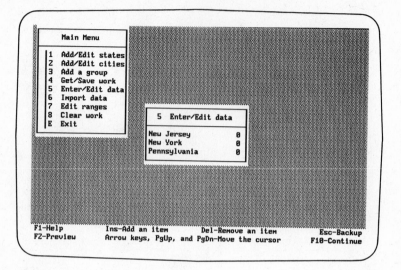

2. Type the sales figures for each state and press Enter.

Enter the following sales figures:

New Jersey 750000
New York 480000
Pennsylvania 622000

Editing the Ranges

Now you can define the ranges and associate those ranges with colors so that the states can fall into the ranges based on the data you entered in the preceding section. You do not have to enter the minimum value for any range because MapMaker calculates the minimum value based on the preceding range. The minimum value of the first range is displayed as less than.

In this example, you can show all of the states with sales greater than 500,000 in one color, and those with less than 500,000 in another color.

Color-coding a map works only when the colors of the state are set to Color Code on the colors list. This choice sets MapMaker to determine the color of that state based on the range set and actual value for that range, rather than by individual settings for that state. To set the color options for each state in this map to Color Code, refer to the procedures in the section "Adding a State," earlier in this appendix.

To add or edit a range, follow these steps:

1. Select Edit Ranges from the main menu to summon the ranges form. The Range overlay appears.

2. Type the maximum of the first range you want to color-code, 499999, and press Enter.

3. Press Enter to select a color for the inside of the states that fall into this range. Highlight Yellow and press Enter to move to the Border Color option.

4. Press Enter to select a color for the border of the states that fall into this range. Highlight Royal Blue and press Enter to move to the Legend option.

5. Type the text you want to appear at the bottom of the map as the legend describing this range, Sales ‹ $500,000, and press Enter to add the range to the Range Form. Figure D.14 shows the completed range overlay.

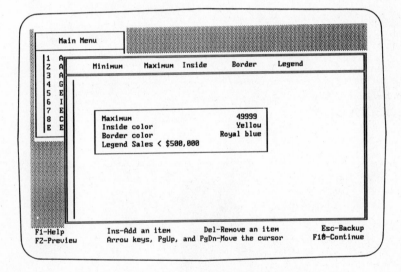

Fig. D.14.

The completed Range overlay.

6. Press Ins (Add an Item) to insert another range.

7. Type the maximum of the second range you want to color-code, 999999, and press Enter.

8. Press Enter to select a color for the inside of the states that fall into this range. Highlight Not Drawn and press Enter to move to the Border Color option.

9. Press Enter to select a color for the border of the states that fall into this range. Highlight Royal Blue and press Enter to move to the Legend option.

10. Type the text you want to appear at the bottom of the map as the legend describing this range, Sales = $500,000 to $1,000,000, and press Enter to add the range to the Range form. Figure D.15 shows the completed Range screen, and figure D.16 shows the completed map.

Fig. D.15.

The completed Range list.

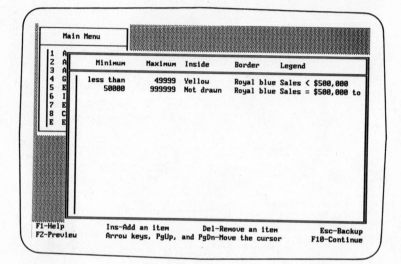

Fig. D.16.

The map with sales ranges color coded.

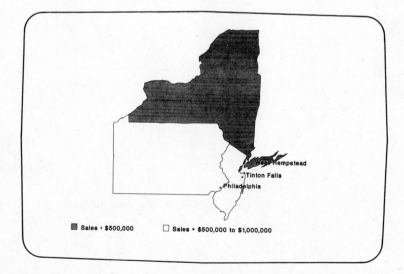

11. Press Esc to return to the main menu.

Adding a Group

You can add states and cities by groups. Adding by groups is quicker than adding one state at a time and is especially useful if you want to create maps of standard regions of the country. To add a group, press 3 (Add a Group) from the main menu. The group list appears, with groups of states first, followed by groups of cities. Highlight the group you want to add and press Enter. You can change the state or city options for the entire group at this point, or press F10 (Continue) to add the group with the default options.

Creating Your Own Group

You are not limited to using the standard groups. You can create your own groups of states, cities, or combinations of the two, and you can even edit existing groups to tailor them to your particular needs. For example, if your company considers Delaware a Mid-Atlantic State, you can permanently delete it from Southern Atlantic States and add it to the Mid-Atlantic States group.

To create your own groups or edit existing groups, you must exit U.S. MapMaker and use a word processor that can read and save a file in ASCII file format. With your word processor, load the ASCII file called USMAP.GRP. At the beginning of the file are instructions on how to add groups to the file. Figure D.17 shows the U.S. MapMaker ASCII file.

```
1 L[·········1·········2·········3·········4·········5·········]·········7·····
       # This file defines the groups you can add to a map using
   Add a group
       # (Main Menu option 3).

       # To add a group to this file:

       # 1.   Move to the bottom of the file and type the group name
       #      beginning in the first column of a new line.

       # 2.   Then type each item in the group on a separate line,
       #      indented at least one space or tab.

       #      To add a state, type its full name; to add a city,
   type
       #      the full city name, a comma, and the two-character
   state
       #      abbreviation.

       #      You can mix cities and states within a group.
   (Remember
       #      that if you add a city, U.S. MapMaker automatically
   adds
                                                    ══USMAP.GRP══
```

Fig. D.17.

The USMAP.GRP ASCII file.

To add a new group, go to the end of the group list and on a blank line, starting in column 1, type the name of the group (up to 40 characters long). Press Enter. Then add the states and cities you want to include in this group by typing each name on a separate line, starting in column 3. You also can use the add, delete, move, and copy features of your word processor to copy or move states or cities to your new group or to change the composition of existing groups.

When you finish editing the file, save the file in ASCII format. When you return to MapMaker, your new groups and modified groups appear on the Groups list.

Importing Data

Just as you can import data into Harvard Graphics, you also can import data into MapMaker. The data is interpreted, and the map is color-coded based on the ranges you specify. You can import data in ASCII format into MapMaker by selecting the Import Data option from the main menu.

The data in the imported ASCII file must be in a format that has two-letter state abbreviations, followed by at least two spaces or a tab and ending with their values in integer form. Only one state can appear on each line. For example, the data file may look like this:

```
NJ    43455
NY    57899
DE    12435
```

If you import a data file that contains states that do not yet appear on the states list, MapMaker adds those states automatically.

Saving a Map

When you finish working with a map, you should save it. To save a map, select the Get/Save Work option on the main menu. Three formats for saving a map exist:

Save Map. This option saves the map as a map. MapMaker saves the file with the extension MAP so that you can work with it again in MapMaker but not in Harvard Graphics.

Create HG Chart. This option saves the map as a Harvard Graphics chart so that you can print the map chart in Harvard Graphics. (MapMaker has no print capabilities.) This option saves the file with extension CHT.

Create HG Symbol. This option saves the map as a Harvard Graphics symbol. This option enables you to bring the map into Draw/Annotate, ungroup it, and modify the different graphic elements of the map. This option also enables you to use Harvard Graphics to print the chart. This option saves the file with extension SYM.

Clearing Work

Choose the Clear Work option from the main menu to create a map from scratch. This process erases all the selections of states and cities, all the values and ranges entered, and so on. The Clear Work option is particularly useful if you need to create a batch of maps of different regions.

Index

100% bar style, 178-179
3D effect
    bar charts, 182-184
    pie chart, 239
@REDUC (data reduction), 260-263

A

accessory products
    Draw Partner, 602
    Screenshow Utilities, 602
accessory programs, 601-655
    Business Symbols, 601
    Designer Galleries, 601, 623-638
    Military Symbols, 601
    Quick Charts, 601-623
    U.S. MapMaker, 60
Add Draw menu option, 291
addresses
    adding text, 371-373
align
    Draw menu option, 291
    Text Options menu, 300
    menu options, 423
    graphical objects, 421, 439
All Files Except VDI Devices
    INSTALL program menu option, 24

animated sequences
    Harvard Graphics 2.3, 599
    in screenshows, 532-535
animating charts
    screenshows, 520
applications
    installing DOS, 47
Applications (F3) function key, 46-47, 342
Applications menu
    Harvard Graphics 2.3, 598-599
    setting up, 46-47
Applications option
    Setup main menu, 46-47
approach of Harvard Graphics, 20-21
arcs
    definition, 350
    drawing, 350-352
    drawing with Draw Partner, 393-395
area charts, 146
    creating, 215-223
    entering data, 217-222
    Titles & Options pages, 218-222
arrow keys, 30, 52
arrows
    adding to a chart, 309
ASCII data
    importing, 274-277
    customizing columns, 278-283
    screen functions, 275-277

G

Free Catalog!

Mail us this registration form today, and we'll send you a free catalog featuring Que's complete line of best-selling books.

Name of Book _____

Name _____

Title _____

Phone (___) _____

Company _____

Address _____

City _____

State _____ ZIP _____

Please check the appropriate answers:

1. Where did you buy your Que book?
   - ☐ Bookstore (name: _____)
   - ☐ Computer store (name: _____)
   - ☐ Catalog (name: _____)
   - ☐ Direct from Que
   - ☐ Other: _____

2. How many computer books do you buy a year?
   - ☐ 1 or less
   - ☐ 2-5
   - ☐ 6-10
   - ☐ More than 10

3. How many Que books do you own?
   - ☐ 1
   - ☐ 2-5
   - ☐ 6-10
   - ☐ More than 10

4. How long have you been using this software?
   - ☐ Less than 6 months
   - ☐ 6 months to 1 year
   - ☐ 1-3 years
   - ☐ More than 3 years

5. What influenced your purchase of this Que book?
   - ☐ Personal recommendation
   - ☐ Advertisement
   - ☐ In-store display
   - ☐ Price
   - ☐ Que catalog
   - ☐ Que mailing
   - ☐ Que's reputation
   - ☐ Other: _____

6. How would you rate the overall content of the book?
   - ☐ Very good
   - ☐ Good
   - ☐ Satisfactory
   - ☐ Poor

7. What do you like *best* about this Que book?
   _____
   _____

8. What do you like *least* about this Que book?
   _____
   _____

9. Did you buy this book with your personal funds?
   - ☐ Yes   ☐ No

10. Please feel free to list any other comments you may have about this Que book.
   _____
   _____
   _____

que

Order Your Que Books Today!

Name _____

Title _____

Company _____

City _____

State _____ ZIP _____

Phone No. (___) _____

Method of Payment:

Check ☐   (Please enclose in envelope.)

Charge My: VISA ☐   MasterCard ☐

American Express ☐

Charge # _____

Expiration Date _____

Order No.	Title	Qty.	Price	Total

You can **FAX** your order to **1-317-573-2583**. Or call **1-800-428-5331, ext. ORDR** to order direct.
Please add $2.50 per title for shipping and handling.

Subtotal _____

Shipping & Handling _____

Total _____

que

BUSINESS REPLY MAIL

First Class Permit No. 9918   Indianapolis, IN

Postage will be paid by addressee

11711 N. College
Carmel, IN 46032

BUSINESS REPLY MAIL

First Class Permit No. 9918   Indianapolis, IN

Postage will be paid by addressee

11711 N. College
Carmel, IN 46032

Que Corporation
11711 N. College Avenue
Carmel, IN 46032
1-800-428-5331

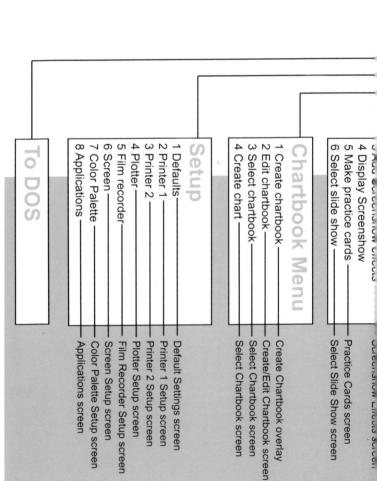

Chartbook Menu

1 Create chartbook ———————— Create Chartbook overlay
2 Edit chartbook ———————————— Create/Edit Chartbook screen
3 Select chartbook ————————— Select Chartbook screen
4 Create chart ——————————————— Select Chartbook screen

3 Add Slideshow Effects
4 Display Screenshow
5 Make practice cards ———————— Practice Cards screen
6 Select slide show ——————————— Select Slide Show screen

Setup

1 Defaults ——————————————————— Default Settings screen
2 Printer 1 ———————————————————— Printer 1 Setup screen
3 Printer 2 ———————————————————— Printer 2 Setup screen
4 Plotter ——————————————————————— Plotter Setup screen
5 Film recorder ————————————— Film Recorder Setup screen
6 Screen ———————————————————————— Screen Setup screen
7 Color Palette ——————————————— Color Palette Setup screen
8 Applications ————————————————— Applications screen

To DOS

Using Harvard™ Graphics

MENU MAP

Harvard Graphics 2.3

MAIN MENU

1 Create new chart
2 Enter/Edit chart
3 Draw/Annotate
4 Get/Save/Remove
5 Import/Export
6 Produce output
7 Slide show menu
8 Chartbook menu
9 Setup
E Exit

Import/Export

1 Import Lotus Graph —— Select Worksheet screen
2 Import Lotus data —— Select Worksheet screen
3 Import ASCII data —— Select File screen
4 Import delimited ASCII —— Select File screen
5 Import Excel chart —— Select Excel Chart screen
6 Import Excel data —— Select Excel Worksheet screen
7 Import CGM metafile —— Select CGM Metafile screen
8 Export picture —— Export Picture overlay
9 Export CGM metafile —— Export Metafile overlay

Produce Output

1 Printer —— Print Chart Options overlay
2 Plotter —— Plot Chart Options overlay
3 Film recorder —— Record Chart Options overlay
4 Print chart data
5 Print slide show
6 Plot slide show
7 Record slide show
8 Print practice cards
9 Print slide show list

Slide Show Menu

1 Create slide show —— Create Slide Show overlay
2 Edit slide show —— Create/Edit Slide Show screen